Another Way

Small steps can lead to big change

Walk with us as we take small steps in our everyday lives for the good of our global neighbours.

Find out how we can give, act, live an
christianaid.org.uk/anotherway

D1078721

Take your church on an adventure with MAF

We would like to invite you and your church to partner with us and, in return, we'll bring you right to the heart of MAF's work

Take part in a Country Lifeline for 12 months, we'll provide you with display materials, events and community outreach resources, updates and a MAF representative.

For more information, please phone **0141 332 5222** or email **scottishoffice@maf-uk.org**

Come with us on an adventure
www.maf-uk.org/**adventure**

Registered charity in England and Wales (1064598) and in Scotland (SC039107)
® Registered trademark 3026860, 3026908, 3026915

You don't have to give blood to volunteer with Mercy Ships

Mercy
Ships
Bringing Hope and Healing...

Some do! Lalao received free surgery to remove a goiter on board the hospital-ship, *Africa Mercy*. Nurse Megan gave blood to help in her recovery.

Can your church help our patients?

Find out more about the inspiring work of *Africa Mercy*. Would any of your members join this extraordinary crew? We need all kinds of volunteers for all kinds of roles!

Join our journey at **www.mercyships.org.uk** or **www.mercyships.org/volunteer** or ring 01438 727800 to ask for charity information and a visiting speaker

Mercy Ships UK, 12 Meadway Court, Stevenage SG1 2EF

/mercyshipsuk   @mercyshipsuk

Registered Charity Numbers: 1053055 (England & Wales) and SCO39743
(Scotland) Company No. 3147724 (England & Wales)

The Church of Scotland

HOUSING & LOAN FUND FOR RETIRED MINISTERS AND WIDOWS AND WIDOWERS OF MINISTERS

The Church of Scotland Housing and Loan Fund's primary objective is to assist Ministers who have the need of help with housing upon their retirement. Ministers live in manses during their years of service, but as these are tied houses, the manse families must move and put down new roots when the Minister retires. At all times, widow(er)s of Ministers are also a main concern for support.

The Fund owns and acquires houses for renting, or gives loans, which make it possible for the manse family to secure a home in retirement.

The Fund can also provide similar assistance to retired Ministers and their widow(er)s who wish to move to more suitable accommodation.

Over the years the favourable terms which the Fund offers have been greatly valued by Ministers and their families. The generosity of those who remember the Fund in their wills greatly supports ongoing work. Gifts to the Fund are always much appreciated.

Donations, Legacies and Gift Aid Contributions will be welcomed with gratitude. Applications for assistance should be directed to: The Secretary, Miss Lin J. Macmillan, MA, The Church of Scotland Housing and Loan Fund for Retired Ministers and Widows and Widowers of Ministers, 121 George Street, Edinburgh EH2 4YN. Tel: 0131 225 5722 Email: lmacmillan@cofscotland.org.uk

THE CHURCH OF SCOTLAND

CHARITY No. SCO 11353

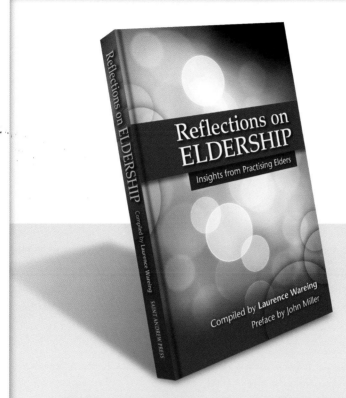

The Right Reverend Dr Russell Barr
MODERATOR

The Church of Scotland
YEAR BOOK
2016/2017

Editor
Douglas Galbraith

Published on behalf of
THE CHURCH OF SCOTLAND
by SAINT ANDREW PRESS
121 George Street, Edinburgh EH2 4YN

THE OFFICES OF THE CHURCH

121 George Street
Edinburgh EH2 4YN

Tel: 0131-225 5722
Fax: 0131-220 3113
Website: www.churchofscotland.org.uk/

Office Hours:
Facilities Manager:

Monday–Friday 9:00am–5:00pm
Carole Tait 0131-240 2214

THE COUNCILS OF THE CHURCH
The following five Councils of the Church operate from the Church Offices, 121 George Street, Edinburgh
EH2 4YN (Tel: 0131-225 5722):

- The Council of Assembly
- The Church and Society Council   E-mail: churchandsociety@churchofscotland.org.uk
- The Ministries Council   E-mail: ministries@churchofscotland.org.uk
- The Mission and Discipleship Council   E-mail: mandd@churchofscotland.org.uk
- The World Mission Council   E-mail: world@churchofscotland.org.uk

The Social Care Council (CrossReach) operates from Charis House, 47 Milton Road East, Edinburgh
EH15 2SR

Tel: 0131-657 2000
Fax: 0131-657 5000
E-mail: info@crossreach.org.uk
Website: www.crossreach.org.uk

SCOTTISH CHARITY NUMBERS
The Church of Scotland: unincorporated Councils and Committees	SC011353
The Church of Scotland General Trustees	SC014574
The Church of Scotland Investors Trust	SC022884
The Church of Scotland Trust	SC020269

(For the Scottish Charity Numbers of congregations, see Section 7)

First published in 2016 by SAINT ANDREW PRESS, 121 George Street, Edinburgh EH2 4YN on behalf of THE CHURCH of SCOTLAND

Copyright © THE CHURCH of SCOTLAND, 2016

ISBN 978-0-86153-966-6

It is the Publisher's policy only to use papers that are natural and recyclable and that have been manufactured from timber grown in renewable, properly managed forests. All of the manufacturing processes of the papers are expected to conform to the environmental regulations of the country of origin.

Acceptance of advertisements for inclusion in the *Church of Scotland Year Book* does not imply endorsement of the goods or services or of any views expressed within the advertisements.

British Library Cataloguing in Publication Data
A catalogue record for this book is available from the British Library.

Printed and bound by Bell and Bain Ltd, Glasgow

QUICK DIRECTORY

Action of Churches Together in Scotland (ACTS)	01259 216980
Christian Aid London	020 7620 4444
Christian Aid Scotland	0141-221 7475
Church and Society Council	0131-240 2206
Church of Scotland Insurance Co. Ltd	0131-220 4119
Conforti Institute	01236 607120
Council of Assembly	0131-240 2229
CrossReach	0131-657 2000
Eco-Congregation Scotland	0131-240 2274
Ecumenical Officer	0131-240 2208
Gartmore House	01877 382991
Glasgow Lodging House Mission	0141-552 0285
Iona Community	0141-429 7281
Media Relations Team (Press Office)	0131-240 2278
Media Relations Team (after hours)	07854 783539
Old Churches House, Dunblane (Scottish Churches House)	01786 823663
Pension Trustees (E-mail: pensions@churchofscotland.org.uk)	0131-240 2255
Place for Hope	07884 580359
Principal Clerk (E-mail: pcoffice@churchofscotland.org.uk)	0131-240 2240
Priority Areas Office	0141-248 2905
Safeguarding Service (item 31 in Assembly Committee list)	0131-240 2276
Scottish Churches Organist Training Scheme (SCOTS)	01592 752403
Scottish Churches Parliamentary Office	0131-220 0246
Scottish Storytelling Centre/John Knox House/Netherbow	0131-556 9579
Year Book Editor	01592 752403

Pulpit Supply: Fee and Expenses
See www.churchofscotland.org.uk > Resources > Yearbook > Section 3F

**All correspondence regarding the *Year Book* should be sent to
The Editor, *Church of Scotland Year Book*,
Saint Andrew Press, 121 George Street, Edinburgh EH2 4YN
[E-mail: yearbookeditor@churchofscotland.org.uk]
Tel: 01592 752403**

GENERAL ASSEMBLY OF 2017
The General Assembly of 2017 will convene on
Saturday, 20 May 2017

CONTENTS

		Page
Prefaces		xxvi

1 Assembly Councils, Committees, Departments and Agencies 1

Alphabetical listing of Councils, Committees, Departments and Agencies 1

2 General Information 17

   (1) Other Churches in the United Kingdom............................... 18
   (2) Overseas Churches 19
   (3) Her Majesty's Household in Scotland Ecclesiastical 20
   (4) Recent Lord High Commissioners to the General Assembly................ 20
   (5) Recent Moderators of the General Assembly......................... 21
   (6) Scottish Divinity Faculties 22
   (7) Societies and Associations 23
   (8) Trusts and Funds.................................... 30
   (9) Long Service Certificates 36
  (10) Records of the Church of Scotland................................ 37

3 Church Procedure 39

  (A) The Minister and Baptism 40
  (B) The Minister and Marriage 40
  (C) Conduct of Marriage Services (Code of Good Practice) 40
  (D) Marriage and Civil Partnership (Scotland) Act 2014 40
  (E) Conduct of Funeral Services: Fees.............................. 40
  (F) Pulpit Supply Fees and Expenses.............................. 40
  (G) Procedure in a Vacancy 40

4 The General Assembly of 2016.. 41

  A General Assembly 2016 42
  B The Church of Scotland and the Gaelic Language....................... 44

5 Presbytery Lists 47

Introduction and explanation................................. 48
Key to abbreviations 48
Numerical listing, 1–49, of Presbyteries............................ 48

6 Additional Lists of Personnel 241

  A Ordained Local Ministers 242
    Ordained Local Ministers (Retired List)........................... 243
  B Auxiliary Ministers.................................... 244
    Auxiliary Ministers (Retired List)............................. 245
  C The Diaconate 246
    The Diaconate (Retired List)................................ 247

    The Diaconate (Supplementary List) 249
D Ministers Not in Presbyteries (Practising Certificate) 249
E Ministers Not in Presbyteries (Without Certificate)........................ 254
F Chaplains, Health and Social Care 257
G Chaplains to HM Forces 260
H Readers 262
I Ministries Development Staff.. 277
J Overseas Locations 280
K Overseas Resigned and Retired Mission Partners 281
L Chaplains, Full-time Workplace 281
M Chaplains, Prison.. 282
N Chaplains, University 282
O Representatives on Council Education Committees........................ 282
P Retired Lay Agents 282
Q Ministers Ordained for Sixty Years and Upwards 282
R Deceased Ministers 283

7 **Legal Names and Scottish Charity Numbers for Individual Congregations 285**

8 **Church Buildings: Ordnance Survey National Grid References 287**

9 **Discontinued Parish and Congregational Names........................... 289**

10 **Congregational Statistics – 2015 .... 293**

Index of ADVERTISERS 325
Index of MINISTERS 326
Index of PARISHES AND PLACES 337
Index of SUBJECTS 343

FROM THE MODERATOR

Welcome to the 2016–17 edition of the *Church of Scotland Year Book*, an invaluable resource which will help you make connections with the people of the church, the courts, councils, committees and agencies of the church, the procedures and processes of the church, the practices and beliefs of the church and something of the history of the church.

Connections matter and if the Christian faith is centred on the connection God made with the world through the life and teaching, death and rising again of Jesus of Nazareth, making connections remains at the heart of the church's ministry in all its many shapes and forms.

Having worked as a parish minister in Glasgow, Greenock and Edinburgh, so much of my time has been spent making connections with the people of my congregation and community, and in my role as a minister of Word and Sacrament so much of my ministry has been devoted to helping connect people with the hopes and promises of the Christian faith and with God.

Although much will have changed since the first edition of the *Year Book* was published in 1886, not least the fact that much of the material can now be accessed online, one hundred and thirty years later the basic principle of helping those of us who use the *Year Book* to make connections with all the various aspects and people of the church remains the same.

There is a wealth of information and detail to be found in the pages of the *Year Book* and I would like to express my gratitude to the editor, Douglas Galbraith, for his painstaking work in producing this latest edition.

I have much pleasure in commending the 2016–17 edition of *Church of Scotland Year Book* and I am quite sure it will help you make connections.

G Russell Barr

FACAL O'N MHODERATOR

Fàilte oirbh gu iris 2016/17 de *Leabhar Bliadhnail Eaglais na h-Alba*, goireas ro-luachmhor a bhios 'na chuideachadh airson ceanglaichean a dhèanamh ri muinntir na h-eaglais, cùirtean, comhairlean, comataidhean agus buidhnean na h-eaglais, dòighean-obrachaidh agus iomairtean na h-eaglais, cleachdaidhean agus creideamh na h-eaglais agus beagan mu eachdraidh na h-eaglais.

Tha ceanglaichean cudthromach agus ma tha an creideamh Crìosdail stèidhte air a' cheangal a rinn Dia tre bheatha agus teagasg, bàs agus aiseirigh Iosa o Nàsaret, tha a' dèanamh ceanglaichean fhathast aig cridhe ministrealachd na h-eaglais anns a h-uile cruth agus dòigh.

Nuair a bha mi 'nam mhinistear-sgìre ann an Glaschu, ann an Grianaig agus ann an Dùn Eideann, bha mòran dem ùine air a caitheamh ann a bhith a' dèanamh cheanglaichean ri muinntir mo choitheanail agus mo choimhearsnachd, agus 'nam obair mar mhinistear an Fhacail agus nan Sàcramaid bha cuid mhath dem mhinistrealachd air a gabhail a-steach ann a bhith a' cuideachadh dhaoine gu bhith air an ceangal ri dòchas agus geallaidhean a' chreidimh Chrìosdail agus ri Dia.

Ged a tha iomadh nì air atharrachadh bho chaidh a' cheud dheasachadh den *Leabhar Bhliadhnail* fhoillseachadh ann an 1886, gu h-àraidh a chionn gum faighear mòran den stuth air loidhne, an dèidh sia fichead bliadhna agus deich tha am prìomh amas a' seasamh, a bhith gar cuideachadh-ne a tha a' cleachdadh an *Leabhair Bhliadhnail* ann a bhith a' dèanamh cheanglaichean ri na cuspairean agus na daoine eadar-dhealaichte a bhuineas don eaglais.

Tha beairteas fiosrachaidh agus mion-fhiosrachaidh ri fhaotainn air duilleagan An *Leabhair Bhliadhnail* agus bu toigh leam taing mhòr a thoirt don fhear-dheasachaidh, Dùghlas Mac a' Bhreatnaisch, a tha air obair cho mionaideach a dhèanamh ann a bhith a' toirt leabhar na bliadhna seo gu buil.

Tha e a' toirt mòran toileachaidh dhomh ann a bhith a' moladh dhuibh iris 2016/17 de *Leabhar Bliadhnail Eaglais na h-Alba* agus tha mi làn chinnteach gum bi e 'na chuideachadh ann a bhith a' dèanamh cheanglaichean.

Seòras Ruiseil Barr
translation by the Revd Dr Roderick MacLeod

EDITOR'S PREFACE

It is quite possible that this is the 130th edition of the Year Book. The winning formula of 1886 has changed little in the time. Last year's edition was notable in embracing the electronic media, referring those items that could be looked up at leisure to web pages – our own and those of other councils and committees on the Church's own very comprehensive site as well as the websites of several other bodies where fuller information might be found – and keeping in print such material as might be required on the run. This new edition of the Year Book retains the format introduced last year. What is lost in having everything to hand on the page is amply made up for by the greater breadth of information, continuously brought up to date, that such locations provide, together with the undeniable attractiveness of the presentation. It is hoped that the pathways we offer through the electronic thicket are clear; please tell us if not.

We were encouraged that no great outcry attended last year's innovations, perhaps less than that fielded by my predecessor in 2004 when a cover redesign seemed to some to compromise the 'redness' of the Red Book (by which this publication is often known, to distinguish it from the Blue Book of Assembly reports). For some, the new jacket was neither red enough, for others the red in aggregate insufficiently generous. However, the discussion about the content continues, some favouring the sole use of electronic media, others valuing a print version, both for its handiness and its archival advantages. Some did make contact with concerns and suggestions; we thank them and have taken account of their views where we were able to do so (at what is still an in-between stage – editing the book is an example of interim, if not transitional, ministry!).

One feature that slips quietly away this year is the time-honoured report, albeit sometimes rather idiosyncratic, of the previous General Assembly. For long, those not Commissioners in a particular year were able to learn what transpired, as were those who no doubt intended to be present throughout but whose resolve was not steeled by the danger of forfeiting expenses, as so recently has become the case. (One year during his editorship, Andrew Herron noted that a vote took place with only 59 present in the chamber.) The current incumbent, although his own experience of the debates was always augmented in recollection by the concise but inclusive twice-daily podcasts from old BBC-hand Douglas Aitken, had at least been present in person at Assemblies about which he has written, but retiral last year from the role which required such attendance now precludes an eyewitness account. This, I venture to suggest, is no great loss since in very recent years we (and the rest of the world) have enjoyed thorough and engaging coverage of every minute of the proceedings through the skills and flair of the Church's Communications Department. This material, with that of past years, remains accessible on the website for all to find.

One feature has been partly re-instated. For some time church historian Roy Pinkerton has charted the changes in parish names and recorded these in a way that no name has been lost, and that the successor parish can be found – a benefit not just for the historical record but for legal reasons and for facilitating research into family history. Although this list, continuously updated, remains accessible on our own pages on the Church's website, we also this year offer a record of very recent changes, both to keep track but also so that it can be seen how the Church is regrouping to meet new situations.

Another change this year is to have included the new 'corporate' @churchofscotland email addresses, except where they have not been activated. Some regret this 'globalisation' of their identity, and certainly individual creativity has been compromised. Gone are the wry or the the whimsical, the cosy or the recondite, the literary or the geographical, the intimate or the too-much-information, the nick names and the numbers. Welcome to the corporate, invariable singleinitial-no-dot-surname. Except of course for the favoured few with common names where confusion might occur and so variety and distinctiveness has crept in by the back door. These may surely walk a little taller amongst their colleagues. Most distinctive of all are the two rare ministers, unnamed here, who sport an intrusive dot between initial and surname (typist's error?) who could probably sell them on eBay, like penny blacks printed with the wrong colour of ink!

It is hoped that the Year Book, with its recent changes and perhaps more to come, will not be seen as a book where things have gone missing, a mere skeleton of what once was, but rather as a whole work approached in two dimensions, print and pixel. We may recall the moment in this year's Assembly, as the Columba Declaration debate was about to begin, when the Convener of the Business Committee, whose quips enliven many a day at the Assembly, 'spied' among the Lord High Commissioner's guests in the gallery the Archbishop of Canterbury. That morning the Scotsman had reported the arrival in England of a bone fragment of one of his predecessors, Thomas Becket. 'I can do better', said Dr Browning; 'I bring you the whole Archbishop!'

Douglas Galbraith
yearbookeditor@churchofscotland.org.uk

SECTION 1

Assembly Councils, Committees, Departments and Agencies

Page

The Department of the General Assembly | 2

1.	**Councils**	3
1.1	The Council of Assembly	3
1.2	The Church and Society Council	3
1.3	The Ministries Council	3
1.4	The Mission and Discipleship Council	4
1.5	The Social Care Council	5
1.6	The World Mission Council	6
2.	**Departments, Committees and Agencies**	6
2.1	Assembly Arrangements Committee	6
2.2	Central Properties Department	7
2.3	Central Services Committee	7
2.4	Church of Scotland Trust	7
2.5	Communications Department	8
2.6	Ecumenical Relations Committee	8
2.7	Forces Chaplains Committee	9
2.8	General Trustees	9
2.9	The Guild	10
2.10	Housing and Loan Fund	10
2.11	Human Resources Department	10
2.12	Information Technology Department	11
2.13	Investors Trust	11
2.14	Law Department	11
2.15	Legal Questions Committee	12
2.16	Life and Work	12
2.17	Nomination Committee	12
2.18	Office Management Department	13
2.19	Panel on Review and Reform	13
2.20	Pension Trustees	13
2.21	Safeguarding Service	14
2.22	Saint Andrew Press	14
2.23	Scottish Churches Parliamentary Office	15
2.24	Scottish Storytelling Centre (The Netherbow)	15
2.25	Stewardship and Finance Department	15
2.26	Theological Forum	16

The symbol > used in website information indicates the headings to be selected as they appear

---

THE DEPARTMENT OF THE GENERAL ASSEMBLY

The Department of the General Assembly supports the General Assembly and the Moderator, the Council of Assembly and the Ecumenical Relations Committee. In addition, Departmental staff service the following Committees (qv): Assembly Arrangements, Legal Questions, the Committee to Nominate the Moderator, the Nomination Committee, the Committee on Overtures and Cases, the Committee on Classifying Returns to Overtures and the Central Services Committee. The Clerks of Assembly are available for consultation on matters of Church Law, Practice and Procedure.

Principal Clerk:	Very Rev. John P. Chalmers BD CPS DD
Depute Clerk of the General Assembly:	Rev. George J. Whyte BSc BD DMin
Personal Assistant to the Principal Clerk and Depute Clerk:	Mrs Linda Jamieson Tel. 0131-240 2240
Senior Administration Officer: (Assembly Arrangements and Moderatorial Support)	Mrs Alison Murray MA 0131-225 5722 ext. 2250
Legal and Learning Resources Officer:	Ms Christine Paterson LLB DipLP Tel: 0131-225 5722 ext. 2263
Interfaith Programme Officer:	Ms Mirella Yandoli MDiv MSt
Secretary to the Council of Assembly:	Rev. Martin Scott DipMusEd RSAM BD PhD
Executive Officer:	Mrs Catherine Forsyth MA
Audit and Compliance Officer:	Mrs Debra Livingstone MA FCCA
Senior Administration Officer: (Council of Assembly, Central Services Committee and Nomination Committee)	Mrs Pauline Wilson BA Tel: 0131-240 2229
Worship Development and Mission Statistics Co-ordinator:	Rev. Fiona Tweedie BSc PhD Tel: 0131-240 3007
Ecumenical Officer:	Vacant
Senior Administrator: (Ecumenical Relations)	Miss Rosalind Milne Tel: 0131-225 5722 ext. 2370

Personnel in this department are also listed with the Councils and Committees that they serve

Contact: Tel: 0131-240 2240
　　　　　　Fax: 0131-240 2239
　　　　　　E-mail: pcoffice@churchofscotland.org.uk
Further information:
www.churchofscotland.org.uk > About us > Councils, committees > Departments > General Assembly

1. COUNCILS

1.1 THE COUNCIL OF ASSEMBLY

The function of the Council is to co-ordinate, support and evaluate the work of the Councils and Committees of the Church, to assist the General Assembly in determining and implementing policies, and to take necessary administrative decisions in between General Assemblies. The voting members of the Council of Assembly act as the Charity Trustees for the Unincorporated Councils and Committees of the General Assembly: Scottish Charity No. SC011353.

Convener: Dr Sally E. Bonnar MB ChB FRCPsych
Vice-Convener: Miss Catherine Coull LLB
Secretary: Rev. Martin Scott DipMusEd RSAM BD PhD

Contact: Mrs. Pauline Wilson BA, Senior Administrative Officer
                Tel: 0131-240 2229, E-mail: pwilson@churchofscotland.org.uk
Further information:
www.churchofscotland.org.uk > About us > Councils, committees > Councils > Council of Assembly

1.2 THE CHURCH AND SOCIETY COUNCIL

The Council seeks to engage on behalf of the Church in national, political and social issues through research, theological reflection, resourcing the local church, and by engaging with leaders in civic society, public bodies, professional associations and other networks. The Council seeks to put the wisdom of local congregations and those with lived experience of poverty and injustice at the heart of its work. Its focus for the next decade, after a consultation involving 10,000 respondents: investing in young people, local communities where people flourish, the health and wellbeing of all, caring for creation, global friendships, an economy driven by equality, doing politics differently.

Convener: Rev. Richard E. Frazer BA BD DMin
Vice-Conveners: Wendy Young BSc PGCE MLitt
                Pauline Edmiston BD
Secretary: Rev. H. Martin J. Johnstone MA BD MTh PhD
                mjohnstone@churchofscotland.org.uk

Contact: churchandsociety@churchofscotland.org.uk   Tel: 0131-240 2206
Further information:
www.churchofscotland.org.uk > About us > Councils, committees > Councils > Church and Society
www.churchofscotland.org.uk > speak out

1.3   THE MINISTRIES COUNCIL

The Council's remit is to recruit, train and support ministries in every part of Scotland, to monitor their deployment, working in partnership with ecumenical, inter-faith and statutory agencies, and giving priority to the poorest and most marginalised sections of the community.

Convener:	Rev. Neil M Glover
Vice-Conveners:	Rev. Colin M. Brough BSc BD
	Dr John Dent MB ChB MMEd
	Rev. Marjory A. MacLean LLB BD PhD RNR
	Rev. Derek H.N. Pope BD

Council Secretary:	Rev Jayne E. Scott BA MEd MBA
Depute:	Ms Catherine Skinner BA MA
Priority Areas:	Ms Shirley Grieve BA PGCE (0141-248 2905)
Education and Support:	Rev. Marjory McPherson LLB BD
Partnership Development:	Rev. Angus R. Mathieson MA BD
Human Resources:	Mr Daran Golby BA CIPD
Training Development:	Mr David Plews MA MTh
Pastoral Support:	Mrs Gabrielle Dench LLB BA MPC
Go For It:	Vacant
Contact:	Tel: 0131-225 5722; Fax: 0131 240 2201; E-mail: ministries@ churchofscotland.org.uk

Further information:
www.churchofscotland.org.uk > About us > Councils, committees > Councils > Ministries Council
www.churchofscotland.org.uk > Serve > Ministries Council > Ministries in the Church
Pulpit Supply Fees:
www.churchofscotland.org.uk/yearbook > Section 3F

1.4   THE MISSION AND DISCIPLESHIP COUNCIL

The Council's remit is to stimulate and support the Church by the provision of resources nationally, regionally and locally in worship, witness, mission and discipleship. This includes the development of strategies and materials in the areas of adult education, resourcing elders, work with young adults, young people and children (including those with particular needs and disabilities), as well as in liturgy, and church art and architecture.

Convener:	Rev. Norman A. Smith MA BD
Vice-Conveners:	Rev. Daniel J.M. Carmichael MA BD
	Rev. W. Martin Fair BA BD DMin
	Rev. Jamie Milliken BD

Council Secretary:	Rev. Dr Alister W. Bull BD (Hons) DipMin MTh

Church Without Walls: Mrs Lesley Hamilton-Messer MA
Congregational Learning: Mr Ronald H. Clarke BEng MSc PGCE
Resourcing Worship: Mr Graham Fender-Allison BA

Church Art and Architecture:
Convener: Rev. William T. Hogg MA BD
Contact: bwaller@churchofscotland.org.uk

Contact: Eva Elder
         (E-mail: mandd@churchofscotland.org.uk)
Further information:
www.churchofscotland.org.uk > About us > Councils, committees > Mission and Discipleship
www.resourcingmission.org.uk

Church Art and Architecture www.resourcingmission.org.uk > CARTA

For The Netherbow: Scottish Storytelling Centre see below 2.24
For Life and Work see below 2.16
For Saint Andrew Press see below 2.22

1.5 THE SOCIAL CARE COUNCIL
(CrossReach)
Charis House, 47 Milton Road East, Edinburgh EH15 2SR
Tel: 0131-657 2000; Fax: 0131-657 5000
E-mail: info@crossreach.org.uk; Website: www.crossreach.org.uk

The Social Care Council, known as CrossReach, provides social-care services as part of the Christian witness of the Church to the people of Scotland, and engages with other bodies in responding to emerging areas of need. CrossReach operates 75 services across the country.

Convener: Mr Bill Steele
Vice-Conveners: Rev. Richard Begg
                   Rev. Hugh M Stewart

Chief Executive Officer: Peter Bailey (peter.bailey@crossreach.org.uk)

Director of Services to Older People: Allan Logan (allan.logan@crossreach.org.uk)
Director of Adult Care Services: Calum Murray (calum.murray@crossreach.org.uk)
Director of Children and Families: Viv Dickenson (viv.dickenson@crossreach.org.uk)
Director of Finance and Resources: Ian Wauchope (ian.wauchope@crossreach.org.uk)
Director of Human Resources and
   Organisational Development: Mari Rennie (mari.rennie@crossreach.org.uk)

Further information:
www.crossreach.org.uk

For sharing local experience and inititatives:
www.socialcareforum.scot

1.6   THE WORLD MISSION COUNCIL

The Council's remit is to enable and encourage the Church of Scotland to accompany partner churches around the world and to keep the Church informed about issues and engaged in this endeavour as together we seek to live the Christian life and offer support to each other in our witness to Christ in the world. The Council is also the principal link with Christian Aid.

Convener: Rev. Iain D. Cunningham MA BD
Vice-Conveners: Rev. Susan M. Brown BD DipMin
                  Mrs Valerie Brown

Council Secretary: Rev. Ian W. Alexander BA BD STM
Secretaries: Mrs Jennie Chinembiri (Africa and Caribbean)
                  Ms Carol Finlay (Twinning and Local Development)
                  Mr Kenny Roger (Middle East Secretary)
                  Mr Sandy Sneddon (Asia)
Administration:

Contact: Tel: 0131-225 5722
              E-mail: world@churchofscotland.org.uk
Further Information:
www.churchofscotland.org.uk > About us > Councils, committees > Councils > World Mission
www.churchofscotland.org.uk > Serve > World Mission

---

2.   DEPARTMENTS, COMMITTEES AND AGENCIES

2.1   ASSEMBLY ARRANGEMENTS COMMITTEE

Convener: Rev. Derek Browning MA BD DMin
Vice-Convener: Mrs Judith J.H. Pearson LLB LLM
Secretary: Principal Clerk
                Tel. 0131-240 2240
                E-mail: pc@churchofscotland.org.uk

Further information:
www.churchofscotland.org.uk > About us > General Assembly
www.churchofscotland.org.uk > About us > Councils, committees > Committees > Assembly Arrangements

2.2   CENTRAL PROPERTIES DEPARTMENT

Remit: to provide property, facilities and health and safety services to the Councils and Departments of the central administration of the Church.

Property, Health and Safety Manager: Colin Wallace
Property, Health and Safety Officer: Jacqueline Collins
Property Officer: Eunice Hessell
Support Assistant: Joyce Anderson

Contact: Tel: 0131-240 2254
              E-mail: cpd@churchofscotland.org.uk

2.3 CENTRAL SERVICES COMMITTEE

The remit of this committee draws together departments which carry out the central day-to-day service work of the Church: Office Management, Central Properties, Information Technology and Human Resources Departments.

Convener: Mr David Brackenridge BSc
Vice-Convener: Mrs Mary Sweetland BSc MBA CStat
Administrative Secretary: Mrs Pauline Wilson BA

Contact: Tel: 0131-240 2229
                             E-mail: pwilson@churchofscotland.org.uk

Further Information:
www.churchofscotland.org.uk > About us > Councils, committees > Central Services

2.4   CHURCH OF SCOTLAND TRUST

Chairman: Mr John M. Hodge WS
Vice-Chairman: Mr Thomas C Watson
Treasurer: Mrs Anne F. Macintosh BA CA
Secretary and Clerk: Mrs Jennifer M. Hamilton BA
                        Tel: 0131-240 2222
                        E-mail: jhamilton@churchofscotland.org.uk

Further information:
www.churchofscotland.org.uk > About us > Councils, committees > Departments > Church of Scotland Trust

2.5   COMMUNICATIONS DEPARTMENT

Head of Communications: Seonag Mackinnon
Communications Manager: Rob Flett
Communications and Media Relations Team
    Senior Communications Officer: Helen Silvis
    Communications Officer: Cameron Brooks
    Communications Assistant: Jane Bristow
Web Editor: Jason Derr
Web Developer: Alan Murray
Design Team Leader: Chris Flexen
Senior Designer: Steve Walker

Contact Media Relations: Tels. 0131-240 2278, 0131-240 2268
                            (After hours) 07854 783539
Contact department: 0131-240 2204
Further information:
www.churchofscotland.org.uk > About us > Councils, committees > Departments > Communications

---

2.6   ECUMENICAL RELATIONS COMMITTEE

The Committee includes five members who are each a member of one of the five Councils, plus representatives of other denominations in Scotland, Church of Scotland representatives on British and international ecumenical bodies, with the General Secretary of ACTS as a corresponding member.

Convener: Rev. Alison P. McDonald MA BD
Vice-Convener: Rev. Calum I. MacLeod BA BD
Secretary and Ecumenical Officer: Vacant
Senior Administrator: Miss Rosalind Milne

Contact: ecumenical@churchofscotland.org.uk
            Tel. 0131-240 2208

Further information:
www.churchofscotland.org.uk > About us > Councils, committees > Committees > Ecumenical Relations Committee
www.churchofscotland.org.uk > Connect > Ecumenism
www.churchofscotland.org.uk > Resources > Subjects > Ecumenical Resources
World Council of Churches:
www.oikumene.org
Churches Together in Britain and Ireland:
www.ctbi.org.uk

Action of Churches Together in Scotland:
www.acts-scotland.org
For other international ecumenical bodies see Committee's web pages as above
See also 'Other Churches in the United Kingdom' page 18

2.7   FORCES CHAPLAINS COMMITTEE

Convener: Rev. Gordon T. Craig BD DipMin
Vice-Convener: Rev. John A.H. Murdoch BA BD DPSS
Secretary: Mr John K. Thomson, Ministries Council
                       Tel: 0131-225 5722
                       E-mail: jthomson@churchofscotland.org.uk

Further information:
www.churchofscotland.org.uk > About us > Councils, committees > Forces Chaplains
Committee
A list of Chaplains is found on page 260

2.8   GENERAL TRUSTEES

Chairman: Mr Iain C. Douglas RD BArch FRIAS
Vice-Chairman: Mr Roger G.G. Dodd DipBldgCons(RICS) FRICS
Secretary and Clerk: Mr David D. Robertson LLB NP
Depute Secretary and Clerk: Mr Keith S. Mason LLB NP
Assistant Secretaries: Ms Claire L. Cowell LLB (Glebes)
                                            Mrs Morag J. Menneer BSc MRICS (Glebes)
                                            Mr Brian D. Waller LLB (Ecclesiastical Buildings)
                                            Mr. Neil Page BSc MCIOB
Safe Buildings Consultant: Mr Brian Auld ChEHO MREHIS FRSPH GradIOSH
Energy Conservation: Mr Robert Lindores FInstPa
Treasurer: Mrs Anne F. Macintosh BA CA
Finance Manager: Mr Alex Semple FCCA

Buildings insurance,   Church of Scotland Insurance Services Ltd.
all enquiries to   121 George Street, Edinburgh EH2 4YN
                                            Tel: 0131-220 4119, Fax: 0131-220 4120
                                            E-mail: enquiries@cosic.co.uk

Contact: gentrustees@churchofscotland.org.uk   0131-225 5722 ext. 2261
Further information:
www.churchofscotland.org.uk > About us > Councils, committees > Departments > General
Trustees

2.9   THE GUILD

The Church of Scotland Guild is a movement within the Church of Scotland whose aim is 'to invite and encourage both women and men to commit their lives to Jesus Christ and to enable them to express their faith in worship, prayer and action'.

Convener: Rosemary Johnston BA
Vice-Convener: Marge Paterson
General Secretary: Iain W. Whyte BA DCE DMS

Contact: Tel: 0131-240 2217
E-mail: guild@churchofscotland.org.uk

Further information:
www.cos-guild.org.uk
www.churchofscotland.org.uk > Serve > The Guild

2.10   HOUSING AND LOAN FUND

Chairman: Rev. Ian Taylor BD ThM
Deputy Chairman: Rev. MaryAnn R. Rennie BD MTh
Secretary: Lin J. Macmillan MA
                     Tel: 0131-225 5722 ext. 2310
                     E-mail: lmacmillan@churchofscotland.org.uk
Property Manager: Hilary J. Hardy
Property Assistant: John Lunn

Further information:
www.churchofscotland.org.uk > About us > Councils, committees > Departments > Housing and Loan Fund

2.11   HUMAN RESOURCES DEPARTMENT

Interim Head of Support Services: Lynn Haemmerie
Human Resources Manager: Daran Golby (Ministries)
                                    Karen Smith (Operations)
                                    Elaine McCloghry (Organisational Development)

Contact: Tel: 0131-240 2270
E-mail: hr@churchofscotland.org.uk

2.12   INFORMATION TECHNOLOGY DEPARTMENT

Information Technology Manager: David Malcolm
Tel: 0131-240 2247

Contact: Tel: 0131-240 2245
E-mail: itdept@churchofscotland.org.uk
Further information:
www.churchofscotland.org.uk > About us > Councils, committees > Committees > IT

2.13   INVESTORS TRUST

Chairman: Ms Catherine Y. Alexander
Vice-Chairman: Mr Brian J. Duffin
Treasurer: Mrs Anne F. Macintosh BA CA
Secretary: Mrs Nicola Robertson
                  E-mail: investorstrust@churchofscotland.org.uk

Further information:
www.churchofscotland.org.uk > About us > Councils, committees > Departments > Investors Trust

2.14   LAW DEPARTMENT

Solicitor of the Church
and of the General Trustees: Miss Mary Macleod LLB NP
Depute Solicitor: Mrs Jennifer Hamilton BA NP
Solicitors: Mrs Elspeth Annan LLB NP
                              Miss Susan Killean LLB NP
                              Mrs Anne Steele LLB NP
                              Mrs Jennifer Campbell LLB LLM NP
                              Gregor Buick LLB WS NP
                              Mrs Madelaine Sproule LLB NP
                              Gordon Barclay LLB BSc MSc MPhil PhD
                              David Stihler LLB MA

Contact: Tel: 0131-225 5722 ext. 2230; Fax: 0131-240 2246.
E-mail: lawdept@churchofscotland.org.uk

Further information:
www.churchofscotland.org.uk > About us > Councils, committees > Committees > Law

2.15   LEGAL QUESTIONS COMMITTEE

The Committee's remit is to advise the General Assembly on questions of Church and Constitutional Law, assist Agencies of the Assembly in preparing and interpreting legislation, compile statistics and arrange for the care of Church Records.

Convener: Rev. George S. Cowie BSc BD
Vice-Convener: Rev. Alistair S. May LLB BD PhD
Secretary: Principal Clerk
Legal and Learning Resources Officer: Ms Christine Paterson LLB DipLP

Contact: Tel. 0131-240 2240
                    E-mail: pc@churchofscotland.org.uk

Further information:
www.churchofscotland.org.uk > About us > Councils, committees > Committees > Legal Questions

---

2.16   LIFE AND WORK
the Church of Scotland's monthly magazine

The magazine's purpose is to keep the Church informed about events in church life at home and abroad and to provide a forum for Christian opinion and debate on a variety of topics. It has an independent editorial policy. Contributions which are relevant to any aspect of the Christian faith are welcome. The magazine has a cover price of £2.20 and an audited sale of 18,475 in 2105 – a opportunity also for advertisers to reach a discerning readership in all parts of Scotland, and via the website.

Editor: Lynne McNeil
        Tel: 0131-225 5722; Fax: 0131-240 2207
        E-mail: magazine@lifeandwork.org

Further information:
www.lifeandwork.org (where subscriptions may be taken out)
www.churchofscotland.org.uk > News and Events > Life and Work

---

2.17   NOMINATION COMMITTEE

Convener: Rev. Kenneth Stott MA BD
Vice-Convener: Miss Ann Lyall DCS
Secretary: Rev. Martin Scott DipMusEd RSAM BD PhD

Contact: Mrs Pauline Wilson BA, Senior Administration Officer
Tel: 0131-240 2229
E-mail: pwilson@churchofscotland.org.uk

Further information:
www.churchofscotland.org.uk > About us > Councils, committees > Committees > Nomination Committee

2.18   OFFICE MANAGEMENT DEPARTMENT

Facilities Manager: Carole Tait
Tel: 0131-240 2214, E-mail: ctait@churchofscotland.org.uk

Further information:
www.churchofscotland.org.uk > About us > Councils, committees > Committees > Office management

2.19   PANEL ON REVIEW AND REFORM

Convener: Rev. Graham Duffin BSc BD DipEd
Vice-Convener: Rev. David C. Cameron BD CertMin

Contact: Tel: 0131-225 5722 ext. 2336

Further information:
www.churchofscotland.org.uk > About us > Councils, committees > Committees > Panel on Review and Reform

2.20   PENSION TRUSTEES

Chairman: Mr W. John McCafferty ACII APFS TEP
Vice-Chairman: Mr Graeme R. Caughey BSc FFIA
Secretary and
Pensions Manager: Mr Steven D. Kaney BSc DipPMI Dip IEB
Pensions Administrators: Mrs Fiona McCulloch-Stevenson
                         Miss Marshall Paterson
                         Ms Birgit Mosemann
Administrative Assistant: Mrs Diana Knowles

Contact: Tel: 0131-240 2255
E-mail: pensions@churchofscotland.org.uk

Further information:
www.churchofscotland.org.uk > About us > Councils, committees > Departments > Pension Trustees

2.21   SAFEGUARDING SERVICE

The service ensures that the Church has robust structures and policies in place for the prevention of harm and abuse of children and adults at risk; and to ensure a timely and appropriate response when harm or abuse is witnessed, suspected or reported.

Convener: Rev. Karen K. Campbell BD MTh DMin
Vice-Convener: Sheila Ritchie MSc DipSW MSc (Criminal Justice Social Work)
Head of Safeguarding: Richard Crosse MA (Cantab) MSW CQSW
Assistant Head of Safeguarding: Jennifer Milligan CQSW DipSW

Contact: Tel: 0131-240 2256; Fax: 0131-220 3113
E-mail: safeguarding@churchofscotland.org.uk

Further Information:
www.churchofscotland.org.uk > About us > Councils, committees > Departments > Safeguarding Service

2.22   SAINT ANDREW PRESS

Saint Andrew Press is managed on behalf of the Church of Scotland by Hymns Ancient and Modern Ltd and publishes a broad range of books and resources, ranging from the much-loved William Barclay series of New Testament *Daily Study Bible* commentaries to the *Pilgrim Guide to Scotland*. The full catalogue can be viewed on the Saint Andrew Press website (see below).

Contact: Christine Smith, Publishing Director (Tel: 0207 776 7546; E-mail: christine@ hymnsam.co.uk)

Further information: www.standrewpress.com

2.23 SCOTTISH CHURCHES PARLIAMENTARY OFFICE
121 George Street, Edinburgh EH2 4YN

The Office exists to build fruitful relationships between the Churches and the Scottish and UK Parliaments and Governments, seeking to engage reflectively in the political process, translate their commitment to the welfare of Scotland into parliamentary debate, and contribute their experience and faith-based reflection on it to the decision-making process.

Scottish Churches Parliamentary Officer: Chloe Clemmons MA MA (Human Rights)

Contact: Tel: 0131-220 2276
E-mail: chloe@actsparl.org

Further information:
www.churchofscotland.org.uk > Speak out > Politics and Government
www.actsparl.org

2.24 SCOTTISH STORYTELLING CENTRE (THE NETHERBOW)

The integrated facilities of the **Netherbow Theatre** and the **John Knox House Museum**, together with the outstanding conference and reception areas, form an important cultural and visitor centre on the Royal Mile in Edinburgh and provide advice and assistance nationally in the use of the arts in a diversity of settings. Mission and Discipleship Council are pleased to host TRACS (Traditional Arts and Culture Scotland), a grant-funded body who provide an extensive cultural and literary programme.

Contact: Tel: 0131-556 9579, Fax: 0131-557 5224
E-mail: reception@scottishstorytellingcentre.com

Further information:
www.scottishstorytellingcentre.co.uk

2.25 STEWARDSHIP AND FINANCE DEPARTMENT

General Treasurer:	Mrs Anne F. Macintosh BA CA
Head of Stewardship:	
Deputy Treasurer (Congregational Finance):	Mr Archie McDowall BA CA
Deputy Treasurer (Unincorporated Councils and Committees):	Mr Bob Cowan BCom CA
Finance Managers:	Alex Semple FCCA
	Mrs Elaine Macadie BA CA
	Mrs Catriona M. Scrimgeour BSc ACA
Pensions Accountant:	Mrs Kay C. Hastie BSc CA

Contact: E-mail: sfadmin@churchofscotland.org.uk
Further information and details of local consultants:
www.churchofscotland.org.uk > About us > Councils, committees > Departments > Stewardship
and Budget
www.churchofscotland.org.uk > Resources > Subjects > National Stewardship Programme

2.26   THEOLOGICAL FORUM

The purpose of the Forum is to continue to develop and bring to expression doctrinal understanding of the Church with reference to Scripture and to the confessional standards of the
Church of Scotland, and the implications of this for worship and witness in and beyond
contemporary Scotland. It responds to requests to undertake enquiries as they arise, draws the
Church's attention to particular matters requiring theological work, and promotes theological
reflection throughout the Church.

Convener:	Very Rev. Prof. Iain R. Torrance TD DPhil DD DTheol LHD FRSE
Vice-Convener:	Rev. Donald G. MacEwan MA BD PhD
Secretary:	Vacant

Further Information:
www.churchofscotland.org.uk > About us > Councils, committees > Committees > Theological
Forum

SECTION 2

General Information

		Page
(1)	Other Churches in the United Kingdom	18
(2)	Overseas Churches	19
(3)	Her Majesty's Household in Scotland Ecclesiastical	20
(4)	Recent Lord High Commissioners to the General Assembly	20
(5)	Recent Moderators of the General Assembly	21
(6)	Scottish Divinity Faculties	22
(7)	Societies and Associations	23
(8)	Trusts and Funds	30
(9)	Long Service Certificates	36
(10)	Records of the Church of Scotland	37

(1) OTHER CHURCHES IN THE UNITED KINGDOM

ACTION OF CHURCHES TOGETHER IN SCOTLAND (ACTS)
Eaglaisean Còmhla n Gnìomh an Alba
General Secretary: Rev Matthew Z. Ross LLB BD MTh FSAScot, Jubilee House, Forthside Way, Stirling FK8 1QZ (Tel: 01259 216980; E-mail: matthewross@acts-scotland.org; Website: www.acts-scotland.org).

THE UNITED FREE CHURCH OF SCOTLAND
General Secretary: Rev. John Fulton BSc BD, United Free Church Offices, 11 Newton Place, Glasgow G3 7PR (Tel: 0141-332 3435; E-mail: office@ufcos.org.uk).

THE FREE CHURCH OF SCOTLAND
Principal Clerk: Rev. Callum Macleod, 15 North Bank Street, The Mound, Edinburgh EH1 2LS (Tel: 0131-226 5286; E-mail: offices@freechurch.org).

FREE CHURCH OF SCOTLAND (CONTINUING)
Principal Clerk: Rev. John MacLeod, Free Church Manse, Portmahomack, Tain IV20 1YL (Tel: 01862 871467; E-mail: principalclerk@fccontinuing.org).

THE FREE PRESBYTERIAN CHURCH OF SCOTLAND
Clerk of Synod: Rev. John MacLeod, 6 Church Avenue, Sidcup, Kent DA14 6BU (E-mail: jmacl265@aol.com).

ASSOCIATED PRESBYTERIAN CHURCHES
Clerk of Presbytery: Rev. J.R. Ross Macaskill, Bruach Taibh, 2 Borve, Arnisort, Isle of Skye IV51 9PS (Tel: 01470 582264; E-mail: emailjrrm@gmail.com).

THE REFORMED PRESBYTERIAN CHURCH OF SCOTLAND
Clerk of Presbytery: Rev. Andrew Quigley, Church Offices, 48 North Bridge Street, Airdrie ML6 6NE (Tel: 01236 620107; E-mail: sandrewq@aol.com).

THE PRESBYTERIAN CHURCH IN IRELAND
Clerk of the General Assembly and General Secretary: Rev. Trevor Gribben, Assembly Buildings, 2–10 Fisherwick Place, Belfast BT1 6DW (Tel: 028 9041 7208; E-mail: clerk@presbyterianireland.org).

THE PRESBYTERIAN CHURCH OF WALES
General Secretary: Rev. Meiron Morris, Tabernacle Chapel, 81 Merthyr Road, Whitchurch, Cardiff CF14 1DD (Tel: 02920 627465; E-mail: swyddfa.office@ebcpcw.org.uk).

THE UNITED REFORMED CHURCH
General Secretary: Rev. John Proctor, 86 Tavistock Place, London WC1H 9RT (Tel: 020 7916 8646; Fax: 020 7916 2021; E-mail: john.proctor@urc.org.uk).

UNITED REFORMED CHURCH SYNOD OF SCOTLAND
Synod Clerk: Mr Bill Robson, United Reformed Church, 113 West Regent Street, Glasgow G1 2RU (Tel: 0141-248 5382; E-mail: brobson@urcscotland.org.uk).

BAPTIST UNION OF SCOTLAND
General Director: Rev. Alan Donaldson, 48 Speirs Wharf, Glasgow G4 9TH (Tel: 0141-423 6169; E-mail: admin@scottishbaptist.org.uk).

CONGREGATIONAL FEDERATION IN SCOTLAND
Chair: Rev. May-Kane Logan, 93 Cartside Road, Busby, Glasgow G76 8QD (Tel: 0141-237 1349; E-mail: maycita@talktalk.net).

RELIGIOUS SOCIETY OF FRIENDS (QUAKERS)
Martin Burnell, Clerk to the General Meeting for Scotland, 25 Learmonth Grove, Edinburgh EH4 1BR (Tel: 0131-343 2592; E-mail: mburnell@mbees.net). From January 2017, Adwoa Bittle, 4 Burnside Park, Pitcairngreen, Perth PH1 3BF (Tel: 01738 583108; E-mail: adwoabittle@hotmail.co.uk).

ROMAN CATHOLIC CHURCH
Mgr Hugh Bradley, General Secretary, Bishops' Conference of Scotland, 64 Aitken Street, Airdrie ML6 6LT (Tel: 01236 764061; E-mail: gensec@bpsconfscot.com).

THE SALVATION ARMY
Lt-Col. Carol Bailey, Secretary for Scotland and Divisional Commander East Scotland Division, Headquarters and Scotland Secretariat, 12A Dryden Road, Loanhead EH20 9LZ (Tel: 0131-440 9101; E-mail: carol.bailey@salvationarmy.org.uk).

SCOTTISH EPISCOPAL CHURCH
Secretary General: Mr John F. Stuart, 21 Grosvenor Crescent, Edinburgh EH12 5EL (Tel: 0131-225 6357; E-mail: secgen@scotland.anglican.org).

THE SYNOD OF THE METHODIST CHURCH IN SCOTLAND
District Administrator: Mrs Fiona Inglis, Methodist Church Office, Old Churches House, Kirk Street, Dunblane FK15 0AJ (Tel/Fax: 01786 820295; E-mail: fiona@methodistchurchinscotland.net).

GENERAL SYNOD OF THE CHURCH OF ENGLAND
Secretary General: Mr William Nye, Church House, Great Smith Street, London SW1P 3NZ (Tel: 020 7898 1360; E-mail: enquiry@churchofengland.org).

---

(2) OVERSEAS CHURCHES

See www.churchofscotland.org.uk > Serve > World Mission > Our partner churches

(3) HER MAJESTY'S HOUSEHOLD IN SCOTLAND
ECCLESIASTICAL

Dean of the Order of the Thistle and Dean of the Chapel Royal:

Very Rev. Prof. Iain R. Torrance
  TD DPhil DD DTheol LHD FRSE

Domestic Chaplains:

Rev. Kenneth I. Mackenzie DL BD CPS
Rev. Neil N. Gardner MA BD RNR

Chaplains in Ordinary:

Rev. Norman W. Drummond CBE MA BD DUniv FRSE
Rev. Alastair H. Symington MA BD
Rev. James M. Gibson TD LTh LRAM
Very Rev. Angus Morrison MA BD PhD
Very Rev. E. Lorna Hood MA BD DD
Rev. Alistair G. Bennett BSc BD
Rev. Susan M. Brown BD DipMin
Very Rev. John P. Chalmers BD CPS DD
Rev. Prof. David A.S. Fergusson
  OBE MA BD DPhil DD FBA FRSE

Extra Chaplains:

Rev. Kenneth MacVicar MBE DFC TD MA
Rev. Alwyn J.C. Macfarlane MA
Rev. John MacLeod MA
Very Rev. James L. Weatherhead CBE MA LLB DD
Very Rev. James A. Simpson BSc BD STM DD
Very Rev. James Harkness KCVO CB OBE MA DD
Rev. John L. Paterson MA BD STM
Rev. Charles Robertson LVO MA
Very Rev. John B. Cairns KCVO LTh LLB LLD DD
Very Rev. Gilleasbuig I. Macmillan
  KCVO MA BD Drhc DD FRSE HRSA FRCSEd
Very Rev. Finlay A.J. Macdonald MA BD PhD DD

---

(4) RECENT LORD HIGH COMMISSIONERS
TO THE GENERAL ASSEMBLY

1990/91	The Rt Hon. Donald MacArthur Ross FRSE
1992/93	The Rt Hon. Lord Macfarlane of Bearsden KT FRSE
1994/95	Lady Marion Fraser LT
1996	Her Royal Highness the Princess Royal LT LG GCVO
1997	The Rt Hon. Lord Macfarlane of Bearsden KT FRSE
1998/99	The Rt Hon. Lord Hogg of Cumbernauld
2000	His Royal Highness the Prince Charles, Duke of Rothesay KG KT GCB OM

2001/02	The Rt Hon. Viscount Younger of Leckie
	Her Majesty the Queen attended the opening of the General Assembly of 2002
2003/04	The Rt Hon. Lord Steel of Aikwood KT KBE
2005/06	The Rt Hon. Lord Mackay of Clashfern KT
2007	His Royal Highness the Prince Andrew, Duke of York KG KCVO
2008/09	The Rt Hon. George Reid KT MA
2010/11	Lord Wilson of Tillyorn KT GCMG PRSE
2012/13	The Rt Hon. Lord Selkirk of Douglas QC MA LLB
2014	His Royal Highness the Prince Edward, Earl of Wessex KG GCVO
2015	The Rt Hon. Lord Hope of Craighead KT PC FRSE
2016	The Rt Hon. Lord Hope of Craighead KT PC FRSE

For Lord High Commissioners prior to 1990 see www.churchofscotland.org.uk/resources/yearbook > Section 2.4

(5) RECENT MODERATORS
OF THE GENERAL ASSEMBLY

1987	Duncan Shaw of Chapelverna Bundesverdienstkreutz PhD ThDr Drhc, Edinburgh: Craigentinny St Christopher's
1988	James A. Whyte MA LLD DD DUniv, University of St Andrews
1989	William J.G. McDonald MA BD DD, Edinburgh: Mayfield
1990	Robert Davidson MA BD DD FRSE, University of Glasgow
1991	William B.R. Macmillan MA BD LLD DD, Dundee: St Mary's
1992	Hugh R. Wyllie MA DD FCIBS, Hamilton: Old Parish Church
1993	James L. Weatherhead CBE MA LLB DD, Principal Clerk of Assembly
1994	James A. Simpson BSc BD STM DD, Dornoch Cathedral
1995	James Harkness KCVO CB OBE MA DD, Chaplain General (Emeritus)
1996	John H. McIndoe MA BD STM DD, London: St Columba's linked with Newcastle: St Andrew's
1997	Alexander McDonald BA DUniv CMIWSc, General Secretary, Department of Ministry
1998	Alan Main TD MA BD STM PhD DD, University of Aberdeen
1999	John B. Cairns KCVO LTh LLB LLD DD, Dumbarton: Riverside
2000	Andrew R.C. McLellan CBE MA BD STM DD, Edinburgh: St Andrew's and St George's
2001	John D. Miller BA BD DD, Glasgow: Castlemilk East
2002	Finlay A.J. Macdonald MA BD PhD DD, Principal Clerk of Assembly
2003	Iain R. Torrance TD DPhil DD DTheol LHD FRSE, University of Aberdeen
2004	Alison Elliot OBE MA MSc PhD LLD DD FRSE, Associate Director CTPI
2005	David W. Lacy BA BD DLitt DL, Kilmarnock: Henderson
2006	Alan D. McDonald LLB BD MTh DLitt DD, Cameron linked with St Andrews: St Leonard's
2007	Sheilagh M. Kesting BA BD DD, Secretary of Ecumenical Relations Committee
2008	David W. Lunan MA BD DUniv DLitt DD, Clerk to the Presbytery of Glasgow

2009	William C. Hewitt BD DipPS, Greenock: Westburn
2010	John C. Christie BSc BD MSB CBiol, Interim Minister
2011	A. David K. Arnott MA BD, St Andrews: Hope Park with Strathkinness
2012	Albert O. Bogle BD MTh, Bo'ness: St Andrew's
2013	E. Lorna Hood MA BD DD, Renfrew: North
2014	John P. Chalmers BD CPS DD, Principal Clerk of Assembly
2015	Angus Morrison MA BD PhD, Orwell and Portmoak
2016	G. Russell Barr BA BD MTh DMin, Edinburgh: Cramond

For Moderators prior to 1988 see www.churchofscotland.org.uk/yearbook > Section 2.5

MATTER OF PRECEDENCE
The Lord High Commissioner to the General Assembly of the Church of Scotland (while the Assembly is sitting) ranks next to the Sovereign and the Duke of Edinburgh and before the rest of the Royal Family.

The Moderator of the General Assembly of the Church of Scotland ranks next to the Lord Chancellor of Great Britain and before the Keeper of the Great Seal of Scotland (the First Minister) and the Dukes.

---

(6) SCOTTISH DIVINITY FACULTIES
[* denotes a Minister of the Church of Scotland]

ABERDEEN
(School of Divinity, History and Philosophy)
50–52 College Bounds, Old Aberdeen AB24 3DS
(Tel: 01224 272366; Fax: 01224 273750; E-mail: divinity@abdn.ac.uk)

Master of Christ's College: Rev. Prof. John Swinton* BD PhD RNM RNMD
  (E-mail: christs-college@abdn.ac.uk)
Head of School: Prof. John Morrison MA PhD
Deputy Head of School: Prof. Paul Nimmo MA DipIA, BD ThM PhD

For teaching staff and further information see www.abdn.ac.uk/sdhp/

ST ANDREWS
(University College of St Mary)
St Mary's College, St Andrews, Fife KY16 9JU
(Tel: 01334 462850/1; Fax: 01334 462852; E-mail: divinity@st-andrews.ac.uk)

Principal: Very Rev. Ian C. Bradley* BA MA DPhil
Head of School: Rev. Stephen Holmes BA MA MTh PhD

For teaching staff and further information see www.st-andrews.ac.uk/divinity/

EDINBURGH
(School of Divinity and New College)
New College, Mound Place, Edinburgh EH1 2LX
(Tel: 0131-650 8959; Fax: 0131-650 7952; E-mail: divinity@ed.ac.uk)

Head of School: Prof. Graham Paul Foster BD MSt PhD
Principal of New College: Rev. Professor David A.S. Fergusson* OBE MA BD DPhil DD
                             FBA FRSE
Assistant Principal of
New College: Rev. Alison M. Jack* MA BD PhD

For teaching staff and further information see www.ed.ac.uk/schools-departments/divinity/

GLASGOW
School of Critical Studies
Theology and Religious Studies Subject Area
4 The Square, University of Glasgow, Glasgow G12 8QQ
(Tel: 0141-330 6526; Fax: 0141-330 4943)

Head of Subject: Rev. Canon Dr Charlotte Methuen
Principal of Trinity College: Rev. Doug Gay* MA BD PhD

For teaching staff and further information see www.gla.ac.uk Subjects A-Z. Theology and
Religious Studies

HIGHLAND THEOLOGICAL COLLEGE UHI
High Street, Dingwall IV15 9HA
(Tel: 01349 780000; Fax: 01349 780001;
E-mail: htc@uhi.ac.uk)

Principal of HTC: Rev. Hector Morrison* BSc BD MTh
Vice-Principal of HTC: Jamie Grant PhD MA LLB

For teaching staff and further information see www.htc.uhi.ac.uk

(7) SOCIETIES AND ASSOCIATIONS

The undernoted list shows the name of the Association, along with the name and address of the
Secretary.

1. INTER-CHURCH ASSOCIATIONS

ACTION OF CHURCHES TOGETHER IN SCOTLAND (ACTS) – Eaglaisean Còmhla an Gnìomh an Alba – was formed in 1990 as Scotland's national ecumenical instrument. It brings together nine denominations in Scotland who share a desire for greater oneness between churches, a growth of understanding and common life between churches, and unified action in proclaiming and responding to the gospel in the whole of life. General Secretary: Rev Matthew Z. Ross LLB BD MTh FSAScot, Jubilee House, Forthside Way, Stirling, FK8 1QZ (Tel: 01259 216980; E-mail: matthewross@actsscotland.org; Website: www.acts-scotland.org).

The FELLOWSHIP OF ST ANDREW: The fellowship promotes dialogue between Churches of the east and the west in Scotland. Further information available from the Secretary, Rev. John G. Pickles, 1 Annerley Road, Annan DG12 6HE (Tel: 01461 202626; E-mail: jgpickles@hotmail.com).

The FELLOWSHIP OF ST THOMAS: An ecumenical association formed to promote informed interest in and to learn from the experience of Churches in South Asia (India, Pakistan, Bangladesh, Nepal, Sri Lanka and Burma (Myanmar)). Secretary: Rev. Val Nellist, 28 Glamis Gardens, Dalgety Bay, Dunfermline KY11 5TD (Tel: 01383 824066; E-mail: valnellist@btinternet.com; Website: www.fost.org.uk).

FRONTIER YOUTH TRUST: Encourages, resources and supports churches, organisations and individuals working with young people (in particular, disadvantaged young people). Through the StreetSpace initiative, the Trust is able to help churches to explore new ways of engaging young people in the community around mission and fresh expressions of church. All correspondence to: Frontier Youth Trust, 202 Bradford Court, 123/131 Bradford Street, Birmingham B12 0NS (Tel: 0121-771 2328; E-mail: frontier@fyt.org.uk; Website: www. fyt.org.uk). For information on StreetSpace, contact Clare McCormack (E-mail: scotland@ streetspace.org.uk).

INTERSERVE SCOTLAND: We are part of Interserve, an international, evangelical and interdenominational organisation with 160 years of Christian service. The purpose of Interserve is 'to make Jesus Christ known through *wholistic* ministry in partnership with the global church, among the neediest peoples of Asia and the Arab world', and our vision is 'Lives and communities transformed through encounter with Jesus Christ'. Interserve supports over 800 people in cross-cultural ministry in a wide range of work including children and youth, the environment, evangelism, Bible training, engineering, agriculture, business development and health. We rely on supporters in Scotland and Ireland to join us. Director: Grace Penney, 4 Blairtummock Place, Panorama Business Village, Queenslie, Glasgow G33 4EN (Tel: 0141-781 1982; Fax: 0141-781 1572; E-mail: info@issi.org.uk; Website: www.interservescotlandandireland.org).

IONA COMMUNITY: We are an ecumenical Christian community with a dispersed worldwide membership of Full Members, Associate Members and Friends. Inspired by our faith and loving concern for the world and its people, we pursue justice and peace in and through community. Our new Glasgow centre hosts a growing programme of events, our work with young people, Wild Goose Publications and the Wild Goose Resource Group. The Iona Community also welcomes guests to share in the common life in the Abbey and MacLeod

Centre, Iona and Camas outdoor adventure centre, Mull. Leader: Rev. Peter Macdonald, 21 Carlton Court, Glasgow, G5 9JP (Tel: 0141 429 7281, Website: www.iona.org.uk; E-mail: admin@iona.org.uk; Facebook: Iona Community; Twitter: @ionacommunity). Island Centres Director: Rev Rosie Magee, Iona Abbey, Isle of Iona, Argyll, PA76 6SN (Tel: 01681 700404, E-mail: enquiries@iona.org.uk).

PLACE FOR HOPE: A body with its roots in the Church of Scotland and now an independent charity, its vision is for a world where people embrace the transformational potential of conflict and nurture the art of peacebuilding. Place for Hope accompanies and equips people and faith communities where relationships have become impaired and helps them move towards living well with difference. Through a skilled and highly trained team we aim to accompany groups navigating conflict and difficult conversations and to resource the church and wider faith communities with peacemakers. If you are aware of conflict or difficulty within your faith community and would appreciate support, or wish to encourage your church or faith group to host a community dialogue, invite us to deliver a training or workshop session to your Kirk Session or Presbytery – it is never too early for a conversation about how we may help; you may also develop your own skills through our open access training courses. (Tel: 07884 580359; E-mail: info@placeforhope.org.uk; Website: www.placeforhope.org.uk).

The ST COLM'S FELLOWSHIP: An association for all from any denomination who have trained, studied or been resident at St Colm's, either when it was a college or later as International House. There is an annual retreat and a meeting for Commemoration; and some local groups meet on a regular basis. Hon. Secretary: Margaret Nutter, 'Kilmorich', 14 Balloch Road, Balloch G83 8SR (Tel: 01389 754505; E-mail: maenutter@gmail.com).

SCOTTISH CHURCHES HOUSING ACTION: Unites the Scottish Churches in tackling homelessness; supports local volunteering to assist homeless people; advises on using property for affordable housing. Chief Executive: Alastair Cameron, 44 Hanover Street, Edinburgh EH2 2DR (Tel: 0131-477 4500; E-mail: info@churches-housing.org; Website: www.churches-housing.org).

SCOTTISH CHURCHES ORGANIST TRAINING SCHEME (SCOTS): Established in 1997 as an initiative of the then Panel on Worship, along with the Royal School of Church Music's Scottish Committee and the Scottish Federation of Organists, this is a self-propelled scheme by which a pianist who seeks competence on the organ – and organists who wish to develop their skills – can follow a three-stage syllabus, receiving a certificate at each stage. Participants each have an Adviser whom they meet occasionally for assessment, and also take part in one of the three or four Local Organ Workshops which are held in different parts of Scotland each year. There is a regular e-newsletter, *Scots Wha Play*. Costs are kept low. SCOTS is an ecumenical scheme. Information from Douglas Galbraith (Tel: 01592 752403; E-mail: dgalbraith@hotmail.com; Website: www.scotsorgan.org.uk > SCOTS).

SCOTTISH JOINT COMMITTEE ON RELIGIOUS AND MORAL EDUCATION: This is an interfaith body that began as a joint partnership between the Educational Institute of Scotland and the Church of Scotland to provide resources, training and support for the work of religious and moral education in schools. Mr Andrew Tomlinson, 121 George Street, Edinburgh EH2 4YN (Tel: 0131-225 5722; E-mail: atomlinson@churchofscotland.org.uk), and Mr Lachlan Bradley, 6 Clairmont Gardens, Glasgow G3 7LW (Tel: 0141-353 3595).

SCRIPTURE UNION SCOTLAND: 70 Milton Street, Glasgow G4 0HR (Tel: 0141-332 1162; Fax: 0141-352 7600; E-mail: info@suscotland.org.uk; Website: www.suscotland.org. uk). Scripture Union Scotland's vision is to see the children and young people of Scotland exploring the Bible and responding to the significance of Jesus. SU Scotland works in schools running SU groups and supporting Curriculum for Excellence. Its two activity centres, Lendrick Muir and Alltnacriche, accommodate school groups and weekends away during term-time. During the school holidays it runs an extensive programme of events for school-age children – including residential holidays (some focused on disadvantaged children and young people), missions and church-based holiday clubs. In addition, it runs discipleship and training programmes for young people and is committed to promoting prayer for, and by, the young people of Scotland through a range of national prayer events and the *Pray for Schools Scotland* initiative.

STUDENT CHRISTIAN MOVEMENT: National Co-ordinator: Hilary Topp, SCM, Grays Court, 3 Nursery Road, Edgbaston, Birmingham B15 3JX (Tel: 0121-426 4918; E-mail: scm@movement.org.uk; Website: www.movement.org.uk). SCM is a student-led movement inspired by Jesus to act for justice and show God's love in the world. As a community we come together to pray, worship and explore faith in an open and non-judgemental environment. The movement is made up of a network of groups and individual members across Britain, as well as link churches and affiliated chaplaincies. As a national movement we come together at regional and national events to learn more about our faith and spend time as a community, and we take action on issues of social justice chosen by our members. SCM provides resources and training to student groups, churches and chaplaincies on student outreach and engagement, leadership and social action.

UCCF: THE CHRISTIAN UNIONS: Blue Boar House, 5 Blue Boar Street, Oxford OX1 4EE (Tel: 01865 253678; E-mail: email@uccf.org.uk). UCCF is a fellowship of students, staff and supporters. Christian Unions are mission teams operating in universities and colleges, supported by the local church, and resourced by UCCF staff. This fellowship exists to proclaim the gospel of Jesus Christ in the student world.

WORLD DAY OF PRAYER: SCOTTISH COMMITTEE: Convener: Christian Williams, 61 McCallum Gardens, Strathview Estate, Bellshill ML4 2SR. Secretary: Marjorie Paton, Muldoanich, Stirling Street, Blackford, Auchterarder PH4 1QG (Tel: 01764 682234; E-mail: marjoriepaton.wdp@btinternet.com; Website: www.wdpscotland.org.uk).

YMCA SCOTLAND: Offers support, training and guidance to churches seeking to reach out to love and serve young people's needs. Chief Executive – National General Secretary: Mrs Kerry Reilly, James Love House, 11 Rutland Street, Edinburgh EH1 2DQ (Tel: 0131-228 1464; E-mail: kerry@ymcascotland.org; Website: www.ymcascotland.org).

YOUTH FOR CHRIST INTERNATIONAL: Youth for Christ is a national Christian charity committed to taking the Good News of Jesus Christ relevantly to every young person in Great Britain. In Scotland there are 5 locally governed, staffed and financed centres, communicating and demonstrating the Christian faith. Local Ministries Director: Lauren Fox (Tel: 0121 502 9620; E-mail: lauren.fox@yfc.co.uk; Website: www.yfc.co.uk/local-centres/scotland).

2. CHURCH OF SCOTLAND SOCIETIES

CHURCH OF SCOTLAND ABSTAINERS' ASSOCIATION: Recognising that alcohol is a major – indeed a growing – problem within Scotland, the aim of the Church of Scotland Abstainers' Association, with its motto 'Abstinence makes sense', is to encourage more people to choose a healthy alcohol-free lifestyle. Further details are available from 'Blochairn', 17A Culduthel Road, Inverness IV24 4AG (Website: www.kirkabstainers.org.uk).

The CHURCH OF SCOTLAND CHAPLAINS' ASSOCIATION: The Association consists of serving and retired chaplains to HM Forces. It holds an annual meeting and lunch on Shrove Tuesday, and organises the annual Service of Remembrance in St Giles' Cathedral on Chaplains' Day of the General Assembly. Hon. Secretary: Rev. Neil N. Gardner MA BD RNR, The Manse of Canongate, Edinburgh EH8 8BR (Tel: 0131-556 3515; E-mail: nng22@btinternet.com).

The CHURCH OF SCOTLAND RETIRED MINISTERS' ASSOCIATION: Hon. Secretary: Rev. David Dutton, 13 Acredales, Haddington EH41 4NT (Tel: 01620 825999; E-mail: duttondw@gmail.com).

The CHURCH SERVICE SOCIETY: Founded in 1865 to study the development of Christian worship through the ages and in the Reformed tradition, and to work towards renewal in contemporary worship. It has published since 1928, and continues to publish, a liturgical journal, archived on its website. Secretary: Rev. Dr Douglas Galbraith (Tel: 01592 752403; E-mail: dgalbraith@hotmail.com; Website: www.churchservicesociety.org).

FORUM OF GENERAL ASSEMBLY AND PRESBYTERY CLERKS: Secretary: Rev. David W. Clark, 3 Ritchie Avenue, Cardross, Dumbarton G82 5LL (Tel: 01389 849319; E-mail: dumbarton@churchofscotland.org.uk).

COVENANT FELLOWSHIP SCOTLAND (formerly FORWARD TOGETHER): An organisation for evangelicals within the Church of Scotland. Contact the Director, Mr Eric C. Smith (Tel: 07715 665728; E-mail: director@covenantfellowshipscotland.com), or the Chairman, Rev. Prof. Andrew T.B. McGowan (Tel: 01463 238770; E-mail: amcgowan@churchofscotland.org.uk; Website: http://covenantfellowshipscotland.com).

The FRIENDS OF TABEETHA SCHOOL, JAFFA: President: Rev. Elinor Gordon. Hon. Secretary: Rev. Iain F. Paton, Muldoanich, Stirling Street, Blackford, Auchterarder PH4 1QG (Tel: 01764 682234; E-mail: iain.f.paton@btinternet.com).

The IRISH GATHERING: Secretary: Rev. William McLaren, 23 Shamrock Street, Dundee DD4 7AH (Tel: 01382 459119; E-mail: WMcLaren@churchofscotland.org.uk).

SCOTTISH CHURCH SOCIETY: Founded in 1892 to 'defend and advance Catholic doctrine as set forth in the Ancient Creeds and embodied in the Standards of the Church of Scotland', the Society meets for worship and discussion at All Saints' Tide, holds a Lenten Quiet Day, an AGM, and other meetings by arrangement; all are open to non members. Secretary: Rev. W. Gerald Jones MA BD MTh, The Manse, Patna Road, Kirkmichael, Maybole KA19 7PJ (Tel: 01655 750286; E-mail: revgerald@jonesg99.freeserve.co.uk).

SCOTTISH CHURCH THEOLOGY SOCIETY: Rev. Alexander Shuttleworth, 62 Toll Road, Kincardine, Alloa FK10 4QZ (Tel: 01259 731002; E-mail: AShuttleworth@churchofscotland. org.uk). The Society encourages theological exploration and discussion of the main issues confronting the Church in the twenty-first century.

SOCIETY OF FRIENDS OF ST ANDREW'S JERUSALEM: Hon. Secretary: Major J.M.K. Erskine MBE, World Mission Council, 121 George Street, Edinburgh EH2 4YN. Membership Secretary: Walter T. Dunlop, 50 Oxgangs Road North, Edinburgh EH13 9DR (Tel: 07925 481523); E-mail: oxgangs9586@hotmail.com).

3. BIBLE SOCIETIES

The SCOTTISH BIBLE SOCIETY: Chief Executive: Elaine Duncan, 7 Hampton Terrace, Edinburgh EH12 5XU (Tel: 0131-337 9701; E-mail: info@scottishbiblesociety.org).

WEST OF SCOTLAND BIBLE SOCIETY: Secretary: Rev. Finlay Mackenzie, 6 Shaw Road, Milngavie, Glasgow G62 6LU (Tel: 07817 680011; E-mail: f.c.mack51@gmail.com; Website: www.westofscotlandbiblesociety.com).

4. GENERAL

The BOYS' BRIGADE: Scottish Headquarters, Carronvale House, Carronvale Road, Larbert FK5 3LH (Tel: 01324 562008; Fax: 01324 552323; E-mail: scottishhq@boys-brigade.org.uk).

BROKEN RITES: Support group for divorced and separated clergy spouses (Tel: 01896 759254 or 01309 641526; E-mail: eshirleydouglas@hotmail.co.uk; Website: www.brokenrites.org).

CHRISTIAN AID SCOTLAND: Sally Foster-Fulton, Head of Christian Aid Scotland, Sycamore House, 290 Bath Street, Glasgow G2 4JR (Tel: 0141-221 7475; E-mail: glasgow@ christian-aid.org). Edinburgh Office: Tel: 0131-220 1254. Perth Office: Tel: 01738 643982.

CHRISTIAN ENDEAVOUR IN SCOTLAND: Challenging and encouraging children and young people in the service of Christ and the Church, especially through the CE Award Scheme: 16 Queen Street, Alloa FK10 2AR (Tel: 01259 215101; E-mail: admin@cescotland.org; Website: www.cescotland.org).

DAYONE CHRISTIAN MINISTRIES (THE LORD'S DAY OBSERVANCE SOCIETY): Ryelands Road, Leominster, Herefordshire HR6 8NZ. Contact Mark Roberts for further information (Tel: 01568 613740; E-mail: info@dayone.co.uk).

ECO-CONGREGATION SCOTLAND: 121 George Street, Edinburgh EH2 4YN (Tel: 0131-240 2274; E-mail: manager@ecocongregationscotland.org; Website: www.ecocongregationscotland.org). Eco-Congregation Scotland is the largest movement of community-based environment groups in Scotland. We offer a programme to help congregations reduce their impact on climate change and live sustainably in a world of limited resources.

GIRLGUIDING SCOTLAND: 16 Coates Crescent, Edinburgh EH3 7AH (Tel: 0131-226 4511; Fax: 0131-220 4828; E-mail: administrator@girlguiding-scot.org.uk; Website: www. girlguidingscotland.org.uk).

GIRLS' BRIGADE SCOTLAND: 11A Woodside Crescent, Glasgow G3 7UL (Tel: 0141-332 1765; E-mail: enquiries@girls-brigade-scotland.org.uk; Website: www.girls-brigade-scotland.org.uk).

The LEPROSY MISSION SCOTLAND: Suite 2, Earlsgate Lodge, Livilands Lane, Stirling FK8 2BG (Tel: 01786 449266; E-mail: contactus@tlmscotland.org.uk; Website: www.tlmscotland.org.uk). Working in over 30 countries, the Leprosy Mission is a global fellowship united by our Christian faith and commitment to seeing leprosy defeated and lives transformed.

RELATIONSHIPS SCOTLAND: Chief Executive: Mr Stuart Valentine, 18 York Place, Edinburgh EH1 3EP (Tel: 0845 119 2020; Fax: 0845 119 6089; E-mail: enquiries@relationships-scotland.org.uk; Website: www.relationships-scotland.org.uk).

SCOTTISH CHURCH HISTORY SOCIETY: Secretary: Dr Eleanor M. Harris, E-mail: eleanormharris@gmail.com.

SCOTTISH EVANGELICAL THEOLOGY SOCIETY: Secretary: Rev. M.G. Smith, 0/2, 2008 Maryhill Road, Glasgow G20 0AB (Tel: 0141 570 8680; E-mail: sets.secretary@gmail.com; Website: www.s-e-t-s.org.uk).

The SCOTTISH REFORMATION SOCIETY: Chairman: Rev. Dr S. James Millar. Vice-Chairman: Rev. John J. Murray. Secretary: Rev. Dr Douglas Somerset. Treasurer: Rev. Andrew W.F. Coghill, The Magdalen Chapel, 41 Cowgate, Edinburgh EH1 1JR (Tel: 0131-220 1450; E-mail: info@scottishreformationsociety.org; Website: www.scottishreformationsociety.org).

SCOUTS SCOTLAND: Scottish Headquarters, Fordell Firs, Hillend, Dunfermline KY11 7HQ (Tel: 01383 419073; E-mail: shq@scouts.scot; Website: www.scouts.scot).

The SOCIETY IN SCOTLAND FOR PROPAGATING CHRISTIAN KNOWLEDGE: Chairman: Rev. Scott McKenna; Secretary: Tom Hamilton, SSPCK, c/o Shepherd and Wedderburn LLP, 1 Exchange Crescent, Edinburgh EH3 8UL (Tel: 0131-228 9900; Website: www.sspck.co.uk; E-mail: SSPCK@shepwedd.co.uk).

TEARFUND: 100 Church Road, Teddington TW11 8QE (Tel: 0208 977 9144). Director: Lynne Paterson, Tearfund Scotland, Challenge House, 29 Canal Street, Glasgow G4 0AD (Tel: 0141-332 3621; E-mail: scotland@tearfund.org; Website: www.tearfund.org).

THEATRE CHAPLAINCY UK (formerly the Actor's Church Union) is an ecumenical scheme providing a Church contact and support to staff and travelling theatre groups in theatres and concert halls throughout the UK. Area Chaplain Scotland: Rev. Thomas Coupar (Tel: 07814 588904; E-mail: chaplain@robinchapel.org.uk).

The WALDENSIAN MISSIONS AID SOCIETY FOR WORK IN ITALY: David A. Lamb SSC, 36 Liberton Drive, Edinburgh EH16 6NN (Tel: 0131-664 3059; E-mail: david@dlamb.co.uk; Website: www.scottishwaldensian.org.uk).

YOUTH SCOTLAND: Balfour House, 19 Bonnington Grove, Edinburgh EH6 4BL (Tel: 0131-554 2561; Fax: 0131-454 3438; E-mail: office@youthscotland.org.uk; Website: www.youthscotland.org.uk).

THE YOUNG WOMEN'S MOVEMENT: Director: Jackie Scutt, Third Floor, Princes House, 5 Shandwick Place, Edinburgh EH2 4RG (Tel: 0330 121 0002; E-mail: admin@ywcascotland. org; Website: www.ywcascotland.org).

(8) TRUSTS AND FUNDS

ABERNETHY ADVENTURE CENTRES: Full board residential accommodation and adventure activities available for all Church groups, plus a range of Christian summer camps at our four centres across Scotland. Tel: 01479 818005; E-mail: marketing@abernethy.org.uk; Website: www.abernethy.org.uk).

The ARROL TRUST: The Arrol Trust gives small grants to young people between the ages of 16 and 25 for the purposes of travel which will provide education or work experience. Potential recipients would be young people with disabilities or who would for financial reasons be otherwise unable to undertake projects. It is expected that projects would be beneficial not only to applicants but also to the wider community. Application forms are available from Callum S. Kennedy WS, Lindsays WS, Caledonian Exchange, 19A Canning Street, Edinburgh EH3 8HE (Tel: 0131-229 1212).

The BAIRD TRUST: Assists in the building and repair of churches and halls, and generally assists the work of the Church of Scotland. Apply to Iain A.T. Mowat CA, 182 Bath Street, Glasgow G2 4HG (Tel: 0141-332 0476; E-mail: info@bairdtrust.org.uk; Website: www.bairdtrust.org.uk).

The Rev. Alexander BARCLAY BEQUEST: Assists a family member of a deceased minister of the Church of Scotland who at the time of his/her death was acting as his/her housekeeper and who is in needy circumstances, and in certain circumstances assists Ministers, Deacons, Ministries Development Staff and their spouses facing financial hardship. Applications should be made to the Secretary and Clerk, The Church of Scotland Trust, 121 George Street, Edinburgh EH2 4YN (Tel: 0131-240 2222; E-mail: jhamilton@churchofscotland.org.uk) or the Pastoral Support Team, 121 George Street, Edinburgh EH2 4YN (Tel: 0131-225 5722).

BELLAHOUSTON BEQUEST FUND: Gives grants to Protestant evangelical denominations in the City of Glasgow and certain areas within five miles of the city boundary for building and repairing churches and halls and the promotion of religion. Apply to Mr Donald B. Reid, Mitchells Roberton, 36 North Hanover Street, Glasgow G1 2AD (Tel: 0141-552 3422; E-mail: info@mitchells-roberton.co.uk).

BEQUEST FUND FOR MINISTERS: Provides financial assistance to ministers in outlying districts towards the cost of manse furnishings, pastoral efficiency aids, and personal and family medical or educational (including university) costs. Apply to A. Linda Parkhill CA, 60 Wellington Street, Glasgow G2 6HJ (Tel: 0141-226 4994; E-mail: mail@parkhillmackie.co.uk).

CARNEGIE TRUST FOR THE UNIVERSITIES OF SCOTLAND: In cases of hardship, the Carnegie Trust is prepared to consider applications by students of Scottish birth or extraction (at least one parent born in Scotland), or who have had at least two years' education at a secondary school in Scotland, for financial assistance with the payment of their fees for a first degree at a Scottish university. For further details, students should apply to the Secretary, Carnegie Trust for the Universities of Scotland, Andrew Carnegie House, Pittencrieff Street, Dunfermline KY12 8AW (Tel: 01383 724990; E-mail: admin@carnegie-trust.org; Website: www.carnegie-trust.org).

CHURCH OF SCOTLAND INSURANCE SERVICES LTD: Arranges Church property and liabilities insurance in its capacity of Insurance Intermediary; also arranges other classes of business including household insurance for members and adherents of the Church of Scotland and insurances for charities. It pays its distributable profits to the Church of Scotland through Gift Aid. It is authorised and regulated by the Financial Conduct Authority. Contact 121 George Street, Edinburgh EH2 4YN (Tel: 0131-220 4119; Fax: 0131-220 3113; E-mail: enquiries@cosic.co.uk; Website: www.cosic.co.uk).

CHURCH OF SCOTLAND MINISTRY BENEVOLENT FUND: Makes grants to retired men and women who have been ordained or commissioned for the ministry of the Church of Scotland and to widows, widowers, orphans, spouses or children of such, who are in need. Apply to Elaine Macadie BA CA, Assistant Treasurer (Ministries), 121 George Street, Edinburgh EH2 4YN (Tel: 0131-225 5722).

The CINTRA BEQUEST: See 'Tod Endowment Trust ...' entry below.

CLARK BURSARY: Awarded to accepted candidate(s) for the ministry of the Church of Scotland whose studies for the ministry are pursued at the University of Aberdeen. Applications or recommendations for the Bursary to the Clerk to the Presbytery of Aberdeen, Mastrick Church, Greenfern Road, Aberdeen AB16 6TR by 16 October annually.

CRAIGCROOK MORTIFICATION: Pensions are paid to poor men and women over 60 years old, born in Scotland or who have resided in Scotland for not less than ten years. At present, pensions amount to £1,000–£1,500 p.a. Ministers are invited to notify the Clerk and Factor, Mrs Fiona M.M. Watson CA, Exchange Place 3, Semple Street, Edinburgh EH3 8BL (Tel: 0131-473 3500; E-mail: charity@scott-moncrieff.com) of deserving persons and should be prepared to act as a referee on the application form.

CROMBIE SCHOLARSHIP: Provides grants annually on the nomination of the Deans of Faculty of Divinity of the Universities of St Andrews, Glasgow, Aberdeen and Edinburgh, who each nominate one matriculated student who has taken a University course in Greek (Classical or Hellenistic) and Hebrew. Award by recommendation only.

The DRUMMOND TRUST: Makes grants towards the cost of publication of books of 'sound Christian doctrine and outreach'. The Trustees are also willing to receive grant requests towards the cost of audio-visual programme material, but not equipment, software but not hardware. Requests for application forms should be made to the Secretaries, Hill and Robb Limited, 3 Pitt Terrace, Stirling FK8 2EY (Tel: 01786 450985; E-mail: douglaswhyte@hillandrobb.co.uk). Manuscripts should *not* be sent.

The David DUNCAN TRUST: Makes grants annually to students for the ministry and students in training to become deacons in the Church of Scotland in the Faculties of Arts and Divinity. Preference is given to those born or educated within the bounds of the former Presbytery of Arbroath. Applications not later than 31 October to Thorntons Law LLP, Brothockbank House,

Arbroath DD11 1NE (reference: G.J.M. Dunlop; Tel: 01241 872683; E-mail: gdunlop@ thorntons-law.co.uk).

ERSKINE CUNNINGHAM HILL TRUST: Donates 50% of its annual income to the central funds of the Church of Scotland and 50% to other charities. Individual donations are in the region of £1,000. Priority is given to charities administered by voluntary or honorary officials, in particular charities registered and operating in Scotland and relating to the elderly, young people, ex-service personnel or seafarers. Application forms from the Secretary, Nicola Robertson, 121 George Street, Edinburgh EH2 4YN (Tel: 0131-225 5722; E-mail: nrobertson@cofscotland.org.uk).

ESDAILE TRUST: Assists the education and advancement of daughters of ministers, missionaries and widowed deaconesses of the Church of Scotland between 12 and 25 years of age. Applications are to be lodged by 31 May in each year with the Clerk and Treasurer, Mrs Fiona M.M. Watson CA, Exchange Place 3, Semple Street, Edinburgh EH3 8BL (Tel: 0131-473 3500; E-mail: charity@scott-moncrieff.com).

FERGUSON BEQUEST FUND: Assists with the building and repair of churches and halls and, more generally, with the work of the Church of Scotland. Priority is given to the Counties of Ayr, Kirkcudbright, Wigtown, Lanark, Dunbarton and Renfrew, and to Greenock, Glasgow, Falkirk and Ardrossan; applications are, however, accepted from across Scotland. Apply to Iain A.T. Mowat CA, 182 Bath Street, Glasgow G2 4HG (Tel: 0141-332 0476; E-mail: info@ fergusonbequestfund.org.uk; Website: www.fergusonbequestfund.org.uk).

GEIKIE BEQUEST: Makes small grants to students for the ministry, including students studying for entry to the University, preference being given to those not eligible for SAAS awards. Apply to Elaine Macadie BA CA, Assistant Treasurer (Ministries), 121 George Street, Edinburgh EH2 4YN by September for distribution in November each year.

James GILLAN'S BURSARY FUND: Bursaries are available for male or female students for the ministry who were born or whose parents or parent have resided and had their home for not less than three years continually in the old counties of Moray or Nairn. Apply to Mr Donald Prentice, St Leonard's, Nelson Road, Forres IV36 IDR (Tel: 01309 672380).

The GLASGOW SOCIETY OF THE SONS AND DAUGHTERS OF MINISTERS OF THE CHURCH OF SCOTLAND: The Society's primary purpose is to grant financial assistance to children (no matter what age) of deceased ministers of the Church of Scotland. Applications are to be submitted by 1 February in each year. To the extent that funds are available, grants are also given for the children of ministers or retired ministers, although such grants are normally restricted to university and college students. These latter grants are considered in conjunction with the Edinburgh-based Society. Limited funds are also available for individual application for special needs or projects. Applications are to be submitted by 31 May in each year. Emergency applications can be dealt with at any time when need arises. Application forms may be obtained from the Secretary and Treasurer, Mrs Fiona M.M. Watson CA, Exchange Place 3, Semple Street, Edinburgh EH3 8BL (Tel: 0131-473 3500; E-mail: charity@scott-moncrieff.com).

HAMILTON BURSARY TRUST: Awarded, subject to the intention to serve overseas under the Church of Scotland World Mission Council or to serve with some other Overseas Mission Agency approved by the Council, to a student at the University of Aberdeen. Preference is given to a student born or residing in (1) Parish of Skene, (2) Parish of Echt, (3) the Presbytery of Aberdeen, Kincardine and Deeside, or Gordon; failing which to Accepted Candidate(s) for the Ministry of the Church of Scotland whose studies for the Ministry are pursued at Aberdeen University. Applications or recommendations for the Bursary to the Clerk to the Presbytery of Aberdeen, Mastrick Church, Greenfern Road, Aberdeen AB16 6TR by 16 October annually.

Martin HARCUS BEQUEST: Makes annual grants to candidates for the ministry resident within the Presbytery of Edinburgh and currently under the jurisdiction of the Presbytery. Applications to the Principal's Secretary, New College, Mound Place, Edinburgh EH1 2LX (E-mail: k.mclean@ed.ac.uk) by 15 October.

The HOPE TRUST: Gives some support to organisations involved in combating drink and drugs, and has as its main purpose the promotion of the Reformed tradition throughout the world. There is also a Scholarship programme for Postgraduate Theology Study in Scotland. Apply to Robert P. Miller SSC LLB, 31 Moray Place, Edinburgh EH3 6BY (Tel: 0131-226 5151).

KEAY THOM TRUST: The principal purposes of the Keay Thom Trust are:
1. To benefit the widows, daughters or other dependent female relatives of deceased ministers, or wives of ministers who are now divorced or separated, all of whom have supported the minister in the fulfilment of his duties and who, by reason of death, divorce or separation, have been required to leave the manse. The Trust can assist them in the purchase of a house or by providing financial or material assistance whether it be for the provision of accommodation or not.
2. To assist in the education or training of the above female relatives or any other children of deceased ministers.
Further information and application forms are available from Miller Hendry, Solicitors, 10 Blackfriars Street, Perth PH1 5NS (Tel: 01738 637311).

LADIES' GAELIC SCHOOLS AND HIGHLAND BURSARY ASSOCIATION: Distributes money to students, preferably with a Highland/Gaelic background, who are training to be ministers in the Church of Scotland. Apply by 15 October in each year to the Secretary, Mrs Marion McGill, 61 Ladysmith Road, Edinburgh EH9 3EY (Tel: 0131 667 4243; E-mail: marionmcgill61@gmail.com).

The LYALL BEQUEST (Scottish Charity Number SC005542): Offers grants to ministers:
1. Grants to individual ministers and to couples for a holiday for a minimum of one week. No reapplication within a three-year period; and thereafter a 50 per cent grant to those reapplying.
2. Grants towards sickness and convalescence costs so far as not covered by the National Health Service. Applications should be made to the Secretary and Clerk, The Church of Scotland Trust, 121 George Street, Edinburgh EH2 4YN (Tel: 0131-240 2222; E-mail: jhamilton@churchofscotland.org.uk).

REV DR MACINNES AND MRS MACINNES TRUST: Provides grants to (1) retired ministers who have spent part of their ministry in the Counties of Nairn, Ross & Cromarty or Argyll and are solely dependent upon their pensions and preaching fees and (2) widows or widowers of such ministers solely dependent on their pensions. Applications should be made to the Secretary and Clerk, The Church of Scotland Trust, 121 George Street, Edinburgh EH2 4YN (Tel: 0131-240 2222; E-mail: jhamilton@churchofscotland.org.uk).

Gillian MACLAINE BURSARY FUND: Open to candidates for the ministry of the Church of Scotland of Scottish or Canadian nationality. Preference is given to Gaelic-speakers. Application forms available from Dr Christopher T. Brett MA PhD, Clerk to the Presbytery of Argyll, Minahey Cottage, Kames, Tighnabruaich PA21 2AD (Tel: 01700 811142; E-mail: argyll@ churchofscotland.org.uk). Closing date for receipt of applications is 31 October.

The E. McLAREN FUND: The persons intended to be benefited are widows and unmarried ladies, preference being given to ladies above 40 years of age in the following order:
(a) Widows and daughters of Officers in the Highland Regiment, and
(b) Widows and daughters of Scotsmen.
Further details from the Secretary, The E. McLaren Fund, Messrs BMK Wilson, Solicitors, 90 St Vincent Street, Glasgow G2 5UB (Tel: 0141-221 8004; Fax: 0141-221 8088; E-mail: rrs@bmkwilson.co.uk).

MORGAN BURSARY FUND: Makes grants to candidates for the Church of Scotland ministry studying at the University of Glasgow. Apply to the Clerk to the Presbytery of Glasgow, 260 Bath Street, Glasgow G2 4JP (Tel: 0141-332 6606). Closing date October 31.

NEW MINISTERS' FURNISHING LOAN FUND: Makes loans (of £1,000) to ministers in their first charge to assist with furnishing the manse. Apply to Elaine Macadie, Assistant Treasurer (Ministries), 121 George Street, Edinburgh EH2 4YN.

NOVUM TRUST: Provides small short-term grants – typically between £200 and £2,500 – to initiate projects in Christian action and research which cannot readily be financed from other sources. Trustees welcome applications from projects that are essentially Scottish, are distinctively new, and are focused on the welfare of young people, on the training of lay people or on new ways of communicating the Christian faith. The Trust cannot support large building projects, staff salaries or individuals applying for maintenance during courses or training. Application forms and guidance notes from novumt@cofscotland.org.uk or Mrs Susan Masterton, Blair Cadell WS, The Bond House, 5 Breadalbane Street, Edinburgh EH6 5JH (Tel: 0131-555 5800; Website: www.novum.org.uk).

PARK MEMORIAL BURSARY FUND: Provides grants for the benefit of candidates for the ministry of the Church of Scotland from the Presbytery of Glasgow under full-time training. Apply to the Clerk to the Presbytery of Glasgow, 260 Bath Street, Glasgow G2 4JP (Tel: 0141-332 6606). Closing date November 15.

PATON TRUST: Assists ministers in ill health to have a recuperative holiday outwith, and free from the cares of, their parishes. Apply to Alan S. Cunningham CA, Alexander Sloan, Chartered Accountants, 38 Cadogan Street, Glasgow G2 7HF (Tel: 0141-204 8989; Fax: 0141-248 9931; E-mail: alan.cunningham@alexandersloan.co.uk).

PRESBYTERY OF ARGYLL BURSARY FUND: Open to students who have been accepted as candidates for the ministry and the readership of the Church of Scotland. Preference is given to applicants who are natives of the bounds of the Presbytery, or are resident within the bounds of the Presbytery, or who have a strong connection with the bounds of the Presbytery. Application forms available from Dr Christopher T. Brett MA PhD, Clerk to the Presbytery of Argyll, Minahey Cottage, Kames, Tighnabruaich PA21 2AD (Tel: 01700 811142; E-mail: argyll@churchofscotland.org.uk). Closing date for receipt of applications is 31 October.

Margaret and John ROSS TRAVELLING FUND: Offers grants to ministers and their spouses for travelling and other expenses for trips to the Holy Land where the purpose is recuperation or relaxation. Applications should be made to the Secretary and Clerk, The Church of Scotland Trust, 121 George Street, Edinburgh EH2 4YN (Tel: 0131-240 2222; E-mail: jhamilton@churchofscotland.org.uk).

SCOTLAND'S CHURCHES TRUST: Assists, through grants, with the preservation of the fabric of buildings in use for public worship by any denomination. Also supports the playing of church organs by grants for public concerts, and through tuition bursaries for suitably proficient piano or organ players wishing to improve skills or techniques. SCT promotes visitor interest in churches through the trust's Pilgrim Journeys covering Scotland. Criteria and how to apply at www.scotlandschurchestrust.org.uk. Scotland's Churches Trust, 15 North Bank Street, Edinburgh EH1 2LP (E-mail: info@scotlandschurchestrust.org.uk).

SCOTTISH CHURCHES HOUSE LEGACY RESERVE: Aim – to enable Scotland's churches and Christian organisations to resource new ways of ecumenical working. Between 1960 and 2011, the former Scottish Churches House in Dunblane was a centre for ecumenical encounter, sharing, challenge and development – the Legacy Reserve aims to continue this ethos. Applications are invited for the funding of projects; completed application forms must be submitted no later than 5th January or 5th August in any year. Property schemes (such as repairs or purchase) are not eligible. Further details and application forms are available from the General Secretary, Action of Churches Together in Scotland, Jubilee House, Forthside Way, STIRLING FK8 1QZ. Telephone 01259 216980. E-mail: matthewross@acts-scotland.org.

SMIETON FUND: Makes small holiday grants to ministers. Administered at the discretion of the pastoral staff, who will give priority in cases of need. Applications to the Education and Support Secretary, Ministries Council, 121 George Street, Edinburgh EH2 4YN.

Mary Davidson SMITH CLERICAL AND EDUCATIONAL FUND FOR ABERDEENSHIRE: Assists ministers who have been ordained for five years or over and are in full charge of a congregation in Aberdeen, Aberdeenshire and the north, to purchase books, or to travel for educational purposes, and assists their children with scholarships for further education or vocational training. Apply to Alan J. Innes MA LLB, 100 Union Street, Aberdeen AB10 1QR (Tel: 01224 428000).

The SOCIETY FOR THE BENEFIT OF THE SONS AND DAUGHTERS OF THE CLERGY OF THE CHURCH OF SCOTLAND: Annual grants are made to assist in the education of the children (normally between the ages of 12 and 25 years) of ministers of the Church of Scotland. The Society also gives grants to aged and infirm daughters of ministers and ministers' unmarried daughters and sisters who are in need. Applications are to be lodged by 31 May in each year with the Secretary and Treasurer, Mrs Fiona M.M. Watson CA, Exchange Place 3, Semple Street, Edinburgh EH3 8BL (Tel: 0131-473 3500; E-mail: charity@scott-moncrieff.com).

The Nan STEVENSON CHARITABLE TRUST FOR RETIRED MINISTERS: Provides houses, or loans to purchase houses, on similar terms to the Housing and Loan Fund, for any retired paid church worker with a North Ayrshire connection. Secretary and Treasurer: Mrs Ann Turner, 42 Keir Hardie Drive, Ardrossan KA22 8PA (Tel: 01294 462834; E-mail: annturner62@btopenworld.com).

Miss M.E. SWINTON PATERSON'S CHARITABLE TRUST: The Trust can give modest grants to support smaller congregations in urban or rural areas who require to fund essential maintenance or improvement works at their buildings. Apply to Mr Callum S. Kennedy WS, Messrs Lindsays WS, Caledonian Exchange, 19A Canning Street, Edinburgh EH3 8HE (Tel: 0131-229 1212).

SYNOD OF GRAMPIAN CHILDREN OF THE CLERGY FUND: Makes annual grants to children of deceased ministers. Apply to Rev. Iain U. Thomson, Clerk and Treasurer, 4 Keirhill Gardens, Westhill AB32 6AZ (Tel: 01224 746743).

SYNOD OF GRAMPIAN WIDOWS' FUND: Makes annual grants (currently £240 p.a.) to widows or widowers of deceased ministers who have served in a charge in the former Synod. Apply to Rev. Iain U. Thomson, Clerk and Treasurer, 4 Keirhill Gardens, Westhill AB32 6AZ (Tel: 01224 746743).

TOD ENDOWMENT TRUST; CINTRA BEQUEST; TOD ENDOWMENT SCOTLAND HOLIDAY FUND: The Trustees of the Cintra Bequest and of the Tod Endowment Scotland Holiday Fund can consider an application for a grant from the Tod Endowment funds from any ordained or commissioned minister or deacon in Scotland of at least two years' standing before the date of application, to assist with the cost of the beneficiary and his or her spouse or partner and dependants obtaining rest and recuperation in Scotland. The Trustees of the Tod Endowment Scotland Holiday Fund can also consider an application from an ordained or commissioned minister or deacon who has retired. Application forms are available from Mrs J.S. Wilson, Solicitor (for the Cintra Bequest), and from Elaine Macadie BA CA, Assistant Treasurer (Ministries) (for the Tod Endowment Scotland Holiday Fund). The address in both cases is 121 George Street, Edinburgh EH2 4YN (Tel: 0131-225 5722). (Attention is drawn to the separate entry above for the Church of Scotland Ministry Benevolent Fund.)

STEPHEN WILLIAMSON & ALEX BALFOUR FUND: Offers grants to Ministers in the Presbyteries of Angus, Dunfermline, Kirkcaldy and St Andrews to assist with the cost of educational school trips for children. Applications should be made to the Secretary and Clerk, The Church of Scotland Trust, 121 George Street, Edinburgh EH2 4YN (Tel: 0131-240 2222; E-mail: jhamilton@churchofscotland.org.uk).

The undernoted hotels provide special terms as described. Fuller information may be obtained from the establishments:

CRIEFF HYDRO Ltd and MURRAYPARK HOTEL: The William Meikle Trust Fund and Paton Fund make provision whereby active ministers and their spouses and members of the Diaconate may enjoy the hotel and self-catering accommodation all year round at a supplemented rate, subject to availability and a maximum number of stays per year. Crieff Hydro offers a wide range of inclusive leisure facilities including leisure pool, gym, cinema and entertainment programme. BIG Country also provides free daily childcare for Crieff Hydro guests only. Over-60 on-site activities and five places to eat are also available at great prices. Currently, a moratorium has been placed on benefits from the Trust.

(9) LONG SERVICE CERTIFICATES

Long Service Certificates, signed by the Moderator, have to date been available for presentation to elders and others in respect of not less than thirty years of service. At the General Assembly of 2015, it was agreed that further certificates could be issued at intervals of ten years thereafter. It should be noted that the period is years of *service*, not (for example) years of ordination in the case of an elder. In the case of Sunday School teachers and Bible Class leaders, the qualifying period is twenty-one years of service. Certificates are not issued posthumously, nor is it possible to make exceptions to the rules, for example by recognising quality of service in order to reduce the qualifying period, or by reducing the qualifying period on compassionate grounds, such as serious illness. Applications for Long Service Certificates should be made in writing to the Principal Clerk at 121 George Street, Edinburgh EH2 4YN by the parish minister, or by the session clerk on behalf of the Kirk Session. Certificates are not issued from this office to the individual recipients, nor should individuals make application themselves.

(10) RECORDS OF THE CHURCH OF SCOTLAND

Church records more than fifty years old, unless still in use, should be sent or delivered to the Principal Clerk for onward transmission to the National Records of Scotland. Where ministers or session clerks are approached by a local repository seeking a transfer of their records, they should inform the Principal Clerk, who will take the matter up with the National Records of Scotland.

Where a temporary retransmission of records is sought, it is extremely helpful if notice can be given three months in advance so that appropriate procedures can be carried out satisfactorily.

SECTION 3

Church Procedure

A. THE MINISTER AND BAPTISM

See www.churchofscotland.org.uk > Resources > Yearbook > Section 3A

B. THE MINISTER AND MARRIAGE

See www.churchofscotland.org.uk > Resources > Yearbook > Section 3B

C. CONDUCT OF MARRIAGE SERVICES (CODE OF GOOD PRACTICE)

See www.churchofscotland.org.uk > Resources > Yearbook > Section 3C

D. MARRIAGE AND CIVIL PARTNERSHIP (SCOTLAND) ACT 2014

See www.churchofscotland.org.uk > Resources > Yearbook > Section 3D

E. CONDUCT OF FUNERAL SERVICES: FEES

See www.churchofscotland.org.uk > Resources > Yearbook > Section 3E

F. PULPIT SUPPLY FEES AND EXPENSES

See www.churchofscotland.org.uk > Resources > Yearbook > Section 3F

G. PROCEDURE IN A VACANCY

A full coverage can be found in two handbooks listed under *Interim Moderators and Nominating Committees* on the Ministries Resources pages on the Church of Scotland website: www.churchofscotland.org.uk > Resources > Subjects > Ministries resources > Interim Moderators and Nominating Committees
See also www.churchofscotland.org.uk > Serve > Ministries Council > Partnership Development > Locum Appointment Guidance

SECTION 4

A. General Assembly 2016
B. The Church of Scotland and the Gaelic Language

A. General Assembly 2016

OFFICE-BEARERS OF THE GENERAL ASSEMBLY

The Lord High Commissioner:	The Right Honourable The Lord Hope of Craighead KT PC FRSE
Moderator:	The Right Rev. Dr G. Russell Barr
Chaplains to the Moderator:	Rev. Ian Y Gilmour Rev. Moira McDonald
Acting Principal Clerk:	Very Rev. Dr John P. Chalmers
Acting Depute Clerk:	Rev. Dr George Whyte
Procurator:	Ms Laura Dunlop QC
Law Agent:	Mrs Janette S. Wilson
Law Agent Nominate:	Miss Mary Macleod
Convener of the Business Committee:	Rev. Dr Derek Browning
Vice-Convener of the Business Committee:	Ms Judith Pearson
Precentor:	Rev. Dr Martin C. Scott
Chief Steward:	Mr. Alexander F. Gemmill
Assembly Officer:	Mr David McColl
Assistant Assembly Officer:	Mr Craig Marshall

THE MODERATOR

The Right Reverend G. Russell Barr BA BD MTh DMin

Russell Barr, the son of a GP and a theatre nurse, was born and brought up in Kilmarnock, a brother to Robert and Jeanie. Russell's Kilmarnock connection is important in his story as, being the son of a GP, he learned at first hand the art of caring for people – Dr Barr told his son that medicine was an art rather than a science, and Russell's pastoral skills surely owe something to his father's care as a local doctor. Being a supporter of Kilmarnock FC also led to a resilience in life, celebrating victories where they occurred, and learning from mistakes as they happened.

Russell was one of five recent Moderators to attend Kilmarnock Academy, a time in his life when he played golf and rugby as well as being an active member of the Boys' Brigade. Russell's ambition in life was to play golf professionally but the wise counsel of his parents told him to get an education to fall back on, and having gained qualifications at Langside College, Glasgow, he then went to Edinburgh University to study history, and later Divinity when his call to the ministry of Word and Sacrament became clear. Russell experienced many voices of encouragement and guidance in his own path to ministry and subsequently became a similar voice for many others as they too considered where God was leading them. He and Margaret were students at the same time and after graduation they married in 1978 and moved to Jedburgh where Margaret taught Biology and Chemistry at Kelso High School and Russell served his probationary period at the linked charge of Jedburgh Old with Ancrum with Edgerston.

A year later they found themselves in Glasgow's East End, in Garthamlock and Craigend East, where their son Robert and then daughter Lindsey were born. In 1988 Russell was called to Greenock St Luke's and then in 1993 to Cramond Kirk in Edinburgh.

The art of being a minister gives Russell a real heart for the people he has served and worked with in all the challenges they face in life. His sense of humour, of community, of social justice lead him to hear the stories, often unspoken, of all he meets and to recognise the needs and worries being expressed. During his time in Cramond Russell wondered what might be done to mark the birth of the new millennium and Fresh Start was born, a local charity aimed at helping people who had been homeless make a home for themselves. It is a charity that has captured the imagination and hearts of many congregations in Edinburgh and hundreds of church members volunteer their time and skills every week, and the two sides of Edinburgh, the secure and wealthy living side by side with people in poverty and need, is a subject Russell continues to speak about in his role as Moderator.

Always a keen reader, Russell completed his MTh in 1993 and then his DMin from Princeton Theological Seminary in 2000. He has served on both the Assembly Church and Nation Committee and the World Mission Council, where he was Convener of the Africa and Caribbean Committee, and as Moderator of Edinburgh Presbytery and Convener of Superintendence. Russell has also throughout his years of ministry supervised and trained many future ministers, proving an example of hard work, thoughtfulness, pastoral care, and community building – his two chaplains during his Moderatorial year are both former students and have benefited hugely from Russell's patience and example, as well as from his and Margaret's hospitality and friendship.

Russell's year as Moderator will be one where he and Margaret can explore and enjoy their many social and theological interests, as well as enjoying the occasional game of golf. They have recently enjoyed the addition of a third grandchild to their family and were delighted that Robert was able to fly home from Australia and Lindsey and her family from Brussels to be with them at the opening of the General Assembly.

As his chaplains, we are delighted and honoured that Russell has been invited to serve in his role as Moderator of the General Assembly, and that he has trusted us to be his chaplains. We ask God's blessing on both Russell and Margaret as they serve the wider church in this year, confident that the care, thoughtfulness, and energy that has characterised Russell's ministry thus far will continue to serve him well.

Ian Gilmour and Moira McDonald
Moderator's Chaplains

B. THE CHURCH OF SCOTLAND AND THE GAELIC LANGUAGE

Rev. Dr Roderick MacLeod

Seirbheis Ghàidhlig an Ard-sheanaidh

Mar as àbhaist, chumadh seirbheis Ghàidhlig ann an Eaglais nam Manach Liath ann an Dùn Eideann air Didòmhnaich an Ard-sheanaidh. Air ceann an adhraidh am bliadhna agus a' searmonachadh bha an t-Urr. Iain Murchadh MacDhòmhnaill, ministear Tairbeart na Hearadh. A' togail an fhuinn bha Alasdair MacLeòid. Chaidh na Sgriobtaran a leughadh le dithis o choitheanal Gàidhlig Eaglais nam Manach Liath, Dòmhnall Iain MacDòmhnaill agus Màiri NicRath. Mar a tha air tachairt bho chionn grunn bhliadhnachan a-nis, sheinn Còisir Ghàidhlig Lodainn aig toiseach agus deireadh na seirbheis. Rinn Moderàtor an Ard-sheanaidh, an t-Oll. Urr. Ruiseil Barr, am Beannachadh.

An dèidh an adhraidh fhuair an luchd-adhraidh cuireadh gu greim-bìdh agus bha cothrom aca a bhith a' còmhradh agus a' conaltradh.

Tha Eaglais nam Manach Liath air tè de na h-eaglaisean aig Eaglais na h-Alba anns na bailtean mòra far a bheil seirbheis Ghàidhlig air a cumail a h-uile seachdain. Tha seirbheis Ghàidhlig gach Sàbaid cuideachd ann an Eaglais Chaluim Chille ann an Glaschu.

Anns na Meadhanan

Bidh ministearan agus buill eile o Eaglais na h-Alba a' gabhail compàirt ann am prògraman spioradail air an ràdio agus air an telebhisean.

Bidh mòran ag èisdeachd ri Dèanamaid Adhradh air an ràdio madainn agus feasgar na Sàbaid. Air an oidhche bidh seirbheisean à tasglan a' BhBC air an craobh-sgaoileadh, cuid mhath dhiùbh, cuid mhath dhiùbh o Eaglais na h-Alba. Gach latha tron t-seachdain tha Smuain na Maidne a' tighinn a-mach air Ràdio nan Gàidheal. Tha daoine nach eil air chomas seirbheisean eaglais a fhrithealadh a' dèanamh fiughair ris na prògraman spioradail seo.

Bidh am BBC a' toirt fiosrachaidh seachad mu sheirbheisean Gàidhlig a tha air an cumail air feadh na dùthcha.

Na Duilleagan Gàidhlig

A h-uile mìos o tha Eaglais na h-Alba air a bhith a' foillseachadh dhuilleagan Gàidhlig an lùib na h-iris mhìosail Life and Work. Bidh cuid mhath de luchd-ionnsachaidh agus feadhainn o eaglaisean eile a' leughadh nan Duilleag.

An Ath Cheum

Anns a' bhliadhna a bha an t-Oll. Urr. Aonghas Moireasdan 'na Mhoderàtor air an Ard-sheanadh rinn e mòran as leth na Gàidhlig. Chumadh Co-labhairt chudthromach an-uiridh anns an robh rannsachadh ga dhèanamh air suidheachadh na Gàidhlig ann an Eaglais na h-Alba. Thugadh An Ciad Ceum air a' cho-labhairt seo agus tha sinn a' dèanamh fiughair ris an ath cheum.

General Assembly Gaelic Service

As always there was a Gaelic service on the Sunday of the General Assembly in Greyfriars Kirk in Edinburgh. Conducting the service and preaching the sermon was Rev. Ian Murdo Macdonald, minister of Tarbert Harris. The precentor was Alasdair Macleod. Two members of Greyfriars Gaelic congregation read the Scriptures, Donald John Macdonald and Mairi

Macrae. As has happened for a number of years, Lothian Gaelic Choir sang at the beginning and conclusion of the service. The Moderator, Rev. Dr G. Russell Barr pronounced the Benediction.

Following the service, worshippers were invited to a light lunch when worshippers had an opportunity for conversation and fellowship.

Greyfriars Kirk is one of the Church of Scotland congregations in the city which hold weekly Gaelic services. A Gaelic service is also held each Sunday in St. Columba's church in Glasgow.

The Media
Ministers and members of the Church of Scotland regularly take part in Gaelic religious programmes on radio and television. The weekly Gaelic service on radio, Dèanamaid Adhradh, broadcast each Sunday morning and repeated in the afternoon, attracts a large audience. Each Sunday evening services are broadcast from the BBC archives, a good number of them from the Church of Scotland.

The BBC gives information about Gaelic services taking place in different parts of the country.

The Gaelic Supplement
The Church of Scotland publishes a Gaelic supplement each month which is distributed free of charge with *Life and Work*. Learners of Gaelic and members of other churches are regular readers of the Gaelic supplement.

The Next Step
During his moderatorial year Rev. Dr. Angus Morrison did much to raise the profile of Gaelic. Last year an important conference was held to consider the place of Gaelic within the Church of Scotland. The seminar was called An Ciad Ceum (The First Step), and we look forward to the next step.

SECTION 5

Presbytery Lists

See overleaf for an explanation of the two parts of each list; a Key to Abbreviations; and a list of the Presbyteries in their numerical order.

SECTION 5 – PRESBYTERY LISTS

In each Presbytery list, the congregations ('charges') are listed in alphabetical order. In a linked charge, the names appear under the first named congregation. Under the name of the congregation will be found the name of the minister and, where applicable, that of an associate minister, ordained local minister, auxiliary minister and member of the Diaconate. The years indicated after a minister's name in the congregational section of each Presbytery list are the year of ordination (column 1) and the year of current appointment (column 2). Where only one date is given, it is both the year of ordination and the year of appointment. For an ordained local minister, the date is of ordination.

In the second part of each Presbytery list, those named, who are either engaged in ministry other than parish or are retired, are listed alphabetically. The first date is the year of ordination, and the following date is the year of appointment or retirement. If the person concerned is retired, then the appointment last held will be shown in brackets.

KEY TO ABBREVIATIONS

(E) Indicates a Church Extension charge. New Charge Developments are separately indicated.
(GD) Indicates a charge where it is desirable that the minister should have a knowledge of Gaelic.
(GE) Indicates a charge where public worship must be regularly conducted in Gaelic.
(H) Indicates that a Hearing Aid Loop system has been installed. In Linked charges, the (H) is placed beside the appropriate building as far as possible.
(L) Indicates that a Chair Lift has been installed.
(R) Indicates that the minister has been appointed on the basis of Reviewable Tenure.

PRESBYTERY NUMBERS

1	Edinburgh	18	Dumbarton
2	West Lothian	19	Argyll
3	Lothian	20	
4	Melrose and Peebles	21	
5	Duns	22	Falkirk
6	Jedburgh	23	Stirling
7	Annandale and Eskdale	24	Dunfermline
8	Dumfries and Kirkcudbright	25	Kirkcaldy
9	Wigtown and Stranraer	26	St Andrews
10	Ayr	27	Dunkeld and Meigle
11	Irvine and Kilmarnock	28	Perth
12	Ardrossan	29	Dundee
13	Lanark	30	Angus
14	Greenock and Paisley	31	Aberdeen
15		32	Kincardine and Deeside
16	Glasgow	33	Gordon
17	Hamilton	34	Buchan
		35	Moray
		36	Abernethy
		37	Inverness
		38	Lochaber
		39	Ross
		40	Sutherland
		41	Caithness
		42	Lochcarron – Skye
		43	Uist
		44	Lewis
		45	Orkney
		46	Shetland
		47	England
		48	International Charges
		49	Jerusalem

(1) EDINBURGH

The Presbytery meets:
- at Palmerston Place Church, Edinburgh, on 13 September, 1 November and 6 December 2016, and on 7 February, 28 March, 16 May and 27 June 2017;
- in the church of the Moderator on 4 October 2016.

Clerk: REV. GEORGE J. WHYTE BSc BD DMin   10/1 Palmerston Place, Edinburgh EH12 5AA   0131-225 9137
[E-mail: edinburgh@churchofscotland.org.uk]

Depute Clerk: HAZEL HASTIE MA CQSW PhD AIWS   17 West Court, Edinburgh EH16 4EB   07827 314374 (Mbl)
[E-mail: HHastie@churchofscotland.org.uk]

1 **Edinburgh: Albany Deaf Church of Edinburgh (H) (0131-444 2054)**
Rosemary A. Addis (Mrs) BD   2014   c/o Ministries Council, 121 George Street, Edinburgh EH2 4YN   07738 983393 (Mbl)
[E-mail: RAddis@churchofscotland.org.uk]
(Albany Deaf Church is a Mission Initiative of Edinburgh: St Andrew's and St George's West)

2 **Edinburgh: Balerno (H)**
Vacant

3 **Edinburgh: Barclay Viewforth (0131-229 6810) (E-mail: admin@barclaychurch.org.uk)**
Samuel A.R. Torrens BD   1995   2005   113 Meadowspot, Edinburgh EH10 5UY   0131-478 2376
[E-mail: STorrens@churchofscotland.org.uk]

4 **Edinburgh: Blackhall St Columba's (0131-332 4431) (E-mail: secretary@blackhallstcolumba.org.uk)**
Benjamin J.A. Abeledo BTh DipTh   1991   2016   5 Blinkbonny Crescent, Edinburgh EH4 3NB   0131-343 3708
[E-mail: BAbeledo@churchofscotland.org.uk]

5 **Edinburgh: Bristo Memorial Craigmillar**
Drausio P. Goncalves   2008   2013   72 Blackchapel Close, Edinburgh EH15 3SL   0131-657 3266
[E-mail: DGoncalves@churchofscotland.org.uk]

6 **Edinburgh: Broughton St Mary's (H) (0131-556 4786)**
Graham G. McGeoch MA BTh MTh   2009   2013   103 East Claremont Street, Edinburgh EH7 4JA   0131-556 7313
[E-mail: GMcGeoch@churchofscotland.org.uk]

7 **Edinburgh: Canongate (H)**
Neil N. Gardner MA BD   1991   2006   The Manse of Canongate, Edinburgh EH8 8BR   0131-556 3515
[E-mail: NGardner@churchofscotland.org.uk]

8 **Edinburgh: Carrick Knowe (H) (0131-334 1505) (E-mail: ckchurch@talktalk.net)**
Fiona M. Mathieson (Mrs)   1988   2001
BEd BD PGCommEd MTh
21 Traquair Park West, Edinburgh   EH12 7AN
[E-mail: FMathieson@churchofscotland.org.uk]
0131-334 9774

9 **Edinburgh: Colinton (H) (0131-441 2232) (E-mail: church.office@colinton-parish.com)**
Rolf H. Billes BD   1996   2009
The Manse, Colinton, Edinburgh   EH13 0JR
[E-mail: RBilles@churchofscotland.org.uk]
0131-466 8384

Gayle J.A. Taylor (Mrs) MA BD   1999   2009
(Associate Minister)
Colinton Parish Church, Dell Road, Edinburgh   EH13 0JR
[E-mail: GTaylor@churchofscotland.org.uk]
0131-441 2232

10 **Edinburgh: Corstorphine Craigsbank (H) (0131-334 6365)**
Stewart M. McPherson BD CertMin   1991   2003
17 Craigs Bank, Edinburgh   EH12 8HD
[E-mail: SMcPherson@churchofscotland.org.uk]
0131-467 6826
07814 901429 (Mbl)

11 **Edinburgh: Corstorphine Old (H) (0131-334 7864) (E-mail: corold@aol.com)**
Moira McDonald MA BD   1997   2005
23 Manse Road, Edinburgh   EH12 7SW
[E-mail: MMcDonald@churchofscotland.org.uk]
0131-476 5893

12 **Edinburgh: Corstorphine St Anne's (0131-316 4740) (E-mail: office@stannes.corstorphine.org.uk)**
James J. Griggs BD MTh   2011   2013
1/5 Morham Gait, Edinburgh   EH10 5GH
[E-mail: JGriggs@churchofscotland.org.uk]
0131-466 3269

13 **Edinburgh: Corstorphine St Ninian's (H) (0131-539 6204) (E-mail: office@st-ninians.co.uk)**
Alexander T. Stewart MA BD FSAScot   1975   1995
17 Templeland Road, Edinburgh   EH12 8RZ
[E-mail: AStewart@churchofscotland.org.uk]
0131-334 2978

14 **Edinburgh: Craiglockhart (H) (E-mail: office@craiglockhartchurch.org)**
Gordon Kennedy BSc BD MTh   1993   2012
20 Craiglockhart Quadrant, Edinburgh   EH14 1HD
[E-mail: GKennedy@churchofscotland.org.uk]
0131-444 1615

15 **Edinburgh: Craigmillar Park (H) (0131-667 5862) (E-mail: cpkirk@btinternet.com)**
John C.C. Urquhart MA MA BD   2010
14 Hallhead Road, Edinburgh   EH16 5QJ
[E-mail: JCUrquhart@churchofscotland.org.uk]
0131-667 1623

16 **Edinburgh: Cramond (H) (E-mail: cramond.kirk@blueyonder.co.uk)**
G. Russell Barr BA BD MTh DMin   1979   1993
Manse of Cramond, Edinburgh   EH4 6NS
[E-mail: GBarr@churchofscotland.org.uk]
0131-336 2036

17   Edinburgh: Currie (H) (0131-451 5141) (E-mail: currie_kirk@btconnect.com)
V. Easter Smart BA MDiv DMin   1996   2015   43 Lanark Road West, Currie EH14 5JX   0131-449 4719
[E-mail: ESmart@churchofscotland.org.uk]

18   Edinburgh: Dalmeny linked with Edinburgh: Queensferry
David C. Cameron BD CertMin   1993   2009   1 Station Road, South Queensferry EH30 9HY   0131-331 1100
[E-mail: DavidCCameron@churchofscotland.org.uk]

19   Edinburgh: Davidson's Mains (H) (0131-312 6282) (E-mail: life@dmainschurch.plus.com)
Daniel Robertson BA BD   2009   2016   1 Hillpark Terrace, Edinburgh EH4 7SX   0131-336 3078
[E-mail: Daniel.Robertson@churchofscotland.org.uk]   07909 840654 (Mbl)

20   Edinburgh: Dean (H)
Guardianship of the Presbytery   1 Ravelston Terrace, Edinburgh EH4 3EF   0131-332 5736

21   Edinburgh: Drylaw (0131-343 6643)
Vacant   15 House o' Hill Gardens, Edinburgh EH4 2AR   0131-531 5786

22   Edinburgh: Duddingston (H) (E-mail: dodinskirk@aol.com)
James A.P. Jack   1989   2001   Manse of Duddingston, Old Church Lane, Edinburgh EH15 3PX   0131-661 4240
BSc BArch BD DMin RIBA ARIAS   [E-mail: JJack@churchofscotland.org.uk]

23   Edinburgh: Fairmilehead (H) (0131-445 2374) (E-mail: office@fhpc.org.uk)
John R. Munro BD   1976   1992   c/o Fairmilehead Parish Church, 1 Frogston Road West,   0131-446 9363
Edinburgh EH10 7AA
[E-mail: JMunro@churchofscotland.org.uk]
Hayley O'Connor BS MDiv   2009   19 Caiystane Terrace, Edinburgh EH10 6SR   0131-629 1610
(Assistant Minister)   [E-mail: oconnorhe@gmail.com]

24   Edinburgh: Gorgie Dalry Stenhouse (H) (0131-337 7936)
Peter I. Barber MA BD   1984   1995   90 Myreside Road, Edinburgh EH10 5BZ   0131-337 2284
[E-mail: PBarber@churchofscotland.org.uk]

25   Edinburgh: Gracemount linked with Edinburgh: Liberton
John N. Young MA BD PhD   1996   7 Kirk Park, Edinburgh EH16 6HZ   0131-664 3067
[E-mail: JYoung@churchofscotland.org.uk]
(Gracemount is the new designation for Kaimes Lockhart Memorial)

26 Edinburgh: Granton (H) (0131-552 3033)

Norman A. Smith MA BD — 1997 2005 — 8 Wardie Crescent, Edinburgh EH5 1AG — 0131-551 2159
[E-mail: NSmith@churchofscotland.org.uk]

27 Edinburgh: Greenbank (H) (0131-447 9969) (E-mail: greenbankchurch@btconnect.com; Website: www.greenbankchurch.org)

Alison I. Swindells (Mrs) LLB BD — 1998 2007 — 112 Greenbank Crescent, Edinburgh EH10 5SZ — 0131-447 4032
[E-mail: ASwindells@churchofscotland.org.uk]

William H. Stone BA MDiv ThM — 2012 — 19 Caiystane Terrace, Edinburgh EH10 6SR — 0131-629 1610 / 07883 815598 (Mbl)
(Youth Minister)
[E-mail: billstoneiii@ gmail.com]

28 Edinburgh: Greenside (H) (0131-556 5588)

Guardianship of the Presbytery — 80 Pilrig Street, Edinburgh EH6 5AS — 0131-554 3277 (Tel/Fax)

29 Edinburgh: Greyfriars Kirk (GE) (H) (0131-225 1900) (E-mail: enquiries@greyfriarskirk.com)

Richard E. Frazer BA BD DMin — 1986 2003 — 12 Tantallon Place, Edinburgh EH9 1NZ — 0131-667 6610
[E-mail: RFrazer@churchofscotland.org.uk]

Lezley J. Stewart BD ThM MTh — 2000 2014 — Greyfriars Kirk, 1 Greyfriars Place, Edinburgh EH1 2QQ — 0131-225 1900 / 07713 974423 (Mbl)
(Associate Minister)
[E-mail: LStewart@churchofscotland.org.uk]

30 Edinburgh: High (St Giles') (0131-225 4363) (E-mail: info@stgilescathedral.org.uk)

Calum I. MacLeod BA BD — 1996 2014 — St Giles' Cathedral, Edinburgh EH1 1RE — 0131-225 4363
[E-mail: CMacLeod@churchofscotland.org.uk]

Helen J.R. Alexander BD DipSW — 1981 2012 — 7 Polwarth Place, Edinburgh EH11 1LG — 0131-346 0685
(Assistant Minister)
[E-mail: st_giles_cathedral@btconnect.com]

31 Edinburgh: Holyrood Abbey (H) (0131-661 6002)

Vacant — 100 Willowbrae Avenue, Edinburgh EH8 7HU

32 Edinburgh: Holy Trinity (H) (0131-442 3304)

Vacant — 16 Thorburn Road, Edinburgh EH13 0BQ — 0131-441 1403

Ian MacDonald BD MTh — 2005 — 5 Baberton Mains Terrace, Edinburgh EH14 3DG — 0131-281 6153
(Associate Minister)
[E-mail: ianafrica@hotmail.com]

Oliver M.H. Clegg BD (Youth Minister) — 2003 — 4 Blinkbonny Steading, Blinkbonny Road, Currie EH14 6AE — 0131-478 5341
[E-mail: ollieclegg@btinternet.com]

33 Edinburgh: Inverleith St Serf's (H)

Joanne G. Foster (Mrs) — 1996 2012 — 78 Pilrig Street, Edinburgh EH6 5AS — 0131-561 1392
DipTMus BD AdvDipCouns
[E-mail: JFoster@churchofscotland.org.uk]

34   Edinburgh: Juniper Green (H)
James S. Dewar MA BD   1983   2000
476 Lanark Road, Juniper Green, Edinburgh EH14 5BQ
[E-mail: JDewar@churchofscotland.org.uk]
0131-453 3494

35   Edinburgh: Kirkliston
Margaret R. Lane (Mrs) BA BD MTh   2009
43 Main Street, Kirkliston EH29 9AF
[E-mail: MLane@churchofscotland.org.uk]
0131-333 3298
07795 481441   (Mbl)

36   Edinburgh: Leith North (H) (0131-553 7378) (E-mail: nlpc-office@btinternet.com)
Alexander T. McAspurren BD MTh   2002   2011
6 Craighall Gardens, Edinburgh EH6 4RJ
[E-mail: AMcAspurren@churchofscotland.org.uk]
0131-551 5252

37   Edinburgh: Leith St Andrew's (H)
A. Robert A. Mackenzie LLB BD   1993   2013
30 Lochend Road, Edinburgh EH6 8BS
[E-mail: AMacKenzie@churchofscotlandorg.uk]
0131-553 2122

38   Edinburgh: Leith South (H) (0131-554 2578) (E-mail: slpc@dial.pipex.com)
John S. (Iain) May BSc MBA BD   2012
37 Claremont Road, Edinburgh EH6 7NN
[E-mail: JMay@churchofscotland.org.uk]
0131-554 3062

Pauline Robertson (Mrs) DCS BA CertTheol
6 Ashville Terrace, Edinburgh EH6 8DD
[E-mail: PRobertson@churchofscotland.org.uk]
0131-554 6564
07759 436303   (Mbl)

39   Edinburgh: Leith Wardie (H) (0131-551 3847) (E-mail: churchoffice@wardie.org.uk)
Ute Jaeger-Fleming MTh CPS   2008   2015
35 Lomond Road, Edinburgh EH5 3JN
[E-mail: UJaeger-Fleming@churchofscotland.org.uk]
0131-552 0190

40   Edinburgh: Liberton (H) See Edinburgh: Gracemount

41   Edinburgh: Liberton Northfield (H) (0131-551 3847)
Michael A. Taylor DipTh MPhil   2006   2015
9 Claverhouse Drive, Edinburgh EH16 6BR
[E-mail: MTaylor@churchofscotland.org.uk]
0131-664 5490
07479 985075   (Mbl)

42   Edinburgh: London Road (H) (0131-661 1149)
Vacant
26 Inchview Terrace, Edinburgh EH7 6TQ
0131-669 5311

43   Edinburgh: Marchmont St Giles' (H) (0131-447 4359)
Karen K. Campbell BD MTh DMin   1997   2002
2 Trotter Haugh, Edinburgh EH9 2GZ
[E-mail: KKCampbell@churchofscotland.org.uk]
0131-447 2834

44 Edinburgh: Mayfield Salisbury (0131-667 1522)
Scott S. McKenna BA BD MTh MPhil 1994 2000
26 Seton Place, Edinburgh EH9 2JT
[E-mail: SMcKenna@churchofscotland.org.uk]
0131-667 1286

45 Edinburgh: Morningside (H) (0131-447 6745) (E-mail: office@morningsideparishchurch.org.uk)
Derek Browning MA BD DMin 1987 2001
20 Braidburn Crescent, Edinburgh EH10 6EN
[E-mail: Derek.Browning@churchofscotland.org.uk]
0131-447 1617

46 Edinburgh: Morningside United (H) (0131-447 3152)
Steven Manders LLB BD STB MTh 2008 2015
1 Midmar Avenue, Edinburgh EH10 6BS
[E-mail: stevenmanders@hotmail.com]
0131-447 7943
07808 476733 (Mbl)
Morningside United is a Local Ecumenical Project shared with the United Reformed Church

47 Edinburgh: Murrayfield (H) (0131-337 1091) (E-mail: mpchurch@btconnect.com)
Keith Edwin Graham MA PGDip BD 2008 2014
45 Murrayfield Gardens, Edinburgh EH12 6DH
[E-mail: KEGraham@churchofscotland.org.uk]
0131-337 1364

48 Edinburgh: Newhaven (H)
Peter Bluett 2007
158 Granton Road, Edinburgh EH5 3RF
[E-mail: PBluett@churchofscotland.org.uk]
0131-476 5212

49 Edinburgh: Old Kirk and Muirhouse (H)
Stephen Ashley-Emery BD DPS 2006 2016
2 Thornyhall, Dalkeith EH22 2ND
[E-mail: SEmery@churchofscotland.org.uk]
07713 613069 (Mbl)

50 Edinburgh: Palmerston Place (H) (0131-220 1690) (E-mail: admin@palmerstonplacechurch.com)
Colin A.M. Sinclair BA BD 1981 1996
30B Cluny Gardens, Edinburgh EH10 6BJ
[E-mail: CSinclair@churchofscotland.org.uk]
0131-447 9598
0131-225 3312 (Fax)

51 Edinburgh: Pilrig St Paul's (0131-553 1876)
Mark M. Foster BSc BD 1998 2013
78 Pilrig Street, Edinburgh EH6 5AS
[E-mail: MFoster@churchofscotland.org.uk]
0131-332 5736

52 Edinburgh: Polwarth (H) (0131-346 2711) (E-mail: polwarthchurch@tiscali.co.uk)
Jack Holt BSc BD MTh 1985 2011
88 Craiglockhart Road, Edinburgh EH14 1EP
[E-mail: JHolt@churchofscotland.org.uk]
0131-441 6105

53 Edinburgh: Portobello and Joppa (H) (0131-669 3641)
Stewart G. Weaver BA BD PhD   2003   2014
6 St Mary's Place, Edinburgh EH15 2QF
[E-mail: SWeaver@churchofscotland.org.uk]
0131-669 2410

Laurens De Jager PgDip MDiv BTh   2013   2015
1 Brunstane Road North, Edinburgh EH15 2DL
[E-mail: LDeJager@churchofscotland.org.uk]
07521 426644 (Mbl)

54 Edinburgh: Priestfield (H) (0131-667 5644)
Jared W. Hay BA MTh DipMin DMin   1987   2009
13 Lady Road, Edinburgh EH16 5PA
[E-mail: JHay@churchofscotland.org.uk]
0131-468 1254

55 Edinburgh: Queensferry (H) See Edinburgh: Dalmeny

56 Edinburgh: Ratho
Ian J. Wells BD   1999
2 Freelands Road, Ratho, Newbridge EH28 8NP
[E-mail: IWells@churchofscotland.org.uk]
0131-333 1346

57 Edinburgh: Reid Memorial (H) (0131-662 1203) (E-mail: reid.memorial@btinternet.com)
Vacant
20 Wilton Road, Edinburgh EH16 5NX
0131-667 3981

58 Edinburgh: Richmond Craigmillar (H) (0131-661 6561)
Elizabeth M. Henderson MA BD MTh   1985   1997
Manse of Duddingston, Old Church Lane, Edinburgh EH15 3PX
[E-mail: EHenderson@churchofscotland.org.uk]
0131-661 4240

59 Edinburgh: St Andrew's and St George's West (H) (0131-225 3847) (E-mail: info@standrewsandstgeorges.org.uk)
Ian Y. Gilmour BD   1985   2011
25 Comely Bank, Edinburgh EH4 1AJ
[E-mail: IGilmour@churchofscotland.org.uk]
0131-332 5848

60 Edinburgh: St Andrew's Clermiston
Alistair H. Keil BD DipMin   1989
87 Drum Brae South, Edinburgh EH12 8TD
[E-mail: AKeil@churchofscotland.org.uk]
0131-339 4149

61 Edinburgh: St Catherine's Argyle (H) (0131-667 7220)
Stuart D. Irvin BD   2013   2016
5 Palmerston Road, Edinburgh EH9 1TL
[E-mail: SIrvin@churchofscotland.org.uk]
0131-667 9344

62 Edinburgh: St Cuthbert's (H) (0131-229 1142) (E-mail: office@st-cuthberts.net)
Vacant
Stark, Suzie BD   St Cuthbert's Church, 5 Lothian Road, Edinburgh EH1 2EP   0131-229 1142
  (Assistant Minister)   [E-mail: SStark@churchofscotland.org.uk]   07888 942561 (Mbl)

63 Edinburgh: St David's Broomhouse (H) (0131-443 9851)
Michael J. Mair BD   2014   33 Traquair Park West, Edinburgh EH12 7AN   0131-334 1730
                                           [E-mail: MMair@churchofscotland.org.uk]

64 Edinburgh: St John's Colinton Mains
Peter Nelson BSc BD   2015   2 Caiystane Terrace, Edinburgh EH10 6SR   07500 057889 (Mbl)
                                           [E-mail: PNelson@churchofscotland.org.uk]

65 Edinburgh: St Margaret's (H) (0131-554 7400) (E-mail: stm.parish@virgin.net)
Carolyn (Carol) H.M. Ford DSD   2003   43 Moira Terrace, Edinburgh EH7 6TD   0131-669 7329
  RSAMD BD   [E-mail: CFord@churchofscotland.org.uk]
Pauline Robertson (Mrs) DCS BA CertTheol 6 Ashville Terrace, Edinburgh EH6 8DD   0131-554 6564
                                           [E-mail: PRobertson@churchofscotland.org.uk]   07759 436303 (Mbl)

66 Edinburgh: St Martin's
Russel Moffat BD MTh PhD   1986 2008   5 Duddingston Crescent, Edinburgh EH15 3AS   0131-657 9894
                                           [E-mail: Russell.Moffat@churchofscotland.org.uk]

67 Edinburgh: St Michael's (H) (E-mail: office@stmichaels-kirk.co.uk)
James D. Aitken BD   2002 2005   9 Merchiston Gardens, Edinburgh EH10 5DD   0131-346 1970
                                           [E-mail: JAitken@churchofscotland.org.uk]

68 Edinburgh: St Nicholas' Sighthill
Thomas M. Kisitu MTh PhD   2015   122 Sighthill Loan, Edinburgh EH11 4NT   0131-442 3978
                                           [E-mail: TMKisitu@churchofscotland.org.uk]

69 Edinburgh: St Stephen's Comely Bank (0131-315 4616)
George Vidits BD MTh   2000 2015   8 Blinkbonny Crescent, Edinburgh EH4 3NB   0131-332 3364
                                           [E-mail: GVidits@churchofscotland.org.uk]

70 Edinburgh: Slateford Longstone
Michael W. Frew BSc BD   1978 2005   50 Kingsknowe Road South, Edinburgh EH14 2JW   0131-466 5308
                                           [E-mail: MFrew@churchofscotland.org.uk]

71 Edinburgh: Stockbridge (H) (0131-552 8738) (E-mail: stockbridgechurch@btconnect.com)

John A. Cowie BSc BD   1983   2013   19 Eildon Street, Edinburgh EH3 5JU   0131-557 6052
                                                                           07506 104416 (Mbl)
[E-mail: JCowie@churchofscotland.org.uk]

72 Edinburgh: The Tron Kirk (Gilmerton and Moredun)

Cameron Mackenzie BD   1997   2010   467 Gilmerton Road, Edinburgh EH17 7JG   0131-664 7538
[E-mail: Cammy.Mackenzie@churchofscotland.org.uk]

Liz Crocker DipComEd DCS   77c Craigcrook Road, Edinburgh EH4 3PH   0131-332 0227
[E-mail: ECrocker@churchofscotland.org.uk]

73 Edinburgh: Willowbrae (H) (0131-661 5676)

Vacant

(Edinburgh: Willowbrae is a new charge formed by the union of Edinburgh: Craigentinny St Christopher's and Edinburgh: New Restalrig)

Abernethy, William LTh	1979	1993	(Glenrothes: St Margaret's)	120/1 Willowbrae Road, Edinburgh EH8 7HW	0131-661 0390
Aitken, Alexander R. MA	1965	1997	(Newhaven)	36 King's Meadow, Edinburgh EH16 5JW	0131-667 1404
Alexander, Ian W. BA BD STM	1990	2010	World Mission Council	121 George Street, Edinburgh EH2 4YN [E-mail: IAlexander@churchofscotland.org.uk]	0131-225 5722
Anderson, Robert S. BD	1988	1997	(Scottish Churches World Exchange)		
Armitage, William L. BSc BD	1976	2006	(Edinburgh: London Road)	Flat 7, 4 Papermill Wynd, Edinburgh EH7 4GJ [E-mail: bill@billarm.plus.com]	0131-558 8534
Baird, Kenneth S. MSc PhD BD MIMarEST	1998	2009	(Edinburgh: Leith North)	3 Maule Terrace, Gullane EH31 2DB	01620 843447
Barrington, Charles W.H. MA BD	1997	2007	(Associate: Edinburgh: Balerno)	502 Lanark Road, Edinburgh EH14 5DH	0131-453 4826
Beckett, David M. BA BD	1964	2002	(Edinburgh: Greyfriars, Tolbooth and Highland Kirk)	1F1, 31 Sciennes Road, Edinburgh EH9 1NT [E-mail: davidbeckett3@aol.com]	0131-667 2672
Blakey, Ronald S. MA BD MTh	1962	2000	(Assembly Council)	24 Kimmerghame Place, Edinburgh EH4 2GE [E-mail: kathleen.blakey@gmail.com]	0131-343 6352 / 07851 598101 (Mbl)
Booth, Jennifer (Mrs) BD	1996	2004	(Associate: Leith South)	39 Lilyhill Terrace, Edinburgh EH8 7DR	0131-661 3813
Borthwick, Kenneth S. MA BD	1983	2016	(Edinburgh: Holy Trinity)	[E-mail: kennysamuel@aol.com]	07735 749594 (Mbl)
Boyd, Kenneth M. MA BD PhD FRCPE	1970	1996	University of Edinburgh: Medical Ethics	1 Doune Terrace, Edinburgh EH3 6DY	0131-225 6485
Brady, Ian D. BSc ARCST BD	1967	2001	(Edinburgh: Corstorphine Old)	28 Frankfield Crescent, Dalgety Bay, Dunfermline KY11 9LW [E-mail: pidb@dbay28.fsnet.co.uk]	01383 825104
Brook, Stanley A. BD MTh	1977	2016	(Newport-on-Tay)	4 Scotstoun Green, South Queensferry EH30 9YA [E-mail: stan_brook@btinternet.com]	0131-331 4237
Brown, William D. MA	1963	1989	(Wishaw: Thornlie)	9/3 Craigend Park, Edinburgh EH16 5XY [E-mail: wdbrown@surefish.co.uk]	0131-672 2936
Brown, William D. BD CQSW	1987	2013	(Edinburgh: Murrayfield)	79 Carnbee Park, Edinburgh EH16 6GG [E-mail: wdb@talktalk.net]	0131-261 7297
Cameron, G. Gordon MA BD STM	1957	1997	(Juniper Green)	10 Beechwood Gardens, Stirling FK8 2AX	01786 472934
Cameron, John W.M. MA BD	1957	1996	(Liberton)	10 Plewlands Gardens, Edinburgh EH10 5JP	0131-447 1277
Chalmers, Murray MA	1965	2006	(Hospital Chaplain)	8 Easter Warriston, Edinburgh EH7 4QX	0131-552 4211

Clark, Christine M. (Mrs) BA BD MTh	2006	2013	(Aberlady with Gullane)	40 Pentland Avenue, Edinburgh EH13 0HY [E-mail: christine.clark7@aol.co.uk]	0131-312 8447
Clinkenbeard, William W. BSc BD STM	1966	2000	(Edinburgh: Carrick Knowe)	3/17 Western Harbour Breakwater, Edinburgh EH6 6PA [E-mail: bjclinks@compuserve.com]	0131-664 1358
Cook, John MA BD	1967	2005	(Edinburgh: Leith St Andrew's)	26 Silverknowes Court, Edinburgh EH4 5NR	0131-476 3864
Curran, Elizabeth M. (Miss) BD	1995	2008	(Aberlour)	Blackford Grange, 39/2 Blackford Avenue, Edinburgh EH9 3HN [E-mail: ecurran8@aol.com]	
Cuthell, Tom C. MA BD MTh	1965	2007	(Edinburgh: St Cuthbert's)	Flat 10, 2 Kingsburgh Crescent, Waterfront, Edinburgh EH5 1JS	
Davidson, D. Hugh MA	1965	2009	(Edinburgh: Inverleith)	Flat 1/2, 22 Summerside Place, Edinburgh EH6 4NZ [E-mail: hdavidson35@btinternet.com]	0131-554 8420
Davidson, Ian M.P. MBE MA BD	1954	1994	(Stirling: Allan Park South with Church of the Holy Rude)	13/8 Craigend Park, Edinburgh EH16 5XX	0131-664 0074
Dawson, Michael S. BTech BD	1979	2005	(Associate: Edinburgh: Holy Trinity)	9 The Broich, Alva FK12 5NR [E-mail: mixpen.dawson@btinternet.com]	01259 769309
Dilbey, Mary D. (Miss) BD	1997	2002	(West Kirk of Calder)	41 Bonaly Rise, Edinburgh EH13 0QU	0131-441 9092
Donald, Alistair P. MA PhD BD	1999	2009	Chaplain: Heriot-Watt University	The Chaplaincy, Heriot-Watt University, Edinburgh EH14 4AS [E-mail: a.p.donald@hw.ac.uk]	0131-451 4508
Dougall, Elspeth G. (Mrs) MA BD	1989	2001	(Edinburgh: Marchmont St Giles')	60B Craigmillar Park, Edinburgh EH16 5PU	0131-668 1342
Douglas, Alexander B. BD	1979	2014	(Edinburgh: Blackhall St Columba's)	15 Inchview Gardens, Dalgety Bay, Dunfermline KY11 9SA [E-mail: alexandjill@douglas.net]	01383 242872
Douglas, Colin R. MA BD STM	1969	2007	(Livingston Ecumenical Parish)	34 West Pilton Gardens, Edinburgh EH4 4EQ [E-mail: colinrdouglas@btinternet.com]	0131-551 3808
Doyle, Ian B. MA BD PhD	1946	1991	(Department of National Mission)	21 Lygon Road, Edinburgh EH16 5QD	0131-667 2697
Drummond, Rhoda (Miss) DCS			(Deacon)	Flat K, 23 Grange Loan, Edinburgh EH9 2ER	0131-668 3631
Dunn, W. Iain C. DA LTh	1983	1998	(Pilrig and Dalmeny Street)	10 Fox Covert Avenue, Edinburgh EH12 6UQ	0131-334 1665
Embleton, Brian M. BD	1976	2015	(Edinburgh: Reid Memorial)	54 Edinburgh Road, Peebles EH45 8EB [E-mail: bmembleton@gmail.com]	01721 602157
Embleton, Sara R. (Mrs) BA BD MTh	1988	2010	(Edinburgh: Leith St Serf's)	54 Edinburgh Road, Peebles EH45 8EB [E-mail: srembleton@gmail.com]	01721 602157
Evans, Mark BSc MSc DCS	2006		Head of Spiritual Care NHS Fife	13 Easter Drylaw Drive, Edinburgh EH4 2QA [E-mail: mark.evans59@nhs.net]	(Home) 0131-343 3089 (Office) 01383 674136
Farquharson, Gordon MA BD DipEd	1998	2007	(Stonehaven: Dunnottar)	26 Learmonth Court, Edinburgh EH4 1PB [E-mail: gfarqu@talktalk.net]	0131-343 1047
Faulds, Norman L. MA BD FSAScot	1968	2000	(Aberlady with Gullane)	10 West Fenton Court, West Fenton, North Berwick EH39 5AE	01620 842331
Fergusson, David A.S. OBE MA BD DPhil DD FBA FRSE (Prof.)	1984	2000	University of Edinburgh	23 Riselaw Crescent, Edinburgh EH10 6HN	0131-447 4022
Forrester, Margaret R. (Mrs) MA BD	1974	2003	(Edinburgh: St Michael's)	25 Kingsburgh Road, Edinburgh EH12 6DZ [E-mail: margaret@rosskeen.org.uk]	0131-337 5646
Fraser, Shirley A. (Miss) MA BD	1992	2008	(Scottish Field Director: Friends International)	6/50 Roseburn Drive, Edinburgh EH12 5NS	0131-347 1400
Gardner, John V.	1997	2003	(Glamis, Inverarity and Kinnettles)	75/1 Lockharton Avenue, Edinburgh EH14 1BD [E-mail: jvgardnerf66@googlemail.com]	0131-443 7126
Gordon, Margaret (Mrs) DCS			(Edinburgh: Currie)	92 Lanark Road West, Currie EH14 5LA	0131-449 2554

Gordon, Tom MA BD	1974	2009	(Chaplain: Marie Curie Hospice, Edinburgh)	22 Gosford Road, Port Seton, Prestonpans EH32 0HF	01875 812262
Graham, W. Peter MA BD	1967	2008	(Presbytery Clerk)	23/6 East Comiston, Edinburgh EH10 6RZ	0131-445 5763
Hardman Moore, Susan (Prof.) BA PGCE MA PhD		2013	Ordained Local Minister	c/o New College, Mound Place, Edinburgh EH1 2LX [E-mail: SHardman-Moore@churchofscotland.org.uk]	0131-650 8908 (Mbl) 07811 345699
Harkness, James CB OBE QHC MA DD	1961	1995	(Chaplain General: Army)	13 Saxe Coburg Place, Edinburgh EH3 5BR	0131-343 1297
Herbold Ross, Kristina M.	2008	2016	Workplace Chaplain	Old Parish Church Office, 2a Costorphine High Street, Edinburgh EH12 7ST [E-mail: kristina.ross@wpcscotland.co.uk]	(Mbl) 07702 863342
Hill, J. William BA BD	1967	2001	(Edinburgh: Corstorphine St Anne's)	33/9 Murrayfield Road, Edinburgh EH12 6EP	
Inglis, Ann (Mrs) LLB BD	1986	2015	(Langton and Lammermuir Kirk)	34 Echline View, South Queensferry EH30 9XL [E-mail: revainglis@gmail.com]	0131-629 0233
Irving, William D. LTh	1985	2005	(Golspie)	122 Swanston Muir, Edinburgh EH10 7HY	0131-441 3384
Jeffrey, Eric W.S. JP MA	1954	1994	(Edinburgh: Bristo Memorial)	18 Gillespie Crescent, Edinburgh EH10 4HT	0131-229 7815
Kingston, David V.F. BD DipPTh	1993	2015	(Chaplain: Army)	2 Cleuch Avenue, North Middleton, Gorebridge EH23 4RP	01875 822026
Lawson, Kenneth C. MA BD	1963	1999	(Adviser in Adult Education)	56 Easter Drylaw View, Edinburgh EH4 2QP	0131-539 3311
Logan, Anne T. (Mrs) MA BD MTh DMin	1981	2012	(Edinburgh: Stockbridge)	Sunnyside Cottage, 18 Upper Broomieknowe, Lasswade EH18 1LP [E-mail: annetlogan@blueyonder.co.uk]	0131-663 9550
McCaskill, George I.L. MA BD	1953	1990	(Religious Education)	19 Tyler's Acre Road, Edinburgh EH12 7HY	0131-334 7451
Macdonald, Finlay A.J. MA BD PhD DD	1971	2010	(Principal Clerk)	8 St Ronan's Way, Innerleithen EH44 6RG [E-mail: finlay_macdonald@btinternet.com]	01896 831631
Macdonald, Peter J. BD	1986	2009	Leader of the Iona Community	63 Jim Bush Drive, Prestonpans EH32 9GB [E-mail: petermacdonald@iona.org.uk] [E-mail: petermacdonald166@btinternet.com]	(Office) 0141-429 7281 (Mbl) 07946 715166 01875 819655
Macdonald, William J. BD	1976	2002	(Board of National Mission: New Charge Development)	1/13 North Werber Park, Edinburgh EH4 1SY	0131-332 0254
MacGregor, Margaret S. (Miss) MA BD DipEd	1985	1994	(Calcutta)	16 Learmonth Court, Edinburgh EH4 1PB	0131-332 1089
McGregor, Alistair G.C. QC BD	1987	2002	(Edinburgh: Leith North)	22 Primrose Bank Road, Edinburgh EH5 3JG	0131-551 2802
McGregor, T. Stewart MBE MA BD	1957	1998	(Chaplain: Edinburgh Royal Infirmary)	19 Lonsdale Terrace, Edinburgh EH3 9HL [E-mail: cetsm@uwclub.net]	0131-229 5332
MacKay, Stewart A.		2009	Chaplain: Army	3 Bn Black Watch, Royal Regiment of Scotland, Fort George, Ardersier, Inverness IV1 2TD	
Mackenzie, James G. BA BD	1980	2005	(Jersey: St Columba's)	26 Drylaw Crescent, Edinburgh EH4 2AU [E-mail: jgmackenzie@jerseymail.co.uk]	0131-332 3720
MacLaughlan, Grant BA BD	1998	2013	Workplace Chaplain	54 Crieff Road, Perth PH1 2RS [E-mail: grm6871@gmail.com]	
Maclean, Ailsa G. (Mrs) BD DipCE	1979	1988	(Chaplain: George Heriot's School)	28 Swan Spring Avenue, Edinburgh EH10 6NJ	0131-445 1320
Macmillan, Gilleasbuig I. KCVO MA BD Drhc DD FRSE HRSA FRCSEd	1969	2013	(Edinburgh: High (St Giles'))	207 Dalkeith Road, Edinburgh EH16 5DS [E-mail: gmacmillan1@btinternet.com]	0131-667 5732
MacMurchie, F. Lynne LLB BD	1998	2003	Healthcare Chaplain	Edinburgh Community Mental Health Chaplaincy, 41 George IV Bridge, Edinburgh EH1 1EL	0131-220 5150
McNab, John L. MA BD	1997	2014	Ministries Council	121 George Street, Edinburgh EH2 4YN	0131-225 5722
McPake, John M. LTh	2000	2014	(Edinburgh: Liberton Northfield)	9 Claverhouse Drive, Edinburgh EH16 6BR [E-mail: john_mcpake9@yahoo.co.uk]	0131-658 1754

Name	Ord.	Ind.	Role	Address	Telephone
McPheat, Elspeth DCS			Deaconess: CrossReach	11/5 New Orchardfield, Edinburgh EH6 5ET [E-mail: elspeth176@sky.com]	0131-554 4143
McPhee, Duncan C. MA BD	1953	1993	(Department of National Mission)	8 Belvedere Park, Edinburgh EH6 4LR	0131-552 6784
Macpherson, Colin C.R. MA BD	1958	1996	(Dunfermline St Margaret's)	7 Eva Place, Edinburgh EH9 3ET	0131-667 1456
McPherson, Marjory (Mrs) LLB BD MTh	1990	2012	Ministries Council	17 Craigs Bank, Edinburgh EH12 8HD [E-mail: MMcPherson@churchofscotland.org.uk]	0131-467 6826
Mathieson, Angus R. MA BD	1988	1998	Ministries Council	21 Traquair Park West, Edinburgh EH12 7AN	0131-334 9774
Moir, Ian A. MA BD	1962	2000	(Adviser for Urban Priority Areas)	28/6 Comely Bank Avenue, Edinburgh EH4 1EL	0131-332 2748
Monteith, W. Graham BD PhD	1974	1994	(Flotta and Fara with Hoy and Walls)	20/3 Grandfield, Edinburgh EH6 4TL	0131-552 2564
Morrice, William G. MA BD STM PhD	1957	1991	(St John's College, Durham)	Flat 37, The Cedars, 2 Manse Road, Edinburgh EH12 7SN [E-mail: w.g.morrice@btinternet.com]	0131-316 4845
Morrison, Mary B. (Mrs) MA BD DipEd	1978	2000	(Edinburgh: Stenhouse St Aidan's)	174 Craigcrook Road, Edinburgh EH4 3PP	0131-336 4706
Moyes, Sheila A. (Miss) DCS			(Deacon)	158 Pilton Avenue, Edinburgh EH5 2JZ [E-mail: sheilamoyes@btinternet.com]	0131-551 1731
Mulligan, Anne MA DCS			(Deacon: Hospital Chaplain)	27A Craigour Avenue, Edinburgh EH17 1NH [E-mail: mulliganne@aol.com]	0131-664 3426
Munro, George A.M.	1968	2000	(Edinburgh: Cluny)	108 Caiyside, Edinburgh EH10 7HR	0131-445 5829
Munro, John P.L. MA BD PhD	1977	2007	(Kinross)	5 Marchmont Crescent, Edinburgh EH9 1HN [E-mail: jplmunro@yahoo.co.uk]	0131-623 0198
Murrie, John BD	1953	1996	(Kirkliston)	31 Nicol Road, The Whins, Broxburn EH52 6JJ	01506 852464
Orr, Sheena BA MSc MBA BD	2011	2015	Prison Chaplain	HM Prison, Edinburgh EH11 3LN [E-mail: sheens59@gmail.com]	0131-444 3115 / 07922 649160 (Mbl)
Paterson, Douglas S. MA BD	1976	2010	(Edinburgh: St Colm's)	4 Ards Place, High Street, Aberlady EH32 0DB	01875 870192
Plate, Maria A.G. (Miss) LTh BA	1983	2000	(South Ronaldsay and Burray)	Flat 29, 77 Barnton Park View, Edinburgh EH4 6EL	0131-339 8539
Rennie, Agnes M. (Miss) DCS			(Deacon)	3/1 Craigmillar Court, Edinburgh EH16 4AD	0131-661 8475
Ridland, Alistair K. MA BD	1982	2000	Chaplain: Western General Hospital	13 Stewart Place, Kirkliston EH29 0BQ	0131-333 2711
Robertson, Charles LVO MA	1965	2005	(Edinburgh: Canongate)	3 Ross Gardens, Edinburgh EH9 3BS [E-mail: canongate1@aol.com]	0131-662 9025
Robertson, Norma P. (Miss) BD DMin MTh	1993	2002	(Kincardine O'Neil with Lumphanan)	Flat 5, 2 Burnbrae Drive, Grovewood Hill, Edinburgh EH12 8AS	0131-339 6701
Ronald, Norma A. (Miss) MBE DCS			(Deacon)	2B Saughton Road North, Edinburgh EH12 7HG	0131-334 8736
Ross, Matthew Z. LLB BD MTh FSAScot	1998	2014	General Secretary, Action of Churches Together in Scotland (ACTS)	Jubilee House, Forthside Way, Stirling FK8 1QZ [E-mail: matthewross@acts-scotland.org]	01259 222360 / 07111 706950 (Mbl)
Schofield, Melville F. MA	1960	2000	(Chaplain: Western General Hospital)	25 Rowantree Grove, Currie EH14 5AT	0131-449 4745
Scott, Ian G. BSc BD STM	1965	2006	(Edinburgh: Greenbank)	50 Forthview Walk, Tranent EH33 1FE [E-mail: igscott50@btinternet.com]	01875 612907
Scott, Jayne E. BA MEd MBA	1988	2016	Secretary, Ministries Council	121 George Street, Edinburgh EH2 4YN [E-mail: JScott@churchofscotland.org.uk]	0131-225 5722
Scott, Martin DipMusEd RSAM BD PhD	1986	2016	Secretary, Council of Assembly	121 George Street, Edinburgh EH2 4YN [E-mail: MScott@churchofscotland.org.uk]	0131-225 5722
Shewan, Frederick D.F. MA BD	1970	2005	(Edinburgh: Muirhouse St Andrew's)	36 Glendinning Road, Kirkliston EH29 9HE	0131-333 2631
Smith, Angus MA LTh	1965	2006	(Chaplain to the Oil Industry)	3/7 West Powburn, West Savile Gait, Edinburgh EH9 3EW	0131-667 1761

Name	Description	Ord.	Ind.	Address	Phone
Steele, Marilynn J. (Mrs) BD DCS	(Deacon)			2 Northfield Gardens, Prestonpans EH32 9LQ [E-mail: marilynmsteele@aol.com]	01875 811497
Stephen, Donald M. TD MA BD ThM	(Edinburgh: Marchmont St Giles')	1962	2001	10 Hawkhead Crescent, Edinburgh EH16 6LR [E-mail: donaldmstephen@gmail.com]	0131-658 1216
Stevenson, John MA BD PhD	(Department of Education)	1963	2001	12 Swanston Gardens, Edinburgh EH10 7DL	0131-445 3960
Stirling, A. Douglas BSc	(Rhu and Shandon)	1956	1994	162 Avontoun Park, Linlithgow EH49 6QH	01506 845021
Stitt, Ronald J. Maxwell LTh BA ThM BREd DMin FSAScot	(Hamilton: Gilmour and Whitehill)	1977	2012	413 Gilmerton Road, Edinburgh EH17 7JJ	
Tait, John M. BSc BD	(Edinburgh: Pilrig St Paul's)	1985	2012	82 Greenend Gardens, Edinburgh EH17 7QH [E-mail: johnmtait@me.com]	0131-258 9105
Taylor, William R. MA BD MTh	Chaplaincy Adviser (Church of Scotland): Scottish Prison Service	1983	2004	Calton House, 5 Redheughs Rigg, South Gyle, Edinburgh EH12 9DQ [E-mail: bill.taylor@sps.pnn.gov.uk]	0131-244 8640
Teague, Yvonne (Mrs) DCS	(Board of Ministry)			46 Craigcrook Avenue, Edinburgh EH4 3PX [E-mail: y.teague.1@blueyonder.co.uk]	0131-336 3113
Telfer, Iain J.M. BD DPS	Chaplain: Royal Infirmary	1978	2001	Royal Infirmary of Edinburgh, 51 Little France Crescent, Edinburgh EH16 4SA	0131-242 1997
Thom, Helen (Miss) BA DipEd MA DCS	(Deacon)			84 Great King Street, Edinburgh EH3 6QU	0131-556 5687
Thomson, Donald M. BD	(Tullibody: St Serf's)	1975	2013	50 Sighthill Road, Edinburgh EH11 4NY [E-mail: donniethomson@tiscali.co.uk]	
Tweedie, Fiona BSc PhD	Ordained Local Minister: Mission Statistics Co-ordinator	2011		121 George Street, Edinburgh EH2 4YN [E-mail: ftweedie@churchofscotland.org.uk]	0131-225 5722
Watson, Nigel G. MA	(Associate: East Kilbride: Old/Stewartfield/West)	1998	2012	7 St Catherine's Place, Edinburgh EH9 1NU [E-mail: nigel.g.watson@gmail.com]	0131-662 4191
Webster, Peter BD	(Edinburgh: Portbello St James')	1977	2014	51 Kempock Street, Gourock PA19 1NF [E-mail: peterwebster101@hotmail.com]	01475 321916
Whyte, George J. BSc BD DMin	Presbytery Clerk	1981	2008	4 Baberton Mains Lea, Edinburgh EH14 3HB [E-mail: edinburgh@churchofscotland.org.uk]	0131-466 1674
Whyte, Iain A. BA BD STM PhD	(Community Mental Health Chaplain)	1968	2005	14 Carlingnose Point, North Queensferry, Inverkeithing KY11 1ER [E-mail: iainisabel@whytes28.fsnet.co.uk]	01383 410732
Wigglesworth, J. Christopher MBE BSc PhD BD	(St Andrew's College, Selly Oak)	1968	1999	12 Leven Terrace, Edinburgh EH3 9LW [E-mail: wiggles@talk21.com]	0131-228 6335
Williams, Jenny M. BSc CQSW BD	Health, healing, spirituality	1996	1997	16 Blantyre Terrace, Edinburgh EH10 5AE [E-mail: butterfly.greenleaf@gmx.net]	0131-447 0050
Wilson, John M. MA	(Adviser in Religious Education)	1964	1995	27 Bellfield Street, Edinburgh EH15 2BR	0131-669 5257
Wishart, William DCS	(Deacon)			1 Brunstane Road North, Edinburgh EH15 2DL [E-mail: bill@wishartfamily.co.uk]	07846 555654 (Mbl)
Wynne, Alistair T.E. BA BD	(Nicosia Community Church, Cyprus)	1982	2009	Flat 6, 14 Burnbrae Drive, Edinburgh EH12 8AS [E-mail: awynne2@googlemail.com]	0131-339 6462
Young, Alexander W. BD DipMin	(Head of Spiritual Care: NHS Lothian)	1988	2016	32 Lindsay Circus, The Hawthorns, Rosewell EH24 9EP	

EDINBURGH ADDRESSES

Albany	82 Montrose Terrace
Balerno	Johnsburn Road, Balerno
Barclay Viewforth	Barclay Place
Blackhall St Columba's	Queensferry Road
Bristo Memorial	Peffermill Road, Craigmillar
Broughton St Mary's	Bellevue Crescent
Canongate	Canongate
Carrick Knowe	North Saughton Road
Colinton	Dell Road
Corstorphine	
Craigsbank	Craig's Crescent
Old	Kirk Loan
St Anne's	Kaimes Road
St Ninian's	St John's Road
Craiglockhart	Craiglockhart Avenue
Craigmillar Park	Craigmillar Park
Cramond	Cramond Glebe Road
Currie	Kirkgate, Currie
Davidson's Mains	Quality Street
Dean	Dean Path
Drylaw	Groathill Road North
Duddingston	Old Church Lane, Duddingston
Fairmilehead	Frogston Road West, Fairmilehead
Gorgie Dalry Stenhouse	Gorgie Road
Edgar Hall	Chesser Avenue
Gracemount	Gracemount Drive
Granton	Boswall Parkway
Greenbank	Braidburn Terrace
Greenside	Royal Terrace
Greyfriars Kirk	Greyfriars Place
High (St Giles')	High Street
Holyrood Abbey	Dalziel Place x London Road
Holy Trinity	Hailesland Place, Wester Hailes
Inverleith St Serf's	Ferry Road
Juniper Green	Lanark Road, Juniper Green
Kirkliston	The Square, Kirkliston
Leith	
North	Madeira Street off Ferry Road
St Andrew's	Easter Road
South	Kirkgate, Leith
Wardie	Primrosebank Road
Liberton	Kirkgate, Liberton
Northfield	Gilmerton Road, Liberton
London Road	London Road
Marchmont St Giles'	Kilgraston Road
Mayfield Salisbury	Mayfield Road x West Mayfield
Morningside	Cluny Gardens
Morningside United	Bruntsfield Place x Chamberlain Rd
Murrayfield	Abinger Gardens
Newhaven	Craighall Road
Old Kirk and Muirhouse	Pennywell Gardens
Palmerston Place	Palmerston Place
Pilrig St Paul's	Pilrig Street
Polwarth	Polwarth Terrace x Harrison Road
Portobello and Joppa	Abercorn Terrace
Priestfield	Dalkeith Road x Marchhall Place
Queensferry	The Loan, South Queensferry
Ratho	Baird Road, Ratho
Reid Memorial	West Savile Terrace
Richmond Craigmillar	Niddrie Mains Road
St Andrew's and	
St George's West	George Street
St Andrew's Clermiston	Clermiston View
St Catherine's Argyle	Grange Road x Chalmers Crescent
St Cuthbert's	Lothian Road
St David's Broomhouse	Broomhouse Crescent
St John's Colinton Mains	Oxgangs Road North
St Margaret's	Restalrig Road South
St Martin's	Magdalene Drive
St Michael's	Slateford Road
St Nicholas' Sighthill	Calder Road
St Stephen's Comely Bank	Comely Bank
Slateford Longstone	Kingsknowe Road North
Stockbridge	Saxe Coburg Street
The Tron Kirk (Gilmerton and Moredun)	Craigour Gardens and Ravenscroft Street
Willowbrae	Willowbrae Road

(2) WEST LOTHIAN

Meets in the church of the incoming Moderator on the first Tuesday of September and in St John's Church Hall, Bathgate, on the first Tuesday of every other month, except December, when the meeting is on the second Tuesday, and January, July and August, when there is no meeting.

Clerk: REV. DUNCAN SHAW BD MTh   St John's Manse, Mid Street, Bathgate **EH48 1QD**   **01506 653146**
[E-mail: westlothian@churchofscotland.org.uk]

Abercorn (H) linked with Pardovan, Kingscavil (H) and Winchburgh (H)
A. Scott Marshall DipComm BD   1984   1998   The Manse, Winchburgh, Broxburn EH52 6TT   01506 890919
[E-mail: SMarshall@churchofscotland.org.uk]

Armadale (H) Julia C. Wiley (Ms) MA(CE) MDiv	1998	2010	70 Mount Pleasant, Armadale, Bathgate EH48 3HB [E-mail: JWiley@churchofscotland.org.uk]	01501 730358
Margaret Corrie (Miss) DCS			44 Sunnyside Street, Camelon, Falkirk FK1 4BH [E-mail: MCorrie@churchofscotland.org.uk]	07955 633969 (Mbl)
Avonbridge (H) linked with Torphichen (H) Vacant			Manse Road, Torphichen, Bathgate EH48 4LT	01506 676803
Bathgate: Boghall (H) Christopher Galbraith BA LLB BD	2012		1 Manse Place, Ash Grove, Bathgate EH48 1NJ [E-mail: CGalbraith@churchofscotland.org.uk]	01506 652715
Bathgate: High (H) Emma McDonald BD	2013	2015	19 Hunter Grove, Bathgate EH48 1NN [E-mail: EMcDonald@churchofscotland.org.uk]	01506 650038
Bathgate: St John's (H) Duncan Shaw BD MTh	1975	1978	St John's Manse, Mid Street, Bathgate EH48 1QD [E-mail: westlothian@churchofscotland.org.uk]	01506 653146
Blackburn and Seafield (H) Robert A. Anderson MA BD DPhil	1980	1998	The Manse, 5 MacDonald Gardens, Blackburn, Bathgate EH47 7RE [E-mail: RAnderson@churchofscotland.org.uk]	01506 652825
Blackridge (H) linked with Harthill: St Andrew's (H) Vacant			East Main Street, Harthill, Shotts ML7 5QW	01501 751239
Breich Valley (H) Robert J. Malloch BD	1987	2013	Breich Valley Manse, Stoneyburn, Bathgate EH47 8AU [E-mail: RMalloch@churchofscotland.org.uk]	01501 763142
Broxburn Jacobus Boonzaaier BA BCom(OR) BD MDiv PhD	1995	2015	2 Church Street, Broxburn EH52 5EL [E-mail: JBoonzaaier@churchofscotland.org.uk]	01506 337560
Fauldhouse: St Andrew's (H) Vacant			7 Glebe Court, Fauldhouse, Bathgate EH47 9DX	01501 771190

Harthill: St Andrew's See Blackridge

Kirknewton (H) and East Calder (H)

Name	Ord.	Ind.	Address	Phone
Andre Groenewald BA BD MDiv DD	1994	2009	8 Manse Court, East Calder, Livingston EH53 0HF [E-mail: AGroenewald@churchofscotland.org.uk]	01506 884585 / 07588 845814 (Mbl) / 0131-333 2746
Brenda Robson PhD (Auxiliary Minister)	2005	2014	2 Baird Road, Ratho, Newbridge EH28 8RA [E-mail: BRobson@churchofscotland.org.uk]	

Kirk of Calder (H)

Name	Ord.	Ind.	Address	Phone
John M. Povey MA BD	1981		19 Maryfield Park, Mid Calder, Livingston EH53 0SB [E-mail: JPovey@churchofscotland.org.uk]	01506 882495
Kay McIntosh (Mrs) DCS			4 Jacklin Green, Livingston EH54 8PZ [E-mail: kay@backedge.co.uk]	01506 440543

Linlithgow: St Michael's (H) (E-mail: info@stmichaels-parish.org.uk)

Name	Ord.	Ind.	Address	Phone
D. Stewart Gillan BSc MDiv PhD	1985	2004	St Michael's Manse, Kirkgate, Linlithgow EH49 7AL [E-mail: SGillan@churchofscotland.org.uk]	01506 842195
Cheryl McKellar-Young (Mrs) BA BD (Associate Minister)		2013	c/o Cross House, The Cross, Linlithgow EH49 7AL [E-mail: CMcKellarYoung@churchofscotland.org.uk]	01506 842188
Thomas S. Riddell BSc CEng FIChemE (Auxiliary Minister)	1993	1994	4 The Maltings, Linlithgow EH49 6DS [E-mail: TRiddell@churchofscotland.org.uk]	01506 843251

Linlithgow: St Ninian's Craigmailen (H)

Name	Ord.	Ind.	Address	Phone
W. Richard Houston BSc BD	1998	2004	29 Philip Avenue, Linlithgow EH49 7BH [E-mail: WHouston@churchofscotland.org.uk]	01506 202246

Livingston: Old (H)

Vacant

Name	Ord.	Ind.	Address	Phone
Gordon J. Pennykid BD DCS		2015	Manse of Livingston, Charlesfield Lane, Livingston EH54 7AJ / 8 Glenfield, Livingston EH54 7BG [E-mail: GPennykid@churchofscotland.org.uk]	01506 420227 / 07747 652652 (Mbl)

Livingston United

Name	Ord.	Ind.	Address	Phone
Ronald G. Greig MA BD	1987	2008	2 Eastcroft Court, Livingston EH54 7ET [E-mail: RGreig@churchofscotland.org.uk]	01506 467426
Stephanie Njeru BA			13 Eastcroft Court, Livingston EH54 7ET [E-mail: stephanie.njeru@methodist.org.uk]	01506 461020

Livingston United is a Local Ecumenical Project shared with the Scottish Episcopal, Methodist and United Reformed Churches

Pardovan, Kingscavil and Winchburgh See Abercorn

Polbeth Harwood linked with West Kirk of Calder (H)

Jonanda Groenewald BA BD MTh DD	1999 2014	8 Manse Court, East Calder, Livingston EH53 0HF [E-mail: JGroenewald@churchofscotland.org.uk]	01506 884802

Strathbrock (H)

Marc B. Kenton BTh MTh	1997 2009	1 Manse Park, Uphall, Broxburn EH52 6NX [E-mail: MKenton@churchofscotland.org.uk]	01506 852550

Torphichen See Avonbridge

Uphall: South (H)

Ian D. Maxwell MA BD PhD	1977 2013	8 Fernlea, Uphall, Broxburn EH52 6DF [E-mail: IMaxwell@churchofscotland.org.uk]	01506 239840

West Kirk of Calder (H) See Polbeth Harwood

Whitburn: Brucefield (H)

Alexander M. Roger BD PhD	1982 2014	48 Gleneagles Court, Whitburn, Bathgate EH47 8PG [E-mail: ARoger@churchofscotland.org.uk]	01501 229354

Whitburn: South (H)

Angus Kerr BD CertMin ThM DMin	1983 2013	5 Mansewood Crescent, Whitburn, Bathgate EH47 8HA [E-mail: AKerr@churchofscotland.org.uk]	01501 740333

Black, David W. BSc BD	1968	2008	(Strathbrock)	66 Bridge Street, Newbridge EH28 8SH [E-mail: dw.black666@yahoo.co.uk]	0131-333 2609
Cameron, Ian MA BD	1953	1981	(Kilbrandon and Kilchattan)	Craigellen, West George Street, Blairgowrie PH10 6DZ	01250 872087
Darroch, Richard J.G. BD MTh MA(CMS)	1993	2010	(Whitburn: Brucefield)	23 Barnes Green, Livingston EH54 8PP [E-mail: richdarr@aol.com]	01506 436648
Dunleavy, Suzanne BD DipEd	1990	2016		44 Tantallon Gardens, Bellsquarry, Livingston EH54 9AT [E-mail: suzanne.dunleavy@btinternet.com]	
Dunphy, Rhona (Mrs) BD DPTheol	2005	2016	Ministries Council	8 Chalmers Buildings, Linlithgow Bridge, Linlithgow EH49 7PR RDunphy@churchofscotland.org.uk	01506 844360 (Mbl) 07791 007158
Jamieson, Gordon D. MA BD	1974	2012	(Head of Stewardship)	41 Goldpark Place, Livingston EH54 6LW [E-mail: gdj1949@talktalk.net]	01506 412020
Mackay, Kenneth J. MA BD	1971	2007	(Edinburgh: St Nicholas' Sighthill)	46 Chuckethall Road, Livingston EH54 8FB [E-mail: kmth_mackay@yahoo.co.uk]	01506 410884
MacLaine, Marilyn (Mrs) LTh	1995	2009	(Inchinnan)	37 Bankton Brae, Livingston EH54 9LA [E-mail: marilynmaclaine@btinternet.com]	01506 400619
MacRae, Norman I. LTh	1966	2003	(Inverness: Trinity)	144 Hope Park Gardens, Bathgate EH48 2QX [E-mail: normanmacrae@talktalk.com]	01506 635254
Merrilees, Ann (Miss) DCS			(Deacon)	23 Cuthill Brae, West Calder EH55 8QE [E-mail: ann@merrilees.freeserve.co.uk]	01501 762909
Morrison, Iain C. BA BD	1990	2003	(Linlithgow: St Ninian's Craigmailen)	Whaligoe, 53 Eastcroft Drive, Polmont, Falkirk FK2 0SU	01324 713249

[E-mail: iain@kirkweb.org]

Nelson, Georgina MA BD PhD DipEd	1990	1995	Hospital Chaplain	63 Hawthorn Bank, Seafield, Bathgate EH47 7EB	
Nicol, Robert M.	1984	1996	(Jersey: St Columba's)	59 Kinloch View, Blackness Road, Linlithgow EH49 7HT [E-mail: revrob.nicol@tiscali.co.uk]	01506 670391
Orr, J. McMichael MA BD PhD	1949	1986	(Aberfoyle with Port of Menteith)	17a St Ninians Way, Linlithgow EH49 7HL [E-mail: mikeandmargorr@googlemail.com]	01506 840515
Smith, Graham W. BA BD FSAScot	1995	2016	(Livingston: Old)	76 Bankton Park East, Livingston EH54 9BN [E-mail: gsmith2014@hotmail.com]	
Thomson, Phyllis (Miss) DCS	2003	2010	(Deacon)	63 Caroline Park, Mid Calder, Livingston EH53 0SJ	01506 883207
Trimble, Robert DCS			(Deacon)	5 Templar Rise, Dedridge, Livingston EH54 6PJ	01506 412504
Walker, Ian BD MEd DipMS	1973	2007	(Rutherglen: Wardlawhill)	92 Carseknowe, Linlithgow EH49 7LG [E-mail: walk102822@aol.com]	01506 844412

(3) LOTHIAN

Meets at Musselburgh: St Andrew's High Parish Church at 7pm on the last Thursday in February, April, June and November, and in a different church on the last Thursday in September.

Clerk: MR JOHN D. McCULLOCH DL   20 Tipperwell Way, Howgate, Penicuik EH26 8QP   **01968 676300**
[E-mail: lothian@churchofscotland.org.uk]

Aberlady (H) linked with Gullane (H)
Brian C. Hilsley LLB BD   1990   2015   The Manse, Hummel Road, Gullane EH31 2BG   01620 843192
[E-mail: BHilsley@churchofscotland.org.uk]

Athelstaneford linked with Whitekirk and Tyninghame
Joanne H.G. Evans-Boiten BD   2004   2009   The Manse, Athelstaneford, North Berwick EH39 5BE   01620 880378
[E-mail: JEvansBoiten@churchofscotland.org.uk]

Belhaven (H) linked with Spott
Laurence H. Twaddle MA BD MTh   1977   1978   The Manse, Belhaven Road, Dunbar EH42 1NH   01368 863098
[E-mail: LTwaddle@churchofscotland.org.uk]

Bilston linked with Glencorse (H) linked with Roslin (H)
John R. Wells BD DipMin   1991   2005   31A Manse Road, Roslin EH25 9LG   0131-440 2012
[E-mail: JWells@churchofscotland.org.uk]

Bonnyrigg (H)
John Mitchell LTh CertMin   1991   9 Viewbank View, Bonnyrigg EH19 2HU
[E-mail: JMitchell@churchofscotland.org.uk]   0131-663 8287 (Tel/Fax)

Cockenzie and Port Seton: Chalmers Memorial (H)
Vacant   2 Links Road, Port Seton, Prestonpans EH32 0HA   01875 819254

Cockenzie and Port Seton: Old (H)
Guardianship of the Presbytery

Cockpen and Carrington (H) linked with Lasswade (H) and Rosewell (H)
Lorna M. Souter MA BD MSc   2016   11 Pendreich Terrace, Bonnyrigg EH19 2DT
[E-mail: LSouter@churchofscotland.org.uk]   07889 566418 (Mbl)

Dalkeith: St John's and King's Park (H)
Keith L. Mack BD MTh DPS   2002   13 Weir Crescent, Dalkeith EH22 3JN
[E-mail: KMack@churchofscotland.org.uk]   0131-454 0206

Dalkeith: St Nicholas' Buccleuch (H)
Alexander G. Horsburgh MA BD   1995   2004   16 New Street, Musselburgh EH21 6JP
[E-mail: AHorsburgh@churchofscotland.org.uk]   0131-653 3318

Dirleton (H) linked with North Berwick: Abbey (H) (Office: 01620 892800) (E-mail: abbeychurch@btconnect.com)
David J. Graham BSc BD PhD   1982   1998   Sydserff, Old Abbey Road, North Berwick EH39 4BP
[E-mail: DGraham@churchofscotland.org.uk]   01620 840878

Dunbar (H)
Gordon Stevenson BSc BD   2010   The Manse, 10 Bayswell Road, Dunbar EH42 1AB
[E-mail: GStevenson@churchofscotland.org.uk]   01368 865482

Dunglass
Suzanne G. Fletcher (Mrs) BA MDiv MA   2001   2011   The Manse, Cockburnspath TD13 5XZ
[E-mail: SFletcher@churchofscotland.org.uk]   01368 830713

Garvald and Morham linked with Haddington: West (H)
John Vischer   1993   2011   15 West Road, Haddington EH41 3RD
[E-mail: JVischer@churchofscotland.org.uk]   01620 822213

Gladsmuir linked with Longniddry (H)
Robin E. Hill LLB BD PhD   2004   The Manse, Elcho Road, Longniddry EH32 0LB
[E-mail: RHill@churchofscotland.org.uk]   01875 853195

Glencorse (H) See Bilston

Gorebridge (H)
Mark S. Nicholas MA BD   1999   100 Hunterfield Road, Gorebridge EH23 4TT
[E-mail: MNicholas@churchofscotland.org.uk]   01875 820387

Gullane See Aberlady

Haddington: St Mary's (H)
Jennifer Macrae (Mrs) MA BD   1998   2007   1 Nungate Gardens, Haddington EH41 4EE
[E-mail: JMacrae@churchofscotland.org.uk]   01620 823109

Haddington: West See Garvald and Morham

Howgate (H) linked with Penicuik: South (H)
Ian A. Cathcart BSc BD   1994   2007   15 Stevenson Road, Penicuik EH26 0LU
[E-mail: ICathcart@churchofscotland.org.uk]   01968 674692
Frederick Harrison
(Ordained Local Minister)   2013   33 Castle Avenue, Gorebridge EH23 4TH
[E-mail: FHarrison@churchofscotland.org.uk]   01875 820908

Humbie linked with Yester, Bolton and Saltoun
Anikó Schuetz Bradwell MA BD   2015   The Manse, Tweeddale Avenue, Gifford, Haddington EH41 4QN
[E-mail: ASchuetzBradwell@churchofscotland.org.uk]   01620 811193

Lasswade and Rosewell See Cockpen and Carrington

Loanhead
Graham L. Duffin BSc BD DipEd   1989   2001   120 The Loan, Loanhead EH20 9AJ
[E-mail: GDuffin@churchofscotland.org.uk]   0131-448 2459

Longniddry See Gladsmuir

Musselburgh: Northesk (H)
Alison P. McDonald MA BD   1991   1998   16 New Street, Musselburgh EH21 6JP
[E-mail: Alison.McDonald@churchofscotland.org.uk]   0131-665 2128

Musselburgh: St Andrew's High (H) (0131-665 7239)
Yvonne E.S. Atkins (Mrs) BD   1997   8 Ferguson Drive, Musselburgh EH21 6XA   0131-665 1124
[E-mail: YAtkins@churchofscotland.org.uk]

Musselburgh: St Clement's and St Ninian's
Guardianship of the Presbytery   The Manse, Wallyford Loan Road, Wallyford,
                                        Musselburgh EH21 8BU

Musselburgh: St Michael's Inveresk
Vacant

Newbattle (H) (Website: http://freespace.virgin.net/newbattle.focus)
Sean Swindells BD DipMin MTh   1996   2011   112 Greenbank Crescent, Edinburgh EH10 5SZ   0131-447 4032
                                                       [E-mail: SSwindells@churchofscotland.org.uk]   07791 755976 (Mbl)
Michael D. Watson   2013   47 Crichton Terrace, Pathhead EH37 5QZ   01875 320043
  (Ordained Local Minister)   [E-mail: MWatson@churchofscotland.org.uk]
Malcolm T Muir   2001   2015   Mayfield and Easthouses Church, Bogwood Court, Mayfield,   0131-663 3245
  (Associate Minister)   EH22 5DG   07920 855467 (Mbl)
                                                       [E-mail: MMuir@churchofscotland.org.uk]

Newton
Guardianship of the Presbytery   The Manse, Newton, Dalkeith EH22 1SR   0131-663 3845
Andrew Don MBA   2006   5 Eskvale Court, Penicuik EH26 8HT   01968 675766
  (Ordained Local Minister)   [E-mail: ADon@churchofscotland.org.uk]

North Berwick: Abbey See Dirleton

North Berwick: St Andrew Blackadder (H) (E-mail: admin@standrewblackadder.org.uk) (Website: www.standrewblackadder.org.uk)
Neil J. Dougall BD   1991   2003   7 Marine Parade, North Berwick EH39 4LD   01620 892132
                                                       [E-mail: NDougall@churchofscotland.org.uk]

Ormiston linked with Pencaitland
David J. Torrance BD DipMin   1993   2009   The Manse, Pencaitland, Tranent EH34 5DL   01875 340963
                                                       [E-mail: DTorrance@churchofscotland.org.uk]

Pencaitland See Ormiston

Penicuik: North (H) (Website: www.pnk.org.uk)
Ruth D. Halley BEd BD PGCM   2012   93 John Street, Penicuik EH26 8AG   01968 675761
                                                       [E-mail: RHalley@churchofscotland.org.uk]   07530 307413 (Mbl)

Penicuik: St Mungo's (H)
Vacant

Penicuik: South See Howgate

Prestonpans: Prestongrange
Kenneth W Donald BA BD   1982 2014   The Manse, East Loan, Prestonpans EH32 9ED   01875 571579
[E-mail: KDonald@churchofscotland.org.uk]

Roslin See Bilston
Spott See Belhaven

Tranent
Erica M Wishart (Mrs) MA BD   2014   1 Toll House Gardens, Tranent EH33 2QQ   01875 704071
[E-mail: EWishart@churchofscotland.org.uk]

Traprain
David D. Scott BSc BD   1981 2010   The Manse, Preston Road, East Linton EH40 3DS   01620 860227 (Tel/Fax)
[E-mail: DDScott@churchofscotland.org.uk]

Tyne Valley Parish (H)
Alan R. Cobain BD   2000 2013   Cranstoun Cottage, Ford, Pathhead EH37 5RE   01875 320314
[E-mail: ACobain@churchofscotland.org.uk]

Whitekirk and Tyninghame See Athelstaneford
Yester See Humbie

Andrews, J. Edward   1985 2005   (Armadale)   Dunnichen, 1B Cameron Road, Nairn IV12 5NS   01667 459466
MA BD DipCG FSAScot   [E-mail: edward.andrews@btinternet.com]

Bayne, Angus L. LTh BEd MTh   1969 2005   (Edinburgh: Bristo Memorial Craigmillar)   14 Myredale, Bonnyrigg EH19 3NW   (Mbl) 07808 720708
[E-mail: angus@mccookies.com]   0131-663 6871

Berry, Geoff T. BD BSc   2009 2011   Chaplain: Army   38 Muirfield Drive, Gullane EH31 2HJ
[E-mail: geofftalk@yahoo.co.uk]

Black, A. Graham MA   1964 2003   (Gladsmuir with Longniddry)   26 Hamilton Crescent, Gullane EH31 2HR   01620 843899
[E-mail: grablack@btinternet.com]

Brown, Ronald H.   1974 1998   (Musselburgh: Northesk)   6 Monktonhall Farm Cottages, Musselburgh EH21 6RZ   0131-653 2531

Brown, William BD   1972 1997   (Edinburgh: Polwarth)   13 Thornyhall, Dalkeith EH22 2ND   0131-654 0929

Buchanan, John DCS   1982 2013   (Deacon)   19 Gillespie Crescent, Edinburgh EH10 4HZ   0131-229 0794

Burt, Thomas W. BD   (Carlops with Kirkurd and Newlands with West Linton: St Andrew's)   7 Arkwright Court, North Berwick EH39 4RT   01620 895494
[E-mail: tomburt@westlinton.com]

Cairns, John B.   1974 2009   (Aberlady with Gullane)   Bell House, Roxburghe Park, Dunbar EH42 1LR   01368 862501
KCVO LTh LLB LLD DD   [E-mail: johncairns@mail.com]

Coltart, Ian O. CA BD   1988 2010   (Arbirlot with Carmyllie)   25 Bothwell Gardens, Dunbar EH42 1PZ   01368 860064

Name	Dates	Position	Address	Telephone
Dick, Andrew B. BD DipMin	1986 2015	(Musselburgh: St Michael's Inveresk)	4 Kirkhill Court, Gorebridge EH23 4TW [E-mail: dixbit@aol.com]	01875 571223
Frail, Nicola R. BLE MBA MDiv	2000	Army Chaplain	32 Engineer Regiment, Marne Barracks, Catterick Garrison DL10 7NP [E-mail: nrfscot@hotmail.com]	
Fraser, John W. MA BD	1974 2011	(Penicuik: North)	66 Camus Avenue, Edinburgh EH10 6QX [E-mail: jjjj2005@hotmail.co.uk]	0131-623 0647
Glover, Robert L. BMus BD MTh ARCO	1971 2010	(Cockenzie and Port Seton: Chalmers Memorial)	12 Seton Wynd, Port Seton, Prestonpans EH32 0TY [E-mail: rlglover@btinternet.com]	01875 818759
Hutchison, Alan E.W.		(Deacon)	132 Lochbridge Road, North Berwick EH39 4DR	01620 894077 (Mbl) 0775 444 8889
Johnston, June E. BSc MEd BD	2013	Ordained Local Minister	Tarmacann, Main Street, Killin FK21 8TN [E-mail: johnston330@btinternet.com]	
Jones, Anne M. (Mrs) BD	1998 2002	(Hospital Chaplain)	7 North Elphinstone Farm, Tranent EH33 2ND [E-mail: revamjones@aol.com]	01875 614442
Kellock, Chris N. MA BD	1998 2012	Army Chaplain	1 Plantation Road, Tidworth SP9 7SJ	01980 601070
Manson, James A. LTh	1981 2004	(Glencorse with Roslin)	31 Nursery Gardens, Kilmarnock KA1 3JA [E-mail: james.manson@virgin.net]	01563 535430
Pirie, Donald LTh	1975 2006	(Bolton and Saltoun with Humbie with Yester)	46 Caiystane Avenue, Edinburgh EH10 6SH	0131-445 2654
Ritchie, James McL. MA BD MPhil	1950 1985	(Coalsnaughton)	Flat 2/25, Croft-an-Righ, Edinburgh EH8 8EG [E-mail: jasritch_77@msn.com]	0131-557 1084
Simpson, Robert R. BA BD	1994 2014	(Callander)	10 Bellsmains, Gorebridge EH23 4QD [E-mail: robert@pansmanse.co.uk]	01875 820843
Stein, Jock MA BD	1973 2008	(Tulliallan and Kincardine)	35 Dunbar Road, Haddington EH41 3PJ [E-mail: jstein@handselpress.org.uk]	01620 824896
Stein, Margaret E. (Mrs) DA BD DipRE	1984 2008	(Tulliallan and Kincardine)	35 Dunbar Road, Haddington EH41 3PJ [E-mail: margaretestein@hotmail.com]	01620 824896
Steven, Gordon R. BD DCS		(Deacon)	51 Nantwich Drive, Edinburgh EH7 6RB [E-mail: grsteven@btinternet.com]	0131-669 2054 (Mbl) 07904 385256
Swan, Andrew F. BD	1983 2000	(Loanhead)	Park View, 2 Park Place, Lanark ML11 9HH	
Torrance, David W. MA BD	1955 1991	(Earlston)	38 Forth Street, North Berwick EH39 4IQ [E-mail: torrance103@btinternet.com]	(Tel/Fax) 01620 895109
Underwood, Florence A. (Mrs) BD	1992 2006	(Assistant: Gladsmuir with Longniddry)	18 Covenanters Rise, Pitreavie Castle, Dunfermline KY11 8SQ [E-mail: gunderwood@tesco.net]	01383 740745
Underwood, Geoffrey H. BD DipTh FPhS	1964 1992	(Cockenzie and Port Seton: Chalmers Memorial)	18 Covenanters Rise, Pitreavie Castle, Dunfermline KY11 8SQ [E-mail: gunderwood@tesco.net]	01383 740745

(4) MELROSE AND PEEBLES

Meets at Innerleithen on the first Tuesday of February, March, May, October, November and December, and on the fourth Tuesday of June, and in places to be appointed on the first Tuesday of September.

Clerk: REV. VICTORIA LINFORD LLB BD   The Manse, 209 Galashiels Road, Stow, Galashiels TD1 2RE   01578 730237
[E-mail: melrosepeebles@churchofscotland.org.uk]

Ashkirk linked with Selkirk (H)
Margaret D.J. Steele (Miss) BSc BD   2000   2011   1 Loanside, Selkirk TD7 4DJ   01750 23308
[E-mail: MSteele@churchofscotland.org.uk]

Bowden (H) and Melrose (H)
Vacant

Broughton, Glenholm and Kilbucho (H) linked with Skirling linked with Stobo and Drumelzier linked with Tweedsmuir (H)
Robert B. Milne BTh   1999   2009   The Manse, Broughton, Biggar ML12 6HQ   01899 830331
[E-mail: Robert.Milne@churchofscotland.org.uk]

Caddonfoot (H) linked with Galashiels: Trinity (H) (01896 752967)
Elspeth Harley BA MTh   1991   2014   8 Mossilee Road, Galashiels TD1 1NF   01896 758485
[E-mail: EHarley@churchofscotland.org.uk]

Carlops linked with Kirkurd and Newlands (H) linked with West Linton: St Andrew's (H)
Linda J. Dunbar BSc BA BD PhD FRHS   2000   2013   The Manse, Main Street, West Linton EH46 7EE   01968 660221
07939 496360 (Mbl)
[E-mail: LDunbar@churchofscotland.org.uk]

Channelkirk and Lauder
Marion (Rae) Clark MA BD   2014   The Manse, Brownsmuir Park, Lauder TD2 6QD   01578 718996
[E-mail: RClark@churchofscotland.org.uk]

Earlston
Julie M. Woods (Ms) BTh   2005   2011   The Manse, High Street, Earlston TD4 6DE   01896 849236
[E-mail: JWoods@churchofscotland.org.uk]

Eddleston (H) linked with Peebles: Old (H)
Malcolm M. Macdougall BD MTh DipCE   1981   2001   7 Clement Gunn Square, Peebles EH45 8LW   01721 720568
[E-mail: MMacdougall@churchofscotland.org.uk]
Pamela D. Strachan (Lady) MA (Cantab)   2015   Glenhighton, Broughton, Biggar ML12 6JF   01899 830423
(Ordained Local Minister)   07837 873688 (Mbl)
[E-mail: PStrachan@churchofscotland.org.uk]

Ettrick and Yarrow
Samuel Siroky BA MTh   2003   Yarrow Manse, Yarrow, Selkirk TD7 5LA   01750 82336
[E-mail: SSiroky@churchofscotland.org.uk]

Galashiels: Old Parish and St Paul's (H) linked with Galashiels: St John's (H)
Leon Keller BA BD DipTheol PhD   1988   2015   Woodlea, Abbotsview Drive, Galashiels TD1 3SL   01896 753029
[E-mail: LKeller@churchofscotland.org.uk]

Galashiels: St John's See Galashiels: Old Parish and St Paul's
Galashiels: Trinity See Caddonfoot

Innerleithen (H), Traquair and Walkerburn
Janice M. Faris (Mrs) BSc BD   1991   2001   The Manse, 1 Millwell Park, Innerleithen, Peebles EH44 6JF   01896 830309
[E-mail: JFaris@churchofscotland.org.uk]

Kirkurd and Newlands See Carlops

Lyne and Manor linked with Peebles: St Andrew's Leckie (H) (01721 723121)
Malcolm S. Jefferson   2012   Mansefield, Innerleithen Road, Peebles EH45 8BE   01721 725148
[E-mail: MJefferson@churchofscotland.org.uk]

Maxton and Mertoun linked with Newtown linked with St Boswells
Sheila W. Moir (Ms) MTheol   2008   7 Strae Brigs, St Boswells, Melrose TD6 0DH   01835 822255
[E-mail: SMoir@churchofscotland.org.uk]

Newtown See Maxton and Mertoun
Peebles: Old See Eddleston
Peebles: St Andrew's Leckie See Lyne and Manor
St Boswells See Maxton and Mertoun
Selkirk See Ashkirk
Skirling See Broughton, Glenholm and Kilbucho
Stobo and Drumelzier See Broughton, Glenholm and Kilbucho

Stow: St Mary of Wedale and Heriot
Victoria J. Linford (Mrs) LLB BD   2010   The Manse, 209 Galashiels Road, Stow, Galashiels TD1 2RE   01578 730237
[E-mail: VLinford@churchofscotland.org.uk]

Tweedsmuir See Broughton, Glenholm and Kilbucho
West Linton: St Andrew's See Carlops

Arnott, A. David K. MA BD	1971	2010	(St Andrews: Hope Park with Strathkinness)	53 Whitehaugh Park, Peebles EH45 9DB [E-mail: adka53@btinternet.com]	01721 725979 (Mbl) 07759 709205
Bowie, Adam McC.	1976	1996	(Cavers and Kirkton with Hobkirk and Southdean)	Glenbield, Redpath, Earlston TD4 6AD	01896 848173
Cashman, P. Hamilton BSc	1985	1998	(Dirleton with North Berwick: Abbey)	38 Abbotsford Road, Galashiels TD1 3HR [E-mail: mcashman@tiscali.co.uk]	01896 752711
Cutler, James S.H. BD CEng MIStructE	1986	2011	(Black Mount with Culter with Libberton and Quothquan)	12 Kittlegairy Place, Peebles EH45 9LW [E-mail: revjc@btinternet.com]	01721 723950
Devenny, Robert P.		2002	Head of Spiritual Care, NHS Borders (Hospital Chaplain)	Blakeburn Cottage, Wester Housebyres, Melrose TD6 9BW	01896 822350
Dick, J. Ronald BD	1973	1996	(Broughton, Glenholm and Kilbucho with Skirling with Stobo and Drumelzier with Tweedsmuir)	5 Georgefield Farm Cottages, Earlston TD4 6BH	01896 848956
Dobie, Rachel J.W. (Mrs) LTh	1991	2008	(Kelso: Old and Sprouston)	20 Moss Side Crescent, Biggar ML12 6GE [E-mail: revracheldobie@talktalk.net]	01899 229244
Dodd, Marion E. (Miss) MA BD LRAM	1988	2010	(Heriot with Stow: St Mary of Wedale)	Esdaile, Tweedmount Road, Melrose TD6 9ST [E-mail: mariondodd@btinternet.com]	01896 822446
Duncan, Charles A. MA	1956	1992	(Blackridge with Harthill: St Andrew's)	10 Elm Grove, Galashiels TD1 3JA	01896 753261
Hardie, H. Warner BD	1979	2005	(Tranent)	Keswick Cottage, Kingsmuir Drive, Peebles EH45 9AA [E-mail: hardies@bigfoot.com]	01721 724003
Hogg, Thomas M. BD	1986	2007		22 Douglas Place, Galashiels TD1 3BT	01896 759381
Hughes, Barry MA		2011	Ordained Local Minister	Dunslair, Cardrona Way, Cardrona, Peebles EH45 9LD [E-mail: BHughes@churchofscotland.org.uk]	01896 831197
Kellet, John M. MA	1962	1995	(Leith: South)	4 High Cottages, Walkerburn EH43 6AZ	01896 870351
Kennon, Stanley BA BD RN	1992	2000	Chaplain: Royal Navy	Britannia Royal Naval College, Dartmouth TO6 0HJ [E-mail: bmc-csf@fleetfost.mod.uk]	
Lawrie, Bruce B. BD	1974	2012	(Duffus, Spynie and Hopeman)	5 Thorncroft, Scotts Place, Selkirk TD7 4LN [E-mail: thorncroft54@gmail.com]	01750 725427
MacFarlane, David C. MA	1957	1997	(Eddleston with Peebles: Old)	Lorimer House Nursing Home, 491 Lanark Road, Edinburgh EH14 5DQ	
Milloy, A. Miller DPE LTh DipTrMan	1979	2012	General Secretary: United Bible Societies	18 Kittlegairy Crescent, Peebles EH45 9NJ [E-mail: ammilloy@aol.com]	01721 723380
Moore, W. Haisley MA	1966	1996	(Secretary: The Boys' Brigade)	26 Tweedbank Avenue, Tweedbank, Galashiels TD1 3SP	01896 668577
Munson, Winnie (Ms) BD	1996	2006	(Delting with Northmavine)	6 St Cuthbert's Drive, St Boswells, Melrose TD6 0DF	01835 823375
Norman, Nancy M. (Miss) BA MDiv MTh	1988	2012	(Lyne and Manor)	25 March Street, Peebles EH45 8EP [E-mail: nancy.norman1@googlemail.com]	01721 721699
Rae, Andrew W.	1951	1987	(Annan: St Andrew's Greenknowe Erskine)	Roseneuk, Tweedside Road, Newtown St Boswells TD6 0PQ	01835 823783
Rennie, John D. MA	1962	1996	(Broughton, Glenholm and Kilbucho with Skirling with Stobo and Drumelzier with Tweedsmuir)	29/1 Rosetta Road, Peebles EH45 8HJ [E-mail: tworennies@talktalk.net]	01721 720963
Riddell, John A. MA BD	1967	2006	(Jedburgh: Trinity)	Orchid Cottage, Gingham Row, Earlston TD4 6ET	01896 848784
Steele, Leslie M. MA BD	1973	2013	(Galashiels: Old and St Paul's)	25 Bardfield Road, Colchester CO2 8LW [E-mail: lms@hotmail.co.uk]	01206 621939 (Mbl) 07786 797974
Taverner, Glyn R. MA BD	1957	1995	(Maxton and Mertoun with St Boswells)	Woodcot Cottage, Waverley Road, Innerleithen EH44 6QW	01896 830156
Wallace, James H. MA BD	1973	2011	(Peebles: St Andrew's Leckie)	52 Waverley Mills, Innerleithen EH44 6RH [E-mail: jimwallace121@btinternet.com]	01896 831637

(5) DUNS

Meets at Duns, in the Parish Church hall, normally on the first Saturday of February, the first Tuesdays of September and December, and in places to be appointed on the first Tuesday of May. It meets for conference, worship and training events throughout the year.

| Clerk: | DR H. DANE SHERRARD | Mount Pleasant Granary, Mount Pleasant Farm, Duns TD11 3HU
[E-mail: duns@churchofscotland.org.uk] | 01361 882254
07582 468468 |

Ayton (H) and District Church

| Norman R. Whyte BD MTh DipMin | 1982 | 2006 | The Manse, Beanburn, Ayton, Eyemouth TD14 5QY
[E-mail: NWhyte@churchofscotland.org.uk] | 01890 781333 |

(New charge formed by the union of Ayton and Burnmouth, Foulden and Mordington, and Grantshouse, Houndwood and Reston)

Berwick-upon-Tweed: St Andrew's Wallace Green (H) and Lowick

| Adam J.J. Hood MA BD DPhil | 1989 | 2012 | 3 Meadow Grange, Berwick-upon-Tweed TD15 1NW
[E-mail: AHood@churchofscotland.org.uk] | 01289 332787 |

Chirnside linked with Hutton and Fishwick and Paxton

| Vacant | | | Parish Church Manse, The Glebe, Chirnside, Duns TD11 3XL | 01890 819109 |

Coldingham and St Abbs linked with Eyemouth

| Andrew Haddow BEng BD | 2012 | The Manse, Victoria Road, Eyemouth TD14 5JD
[E-mail: AHaddow@churchofscotland.org.uk] | 01890 750327 |

Coldstream and District Parishes (H) linked with Eccles and Leitholm

| David J. Taverner MCIBS ACIS BD | 1996 | 2011 | 36 Bennecourt Drive, Coldstream TD12 4BY
[E-mail: DTaverner@churchofscotland.org.uk] | 01890 883887 |

(The charge of Coldstream and District Parishes is formed by a union between Coldstream, Swinton and Ladykirk with Whitsome)

Duns and District Parishes

| Stephen A. Blakey BSc BD | 1977 | 2012 | The Manse, Castle Street, Duns TD11 3DG
[E-mail: SBlakey@churchofscotland.org.uk] | 01361 883755 |

(New charge formed by the union between Duns and District Parishes and Langton and Lammermuir Kirk)

Eccles and Leitholm See Coldstream   (New charge formed by the union of Eccles and Leitholm)

Eyemouth See Coldingham and St Abbs

Fogo
Guardianship of the Presbytery

Gordon: St Michael's linked with Greenlaw (H) linked with Legerwood linked with Westruther   1982   1995
Thomas S. Nicholson BD DPS   The Manse, Todholes, Greenlaw, Duns TD10 6XD   01361 810316
                                                           [E-mail: TNicholson@churchofscotland.org.uk]

Greenlaw See Gordon: St Michael's
Hutton and Fishwick and Paxton See Chirnside
Legerwood See Gordon: St Michael's
Westruther See Gordon: St Michael's

Name		Years	Charge	Address	Phone
Cartwright, Alan C.D. BSc BD	1976	2016	(Fogo and Swinton with Ladykirk and Whitsome with Leithholm)	Drumgray, Edrom, Duns TD11 3PX [E-mail: merse.minister@btinternet.com]	01890 819191
Gaddes, Donald R.	1961	1994	(Kelso: North and Ednam)	2 Teindhill Green, Duns TD11 3DX [E-mail: drgaddes@btinternet.com]	01361 883172
Gale, Ronald A.A. LTh	1982	1995	(Dunoon: Old and St Cuthbert's)	55 Lennel Mount, Coldstream TD12 4NS [E-mail: rgale89@aol.com]	01890 883699
Graham, Jennifer D. (Mrs) BA MDiv PhD	2000	2011	(Eday with Stronsay: Moncur Memorial)	Lodge, Stronsay, Orkney KW17 2AN [E-mail: jdgraham67@gmail.com]	01857 616487
Higham, Robert D. BD	1985	2002	(Tiree)	36 Low Greens, Berwick-upon-Tweed TD15 1LZ	01289 302392
Hope, Geraldine H. (Mrs) MA BD	1986	2007	(Foulden and Mordington with Hutton and Fishwick and Paxton)	4 Well Court, Chirnside, Duns TD11 3UD [E-mail: geraldine.hope@virgin.net]	01890 818134
Kerr, Andrew MA BLitt	1948	1991	(Kilbarchan: West)	4 Lairds Gate, Port Glasgow Road, Kilmacolm PA13 4EX	01507 874852
Landale, William S.	2005		Auxiliary Minister	Green Hope Guest House, Ellemford, Duns TD11 3SG [E-mail: WLandale@churchofscotland.org.uk]	01361 890242
Lindsay, Daniel G. BD	1978	2011	(Coldingham and St Abbs with Eyemouth)	18 Hallidown Crescent, Eyemouth TD14 5TB	01890 751389
Murray, Duncan E. BA BD	1970	2012	(Bonkyl and Preston with Chirnside with Edrom Allanton)	Beech Cottage, York Road, Knaresborough HG5 0TT [E-mail: duncanemurray@tiscali.co.uk]	01423 313287
Neill, Bruce F. MA BD	1966	2007	(Maxton and Mertoun with Newtown with St Boswells)	18 Brierydean, St Abbs, Eyemouth TD14 5PQ [E-mail: bneill@phonecoop.coop]	01890 771569
Paterson, William BD	1977	2001	(Bonkyl and Preston with Chirnside with Edrom Allanton)	Benachie, Gavinton, Duns TD11 3QT [E-mail: billdm.paterson@btinternet.com]	01361 882727
Sherrard, H. Dane BD DMin	1971	2013	Presbytery Clerk	Mount Pleasant Granary, Mount Pleasant Farm, Duns TD11 4HU [E-mail: dane@mountpleasantgranary.net] (Mbl)	01361 882254 07801 939138
Shields, John M. MBE LTh	1972	2007	(Channelkirk and Lauder)	12 Eden Park, Ednam, Kelso TD5 7RG [E-mail: john.shields118@btinternet.com]	01573 229015
Walker, Kenneth D.F. MA BD PhD	1976	2008	(Athelstaneford with Whitekirk and Tyninghame)	Allanbank Kothi, Allanton, Duns TD11 3PY [E-mail: walkerkenneth49@gmail.com]	01890 817102

(6) JEDBURGH

Meets at various venues on the first Wednesday of February, March, May, September, October, November and December and on the last Wednesday of June.

Clerk	REV. FRANK CAMPBELL	22 The Glebe, Ancrum, Jedburgh TD8 6UX [E-mail: jedburgh@churchofscotland.org.uk]	01835 830318

Ale and Teviot United (H) (Website: www.aleandteviot.org.uk)
Frank Campbell   1989   1991   22 The Glebe, Ancrum, Jedburgh TD8 6UX   01835 830318
[E-mail: jedburgh@churchofscotland.org.uk]

Cavers and Kirkton linked with Hawick: Trinity (H)
Michael D. Scouler MBE BSc BD   1988   2009   Trinity Manse, Howdenburn, Hawick TD9 8PH   01450 378248
[E-mail: MScouler@churchofscotland.org.uk]

Cheviot Churches (H) (Website: www.cheviotchurches.org)
Vacant

Hawick: Burnfoot (Website: www.burnfootparishchurch.org.uk)
Charles J. Finnie LTh DPS   1991   1997   29 Wilton Hill, Hawick TD9 8BA   01450 373181
[E-mail: CFinnie@churchofscotland.org.uk]

Hawick: St Mary's and Old (H) linked with Hawick: Teviot (H) and Roberton
Vacant   The Manse, Buccleuch Road, Hawick TD9 0EL   01450 372150

Hawick: Teviot and Roberton See Hawick: St Mary's and Old
Hawick: Trinity See Cavers and Kirkton

Hawick: Wilton linked with Teviothead
Lisa-Jane Rankin BD CPS   2003   4 Wilton Hill Terrace, Hawick TD9 8BE   01450 370744
[E-mail: LRankin@churchofscotland.org.uk]

Hobkirk and Southdean (Website: www.hobkirkruberslaw.org) linked with Ruberslaw (Website: www.hobkirkruberslaw.org)
Douglas A.O. Nicol MA BD   1974   2009   The Manse, Denholm, Hawick TD9 8NB   01450 870268
[E-mail: Douglas.Nicol@churchofscotland.org.uk]

Jedburgh: Old and Trinity (Website: www.jedburgh-parish.org.uk)

Graham D. Astles BD MSc   2007   The Manse, Honeyfield Drive, Jedburgh TD8 6LQ   01835 863417
[E-mail: GAstles@churchofscotland.org.uk]   07906 290568 (Mbl)

Kelso Country Churches linked with Oxnam
Vacant

Kelso: North (H) and Ednam (H) (01573 224154) (E-mail: office@kelsonorthandednam.org.uk) (Website: www.kelsonorthandednam.org.uk)
Vacant

Kelso: Old and Sprouston
Vacant

Ruberslaw See Hobkirk and Southdean
Teviothead See Hawick: Wilton

Combe, Neil R. BSc MSc BD	1984	2015	(Hawick: St Mary's and Old with Hawick: Teviot and Roberton)	2 Abbotsview Gardens, Galashiels TD1 3ER [E-mail: neil.combe@btinternet.com]	01896 755869
Earl, Jenny MA BD	2007	2015	(Kelso Country Churches with Kelso: Old and Sprouston)	1 The Steadings, Achavaich, Isle of Iona PA76 6SW [E-mail: jennyearl@btinternet.com]	(Mbl) 07769 994680
McHaffie, Robin D. BD	1979	2016	(Cheviot Churches)	Shepherd's Cottage, Castle Heaton, Cornhill-on-Tweed TD12 4XQ	
McNicol, Bruce	1967	2006	(Jedburgh: Old and Edgerston)	42 Dounehill, Jedburgh TD8 6LJ [E-mail: mcnicol942@gmail.com]	01835 862991
Rodwell, Anna S. BD DipMin	1998	2003	(Langbank)	The Old Mill House, Hownam Howgate, Kelso TD5 8AJ [E-mail: ARodwell@churchofscotland.org.uk]	01573 440761

HAWICK ADDRESSES

Burnfoot	Fraser Avenue
St Mary's and Old	Kirk Wynd
Teviot	off Buccleuch Road
Trinity	Central Square
Wilton	Princes Street

(7) ANNANDALE AND ESKDALE

Meets on the first Tuesday of February, May, September and December, and the third Tuesday of March, June and October. The September meeting is held in the Moderator's charge. The other meetings are held in Dryfesdale Church Hall, Lockerbie, except for the June meeting, which is separately announced.

| Clerk: | REV. C. BRYAN HASTON LTh | The Manse, Gretna Green, Gretna DG16 5DU
[E-mail: annandaleeskdale@cofscotland.org.uk] | 01461 338313 |

Annan: Old (H) linked with Dornock
Vacant — 12 Plumdon Park Avenue, Annan DG12 6EY — 01461 201405

Annan: St Andrew's (H) linked with Brydekirk
John G. Pickles BD MTh MSc — 2011 — 1 Annerley Road, Annan DG12 6HE — 01461 202626
[E-mail: JPickles@churchofscotland.org.uk]

Applegarth, Sibbaldbie (H) and Johnstone linked with Lochmaben (H)
Paul R. Read BSc MA(Th) — 2000 2013 — The Manse, Barrashead, Lochmaben, Lockerbie DG11 1QF — 01387 810640
[E-mail: PRead@churchofscotland.org.uk]

Brydekirk See Annan: St Andrew's

Canonbie United (H) linked with Liddesdale (H)
Brian Ian Murray — 2002 2016 — 23 Langholm Street, Newcastleton TD9 0QX — 01387 375242
[E-mail: BMurray@churchofscotland.org.uk]
Canonbie United is a Local Ecumenical Project shared with the United Free Church

Dalton and Hightae linked with St Mungo
Vacant — The Manse, Hightae, Lockerbie DG11 1JL — 01387 811499

Dornock See Annan: Old

Gretna: Old (H), Gretna: St Andrew's (H), Half Morton and Kirkpatrick Fleming
C. Bryan Haston LTh — 1975 — The Manse, Gretna Green, Gretna DG16 5DU — 01461 338313
[E-mail: CBHaston@churchofscotland.org.uk]
Eric T. Dempster — 2016 — Annanside, Wamphray, Moffat DG10 9LZ — 01576 470496
(Ordained Local Minister) [E-mail: EDempster@churchofscotland.org.uk]

Hoddom, Kirtle-Eaglesfield and Middlebie
Frances M. Henderson BA BD PhD   2006   2013   The Manse, Main Road, Ecclefechan, Lockerbie DG11 3BU   01576 300108
[E-mail: FHenderson@churchofscotland.org.uk]

Kirkpatrick Juxta linked with Moffat: St Andrew's (H) linked with Wamphray
Adam J. Dillon BD ThM   2003   2008   The Manse, 1 Meadowbank, Moffat DG10 9LR   01683 220128
[E-mail: ADillon@churchofscotland.org.uk]

Langholm Eskdalemuir Ewes and Westerkirk
I. Scott McCarthy BD   2010   The Manse, Langholm DG13 0BL   01387 380252
[E-mail: ISMcCarthy@churchofscotland.org.uk]

Liddesdale See Canonbie United
Lochmaben See Applegarth, Sibbaldbie and Johnstone

Lockerbie: Dryfesdale, Hutton and Corrie
Vacant

Moffat: St Andrew's See Kirkpatrick Juxta
St Mungo See Dalton

The Border Kirk (Church office: Chapel Street, Carlisle CA1 1JA; Tel: 01228 591757)
David G. Pitkeathly LLB BD   1996   2007   95 Pinecroft, Carlisle CA3 0DB   01228 593243
[E-mail: DPitkeathly@churchofscotland.org.uk]

Tundergarth
Guardianship of the Presbytery

Wamphray See Kirkpatrick Juxta

Annand, James M. MA BD   1955 1995 (Lockerbie: Dryfesdale)   Dere Cottage, 48 Main Street, Newstead, Melrose TD6 9DX   0131-225 3393
Beveridge, S. Edwin P. BA   1959 2004 (Brydekirk with Hoddom)   19 Rothesay Terrace, Edinburgh EH3 7RY   (Mbl) 07543 796820
Brydson, Angela (Mrs) DCS   Deacon   52 Victoria Park, Lockerbie DG11 2AY
[E-mail: ABrydson@churchofscotland.org.uk]
Byers, Mairi C. (Mrs) BTh CPS   1992 1998 (Jura)   Meadowbank, Plumdon Road, Annan DG12 6SJ   01461 206512
[E-mail: aljbyers@hotmail.com]

Dawson, Morag A. BD MTh	1999 2016	(Dalton l/w Hightae l/w St Mungo)	MDawson@churchofscotland.org.uk	
Gibb, J. Daniel M. BA LTh	1994 2006	(Aberfoyle with Port of Menteith)	1 Beechfield, Newton Aycliffe DL5 7AX [E-mail: dannygibb@hotmail.co.uk]	01768 840749 07403 638339 (Mbl)
Harvey, P. Ruth (Ms) MA BD	2009 2012	Place for Hope	Croslands, Beacon Street, Penrith CA11 7TZ [E-mail: ruth.harvey@placeforhope.org.uk]	01387 811528
MacMillan, William M. LTh	1980 1998	(Kilmory with Lamlash)	Balskia, 61 Queen Street, Lochmaben, Lockerbie DG11 1PP	
MacPherson, Duncan J. BSc BD	1993 2002	Chaplain: Army	MP413, Kentigern House, 65 Brown Street, Glasgow G2 8EX	01750 52324
Ross, Alan C. CA BD	1988 2007	(Eskdalemuir with Hutton and Corrie with Tundergarth)	Yarra, Ettrickbridge, Selkirk TD7 5JN [E-mail: alkaross@aol.com]	
Seaman, Ronald S. MA	1967 2007	(Dornock)	1 Springfield Farm Court, Springfield, Gretna DG16 5EH	01461 337228
Steenbergen, Pauline (Ms) MA BD	1996 2012	Hospice Chaplain	Eden Valley Hospice, Durdar Road, Carlisle CA2 4SD [E-mail: pauline.steenbergen@edenvalleyhospice.co.uk]	01228 817609
Swinburne, Norman BA	1960 1993	(Sauchie)	Damerosehay, Birch Hill Lane, Kirkbride, Wigton CA7 5HZ	01697 351497
Vivers, Katherine A.	2004	Auxiliary Minister	Blacket House, Eaglesfield, Lockerbie DG11 3AA [E-mail: KVivers@churchofscotland.org.uk]	01461 500412
Williams, Trevor C. LTh	1990 2007	(Hoddom with Kirtle-Eaglesfield with Middlebie with Waterbeck)	c/o Presbytery Clerk [E-mail: revtrev@btinternet.com]	07748 233011 (Mbl)

(8) DUMFRIES AND KIRKCUDBRIGHT

Meets at Dumfries on the last Wednesday of February, April, June, September and November.

Clerk: **REV. WILLIAM T. HOGG MA BD**   **St Bride's Manse, Glasgow Road, Sanquhar DG4 6BZ**   **01659 50247**
[E-mail: dumfrieskirkcudbright@churchofscotland.org.uk]

Balmaclellan and Kells (H) linked with Carsphairn (H) linked with Dalry (H)
David S. Bartholomew BSc MSc PhD BD   1994   The Manse, Dalry, Castle Douglas DG7 3PJ   01644 430380
[E-mail: DBartholomew@churchofscotland.org.uk]

Caerlaverock linked with Dumfries: St Mary's-Greyfriars' (H)
David D.J. Logan MStJ BD MA Cf(V) FRSA   2009   2015   4 Georgetown Crescent, Dumfries DG1 4EQ   01387 253877
[E-mail: DLogan@churchofscotland.org.uk]   07797 742012 (Mbl)

Carsphairn See Balmaclellan and Kells

Castle Douglas (H) linked with The Bengairn Parishes
Vacant
Oonagh Dee   2016   1 Castle View, Castle Douglas DG7 1BG   01556 505983
(Ordained Local Minister)   Kendoon, Merse Way, Kippford, Dalbeattie DG5 4LL   01556 620001
                                          [E-mail: ODee@churchofscotland.org.uk]

Closeburn linked with Kirkmahoe
Vacant   The Manse, Kirkmahoe, Dumfries DG1 1ST   01387 710572

Colvend, Southwick and Kirkbean
James F. Gatherer BD   1984   2003   The Manse, Colvend, Dalbeattie DG5 4QN   01556 630255
                                          [E-mail: JGatherer@churchofscotland.org.uk]

Corsock and Kirkpatrick Durham linked with Crossmichael, Parton and Balmaghie
Sally Russell BTh MTh   2006   Knockdrocket, Clarebrand, Castle Douglas DG7 3AH   01556 503645
                                          [E-mail: SRussell@churchofscotland.org.uk]

Crossmichael and Parton See Corsock and Kirkpatrick Durham

Cummertrees, Mouswald and Ruthwell (H)
Vacant   The Manse, Ruthwell, Dumfries DG1 4NP   01387 870217

Dalbeattie (H) and Kirkgunzeon linked with Urr (H)
Fiona A. Wilson (Mrs) BD   2008   2014   36 Mill Street, Dalbeattie DG5 4HE   01556 610708
                                          [E-mail: FWilson@churchofscotland.org.uk]

Dalry See Balmaclellan and Kells

Dumfries: Maxwelltown West (H)
David A. Sutherland BD   2001   2014   Maxwelltown West Manse, 11 Laurieknowe, Dumfries DG2 7AH   01387 247538
                                          [E-mail: DSutherland@churchofscotland.org.uk]

Dumfries: Northwest
Neil G. Campbell BA BD   1988   2006   c/o Church Office, Dumfries Northwest Church, Lochside Road, 01387 249964
                                          Dumfries DG2 0DZ
                                          [E-mail: NCampbell@churchofscotland.org.uk]

Dumfries: St George's (H)
Donald Campbell BD   1997   9 Nunholm Park, Dumfries DG1 1JP   01387 252965
                                          [E-mail: DCampbell@churchofscotland.org.uk]

Dumfries: St Mary's-Greyfriars' See Caerlaverock

Dumfries: St Michael's and South			
Maurice S. Bond MTh BA DipEd PhD	1981	39 Cardoness Street, Dumfries DG1 3AL	01387 253849
		[E-mail: MBond@churchofscotland.org.uk]	
Dumfries: Troqueer (H)			
John R. Notman BSc BD	1990 2015	Troqueer Manse, Troqueer Road, Dumfries DG2 7DF	01387 253043
		[E-mail: JNotman@churchofscotland.org.uk]	
Dunscore linked with Glencairn and Moniaive			
Joachim J.H. du Plessis BA BD MTh	1975 2013	Wallaceton, Auldgirth, Dumfries DG2 0TJ	01387 820245
		[E-mail: JduPlessis@churchofscotland.org.uk]	
Durisdeer linked with Penpont, Keir and Tynron linked with Thornhill (H)			
J. Stuart Mill MA MBA BD	1976 2013	The Manse, Manse Park, Thornhill DG3 5ER	01848 331191
		[E-mail: JMill@churchofscotland.org.uk]	
Gatehouse and Borgue linked with Tarff and Twynholm			
Valerie J. Ott (Mrs) BA BD	2002	The Manse, Planetree Park, Gatehouse of Fleet, Castle Douglas DG7 2EQ	01557 814233
		[E-mail: VOtt@churchofscotland.org.uk]	
Glencairn and Moniaive See Dunscore			
Irongray, Lochrutton and Terregles			
Gary J. Peacock MA BD MTh	2015	The Manse, Shawhead, Dumfries DG2 9SJ	01387 730759
		[E-mail: GPeacock@churchofscotland.org.uk]	
Kirkconnel (H)			
Vacant			
Kirkcudbright (H)			
Douglas R. Irving LLB BD WS	1984 1998	6 Bourtree Avenue, Kirkcudbright DG6 4AU	01557 330489
		[E-mail: DIrving@churchofscotland.org.uk]	
Kirkmahoe See Closeburn			

Kirkmichael, Tinwald and Torthorwald
Vacant
Manse of Tinwald, Tinwald, Dumfries DG1 3PL   01387 710246

Lochend and New Abbey
Maureen M. Duncan (Mrs) BD   1996   2014
New Abbey Manse, 32 Main Street, New Abbey, Dumfries DG2 8BY   01387 850490
[E-mail: revmo@talktalk.net]

Penpont, Keir and Tynron See Durisdeer

Sanquhar: St Bride's (H)
William T. Hogg MA BD   1979   2000
St Bride's Manse, Glasgow Road, Sanquhar DG6 6BZ   01659 50247
[E-mail: WHogg@churchofscotland.org.uk]

Tarff and Twynholm See Gatehouse and Borgue
The Bengairn Parishes See Castle Douglas
Thornhill See Durisdeer
Urr See Dalbeattie and Kirkgunzeon

Name				Contact	Phone
Bennett, David K.P. BA	1974	2000	(Kirkpatrick Irongray with Lochrutton with Terregles)	53 Anne Arundel Court, Heathhall, Dumfries DG1 3SL	01387 257755
Finch, Graham S. MA BD	1977	2016	(Cadder)	32a St Mary Street, Kirkcudbright DG6 4DN [E-mail: gsf231@gmail.com]	01557 620123
Greer, A. David C. LLB DMin DipAdultEd	1956	1996	(Barra)	17 Duthac Wynd, Tain IV19 1LP [E-mail: greer2@talktalk.net]	01862 892065
Hammond, Richard J. BA BD	1993	2007	(Kirkmahoe)	3 Marchfield Mount, Marchfield, Dumfries DG1 1SE [E-mail: libby.hammond@virgin.net]	(Mbl) 07764 465783
Holland, William MA	1967	2009	(Lochend and New Abbey)	Ardshean, 55 Georgetown Road, Dumfries DG1 4DD [E-mail: billholland55@btinternet.com]	01387 256131
Kelly, William W. BSc BD	1994	2014	(Dumfries: Troqueer)	6 Vitality Way, Craigie, Perth, WA 6025, Australia [E-mail: ww.kelly@btinternet.com]	(Mbl) 07766 531732
Kirk, W. Logan MA BD MTh	1988	2000	(Dalton with Hightae with St Mungo)	2 Raecroft Avenue, Collin, Dumfries DG1 4LP	01387 750489
Mack, Elizabeth A. (Miss) DipEd	1994	2011	(Auxiliary Minister)	24 Roberts Crescent, Dumfries DG2 7RS [E-mail: mackliz@btinternet.com]	01387 264847
McKay, David M. MA BD	1979	2007	(Kirkpatrick Juxta with Moffat: St Andrew's with Wamphray)	20 Auld Brig View, Auldgirth, Dumfries DG2 0XE [E-mail: davidmckay20@tiscali.co.uk]	01387 740013
McKenzie, William M. DA	1958	1993	(Dumfries: Troqueer)	41 Kingholm Road, Dumfries DG1 4SR [E-mail: mckenzie.dumfries@btinternet.com]	01387 253688

Name	Dates	Congregation	Address	Tel
McKichan, Alistair J. MA BD	1984 2015	(Kirkconnel)	The Wyld, Horndean, Berwick-upon-Tweed TD15 1XJ [E-mail: alistairjmck@btinternet.com]	01289 382745
McLauchlan, Mary C. (Mrs) LTh	1997 2013	(Mochrum)	3 Ayr Street, Moniaive, Thornhill DG3 4HP [E-mail: mary@revmother.co.uk]	01848 200786
Owen, John J.C. LTh	1967 2001	(Applegarth and Sibbaldbie with Lochmaben)	5 Galla Avenue, Dalbeattie DG5 4JZ [E-mail: jj.owen@onetel.net]	01556 612125
Robertson, Ian W. MA BD	1956 1995	(Colvend, Southwick and Kirkbean)	10 Marjoriebanks, Lochmaben, Lockerbie DG11 1QH	01387 810541
Sutherland, Colin A. LTh	1995 2007	(Blantyre: Livingstone Memorial)	71 Caulstran Road, Dumfries DG2 9FJ [E-mail: colin.csutherland@btinternet.com]	01387 279954
Wallace, Mhairi (Mrs)	2013	Ordained Local Minister	5 Dee Road, Kirkcudbright DG6 4HQ [E-mail: MWallace@churchofscotland.org.uk]	(Mbl) 07701 375064
Williamson, James BA BD	1986 2009	(Cummertrees with Mouswald with Ruthwell)	12 Mulberry Drive, Dunfermline KY11 8BZ [E-mail: jimwill@remkirk.fsnet.co.uk]	01383 734872
Wotherspoon, Robert C. LTh	1976 1998	(Corsock and Kirkpatrick Durham with Crossmichael and Parton)	7 Hillowton Drive, Castle Douglas DG7 1LL [E-mail: robert.wotherspoon@tiscali.co.uk]	01556 502267
Young, John MTh DipMin	1963 1999	(Airdrie: Broomknoll)	Craigview, North Street, Moniaive, Thornhill DG3 4HR	01848 200318

DUMFRIES ADDRESSES

Maxwelltown West	Laurieknowe	
Northwest	Lochside Road	
St George's	George Street	
St Mary's-Greyfriars	St Mary's Street	
St Michael's and South	St Michael's Street	
Troqueer	Troqueer Road	

(9) WIGTOWN AND STRANRAER

Meets at Glenluce, in the church hall, on the first Tuesday of March, October and December for ordinary business; on the first Tuesday of September for formal business followed by meetings of committees; on the first Tuesday of November, February and May for worship followed by meetings of committees; and at a church designated by the Moderator on the first Tuesday of June for Holy Communion followed by ordinary business.

Clerk: MR SAM SCOBIE 40 Clenoch Parks Road, Stranraer DG9 7QT [E-mail: wigtownstranraer@churchofscotland.org.uk] 01776 703975

Ervie Kirkcolm linked with Leswalt
Michael J. Sheppard BD 1997 Ervie Manse, Stranraer DG9 0QZ [E-mail: MSheppard@churchofscotland.org.uk] 01776 854225

Glasserton and Isle of Whithorn linked with Whithorn: St Ninian's Priory
Alexander I. Currie BD CPS   1990   The Manse, Whithorn, Newton Stewart DG8 8PT   01988 500267
                                                         [E-mail: ACurrie@churchofscotland.org.uk]

Inch linked with Portpatrick linked with Stranraer: Trinity (H)
John H. Burns BSc BD   1985   1988   Bayview Road, Stranraer DG9 8BE   01776 702383
                                                         [E-mail: JBurns@churchofscotland.org.uk]

Kirkcowan (H) linked with Wigtown (H)
Eric Boyle BA MTh   2006   Seaview Manse, Church Lane, Wigtown, Newton Stewart DG8 9HT   01988 402314
                                                         [E-mail: EBoyle@churchofscotland.org.uk]

Kirkinner linked with Mochrum linked with Sorbie (H)
Jeffrey M. Mead BD   1978   1986   The Manse, Kirkinner, Newton Stewart DG8 9AL   01988 840643
                                                         [E-mail: JMead@churchofscotland.org.uk]

Kirkmabreck linked with Monigaff (H)
Stuart Farmes   2011   2014   Creebridge, Newton Stewart DG8 6NR   01671 403361
                                                         [E-mail: SFarmes@churchofscotland.org.uk]

Kirkmaiden (H) linked with Stoneykirk
Christopher Wallace BD DipMin   1988   2016   Church Road, Sandhead, Stranraer DG9 9JJ   01776 830757
                                                         [E-mail: Christopher.Wallace@churchofscotland.org.uk]

Leswalt See Ervie Kirkcolm

Luce Valley
Vacant   Glenluce, Newton Stewart DG8 0PU   01581 300319
                                            (New charge formed by the union between Old Luce and New Luce)

Monigaff See Kirkmabreck

Penninghame (H)
Edward D. Lyons BD MTh   2007   The Manse, 1A Corvisel Road, Newton Stewart DG8 6LW   01671 404425
                                                         [E-mail: ELyons@churchofscotland.org.uk]

Portpatrick See Inch

Sorbie See Kirkinner
Stoneykirk See Kirkmaiden

Stranraer: High Kirk (H)
Ian McIlroy BSS BD 1996 2009 Stoneleigh, Whitehouse Road, Stranraer DG9 0JB 01776 700616
[E-mail: IMcIlroy@churchofscotland.org.uk]

Stranraer: Trinity See Inch
Whithorn: St Ninian's Priory See Glasserton and Isle of Whithorn
Wigtown See Kirkcowan

Aiken, Peter W.I.	1996 2013	(Kirkmabreck with Monigaff)	Garroch, Viewhills Road, Newton Stewart DG8 6JA [E-mail: revpetevon@gmail.com]	
Baker, Carolyn M. (Mrs) BD	1997 2008	(Ochiltree with Stair)	Clanary, 1 Maxwell Drive, Newton Stewart DG8 6EL [E-mail: cncbaker@btinternet.com]	
Bellis, Pamela A. BA	2014	Ordained Local Minister	Maughold, Low Killantrae, Port William, Newton Stewart DG8 9QR	01988 700590
			[E-mail: pam@bellisconsultancy.co.uk]	
Cairns, Alexander B. MA	1957 2009	(Turin)	Beechwood, Main Street, Sandhead, Stranraer DG9 9JG	01776 830389
			[E-mail: dorothycairns@aol.com]	
Harvey, Joyce (Mrs)	2013	Ordained Local Minister	4A Allanfield Place, Newton Stewart DG8 6BS	01671 403693
			[E-mail: JHarvey@churchofscotland.org.uk]	
Munro, Mary (Mrs) BA	1993 2004	(Auxiliary Minister)	14 Auchneel Crescent, Stranraer DG9 0JH	01776 702305

(10) AYR

Meets in Alloway Church Hall on the first Tuesday of every month from September to May, excluding January and April. The June meeting takes place on the third Tuesday of the month in the newly installed Moderator's church. The October meeting is held in a venue determined by the Business Committee.

Clerk:	**REV. KENNETH C. ELLIOTT** **BD BA CertMin**	68 St Quivox Road, Prestwick KA9 1JF [E-mail: ayr@churchofscotland.org.uk]	01292 478788
Presbytery Office:		Prestwick South Parish Church, 50 Main Street, Prestwick KA9 1NX	01292 678556

Alloway (H)
Neil A. McNaught BD MA 1987 1999 1A Parkview, Alloway, Ayr KA7 4QG 01292 441252
[E-mail: NMcNaught@churchofscotland.org.uk]

Annbank (H) linked with Tarbolton P. Jill Clancy (Mrs) BD DipMin	2000	2014	The Manse, Tarbolton, Mauchline KA5 5QL [E-mail: JClancy@churchofscotland.org.uk]	01292 540969
Auchinleck (H) linked with Catrine Stephen F. Clipston MA BD	1982	2006	28 Mauchline Road Auchinleck KA18 2BN [E-mail: SClipston@churchofscotland.org.uk]	01290 424776
Ayr: Auld Kirk of Ayr (St John the Baptist) (H) David R. Gemmell MA BD	1991	1999	58 Monument Road, Ayr KA7 2UB [E-mail: DGemmell@churchofscotland.org.uk]	01292 262580 (Tel/Fax)
Ayr: Castlehill (H) Vacant			3 Old Hillfoot Road, Ayr KA7 3LW	01292 263001
Ayr: Newton Wallacetown (H) Abi T. Ngunga GTh LTh MDiv MTh PhD	2001	2014	9 Nursery Grove, Ayr KA7 3PH [E-mail: ANgunga@churchofscotland.org.uk]	01292 264251
Ayr: St Andrew's (H) Morag Garrett (Mrs) BD	2011	2013	31 Bellevue Crescent, Ayr KA7 2DP [E-mail: MGarrett@churchofscotland.org.uk]	01292 261472
Ayr: St Columba (H) Fraser R. Aitken MA BD	1978	1991	3 Upper Crofts, Alloway, Ayr KA7 4QX [E-mail: FAitken@churchofscotland.org.uk]	01292 443747
Ayr: St James' (H) Vacant			1 Prestwick Road, Ayr KA8 8LD	01292 262420
Ayr: St Leonard's (H) linked with Dalrymple Brian Hendrie BD	1992	2015	35 Roman Road, Ayr KA7 3SZ [E-mail: BHendrie@churchofscotland.org.uk]	01292 283825
Ayr: St Quivox (H) Vacant			11 Springfield Avenue, Prestwick KA9 2HA	01292 478306
Ballantrae (H) linked with St Colmon (Arnsheen Barrhill and Colmonell) Stephen Ogston MPhys MSc BD	2009		The Manse, 1 The Vennel, Ballantrae, Girvan KA26 0NH [E-mail: SOgston@churchofscotland.org.uk]	01465 831252

Barr linked with Dailly linked with Girvan: South
Ian K. McLachlan MA BD   1999   30 Henrietta Street, Girvan KA26 9AL   01465 713370
[E-mail: IMcLachlan@churchofscotland.org.uk]

Catrine See Auchinleck

Coylton linked with Drongan: The Schaw Kirk
Vacant   4 Hamilton Place, Coylton, Ayr KA6 6JQ   01292 571442
Douglas T. Moore   2003   9 Midton Avenue, Prestwick KA9 1PU   01292 671352
(Auxiliary Minister)   [E-mail: douglastmoore@hotmail.com]

Craigie Symington linked with Prestwick South (H) (E-mail: office@pwksouth.plus.com)
Kenneth C. Elliott BD BA Cert Min   1989   68 St Quivox Road, Prestwick KA9 1JF   01292 478788
[E-mail: KElliott@churchofscotland.org.uk]
Tom McLeod   2014   2015   3 Martnaham Drive, Coylton KA6 6JE   01292 570100
(Ordained Local Minister)   [E-mail: tamlin410@btinternet.com]

Crosshill (H) linked with Maybole
Vacant   The Manse, 16 McAdam Way, Maybole KA19 8FD   01655 883710

Dailly See Barr

Dalmellington linked with Patna Waterside
Eleanor J. McMahon BEd BD   1994   4 Carsphairn Road, Dalmellington, Ayr KA6 7RE   01292 551503
(Interim Minister)   [E-mail: EMcMahon@churchofscotland.org.uk]   07974 116539 (Mbl)

Dalrymple See Ayr: St Leonard's
Drongan: The Schaw Kirk See Coylton

Dundonald (H)
Robert Mayes BD   1982   1988   64 Main Street, Dundonald, Kilmarnock KA2 9HG   01563 850243
[E-mail: RMayes@churchofscotland.org.uk]

Fisherton (H) linked with Kirkoswald (H)
Ian R. Stirling BSc BD   1990   2016   The Manse, Kirkoswald, Maybole KA19 8HZ   01655 760210
[E-mail: IStirling@churchofscotland.org.uk]

Girvan: North (Old and St Andrew's) (H)
Richard G. Moffat BD   1994   2013   38 The Avenue, Girvan KA26 9DS   01465 713203
[E-mail: RMoffat@churchofscotland.org.uk]

Girvan: South See Barr

Kirkmichael linked with Straiton: St Cuthbert's
W. Gerald Jones MA BD MTh   1984   The Manse, Patna Road, Kirkmichael, Maybole KA19 7PJ   01655 750286
[E-mail: WJones@churchofscotland.org.uk]

Kirkoswald See Fisherton

Lugar linked with Old Cumnock: Old (H)
John W. Paterson BSc BD DipEd   1994   33 Barrhill Road, Cumnock KA18 1PJ   01290 420769
[E-mail: JPaterson@churchofscotland.org.uk]

Mauchline (H) linked with Sorn
David A. Albon BA MCS   1991 2011   4 Westside Gardens, Mauchline KA5 5DJ   01290 518528
[E-mail: DAlbon@churchofscotland.org.uk]

Maybole See Crosshill

Monkton and Prestwick: North (H)
David Clarkson BSc BA MTh   2010   40 Monkton Road, Prestwick KA9 1AR   01292 471379
[E-mail: DClarkson@churchofscotland.org.uk]

Muirkirk (H) linked with Old Cumnock: Trinity
Scott M. Rae MBE BD CPS   1976 2008   46 Ayr Road, Cumnock KA18 1DW   01290 422145
[E-mail: SRae@churchofscotland.org.uk]

New Cumnock (H)
Helen E. Cuthbert MA MSc BD   2009   37 Castle, New Cumnock, Cumnock KA18 4AG   01290 338296
[E-mail: HCuthbert@churchofscotland.org.uk]

Ochiltree linked with Stair
Vacant   10 Mauchline Road, Ochiltree, Cumnock KA18 2PZ   01290 700365

Old Cumnock: Old See Lugar
Old Cumnock: Trinity See Muirkirk
Patna Waterside See Dalmellington

Prestwick: Kingcase (H) (E-mail: office@kingcase.freeserve.co.uk)
Ian Wiseman BTh DipHSW — 1993 2015
15 Bellrock Avenue, Prestwick KA9 1SQ
[E-mail: IWiseman@churchofscotland.org.uk]
01292 479571

Prestwick: St Nicholas' (H)
George R. Fiddes BD — 1979 1985
3 Bellevue Road, Prestwick KA9 1NW
[E-mail: GFiddes@churchofscotland.org.uk]
01292 477613

Prestwick: South See Craigie Symington
St Colmon (Arnsheen Barrhill and Colmonell) See Ballantrae
Sorn See Mauchline
Stair See Ochiltree
Straiton: St Cuthbert's See Kirkmichael
Tarbolton See Annbank

Troon: Old (H)
David B. Prentice-Hyers BA MDiv — 2003 2013
85 Bentinck Drive, Troon KA10 6HZ
[E-mail: DPrentice-Hyers@churchofscotland.org.uk]
01292 313644

Troon: Portland (H)
Jamie Milliken BD — 2005 2011
89 South Beach, Troon KA10 6EQ
[E-mail: JMilliken@churchofscotland.org.uk]
01292 318929
07929 349045 (Mbl)

Troon: St Meddan's (H) (E-mail: st.meddan@virgin.net)
Derek Peat BA BD MTh — 2013
27 Bentinck Drive, Troon KA10 6HX
[E-mail: DPeat@churchofscotland.org.uk]
01292 319163

Name	Ordained	Inducted	Charge / Note	Address	Telephone
Birse, G. Stewart CA BD BSc	1980	2013	(Ayr: Newton Wallacetown)	9 Calvinston Road, Prestwick KA9 2EL [E-mail: stewart.birse@gmail.com]	01292 864975
Black, Sandra (Mrs)	2013		Ordained Local Minister	5 Doon Place, Troon KA10 7EQ [E-mail: Sandra.Black@churchofscotland.org.uk]	01292 220075
Blyth, James G.S. BSc BD	1963	1986	(Glenmuick)	40 Robsland Avenue, Ayr KA7 2RW	01292 261276
Bogle, Thomas C. BD	1983	2003	(Fisherton with Maybole: West)	38 McEwan Crescent, Mossblown, Ayr KA6 5DR	01292 521215
Brown, Jack M. BSc BD	1977	2012	(Applegarth, Sibbaldbie and Johnstone with Lochmaben)	69 Berelands Road, Prestwick KA9 1ER [E-mail: jackm.brown@tiscali.co.uk]	01292 477151
Crichton, James MA BD MTh	1969	2010	(Crosshill with Dalrymple)	4B Garden Court, Ayr KA8 0AT [E-mail: crichton.james@btinternet.com]	01292 288978
Crumlish, Elizabeth A. BD	1995	2015	Path of Renewal Co-ordinator	53 Ayr Road, Prestwick KA9 1SY [E-mail: ECrumlish@churchofscotland.org.uk]	(Mbl) 07464 675434
Dickie, Michael M. BSc	1955	1994	(Ayr: Castlehill)	8 Noltmire Road, Ayr KA8 9ES	01292 618512

Name	Charge / Role	Years	Address & E-mail	Telephone
Geddes, Alexander J. MA BD	(Stewarton: St Columba's)	1960 1998	2 Gregory Street, Mauchline KA5 6BY [E-mail: sandy270736@gmail.com]	01290 518597
Glencross, William M. LTh	(Bellshill: Macdonald Memorial)	1968 1999	1 Lochay Place, Troon KA10 7HH	01292 317097
Grant, J. Gordon MA BD PhD	(Edinburgh: Dean)	1957 1997	33 Fullarton Drive, Troon KA10 6LE	01292 311852
Guthrie, James A.	(Corsock and Kirkpatrick Durham with Crossmichael and Parton)	1969 2005	2 Barrhill Road, Pinwherry, Girvan KA26 0QE [E-mail: p.h.m.guthrie@btinternet.com]	01465 841236
Hannah, William BD MCAM MIPR	(Muirkirk)	1987 2001	8 Dovecote View, Kirkintilloch, Glasgow G66 3HY [E-mail: revbillnews@btinternet.com]	0141-776 1337
Harper, David L. BSc BD	(Troon: St Meddan's)	1972 2012	19 Calder Avenue, Troon KA10 7JT [E-mail: d.l.harper@btinternet.com]	01292 312626
Harris, Samuel McC. OStJ BA BD	(Rothesay: Trinity)	1974 2010	36 Adam Wood Court, Troon KA10 6BP	01292 319603
Hickman, Mandy R. RGN	Presbytery Mission Development Officer	2013	Lagnaleon, 4 Wilson Street, Largs KA30 9AQ [E-mail: MHickman@churchofscotland.org.uk]	01475 675347 (Mbl) 07743 760792
Jackson, Nancy	Auxiliary Minister	2009 2013	35 Auchentrae Crescent, Ayr KA7 4BD [E-mail: NJackson@churchofscotland.org.uk]	01292 262034
Johnston, William R. BD	(Ochiltree linked with Stair)	1998 2016	30 Annfield Glen Road, Ayr KA7 3RP	01292 282663
Kent, Arthur F.S.	(Monkton and Prestwick: North)	1966 1999	17 St David's Drive, Evesham, Worcs WR11 2AS [E-mail: afskent@onetel.com]	01386 421562
Laing, Iain A. MA BD	(Bishopbriggs: Kenmuir)	1971 2009	9 Annfield Road, Prestwick KA9 1PP [E-mail: iandrlaing@yahoo.co.uk]	01292 471732
Lennox, Lawrie I. MA BD DipEd	(Cromar)	1991 2006	7 Carwinshoch View, Ayr KA7 4AY [E-mail: lennox127@btinternet.com]	01465 811262
Lochrie, John S. BSc BD MTh PhD	(St Colmon)	1967 2008	Cosyglen, Kilkerran, Maybole KA19 8LS	(Mbl) 07771 481698
Lynn, Robert MA BD	(Ayr: St Leonard's with Dalrymple)	1984 2011	8 Kirkbrae, Maybole KA19 7ER	
McCrorie, William	(Free Church Chaplain: Royal Brompton Hospital)	1965 1999	20 Bellevue Crescent, Ayr KA7 2BR [E-mail: billevemcrorie@btinternet.com]	01292 288854
McGurk, Andrew F. BD	(Largs: St John's)	1983 2011	15 Fraser Avenue, Troon KA10 6XF [E-mail: afmcg.largs@talk21.com]	01292 676008
McNidder, Roderick H. BD	Chaplain: NHS Ayrshire and Arran Trust	1987 1997	6 Hollow Park, Alloway, Ayr KA7 4SR [E-mail: roddymcnidder@sky.com]	01292 442554
McPhail, Andrew M. BA	(Ayr: Wallacetown)	1968 2002	25 Maybole Road, Ayr KA7 2QA	01292 282108
Matthews, John C. MA BD OBE	(Glasgow: Ruchill Kelvinside)	1992 2010	12 Arrol Drive, Ayr KA7 4AF [E-mail: mejohnmatthews@gmail.com]	01292 264382
Mealyea, Harry B. BArch BD	(Ayr: St Andrew's)	1984 2011	38 Rosamunde Pilcher Drive, Longforgan, Dundee DD2 5EF [E-mail: mealyeal@sky.com]	
Mitchell, Sheila M. (Miss) BD MTh	Healthcare Chaplaincy Director Scotland	1995 2015	3rd Floor, 2 Central Quay, 89 Hydepark Street, Glasgow G3 8BW [E-mail: sheila.mitchell@nes.scot.nhs.uk]	(Mbl) 07769 367615
Morrison, Alistair H. BTh DipYCS	(Paisley: St Mark's Oldhall)	1985 2004	92 St Leonard's Road, Ayr KA7 2PU [E-mail: alistairmorrison@supanet.com]	01292 266021
Ness, David T. LTh	(Ayr: St Quivox)	1972 2008	17 Winston Avenue, Prestwick KA9 2EZ [E-mail: dtness@tiscali.co.uk]	
Russell, Paul R. MA BD	Hospital Chaplain	1984 2006	23 Nursery Wynd, Ayr KA7 3NZ	01292 618020

Sanderson, Alastair M. BA LTh	1971 2007	(Craigie with Symington)	26 Main Street, Monkton, Prestwick KA9 2QL [E-mail: alel@sanderson29.fsnet.co.uk]	01292 475819
Simpson, Edward V. BSc BD	1972 2009	(Glasgow: Giffnock South)	8 Paddock View, Thorntoun, Crosshouse, Kilmarnock KA2 0BH [E-mail: eddie.simpson3@talktalk.net]	01563 522841
Smith, Elizabeth (Mrs) BD	1996 2009	(Fauldhouse: St Andrew's)	16 McIntyre Road, Prestwick KA9 1BE [E-mail: smithrevb@btinternet.com]	01292 471588
Stirling, Ian R. BSc BD	1990 2002	Chaplain: The Ayrshire Hospice	Ayrshire Hospice, 35–37 Racecourse Road, Ayr KA7 2TG [E-mail: IStirling@churchofscotland.org.uk]	01292 269200
Symington, Alastair H. MA BD	1972 2012	(Troon: Old)	1 Cavendish Place, Troon KA10 6JG [E-mail: revdahs@virginmedia.com]	01292 312556
Wilkinson, Arrick D. BSc BD	2000 2013	(Fisherton with Kirkoswald)	Dunwhinny, Main Street, Ballantrae, Girvan KA26 0NB [E-mail: arrick@dunwhinny.plus.com]	01465 831704
Young, Rona M. (Mrs) BD DipEd	1991 2015	(Ayr: St Quivox)	16 Macintyre Road, Prestwick KA9 1BE [E-mail: revronyoung@hotmail.com]	
Yorke, Kenneth B.	1982 2009	(Dalmellington with Patna Waterside)	13 Amfield Terrace, Prestwick KA9 1PS [E-mail: kenneth.yorke@googlemail.com]	(Mbl) 07766 320525

AYR ADDRESSES

Ayr			
Auld Kirk	Kirkport (116 High Street)		
Castlehill	Castlehill Road x Hillfoot Road		
Newton Wallacetown	Main Street		
St Andrew's	Park Circus		
St Columba	Midton Road x Carrick Park		
St James'	Prestwick Road x Falkland Park Road		
St Leonard's	St Leonard's Road x Monument Road		
Girvan			
North	Montgomerie Street		
South	Stair Park		
Prestwick		Monkton and Prestwick North	Monkton Road
Kingcase	Waterloo Road	St Nicholas	Main Street
		South	Main Street
		Troon	
		Old	Ayr Street
		Portland	St Meddan's Street
		St Meddan's	St Meddan's Street

(11) IRVINE AND KILMARNOCK

The Presbytery meets ordinarily at 7:00pm in the Howard Centre, Portland Road, Kilmarnock, on the first Tuesday in September, December and March and on the fourth Tuesday in June for ordinary business, and at different locations on the first Tuesday in October, November, February and May for mission. The September meeting commences with the celebration of Holy Communion.

Clerk:	MR I. STEUART DEY LLB	72 Dundonald Road, Kilmarnock KA1 1RZ [E-mail: irvinekilmarnock@churchofscotland.org.uk] [E-mail: steuart.dey@btinternet.com]	01563 521686 (Home) 01563 526295 (Office)
Treasurer:	MR JAMES McINTOSH BA CA	15 Dundonald Road, Kilmarnock KA1 1RU	01563 523552

The Presbytery office is staffed each Tuesday, Wednesday and Thursday from 9am until 12:30pm. The office telephone number is 01563 526295.

Caldwell linked with Dunlop
Vacant — 4 Dampark, Dunlop, Kilmarnock KA3 4BZ — 01560 483268

Crosshouse (H)
T. Edward Marshall BD — 1987 2007 — 27 Kilmarnock Road, Crosshouse, Kilmarnock KA2 0EZ
[E-mail: TMarshall@churchofscotland.org.uk] — 01563 524089

Darvel (01560 322924)
Charles Lines BA — 2010 — 46 West Main Street, Darvel KA17 0AQ
[E-mail: CLines@churchofscotland.org.uk] — 01560 322924

Dreghorn and Springside
Vacant — 96A Townfoot, Dreghorn, Irvine KA11 4EZ — 01294 217770

Dunlop See Caldwell

Fenwick (H)
Geoffrey Redmayne BSc BD MPhil — 2000 — 2 Kirkton Place, Fenwick, Kilmarnock KA3 6DW
[E-mail: GRedmayne@churchofscotland.org.uk] — 01560 600217

Galston (H) (01563 820136)
Vacant — 60 Brewland Street, Galston KA4 8DX

Hurlford (H)
Vacant — 12 Main Road, Crookedholm, Kilmarnock KA3 6JT — 01563 535673

Irvine: Fullarton (H) (Website: www.fullartonchurch.co.uk)
Neil Urquhart BD DipMin — 1989 — 48 Waterside, Irvine KA12 8QJ
[E-mail: NUrquhart@churchofscotland.org.uk] — 01294 279909

Irvine: Girdle Toll (H) (Website: www.girdletoll.fsbusiness.co.uk)
Vacant — 2 Littlestane Rise, Irvine KA11 2BJ — 01294 213565

Irvine: Mure (H)
Vacant — 9 West Road, Irvine KA12 8RE — 01294 279916

Irvine: Old (H) (01294 273503)
Vacant
22 Kirk Vennel, Irvine KA12 0DQ
01294 279265

Irvine: Relief Bourtreehill (H)
Andrew R. Black BD
1987 2003
4 Kames Court, Irvine KA11 1RT
[E-mail: ABlack@churchofscotland.org.uk]
01294 216939

Irvine: St Andrew's (H) (01294 276051)
Ian W. Benzie BD
1999 2008
St Andrew's Manse, 206 Bank Street, Irvine KA12 0YD
[E-mail: Ian.Benzie@churchofscotland.org.uk]
01294 216139

Kilmarnock: Kay Park (H) (07818 550606) (Website: www.kayparkparishchurch.co.uk)
David W. Lacy BA BD DLitt DL
1976 2012
52 London Road, Kilmarnock KA3 7AJ
[E-mail: DLacy@churchofscotland.org.uk]
01563 523113 (Tel/Fax)

Kilmarnock: New Laigh Kirk (H)
David S. Cameron BD
2001 2009
1 Holmes Farm Road, Kilmarnock KA1 1TP
[E-mail: David.Cameron@churchofscotland.org.uk]
01563 525416

Barbara Urquhart (Mrs) DCS
9 Standalane, Kilmaurs, Kilmarnock KA3 2NB
[E-mail: BUrquhart@churchofscotland.org.uk]
01563 538289

Kilmarnock: Riccarton (H)
Colin A. Strong BSc BD
1989 2007
2 Jasmine Road, Kilmarnock KA1 2HD
[E-mail: CStrong@churchofscotland.org.uk]
01563 549490

Kilmarnock: St Andrew's and St Marnock's
James McNaughtan BD DipMin
1983 2008
35 South Gargieston Drive, Kilmarnock KA1 1TB
[E-mail: JMcNaughtan@churchofscotland.org.uk]
01563 521665

Alison McBrier MA BD
(Associate Minister)
2011 2015
The Howard Centre, 5 Portland Road, Kilmarnock KA1 2BT
[E-mail: AMcBrier@churchofscotland.org.uk]
01563 541337
07478 937628 (Mbl)

Kilmarnock: St John's Onthank (H)
Vacant
84 Wardneuk Drive, Kilmarnock KA3 2EX
01563 521815

Kilmarnock: St Kentigern's (Website: www.stkentigern.org.uk)
Vacant
1 Thirdpart Place, Kilmarnock KA1 1UL
01563 571280

Kilmarnock: South (01563 524705)

H. Taylor Brown BD CertMin	1997 2012	14 McLelland Drive, Kilmarnock KA1 1SE [E-mail: HBrown@churchofscotland.org.uk]	01563 529920

Kilmaurs: St Maur's Glencairn (H)

John A. Urquhart BD	1993	9 Standalane, Kilmaurs, Kilmarnock KA3 2NB [E-mail: John.Urquhart@churchofscotland.org.uk]	01563 538289

Newmilns: Loudoun (H)

Vacant		Loudoun Manse, 116A Loudoun Road, Newmilns KA16 9HH	01560 320174

Stewarton: John Knox

Gavin A. Niven BSc MSc BD	2010	27 Avenue Street, Stewarton, Kilmarnock KA3 5AP [E-mail: GNiven@churchofscotland.org.uk]	01560 482418

Stewarton: St Columba's (H)

George K. Lind BD MCIBS	1998 2010	1 Kirk Glebe, Stewarton, Kilmarnock KA3 5BJ [E-mail: GLind@churchofscotland.org.uk]	01560 485113

Ayrshire Mission to the Deaf

Richard C. Durno DSW CQSW	1989 2013	31 Springfield Road, Bishopbriggs, Glasgow G64 1PJ [E-mail: richard.durno@btinternet.com]	(Voice/Text/Fax) 0141-772 1052 (Voice/Text/Voicemail) (Mbl) 07748 607721

Brockie, Colin G.F. BSc(Eng) BD SOSc	1967 2007	(Presbytery Clerk)	36 Braehead Court, Kilmarnock KA3 7AB [E-mail: revcol@revcol.demon.co.uk]	01563 559960
Campbell, John A. JP FIEM	1984 1998	(Irvine: St Andrew's)	Flowerdale, Balmoral Road, Rattray, Blairgowrie PH10 7AF [E-mail: exrevjack@aol.com]	01250 872795
Cant, Thomas M. MA BD	1965 2004	(Paisley: Laigh Kirk)	3 Meikle Cutstraw, Stewarton, Kilmarnock KA3 5HU [E-mail: revtmcant@aol.com]	01560 480566
Christie, Robert S. MA BD ThM	1964 2001	(Kilmarnock: West High)	24 Homeroyal House, 2 Chalmers Crescent, Edinburgh EH9 1TP	01294 312515
Davidson, James BD DipAFH	1989 2002	(Wishaw: Old)	13 Redburn Place, Irvine KA12 9BQ	01563 402622
Davidson Kelly, Thomas A. MA BD FSAScot	1975 2002	(Glasgow: Govan Old)	2 Springhill Stables, Portland Road, Kilmarnock KA1 2EJ [E-mail: ktdks33@aol.com]	
Garrity, T. Alan W. BSc BD MTh	1969 2008	(Bermuda)	17 Solomon's View, Dunlop, Kilmarnock KA3 4ES [E-mail: alangarrity@btinternet.com]	01560 486879
Gillon, C. Blair BD	1975 2007	(Glasgow: Ibrox)	East Muirshiel Farmhouse, Dunlop, Kilmarnock KA3 4EJ [E-mail: blairg2011@hotmail.co.uk]	01560 483778

Godfrey, Linda BSc BD	2012	2014	(Ayr: St Leonard's with Dalrymple)	9 Taybank Drive, Ayr KA7 4RL [E-mail: godfreykayak@aol.com]	(Mbl) 07825 663866
Hall, William M. BD	1972	2010	(Kilmarnock: Old High Kirk)	33 Cairns Terrace, Kilmarnock KA1 2JG [E-mail: revwillie@talktalk.net]	01563 525080
Hare, Malcolm M.W. BA BD	1956	1994	(Kilmarnock: St Kentigern's)	Flat 5, The Courtyard, Auchlochan, Lesmahagow, Lanark ML11 0GS	
Horsburgh, Gary E. BA	1977	2015	(Dreghorn and Springside)	1 Woodlands Grove, Kilmarnock KA3 1TY [E-mail: garyhorsburgh@hotmail.co.uk]	01563 624508
Hosain Lamarti, Samuel BD MTh PhD	1979	2006	(Stewarton: John Knox)	7 Dalwhinnie Crescent, Kilmarnock KA3 1QS [E-mail: samlamar@pobroadband.co.uk]	01563 529632
Huggett, Judith A. (Miss) BA BD	1990	1998	Lead Chaplain, NHS Ayrshire and Arran	4 Westmoor Crescent, Kilmarnock KA1 1TX [E-mail: judith.huggett@aaaht.scotnhs.uk]	
Keating, Glenda K. (Mrs) MTh	1996	2015	(Craigie Symington)	8 Wardlaw Gardens, Irvine KA11 2EW [E-mail: kirkglen@btinternet.com]	
McAllister, Anne C. BSc DipEd CCS	2013		Ordained Local Minister	39 Bowes Rigg, Stewarton, Kilmarnock KA3 5EN [E-mail: AMcAllister@churchofscotland.org.uk]	01560 483191
McAlpine, Richard H.M. BA FSAScot	1968	2000	(Lochgoilhead and Kilmorich)	7 Kingsford Place, Kilmarnock KA3 6FG	01563 572075
McCulloch, James D. BD MIOP MIP3 FSAScot	1996	2016	(Hurlford)	18 Edradour Place, Dunsmuir Park, Kilmarnock KA3 1US [E-mail: mccullochmanse1@btinternet.com]	01563 535833
MacDonald, James M. BD ThM	1964	1987	(Kilmarnock: St John's Onthank)	29 Carmel Place, Kilmaurs, Kilmarnock KA3 2QU	01563 525254
Scott, Thomas T.	1968	1989	(Kilmarnock: St Marnock's)	6 North Hamilton Place, Kilmarnock KA1 2QN [E-mail: tomtscott@btinternet.com]	01563 531415
Shaw, Catherine A.M. MA	1998	2006	(Auxiliary Minister)	40 Merrygreen Place, Stewarton, Kilmarnock KA3 5EP [E-mail: catherine.shaw@tesco.net]	01560 483352
Watt, Kim	2015		Ordained Local Minister	Reddans Park Gate, The Crescent, Stewarton, Kilmarnock KA3 5AY [E-mail: KWatt@churchofscotland.org.uk]	01560 482267
Welsh, Alex M. MA BD	1979	2007	Hospital Chaplain	8 Greenside Avenue, Prestwick KA9 2HB [E-mail: alexandevelyn@hotmail.com]	01292 475341

IRVINE and KILMARNOCK ADDRESSES

Irvine

Dreghorn and Springside	Townfoot x Station Brae
Fullarton	Marress Road x Church Street
Girdle Toll	Bryce Knox Court
Mure	West Road
Old	Kirkgate
Relief Bourtreehill	Crofthead, Bourtreehill
St Andrew's	Caldon Road x Oaklands Ave

Kilmarnock

Ayrshire Mission to the Deaf	10 Clark Street
Kay Park	London Road
Kilmarnock South	Whatriggs Road
New Laigh Kirk	John Dickie Street
Riccarton	Old Street
St Andrew's and St Marnock's	St Marnock Street
St John's Onthank	84 Wardneuk Street

(12) ARDROSSAN

Meets at Saltcoats, New Trinity, on the first Tuesday of February, March, April, May, September, October, November and December, and on the second Tuesday of June.

Clerk:	Vacant		[E-mail: ardrossan@churchofscotland.org.uk]	

Ardrossan: Park (01294 463711)
Tanya Webster BCom DipAcc BD	2011	35 Ardneil Court, Ardrossan KA22 7NQ	01294 538903
		[E-mail: TWebster@churchofscotland.org.uk]	

Ardrossan and Saltcoats: Kirkgate (H) (01294 472001) (Website: www.kirkgate.org.uk)
Dorothy A. Granger BA BD	2009	10 Seafield Drive, Ardrossan KA22 8NU	01294 463571
		[E-mail: DGranger@churchofscotland.org.uk]	07918 077877 (Mbl)

Beith (H) (01505 502686)
Roderick I.T. MacDonald BD CertMin	1992	2005	2 Glebe Court, Beith KA15 1ET	01505 503858
			[E-mail: RMacDonald@churchofscotland.org.uk]	
Fiona Blair DCS			9 West Road, Irvine KA12 8RE	07495 673428 (Mbl)
			[E-mail: FBlair@churchofscotland.org.uk]	

Brodick linked with Corrie linked with Lochranza and Pirnmill linked with Shiskine (H)
R. Angus Adamson BD	2006	4 Manse Crescent, Brodick, Isle of Arran KA27 8AS	01770 302334
		[E-mail: RAdamson@churchofscotland.org.uk]	

Corrie See Brodick

Cumbrae linked with Largs: St John's (H) (01475 674468)
Vacant	1 Newhaven Grove, Largs KA30 8NS	01475 329933

Dalry: St Margaret's
Vacant	33 Templand Crescent, Dalry KA24 5EZ	01294 832747

Charge / Minister	Ord.	Ind.	Address / E-mail	Tel
Dalry: Trinity (H) Martin Thomson BSc DipEd BD	1988	2004	Trinity Manse, West Kilbride Road, Dalry KA24 5DX [E-mail: MThomson@churchofscotland.org.uk]	01294 832363
Fairlie (H) linked with Largs: St Columba's Christian J. Vermeulen DipLT BTh MA	1986	2015	14 Fairlieburne Gardens, Fairlie, Largs KA29 0ER [E-mail: CVermeulen@churchofscotland.org.uk]	01475 568515
Kilbirnie: Auld Kirk (H) David Whiteman BD	1998	2015	49 Holmhead, Kilbirnie KA25 6BS [E-mail: DWhiteman@churchofscotland.org.uk]	01505 682342
Kilbirnie: St Columba's (H) (01505 685239) Fiona C. Ross (Miss) BD DipMin	1996	2004	Manse of St Columba's, Dipple Road, Kilbirnie KA25 7JU [E-mail: FRoss@churchofscotland.org.uk]	01505 683342
Kilmory linked with Lamlash Lily F McKinnon (Mrs) MA BD PGCE	1993	2015	The Manse, Lamlash, Isle of Arran KA27 8LE [E-mail: LMcKinnon@churchofscotland.org.uk]	01770 600074
Kilwinning: Mansefield Trinity (01294 550746) Vacant			47 Meadowfoot Road, West Kilbride KA23 9BU	01294 822224
Kilwinning: Old Jeanette Whitecross BD	2002	2011	54 Dalry Road, Kilwinning KA13 7HE [E-mail: JWhitecross@churchofscotland.org.uk]	01294 552606
Isobel Beck BD DCS			6 Patrick Avenue, Stevenston KA20 4AW [E-mail: IBeck@churchofscotland.org.uk]	07919 193425
Lamlash See Kilmory				
Largs: Clark Memorial (H) (01475 675186) T. David Watson BSc BD	1988	2014	31 Douglas Street, Largs KA30 8PT [E-mail: DWatson@churchofscotland.org.uk]	01475 672370

Largs: St Columba's (01475 686212) See Fairlie
Largs: St John's See Cumbrae
Lochranza and Pirnmill See Brodick

Saltcoats: North (01294 464679)
Alexander B. Noble MA BD ThM   1982   2003   25 Longfield Avenue, Saltcoats KA21 6DR   01294 604923
[E-mail: ANoble@churchofscotland.org.uk]

Saltcoats: St Cuthbert's (H)
Vacant   10 Kennedy Road, Saltcoats KA21 5SF   01294 696030

Shiskine See Brodick

Stevenston: Ardeer linked with Stevenston: Livingstone (H)
Vacant   32 High Road, Stevenston KA20 3DR   01294 464180

Stevenston: High (H) (Website: www.highkirk.com)
M. Scott Cameron MA BD   2002   Glencairn Street, Stevenston KA20 3DL   01294 463356
[E-mail: Scott.Cameron@churchofscotland.org.uk]

Stevenston: Livingstone See Stevenston: Ardeer

West Kilbride (H) (Website: www.westkilbrideparishchurch.org.uk)
James J. McNay MA BD   2008   The Manse, Goldenberry Avenue, West Kilbride KA23 9LJ   01294 823186
[E-mail: JMcNay@churchofscotland.org.uk]
Mandy R. Hickman RGN   2013   Lagnaleon, 4 Wilson Street, Largs KA30 9AQ   01475 675347
(Ordained Local Minister)   07743 760792 (Mbl)
[E-mail: MHickman@churchofscotland.org.uk]

Whiting Bay and Kildonan
Elizabeth R.L. Watson (Miss) BA BD   1981   1982   The Manse, Whiting Bay, Brodick, Isle of Arran KA27 8RE   01770 700289
[E-mail: EWatson@churchofscotland.org.uk]

Cruickshank, Norman BA BD	1983	2006	(West Kilbride: Overton)	24D Faulds Wynd, Seamill, West Kilbride KA23 9FA 01294 822239
Currie, Ian S. MBE BD	1975	2010	(The United Church of Bute)	15 Northfield Park, Largs KA30 8NZ (Mbl) 07764 254300
				[E-mail: ianscurrie@tiscali.co.uk]
Dailly, John R. BD DipPS	1979	2007	(Chaplain: Army)	2 Curtis Close, Pound Street, Warminster, Wiltshire BA12 9NN
Drysdale, James H. LTh	1987	2006	(Blackbraes and Shieldhill)	10 John Clark Street, Largs KA30 9AH 01475 674870
Falconer, Alan D. MA BD DLitt DD	1972	2011	(Aberdeen: St Machar's Cathedral)	18 North Crescent Road, Ardrossan KA22 8NA 01294 472991
				[E-mail: alanfalconer@gmx.com]
Finlay, William P. MA BD	1968	2000	(Glasgow: Townhead Blochairn)	High Corrie, Brodick, Isle of Arran KA27 8JB 01770 810689
Ford, Alan A. BD	1977	2013	(Glasgow: Springburn)	14 Corsankell Wynd, Saltcoats KA21 6HY 01294 465740
				[E-mail: alan.andy@btinternet.com]

Gordon, David C.	1953	1988	(Gigha and Cara)	South Beach House, South Crescent Road, Ardrossan KA22 8DU	01294 834092
Harbison, David J.H.	1958	1998	(Beith: High with Beith: Trinity)	42 Mill Park, Dalry KA24 5BB [E-mail: djh@harbi.fsnet.co.uk]	
Hebenton, David J. MA BD	1958	2002	(Ayton and Burnmouth with Grantshouse and Houndwood and Reston)	22B Faulds Wynd, Seamill, West Kilbride KA23 9FA	01294 829228
Howie, Marion L.K. (Mrs) MA ACRS	1992		Auxiliary Minister	51 High Road, Stevenston KA20 3DY	01294 466571
				59 Woodcroft Avenue, Largs KA30 9EW [E-mail: MHowie@churchofscotland.org.uk]	01475 670133
McCallum, Alexander D. BD	1987	2005	(Saltcoats: New Trinity)	6A Douglas Place, Largs KA30 8PU [E-mail: sandyandjose@madasafish.com]	01475 673303
McCance, Andrew M. BSc	1986	1995	(Coatbridge: Middle)	4 Golf Road, Millport, Isle of Cumbrae KA28 0HB	01475 530388
Mackay, Marjory H. (Mrs) BD DipEd CCE	1998	2008	(Cumbrae)	[E-mail: marjory.mackay@gmail.com]	
MacLeod, Ian LTh BA MTh PhD	1969	2006	(Brodick with Corrie)	Cronla Cottage, Corrie, Isle of Arran KA27 8JB [E-mail: i.macleod829@btinternet.com]	01770 810237
Mitchell, D. Ross BA BD	1972	2007	(West Kilbride: St Andrew's)	11 Dunbar Gardens, Saltcoats KA21 6GJ [E-mail: ross.mitchell@virgin.net]	
Paterson, John H. BD	1977	2000	(Kirkintilloch: St David's Memorial Park)	Creag Bhan, Golf Course Road, Whiting Bay, Isle of Arran KA27 8QT	01770 700569
Roy, Iain M. MA BD	1960	1997	(Stevenson: Livingstone)	2 The Fieldings, Dunlop, Kilmarnock KA3 4AU	01560 483072
Taylor, Andrew S. BTh FPhS	1959	1992	(Greenock Union)	9 Raillies Avenue, Largs KA30 8QY	01475 674709
				[E-mail: andrew.taylor_123@btinternet.com]	
Thomson, Margaret (Mrs)	1988	1993	(Saltcoats: Erskine)	7 Glen Farg, St Leonards, East Kilbride, Glasgow G74 2JW	01294 279265
Travers, Robert BA BD	1993	2015	(Irvine Old)	74 Caledonian Road, Stevenston KA20 3LF [E-mail: roberttravers@live.co.uk]	
Ward, Alan H. MA BD	1978	2013	(Interim Minister)	47 Meadowfoot Road, West Kilbride KA23 9BU	01475 822224
					(Mbl) 07709 906130

(13) LANARK

Meets on the first Tuesday of February, March, May, September, October, November and December, and on the third Tuesday of June.

Clerk pro tem: REV. BRYAN KERR BA BD   Greyfriars Manse, 3 Bellefield Way, Lanark ML11 7NW   **01555 663363**
[E-mail: lanark@churchofscotland.org.uk]

Biggar (H) linked with Black Mount   1997   2013   'Candlemas', 6C Leafield Road, Biggar ML12 6AY   01899 229291
Mike Fucella BD MTh   [E-mail: MFucella@churchofscotland.org.uk]

Black Mount See Biggar

Cairngryffe linked with Libberton and Quothquan (H) linked with Symington (The Tinto Parishes)
George C. Shand MA BD   1981   2014   16 Abington Road, Symington, Biggar ML12 6JX   01899 309400
[E-mail: George.Shand@churchofscotland.org.uk]

Carluke: Kirkton (H) (Church office: 01555 750778) (Website: www.kirktonchurch.co.uk)
Iain D. Cunningham MA BD   1979   1987   9 Station Road, Carluke ML8 5AA   01555 771262
[E-mail: ICunningham@churchofscotland.org.uk]

Carluke: St Andrew's (H)
Helen E. Jamieson (Mrs) BD DipEd   1989   120 Clyde Street, Carluke ML8 5BG   01555 771218
[E-mail: HJamieson@churchofscotland.org.uk]

Carluke: St John's (H) (Website: www.carluke-stjohns.org.uk)
Elijah O Obinna BA MTh PhD   2016   2016   18 Old Bridgend, Carluke ML8 4HN   01555 752389
[E-mail: EObinna@churchofscotland.org.uk]

Carnwath (H) linked with Carstairs
Maudeen I. MacDougall BA BD MTh   1978   2016   11 Range View, Cleghorn, Carstairs, Lanark ML11 8TF   01555 871258
[E-mail: MMacDougall@churchofscotland.org.uk]

Carstairs See Carnwath

Coalburn (H) linked with Lesmahagow: Old (H) (Church office: 01555 892425)
Vacant   9 Elm Bank, Lesmahagow, Lanark ML11 0EA

Crossford (H) linked with Kirkfieldbank
Steven Reid BAcc CA BD   1989   1997   74 Lanark Road, Crossford, Carluke ML8 5RE   01555 860415
[E-mail: SReid@churchofscotland.org.uk]

Forth: St Paul's (H) (Website: www.forthstpauls.com)
Elspeth J. MacLean (Mrs) BVMS BD   2011   2015   22 Lea Rig, Forth, Lanark ML11 8EA   01555 812832
[E-mail: EMacLean@churchofscotland.org.uk]

Kirkfieldbank See Crossford

Kirkmuirhill (H)
Ann Lyall DCS
(Interim Deacon)   The Manse, 2 Lanark Road, Kirkmuirhill, Lanark ML11 9RB   01555 892409
[E-mail: ALyall@churchofscotland.org.uk]

Lanark: Greyfriars (Church office: 01555 661510) (Website: www.lanarkgreyfriars.com)

| Bryan Kerr BA BD | 2002 | 2007 | Greyfriars Manse, 3 Bellefield Way, Lanark ML11 7NW [E-mail: BKerr@churchofscotland.org.uk] | 01555 663363 |

Lanark: St Nicholas' (H)

| Vacant | 2 Kaimhill Court, Lanark ML11 9HU | 01555 662600 |

Law

| Vacant | 3 Shawgill Court, Law, Carluke ML8 5SJ | 01698 373180 |

Lesmahagow: Abbeygreen

| David S. Carmichael | 1982 | Abbeygreen Manse, Lesmahagow, Lanark ML11 0DB [E-mail: David.Carmichael@churchofscotland.org.uk] | 01555 893384 |

Lesmahagow: Old See Coalburn
Libberton and Quothquan See Cairngryffe
Symington See Cairngryffe

The Douglas Valley Church (Church office: 01555 850000) (Website: www.douglasvalleychurch.org)

| Vacant | The Manse, Douglas, Lanark ML11 0RB | 01555 851213 |

Upper Clyde

| Nikki Macdonald BD MTh PhD | 2014 | 31 Carlisle Road, Crawford, Biggar ML12 6TP [E-mail: NMacdonald@churchofscotland.org.uk] | 01864 502139 |

Clelland, Elizabeth (Mrs) BD	2002	2012	Resident Chaplain, Divine Healing Fellowship (Scotland)	Braehead House Christian Healing and Retreat Centre, Braidwood Road, Crossford, Carluke ML8 5NQ [E-mail: liz_clelland@yahoo.co.uk]	01555 860716
Cowell, Susan G. (Miss) BA BD	1986	1998	(Budapest)	3 Gavel Lane, Regency Gardens, Lanark ML11 9FB	01555 665509
Easton, David J.C. MA BD	1965	2005	(Burnside–Blairbeth)	Rowanbank, Cormiston Road, Quothquan, Biggar ML12 6ND [E-mail: deaston@btinternet.com]	01899 308459
Findlay, Henry J.W. MA BD	1965	2005	(Wishaw: St Mark's)	2 Alba Gardens, Carluke ML8 5US	01555 759995
Houston, Graham R. BSc BD MTh PhD	1978	2011	(Cairngryffe with Symington)	3 Alder Lane, Beechtrees, Lanark ML11 9FT [E-mail: gandih6156@btinternet.com]	01555 678004
MacDougall, Lorna I. (Miss) MA DipGC BD	2003		Auxiliary Minister	11 Range View, Cleghorn, Carstairs, Lanark ML11 8TF [E-mail: LMacDougall@churchofscotland.org.uk]	01555 871258
Paciti, Stephen A. MA	1963	2003	(Black Mount with Culter with Libberton and Quothquan)	157 Nithsdale Road, Glasgow G41 5RD	0141-423 5972
Seath, Thomas J.G.	1980	1992	(Motherwell: Manse Road)	Flat 11, Wallace Court, South Vennel, Lanark ML11 7LL	01555 665399
Young, David A.	1972	2003	(Kirkmuirhill)	110 Carlisle Road, Blackwood, Lanark ML11 9RT [E-mail: david@aol.com]	01555 893357

(14) GREENOCK AND PAISLEY

Meets on the second Tuesday of September, October, November, December, February, March, April and May, and on the third Tuesday of June.

Clerk: REV. PETER McENHILL BD PhD

Presbytery Office: The Presbytery Office (see below)
[E-mail: greenockpaisley@churchofscotland.org.uk]
'Homelea', Faith Avenue, Quarrier's Village, Bridge of Weir PA11 3SX

01505 615033 (Tel)
01505 615088 (Fax)

Barrhead: Bourock (H) (0141-881 9813) Pamela Gordon BD	2006	2014	14 Maxton Avenue, Barrhead, Glasgow G78 1DY [E-mail: PGordon@churchofscotland.org.uk]	0141-881 8736
Barrhead: St Andrew's (H) (0141-881 8442) James S.A. Cowan BD DipMin	1986	1998	10 Arthurlie Avenue, Barrhead, Glasgow G78 2BU [E-mail: JCowan@churchofscotland.org.uk]	0141-881 3457
Bishopton (H) (Office: 01505 862583) Vacant			The Manse, Newton Road, Bishopton PA7 5JP	01505 862161
Bridge of Weir: Freeland (H) (01505 612610) Kenneth N. Gray BA BD	1988		15 Lawmarnock Crescent, Bridge of Weir PA11 3AS [E-mail: aandkgray@btinternet.com]	01505 690918
Bridge of Weir: St Machar's Ranfurly (01505 614364) Vacant			9 Glen Brae, Bridge of Weir PA11 3BH	01505 612975
Elderslie Kirk (H) (01505 323348) Robin N. Allison BD DipMin	1994	2005	282 Main Road, Elderslie, Johnstone PA5 9EF [E-mail: RAllison@churchofscotland.org.uk]	01505 321767
Erskine (0141-812 4620) Jonathan C. Fleming MA BD	2012		The Manse, 7 Leven Place, Linburn, Erskine PA8 6AS [E-mail: JFleming@churchofscotland.org.uk]	0141-570 8103

Gourock: Old Gourock and Ashton (H) David W.G. Burt BD DipMin	1989	2014	331 Eldon Street, Gourock PA16 7QN [E-mail: DBurt@churchofscotland.org.uk]	01475 633914
Gourock: St John's (H) Vacant			6 Barrhill Road, Gourock PA19 1JX	01475 632143
Greenock: East End linked with Greenock: Mount Kirk Francis E. Murphy BEng DipDSE BD	2006		76 Finnart Street, Greenock PA16 8HJ [E-mail: FMurphy@churchofscotland.org.uk]	01475 722338
Greenock: Lyle Kirk Owen Derrick MDiv MASFL	2007	2016	39 Fox Street, Greenock PA16 8PD [E-mail: ODerrick@churchofscotland.org.uk]	01475 717229 07840 983657 (Mbl)
Eileen Manson (Mrs) DipCE (Auxiliary Minister)	1994	2014	1 Cambridge Avenue, Gourock PA19 1XT [E-mail: EManson@churchofscotland.org.uk]	01475 632401
Greenock: Mount Kirk See Greenock: East End				
Greenock: St Margaret's (R) (01475 781953) Morris C. Coull BD	1974		105 Finnart Street, Greenock PA16 8HN [E-mail: MCoull@churchofscotland.org.uk]	01475 892874
Greenock: St Ninian's Allan G. McIntyre BD	1985		5 Auchmead Road, Greenock PA16 0PY [E-mail: AMcIntyre@churchofscotland.org.uk]	01475 631878
Greenock: Wellpark Mid Kirk Alan K. Sorensen BD MTh DipMin FSAScot	1983	2000	101 Brisbane Street, Greenock PA16 8PA [E-mail: ASorensen@churchofscotland.org.uk]	01475 721741
Greenock: Westburn Karen E. Harbison (Mrs) MA BD	1991	2014	50 Ardgowan Street, Greenock PA16 8EP [E-mail: KHarbison@churchofscotland.org.uk]	01475 721048
Houston and Killellan (H) Donald Campbell BD	1998	2007	The Manse of Houston, Main Street, Houston, Johnstone PA6 7EL [E-mail: Donald.Campbell@churchofscotland.org.uk]	01505 612569

Howwood linked with Lochwinnoch
Vacant — The Manse, Beith Road, Howwood, Johnstone PA9 1AS — 01505 703678

Inchinnan (H) (0141-812 1263)
Vacant — The Manse, Inchinnan, Renfrew PA4 9PH — 0141-812 1688

Inverkip (H) linked with Skelmorlie and Wemyss Bay
Archibald Speirs BD — 1995 — 3a Montgomery Terrace, Skelmorlie PA17 5DT [E-mail: ASpeirs@churchofscotland.org.uk] — 01475 529320

Johnstone: High (H) (01505 336303)
Ann C. McCool (Mrs) BD DSD IPA ALCM — 1989 2001 — 76 North Road, Johnstone PA5 8NF [E-mail: AMcCool@churchofscotland.org.uk] — 01505 320006

Johnstone: St Andrew's Trinity
Charles M. Cameron BA BD PhD — 1980 2013 — 45 Woodlands Crescent, Johnstone PA5 0AZ [E-mail: Charles.Cameron@churchofscotland.org.uk] — 01505 672908

Johnstone: St Paul's (H) (01505 321632)
Alistair N. Shaw MA BD MTh — 1982 2003 — 9 Stanley Drive, Brookfield, Johnstone PA5 8UF [E-mail: Alistair.Shaw@churchofscotland.org.uk] — 01505 320060

Kilbarchan
Stephen J. Smith BSc BD — 1993 2015 — The Manse, Church Street, Kilbarchan, Johnstone PA10 2JQ [E-mail: SSmith@churchofscotland.org.uk] — 01505 702621
(New charge formed by the union of Kilbarchan: East and Kilbarchan: West)

Kilmacolm: Old (H) (01505 873911)
Peter McEnhill BD PhD — 1992 2007 — The Old Kirk Manse, Glencairn Road, Kilmacolm PA13 4NJ [E-mail: PMcEnhill@churchofscotland.org.uk] — 01505 873174

Kilmacolm: St Columba (H)
R. Douglas Cranston MA BD — 1986 1992 — 6 Churchill Road, Kilmacolm PA13 4LH [E-mail: RCranston@churchofscotland.org.uk] — 01505 873271

Langbank (R) linked with Port Glasgow: St Andrew's (H)
Vacant — St Andrew's Manse, Barr's Brae, Port Glasgow PA14 5QA — 01475 741486

Linwood (H) (01505 328802)
Eileen M. Ross (Mrs) BD MTh   2005   2008   1 John Neilson Avenue, Paisley PA1 2SX
[E-mail: ERoss@churchofscotland.org.uk]   0141-887 2801

Lochwinnoch   See Howwood

Neilston (0141-881 9445)
Fiona E. Maxwell BA BD   2004   2013   The Manse, Neilston Road, Neilston, Glasgow G78 3NP
[E-mail: FMaxwell@churchofscotland.org.uk]   0141-258 0805

Paisley: Abbey (H) (Tel: 0141-889 7654; Fax: 0141-887 3929)
Alan D. Birss MA BD   1979   1988   15 Main Road, Castlehead, Paisley PA2 6AJ
[E-mail: ABirss@churchofscotland.org.uk]   0141-889 3587

Paisley: Glenburn (0141-884 2602)
Iain M.A. Reid MA BD   1990   2014   10 Hawick Avenue, Paisley PA2 9LD
[E-mail: IReid@churchofscotland.org.uk]   0141-884 4903

Paisley: Lylesland (H) (0141-561 7139)
Alistair W. Cook BSc CA BD   2008   36 Potterhill Avenue, Paisley PA2 8BA
[E-mail: ACook@churchofscotland.org.uk]   0141-561 9277

Paisley: Martyrs' Sandyford (0141-889 6603)
Kenneth A.L. Mayne BA MSc CertEd   1976   2007   27 Acer Crescent, Paisley PA2 9LR
[E-mail: KMayne@churchofscotland.org.uk]   0141-884 7400

Paisley: Oakshaw Trinity (H) (Tel: 0141-889 4010; Fax: 0141-848 5139)
Gordon B. Armstrong BD FIAB BRC   1998   2012   The Manse, 16 Golf Drive, Paisley PA1 3LA
[E-mail: GArmstrong@churchofscotland.org.uk]   0141-887 0884
Oakshaw Trinity is a Local Ecumenical Project shared with the United Reformed Church

Paisley: St Columba Foxbar (H) (01505 812377)
Vacant   13 Corsebar Drive, Paisley PA2 9QD   0141-848 5826

Paisley: St Luke's (H)
D. Ritchie M. Gillon BD DipMin   1994   31 Southfield Avenue, Paisley PA2 8BX
[E-mail: Ritchie.Gillon@churchofscotland.org.uk]   0141-884 6215

Paisley: St Mark's Oldhall (H) (0141-882 2755)
Robert G. McFarlane BD — 2001 2005 — 36 Newtyle Road, Paisley PA1 3JX [E-mail: RMcFarlane@churchofscotland.org.uk] — 0141-889 4279

Paisley: St Ninian's Ferguslie (New Charge Development) (0141-887 9436)
Vacant — 10 Stanely Drive, Paisley PA2 6HE — 0141-884 4177

Paisley: Sherwood Greenlaw (H) (0141-889 7060)
John Murning BD — 1988 2014 — 5 Greenlaw Drive, Paisley PA1 3RX [E-mail: JMurning@churchofscotland.org.uk] — 0141-889 3057

Paisley: Stow Brae Kirk
Robert Craig BA BD DipRS — 2008 2012 — 25 John Neilson Avenue, Paisley PA1 2SX [E-mail: RCraig@churchofscotland.org.uk] — 0141-328 6014

Paisley: Wallneuk North (0141-889 9265)
Peter G. Gill MA BA — 2008 — 5 Glenville Crescent, Paisley PA2 8TW [E-mail: PGill@churchofscotland.org.uk] — 0141-884 4429

Port Glasgow: Hamilton Bardrainney
Vacant — 80 Bardrainney Avenue, Port Glasgow PA14 6HD — 01475 701213

Port Glasgow: St Andrew's See Langbank

Port Glasgow: St Martin's
Sandra Black BSc BD
(Interim Minister) — 1988 2015 — 36 Glencairn Drive, Glasgow G41 4PW [E-mail: SBlack@churchofscotland.org.uk] — 07703 827057 (Mbl)

Renfrew: North (0141-885 2154)
E. Lorna Hood MA BD DD — 1978 1979 — 1 Alexandra Drive, Renfrew PA4 8UB [E-mail: Lorna.Hood@churchofscotland.org.uk] — 0141-886 2074

Renfrew: Trinity (H) (0141-885 2129)
Stuart C. Steell BD CertMin — 1992 2015 — 25 Paisley Road, Renfrew PA4 8JH [E-mail: SSteell@churchofscotland.org.uk] — 0141-387 2464

Skelmorlie and Wemyss Bay See Inverkip

Name	Years	Position	Address / E-mail	Telephone
Alexander, Douglas N. MA BD	1961 1999	(Bishopton)	West Morningside, Main Road, Langbank, Port Glasgow PA4 6XP	01475 540249
Armstrong, William R. BD	1979 2008	(Skelmorlie and Wemyss Bay)	25A The Lane, Skelmorlie PA17 5AR [E-mail: warmstrong17@tiscali.co.uk]	01475 520891
Bell, Ian W. LTh	1990 2011	(Erskine)	40 Brueacre Drive, Wemyss Bay PA18 6HA [E-mail: rviwbepc@ntlworld.com]	01475 529312
Bell, May (Mrs) LTh	1998 2012	(Johnstone: St Andrew's Trinity)	40 Brueacre Drive, Wemyss Bay PA18 6HA [E-mail: may.bell@ntlbusiness.com]	01475 529312
Black, Janette M.K. (Mrs) BD	1993 2006	(Assistant: Paisley: Oakshaw Trinity)	5 Craigiehall Avenue, Erskine PA8 7DB	0141-812 0794
Breingan, Mhairi	2011	Ordained Local Minister	6 Park Road, Inchinnan, Renfrew PA4 4QJ [E-mail: MBreingan@churchofscotland.org.uk]	0141-812 1425
Cameron, Margaret (Miss) DCS		(Deacon)	2 Rowans Gate, Paisley PA2 6RD	0141-840 2479
Cherry, Alastair J. BA BD FPLD	1982 2009	(Glasgow: Penilee St Andrew's)	6 Upper Abbey Road, Belvedere, Kent DA17 5AJ	(Mbl) 07974 826598
Chestnut, Alexander MBE BA	1948 1987	(Greenock: St Mark's Greenbank)	5 Douglas Street, Largs KA30 8PS	01475 674168
Copland, Agnes M. (Mrs) MBE DCS		(Deacon)	3 Craigmuschat Road, Gourock PA19 1SE	01475 631870
Cubie, John P. MA BD	1961 1999	(Caldwell)	36 Winram Place, St Andrews KY16 8XH	01334 474708
Easton, Lilly C. (Mrs)	1999 2012	(Renfrew: Old)	Flat 0/2, 90 Beith Street, Glasgow G11 6DG [E-mail: revlillyeaston@hotmail.co.uk]	0141-586 7628
Erskine, Morag (Miss) DCS		(Deacon)	111 Mains Drive, Park Mains, Erskine PA8 7JJ [E-mail: morag.erskine@ntlworld.com]	0141-812 6096
Forrest, Kenneth P. CBE BSc PhD	2006	Auxiliary Minister	5 Carruth Road, Bridge of Weir PA11 3HQ [E-mail: KForrest@churchofscotland.org.uk]	01505 612651
Fraser, Ian C. BA BD	1983 2008	(Glasgow: St Luke's and St Andrew's)	62 Kingston Avenue, Neilston, Glasgow G78 3JG [E-mail: ianandlindafraser@gmail.com]	0141-563 6794
Geddes, Elizabeth (Mrs)	2013	Ordained Local Minister	9 Shillingworth Place, Bridge of Weir PA11 3DY [E-mail: EGeddes@churchofscotland.org.uk]	01505 612639
Gray, Greta (Miss) DCS		(Deacon)	67 Crags Avenue, Paisley PA3 6SG [E-mail: greta.gray@ntlworld.com]	0141-884 6178
Hamilton, W. Douglas BD	1975 2009	(Greenock: Westburn)	5 Corse Road, Penilee, Glasgow G52 4DG [E-mail: douglas.hamilton44@hotmail.co.uk]	0141-810 1194
Hetherington, Robert M. MA BD	1966 2002	(Barrhead: South and Levern)	31 Brodie Park Crescent, Paisley PA2 6EU [E-mail: r-hetherington@sky.com]	0141-848 6560
Irvine, Euphemia H.C. (Mrs) BD	1972 1988	(Milton of Campsie)	32 Baird Drive, Bargarran, Erskine PA8 6BB	0141-812 2777
Johnston, Mary (Miss) DCS		(Deacon)	19 Lounsdale Drive, Paisley PA2 9ED	0141-849 1615
Kay, David BA BD MTh	1974 2008	(Paisley: Sandyford: Thread Street)	36 Donaldswood Park, Paisley PA2 8RS [E-mail: david.kay500@o2.co.uk]	0141-884 2080
Leitch, Maureen (Mrs) BA BD	1995 2011	(Barrhead: Bourock)	Rockfield, 92 Paisley Road, Barrhead G78 1NW [E-mail: maureen.leitch@ntlworld.com]	0141-580 2927
Lodge, Bernard P. BD	1967 2004	(Glasgow: Govanhill Trinity)	6 Darluith Park, Brookfield, Johnstone PA5 8DD [E-mail: bernardlodge@yahoo.co.uk]	01505 320378
MacColl, James C. BSc BD	1966 2002	(Johnstone: St Andrew's Trinity)	Greenways, Winton, Kirkby Stephen, Cumbria CA17 4HL	01768 372290
MacColl, John BD DipMin	1989 2001	Teacher: Religious Education	1 Birch Avenue, Johnstone PA5 0DD	01505 326506

Name	Years	Role	Address / E-mail	Telephone
McCully, M. Isobel (Miss) DCS		(Deacon)	10 Broadstone Avenue, Port Glasgow PA14 5BB [E-mail: mi.mccully@btinternet.com]	01475 742240
McKaig, William G. BD	1979 2011	(Langbank)	54 Brisbane Street, Greenock PA16 8NT [E-mail: bill.mckaig@virgin.net]	
MacLaine, Marilyn (Mrs) LTh	1995 2009	(Inchinnan)	37 Bankton Brae, Livingston EH54 9LA	01506 400619
Nicol, Joyce M. (Mrs) BA DCS		(Deacon)	93 Brisbane Street, Greenock PA16 8NY [E-mail: joycenicol@hotmail.co.uk]	01475 723235 (Mbl) 07957 642709
Page, John R. BD DipMin	1988 2003	(Gibraltar)	1 The Walton Building, North Street, Mere, Warminster, Wiltshire BA12 6HU	
Palmer, S.W. BD	1980 1991	(Kilbarchan: East)	4 Bream Place, Houston PA6 7ZJ	01505 615280
Prentice, George BA BTh	1964 1997	(Paisley: Martyrs')	46 Victoria Gardens, Corsebar Road, Paisley PA2 9AQ [E-mail: g.prentice04@talktalk.net]	0141-842 1585
Ross, Duncan DCS		(Deacon)	1 John Neilson Avenue, Paisley PA1 2SX [E-mail: ssornacnud@hotmail.com]	0141-887 2801
Simpson, James H. BD LLB	1964 2004	(Greenock: Mount Kirk)	82 Harbourside, Inverkip, Greenock PA16 0BF [E-mail: jameshsimpson@yahoo.co.uk]	01475 520582
Smillie, Andrew M. LTh	1990 2005	(Langbank)	7 Turnbull Avenue, West Freeland, Erskine PA8 7DL [E-mail: andrewsmillie@talktalk.net]	0141-812 7030
Stevenson, Stuart	2011	Ordained Local Minister	143 Springfield Park, Johnstone PA5 8JT [E-mail: SStevenson@churchofscotland.org.uk]	0141-886 2131
Stewart, David MA DipEd BD MTh	1977 2013	(Howwood)	72 Glen Avenue, Largs KA30 8QQ [E-mail: revdavids@aol.com]	
Whiteford, Alexander LTh	1996 2013	(Ardersier with Petty)	Cumbrae, 17 Netherburn Gardens, Houston, Johnstone PA6 7NG [E-mail: alex.whiteford@hotmail.co.uk]	01505 229611
Whyte, John H. MA	1946 1986	(Gourock: Ashton)	6 Castle Levan Manor, Cloch Road, Gourock PA19 1AY	01475 636788
Whyte, Margaret A. (Mrs) BA BD	1988 2011	(Glasgow: Pollokshaws)	4 Springhill Road, Barrhead G78 2AA [E-mail: tdpwhyte@tiscali.co.uk]	0141-881 4942

GREENOCK ADDRESSES

Gourock
Old Gourock and Ashton — 41 Royal Street
St John's — Bath Street x St John's Road

Greenock
Lyle Kirk — 31 Union Street;
Newark Street x Bentinck Street;
Esplanade x Campbell Street
(Lyle Kirk is continuing meantime to retain all three buildings)

Mount Kirk — Dempster Street at Murdieston Park
St Margaret's — Finch Road x Kestrel Crescent
St Ninian's — Warwick Road, Larkfield
Wellpark Mid Kirk — Cathcart Square
Westburn — 9 Nelson Street

Port Glasgow
Hamilton — Bardrainney Avenue x Auchenbothie Road
Bardrainney — Princes Street
St Andrew's — Mansion Avenue
St Martin's

PAISLEY ADDRESSES

Abbey	Town Centre	Oakshaw Trinity	Churchill	Sandyford (Thread St)	Montgomery Road

Abbey — Town Centre
Glenburn — Nethercraigs Drive off Glenburn Road
Lylesland — Rowan Street off Neilston Road
Martyrs' — King Street
Oakshaw Trinity — Churchill
St Columba Foxbar — Amochrie Road, Foxbar
St James' — Underwood Road
St Luke's — Neilston Road
St Mark's Oldhall — Glasgow Road, Ralston
St Ninian's Ferguslie — Blackstoun Road
Sandyford (Thread St) — Montgomery Road
Sherwood Greenlaw — Glasgow Road
Stow Brae Kirk — Causeyside Street
Wallneuk North — off Renfrew Road

(16) GLASGOW

Meets at Govan and Linthouse Parish Church, Govan Cross, Glasgow (unless otherwise intimated), on the following Tuesdays: 2016: 13 September, 11 October, 8 November, 13 December; 2017: 14 February, 14 March, 11 April, 9 May, 20 June.

Joint Clerk: REV. GRAHAM K. BLOUNT LLB BD PhD   **260 Bath Street, Glasgow G2 4JP**
VERY REV. WILLIAM C. HEWITT BD DipPS   [E-mail: glasgow@churchofscotland.org.uk]
[Website: www.presbyteryofglasgow.org.uk]   **0141-332 6606**
0141-352 6646 (Fax)

Treasurer: DOUGLAS BLANEY   [E-mail: treasurer@presbyteryofglasgow.org.uk]

1   Banton linked with Twechar
Vacant

2   Bishopbriggs: Kenmure
James Gemmell BD MTh   1999   2010   5 Marchfield, Bishopbriggs, Glasgow G64 3PP   0141-772 1468
[E-mail: JGemmell@churchofscotland.org.uk]

3   Bishopbriggs: Springfield Cambridge (0141-772 1596)
Ian Taylor BD ThM   1995   2006   64 Miller Drive, Bishopbriggs, Glasgow G64 1FB   0141-772 1540
[E-mail: ITaylor@churchofscotland.org.uk]

4   Broom (0141-639 3528)
James A.S. Boag BD CertMin   1992   2007   3 Laigh Road, Newton Mearns, Glasgow G77 5EX   0141-639 2916 (Tel)
[E-mail: JBoag@churchofscotland.org.uk]   0141-639 3528 (Fax)

5   Burnside Blairbeth (0141-634 4130)
William T.S. Wilson BSc BD   1999   2006   59 Blairbeth Road, Burnside, Glasgow G73 4JD   0141-583 6470
[E-mail: WWilson@churchofscotland.org.uk]

No.	Name	Year	Address	Telephone
6	**Busby (0141-644 2073)** Jeremy C. Eve BSc BD	1998	17A Carmunnock Road, Busby, Glasgow G76 8SZ [E-mail: JEve@churchofscotland.org.uk]	0141-644 3670
7	**Cadder (0141-772 7436)** Vacant		231 Kirkintilloch Road, Bishopbriggs, Glasgow G64 2JB	0141-772 1363
8	**Cambuslang: Flemington Hallside** Neil M. Glover	2005	59 Hay Crescent, Cambuslang, Glasgow G72 6QA [E-mail: NGlover@churchofscotland.org.uk]	0141-641 1049 07779 280074 (Mbl)
9	**Cambuslang Parish Church** A. Leslie Milton MA BD PhD	1996	74 Stewarton Drive, Cambuslang, Glasgow G72 8DG [E-mail: LMilton@churchofscotland.org.uk]	0141-641 2028
	Karen M. Hamilton (Mrs) DCS	2008	6 Beckfield Gate, Glasgow G33 1SW [E-mail: KHamilton@churchofscotland.org.uk]	0141-558 3195 07514 402612 (Mbl)
10	**Campsie (01360 310939)** Jane M. Denniston MA BD MTh	2002	19 Redhill View, Lennoxtown, Glasgow G66 7BL [E-mail: Jane.Denniston@churchofscotland.org.uk]	01360 310846 07738 123101 (Mbl)
11	**Chryston (H) (0141-779 4188)** Mark Malcolm MA BD	1999	The Manse, 109 Main Street, Chryston, Glasgow G69 9LA [E-mail: MMalcolm@churchofscotland.org.uk]	0141-779 1436 07731 737377 (Mbl)
	Mark W.J. McKeown MEng MDiv (Associate Minister)	2013	6 Glenapp Place, Moodiesburn, Glasgow G69 0HS [E-mail: MMcKeown@churchofscotland.org.uk]	01236 263406
12	**Eaglesham (01355 302047)** Andrew J. Robertson BD	2008	The Manse, Cheapside Street, Eaglesham, Glasgow G76 0NS [E-mail: ARobertson@churchofscotland.org.uk]	01355 303495
13	**Fernhill and Cathkin** Margaret McArthur BD DipMin	1995	82 Blairbeth Road, Rutherglen, Glasgow G73 4JA [E-mail: MMcArthur@churchofscotland.org.uk]	0141-634 1508
14	**Gartcosh (H) (01236 873770) linked with Glenboig** David G. Slater BSc BA DipThRS	2011	26 Inchnock Avenue, Gartcosh, Glasgow G69 8EA [E-mail: DSlater@churchofscotland.org.uk]	01236 870331 01236 872274 (Office)

15	**Giffnock: Orchardhill (0141-638 3604)** S. Grant Barclay LLB DipLP BD MSc PhD	1995	2016	23 Huntly Avenue, Giffnock, Glasgow G46 6LW [E-mail: GBarclay@churchofscotland.org.uk]	0141-620 3734
16	**Giffnock: South (0141-638 2599)** Catherine J. Beattie (Mrs) BD	2008	2011	164 Ayr Road, Newton Mearns, Glasgow G77 6EE [E-mail: CBeattie@churchofscotland.org.uk]	0141-258 7804
17	**Giffnock: The Park (0141-620 2204)** Calum D. Macdonald BD	1993	2001	41 Rouken Glen Road, Thornliebank, Glasgow G46 7JD [E-mail: CMacdonald@churchofscotland.org.uk]	0141-638 3023
18	**Glenboig** See Gartcosh				
19	**Greenbank (H) (0141-644 1841)** Jeanne N. Roddick BD	2003		Greenbank Manse, 38 Eaglesham Road, Clarkston, Glasgow G76 7DJ [E-mail: JRoddick@churchofscotland.org.uk]	0141-644 1395
20	**Kilsyth: Anderson** Allan S. Vint BSc BD MTh	1989	2013	Anderson Manse, Kingston Road, Kilsyth, Glasgow G65 0HR [E-mail: AVint@churchofscotland.org.uk]	01236 822345 07795 483070 (Mbl)
21	**Kilsyth: Burns and Old** Vacant				
22	**Kirkintilloch: Hillhead** Guardianship of the Presbytery Bill H Finnie BA PgDipSW CertCRS (Ordained Local Minister)	2015		27 Hallside Crescent, Cambuslang, Glasgow G72 7DY [E-mail: BFinnie@churchofscotland.org.uk]	07518 357138 (Mbl)
23	**Kirkintilloch: St Columba's (H) (0141-578 0016)** Vacant			14 Crossdykes, Kirkintilloch, Glasgow G66 3EU	0141-578 4357
24	**Kirkintilloch: St David's Memorial Park (H) (0141-776 4989)** Bryce Calder MA BD	1995	2001	2 Roman Road, Kirkintilloch, Glasgow G66 1EA [E-mail: BCalder@churchofscotland.org.uk]	0141-776 1434 07986 144834 (Mbl)

25 **Kirkintilloch: St Mary's (0141-775 1166)**
Mark E. Johnstone MA BD 1993 2001 St Mary's Manse, 60 Union Street, Kirkintilloch, Glasgow G66 1DH 0141-776 1252
[E-mail: Mark.Johnstone@churchofscotland.org.uk]

26 **Lenzie: Old (H)**
Louise J.E. McClements BD 2008 2016 41 Kirkintilloch Road, Lenzie, Glasgow G66 4LB 0141-573 5006
[E-mail: LMcClements@churchofscotland.org.uk]

27 **Lenzie: Union (H) (0141-776 1046)**
Daniel J.M. Carmichael MA BD 1994 2003 1 Larch Avenue, Lenzie, Glasgow G66 4HX 0141-776 3831
[E-mail: DCarmichael@churchofscotland.org.uk]

28 **Maxwell Mearns Castle (Tel/Fax: 0141-639 5169)**
Scott R.McL. Kirkland BD MAR 1996 2011 122 Broomfield Avenue, Newton Mearns, Glasgow G77 5JR 0141-560 5603
[E-mail: SKirkland@churchofscotland.org.uk]

29 **Mearns (H) (0141-639 6555)**
Joseph A. Kavanagh BD DipPTh MTh MTh 1992 1998 11 Belford Grove, Newton Mearns, Glasgow G77 5FB 0141-384 2218
[E-mail: JKavanagh@churchofscotland.org.uk]

30 **Milton of Campsie (H)**
Julie H.C. Moody BA BD PGCE 2006 Dunkeld, 33 Birdston Road, Milton of Campsie, Glasgow G66 8BX 01360 310548 / 07787 184800 (Mbl)
[E-mail: JMoody@churchofscotland.org.uk]

31 **Netherlee (H) (0141-637 2503)**
Thomas Nelson BSc BD 1992 2002 25 Ormonde Avenue, Netherlee, Glasgow G44 3QY 0141-585 7502 (Tel/Fax)
[E-mail: TNelson@churchofscotland.org.uk]
David Maxwell 2014 248 Old Castle Road, Glasgow G44 5EZ 0141-569 6379
(Ordained Local Minister)
[E-mail: DMaxwell@churchofscotland.org.uk]

32 **Newton Mearns (H) (0141-639 7373)**
Vacant

33 **Rutherglen: Old (H)**
Vacant

34 Rutherglen: Stonelaw (0141-647 5113)
Alistair S. May LLB BD PhD   2002   80 Blairbeth Road, Rutherglen, Glasgow G73 4JA
[E-mail: AMay@churchofscotland.org.uk]   0141-583 0157

35 Rutherglen: West and Wardlawhill (0844 736 1470)
Vacant   12 Albert Drive, Rutherglen, Glasgow G73 3RT   0141-569 8547

36 Stamperland (0141-637 4999) (H)
Vacant

37 Stepps (H)
Gordon MacRae BD MTh   1985   2014   112 Jackson Drive, Crowwood Grange, Stepps, Glasgow G33 6GF
[E-mail: GMacRae@churchofscotland.org.uk]   0141-779 5742

38 Thornliebank (H)
Mike R. Gargrave BD   2008   2014   19 Arthurlie Drive, Giffnock, Glasgow G46 6UR
[E-mail: MGargrave@churchofscotland.org.uk]   0141-880 5532

39 Torrance (R) (01360 620970)
Nigel L. Barge BSc BD   1991   1 Atholl Avenue, Torrance, Glasgow G64 4JA
[E-mail: NBarge@churchofscotland.org.uk]   01360 622379

40 Twechar See Banton

41 Williamwood (0141-638 2091)
Janet S. Mathieson MA BD   2003   2015   125 Greenwood Road, Clarkston, Glasgow G76 7LL
[E-mail: JMathieson@churchofscotland.org.uk]   0141-579 9997

42 Glasgow: Anderston Kelvingrove (0141-221 9408)
Vacant

43 Glasgow: Baillieston Mure Memorial (0141-773 1216) linked with Glasgow: Baillieston St Andrew's
Malcolm Cuthbertson BA BD   1984   2010   28 Beech Avenue, Baillieston, Glasgow G69 6LF
[E-mail: MCuthbertson@churchofscotland.org.uk]   07740 868181 (Mbl)

Alex P. Stuart   2014   107 Baldorran Crescent, Balloch, Cumbernauld, Glasgow G68 9EX
(Ordained Local Minister)   [E-mail: AStuart@churchofscotland.org.uk]   07901 802967 (Mbl)

44 Glasgow: Baillieston St Andrew's See Glasgow: Baillieston Mure Memorial

45   **Glasgow: Balshagray Victoria Park**
Campbell Mackinnon   BSc BD   1982   2001   20 St Kilda Drive, Glasgow   G14 9JN   0141-954 9780
[E-mail: CMackinnon@churchofscotland.org.uk]

46   **Glasgow: Barlanark Greyfriars (0141-771 6477)**
Willem J. Bezuidenhout   BA BD MHEd MEd   1977   2016   4 Rhindmuir Grove, Baillieston, Glasgow   G69 6NE   0141-771 7103
[E-mail: WBezuidenhout@churchofscotland.org.uk]

47   **Glasgow: Blawarthill**
G. Melvyn Wood   MA BD   1982   2009   46 Earlbank Avenue, Glasgow   G14 9HL   0141-579 6521
[E-mail: GMelvinWood@churchofscotland.org.uk]

48   **Glasgow: Bridgeton St Francis in the East (H) (L) (0141-556 2830) (Church House: Tel: 0141-554 8045)**
Howard R. Hudson   MA BD   1982   1984   10 Albany Drive, Rutherglen, Glasgow   G73 3QN   0141-587 8667
[E-mail: HHudson@churchofscotland.org.uk]

49   **Glasgow: Broomhill (0141-334 2540) linked with Glasgow: Hyndland (H) (Website: www.hyndlandparishchurch.org)**
George C. MacKay   1994   2014   27 St Kilda Drive, Glasgow   G14 9LN   0141-959 3204
BD CertMin CertEd DipPC   [E-mail: GMacKay@churchofscotland.org.uk]

50   **Glasgow: Calton Parkhead (0141-554 3866)**
Alison E.S. Davidge   MA BD   1990   2008   98 Drumover Drive, Glasgow   G31 5RP   07843 625059 (Mbl)
[E-mail: ADavidge@churchofscotland.org.uk]

51   **Glasgow: Cardonald (0141-882 6264)**
Malcolm (Calum) MacLeod   BA BD   1979   2007   133 Newtyle Road, Paisley   PA1 3LB   0141-887 2726
[E-mail: Malcolm.MacLeod@churchofscotland.org.uk]

52   **Glasgow: Carmunnock (0141-644 0655)**
G. Gray Fletcher   BSc BD   1989   2001   The Manse, 161 Waterside Road, Carmunnock, Glasgow   G76 9AJ   0141-644 1578 (Tel/Fax)
[E-mail: GFletcher@churchofscotland.org.uk]

53   **Glasgow: Carmyle linked with Glasgow: Kenmuir Mount Vernon**
Murdo MacLean   BD CertMin   1997   1999   3 Meryon Road, Glasgow   G32 9NW   0141-778 2625
[E-mail: Murdo.MacLean@churchofscotland.org.uk]

54 Glasgow: Carntyne (0141-778 4186)

Joan Ross (Miss) BSc BD PhD	1999	2016	163 Lethamhill Road, Glasgow G33 2SQ [E-mail: JRoss@churchofscotland.org.uk]	0141-770 9247
Patricia A. Carruth (Mrs) BD (Associate Minister)	1998	2014	38 Springhill Farm Road, Baillieston, Glasgow G69 6GW [E-mail: PCarruth@churchofscotland.org.uk]	0141-771 3758

(Glasgow: Carntyne is a new charge formed by the union of Glasgow: High Carntyne and Glasgow: South Carntyne)

55 Glasgow: Carnwadric

Graeme K. Bell BA BD	1983		62 Loganswell Road, Thornliebank, Glasgow G46 8AX [E-mail: GBell@churchofscotland.org.uk]	0141-638 5884
Mary S. Gargrave (Mrs) DCS			12 Parkholm Quad, Glasgow G63 7ZH [E-mail: Mary.Gargrave@churchofscotland.org.uk]	0141-880 5532 07896 866618 (Mbl)

56 Glasgow: Castlemilk (H) (0141-634 1480)

Sarah A. Brown (Ms) MA BD ThM DipYW/Theol PDCCE	2012		156 Old Castle Road, Glasgow G44 5TW [E-mail: Sarah.Brown@churchofscotland.org.uk]	0141-637 5451 07532 457245 (Mbl)

57 Glasgow: Cathcart Old (0141-637 4168)

Neil W. Galbraith BD CertMin	1987	1996	21 Courthill Avenue, Cathcart, Glasgow G44 5AA [E-mail: NGalbraith@churchofscotland.org.uk]	0141-633 5248 (Tel/Fax)

58 Glasgow: Cathcart Trinity (H) (0141-637 6658)

Alasdair MacMillan	2015		82 Merrylee Road, Glasgow G43 2QZ [E-mail: Alasdair.MacMillan@churchofscotland.org.uk]	0141-633 3744
Wilma Pearson (Mrs) BD (Associate Minister)	2004		90 Newlands Road, Glasgow G43 2JR [E-mail: WPearson@churchofscotland.org.uk]	0141-632 2491

59 Glasgow: Cathedral (High or St Mungo's) (0141-552 6891)

Laurence A.B. Whitley MA BD PhD	1975	2007	41 Springfield Road, Bishopbriggs, Glasgow G64 1PL [E-mail: LWhitley@churchofscotland.org.uk]	0141-762 2719

60 Glasgow: Causeway (Tollcross)

Monica Michelin-Salomon BD	1999	2016	228 Hamilton Road, Glasgow G32 9QU [E-mail: MMichelin-Salomon@churchofscotland.org.uk]	0141-778 2413

(New charge formed by the union of Glasgow: Shettleston Old and Glasgow: Shettleston Victoria Tollcross)

61 Glasgow: Clincarthill (H) (0141-632 4206)
Vacant

62 Glasgow: Colston Milton (0141-772 1922)
Christopher J. Rowe BA BD   2008
118 Birsay Road, Milton, Glasgow G22 7QP
[E-mail: CRowe@churchofscotland.org.uk]
0141-564 1138

63 Glasgow: Colston Wellpark (H)
Guardianship of the Presbytery
Leslie Grieve   2014
(Ordained Local Minister)
23 Hertford Avenue, Kelvindale, Glasgow G12 0LG
[E-mail: LGrieve@churchofscotland.org.uk]
07813 255052 (Mbl)

64 Glasgow: Cranhill (H) (0141-774 3344)
Muriel B. Pearson (Ms) MA BD PGCE   2004
31 Lethamhill Crescent, Glasgow G33 2SH
[E-mail: MPearson@churchofscotland.org.uk]
0141-770 6873
07951 888860 (Mbl)

65 Glasgow: Croftfoot (H) (0141-637 3913)
Robert M. Silver BA BD   1995   2011
4 Inchmurrin Gardens, High Burnside, Rutherglen, Glasgow G73 5RU
[E-mail: RSilver@churchofscotland.org.uk]
0141-258 7268

66 Glasgow: Dennistoun New (H) (0141-550 2825)
Ian M.S. McInnes BD DipMin   1995   2008
31 Pencaitland Drive, Glasgow G32 8RL
[E-mail: IMcInnes@churchofscotland.org.uk]
0141-564 6498

67 Glasgow: Drumchapel St Andrew's (0141-944 3758)
John S. Purves LLB BD   1983   1984
6 Firdon Crescent, Old Drumchapel, Glasgow G15 6QQ
[E-mail: JPurves@churchofscotland.org.uk]
0141-944 4566

68 Glasgow: Drumchapel St Mark's
Audrey J. Jamieson BD MTh   2004   2007
146 Garscadden Road, Glasgow G15 6PR
[E-mail: AJamieson@churchofscotland.org.uk]
0141-944 5440

69 Glasgow: Easterhouse St George's and St Peter's (0141-771 8810)
Vacant
3 Barony Gardens, Baillieston, Glasgow G69 6TS
0141-573 8200

70 Glasgow: Eastwood
James R. Teasdale BA BD   2009   2016
54 Mansewood Road, Eastwood, Glasgow G43 1TL
[E-mail: JTeasdale@churchofscotland.org.uk]
0141-649 0463

71	**Glasgow: Gairbraid (H)** Donald Michael MacInnes BD	2002	2011	4 Blackhill Gardens, Summerston, Glasgow G23 5NE [E-mail: DMacInnes@churchofscotland.org.uk]	0141-946 0604
72	**Glasgow: Gallowgate** Peter L.V. Davidge BD MTh	2003	2009	98 Drumover Drive, Glasgow G31 5RP [E-mail: rev_dav46@yahoo.co.uk]	07765 096599 (Mbl)
73	**Glasgow: Garthamlock and Craigend East** Vacant Marion Buchanan (Mrs) MA DCS			16 Almond Drive, East Kilbride, Glasgow G74 2HX [E-mail: MBuchanan@churchofscotland.org.uk]	01355 228776 07999 889817 (Mbl)
74	**Glasgow: Gorbals** Ian F. Galloway BA BD	1976	1996	6 Stirlingfauld Place, Gorbals, Glasgow G5 9QF [E-mail: IGalloway@churchofscotland.org.uk]	0141-649 5250
75	**Glasgow: Govan and Linthouse** Vacant Andrew Thomson BA (Assistant Minister) John Paul Cathcart DCS	1976	2010	19 Dumbreck Road, Glasgow G41 5LJ 3 Laurel Wynd, Drumsagard Village, Cambuslang, Glasgow G72 7BH [E-mail: AThomson@churchofscotland.org.uk] 9 Glen More, East Kilbride, Glasgow G74 2AP [E-mail: John.Cathcart@churchofscotland.org.uk]	0141-419 0308 0141-641 2936 07772 502774 (Mbl) 01355 243970 07708 396074 (Mbl)
76	**Glasgow: Hillington Park (H)** John B. MacGregor BD	1999	2004	61 Ralston Avenue, Glasgow G52 3NB [E-mail: JMacGregor@churchofscotland.org.uk]	0141-882 7000
77	**Glasgow: Hyndland** See Glasgow: Broomhill				
78	**Glasgow: Ibrox (H) (0141-427 0896)** Elisabeth G.B. Spence (Miss) BD DipEd	1995	2008	59 Langhaul Road, Glasgow G53 7SE [E-mail: ESpence@churchofscotland.org.uk]	0141-883 7744
79	**Glasgow: John Ross Memorial Church for Deaf People** **(Voice Text: 0141-420 1391; Fax: 0141-420 3778)** Richard C. Durno DSW CQSW	1989	1998	31 Springfield Road, Bishopbriggs, Glasgow G64 1PJ [E-mail: richard.durno@btinternet.com] (Voice/Text/Fax) (Voice/Text/Voicemail)	0141-772 1052 07748 607721 (Mbl)

80 Glasgow: Jordanhill (Tel: 0141-959 2496)
Bruce H Sinclair BA BD 2009 2015 96 Southbrae Drive, Glasgow G13 1TZ
[E-mail: BSinclair@churchofscotland.org.uk] 0141-959 1310

81 Glasgow: Kelvinbridge (0141-339 1750)
Gordon Kirkwood BSc BD PGCE MTh 1987 2013 Flat 2/2, 94 Hyndland Road, Glasgow G12 9PZ
[E-mail: GKirkwood@churchofscotland.org.uk] 0141-334 5352

Cathie H. McLaughlin (Mrs) 2014 8 Lamlash Place, Glasgow G33 3XH
   (Ordained Local Minister) [E-mail: CMcLaughlin@churchofscotland.org.uk] 0141-774 2483

82 Glasgow: Kelvinside Hillhead (0141-334 2788)
Vacant
Roger D. Sturrock (Prof.) BD MD FCRP 2014 36 Thomson Drive, Bearsden, Glasgow G61 3PA
   (Ordained Local Minister) [E-mail: RSturrock@churchofscotland.org.uk] 0141-942 7412

83 Glasgow: Kenmuir Mount Vernon See Carmyle

84 Glasgow: King's Park (H) (0141-636 8688)
Sandra Boyd (Mrs) BEd BD 2007 1101 Aikenhead Road, Glasgow G44 5SL
[E-mail: SBoyd@churchofscotland.org.uk] 0141-637 2803

85 Glasgow: Kinning Park (0141-427 3063)
Margaret H. Johnston BD 1988 2000 168 Arbroath Avenue, Cardonald, Glasgow G52 3HH
[E-mail: MHJohnston@churchofscotland.org.uk] 0141-810 3782

86 Glasgow: Knightswood St Margaret's (H)
Alexander M. Fraser BD DipMin 1985 2009 26 Airthrey Avenue, Glasgow G14 9LJ
[E-mail: AFraser@churchofscotland.org.uk] 0141-959 7075

87 Glasgow: Langside (0141-632 7520)
David N. McLachlan BD 1985 2004 36 Madison Avenue, Glasgow G44 5AQ
[E-mail: dmclachlan77@hotmail.com] 0141-637 0797

88 Glasgow: Lochwood (H) (0141-771 2649)
Vacant

No.	Charge / Minister	Year(s)	Address	Telephone
89	**Glasgow: Maryhill (H) (0141-946 3512)** Stuart C. Matthews BD MA	2006	251 Milngavie Road, Bearsden, Glasgow G61 3DQ [E-mail: SMatthews@churchofscotland.org.uk]	0141-942 0804
	James Hamilton DCS		6 Beckfield Gate, Glasgow G33 1SW [E-mail: James.Hamilton@churchofscotland.org.uk]	0141-558 3195 07584 137314 (Mbl)
90	**Glasgow: Merrylea (0141-637 2009)** David P. Hood BD CertMin DipIOB(Scot)	1997 2001	4 Pilmuir Avenue, Glasgow G44 3HX [E-mail: DHood@churchofscotland.org.uk]	0141-637 6700
91	**Glasgow: Mosspark (H) (0141-882 2240)** Vacant			
92	**Glasgow: Newlands South (H) (0141-632 3055)** Vacant		24 Monreith Road, Glasgow G43 2NY	0141-632 2588
93	**Glasgow: Partick South (H)** James Andrew McIntyre BD	2010	3 Branklyn Crescent, Glasgow G13 1GJ [E-mail: Andy.McIntyre@churchofscotland.org.uk]	0141-959 3732
94	**Glasgow: Partick Trinity (H)** Vacant		99 Balshagray Avenue, Glasgow G11 7EQ	0141-576 7149
95	**Glasgow: Pollokshaws (0141-649 1879)** Roy J.M. Henderson MA BD DipMin	1987 2013	33 Mannering Road, Glasgow G41 3SW [E-mail: RHenderson@churchofscotland.org.uk]	0141-632 8768
96	**Glasgow: Pollokshields (H)** David R. Black MA BD	1986 1997	36 Glencairn Drive, Glasgow G41 4PW [E-mail: DBlack@churchofscotland.org.uk]	0141-423 4000
97	**Glasgow: Possilpark (0141-336 8028)** Rosalind (Linda) E. Pollock (Miss) BD ThM ThM	2001 2014	108 Erradale Street, Lambhill, Glasgow G22 6PT [E-mail: RPollock@churchofscotland.org.uk]	0141-336 6909
98	**Glasgow: Queen's Park Govanhill (0141-423 3654)** Elijah W. Smith BA MLitt	2015	c/o Presbytery Office [E-mail: E.Smith@churchofscotland.org.uk]	07975 998382 (Mbl)

99 Glasgow: Renfield St Stephen's (Tel: 0141-332 4293; Fax: 0141-332 8482)

Peter M. Gardner MA BD   1988   2002   101 Hill Street, Glasgow G3 6TY
[E-mail: PGardner@churchofscotland.org.uk]

Iain A. MacLeod   2012   6 Hallydown Drive, Glasgow G13 1UF
(Ordained Local Minister)   [E-mail: iain@maximise.com]

0141-353 0349
07795 014889 (Mbl)

100 Glasgow: Robroyston (New Charge Development) (0141-558 8414)

Jonathan A. Keefe BSc BD   2009   7 Beckfield Drive, Glasgow G33 1SR
[E-mail: JKeefe@churchofscotland.org.uk]

0141-558 2952

101 Glasgow: Ruchazie (0141-774 2759)
Vacant

102 Glasgow: Ruchill Kelvinside (0141-946 0466)

Mark Lowey BD DipTh   2012   41 Mitre Road, Glasgow G14 9LE
[E-mail: MLowey@churchofscotland.org.uk]

0141-959 6718

103 Glasgow: St Andrew and St Nicholas

Lyn Peden (Mrs) BD   2010   2015   80 Tweedsmuir Road, Glasgow G52 2RX
[E-mail: LPeden@churchofscotland.org.uk]

0141-883 9873

104 Glasgow: St Andrew's East (0141-554 1485)

Barbara D. Quigley (Mrs)   1979   2011   43 Broompark Drive, Glasgow G31 2JB
MTheol ThM DPS   [E-mail: BQuigley@churchofscotland.org.uk]

0141-237 7982

105 Glasgow: St Christopher's Priesthill and Nitshill (0141-881 6541)

Douglas M. Nicol BD CA   1987   1996   36 Springkell Drive, Glasgow G41 4EZ
[E-mail: DNicol@churchofscotland.org.uk]

0141-427 7877

106 Glasgow: St Columba (GE) (0141-221 3305)
Vacant

107 Glasgow: St David's Knightswood (0141-954 1081)

Graham M. Thain LLB BD   1988   1999   60 Southbrae Drive, Glasgow G13 1QD
[E-mail: GThain@churchofscotland.org.uk]

0141-959 2904

108 Glasgow: St Enoch's Hogganfield (H) (Tel: 0141-770 5694; Fax: 0870 284 0084) (E-mail: church@st-enoch.org.uk)
(Website: www.stenochshogganfield.org.uk)
Vacant   43 Smithycroft Road, Glasgow G33 2RH   0141-770 7593

109 Glasgow: St George's Tron (0141-221 2141)
Alastair S. Duncan MA BD   1989   29 Hertford Avenue, Glasgow G12 0LG   07968 852083 (Mbl)
(Transition Minister)   [E-mail: ADuncan@churchofscotland.org.uk]

110 Glasgow: St James' (Pollok) (0141-882 4984)
John W. Mann BSc MDiv DMin   2004   30 Ralston Avenue, Glasgow G52 3NA   0141-883 7405
                                                          [E-mail: John.Mann@churchofscotland.org.uk]

111 Glasgow: St John's Renfield (0141-339 7021) (Website: www.stjohns-renfield.org.uk)
Fiona L. Lillie (Mrs) BA BD MLitt   1995   2009   26 Leicester Avenue, Glasgow G12 0LU   0141-339 4637
                                                          [E-mail: FLillie@churchofscotland.org.uk]

112 Glasgow: St Margaret's Tollcross Park
Vacant

113 Glasgow: St Paul's (0141-770 8559)
Daniel Manastireanu BA MTh   2010   2014   38 Lochview Drive, Glasgow G33 1QF   0141-770 1561
                                                          [E-mail: DManastireanu@churchofscotland.org.uk]

114 Glasgow: St Rollox (0141-558 1809)
Jane M. Howitt   1996   2016   42 Melville Gardens, Bishopbriggs, Glasgow G64 3DE   0141-581 0050
(Transition Minister)   [E-mail: JHowitt@churchofscotland.org.uk]

115 Glasgow: Sandyford Henderson Memorial (H) (L)
Jonathan de Groot BD MTh CPS   2007   66 Woodend Drive, Glasgow G13 1TG   0141-954 9013
                                                          [E-mail: JdeGroot@churchofscotland.org.uk]

116 Glasgow: Sandyhills (0141-778 3415)
Graham T. Atkinson MA BD MTh   2006   60 Wester Road, Glasgow G32 9JJ   0141-778 2174
                                                          [E-mail: GAtkinson@churchofscotland.org.uk]

117 Glasgow: Scotstoun (R)
Richard Cameron BD DipMin   2000   15 Northland Drive, Glasgow G14 9BE   0141-959 4637
                                                          [E-mail: RCameron@churchofscotland.org.uk]

118 Glasgow: Shawlands (0141-649 1773) linked with Glasgow: South Shawlands (R) (0141-649 4656)
Valerie J. Duff (Miss) DMin   1993   2014   29 St Ronan's Drive, Glasgow G41 3SQ
[E-mail: VDuff@churchofscotland.org.uk]

0141-258 6782

119 Glasgow: Sherbrooke St Gilbert's (H) (0141-427 1968)
Thomas L. Pollock   1982   2003   114 Springkell Avenue, Glasgow G41 4EW
BA BD MTh FSAScot JP   [E-mail: TPollock@churchofscotland.org.uk]

0141-427 2094

120 Glasgow: Shettleston New (0141-778 0857)
Vacant   211 Sandyhills Road, Glasgow G32 9NB

0141-778 1286

121 Glasgow: South Shawlands See Glasgow: Shawlands

122 Glasgow: Springburn (H) (0141-557 2345)
Brian M. Casey MA BD   2014   c/o Springburn Parish Church, 180 Springburn Way,
                                                                 Glasgow G21 1TU
                                                                 [E-mail: BCasey@churchofscotland.org.uk]

07703 166772 (Mbl)

123 Glasgow: Temple Anniesland (0141-959 1814)
Fiona M.E. Gardner (Mrs) BD MA MLitt   1997   2011   76 Victoria Park Drive North, Glasgow G14 9PJ
                                                                 [E-mail: FGardner@churchofscotland.org.uk]

0141-959 5647

124 Glasgow: Toryglen (H)
Ada V. MacLeod MA BD PgCE   2013   2015   133 Newtyle Road, Paisley PA1 3LB
                                                                 [E-mail: AVMacLeod@churchofscotland.org.uk]

07900 254959 (Mbl)

125 Glasgow: Trinity Possil and Henry Drummond
Richard G. Buckley BD MTh   1990   1995   50 Highfield Drive, Glasgow G12 0HL
                                                                 [E-mail: RBuckley@churchofscotland.org.uk]

0141-339 2870

126 Glasgow: Tron St Mary's (0141-558 1011)
Rhona E. Graham BA BD   2015   30 Louden Hill Road, Robroyston, Glasgow G33 1GA
                                                                 [E-mail: RGraham@churchofscotland.org.uk]

0141-389 8816

127 Glasgow: Wallacewell (New Charge Development)
Daniel L. Frank BA MDiv DMin   1984   2011   8 Streamfield Gate, Glasgow G33 1SJ
                                                                 [E-mail: DFrank@churchofscotland.org.uk]

0141-585 0283

128 Glasgow: Wellington (H) (0141-339 0454)

David I. Sinclair BSc BD PhD DipSW	1990	2008	31 Hughenden Gardens, Glasgow G12 9YH [E-mail: DSinclair@churchofscotland.org.uk]	0141-334 2343
Roger Sturrock (Prof.) BD MD FCRP (Ordained Local Minister)	2014		36 Thomson Drive, Bearsden, Glasgow G61 3PA [E-mail: RSturrock@churchofscotland.org.uk]	0141-942 7412

129 Glasgow: Whiteinch (Website: www.whiteinchcofs.co.uk)

Alan McWilliam BD MTh	1993	2000	65 Victoria Park Drive South, Glasgow G14 9NX [E-mail: AMcWilliam@churchofscotland.org.uk]	0141-576 9020

130 Glasgow: Yoker (R)

Karen E. Hendry BSc BD	2005	15 Coldingham Avenue, Glasgow G14 0PX [E-mail: KHendry@churchofscotland.org.uk]	0141-952 3620

Alexander, Eric J. MA BD	1958	1997	(Glasgow: St George's Tron)	77 Norwood Park, Bearsden, Glasgow G61 2RZ	0141-942 4404
Allen, Martin A.W. MA BD ThM	1977	2007	(Chryston)	Lealenge, 85 High Barrwood Road, Kilsyth, Glasgow G65 0EE	01236 826616
Alston, William G.	1961	2009	(Glasgow: North Kelvinside)	Flat 0/2, 5 Knightswood Court, Glasgow G13 2XN [E-mail: williamalston@hotmail.com]	0141-959 3113
Bayes, Muriel C. (Mrs) DCS			(Deacon)	Flat 6, Carlton Court, 10 Fenwick Road, Glasgow G46 6AN	0141-633 0865
Beaton, Margaret S. (Miss) DCS			(Deacon)	64 Gardenside Grove, Carmyle, Glasgow G32 8EZ [E-mail: margaretbeaton54@hotmail.com]	0141-646 2297 (Mbl) 07796 642382
Bell, John L. MA BD FRSCM DUniv	1978	1988	Iona Community	Flat 2/1, 31 Lansdowne Crescent, Glasgow G20 6NH	0141-334 0688
Birch, James PgDip FRSA FIOC	2001	2007	(Auxiliary Minister)	1 Kirkhill Grove, Cambuslang, Glasgow G72 8EH	0141-583 1722
Black, William B. MA BD	1972	2011	(Stornoway: High)	33 Tankerland Road, Glasgow G44 4EN [E-mail: revwillieblack@gmail.com]	0141-637 4717
Blount, A. Sheila (Mrs) BD BA	1978	2010	(Cupar: St John's and Dairsie United)	28 Alcaig Road, Mosspark, Glasgow G52 1NH [E-mail: asblount@orange.net]	
Blount, Graham K. LLB BD PhD	1976	2016	Joint Presbytery Clerk	28 Balcaig Road, Mosspark, Glasgow G52 1NH [E-mail: Graham.Blount@churchofscotland.org.uk]	0131-466 6115
Brain, Isobel J. (Mrs) MA	1987	1997	(Ballantrae)	10/11 Maxwell Street, Edinburgh EH10 5GZ	
Brice, Dennis G. BSc BD	1981		(Taiwan)	8 Parkwood Close, Broxbourne, Herts EN10 7PF [E-mail: dbrice1@comcast.net]	
Bryden, William A. BD	1977	1984	(Yoker: Old with St Matthew's)	145 Bearsden Road, Glasgow G13 1BS	0141-959 5213
Bull, Alister W. BD DipMin MTh PhD	1994	2013	Mission and Discipleship Council	121 George Street, Edinburgh EH2 4YN [E-mail: abull@churchofscotland.org.uk]	0131-225 5722
Campbell, A. Iain MA DipEd	1961	1997	(Busby)	430 Clarkston Road, Glasgow G44 3QF [E-mail: bellmac@sagainternet.co.uk]	0141-637 7460
Campbell, John MA BA BSc	1973	2009	(Caldwell)	96 Boghead Road, Lenzie, Glasgow G66 4BN [E-mail: johncampbell.lenzie@gmail.com]	0141-776 0874
Cartlidge, Graham R.G. MA BD STM	1977	2015	(Glasgow: Eastwood)	5 Briar Grove, Newlands, Glasgow G43 2TG	0141-637 3228

Clark, Douglas W. LTh	1993	2015	(Lenzie: Old)	1/3, 39 Saltmarsh Drive, Lenzie, Glasgow G66 3NR [E-mail: douglaswclark@hotmail.com]	0141-776 1298
Cunningham, Alexander MA BD	1961	2002	(Presbytery Clerk)	18 Lady Jane Gate, Bothwell, Glasgow G71 8BW	01698 811051
Cunningham, James S.A. MA BD BLitt PhD	1992	2000	(Glasgow: Barlanark Greyfriars)	'Kirkland', 5 Inveresk Place, Coatbridge ML5 2DA	01236 421541
Drummond, John W. MA BD	1971	2011	(Rutherglen: West and Wardlawhill)	25 Kingsburn Drive, Rutherglen, Glasgow G73 2AN	0141-571 6002
Duff, T. Malcolm F. MA BD	1985	2009	(Glasgow: Queen's Park)	54 Hawkhead Road, Paisley PA1 3NB	0141-570 0614 (Mbl) 07846 926584
Dutch, Morris M. BD BA Dip BTI	1998	2013	(Costa del Sol)	41 Baronald Drive, Glasgow G12 OHN [E-mail: mmdutch@yahoo.co.uk]	0141-357 2286
Farrington, Alexandra LTh	2003	2015	(Campsie)	'Glenburn', High Banton, Kilsyth G65 0RA [E-mail: revsfarrington@aol.co.uk]	01236 824516
Ferguson, James B. LTh	1972	2002	(Lenzie: Union)	3 Bridgeway Place, Kirkintilloch, Glasgow G66 3HW	0141-588 5868
Ferguson, William B. BA BD	1971	2012	(Glasgow: Broomhill)	20 Swift Crescent, Knightswood Gate, Glasgow G13 4QL [E-mail: revferg@btinternet.com]	0141-954 6655
Fleming, Alexander F. MA BD	1966	1995	(Strathblane)	11 Bankwood Drive, Kilsyth, Glasgow G65 0GZ	01236 821461
Forrest, Martin R. BA MA BD	1988	2012	Prison Chaplain	4/1, 7 Blochairn Place, Glasgow G21 2EB [E-mail: martinrforrest@gmail.com]	0141-552 1132
Forsyth, Sandy LLB BD DipLP PhD	2009	2013	(Associate: Kirkintilloch: St David's Memorial Park)	48 Kerr Street, Kirkintilloch, Glasgow G66 1JZ [E-mail: sandyforsyth67@hotmail.co.uk]	0141-777 8194 (Mbl) 07739 639037
Galloway, Kathy (Mrs) BD DD	1977	2002	(Leader: Iona Community)	20 Hamilton Park Avenue, Glasgow G12 8UU	0141-357 4079
Gay, Douglas C. MA BD PhD	1998	2005	University of Glasgow	1F, 16 Royal Terrace, Glasgow G3 7NY [E-mail: douggay@mac.com]	0141-332 4040 (Mbl) 07971 321452
Getliffe, Dot (Mrs) DCS BA BD DipEd	2006	2013	Families Worker, West Mearns	3 Woodview Terrace, Hamilton ML3 9DP [E-mail: dgetliffe@aol.co.uk]	01698 423504 (Mbl) 07766 910171
Gibson, H. Marshall MA BD	1957	1996	(Glasgow: St Thomas' Gallowgate)	39 Burnthroom Drive, Glasgow G69 7XG	0141-771 0749
Grant, David I.M. MA BD	1969	2003	(Dalry: Trinity)	8 Mossbank Drive, Glasgow G33 1LS	0141-770 7186
Gray, Christine M. (Mrs)			(Deacon)	11 Woodside Avenue, Thornliebank, Glasgow G46 7HR	0141-571 1008
Green, Alex H. MA BD	1986	2010	(Strathblane)	44 Laburnum Drive, Milton of Campsie, Glasgow G66 8HY [E-mail: lesvert@btinternet.com]	01360 313001
Gregson, Elizabeth M. (Mrs) BD	1996	2001	(Glasgow: Drumchapel St Andrew's)	17 Westfields, Bishopbriggs, Glasgow G64 3PL	0141-563 1918
Haley, Derek BD DPS	1960	1999	(Chaplain: Gartnavel Royal)	9 Kinnaird Crescent, Bearsden, Glasgow G61 2BN	0141-942 9281
Harvey, W. John BA BD DD	1965	2002	(Edinburgh: Corstorphine Craigsbank)	501 Shields Road, Glasgow G41 2RF	0141-429 3774
Hazlett, W. Ian P. (Prof.-Emer.) BA BD Dr theol DLitt DD		2009	University of Glasgow	587 Shields Road, Glasgow G41 2RW [E-mail: ian.hazlett@glasgow.ac.uk]	0141-423 7461
Hewitt, William C. BD DipPS	1977	2012	Presbytery Clerk	60 Woodlands Grove, Kilmarnock KA3 1TZ [E-mail: billhewitt1@btinternet.com]	0141-330 5155 01563 533312
Hope, Evelyn P. (Miss) BA BD	1990	1998	(Wishaw: Thornlie)	Flat 0/1, 48 Moss Side Road, Glasgow G41 3UA	(Work) 0141-649 1522
Houston, Thomas C. BA	1975	2004	(Glasgow: Priesthill and Nitshill)	63 Broomhouse Crescent, Uddingston, Glasgow G71 7RE	0141-771 0577
Hughes, Helen (Miss) DCS			(Deacon)	2/2, 43 Burnbank Terrace, Glasgow G20 6UQ [E-mail: helhug35@gmail.com]	0141-333 9459 (Mbl) 07752 604817
Hunter, Alastair G. MSc BD	1976	1980	(University of Glasgow)	487 Shields Road, Glasgow G41 2RG	0141-429 1687
Johnston, Robert W.M. MA BD STM	1964	1999	(Glasgow: Temple Anniesland)	13 Kilmardinny Crescent, Bearsden, Glasgow G61 3NB	0141-931 5862

Name	Role	Ord.	App.	Address	Phone
Johnstone, H. Martin J. MA BD MTh PhD	Church and Society Council	1989	2000	3/1, 952 Pollokshaws Road, Glasgow G41 2ET [E-mail: MJohnstone@churchofscotland.org.uk]	0141-636 5819
Lang, I. Pat (Miss) BSc	(Dunoon: The High Kirk)	1996	2003	37 Crawford Drive, Glasgow G15 6TW	0141-944 2240
Levison, Chris L. MA BD	(Health Care Chaplaincy Training and Development Officer)	1972	1998	Gardenfield, Nine Mile Burn, Penicuik EH26 9LT	01968 674566 (Mbl) 07879 812816
Lloyd, John M. BD CertMin	(Glasgow: Croftfoot)	1984	2009	17 Acacia Way, Cambuslang, Glasgow G72 7ZY	0141-772 0149
Love, Joanna (Ms) BSc DCS	Iona Community: Wild Goose Resource Group			92 Everard Drive, Glasgow G21 1XQ [E-mail: jo@wildgoose.scot]	(Office) 0141-429 7281
Lunan, David W. MA BD DUniv DLitt DD	(Presbytery Clerk)	1970	2002	30 Mill Road, Banton, Glasgow G65 0RD	01236 824110
MacBain, Ian W. BD	(Coatbridge: Coatdyke)	1971	1993	24 Thornyburn Drive, Baillieston, Glasgow G69 7ER	0141-771 7030
McChlery, Lynn M. BA BD	(Eaglesham)	2005	2015	62 Grenville Drive, Cambuslang, Glasgow G72 8DP [E-mail: lmcchlery@btinternet.com]	0141-643 9730 (Mbl) 07748 118008
MacDonald, Anne (Miss) BA DCS	Healthcare Chaplain: Leverndale Hospital			c/o Leverndale Hospital, Glasgow G53 7TU [E-mail: anne.macdonald2@ggc.scot.nhs.uk]	0141-211 6695 (Mbl) 07976 786174
MacDonald, Kenneth MA BA	(Auxiliary Minister)	2001	2006	5 Henderland Road, Bearsden, Glasgow G61 1AH	0141-943 1103
McDougall, Hilary N. (Mrs) MA PGCE BD	Congregational Facilitator: Presbytery of Glasgow	2002	2013	6 Inchmurrin Gardens, High Burnside, Glasgow G73 5RU [E-mail: hilary@presbyteryofglasgow.org.uk]	0141-384 4428 (Mbl) 07539 321832
MacFadyen, Anne M. (Mrs) BSc BD FSAScot	(Auxiliary Minister)	1995		295 Mearns Road, Glasgow G77 5LT	0141-639 3605
Mackenzie, Gordon R. BScAgr BD	(Chapelhall)	1977	2014	16 Crowhill Road, Bishopbriggs, Glasgow G64 1QY [E-mail: rev.g.mackenzie@btopenworld.com]	0141-772 6052
MacKinnon, Charles M. BD	(Kilsyth: Anderson)	1989	2009	36 Hilton Terrace, Bishopbriggs, Glasgow G64 3HB [E-mail: cm.ccmackinnon@tiscali.co.uk]	0141-772 3811
McLachlan, Eric BD MTh	(Glasgow: Cardonald)	1978	2005	16 Kinpurnie Road, Paisley PA1 3HH [E-mail: eric.janis@btinternet.com]	0141-810 5789
McLachlan, T. Alastair BSc	(Craignish with Kilbrandon and Kilchattan with Kilninver and Kilmelford)	1972	2009	9 Alder Road, Milton of Campsie, Glasgow G66 8HH [E-mail: talastair@btinternet.com]	01360 319861
McLaren, D. Muir MA BD MTh PhD	(Glasgow: Mosspark)	1971	2001	House 44, 145 Shawhill Road, Glasgow G43 1SX [E-mail: muir44@yahoo.co.uk]	(Mbl) 07931 155779
McLellan, Margaret DCS	Deacon			18 Broom Road East, Newton Mearns, Glasgow G77 5SD [E-mail: margaretmclellan@rocketmail.com]	0141-639 6853
Macleod, Donald BD LRAM DRSAM	(Blairgowrie)	1987	2008	9 Millersneuk Avenue, Lenzie G66 5HJ [E-mail: donmac2@sky.com]	0141-776 6235
MacLeod-Mair, Alisdair T. MEd DipTheol	(Glasgow: Baillieston St Andrew's)	2001	2012	2/2, 44 Leven Street, Pollokshields, Glasgow G41 2JE [E-mail: revalisdair@hotmail.com]	0141-423 9600
MacMahon, Janet P.H. (Mrs) MSc BD	(Kilmaronock Gartocharn)	1992	2010	14 Hillfoot Drive, Bearsden, Glasgow G61 3QQ [E-mail: janetmacmahon@yahoo.co.uk]	0141-942 8611
Macnaughton, J.A. MA BD	(Glasgow: Hyndland)	1949	1989	Lilyburn Care Home, 100 Birdston Road, Milton of Campsie, Glasgow G66 8BY	(Mbl) 07811 621671
MacPherson, James B. DCS	(Deacon)	1984	2001	0/1, 104 Cartside Street, Glasgow G42 9TQ	0141-616 6468
MacQuarrie, Stuart JP BD BSc MBA	Chaplain: Glasgow University			The Chaplaincy Centre, University of Glasgow, Glasgow G12 8QQ	0141-330 5419
MacQuien, Duncan DCS	(Deacon)	1988		35 Criffel Road, Mount Vernon, Glasgow G32 9JE	0141-575 1137
Martindale, John P.F. BD	(Glasgow: Sandyhills)	1994	2005	Flat 3/2, 25 Albert Avenue, Glasgow G42 8RB	0141-433 4367

Miller, John D. BA BD DD	1971	2007	(Glasgow: Castlemilk East)	98 Kirkcaldy Road, Glasgow G41 4LD [E-mail: rev.john.miller@zol.co.zw]	0141-423 0221
Moffat, Thomas BSc BD	1976	2008	(Culross and Torryburn)	Flat 8/1, 8 Cranston Street, Glasgow G3 8GG [E-mail: tom@gallus.org.uk]	0141-248 1886
Moore, William B.			(Prison Chaplain: Low Moss)	10 South Dumbreck Road, Kilsyth, Glasgow G65 9LX	01236 821918
Muir, Fred C. MA BD ThM ARCM	1961	1997	(Stepps)	20 Alexandra Avenue, Stepps, Glasgow G33 6BP	0141-779 2504
Ninian, Esther J. (Miss) MA BD	1993	2015	(Newton Mearns)	21 St Ronan's Drive, Burnside, Rutherglen G73 3SR [E-mail: estherninian5914@btinternet.com]	0141-647 9720
Philip, George M. MA	1953	1996	(Glasgow: Sandyford Henderson Memorial)	44 Beech Avenue, Bearsden, Glasgow G61 3EX	0141-942 1327
Raeburn, Alan C. MA BD	1971	2010	(Glasgow: Battlefield East)	3 Orchard Gardens, Strathaven ML10 6UN [E-mail: acraeburn@hotmail.com]	(Mbl) 07709 552161
Ramsay, W.G.	1967	1999	(Glasgow: Springburn)	53 Kelvinvale, Kirkintilloch, Glasgow G66 1RD [E-mail: billram@btopenworld.com]	0141-776 2915
Ramsden, Iain R. MStJ BTh	1999	2013	(Killearnan with Knockbain)	Flat 1/1, 15 Cardon Square, Renfrew PA4 8BY [E-mail: s4rev@sky.com]	(Mbl) 07795 972560
Robertson, Archibald MA BD	1957	1999	(Glasgow: Eastwood)	19 Canberra Court, Braidpark Drive, Glasgow G46 6NS	0141-637 7572
Robertson, Blair MA BD ThM	1990	1998	Head of Spiritual Care	The Sanctuary, Queen Elizabeth University Hospital, Govan Road, Glasgow G51 4TF	0141-201 2356
Ross, Donald M. MA	1953	1994	(Industrial Mission Organiser)	14 Cartsbridge Road, Busby, Glasgow G76 8DH	0141-644 2220
Ross, James MA BD	1968	1998	(Kilsyth: Anderson)	53 Turnberry Gardens, Westerwood, Cumbernauld, Glasgow G68 0AY	01236 730501
Shackleton, Scott J.S. QCVS BA BD	1993	2010	Chaplain, Royal Navy	RMB Stonehouse, Dumford Street, Plymouth PL1 3QS [E-mail: shackletonscot@hotmail.com]	
Shackleton, William	1960	1996	(Greenock: Wellpark West)	3 Tynwald Avenue, Burnside, Glasgow G73 4RN	0141-569 9407
Smeed, Alex W. MA BD	2008	2013	(Glasgow: Whiteinch: Associate)	3/1, 24 Thornwood Road, Glasgow G11 7RB [E-mail: alexsmeed@yahoo.co.uk]	0141-337 3878
Smith, G. Stewart MA BD STM	1966	2006	(Glasgow: King's Park)	33 Brent Road, Stewartfield, East Kilbride, Glasgow G74 4RA [E-mail: stewartandmary@googlemail.com]	(Mbl) 07709 756495 (Tel/Fax) 01355 226718
Smith, James S.A.	1956	1991	(Drongan: The Schaw Kirk)	146 Aros Drive, Glasgow G52 1TJ	0141-883 9666
Spencer, John MA BD	1962	2001	(Dumfries: Lincluden with Holywood)	10 Kinkell Gardens, Kirkintilloch, Glasgow G66 2HJ	0141-777 8935
Spiers, John M. LTh MTh	1972	2004	(Giffnock: Orchardhill)	58 Woodlands Road, Thornliebank, Glasgow G46 7JQ	(Tel/Fax) 0141-638 0632
Stewart, Diane E. BD	1988	2006	(Milton of Campsie)	4 Miller Gardens, Bishopbrigs, Glasgow G64 1FG [E-mail: destewart@givemail.co.uk]	0141-762 1358
Stewart, Norma D. (Miss) MA MEd BD MTh	1977	2000	(Glasgow: Strathbungo Queen's Park)	127 Nether Auldhouse Road, Glasgow G43 2YS	0141-637 6956
Sutherland, David A.	2001		Auxiliary Minister	3/1, 145 Broomhill Drive, Glasgow G11 7ND [E-mail: dave.a.sutherland@gmail.com]	0141-357 2058
Sutherland, Denis I.	1963	1995	(Glasgow: Hutchesontown)	56 Lime Crescent, Cumbernauld, Glasgow G67 3PQ	01236 731723
Turner, Angus BD	1976	1998	(Industrial Chaplain)	46 Keir Street, Pollokshields, Glasgow G41 2LA	0141-424 0493
Tuton, Robert M. MA	1957	1995	(Glasgow: Shettleston Old)	6 Holmwood Gardens, Uddingston, Glasgow G71 7BH	01698 321108
Walker, Linda	2008	2013	Auxiliary Minister	18 Valeview Terrace, Glasgow G42 9LA [E-mail: LWalker@churchofscotland.org.uk]	0141-649 1340

Walton, Ainslie MA MEd	1954 1995	(University of Aberdeen)	501 Shields Road, Glasgow G41 2RF [E-mail: revainslie@aol.com]	0141-420 3327
White, C. Peter BVMS BD MRCVS	1974 2011	(Glasgow: Sandyford Henderson Memorial)	2 Hawthorn Place, Torrance, Glasgow G64 4EA [E-mail: revcpw@gmail.com]	01360 622680
Whiteford, John D. MA BD	1989 2016	(Glasgow: Newlands South)	42 Maxwell Drive, East Kilbride, Glasgow G74 4HJ [E-mail: jwhiteford@hotmail.com]	(Mbl) 07809 290806
Whyte, James BD	1981 2011	(Fairlie)	32 Torburn Avenue, Giffnock, Glasgow G46 7RB [E-mail: jameswhyte89@btinternet.com]	
Wilson, John BD	1985 2010	(Glasgow: Temple Anniesland)	4 Carron Crescent, Bearsden, Glasgow G61 1HJ [E-mail: revjwilson@btinternet.com]	0141-931 5609
Younger, Adah (Mrs) BD	1978 2004	(Glasgow: Dennistoun Central)	7 Gartocher Terrace, Glasgow G32 0HE	0141-774 6475

GLASGOW ADDRESSES

Banton	Kelvinhead Road, Banton
Bishopbriggs	
Kenmure	Viewfield Road, Bishopbriggs
Springfield Cambridge	The Leys, off Springfield Road
Broom	Mearns Road, Newton Mearns
Burnside Blairbeth	Church Avenue, Burnside
	Kirkriggs Avenue, Blairbeth
Busby	Church Road, Busby
Cadder	Cadder Road, Bishopbriggs
Cambuslang	
Flemington Hallside	Hutchinson Place
Parish	Arnott Way
Campsie	Main Street, Lennoxtown
Chryston	Main Street, Chryston
Eaglesham	Montgomery Street, Eaglesham
Fernhill and Cathkin	Neilvaig Drive
Gartcosh	113 Lochend Road, Gartcosh
Giffnock	
Orchardhill	Church Road
South	Eastwood Toll
The Park	Ravenscliffe Drive
Glenboig	Main Street, Glenboig
Greenbank	Eaglesham Road, Clarkston
Kilsyth	
Anderson	Kingston Road, Kilsyth
Burns and Old	Church Street, Kilsyth
Kirkintilloch	

Hillhead St Columba's	Newdyke Road, Kirkintilloch
St David's Mem Pk	Waterside Road nr Auld Aisle Road
St Mary's	Alexandra Street Cowgate
Lenzie	
Old	Kirkintilloch Road x Garngaber Ave
Union	65 Kirkintilloch Road
Maxwell	Waterfoot Road
Mearns Castle	
Mearns	Mearns Road, Newton Mearns
Milton of Campsie	Antermony Road, Milton of Campsie
Netherlee	Ormonde Drive x Ormonde Avenue
Newton Mearns	Ayr Road, Newton Mearns
Rutherglen	
Old	Main Street at Queen Street
Stonelaw	Stonelaw Road x Dryburgh Avenue
West and Wardlawhill	3 Western Avenue
Stamperland	Stamperland Gardens, Clarkston
Stepps	Whitehill Avenue
Thornliebank	61 Spiersbridge Road
Torrance	School Road, Torrance
Twechar	Main Street, Twechar
Williamwood	4 Vardar Avenue, Clarkston
Glasgow	
Anderston Kelvingrove	759 Argyle St x Elderslie St

Baillieston	
Mure Memorial	Maxwell Drive, Garrowhill
St Andrew's	Bredisholm Road
Balshagray Victoria Pk	218–230 Broomhill Drive
Barlanark Greyfriars	Edinburgh Rd x Hallhill Rd (365)
Blawarthill	Millbrix Avenue
Bridgeton St Francis in the East	26 Queen Mary Street
Broomhill	64–66 Randolph Rd (x Marlborough Ave)
Calton Parkhead	122 Helenvale Street
Cardonald	2155 Paisley Road West
Carmunnock	Kirk Road, Carmunnock
Carmyle	155 Carmyle Avenue
Carntyne	358 Carntynehall Road
Carnwadric	556 Boydstone Road, Thornliebank
Castlemilk	
Cathcart	Carmunnock Road
Old	119 Carmunnock Road
Trinity	90 Clarkston Road
Cathedral	Cathedral Square, 2 Castle Street
Causeway Church, Tollcross	1134 Tollcross Road
Clincarthill	1216 Cathcart Road
Colston Milton	Egilsay Crescent
Colston Wellpark	1378 Springburn Road
Cranhill	109 Bellrock St (at Bellrock Cr)
Croftfoot	Croftpark Ave x Crofthill Road
Dennistoun New	9 Armadale Street
Drumchapel St Andrew's	153 Garscadden Road
St Mark's	281 Kinfauns Drive

Easterhouse St George's and St Peter's	Boyndie Street
Eastwood	Mansewood Road
Gairbraid	1517 Maryhill Road
Gallowgate	David Street
Garthamlock and Craigend East	46 Porchester Street
Gorbals	1 Errol Gardens
Govan and Linthouse	Govan Cross
Hillington Park	24 Berryknowes Road
Hyndland	79 Hyndland Rd, opp Novar Dr
Ibrox	Carillon Road x Clifford Street
John Ross Memorial	100 Norfolk Street
Jordanhill	28 Woodend Drive (x Munro Road)
Kelvinbridge	Belmont Street at Belmont Bridge
Kelvinside Hillhead	Observatory Road
Kenmuir Mount Vernon	2405 London Road, Mount Vernon
King's Park	242 Castlemilk Road
Kinning Park	Eaglesham Place
Knightswood St Margaret's	2000 Great Western Road
Langside	167–169 Ledard Road (x Lochleven Road)
Lochwood	2A Liff Place, Easterhouse
Maryhill	1990 Maryhill Road
Merrylea	78 Merrylee Road
Mosspark	167 Ashkirk Drive
Newlands South	Riverside Road x Langside Drive
Partick South	259 Dumbarton Road
Trinity	20 Lawrence Street x Elie Street
Pollokshaws	223 Shawbridge Street
Pollokshields	Albert Drive x Shields Road
Possilpark	124 Saracen Street
Queen's Park Govanhill	170 Queen's Drive
Renfield St Stephen's	260 Bath Street
Robroyston	34 Saughs Road
Ruchazie	4 Elibank Street (x Milncroft Road)
Ruchill Kelvinside	Shakespeare Street nr Maryhill Rd and 10 Kelbourne Street (two buildings)
St Andrew and St Nicholas	Bowfield Road x Bowfield Avenue
St Andrew's East	224 Hartlaw Crescent
St Christopher's Priesthill and Nitshill	681 Alexandra Parade
Priesthill building	100 Priesthill Rd (x Muirshiel Cr)
Nitshill building	36 Dove Street
St Christopher's	Meikle Road
St Columba	300 St Vincent Street
St David's Knightswood	66 Boreland Drive (nr Lincoln Avenue)
St Enoch's Hogganfield	860 Cumbernauld Road
St George's Tron	163 Buchanan Street
St James' (Pollok)	Lyoncross Road x Byrebush Road
St John's Renfield	22 Beaconsfield Road
St Margaret's Tollcross Pk	179 Braidfauld Street
St Paul's	30 Langdale St (x Greenrig St)
St Rollox	9 Fountainwell Road
Sandyford Henderson Memorial	Kelvinhaugh Street at Argyle Street
Sandyhills	28 Baillieston Rd nr Sandyhills Rd
Scotstoun	Earlbank Avenue x Ormiston Avenue
Shawlands	Shawlands Cross (1114 Pollokshaws Road)
Sherbrooke St Gilbert's	Nithsdale Rd x Sherbrooke Avenue
Shettleston New	679 Old Shettleston Road
South Shawlands	Regwood Street x Deanston Drive
Springburn	180 Springburn Way
Temple Anniesland	869 Crow Road
Toryglen	Glenmore Ave nr Prospecthill Road
Trinity Possil and Henry Drummond	2 Crowhill Street (x Broadholm Street)
Tron St Mary's	128 Red Road
Wallacewell New Charge Development	no building yet obtained
Wellington	University Ave x Southpark Avenue
Whiteinch	1a Northinch Court
Yoker	10 Hawick Street

(17) HAMILTON

Meets at Motherwell: Dalziel St Andrew's Parish Church Halls, on the first Tuesday of February, March, May, September, October, November and December, and on the third Tuesday of June.

Presbytery Office: 353 Orbiston Street, Motherwell ML1 1QW   01698 259135
[E-mail: hamilton@churchofscotland.org.uk]
[E-mail: clerk@presbyteryofhamilton.co.uk]

Clerk: REV. GORDON A. McCRACKEN BD CertMin DMin   c/o The Presbytery Office

Depute Clerk:　REV. ROBERT A. HAMILTON BA BD
Presbytery Treasurer: MR ROBERT A. ALLAN

c/o The Presbytery Office
7 Graham Place, Ashgill, Larkhall ML9 3BA
[E-mail: Fallan3246@aol.com]

01698 883246

No.	Congregation / Minister	Ord.	Ind.	Address	Tel.
1	**Airdrie: Cairnlea (H) (01236 762101) linked with Calderbank** Vacant (Airdrie: Cairnlea is formed by the union between Airdrie: Broomknoll and Airdrie: Flowerhill)			38 Commonhead Street, Airdrie ML6 6NS	01236 609584
2	**Airdrie: Clarkston** F. Derek Gunn BD	1986	2009	Clarkston Manse, Forrest Street, Airdrie ML6 7BE [E-mail: DGunn@churchofscotland.org.uk]	01236 603146
3	**Airdrie: High linked with Caldercruix and Longriggend** Ian R.W. McDonald BSc BD PhD		2007	17 Etive Drive, Airdrie ML6 9QL [E-mail: IMcDonald@churchofscotland.org.uk]	01236 760023
4	**Airdrie: Jackson** Kay Gilchrist (Miss) BD	1996	2008	48 Dunrobin Road, Airdrie ML6 8LR [E-mail: KGilchrist@churchofscotland.org.uk]	01236 760154
5	**Airdrie: New Monkland (H) linked with Greengairs** William Jackson BD CertMin	1994	2015	3 Dykehead Crescent, Airdrie ML6 6PU [E-mail: WJackson@churchofscotland.org.uk]	01236 761723
6	**Airdrie: St Columba's** Margaret F. Currie BEd BD	1980	1987	52 Kennedy Drive, Airdrie ML6 9AW [E-mail: MCurrie@churchofscotland.org.uk]	01236 763173
7	**Airdrie: The New Wellwynd** Robert A. Hamilton BA BD	1995	2001	20 Arthur Avenue, Airdrie ML6 9EZ [E-mail: RHamilton@churchofscotland.org.uk]	01236 763022
8	**Bargeddie (H)** Vacant			The Manse, Manse Road, Bargeddie, Baillieston, Glasgow G69 6UB	0141-771 1322
9	**Bellshill: Central** Kevin M de Beer BTh	1995	2016	32 Adamson Street, Bellshill ML4 1DT [E-mail: KdeBeer@churchofscotland.org.uk]	01698 841176 07555 265609 (Mbl)

10	**Bellshill: West (H) (01698 747581)** Calum Stark LLB BD	2011	2015	16 Croftpark Street, Bellshill ML4 1EY [E-mail: CStark@churchofscotland.org.uk]	01698 842877
11	**Blantyre: Livingstone Memorial** Vacant			286 Glasgow Road, Blantyre, Glasgow G72 9DB	01698 823794
12	**Blantyre: Old (H)** Sarah L. Ross (Mrs) BD MTh PGDip	2004	2013	The Manse, Craigmuir Road, High Blantyre, Glasgow G72 9UA [E-mail: SRoss@churchofscotland.org.uk]	01698 769046
13	**Blantyre: St Andrew's** Vacant			332 Glasgow Road, Blantyre, Glasgow G72 9LQ	01698 828633
14	**Bothwell (H)** James M. Gibson TD LTh LRAM	1978	1989	Manse Avenue, Bothwell, Glasgow G71 8PQ [E-mail: JGibson@churchofscotland.org.uk]	01698 853189 (Tel) 01698 854903 (Fax)
15	**Calderbank** See Airdrie: Cairnlea				
16	**Caldercruix and Longriggend (H) See Airdrie: High**				
17	**Chapelhall (H)** Vacant			The Manse, Russell Street, Chapelhall, Airdrie ML6 8SG	01236 763439
18	**Chapelton linked with Strathaven: Rankin (H)** Shaw J. Paterson BSc BD MSc	1991		15 Lethame Road, Strathaven ML10 6AD [E-mail: SPaterson@churchofscotland.org.uk]	01357 520019 (Tel) 01357 529316 (Fax)
19	**Cleland (H) linked with Wishaw: St Mark's** Graham Austin BD	1997	2008	The Manse, 302 Coltness Road, Wishaw ML2 7EY [E-mail: GAustin@churchofscotland.org.uk]	01698 384596
20	**Coatbridge: Blairhill Dundyvan (H) linked with Coatbridge: Middle** John K. Collard MA BD (Interim Minister)	1986	2015	1 Nelson Terrace, East Kilbride, Glasgow G74 2EY [E-mail: JCollard@churchofscotland.org.uk]	01355 520093

21	**Coatbridge: Calder (H) linked with Coatbridge: Old Monkland**			
	Vacant		26 Bute Street, Coatbridge ML5 4HF	01236 421516
22	**Coatbridge: Middle** See Coatbridge: Blairhill Dundyvan			
23	**Coatbridge: New St Andrew's**			
	Fiona Nicolson BA BD	1996	2005	77 Eglinton Street, Coatbridge ML5 3JF	01236 437271
				[E-mail: FNicolson@churchofscotland.org.uk]	
24	**Coatbridge: Old Monkland** See Coatbridge: Calder			
25	**Coatbridge: Townhead (H)**			
	Ecilo Selemani LTh MTh	1993	2004	Crinan Crescent, Coatbridge ML5 2LH	01236 702914
				[E-mail: ESelemani@churchofscotland.org.uk]	
26	**Dalserf**			
	Vacant		Manse Brae, Dalserf, Larkhall ML9 3BN	01698 882195
27	**East Kilbride: Claremont (H) (01355 238088)**			
	Gordon R. Palmer MA BD STM	1986	17 Deveron Road, East Kilbride, Glasgow G74 2HR	01355 248526
			[E-mail: GPalmer@churchofscotland.org.uk]	
28	**East Kilbride: Greenhills (E) (01355 221746)**			
	John Brewster MA BD DipEd	1988	21 Turnberry Place, East Kilbride, Glasgow G75 8TB	01355 242564
			[E-mail: JBrewster@churchofscotland.org.uk]	
29	**East Kilbride: Moncreiff (H) (01355 223328)**			
	Neil Buchanan BD	1991	16 Almond Drive, East Kilbride, Glasgow G74 2HX	01355 238639
			[E-mail: NBuchanan@churchofscotland.org.uk]	
30	**East Kilbride: Mossneuk (01355 260954)**			
	John L. McPake BA BD PhD	1987	30 Eden Grove, Mossneuk, East Kilbride, Glasgow G75 8XU	01355 234196
			[E-mail: JMcPake@churchofscotland.org.uk]	
31	**East Kilbride: Old (H) (01355 279004)**			
	Anne S. Paton BA BD	2001	40 Maxwell Drive, East Kilbride, Glasgow G74 4HJ	01355 220732
			[E-mail: APaton@churchofscotland.org.uk]	

32   East Kilbride: South (H)
Vacant
36 Glencairn Drive, Glasgow G41 4PW
0141-423 4000

33   East Kilbride: Stewartfield (New Charge Development)
Douglas W. Wallace MA BD   1981   2001
8 Thistle Place, Stewartfield, East Kilbride, Glasgow G74 4RH
[E-mail: DWallace@churchofscotland.org.uk]
01355 260879

34   East Kilbride: West (H)
Mahboob Masih BA MDiv MTh   1999   2008
4 East Milton Grove, East Kilbride, Glasgow G75 8FN
[E-mail: MMasih@churchofscotland.org.uk]
01355 224469

35   East Kilbride: Westwood (H) (01355 245657)
Kevin Mackenzie BD DPS   1989   1996
16 Inglewood Crescent, East Kilbride, Glasgow G75 8QD
[E-mail: Kevin.MacKenzie@churchofscotland.org.uk]
01355 223992

36   Glassford linked with Strathaven: East
William T. Stewart BD   1980
68 Townhead Street, Strathaven ML10 6DJ
[E-mail: WStewart@churchofscotland.org.uk]
01357 521138

37   Greengairs   See Airdrie: New Monkland

38   Hamilton: Cadzow (H) (01698 428695)
John W. Carswell BS MDiv   1996   2009
3 Carlisle Road, Hamilton ML3 7BZ
[E-mail: JCarswell@churchofscotland.org.uk]
01698 426682

39   Hamilton: Gilmour and Whitehill (H) linked with Hamilton: West
Vacant

40   Hamilton: Hillhouse
Christopher A Rankine MA MTh PgDE   2016
66 Wellhall Road, Hamilton ML3 9BY
[E-mail: CRankine@churchofscotland.org.uk]
01698 327579

41   Hamilton: Old (H) (01698 281905)
I Ross Blackman BSc MBA BD   2015
1 Chateau Grove, Hamilton ML3 7DS
[E-mail: RBlackman@churchofscotland.org.uk]
01698 640185
(This congregation has united with the congregation of Hamilton: North)

42 Hamilton: St John's (H) (01698 283492)
Joanne C. Hood (Miss) MA BD   2003   2012
9 Shearer Avenue, Fermiegair, Hamilton ML3 7FX
[E-mail: JHood@churchofscotland.org.uk]
01698 425002

43 Hamilton: South (H) (01698 281014) linked with Quarter
Donald R. Lawrie   2012
The Manse, Limekilnburn Road, Quarter, Hamilton ML3 7XA
[E-mail: DLawrie@churchofscotland.org.uk]
01698 424511

44 Hamilton: Trinity (01698 284254)
S Lindsay A Turnbull BSc BD   2014
69 Buchan Street, Hamilton ML3 8JY
[E-mail: Lindsay.Turnbull@churchofscotland.org.uk]
01698 284919

45 Hamilton: West (H) (01698 284670) See Hamilton: Gilmore and Whitehill

46 Holytown linked with New Stevenston: Wrangholm Kirk
Caryl A.E. Kyle (Mrs) BD DipEd   2008
The Manse, 260 Edinburgh Road, Holytown, Motherwell ML1 5RU
[E-mail: CKyle@churchofscotland.org.uk]
01698 832622

47 Kirk o' Shotts (H)
Vacant
The Manse, Kirk o' Shotts, Salsburgh, Shotts ML7 4NS
01698 870208

48 Larkhall: Chalmers (H)
Andrea M. Boyes   2013
Quarry Road, Larkhall ML9 1HH
[E-mail: ABoyes@churchofscotland.org.uk]
01698 882238

49 Larkhall: St Machan's (H)
Alastair McKillop BD DipMin   1995   2004
2 Orchard Gate, Larkhall ML9 1HG
[E-mail: AMcKillop@churchofscotland.org.uk]
01698 321976

50 Larkhall: Trinity
Vacant
13 Machan Avenue, Larkhall ML9 2HE
01698 881401

51 Motherwell: Crosshill (H) linked with Motherwell: St Margaret's
Gavin W.G. Black BD   2006
15 Orchard Street, Motherwell ML1 3JE
[E-mail: GBlack@churchofscotland.org.uk]
01698 263410

52	**Motherwell: Dalziel St Andrew's (H) (01698 264097)**				
	Derek W. Hughes BSc BD DipEd	1990	1996	4 Pollock Street, Motherwell ML1 1LP [E-mail: DHughes@churchofscotland.org.uk]	01698 263414
53	**Motherwell: North**				
	Derek H.N. Pope BD	1987	1995	35 Birrens Road, Motherwell ML1 3NS [E-mail: DPope@churchofscotland.org.uk]	01698 266716
54	**Motherwell: St Margaret's** See Motherwell: Crosshill				
55	**Motherwell: St Mary's (H)**				
	Vacant			19 Orchard Street, Motherwell ML1 3JE	
56	**Motherwell: South (H)**				
	Alan W Gibson BA BD	2001	2016	62 Manse Road, Motherwell ML1 2PT [E-mail: Alan.Gibson@churchofscotland.org.uk]	01698 239279
57	**Newarthill and Carfin**				
	Elaine W. McKinnon MA BD	1988	2014	Church Street, Newarthill, Motherwell ML1 5HS [E-mail: EMcKinnon@churchofscotland.org.uk]	01698 296850
58	**Newmains: Bonkle (H) linked with Newmains: Coltness Memorial (H)**				
	Graham Raeburn MTh		2004	5 Kirkgate, Newmains, Wishaw ML2 9BT [E-mail: GRaeburn@churchofscotland.org.uk]	01698 383858
59	**Newmains: Coltness Memorial** See Newmains: Bonkle				
60	**New Stevenston: Wrangholm Kirk** See Holytown				
61	**Overtown**				
	Vacant			The Manse, 146 Main Street, Overtown, Wishaw ML2 0QP	01698 352090
62	**Quarter** See Hamilton: South				
63	**Shotts: Calderhead Erskine**				
	Allan B. Brown BD MTh	1995	2010	The Manse, 9 Kirk Road, Shotts ML7 5ET [E-mail: ABrown@churchofscotland.org.uk]	01501 823204 07578 448655 (Mbl)

64 **Stonehouse: St Ninian's (H)**
    Vacant   4 Hamilton Way, Stonehouse, Larkhall ML9 3PU   01698 792587
    Stonehouse: St Ninian's is a Local Ecumenical Partnership shared with the United Reformed Church

65 **Strathaven: Avendale Old and Drumclog (H) (01357 529748)**
    Alan B. Telfer BA BD   1983   2010   4 Fortrose Gardens, Strathaven ML10 6SH   01357 523031
                                                [E-mail: ATelfer@churchofscotland.org.uk]

66 **Strathaven: East** See Glassford

67 **Strathaven: Rankin** See Chapelton

68 **Uddingston: Burnhead (H)**
    Les N. Brunger BD   2010   90 Laburnum Road, Uddingston, Glasgow G71 5DB   01698 813716
                                                [E-mail: LBrunger@churchofscotland.org.uk]

69 **Uddingston: Old (H) (01698 814015)**
    Fiona L.J. McKibbin (Mrs) MA BD   2011   1 Belmont Avenue, Uddingston, Glasgow G71 7AX   01698 814757
                                                [E-mail: FMcKibbin@churchofscotland.org.uk]

70 **Uddingston: Viewpark (H)**
    Michael G. Lyall BD   1993   2001   14 Holmbrae Road, Uddingston, Glasgow G71 6AP   01698 813113
                                                [E-mail: MLyall@churchofscotland.org.uk]

71 **Wishaw: Cambusnethan North (H)**
    Mhorag Macdonald (Ms) MA BD   1989   350 Kirk Road, Wishaw ML2 8LH   01698 381305
                                                [E-mail: Mhorag.Macdonald@churchofscotland.org.uk]

72 **Wishaw: Cambusnethan Old and Morningside**
    Iain C. Murdoch MA LLB DipEd BD   1995   22 Coronation Street, Wishaw ML2 8LF   01698 384235
                                                [E-mail: IMurdoch@churchofscotland.org.uk]

73 **Wishaw: Craigneuk and Belhaven (H) linked with Wishaw: Old**
    Vacant   130 Glen Road, Wishaw ML2 7NP   01698 375134

74 Wishaw: Old (H) (01698 376080) See Wishaw: Craigneuk and Belhaven

75 Wishaw: St Mark's See Cleland

76 Wishaw: South Wishaw (H) (01698 375306) 1995 2015 3 Walter Street, Wishaw ML2 8LQ 01698 767459
Terence C. Moran BD CertMin

Name	Ordained / Current	Position	Address	Telephone
Barrie, Arthur P. LTh	1973 2007	(Hamilton: Cadzow)	30 Airbles Crescent, Motherwell ML1 3AR [E-mail: elizabethbarrie@ymail.com]	01698 261147
Baxendale, Georgina M. (Mrs) BD	1981 2014	(Motherwell: South)	32 Meadowhead Road, Plains, Airdrie ML6 7HG [E-mail: georgiebaxendale6@tiscali.co.uk]	
Buck, Maxine	2007	Auxiliary Minister	Brownlee House, Mauldslie Road, Carluke ML8 5HW [E-mail: MBuck@churchofscotland.org.uk]	01555 759063
Colvin, Sharon E.F. (Mrs) BD LRAM LTCL	1985 2007	(Airdrie: Jackson)	25 Balblair Road, Airdrie ML6 6GQ [E-mail: dibleycol@hotmail.com]	01236 590796
Cook, J. Stanley BD Dip PSS	1974 2001	(Hamilton: West)	Mansend, 137A Old Manse Road, Netherton, Wishaw ML2 0EW [E-mail: stancook@blueyonder.co.uk]	01698 299600
Currie, R. David BSc BD	1984 2004	(Cambuslang: Flemington Hallside)	69 Kethers Street, Motherwell ML1 3HN	01698 323424
Davidson, Amelia (Mrs) BD	2004 2011	(Coatbridge: Calder)	11 St Mary's Place, Saltcoats KA21 5NY	
Donaldson, George M. MA BD	1984 2015	(Caldercruix and Longriggend)	4 Toul Gardens, Motherwell ML1 2FE [E-mail: g.donaldson505@btinternet.com]	01698 239477
Doyle, David W. MA BD	1977 2014	(Motherwell: St Mary's)	76 Kethers Street, Motherwell ML1 3HN	01698 263472
Dunn, W. Stuart LTh	1970 2006	(Motherwell: Crosshill)	10 Macrostie Gardens, Crieff PH7 4LP	01764 655178
Gordon, Alasdair B. BD LLB EdD	1970 1980	(Aberdeen: Summerhill)	Flat 1, 13 Auchingramont Road, Hamilton ML3 6IP [E-mail: alasdairbgordon@hotmail.com]	01698 200561 (Mbl) 07768 897843
Grant, Paul G.R. BD MTh	2003 2015	Hospital Chaplain	67 Newfield Road, Stonehouse ML9 3HH [E-mail: paul.grant@ggc.scot.nhs.co.uk]	(work) 0141-211 4661
Grier, James BD	1991 2005	(Coatbridge: Middle)	14 Love Drive, Bellshill ML4 1BY	01698 742545
Hunter, James E. LTh	1974 1997	(Blantyre: Livingstone Memorial)	57 Dalwhinnie Avenue, Blantyre, Glasgow G72 9NQ	01698 826177
Kent, Robert M. MA BD	1973 2011	(Hamilton: St John's)	48 Fyne Crescent, Larkhall ML9 2UX [E-mail: robertmkent@talktalk.net]	01698 769244
Lusk, Alastair S. BD	1974 2010	(East Kilbride: Moncreiff)	9 MacFie Place, Stewartfield, East Kilbride, Glasgow G74 4TY	01698 384610
McAlpine, John BSc	1988 2004	(Auxiliary Minister)	Braeside, 201 Bonkle Road, Newmains, Wishaw ML2 9AA	
McCabe, George	1963 1996	(Airdrie: High)	8 Bonaly Road, Edinburgh EH13 0EA	
McCracken, Gordon A. BD CertMin DMin	1988 2015	Presbytery Clerk	1 Kenilworth Road, Lanark ML11 7BL	(Mbl) 07918 600720

Name	Ordained	Inducted	Charge/Position	Address / E-mail	Telephone
McDonald, John A. MA BD	1978	1997	(Cumbernauld: Condorrat)	17 Thomson Drive, Bellshill ML4 3ND	01698 827358
McKee, Norman B. BD	1987	2010	(Uddingston: Old)	148 Station Road, Blantyre, Glasgow G72 9BW [E-mail: normanmckee946@btinternet.com]	
MacKenzie, Ian C. MA BD	1970	2011	(Interim Minister)	21 Wilson Street, Motherwell ML1 1NP [E-mail: iancmac@blueyonder.co.uk]	01698 301230
McKenzie, Raymond D. BD	1978	2012	(Hambank with Hamilton: North)	25 Austine Drive, Hamilton ML3 7YE [E-mail: rdmackenzie@hotmail.co.uk]	
MacLeod, Norman BTh	1999	2013	(Hamilton: St Andrew's)	15 Bent Road, Hamilton ML3 6QB [E-mail: normanmacleod@blueyonder.co.uk]	01698 283264
McPherson, D. Cameron BSc BD DMin	1982	2015	(Dalserf)	6 Moa Court, Blackwood, Lanark ML11 9GF [E-mail: revcam@btinternet.com]	(Mbl) 07852 123956
Martin, James MA BD DD	1946	1987	(Glasgow: High Carntyne)	9 Magnolia Street, Wishaw ML2 7EQ	01698 385825
Melrose, J.H. Loudon MA BD MEd	1955	1996	(Gourock: Old Gourock and Ashton [Assoc])	1 Laverock Avenue, Hamilton ML3 7DD	01698 427958
Moore, Agnes A. (Miss) BD	1987	2014	(Bellshill: West)	10 Carr Quadrant, Mossend, Bellshill ML4 1HZ [E-mail: revamoore2@tiscali.co.uk]	01698 841558
Munton, James G. BA	1969	2002	(Coatbridge: Old Monkland)	2 Moorcroft Drive, Airdrie ML6 8ES [E-mail: jacjim@supanet.com]	01236 754848
Murphy, Jim		2014	Ordained Local Minister	10 Hillview Crescent, Bellshill ML4 1NX [E-mail: JMurphy@churchofscotland.org.uk]	01698 740189
Price, Peter O. CBE QHC BA FPhS	1960	1996	(Blantyre: Old)	22 Old Bothwell Road, Bothwell, Glasgow G71 8AW [E-mail: peteroprice@aol.com]	01698 854032
Rogerson, Stuart D. BSc BD	1980	2001	(Strathaven: West)	17 Westfield Park, Strathaven ML10 6XH [E-mail: srogerson@cnetwork.co.uk]	01357 523321
Ross, Keith W. MA BD	1984	2015	(Congregational Development Officer for the Presbytery of Hamilton)	Easter Bavelaw House, Pentland Hills Regional Park, Balerno EH14 7JS [E-mail: keithwross@outlook.com]	(Mbl) 07855 163449
Salmond, James S. BA BD MTh ThD	1979	2003	(Holytown)	165 Torbothie Road, Shotts ML7 5NE	01698 870598
Spence, Sheila M. (Mrs) MA BD	1979	2010	(Kirk o' Shotts)	6 Drumbowie Crescent, Salsburgh, Shotts ML7 4NP	01698 817582
Stevenson, John LTh	1998	2006	(Cambuslang: St Andrew's)	20 Knowehead Gardens, Uddingston, Glasgow G71 7PY [E-mail: therev20@sky.com]	
Thomson, John M.A. TD JP BD ThM	1978	2014	(Hamilton: Old)	8 Skylands Place, Hamilton ML3 8SB [E-mail: jt@john1949.plus.com]	01698 422511
Waddell, Elizabeth A. (Mrs) BD	1999	2014	(Hamilton: West)	114 Branchalfield, Wishaw ML2 8QD [E-mail: elizabethwaddell@tiscali.co.uk]	01698 382909
Wilson, James H. LTh	1970	1996	(Cleland)	21 Austine Drive, Hamilton ML3 7YE [E-mail: wilsonjh@blueyonder.co.uk]	01698 457042
Wyllie, Hugh R. MA DD FCIBS	1962	2000	(Hamilton: Old)	18 Chantinghall Road, Hamilton ML3 8NP	01698 420002
Zambonini, James LIADip	1997	2015	(Auxiliary Minister)	100 Old Manse Road, Wishaw ML2 0EP	01698 350889

HAMILTON ADDRESSES

Airdrie
Cairnlea — 89 Graham Street
Clarkston — Forrest Street
High — North Bridge Street
Jackson — Glen Road
New Monkland — Glenmavis
St Columba's — Thrashbush Road
The New Wellwynd — Wellwynd

Coatbridge
Blairhill Dundyvan — Blairhill Street
Calder — Calder Street
Middle — Bank Street
New St Andrew's — Church Street
Old Monkland — Woodside Street
Townhead — Crinan Crescent

East Kilbride
Claremont — High Common Road, St Leonard's

Greenhills — Greenhills Centre
Moncreiff — Calderwood Road
Mossneuk — Eden Drive
Old — Montgomery Street
South — Baird Hill, Murray
West — Kittoch Street
Westwood — Belmont Drive, Westwood

Hamilton
Cadzow — Woodside Walk
Gilmour and Whitehill — Glasgow Road, Burnbank
Hillhouse — Abbotsford Road, Whitehill
Old — Clerkwell Road
St John's — Leechlee Road
South — Duke Street
Trinity — Strathaven Road
West — Neilsland Square off Neilsland Road
   Burnbank Road

Motherwell
Crosshill — Windmillhill Street x
   Airbles Street

Dalziel St Andrew's — Merry Street and Muir Street
North — Chesters Crescent
St Margaret's — Shields Road
St Mary's — Avon Street
South — Gavin Street

Uddingston
Burnhead — Laburnum Road
Old — Old Glasgow Road
Viewpark — Old Edinburgh Road

Wishaw
Cambusnethan North — Kirk Road
Old — Kirk Road
Craigneuk and Belhaven — Craigneuk Street
Old — Main Street
St Mark's — Coltness Road
South Wishaw — East Academy Street

(18) DUMBARTON

Meets at Dumbarton, in Riverside Church Halls, on the first Tuesday of February, March, April (if required), May, September, October (if required), November and December, and on the third Tuesday of June at the incoming Moderator's church for the installation of the Moderator.

Clerk: REV. DAVID W. CLARK MA BD   3 Ritchie Avenue, Cardross, Dumbarton G82 5LL   01389 849319
[E-mail: dumbarton@churchofscotland.org.uk]

Alexandria
Elizabeth W. Houston MA BD DipEd   1985   1995   32 Ledrish Avenue, Balloch, Alexandria G83 8JB   01389 751933
[E-mail: WHouston@churchofscotland.org.uk]

Arrochar linked with Luss
Vacant   The Manse, Luss, Alexandria G83 8NZ   01436 860240

Baldernock (H)
Andrew P. Lees BD — 1984 2002 — The Manse, Bardowie, Milngavie, Glasgow G62 6ES [E-mail: ALees@churchofscotland.org.uk] — 01360 620471

Bearsden: Baljaffray (H)
Ian McEwan BSc PhD BD FRSE — 2008 — 5 Fintry Gardens, Bearsden, Glasgow G61 4RJ [E-mail: IMcEwan@churchofscotland.org.uk] — 0141-942 0366

Bearsden: Cross (H)
Graeme R. Wilson MCIBS BD ThM — 2006 2013 — 61 Drymen Road, Bearsden, Glasgow G61 2SU [E-mail: GWilson@churchofscotland.org.uk] — 0141-942 0507

Bearsden: Killermont (H)
Alan J. Hamilton LLB BD PhD — 2003 — 8 Clathic Avenue, Bearsden, Glasgow G61 2HF [E-mail: AHamilton@churchofscotland.org.uk] — 0141-942 0021

Bearsden: New Kilpatrick (H) (0141-942 8827) (E-mail: mail@nkchurch.org.uk)
Roderick G. Hamilton MA BD — 1992 2011 — 51 Manse Road, Bearsden, Glasgow G61 3PN [E-mail: Roddy.Hamilton@churchofscotland.org.uk] — 0141-942 0035

Bearsden: Westerton Fairlie Memorial (H) (0141-942 6960)
Christine M. Goldie LLB BD MTh DMin — 1984 2008 — 3 Canniesburn Road, Bearsden, Glasgow G61 1PW [E-mail: CGoldie@churchofscotland.org.uk] — 0141-942 2672

Bonhill (H) (01389 756516) linked with Renton: Trinity (H)
Barbara O'Donnell BD PGSE — 2007 2016 — Ashbank, 258 Main Street, Alexandria G83 0NU — 01389 752356 / 07889 251912 (Mbl)

Cardross (H) (01389 841322)
Margaret McArthur BD DipMin — 1995 2015 — 16 Bainfield Road, Cardross G82 5JQ [E-mail: MMcArthur@churchofscotland.org.uk] — 01389 849329 / 17799 556367 (Mbl)

Clydebank: Abbotsford linked with Dalmuir: Barclay (0141-941 3988)
Ruth H.B. Morrison MA BD — 2009 2014 — 16 Parkhall Road, Dalmuir, Clydebank G81 3RJ [E-mail: RMorrison@churchofscotland.org.uk] — 0141-941 3317

Clydebank: Faifley
Gregor McIntyre BSc BD — 1991 — Kirklea, Cochno Road, Hardgate, Clydebank G81 6PT [E-mail: Gregor.McIntyre@churchofscotland.org.uk] — 01389 876836

Clydebank: Kilbowie St Andrew's linked with Clydebank: Radnor Park (H)
Margaret J.B. Yule BD   1992
11 Tiree Gardens, Old Kilpatrick, Glasgow G60 5AT   01389 875599
[E-mail: MYule@churchofscotland.org.uk]

Clydebank: Radnor Park See Clydebank: Kilbowie St Andrew's

Clydebank: St Cuthbert's linked with Duntocher (H)
Guardianship of the Presbytery

Craigrownie linked with Garelochhead (01436 810589) linked with Rosneath: St Modan's (H)
Christine M. Murdoch   1999 2015
The Manse, Argyll Road, Kilcreggan, Helensburgh G84 0JW   01436 842274
[E-mail: CMurdoch@churchofscotland.org.uk]   07973 331890 (Mbl)

Margaret A.E. Nutter   2014 2015
Kilmorich, 14 Balloch Road, Balloch, Alexandria G83 8SR   01389 754505
(Ordained Local Minister)
[E-mail: MNutter@churchofscotland.org.uk]

Dalmuir: Barclay See Clydebank: Abbotsford

Dumbarton: Riverside (H) (01389 742551) linked with Dumbarton: West Kirk (H)
C. Ian W. Johnson MA BD   1997 2014
18 Castle Road, Dumbarton G82 1JF   01389 726685
[E-mail: CJohnson@churchofscotland.org.uk]

Dumbarton: St Andrew's (H) linked with Old Kilpatrick Bowling
Vacant
17 Mansewood Drive, Dumbarton G82 3EU   01389 726715
Ishbel A.R. Robertson MA BD   2013 2015
Oakdene, 81 Bonhill Road, Dumbarton G82 2DU   01389 763436
(Ordained Local Minister)
[E-mail: IRobertson@churchofscotland.org.uk]

Dumbarton: West Kirk See Dumbarton: Riverside
Duntocher See Clydebank: St Cuthbert's
Garelochhead See Craigrownie

Helensburgh linked with Rhu and Shandon
David T. Young BA BD MTh   2007
Helensburgh Parish Church, Colquhoun Square, Helensburgh G84 8UP   01436 676880
[E-mail: DYoung@churchofscotland.org.uk]   07508 628133 (Mbl)

Jamestown (H)
Norma Moore MA BD   1995 2004
26 Kessog's Gardens, Balloch, Alexandria G83 8QJ   01389 756447
[E-mail: NMoore@churchofscotland.org.uk]

Kilmaronock Gartocharn
Guardianship of the Presbytery

Luss See Arrochar

Milngavie: Cairns (H) (0141-956 4868)
Andrew Frater BA BD MTh   1987 1994   4 Cairns Drive, Milngavie, Glasgow G62 8AJ   0141-956 1717
[E-mail: AFrater@churchofscotland.org.uk]

Milngavie: St Luke's (0141-956 4226)
Ramsay B. Shields BA BD   1990 1997   70 Hunter Road, Milngavie, Glasgow G62 7BY   0141-577 9171 (Tel)
[E-mail: RShields@churchofscotland.org.uk]   0141-577 9181 (Fax)

Milngavie: St Paul's (H) (0141-956 4405)
Fergus C. Buchanan MA BD MTh   1982 1988   8 Buchanan Street, Milngavie, Glasgow G62 8DD   0141-956 1043
[E-mail: Fergus.Buchanan@churchofscotland.org.uk]

Old Kilpatrick Bowling See Dumbarton: St Andrew's
Renton: Trinity See Bonhill
Rhu and Shandon See Helensburgh
Rosneath: St Modan's See Craigrownie

Booth, Frederick M. LTh	1970	2005	(Helensburgh: St Columba)	Achnashie Coach House, Clynder, Helensburgh G84 0QD [E-mail: boothef@btinternet.com]	01436 831858
Christie, John C. BSc BD MSB CBiol	1990	2014	(Interim Minister)	10 Cumberland Avenue, Helensburgh G84 8QG [E-mail: rev.jcc@btinternet.com]	01436 674078 (Mbl) 07711 336392
Clark, David W. MA BD	1975	2014	(Helensburgh: St Andrew's Kirk with Rhu and Shandon)	3 Ritchie Avenue, Cardross, Dumbarton G82 5LL [E-mail: clarkdw@talktalk.net]	01389 849319
Crombie, William D. MA BD	1947	1987	(Glasgow: Calton New with St Andrew's)	9 Fairview Court, 46 Main Street, Milngavie, Glasgow G62 6BU	0141-956 1898
Dalton, Mark BD DipMin RN	2002		Chaplain: Royal Navy	HM Naval Base Clyde, Faslane, Helensburgh G84 8HL [E-mail: mark.dalton242@mod.uk]	01436 674321 ext. 6216
Donaghy, Leslie G. BD DipMin PGCE FSAScot	1990	2004	(Dumbarton: St Andrew's)	53 Oak Avenue, East Kilbride, Glasgow G75 9ED [E-mail: leslie@donaghy.org.uk]	(Mbl) 07809 484812
Ferguson, Archibald M. MSc PhD CEng FRINA	1989	2004	(Auxiliary Minister)	The Whins, 2 Borrowfield, Station Road, Cardross, Dumbarton G82 5NL [E-mail: drarchieferguson@gmail.com]	01389 841517
Hamilton, David G. MA BD	1971	2004	(Braes of Rannoch with Foss and Rannoch)	79 Finlay Rise, Milngavie, Glasgow G62 6QL [E-mail: davidhamilton40@googlemail.com]	0141-956 4202

Harris, John W.F. MA	1967	2012	(Bearsden: Cross)	68 Mitre Road, Glasgow G14 9LL [E-mail: jwfh@sky.com]	0141-321 1061
Hudson, Eric V. LTh	1971	2007	(Bearsden: Westerton Fairlie Memorial)	2 Murrayfield Drive, Bearsden, Glasgow G61 1JE [E-mail: evhudson@hotmail.co.uk]	0141-942 6110
Kemp, Tina MA	2005		Auxiliary Minister	12 Oaktree Gardens, Dumbarton G82 1EU [E-mail: TKemp@churchofscotland.org.uk]	01389 730477
McCutcheon, John	2014		Ordained Local Minister	Flat 2/6 Parkview, Milton Brae, Milton, Dumbarton G82 2TT [E-mail: JMcCutcheon@churchofscotland.org.uk]	01389 739034
McIntyre, J. Ainslie MA BD	1963	1984	(University of Glasgow)	60 Bonnaughton Road, Bearsden, Glasgow G61 4DB [E-mail: jamcintyre@hotmail.com]	0141-942 5143 (Mbl) 07826 013266
Miller, Ian H. BA BD	1975	2012	(Bonhill)	Derand, Queen Street, Alexandria G83 0AS [E-mail: revianmiller@btinternet.com]	01389 753039
Munro, David P. MA BD STM	1953	1996	(Bearsden: North)	14 Birch Road, Killearn, Glasgow G63 9SQ [E-mail: david.munro1929@btinternet.com]	01360 550098
Ramage, Alastair E. MA BA ADB CertEd	1996		Auxiliary Minister	16 Claremont Gardens, Milngavie, Glasgow G62 6PG [E-mail: sueandalastairramage@btinternet.com]	0141-956 2897
Steven, Harold A.M. MStJ LTh FSA Scot	1970	2001	(Baldernock)	9 Cairnhill Road, Bearsden, Glasgow G61 1AT [E-mail: harold.allison.steven@gmail.com]	0141-942 1598
Stewart, Charles E. BSc BD MTh PhD	1976	2000	(Chaplain of the Fleet)	105 Sinclair Street, Helensburgh G84 9HY [E-mail: c.e.stewart@btinternet.com]	01436 678113
Wright, Malcolm LTh	1970	2003	(Craigrownie with Rosneath: St Modan's)	30 Clairinsh, Drumkinnon Gate, Balloch, Alexandria G83 8SE [E-mail: malcolmcatherine@msn.com]	01389 720338

DUMBARTON ADDRESSES

Bearsden		**Faifley**	Faifley Road	**Helensburgh**	Colquhoun Square
Baljaffray	Grampian Way	Kilbowie St Andrew's	Kilbowie Road		
Cross	Drymen Road	Radnor Park	Radnor Street	**Milngavie**	
Killermont	Rannoch Drive	St Cuthbert's	Linnvale	Cairns	Buchanan Street
New Kilpatrick	Manse Road	**Dumbarton**		St Luke's	Kirk Street
Westerton	Crarae Avenue	Riverside	High Street	St Paul's	Strathblane Road
		St Andrew's	Aitkenbar Circle		
Clydebank		West Kirk	West Bridgend		
Abbotsford	Town Centre				

(19) ARGYLL

Meets in the Village Hall, Tarbert, Loch Fyne, Argyll on the first Tuesday or Wednesday of March, June, September and December. For details, contact the Presbytery Clerk.

| Clerk: | DR CHRISTOPHER T. BRETT MA PhD | Minahey Cottage, Kames, Tighnabruaich PA21 2AD
[E-mail: argyll@churchofscotland.org.uk] | 01700 811142 |
| Treasurer: | MRS PAMELA A. GIBSON | Allt Ban, Portsonachan, Dalmally PA33 1BJ
[E-mail: justpam1@tesco.net] | 01866 833344 |

Appin linked with Lismore

Iain C. Barclay MBE TD MA BD MTh MPhil PhD FRSA	1976	2015	The Manse, Appin PA38 4DD [E-mail: ICBarclay@churchofscotland.org.uk]	01631 730143 01631 760077

Ardchattan (H)

| Jeffrey A. McCormick BD | 1984 | | Ardchattan Manse, North Connel, Oban PA37 1RG
[E-mail: JMcCormick@churchofscotland.org.uk] | 01631 710364 |

Ardrishaig (H) linked with South Knapdale

| David Carruthers BD | 1998 | | The Manse, Park Road, Ardrishaig, Lochgilphead PA30 8HE
[E-mail: DCarruthers@churchofscotland.org.uk] | 01546 603269 |

Barra (GD) linked with South Uist (GD)

| Lindsay Schluter ThE CertMin PhD | 1995 | 2016 | Cuithir, Castlebay, Isle of Barra HS9 5XU
[E-mail: LSchluter@churchofscotland.org.uk] | 01871 810429 |

Campbeltown: Highland (H)

| Vacant | | | Highland Church Manse, Kirk Street, Campbeltown PA28 6BN | 01586 551146 |

Campbeltown: Lorne and Lowland (H)

| Philip D. Wallace BSc BTh DTS | 1998 | 2004 | Lorne and Lowland Manse, Castlehill, Campbeltown PA28 6AN
[E-mail: PWallace@churchofscotland.org.uk] | 01586 552468 |

Coll linked with Connel

| George G. Cringles BD | 1981 | 2002 | St Oran's Manse, Connel, Oban PA37 1PJ
[E-mail: GCringles@churchofscotland.org.uk] | (Connel) 01631 710242
(Coll) 01879 230366 |

Colonsay and Oronsay (Website: www.islandchurches.org.uk)
Guardianship of the Presbytery

Connel See Coll

Craignish linked with Kilbrandon and Kilchattan linked with Kilninver and Kilmelford (Netherlorn)
Kenneth R. Ross BA BD PhD   1982   2010   The Manse, Kilmelford, Oban PA34 4XA   01852 200565
[E-mail: KRoss@churchofscotland.org.uk]

Cumlodden, Lochfyneside and Lochgair linked with Glenaray and Inveraray (West Lochfyneside)
Roderick D.M. Campbell OStJ TD BD   1975   2015   The Manse, Inveraray PA32 8XT   01499 302060
DMin FSAScot   [E-mail: Roderick.Campbell@churchofscotland.org.uk]

Dunoon: St John's linked with Kirn (H) linked with Sandbank (H) (Central Cowal)
Vacant   The Manse, 13 Dhailling Park, Hunter Street, Kirn, Dunoon PA23 8FB   01369 702256

Glenda M. Wilson (Mrs) DCS   5 Allan Terrace, Sandbank, Dunoon PA23 8PR   01369 302295
[E-mail: Glenda.Wilson@churchofscotland.org.uk]   07469 186495 (Mbl)

Dunoon: The High Kirk (H) linked with Innellan (H) linked with Toward (H) (South-East Cowal)
Aileen M. Robson (Miss) BD   2003   2011   7A Mathieson Lane, Innellan, Dunoon PA23 7SH   01369 830276
[E-mail: ARobson@churchofscotland.org.uk]

Ruth I. Griffiths (Mrs)   2004   Kirkwood, Mathieson Lane, Innellan, Dunoon PA23 7TA   01369 830145
(Auxiliary Minister)   [E-mail: RGriffiths@churchofscotland.org.uk]

Gigha and Cara (H) (GD) linked with Kilcalmonell linked with Killean and Kilchenzie (H)
Vacant   The Manse, Muasdale, Tarbert, Argyll PA29 6XD   01583 421432

Glassary, Kilmartin and Ford linked with North Knapdale
Clifford R. Acklam BD MTh   1997   2010   The Manse, Kilmichael Glassary, Lochgilphead PA31 8QA   01546 606926
[E-mail: CAcklam@churchofscotland.org.uk]

Glenaray and Inveraray See Cumlodden, Lochfyneside and Lochgair

Glenorchy and Innishael linked with Strathfillan
Vacant   The Manse, Dalmally PA33 1AA   01838 200207

Innellan See Dunoon: The High Kirk

Iona linked with Kilfinichen and Kilvickeon and the Ross of Mull
Vacant — The Manse, Bunessan, Isle of Mull PA67 6DW — 01681 700227

Jura (GD) linked with Kilarrow (H) linked with Kildalton and Oa (GD) (H)
Vacant — The Manse, Bowmore, Isle of Islay PA43 7LH — 01496 810271

Kilarrow See Jura
Kilbrandon and Kilchattan See Craignish
Kilcalmonell See Gigha and Cara

Kilchoman (GD) linked with Kilmeny linked with Portnahaven (GD)
Valerie G.C. Watson MA BD STM   1987   2013 — The Manse, Port Charlotte, Isle of Islay PA48 7TW — 01496 850241
[E-mail: VWatson@churchofscotland.org.uk]

Kilchrenan and Dalavich linked with Muckairn
Robert E. Brookes BD   2009 — Muckairn Manse, Taynuilt PA35 1HW — 01866 822204
[E-mail: RBrookes@churchofscotland.org.uk]

Kildalton and Oa See Jura

Kilfinan linked with Kilmodan and Colintraive linked with Kyles (H) (West Cowal)
David Mitchell BD DipPTheol MSc   1988   2006 — West Cowal Manse, Kames, Tighnabruaich PA21 2AD — 01700 811045
[E-mail: DMitchell@churchofscotland.org.uk]

Kilfinichen and Kilvickeon and the Ross of Mull See Iona
Killean and Kilchenzie See Gigha and Cara
Kilmeny See Kilchoman
Kilmodan and Colintraive See Kilfinan

Kilmore (GD) and Oban (Website: www.obanchurch.com)
Dugald J.R. Cameron BD DipMin MTh   1990   2007 — Kilmore and Oban Manse, Ganavan Road, Oban PA34 5TU — 01631 566253
[E-mail: Dugald.Cameron@churchofscotland.org.uk]
Christine P. Fulcher BEd   2012   2014 — St Blaan's Manse, Southend, Campbeltown PA28 6RQ — 01586 830504
(Ordained Local Minister)
[E-mail: CFulcher@churchofscotland.org.uk]

Kilmun (St Munn's) (H) linked with Strone (H) and Ardentinny
David Mill KJSJ MA BD 1978 2010 The Manse, Blairmore, Dunoon PA23 8TE 01369 840313
[E-mail: DMill@churchofscotland.org.uk]

**Kilninian and Kilmore linked with Salen (H) and Ulva linked with Tobermory (GD) (H)
linked with Torosay (H) and Kinlochspelvie (North Mull)**
John H. Paton BSc BD 1983 2013 The Manse, Gruline Road, Salen, Aros, Isle of Mull PA72 6XF 01680 300001
[E-mail: JPaton@churchofscotland.org.uk]

Kilninver and Kilmelford See Craignish
Kirn See Dunoon: St John's
Kyles See Kilfinan
Lismore See Appin

Lochgilphead
Hilda C. Smith (Miss) MA BD MSc 1992 2005 Parish Church Manse, Manse Brae, Lochgilphead PA31 8QZ 01546 602238
[E-mail: HSmith@churchofscotland.org.uk]

Lochgoilhead (H) and Kilmorich linked with Strachur and Strathlachlan (Upper Cowal)
Robert K. Mackenzie MA BD PhD 1976 1998 The Manse, Strachur, Cairndow PA27 8DG 01369 860246
[E-mail: RKMackenzie@churchofscotland.org.uk]

Muckairn See Kilchrenan and Dalavich
North Knapdale See Glassary, Kilmartin and Ford
Portnahaven See Kilchoman

Rothesay: Trinity (H) (Website: www.rothesaytrinity.org)
Vacant 12 Crichton Road, Rothesay, Isle of Bute PA20 9JR 01700 503010

Saddell and Carradale (H) linked with Southend (H)
Stephen Fulcher BA MA 1993 2012 St Blaan's Manse, Southend, Campbeltown PA28 6RQ 01586 830504
[E-mail: SFulcher@churchofscotland.org.uk]

Salen and Ulva See Kilninian and Kilmore
Sandbank See Dunoon: St John's

Skipness linked with Tarbert, Loch Fyne and Kilberry (H)
Vacant   The Manse, Cambeltown Road, Tarbert, Argyll PA29 6SX   01880 821012

Southend See Saddell and Carradale
South Knapdale See Ardrishaig
South Uist See Barra
Strachur and Strathlachlan See Lochgoilhead and Kilmorich
Strathfillan See Glenorchy and Innishael
Strone and Ardentinny See Kilmun
Tarbert, Loch Fyne and Kilberry See Skipness

The United Church of Bute
John Owain Jones MA BD FSAScot   1981   2011   10 Bishop Terrace, Rothesay, Isle of Bute PA20 9HF   01700 504502
[E-mail: JJones@churchofscotland.org.uk]

Tiree (GD)
Vacant   The Manse, Scarinish, Isle of Tiree PA77 6TN   01879 220377

Tobermory See Kilninian and Kilmore
Torosay and Kinlochspelvie See Kilninian and Kilmore
Toward See Dunoon: The High Kirk

Beautyman, Paul H. MA BD	1993	2009	Youth Adviser	130b John Street, Dunoon PA23 7BN [E-mail: PBeautyman@churchofscotland.org.uk]	(Mbl) 07596 164112
Bell, Douglas W. MA LLB BD	1975	1993	(Alexandria: North)	3 Cairnbaan Lea, Cairnbaan, Lochgilphead PA31 8BA	01546 606815
Bristow, W.H.G. BEd HDipRE DipSpecEd	1951	2002	(Chaplain: Army)	Cnoc Ban, Southend, Campbeltown PA28 6RQ	01586 830667
Crossan, William		2014	Ordained Local Minister	Gowanbank, Kilkerran Road, Campbeltown PA28 6JL	01586 553453
Dunlop, Alistair J. MA	1965	2004	(Saddell and Carradale)	8 Pipers Road, Cairnbaan, Lochgilphead PA31 8UF [E-mail: dunrevn@btinternet.com]	01546 600316
Forrest, Alan B. MA	1956	1993	(Uphall: South)	126 Shore Road, Innellan, Dunoon PA23 7SX	01369 830424
Gibson, Elizabeth A. (Mrs) MA MLitt BD	2003	2013	Locum Minister	Mo Dhachaidh, Lochdon, Isle of Mull PA64 6AP [E-mail: egibson@churchofscotland.org.uk]	01680 812541
Gibson, Frank S. BL BD STM DSWA DD	1963	1995	(Kilarrow with Kilmeny)	1/7 Joppa Station Place, Edinburgh EH15 2QU [E-mail: scimwest@hotmail.com]	
Goss, Alister J. BD DMin	1975	2009	(Industrial Chaplain)	24 Albert Place, Ardnadam, Sandbank, Dunoon PA23 8QF	01369 704495
Gray, William LTh	1971	2006	(Kilberry with Tarbert)	Lochnagar, Longsdale Road, Oban PA34 5DZ [E-mail: gray98@hotmail.com]	01631 567471

Name	Dates	Charge	Address	Phone
Henderson, Grahame McL. BD	1974 2008	(Kirn)	6 Gerhallow, Bullwood Road, Dunoon PA23 7QB [E-mail: ghende5884@aol.com]	01369 702433
Hood, Catriona A.	2006	Auxiliary Minister	Rose Cottage, Whitehouse, Tarbert PA29 6EP [E-mail: CHood@churchofscotland.org.uk]	01880 730366
Hood, H. Stanley C. MA BD	1966 2000	(London: Crown Court)	10 Dalriada Place, Kilmichael Glassary, Lochgilphead PA31 8QA	01546 606168
Lamont, Archibald MA	1952 1994	(Kilcalmonell with Skipness)	22 Bonnyton Drive, Eaglesham, Glasgow G76 0LU	
Lind, Michael J. LLB BD	1984 2012	(Campbeltown: Highland)	Maybank, Station Road, Conon Bridge, Dingwall IV7 8BJ [E-mail: mijylind@btinternet.com]	
Macfarlane, James PhD	1991 2011	(Lochgoilhead and Kilmorich)	'Lindores', 11 Bullwood Road, Dunoon PA23 7QJ [E-mail: mac.farlane@btinternet.com]	01369 710626
McIvor, Anne (Miss) SRD BD	1996 2013	(Gigha and Cara)	20 Albyn Avenue, Campbeltown PA28 6LY [E-mail: annemcivor@btinternet.com]	(Mbl) 07901 964825
MacLeod, Roderick MA BD PhD(Edin) PhD(Open)	1966 2011	(Cumlodden, Lochfyneside and Lochgair)	Creag-nam-Barnach, Furnace, Inveraray PA32 8XU [E-mail: mail@revroddy.co.uk]	01499 500629
Marshall, Freda (Mrs) BD FCII	1993 2005	(Colonsay and Oronsay with Kilbrandon and Kilchattan)	Allt Mhaluidh, Glenview, Dalmally PA33 1BE [E-mail: mail@freda.org.uk]	01838 200693
Middleton, Jeremy R.H. LLB BD	1981 2015	(Edinburgh: Davidson's Mains)	Innean Mor, Southend, Campbeltown PA28 6RF [E-mail: jmiddleton@churchofscotland.org]	01586 830439
Millar, Margaret R.M. (Miss) BTh	1977 2008	(Kilchrenan and Dalavich with Muckairn)	Fearnoch Cottage, Fearnoch, Taynuilt PA35 1JB [E-mail: macoje@aol.com]	01866 822416
Morrison, Angus W. MA BD	1959 1999	(Kildalton and Oa)	1 Livingstone Way, Port Ellen, Isle of Islay PA42 7EP	01496 300043
Park, Peter B. BD MCIBS	1997 2014	(Fraserburgh: Old)	Hillview, 24 McKelvie Road, Oban PA34 4GB [E-mail: peterpark9@btinternet.com]	01631 565849
Ritchie, Walter M.	1973 1999	(Uphall: South)	Hazel Cottage, Barr Mor View, Kilmartin, Lochgilphead PA31 8UN	01546 510343
Scott, Randolph MA BD	1991 2013	(Jersey: St Columba's)	18 Lochan Avenue, Kirn, Dunoon PA23 8HT [E-mail: rev.rs@hotmail.com]	01369 703175
Shedden, John CBE BD DipPSS	1971 2008	(Fuengirola)	Orchy Cottage, Dalmally PA33 1AX [E-mail: rev.johnshedden@gmx.com]	01838 200535
Stewart, Joseph LTh	1979 2011	(Dunoon: St John's with Sandbank)	7 Glenmorag Avenue, Dunoon PA23 7LG	01369 703438
Taylor, Alan T. BD	1980 2005	(Isle of Mull Parishes)	Erray Road, Tobermory, Isle of Mull PA75 6PS	01688 302496
Wilkinson, W. Brian MA BD	1968 2007	(Glenaray and Inveraray)	3 Achlonan, Taynuilt PA35 1JJ [E-mail: williambrian35@btinternet.com]	01866 822036

ARGYLL Communion Sundays

Ardrishaig	4th Apr, 1st Nov	Kilcalmonell	1st Mar, Jun, Nov
Barra	2nd Mar, June, Sep, Easter, Advent	Kilchoman	1st Feb, Jun, Oct
Campbeltown		Kildalton and Oa	1st May, Nov
Highland	1st May, Nov	Kilfinan	1st Apr, Sep
Lorne and Lowland	1st May, Nov	Killean and Kilchenzie	1st Apr, Jul, Oct, Dec
Craignish	1st Jun, Nov	Kilmeny	1st Mar, Jun, Sep, Dec
Cumlodden, Lochfyneside and Lochgair	1st May, 3rd Nov	Kilmodan and Colintraive	2nd May, Nov
Dunoon		Kilmun	Passion Sun., 2nd Jul, 3rd Nov
St John's	1st Jul, 3rd Nov	Kilninver and Kilmelford	1st Mar, Jun, Sep, Dec
The High Kirk	1st Jul, 2nd Dec, Easter		
Gigha and Cara	Last Apr, Oct		
Glassary, Kilmartin and Ford	1st Mar, Jul, Oct		
Glenaray and Inveraray	2nd May, 3rd Nov		
Innellan	1st Apr, Sep		
Inverlussa and Bellanoch	Last Jun, Nov		
Jura	Last Feb, Jun, Oct		
Kilarrow	2nd Jun, Oct		

Kim   1st May, Nov
Kyles   Last Apr, Oct
Lochgair   2nd Oct (Gaelic)
Lochgilphead   1st Apr, Nov
Lochgoilhead and
   Kilmorich   2nd Mar, Jun, Sep, Nov
North Knapdale   1st Aug, Easter
                                 3rd Oct, 2nd May
Portnahaven   3rd Jul

Rothesay: Trinity   1st Feb, Jun, Nov
Saddell and Carradale   2nd May, 1st Nov
Sandbank   1st Jan, May, Nov
Skipness   2nd May, Nov
Southend   1st Jun, Dec
South Knapdale   4th Apr, 1st Nov
South Uist
   Howmore   1st Jun

Daliburgh   1st Sep
Strachur and Strathlachlan   1st Mar, Jun, Nov
Strone and Ardentinny   Last Feb, Jun, Oct
Tarbert and Kilberry   1st May, Oct
Tayvallich   2nd May, Nov
The United Church of Bute   1st Feb, Jun, Nov
Toward   Last Feb, May, Aug, Nov

(22) FALKIRK

Meets at Falkirk Trinity Parish Church on the first Tuesday of September, December, March and May, on the fourth Tuesday of October and January and on the third Tuesday of June.

Clerk:	To be appointed		[E-mail: falkirk@churchofscotland.org.uk]	
			114 High Station Road, Falkirk FK1 5LN	
Depute Clerk:	REV. ANDREW SARLE BSc BD		[E-mail: depclerk@falkirkpresbytery.org]	01324 621648
Treasurer:	MR ARTHUR PRIESTLY		32 Broomhill Avenue, Larbert FK5 3EH	01324 557142
			[E-mail: treasurer@falkirkpresbytery.org]	

Airth (H)

James F. Todd BD CPS	1984	2012	The Manse, Airth, Falkirk FK2 8LS	01324 831120
			[E-mail: JTodd@churchofscotland.org.uk]	

Blackbraes and Shieldhill linked with Muiravonside

Vacant	81 Stevenson Avenue, Polmont, Falkirk FK2 0GU 01324 717757

Bo'ness: Old (H)

Vacant	10 Dundas Street, Bo'ness EH51 0DG 01506 204585

Bo'ness: St Andrew's (Website: www.standonline.org.uk) (01506 825803)

Vacant	St Andrew's Manse, 11 Erngath Road, Bo'ness EH51 9DP 01506 822195

Bonnybridge: St Helen's (H) (Website: www.bbshnc.com)
George MacDonald BTh	2004	2009	The Manse, 32 Reilly Gardens, High Bonnybridge FK4 2BB [E-mail: GMacDonald@churchofscotland.org.uk]	01324 874807

Bothkennar and Carronshore
Andrew J. Moore BSc BD	2007		11 Hunter Place, Greenmount Park, Carronshore, Falkirk FK2 8QS [E-mail: AMoore@churchofscotland.org.uk]	01324 570525

Brightons (H)
Murdo M. Campbell BD DipMin	1997	2007	The Manse, Maddiston Road, Brightons, Falkirk FK2 0JP [E-mail: MCampbell@churchofscotland.org.uk]	01324 712062

Carriden (H)
Malcolm Lyon BD	2007	2014	The Spires, Foredale Terrace, Carriden, Bo'ness EH51 9LW [E-mail: MLyon@churchofscotland.org.uk]	01506 822141

Cumbernauld: Abronhill (H)
Joyce A. Keyes (Mrs) BD	1996	2003	26 Ash Road, Cumbernauld, Glasgow G67 3ED [E-mail: JKeyes@churchofscotland.org.uk]	01236 723833

Cumbernauld: Condorrat (H)
Grace I.M. Saunders BSc BTh	2007	2011	11 Rosehill Drive, Cumbernauld, Glasgow G67 4EQ [E-mail: GSaunders@churchofscotland.org.uk]	01236 452090
Marion Perry (Mrs) (Auxiliary Minister)	2009	2013	17a Tarbolton Road, Cumbernauld, Glasgow G67 2AJ [E-mail: MPerry@churchofscotland.org.uk]	01236 898519 / 07563 180662 (Mbl)

Cumbernauld: Kildrum (H)
Vacant				
David Nicholson DCS			64 Southfield Road, Balloch, Cumbernauld, Glasgow G68 9DZ / 2D Doonside, Kildrum, Cumbernauld, Glasgow G67 2HX [E-mail: DNicholson@churchofscotland.org.uk]	01236 723204 / 01236 732260

Cumbernauld: Old (H) (Website: www.cumbernauldold.org.uk)
Vacant				
Valerie S. Cuthbertson (Miss) DCS	1999		The Manse, 23 Baronhill, Cumbernauld, Glasgow G67 2SD / 105 Bellshill Road, Motherwell ML1 3SJ [E-mail: VCuthbertson@churchofscotland.org.uk]	01236 721912 / 01698 259001

Cumbernauld: St Mungo's
Vacant			18 Fergusson Road, Cumbernauld, Glasgow G67 1LS	01236 721513

Denny: Old linked with Haggs
Vacant
Alexena (Sandra) Mathers   2015
(Ordained Local Minister)
31 Duke Street, Denny FK6 6NR   01324 824508
10 Ercall Road, Brightons, Falkirk FK2 0RS   01324 872253
[E-mail: SMathers@churchofscotland.org.uk]

Denny: Westpark (H) (Website: www.westparkchurch.org.uk)
Vacant
13 Baxter Crescent, Denny FK6 5EZ   01324 876224

Dunipace (H)
Jean W. Gallacher (Miss)   1989
BD CMin CTheol DMin
The Manse, 239 Stirling Street, Dunipace, Denny FK6 6QJ   01324 824540
[E-mail: JGallacher@churchofscotland.org.uk]

Falkirk: Bainsford
Vacant
Andrew Sarle BSc BD   2013
(Ordained Local Minister)
1 Valleyview Place, Newcarron Village, Falkirk FK2 7JB
114 High Station Road, Falkirk FK1 5LN   01324 621648
[E-mail: ASarle@churchofscotland.org.uk]

Falkirk: Camelon (Church office: 01324 870011)
Stuart W. Sharp MTheol DipPA   2001
30 Cotland Drive, Falkirk FK2 7GE   01324 623631
[E-mail: SSharp@churchofscotland.org.uk]
Amanda MacQuarrie MA PGCE MTh   2014
(Associate Minister)
5 Bethesda Grove, Maddiston, Falkirk FK2 0FR   01324 720514
[E-mail: AMacQuarrie@churchofscotland.org.uk]

Falkirk: Grahamston United (H)
Ian Wilkie BD PGCE   2001   2007
16 Cromwell Road, Falkirk FK1 1SF   01324 624461 / 07877 803280 (Mbl)
[E-mail: IWilkie@churchofscotland.org.uk]
Grahamston United is a Local Ecumenical Project shared with the Methodist and United Reformed Churches

Falkirk: Laurieston linked with Redding and Westquarter
J. Mary Henderson MA BD DipEd PhD   1990   2009
11 Polmont Road, Laurieston, Falkirk FK2 9QQ   01324 621196
[E-mail: JMary.Henderson@churchofscotland.org.uk]

Falkirk: St Andrew's West (H)
Alastair M. Horne BSc BD   1989   1997
1 Maggiewood's Loan, Falkirk FK1 5SJ   01324 623308
[E-mail: AHorne@churchofscotland.org.uk]

Falkirk: St James'
Vacant

Falkirk: Trinity (H)

Robert S.T. Allan LLB DipLP BD	1991	2003	9 Major's Loan, Falkirk FK1 5QF	01324 625124
			[E-mail: RAllan@churchofscotland.org.uk]	
Kathryn Brown (Mrs)	2014		1 Callendar Park Walk, Callendar Grange, Falkirk FK1 1TA	01324 617352
(Ordained Local Minister)			[E-mail: KBrown@churchofscotland.org.uk]	

Grangemouth: Abbotsgrange

Aftab Gohar MA MDiv PgDip	1995	2010	8 Naismith Court, Grangemouth FK3 9BQ	01324 482109
			[E-mail: AGohar@churchofscotland.org.uk]	07528 143784 (Mbl)

Grangemouth: Kirk of the Holy Rood

David J. Smith BD DipMin	1992	2003	The Manse, Bowhouse Road, Grangemouth FK3 0EX	01324 471595
			[E-mail: David.Smith@churchofscotland.org.uk]	

Grangemouth: Zetland (H)

Alison A. Meikle (Mrs) BD	1999	2015	Ronaldshay Crescent, Grangemouth FK3 9JH	01324 336729
			[E-mail: AMeikle@churchofscotland.org.uk]	

Haggs (H) See Denny: Old

Larbert: East

Melville D. Crosthwaite BD DipEd DipMin	1984	1995	1 Cortachy Avenue, Carron, Falkirk FK2 8DH	01324 562402
			[E-mail: MCrosthwaite@churchofscotland.org.uk]	

Larbert: Old (H)
Vacant

The Manse, 38 South Broomage Avenue, Larbert FK5 3ED   01324 872760

Larbert: West (H)
Vacant

11 Carronvale Road, Larbert FK5 3LZ   01324 562878

Muiravonside See Blackbraes and Shieldhill

Polmont: Old
Deborah L. van Welie (Ms) MTheol   2015
3 Orchard Grove, Polmont, Falkirk FK2 0XE   01324 713427
[E-mail: DLVanWelie@churchofscotland.org.uk]

Redding and Westquarter   See Falkirk: Laurieston

Sanctuary First
Albert O. Bogle BD MTh   1981 2016
49a Kenilworth Road, Bridge of Allan FK9 4RS   07715 374557 (Mbl)
[E-mail: albertbogle@mac.com]

Slamannan
Vacant
Monica MacDonald (Mrs)   2014
(Ordained Local Minister)
32 Reilly Gardens, High Bonnybridge, Bonnybridge FK4 2BB   01324 874807
[E-mail: Monica.MacDonald@churchofscotland.org.uk]

Stenhouse and Carron (H)
William Thomson BD   2001 2007
The Manse, 21 Tipperary Place, Stenhousemuir, Larbert FK5 4SX   01324 416628
[E-mail: WThomson@churchofscotland.org.uk]

Black, Ian W. MA BD   1976 2013   (Grangemouth: Zetland)
Flat 1R, 2 Carrickvale Court, Carrickstone, Cumbernauld,
   Glasgow G68 0LA   01236 453370
[E-mail: iwblack@hotmail.com]

Brown, T. John MA BD   1995 2006   (Tullibody: St Serf's)
1 Callendar Park Walk, Callendar Grange, Falkirk FK1 1TA   01324 617352
[E-mail: johnbrown1cpw@talktalk.net]

Campbell-Jack, W.C. BD MTh PhD   1979 2011   (Glasgow: Possilpark)
35 Castle Avenue, Airth, Falkirk FK2 8GA   01324 832011
[E-mail: c.c-j@homecall.co.uk]

Chalmers, George A. MA BD MLitt   1962 2002   (Catrine with Sorn)
3 Cricket Place, Brightons, Falkirk FK2 0HZ   01324 712030
[E-mail: andychristie747@yahoo.com]
Christie, Helen F. (Mrs) BD   1998 2015   (Haggs)
Hardie, Robert K. MA BD   1968 2005   (Stenhouse and Carron)
33 Palace Street, Berwick-upon-Tweed TD15 1HN   01324 832094
Job, Anne J. BSc BD   1993 2010   (Kirkcaldy: Viewforth with Thornton)
5 Carse View, Airth, Falkirk FK2 8NY
[E-mail: aj@ajjob.co.uk]

Kesting, Sheilagh M. BA BD DD   1980 1993   (Ecumenical Officer, Church of Scotland)
12 Glenview Drive, Falkirk FK1 5JU   01324 671489
[E-mail: smkesting@btinternet.com]

Macaulay, Glendon BD   1999 2012   (Falkirk: Erskine)
43 Gavin's Lee, Tranent EH33 2AP   01875 615851
[E-mail: gd.macaulay@btinternet.com]

McCallum, John   1962 1998   (Falkirk: Irving Camelon)
11 Burnbrae Gardens, Falkirk FK1 5SB   01324 619766
McDonald, William G. MA BD   1959 1975   (Falkirk: Grahamston United)
14 Priestden Park, St Andrews KY16 8DL   01334 479770

Name	Dates	Position	Address	Phone
McDowall, Ronald J. BD	1980 2001	(Falkirk: Laurieston with Redding and Westquarter)	'Kailas', Windsor Road, Falkirk FK1 5EJ	01324 871947
MacKinnon, Ronald M. DCS		(Deacon)	12 Mossywood Court, McGregor Avenue, Airdrie ML6 7DY [E-mail: ronnie@ronniemac.plus.com]	01236 763389
Mathers, Daniel L. BD	1982 2001	(Grangemouth: Charing Cross and West)	10 Ercall Road, Brightons, Falkirk FK2 0RS	(Mbl) 07594 427960 / 01324 872253
Maxton, Ronald M. MA	1955 1995	(Dollar: Associate)	5 Rulley View, Denny FK6 6QQ	01324 825441
Miller, Elsie M. (Miss) DCS	1986 1998	(Deacon)	30 Swinton Avenue, Rowansbank, Baillieston, Glasgow G69 6JR	0141-771 0857
Ross, Evan J. LTh		(Cowdenbeath: West with Mossgreen and Crossgates)	5 Arneil Place, Brightons, Falkirk FK2 0NJ	01324 719936
Scott, Donald H. BA BD	1983 2002	Chaplain: HMYOI Polmont	14 Gibsongray Street, Falkirk FK2 0AB [E-mail: donaldhscott@hotmail.com]	01324 722241
Smith, Richard BD	1976 2002	(Denny: Old)	Easter Wayside, 46 Kennedy Way, Airth, Falkirk FK2 8GB [E-mail: richards@uklinux.net]	01324 831386
Wandrum, David C.	1993	Auxiliary Minister	5 Cawder View, Carrickstone Meadows, Cumbernauld, Glasgow G68 0BN [E-mail: DWandrum@churchofscotland.org.uk]	01236 723288
Wilson, Phyllis M. (Mrs) DipCom DipRE	1985 2006	(Motherwell: South Dalziel)	'Landemer', 17 Sneddon Place, Airth, Falkirk FK2 8GH [E-mail: thomas.wilson38@btinternet.com]	01324 832257

FALKIRK ADDRESSES

Blackbraes and Shieldhill	Main St x Anderson Cr
Bo'ness: Old	Panbrae Road
St Andrew's	Grahamsdyke Avenue
Carriden	Carriden Brae
Cumbernauld: Abronhill	Larch Road
Condorrat	Main Road
Kildrum	Clouden Road
Old	Baronhill
St Mungo's	St Mungo's Road
Denny: Old	Denny Cross
Westpark	Duke Street
Dunipace	Stirling Street
Falkirk: Bainsford	Hendry Street, Bainsford
Camelon	Dorrator Road
Grahamston United	Bute Street
Laurieston	Main Falkirk Road
St Andrew's West	Newmarket Street
St James'	Thornhill Road x Firs Street
Trinity	Kirk Wynd
Grangemouth: Abbotsgrange	Abbot's Road
Kirk of the Holy Rood	Bowhouse Road
Zetland	Ronaldshay Crescent
Haggs	Glasgow Road
Larbert: East	Kirk Avenue
Old	Denny Road x Stirling Road
West	Main Street
Muiravonside	off Vellore Road
Polmont: Old	Kirk Entry/Bo'ness Road
Redding and Westquarter	Main Street
Slamannan	Manse Place
Stenhouse and Carron	Church Street

(23) STIRLING

Meets at the Moderator's church on the second Thursday of September, and at Bridge of Allan Parish Church on the second Thursday of February, March, April, May, June, October, November and December.

Clerk:	REV. ALAN F. MILLER BA MA BD	7 Windsor Place, Stirling FK8 2HY [E-mail: AMiller@churchofscotland.org.uk]	01786 465166
Depute Clerk:	MR EDWARD MORTON	22 Torry Drive, Alva FK12 5LN [E-mail: edmort@aol.com]	01259 760861 / 07525 005028 (Mbl)
Treasurer:	MR MARTIN DUNSMORE	60 Brookfield Place, Alva FK12 5AT [E-mail: m.dunsmore53@btinternet.com]	01259 762262
Presbytery Office:		St Columba's Church, Park Terrace, Stirling FK8 2NA [E-mail: stirling@churchofscotland.org.uk]	01786 447575

Aberfoyle (H) linked with Port of Menteith (H) (Website: www.aberfoyleportchurches.org.uk)
Terry Ann Taylor BA MTh   2005   2014   The Manse, Lochard Road, Aberfoyle, Stirling FK8 3SZ   01877 382391
[E-mail: TTaylor@churchofscotland.org.uk]

Alloa: Ludgate (Website: www.alloaludgatechurch.org.uk)
Carol Anne Parker (Mrs) BEd BD   2009   2014   28 Alloa Park Drive, Alloa FK10 1QY   01259 212709
[E-mail: CParker@churchofscotland.org.uk]

Alloa: St Mungo's (H) (Website: www.stmungosparish.org.uk)
Sang Y. Cha BD MTh   2011   37A Claremont, Alloa FK10 2DG   01259 213872
[E-mail: SCha@churchofscotland.org.uk]

Alva (Website: www.alvaparishchurch.org.uk)
James N.R. McNeil BSc BD   1990   1997   34 Ochil Road, Alva FK12 5JT   01259 760262
[E-mail: JMcNeil@churchofscotland.org.uk]

Balfron (Website: www.balfronchurch.org.uk) linked with Fintry (H) (Website: www.fintrykirk.btck.org.uk)
Sigrid Marten   1997   2013   7 Station Road, Balfron, Glasgow G63 0SX   01360 440285
[E-mail: SMarten@churchofscotland.org.uk]

Balquhidder linked with Killin and Ardeonaig (H)
Vacant   The Manse, Killin FK21 8TN
June E. Johnston BSc MEd BD   2013   Tarmachan, Main Street, Killin FK21 8TN   01567 820247 / 0775 444 8889 (Mbl)
(Ordained Local Minister)   [E-mail: June.Johnston@churchofscotland.org.uk]

Bannockburn: Allan (H) (Website: www.allanchurch.org.uk)
Vacant
The Manse, Bogend Road, Bannockburn, Stirling FK7 8NP
01786 814692

Bannockburn: Ladywell (H) (Website: www.ladywellchurch.co.uk)
Elizabeth M.D. Robertson (Miss) BD CertMin   1997
57 The Firs, Bannockburn FK7 0EG
[E-mail: ERobertson@churchofscotland.org.uk]
01786 812467

Bridge of Allan (H) (01786 834155) (Website: www.bridgeofallanparishchurch.org.uk)
Rev. Daniel (Dan) J. Harper BSc BD   2016
29 Keir Street, Bridge of Allan, Stirling FK9 4QJ
[E-mail: DHarper@churchofscotland.org.uk]
01786 832753

Buchanan linked with Drymen (H) (Website: www.drymenchurch.org)
Alexander J. MacPherson BD   1986   1997
Buchanan Manse, Drymen, Glasgow G63 0AQ
[E-mail: AMacPherson@churchofscotland.org.uk]
01360 870212

Buchlyvie (H) linked with Gartmore (H)
Elaine H. MacRae (Mrs) BD   1985   2004
112 Jackson Drive, Crowwood Grange, Stepps, Glasgow G33 6GF
[E-mail: EMacRae@churchofscotland.org.uk]
0141-779 5742
07834 269487 (Mbl)

Callander (H) (Tel/Fax: 01877 331409) (Website: www.callanderkirk.org.uk)
Vacant
3 Aveland Park Road, Callander FK17 8FD
01877 330097

Cambusbarron: The Bruce Memorial (H) (Website: www.cambusbarronchurch.org)
Graham P. Nash MA BD   2006   2012
14 Woodside Court, Cambusbarron, Stirling FK7 9PH
[E-mail: GPNash@churchofscotland.org.uk]
01786 442068

Clackmannan (H) (Website: www.clackmannankirk.org.uk)
Scott Raby LTh   1991   2007
The Manse, Port Street, Clackmannan FK10 4JH
[E-mail: SRaby@churchofscotland.org.uk]
01259 211255

Cowie (H) and Plean linked with Fallin (Website: www.cowiepleanandfallinchurch.com)
Vacant
5 Fincastle Place, Cowie, Stirling FK7 7DS
01786 818413

Dollar (H) linked with Glendevon linked with Muckhart (Website: www.dollarparishchurch.org.uk)
Vacant
2 Princes Crescent East, Dollar FK14 7BU
01259 743593

Drymen See Buchanan

Dunblane: Cathedral (H) (Website: www.dunblanecathedral.org.uk)
Colin C. Renwick BMus BD   1989   2014   Cathedral Manse, The Cross, Dunblane FK15 0AQ   01786 822205
[E-mail: CRenwick@churchofscotland.org.uk]

Dunblane: St Blane's (H) linked with Lecropt (H) (Website: www.lecroptkirk.org.uk)
Gary J. Caldwell BSc BD   2007   2015   46 Kellie Wynd, Dunblane FK15 0NR   01786 825324
[E-mail: GCaldwell@churchofscotland.org.uk]

Fallin See Cowie and Plean
Fintry See Balfron

Gargunnock linked with Kilmadock linked with Kincardine-in-Menteith (Website: blairdrummondchurches.org.uk)
Andrew B. Campbell BD DPS MTh   1979   2011   The Manse, Manse Brae, Gargunnock, Stirling FK8 3BQ   01786 860678
[E-mail: ACampbell@churchofscotland.org.uk]   07523 420079 (Mbl)
Lynne Mack (Mrs)   2013   36 Middleton, Menstrie FK11 7HD   01259 761465
(Ordained Local Minister)   [E-mail: LMack@churchofscotland.org.uk]

Gartmore See Buchlyvie
Glendevon See Dollar

Killearn (H) (Website: www.killearnkirk.org.uk)
Lee Messeder BD PgDipMin   2003   2010   2 The Oaks, Killearn, Glasgow G63 9SF   01360 550045
[E-mail: LMesseder@churchofscotland.org.uk]

Killin and Ardeonaig See Balquhidder
Kilmadock See Gargunnock
Kincardine-in-Menteith See Gargunnock

Kippen (H) linked with Norrieston
Ellen Larson Davidson BA MDiv   2007   2015   The Manse, Main Street, Kippen, Stirling FK8 3DN   01786 871249
[E-mail: ELarsonDavidson@churchofscotland.org.uk]

Lecropt See Dunblane: St Blane's

Logie (H) (Website: sms-test.webplus.net)

Name	Years	Address	Phone
R. Stuart M. Fulton BA BD	1991 2006	21 Craiglea, Causewayhead, Stirling FK9 5EE [E-mail: SFulton@churchofscotland.org.uk]	01786 463060
Anne F. Shearer BA DipEd (Auxiliary Minister)	2010	10 Colsnaur, Menstrie FK11 7HG [E-mail: AShearer@churchofscotland.org.uk]	01259 769176

Menstrie (H) (Website: www.menstrieparishchurch.co.uk)

Name	Years	Address	Phone
Maggie R. Roderick BA BD FRSA FTSI	2010 2015	The Manse, 7 Long Row, Menstrie FK11 7BA [E-mail: MRoderick@churchofscotland.org.uk]	01259 761372

Muckhart See Dollar
Norrieston See Kippen
Port of Menteith See Aberfoyle

Sauchie and Coalsnaughton

Name	Years	Address	Phone
Margaret Shuttleworth MA BD	2013	62 Toll Road, Kincardine, Alloa FK10 4QZ [E-mail: MShuttleworth@churchofscotland.org.uk]	01259 731002

Stirling: Allan Park South (R) (H) (Website: www.apschurch.com)

Name	Years	Address	Phone
Alistair Cowper BSc BD	2011	22 Laurelhill Place, Stirling FK8 2JH [E-mail: ACowper@churchofscotland.org.uk]	01786 358872 / 07791 524504 (Mbl)

Stirling: Church of the Holy Rude (H) (Website: http://holyrude.org) linked with Stirling: Viewfield Erskine (H)

Name	Years	Address	Phone
Alan F. Miller BA MA BD	2000 2010	7 Windsor Place, Stirling FK8 2HY [E-mail: AMiller@churchofscotland.org.uk]	01786 465166

Stirling: North (H) (01786 463376) (Website: www.northparishchurch.com)

Name	Years	Address	Phone
Vacant		18 Shirras Brae Road, Stirling FK7 0BA	01786 357428

Stirling: St Columba's (H) (01786 449516) (Website: www.stcolumbasstirling.org.uk)

Name	Years	Address	Phone
Alexander M. Millar MA BD MBA MCMI	1980 2010	St Columba's Manse, 5 Clifford Road, Stirling FK8 2AQ [E-mail: Alexander.Millar@churchofscotland.org.uk]	01786 469979

Stirling: St Mark's (Website: www.stmarksstirling.org.uk)

Name	Years	Address	Phone
Stuart Davidson BD	2008	44a Causewayhead Road, Stirling FK9 5EY [E-mail: SDavidson@churchofscotland.org.uk]	01786 609237
Jean T. Porter (Mrs) BD DCS		3 Cochrie Place, Tullibody FK10 2RR [E-mail: JPorter@churchofscotland.org.uk]	07729 316321 (Mbl)

Stirling: St Ninians Old (H) (Website: www.stminiansold.org.uk)   1993   1998
Gary J. McIntyre BD DipMin
7 Randolph Road, Stirling FK8 2AJ   01786 474421
[E-mail: GMcIntyre@churchofscotland.org.uk]

Stirling: Viewfield Erskine   See Stirling: Church of the Holy Rude

Strathblane (H) (Website: www.strathblanekirk.org.uk)
Vacant
2 Campsie Road, Strathblane, Glasgow G63 9AB   01360 770226

Tillicoultry (H) (Website: www.tillicoultryparishchurch.co.uk)   1987   2013
Alison E.P. Britchfield (Mrs) MA BD
The Manse, 17 Dollar Road, Tillicoultry FK13 6PD   01259 750340
[E-mail: ABritchfield@churchofscotland.org.uk]

Tullibody: St Serf's (H)   1984   2016
Drew Barrie BSc BD
16 Menstrie Road, Tullibody, Alloa FK10 2RG   01259 729804
[E-mail: DBarrie@churchofscotland.org.uk]

Name	Years	Position	Address / E-mail	Telephone
Aitken, E. Douglas MA	1961 1998	(Clackmannan)	1 Dolan Grove, Saline, Dunfermline KY12 9UP [E-mail: douglasaitken14@btinternet.com]	01383 852730
Allen, Valerie L. (Ms) BMus MDiv DMin	1990 2016	Presbytery Chaplain	16 Pine Court, Doune FK16 6JE [E-mail: vl2allen@btinternet.com]	01786 842577 (Mbl) 07801 291538
Barr, John BSc PhD BD	1958 1979	(Kilmacolm: Old)	6 Ferry Court, Stirling FK9 5GJ [E-mail: kilbrandon@btinternet.com]	01786 472286
Begg, Richard MA BD	2008 2016	Army Chaplain	12 Whiteyetts Drive, Sauchie FK10 3GE [E-mail: rbegg711@aol.com]	
Boyd, Ronald M.H. BD DipTheol	1995 2010	Chaplain, Queen Victoria School	6 Victoria Green, Queen Victoria School, Dunblane FK15 0JY [E-mail:ron.boyd@qvs.org.uk]	(Mbl) 07766 004292
Brown, James H. BD	1977 2005	(Helensburgh: Park)	14 Gullipen View, Callander FK17 8HN [E-mail: revjimhbrown@yahoo.co.uk]	01877 339425
Cloggie, June (Mrs)	1997 2006	(Auxiliary Minister)	11A Tulipan Crescent, Callander FK17 8AR [E-mail: david.cloggie@hotmail.co.uk]	01877 331021
Cochrane, James P.N. LTh	1994 2012	(Tillicoultry)	12 Sandpiper Meadow, Alloa Park, Alloa FK10 1QU [E-mail: jamescochrane@pobroadband.co.uk]	01259 218883
Cook, Helen (Mrs) BD	1974 2012	Hospital Chaplain	60 Pelstream Avenue, Stirling FK7 0BG [E-mail: revhcook@btinternet.com]	01786 464128
Dunnett, Alan L. LLB BD	1994 2016	(Cowie and Plean with Fallin)	9 Tulipan Crescent, Callander FK17 8AR [E-mail: alan.dunnett@sky.com]	01877 339640
Dunnett, Linda BA DCS			9 Tulipan Crescent, Callander FK17 8AR [E-mail: lindadunnett@sky.com]	01877 339640 (Mbl) 07838 041683
Foster-Fulton, Sally BA BD	1999 2016	Head of Christian Aid Scotland	21 Craiglea, Causewayhead, Stirling FK9 5EE [E-mail: sallyfulton01@gmail.com]	01786 463060

Name	Position	Years	Address / E-mail	Telephone
Gaston, A. Ray C. MA BD	(Leuchars: St Athernase)	1969 2002	'Hamewith', 13 Manse Road, Dollar FK14 7AL [E-mail: gaston.arthur@yahoo.co.uk]	01259 743202
Gillespie, Irene C. (Mrs) BD	(Tiree)	1991 2007	39 King O Muirs Drive, Tullibody, Alloa FK10 3AY [E-mail: revicg@btinternet.com]	01259 723937
Gilmour, William M. MA BD	(Lecropt)	1969 2008	14 Pine Court, Doune FK16 6JE	01786 842928
Goodison, Michael J. BSc BD	Chaplain: Army	2013	27 Hunter Crescent, Leuchars KY16 0JP [E-mail: mike.goodison@btinternet.com]	
Goring, Iain M. BSc BD	(Interim Minister)	1976 2015	4 Argyle Grove, Dunblane FK15 9DU [E-mail: imgoring@gmail.com]	01786 821688
Izett, William A.F.	(Law)	1968 2000	1 Duke Street, Clackmannan FK10 4EF [E-mail: william.izett@talktalk.net]	01259 724203
Jack, Alison M. MA BD PhD	Assistant Principal and Lecturer, New College, Edinburgh	1998 2001	5 Murdoch Terrace, Dunblane FK15 9JE [E-mail: alisonmjack809@btinternet.com]	01786 825116
Landels, James BD CertMin	(Bannockburn: Allan)	1990 2015	11 Ardgay Drive, Bonnybridge, Falkirk FK4 2FH [E-mail: revjimlandels@icloud.com]	01324 810685 / 07860 944266 (Mbl)
MacCormick, Moira G. BA LTh	(Buchlyvie with Gartmore)	1986 2003	12 Rankine Wynd, Tullibody, Alloa FK10 2UW [E-mail: mgmaccormick@o2.co.uk]	01259 724619
McIntosh, Hamish N.M. MA	(Fintry)	1949 1987	9 Abbeyfield House, 17 Allan Park, Stirling FK8 2QG	01786 479294
McKenzie, Alan BSc BD	(Bellshill: Macdonald Memorial with Bellshill: Orbiston)	1988 2013	89 Drip Road, Stirling FK8 1RN [E-mail: rev.a.mckenzie@btopenworld.com]	01786 430450
Malloch, Philip R.M. LLB BD	(Killearn)	1970 2009	8 Michael McParland Drive, Torrance, Glasgow G64 4EE [E-mail: pmalloch@mac.com]	01360 620089
Mathew, J. Gordon MA BD	(Buckie: North)	1973 2011	45 Westhaugh Road, Stirling FK9 5GF [E-mail: jg.matthew@btinternet.com]	01786 445951
Millar, Jennifer M. (Mrs) BD DipMin	Teacher: Religious and Moral Education	1986 1995	5 Clifford Road, Stirling FK8 2AQ [E-mail: ajrmillar@blueyonder.co.uk]	01786 469979
Mitchell, Alexander B. BD	(Dunblane: St Blane's)	1981 2014	24 Hebridean Gardens, Crieff PH7 3BP [E-mail: alex.mitchell6@btopenworld.com]	01764 652241
Ogilvie, C. (Mrs)	(Cumbernauld: Old)	1999 2015	Seberham Flat, 1A Bridge Street, Dollar FK14 7DF [E-mail: catriona.ogilvie1@btinternet.com]	01259 742155
Ovens, Samuel B. BD	(Slamannan)	1982 1993	21 Bevan Drive, Alva FK12 5PD	01259 763456
Paterson, John L. MA BD STM	(Linlithgow: St Michael's)	1964 2003	'Kirkmichael', 22 Waterfront Way, Stirling FK9 5GH [E-mail: revianpaterson@hotmail.co.uk]	01786 447165
Picken, Stuart D.B. (Prof.) MA BD PhD	(Ardoch with Blackford)	1966 2014	18C Kilbryde Crescent, Dunblane FK15 9BA [E-mail: picken@eikoku.demon.co.uk]	01786 825947
Pryde, W. Kenneth DA BD	(Foveran)	1994 2012	Corrie, 7 Alloa Road, Woodside, Cambus FK10 2NT [E-mail: wkpryde@hotmail.com]	01259 721562
Rose, Dennis S. LTh	(Arbuthnott, Bervie and Kinneff)	1996 2016	69 Blackthorn Grove, Menstrie FK11 7DX [E-mail: dennis2327@aol.com]	01259 692451
Russell, Kenneth G. BD CCE	Prison Chaplain	1986 2013	Chaplaincy Centre, HM Prison Perth, 3 Edinburgh Road, Perth PH2 7JH [E-mail: kenneth.russell@sps.pnn.gov.uk]	01738 458216
Sangster, Ernest G. MA BD ThM	(Alva)	1958 1997	6 Lawhill Road, Dollar FK14 7BG	01259 742344
Scott, James F.	(Dyce)	1957 1997	5 Gullipen View, Callander FK17 8HN	01877 330565
Scoular, J. Marshall	(Kippen)	1954 1996	6 Buccleuch Court, Dunblane FK15 0AR	01786 825976

Sewell, Paul M.N. MA BD	1970	2010	(Berwick-upon-Tweed: St Andrew's Wallace Green and Lowick)	7 Bohun Court, Stirling FK7 7UT [E-mail: paulmsewell@btinternet.com]	01786 489969
Sherry, George T. LTh	1977	2004	(Menstrie)	4 Woodburn Way, Alva FK12 5LB [E-mail: gandms@btinternet.com]	01259 763779
Sinclair, James H. MA BD DipMin	1966	2004	(Auchencairn and Rerrick with Buittle and Kelton)	16 Delaney Court, Alloa FK10 1RB	01259 729001
Thomson, Raymond BD DipMin	1992	2013	(Slamannan)	8 Rhodders Grove, Alva FK12 5ER	01259 769083
Wilson, Hazel MA BD DMS	1991	2015	(Dundee: Lochee)	2 Boe Court, Springfield Terrace, Dunblane FK15 9LU [E-mail: hmwilson704@gmail.com]	01786 825850

STIRLING ADDRESSES

Allan Park South	Dumbarton Road	North	Springfield Road	St Ninians Old	Kirk Wynd, St Ninians
Holy Rude	St John Street	St Columba's	Park Terrace	Viewfield Erskine	Barnton Street
		St Mark's	Drip Road		

(24) DUNFERMLINE

Meets at Dunfermline in St Andrew's Erskine Church, Robertson Road, on the first Thursday of each month, except January, July and August when there is no meeting, and June when it meets on the last Thursday.

Clerk:	REV. IAIN M. GREENSHIELDS BD DipRS ACMA MSc MTh DD	38 Garvock Hill, Dunfermline KY12 7UU [E-mail: dunfermline@churchofscotland.org.uk]	01383 741495 (Office) 01383 723955 (Home)

Aberdour: St Fillan's (H) (Website: www.stfillans.presbytery.org)

Peter S. Gerbrandy-Baird MA BD MSc FRSA FRGS	2004	St Fillan's Manse, 36 Bellhouse Road, Aberdour, Fife KY3 0TL [E-mail: PGerbrandy-Baird@churchofscotland.org.uk]	01383 861522

Beath and Cowdenbeath: North (H)

David W. Redmayne BSc BD	2001	10 Stuart Place, Cowdenbeath KY4 9BN [E-mail: DRedmayne@churchofscotland.org.uk]	01383 511033

Cairneyhill (H) (01383 882352) linked with Limekilns (H) (01383 873337)

Norman M. Grant BD	1990	The Manse, 10 Church Street, Limekilns, Dunfermline KY11 3HT [E-mail: NGrant@churchofscotland.org.uk]	01383 872341

Carnock and Oakley (H) linked with Saline and Blairingone

| Vacant | | | The Manse, Main Street, Carnock, Dunfermline KY12 9JG | 01383 850327 |

Cowdenbeath: Trinity (H)

| Gavin R. Boswell BTheol | 1993 | 2013 | 2 Glenfield Road, Cowdenbeath KY4 9EL [E-mail: GBoswell@churchofscotland.org.uk] | 01383 510696 |
| John Wyllie (Pastoral Assistant) | | | 51 Seafar Street, Kelty KY4 0JX | 01383 839200 |

Culross and Torryburn (H)

| Vacant | | | The Manse, Culross, Dunfermline KY12 8JD | 01383 880231 |

Dalgety (H) (01383 824092) (E-mail: office@dalgety-church.co.uk) (Website: www.dalgety-church.co.uk)

| Christine Sime (Miss) BSc BD | 1994 | 2012 | 9 St Colme Drive, Dalgety Bay, Dunfermline KY11 9LQ [E-mail: CSime@churchofscotland.org.uk] | 01383 822316 |

Dunfermline: Abbey (H) (Website: www.dunfabbey.freeserve.co.uk)

| MaryAnn R. Rennie (Mrs) BD MTh | 1998 | 2012 | 3 Perdieus Mount, Dunfermline KY12 7XE [E-mail: MARennie@churchofscotland.org.uk] | 01383 727311 |

Dunfermline: East (New Charge Development)

| Andrew A. Morrice MA BD | 1999 | 2010 | 9 Dover Drive, Dunfermline KY11 8HQ [E-mail: AMorrice@churchofscotland.org.uk] | 01383 223144 / 07815 719301 (Mbl) |

Dunfermline: Gillespie Memorial (H) (01383 621253) (E-mail: gillespie.church@btopenworld.com)

| Alan Greig BSc BD (Interim Minister) | 1977 | 2015 | 4 Killin Court, Dunfermline KY12 7XF [E-mail: AGreig@churchofscotland.org.uk] | 01383 723329 |

Dunfermline: North

| Ian G. Thom BSc PhD BD | 1990 | 2007 | 13 Barbour Grove, Dunfermline KY12 9YB [E-mail: IThom@churchofscotland.org.uk] | 01383 733471 |

Dunfermline: St Andrew's Erskine (01383 841660)

| Muriel F. Willoughby (Mrs) MA BD | 2006 | 2013 | 71A Townhill Road, Dunfermline KY12 0BN [E-mail: MWilloughby@churchofscotland.org.uk] | 01383 734657 |

Dunfermline: St Leonard's (01383 620106) (E-mail: office@stleonardsparishchurch.org.uk) (Website: www.stleonardsparishchurch.org.uk)

| Monika R. Redman BA BD | 2003 | 2014 | 12 Torvean Place, Dunfermline KY11 4YY [E-mail: MRedman@churchofscotland.org.uk] | 01383 300092 |

Dunfermline: St Margaret's
Iain M. Greenshields
BD DipRS ACMA MSc MTh DD
1984   2007
38 Garvock Hill, Dunfermline KY12 7UU
[E-mail: IGreenshields@churchofscotland.org.uk]
01383 723955
07427 477575 (Mbl)

Dunfermline: St Ninian's
Elizabeth A. Fisk (Mrs) BD
1996
51 St John's Drive, Dunfermline KY12 7TL
[E-mail: EFisk@churchofscotland.org.uk]
01383 722256

Dunfermline: Townhill and Kingseat (H)
Jean A. Kirkwood BSc PhD BD
2015
7 Lochwood Park, Kingseat, Dunfermline KY12 0UX
[E-mail: JKirkwood@churchofscotland.org.uk]
01383 723691

Inverkeithing linked with North Queensferry (R)
Colin M. Alston BMus BD BN RN
1975   2012
1 Dover Way, Dunfermline KY11 8HR
[E-mail: CAlston@churchofscotland.org.uk]
01383 621050

Kelty (Website: www.keltykirk.org.uk)
Hugh D. Steele LTh DipMin
1994   2013
15 Arlick Road, Kelty KY4 0BH
[E-mail: HSteele@churchofscotland.org.uk]
01383 831362

Limekilns See Cairneyhill

Lochgelly and Benarty: St Serf's
Vacant
82 Main Street, Lochgelly KY5 9AA
01592 780435

North Queensferry See Inverkeithing

Rosyth
Violet C.C. McKay (Mrs) BD
1988   2002
42 Woodside Avenue, Rosyth KY11 2LA
[E-mail: VMcKay@churchofscotland.org.uk]
01383 412776

Morag Crawford (Miss) MSc DCS
118 Wester Drylaw Place, Edinburgh EH4 2TG
[E-mail: MCrawford@churchofscotland.org.uk]
0131-332 2253
07970 982563 (Mbl)

Saline and Blairingone See Carnock and Oakley

Tulliallan and Kincardine
Alexander Shuttleworth MA BD
2004   2013
62 Toll Road, Kincardine, Alloa FK10 4QZ
[E-mail: AShuttleworth@churchofscotland.org.uk]
01259 731002

Almond, David M. BD	1996	2016	(Kirkmahoe)	2 Carlingnose Part, North Queensferry KY11 1EX [E-mail: almonddavid242@gmail.com]	01383 616073
Boyle, Robert P. LTh	1990	2010	(Saline and Blairingone)	43 Dunipace Crescent, Dunfermline KY12 7JE [E-mail: boab.boyle@btinternet.com]	01383 740980
Brown, Peter MA BD FRAScot	1953	1987	(Holm)	24 Inchmickery Avenue, Dalgety Bay, Dunfermline KY11 5NF	01383 822456
Chalmers, John P. BD CPS DD	1979	1995	Principal Clerk	10 Liggars Place, Dunfermline KY12 7XZ	01383 739130
Farquhar, William E. BA BD	1987	2006	(Dunfermline: Townhill and Kingseat)	29 Queens Drive, Middlewich, Cheshire CW10 0DG	01606 835097
Jenkins, Gordon F.C. MA BD PhD	1968	2006	(Dunfermline: North)	20 Lumsden Park, Cupar KY15 5YL [E-mail: jenkinsgordon1@sky.com]	01334 652548
Jessamine, Alistair L. MA BD	1979	2011	(Dunfermline: Abbey)	11 Gallowhill Farm Cottages, Strathaven ML10 6BZ [E-mail: chatty.1@talktalk.net]	01357 520934
Johnston, Thomas N. LTh	1972	2008	(Edinburgh: Priestfield)	71 Main Street, Newmills, Dunfermline KY12 8ST [E-mail: tomjohnston@blueyonder.co.uk]	01383 889240
Kenny, Elizabeth S.S. BD RGN SCM	1989	2010	(Carnock and Oakley)	5 Cobden Court, Crossgates, Cowdenbeath KY4 8AU [E-mail: esskenny@btinternet.com]	(Mbl) 07831 763494
Laidlaw, Victor W.N. BD	1975	2008	(Edinburgh: St Catherine's Argyle)	9 Tern Road, Dunfermline KY11 8GA	01383 620134
Leitch, D. Graham MA BD	1974	2012	(Tyne Valley Parish)	9 St Margaret Wynd, Dunfermline KY12 0UT [E-mail: dgrahamleitch@gmail.com]	01383 249245
McDonald, Tom BD	1994	2015	(Kelso: North and Ednam)	12 Woodmill Grove, Dunfermline KY11 4JR [E-mail: revtomparadise12@gmail.com]	
McLellan, Andrew R.C. CBE MA BD STM DD	1970	2002	(HM Inspector of Prisons)	4 Liggars Place, Dunfermline KY12 7XZ	01383 725959
Paterson, Andrew E. JP	1994		Auxiliary Minister	6 The Willows, Kelty KY4 0FQ [E-mail: APaterson@churchofscotland.org.uk]	01383 830998
Reid, A. Gordon BSc BD	1982	2008	(Dunfermline: Gillespie Memorial)	7 Arkleston Crescent, Paisley PA3 4TG [E-mail: reid501@fsmail.net]	0141-842 1542 (Mbl) 07773 300989
Reid, David MSc LTh FSAScot	1961	1992	(St Monans with Largoward)	North Lethans, Saline, Dunfermline KY12 9TE	01383 733144
Stuart, Anne (Miss) DCS			(Deacon)	1 Murrell Terrace, Aberdour, Burntisland KY3 0XH	01383 860049
Sutherland, Iain A. BSc BD	1996	2014	(Dunfermline: Gillespie Memorial)	64 Beech Crescent, Rosyth KY11 2ZP [E-mail: RevISutherland@aol.com]	(Mbl) 07843 089598
Watt, Robert J. BD	1994	2009	(Dumbarton: Riverside)	101 Birrell Drive, Dunfermline KY11 8FA [E-mail: robertwatt101@gmail.com]	01383 735417 (Mbl) 07753 683717
Whyte, Isabel H. (Mrs) BD	1993		(Chaplain: Queen Margaret Hospital, Dunfermline)	14 Carlingnose Point, North Queensferry, Inverkeithing KY11 1ER [E-mail: iainisabel@whytes28.fsnet.co.uk]	01383 410732

(25) KIRKCALDY

Meets at Kirkcaldy, in the St Bryce Kirk Centre, on the first Tuesday of March, September and December, and on the last Tuesday of June. It meets also on the first Tuesday of November for Holy Communion and a conference at the church of the Moderator.

Clerk:	REV. ROSEMARY FREW (Mrs) MA BD		83 Milton Road, Kirkcaldy KY1 1TP [E-mail: kirkcaldy@churchofscotland.org.uk]	01592 260315
Depute Clerk:	REV. ROBIN J. McALPINE BDS BD MTh		25 Bennochy Avenue, Kirkcaldy KY2 5QE [E-mail: RMcAlpine@churchofscotland.org.uk]	01592 643558

Auchterderran Kinglassie
Vacant

7 Woodend Road, Cardenden, Lochgelly KY5 0NE   01592 720202

Auchtertool linked with Kirkcaldy: Linktown (H) (01592 641080)

Catriona M. Morrison (Mrs) MA BD	1995	2000	16 Raith Crescent, Kirkcaldy KY2 5NN [E-mail: catriona@linktown.org.uk]	01592 265536
Marc Prowe			16 Raith Crescent, Kirkcaldy KY2 5NN [E-mail: marc@linktown.org.uk]	01592 265536

Buckhaven (01592 715577) and Wemyss

Wilma R.C. Cairns (Miss) BD	1999	2004	33 Main Road, East Wemyss, Kirkcaldy KY1 4RE [E-mail: WCairns@churchofscotland.org.uk]	01592 712870
Jacqueline Thomson (Mrs) MTh DCS			16 Aitken Place, Coaltown of Wemyss, Kirkcaldy KY1 4PA [E-mail: Jacqueline.Thomson@churchofscotland.org.uk]	01592 653995 07806 776560 (Mbl)

Burntisland (H)

Alan Sharp BSc BD	1980	2001	21 Ramsay Crescent, Burntisland KY3 9JL [E-mail: ASharp@churchofscotland.org.uk]	01592 874303

Dysart: St Clair (H)
Vacant

1 School Brae, Dysart, Kirkcaldy KY1 2XB   01592 561967

Glenrothes: Christ's Kirk (H)

Scott McCrum BD		2015	12 The Limekilns, Glenrothes KY6 3QJ [E-mail: SMcCrum@churchofscotland.org.uk]	0800 566 8242

Glenrothes: St Columba's (01592 752539) (Rothes Trinity Parish Grouping)

Alan W.D. Kimmitt BSc BD		2013	40 Liberton Drive, Glenrothes KY6 3PB [E-mail: Alan.Kimmitt@churchofscotland.org.uk]	01592 742233

Glenrothes: St Margaret's (H) (01592 328162)
Eileen Miller BD MBACP (Snr. Accred.)   2014   8 Alburne Park, Glenrothes KY7 5RB   01592 752241
DipCouns DipComEd   [E-mail: EMiller@churchofscotland.org.uk]

Glenrothes: St Ninian's (H) (01592 610560) (E-mail: office@stninians.co.uk) (Rothes Trinity Parish Grouping)
Vacant   1 Cawdor Drive, Glenrothes KY6 2HN   01592 611963

Kennoway, Windygates and Balgonie: St Kenneth's (01333 351372) (E-mail: stkennethsparish@gmail.com)
Vacant   2 Fernhill Gardens, Windygates, Leven KY8 5DZ   01333 352329

Kinghorn
James Reid BD   1985   1997   17 Myre Crescent, Kinghorn, Burntisland KY3 9UB   01592 890269
    [E-mail: JReid@churchofscotland.org.uk]

Kirkcaldy: Abbotshall (H) (Website: www.abbotshallchurch.org.uk)
Rosemary Frew (Mrs) MA BD   1988   2005   83 Milton Road, Kirkcaldy KY1 1TP   01592 260315
    [E-mail: RFrew@churchofscotland.org.uk]

Kirkcaldy: Bennochy
Robin J. McAlpine BDS BD MTh   1988   2011   25 Bennochy Avenue, Kirkcaldy KY2 5QE   01592 643518
    [E-mail: RMcAlpine@churchofscotland.org.uk]

Kirkcaldy: Linktown See Auchtertool

Kirkcaldy: Pathhead (H) (Tel/Fax: 01592 204635) (E-mail: pathheadchurch@btinternet.com) (Website: www.pathheadparishchurch.co.uk)
Andrew C. Donald BD DPS   1992   2005   73 Loughborough Road, Kirkcaldy KY1 3DD   01592 652215
    [E-mail: ADonald@churchofscotland.org.uk]

Kirkcaldy: St Bryce Kirk (H) (01592 640016) (E-mail: office@stbrycekirk.org.uk)
J. Kenneth (Ken) Froude MA BD   1979   6 East Fergus Place, Kirkcaldy KY1 1XT   01592 264480
    [E-mail: JFroude@churchofscotland.org.uk]

Kirkcaldy: Templehall (H)
Anthony J.R. Fowler BSc BD   1982   2004   35 Appin Crescent, Kirkcaldy KY2 6EJ   01592 260156
    [E-mail: AFowler@churchofscotland.org.uk]

Kirkcaldy: Torbain
Ian J. Elston BD MTh
1999
91 Sauchenbush Road, Kirkcaldy KY2 5RN
[E-mail: IElston@churchofscotland.org.uk]
01592 263015

Michael Allardyce MA MPhil PGCertTHE FHEA
(Ordained Local Minister)
2014
20 Parbroath Road, Glenrothes KY7 4TH
[E-mail: MAllardice@churchofscotland.org.uk]
01592 772280
07936 203465 (Mbl)

Leslie: Trinity (Rothes Trinity Parish Grouping)
Guardianship of the Presbytery

Leven
Gilbert C. Nisbet CA BD
1993
5 Forman Road, Leven KY8 4HH
[E-mail: GNisbet@churchofscotland.org.uk]
01333 303339

Markinch and Thornton
Carolann Erskine BD
2009   2016
7 Guthrie Crescent, Markinch, Glenrothes KY7 6AY
[E-mail: CErskine@churchofscotland.org.uk]
01592 758264

Methil: Wellesley (H)
Gillian Paterson (Mrs) BD
2010
10 Vettriano Vale, Leven KY8 4GD
[E-mail: GPaterson@churchofscotland.org.uk]
01333 423147

Methilhill and Denbeath
Elisabeth F. Cranfield (Ms) MA BD
1988
9 Chemiss Road, Methilhill, Leven KY8 2BS
[E-mail: ECranfield@churchofscotland.org.uk]
01592 713142

Adams, David G. BD
1991 2011
(Cowdenbeath: Trinity)
13 Fernhill Gardens, Windygates, Leven KY8 5DZ
[E-mail: adams.69@btinternet.com]
01333 351214

Collins, Mitchell BD CPS
1996 2005
(Creich, Flisk and Kilmany with Monimail)
6 Netherby Park, Glenrothes KY6 3PL
[E-mail: collinsmit@aol.com]
01592 742915

Elston, Peter K.
1963 2000
(Dalgety)
6 Cairngorm Crescent, Kirkcaldy KY2 5RF
[E-mail: peterkelston@btinternet.com]
01592 205622

Ferguson, David J.
1966 2001
(Bellie with Speymouth)
4 Russell Gardens, Ladybank, Cupar KY15 7LT
01337 831406

Forrester, Ian L. MA
1964 1996
(Friockheim Kinnell with Inverkeilor and Lunan)

Forsyth, Alexander R. TD BA MTh
1973 2013
(Markinch)
8 Bennochy Avenue, Kirkcaldy KY2 5QE
49 Scaraben Crescent, Formonthills, Glenrothes KY6 3HL
[E-mail: alex@arforsyth.com]
01592 260251
01592 749049
07756 239021 (Mbl)

Galbraith, A. D. Douglas
MA BD BMus MPhil ARSCM PhD
1965 2005
Editor: *The Year Book*
34 Balbirnie Street, Markinch, Glenrothes KY7 6DA
[E-mail: dgalbraith@hotmail.com]
01592 752403

Gatt, David W.
1981 1995
(Thornton)
15 Beech Avenue, Thornton, Kirkcaldy KY1 4AT
01592 774328

Gibson, Ivor MA	1957	1993	(Abercorn with Dalmeny)	15 McInnes Road, Markinch, Glenrothes KY7 6BA	01592 759982
Gisbey, John E. MA BD MSc DipEd	1964	2002	(Thornhill)	Whitemyre House, 28 St Andrews Road, Largoward, Leven KY9 1HZ	01334 840540
Gordon, Ian D. LTh	1972	2001	(Markinch)	2 Somerville Way, Glenrothes KY7 5GE	01592 742487
Houghton, Christine (Mrs) BD	1997	2010	(Whitburn: South)	39 Cedar Crescent, Thornton, Kirkcaldy KY1 4BE [E-mail: c.houghton1@btinternet.com]	01592 772823
McLeod, Alistair G.	1988	2005	(Glenrothes: St Columba's)	13 Greenmantle Way, Glenrothes KY6 3QG [E-mail: alistairmcleod193@gmail.com]	01592 744558
McNaught, Samuel M. MA BD MTh	1968	2002	(Kirkcaldy: St John's)	6 Munro Court, Glenrothes KY7 5GD [E-mail: sjmcnaught@btinternet.com]	01592 742352
Munro, Andrew MA BD PhD	1972	2000	(Glencaple with Lowther)	7 Dunvegan Avenue, Kirkcaldy KY2 5SG [E-mail: am.smm@blueyonder.co.uk]	01592 566129
Nicol, George G. BD DPhil	1982	2013	(Falkland with Freuchie)	48 Fidra Avenue, Burntisland KY3 0AZ [E-mail: ggnicol@totalise.co.uk]	01592 873258
Paterson, Maureen (Mrs) BSc	1992	2010	(Auxiliary Minister)	91 Dalmahoy Crescent, Kirkcaldy KY2 6TA [E-mail: m.e.paterson@blueyonder.co.uk]	01592 262300
Roy, Allistair BD DipSW PgDip	2007	2016	(Glenrothes: St Ninian's)	39 Ravenswood Drive, Glenrothes KY6 2PA [E-mail: minister@revroy.co.uk]	
Templeton, James L. BSc BD	1975	2012	(Innerleven: East)	29 Coldstream Avenue, Leven KY8 5TN [E-mail: jamietempleton@btinternet.com]	01333 427102
Thomson, John D. BD	1985	2005	(Kirkcaldy: Pathhead)	3 Tottenham Court, Hill Street, Dysart, Kirkcaldy KY1 2XY [E-mail: j.thomson10@sky.com]	01592 655313, 07885 414979 (Mbl)
Tomlinson, Bryan L. TD	1969	2003	(Kirkcaldy: Abbotshall)	2 Duddingston Drive, Kirkcaldy KY2 6JP [E-mail: abbkirk@blueyonder.co.uk]	01592 564843
Webster, Elspeth H. (Miss) DCS			(Deacon)	82 Broomhill Avenue, Burntisland KY3 0BP	01592 873616
Wilson, Tilly (Miss) MTh	1990	2012	(Dysart)	6 Citron Glebe, Kirkcaldy KY1 2NF [E-mail: tillywilson@blueyonder.co.uk]	01592 263141
Wright Lynda BEd DCS			Community Chaplaincy Listening (Scotland): National Coordinator	71a Broomhill Avenue, Burntisland KY3 0BP	07835 303395

KIRKCALDY ADDRESSES

Abbotshall	Abbotshall Road	Templehall	Beauly Place
Bennochy	Elgin Street	Torbain	Lindores Drive
Linktown	Nicol Street x High Street	Viewforth	Viewforth Street x Viewforth Terrace
Pathhead	Harriet Street x Church Street		
St Bryce Kirk	St Brycedale Avenue x Kirk Wynd		

(26) ST ANDREWS

Meets at Cupar, in St John's Church Hall, on the first Wednesday of February, May, September, October, November and December, and on the last Wednesday of June.

Clerk: REV. NIGEL J. ROBB FCP MA BD ThM MTh   Presbytery Office, The Basement, 1 Howard Place, St Andrews KY16 9HL   **01334 461300**
[E-mail: standrews@churchofscotland.org.uk]

Depute Clerk: MRS CATHERINE WILSON   5 Taeping Close, Cellardyke, Anstruther KY10 3YL   **01333 310936**
[E-mail: catherine.wilson15@btinternet.com]

Abdie and Dunbog (H) linked with Newburgh (H)
Vacant
2 Guthrie Court, Cupar Road, Newburgh, Cupar KY14 6HA   01337 842228

Anstruther linked with Cellardyke (H) linked with Kilrenny   1997   2009
Arthur A. Christie BD
16 Taeping Close, Cellardyke, Anstruther KY10 3YL   01333 313917
[E-mail: AChristie@churchofscotland.org.uk]

Auchtermuchty (H) linked with Edenshead and Strathmiglo
Vacant
The Manse, Kirk Wynd, Strathmiglo, Cupar KY14 7QS   01337 860256

Balmerino (H) linked with Wormit (H)   1982   2004
James Connolly
DipTh CertMin MA(Theol) DMin
5 Westwater Place, Newport-on-Tay DD6 8NS   01382 542626
[E-mail: JConnolly@churchofscotland.org.uk]

Boarhills and Dunino linked with St Andrews: Holy Trinity   1985   2016
R. Russell McLarty MA BD
(Interim Minister)
13 Lade Braes, St Andrews KY16 9ET   07751 755986 (Mbl)
[E-mail: RussellMcLarty@churchofscotland.org.uk]

Cameron linked with St Andrews: St Leonard's (H) (01334 478702) (E-mail: stlencam@btconnect.com)
Vacant
1 Cairnhill Gardens, St Andrews KY16 8QY   01334 472793

Carnbee linked with Pittenweem   2007
Margaret E.S. Rose BD
29 Milton Road, Pittenweem, Anstruther KY10 2LN   01333 312838
[E-mail: MRose@churchofscotland.org.uk]

Cellardyke See Anstruther

Ceres, Kemback and Springfield James W. Campbell BD	1995	2010	The Manse, St Andrews Road, Ceres, Cupar KY15 5NQ [E-mail: James.Campbell@churchofscotland.org.uk]	01334 829350
Crail linked with Kingsbarns (H) Ann Allison BSc PhD BD	2000	2011	The Manse, St Andrews Road, Crail, Anstruther KY10 3UH [E-mail: AAllison@churchofscotland.org.uk]	01333 451986
Creich, Flisk and Kilmany Vacant				
Cupar: Old (H) and St Michael of Tarvit linked with Monimail Jeffrey A. Martin BA MDiv	1991	2016	76 Hogarth Drive, Cupar KY15 5YU [E-mail: JMartin@churchofscotland.org.uk]	01334 656181
Cupar: St John's and Dairsie United Jan J. Steyn (Mr)	2011		The Manse, 23 Hogarth Drive, Cupar KY15 5YH [E-mail: JSteyn@churchofscotland.org.uk]	01334 650751
Edenshead and Strathmiglo See Auchtermuchty				
Elie (H) Kilconquhar and Colinsburgh (H) Vacant				
Falkland linked with Freuchie (H) Vacant			1 Newton Road, Falkland, Cupar KY15 7AQ	01337 858557
Freuchie See Falkland				
Howe of Fife William F. Hunter MA BD	1986	2011	The Manse, 83 Church Street, Ladybank, Cupar KY15 7ND [E-mail: WHunter@churchofscotland.org.uk]	01337 832717
Kilrenny See Anstruther **Kingsbarns** See Crail				

Largo and Newburn (H) linked with Largo: St David's
Vacant

Largo: St David's See Largo and Newburn

Largoward (H) linked with St Monans (H)
Peter W. Mills CB BD DD CPS 1984 2013 The Manse, St Monans, Anstruther KY10 2DD 01333 730135
[E-mail: PMills@churchofscotland.org.uk]

Leuchars: St Athernase
John C. Duncan BD MPhil 1979 2016 7 David Wilson Park, Balmullo, St Andrews KY16 0NP 01334 870038
[E-mail: JDuncan@churchofscotland.org.uk]

Monimail See Cupar: Old
Newburgh See Abdie and Dunbog

Newport-on-Tay (H)
Vacant

Pittenweem See Carnbee

St Andrews: Holy Trinity See Boarhills and Dunino

St Andrews: Hope Park and Martyrs (H) linked with Strathkinness
Allan McCafferty BSc BD 1993 2011 20 Priory Gardens, St Andrews KY16 8XX 01334 478287 (Tel/Fax)
[E-mail: AMcCafferty@churchofscotland.org.uk]

St Andrews: St Leonard's See Cameron
St Monans See Largoward
Strathkinness See St Andrews: Hope Park and Martyrs

Tayport
Brian H. Oxburgh BSc BD 1980 2011 27 Bell Street, Tayport DD6 9AP 01382 553879
[E-mail: BOxburgh@churchofscotland.org.uk]

Wormit See Balmerino

Name	Years	Position	Address / E-mail	Tel.
Alexander, James S. MA BD BA PhD	1966 1973	(University of St Andrews)	5 Strathkinness High Road, St Andrews KY16 9RP	01334 472680
Barron, Jane L. (Mrs) BA DipEd BD	1999 2013	(Aberdeen: St Machar's Cathedral)	Denhead Old Farm, St Andrews KY16 8PA [E-mail: livialouise888@gmail.com]	01334 850135 (Mbl) 07545 904541
Bradley, Ian C. MA BD DPhil	1990	Principal, St Mary's College	4 Donaldson Gardens, St Andrews KY16 9DN [E-mail: icb@st-andrews.ac.uk]	01334 475389
Brady, Lynn BD DipMin	1996	Interim Minister	10 Howard Place, St Andrews KY16 9HL [E-mail: LBrady@churchofscotland.org.uk]	01334 474474
Cameron, John U. BA BSc PhD BD ThD	1974 2008	(Dundee: Broughty Ferry St Stephen's and West)	2 Cairngreen, Cupar KY15 2SY [E-mail: jucameron@yahoo.co.uk]	
Connolly, Daniel BD DipTheol Dip Min	1983	Army Chaplain	[E-mail: dannyconnolly@hotmail.co.uk]	(Mbl) 07951 078478
Douglas, Peter C. JP	1966 1993	(Boarhills with Dunino)	12 Greyfriars Gardens, St Andrews KY16 8DR	01334 475868
Earnshaw, Philip BA BSc BD	1986 1996	(Glasgow: Pollokshields)	22 Castle Street, St Monans, Anstruther KY10 2AP	01333 730640
Fairlie, George BD BVMS MRCVS	1971 2002	(Crail with Kingsbarns)	41 Warrack Street, St Andrews KY16 8DR	01334 475868
Fraser, Ann G. BD CertMin	1990 2007	(Auchtermuchty)	24 Irvine Crescent, St Andrews KY16 8LG [E-mail: anngilfraser@btinternet.com]	01334 461329
Galloway, Robert W.C. LTh	1970 1998	(Cromarty)	22 Haughgate, Leven KY8 4SG	01333 426223
Gordon, Peter M. MA BD	1958 1995	(Airdrie: West)	3 Cupar Road, Cuparmuir, Cupar KY15 5RH [E-mail: machrie@madasafish.com]	01334 652341
Hamilton, Ian W.F. BD LTh. ALCM AVCM	1978 2012	(Nairn: Old)	Mossneuk, 5 Windsor Gardens, St Andrews KY16 8XL [E-mail: reviwfh@btinternet.com]	01334 477745
Harrison, Cameron	2006	(Auxiliary Minister)	Woodfield House, Priormuir, St Andrews KY16 8LP	
Jeffrey, Kenneth S. BA BD PhD	2002 2014	University of Aberdeen	The North Steading, Dalgairn, Cupar KY15 4PH [E-mail: ksjeffrey@btopenworld.com]	01334 478067 01334 653196
MacEwan, Donald G. MA BD PhD	2001 2012	Chaplain: University of St Andrews	Chaplaincy Centre, 3A St Mary's Place, St Andrews KY16 9UY [E-mail: dgm21@st-andrews.ac.uk]	01334 462865 (Mbl) 07713 322036
McGregor, Duncan J. MIFM	1982 1996	(Channelkirk with Lauder: Old)	14 Mount Melville, St Andrews KY16 8NG	01334 478314
McKimmon, Eric BA BD MTh PhD	1983 2014	(Cargill Burrelton with Collace)	14 Marionfield Place, Cupar KY15 5JN [E-mail: ericmckimmon@gmail.com]	01334 659650
McLean, John P. BSc BPhil BD	1994 2013	(Glenrothes: St Margaret's)	72 Lawmill Gardens, St Andrews KY16 8QS [E-mail: john@mcleanmail.me.uk]	01334 470803
Meager, Peter MA BD CertMgmt(Open)	1971 1998	(Elie with Kilconquhar and Colinsburgh)	7 Lorraine Drive, Cupar KY15 5DY [E-mail: meager52@btinternet.com]	01334 656991
Neilson, Peter MA BD MTh	1975 2006	(Mission Consultant)	Linne Bheag, 2 School Green, Anstruther KY10 3HF [E-mail: neilson.peter@btinternet.com]	01333 310477 (Mbl) 07818 418608
Reid, Alan A.S. MA BD STM	1962 1995	(Bridge of Allan: Chalmers)	Wayside Cottage, Bridgend, Ceres, Cupar KY15 5LS	07818 828509
Robb, Nigel I. FCP MA BD ThM MTh	1981 2014	Presbytery Clerk	Presbytery Office, Hope Park and Martyrs' Church, 1 Howard Place, St Andrews KY16 9UY	(Mbl) 07966 286958
Roy, Alan J. BSc BD	1960 1999	(Aberuthven with Dunning)	14 Comerton Place, Drumoig, Leuchars, St Andrews KY16 0NQ [E-mail: a.roy225@btinternet.com]	01382 542225
Strong, Clifford LTh	1983 1995	(Creich, Flisk and Kilmany with Monimail)	60 Maryknowe, Gauldry, Newport-on-Tay DD6 8SL	
Torrance, Alan J. (Prof.) MA BD DrTheol	1984 1999	University of St Andrews	Kincaple House, Kincaple, St Andrews KY16 9SH	(Home) 01382 330445 01334 850755 (Office) 01334 462843

Unsworth, Ruth BA BD CertMHS	1984		5 Lindsay Gardens, St Andrews KY16 8XB	(Mbl) 07894 802119
PgDipCBP BABCP			[E-mail: RUnsworth@churchofscotland.org.uk]	
Walker, James B. MA BD DPhil	1975 2011	(Chaplain: University of St Andrews)	5 Priestden Park, St Andrews KY16 8DL	01334 472839
Wotherspoon, Ian G. BA LTh	1967 2004	(Coatbridge: St Andrew's)	12 Cherry Lane, Cupar KY15 5DA	01334 650710
			[E-mail: wotherspoonrig@aol.com]	

(27) DUNKELD AND MEIGLE

Meets at Pitlochry on the first Tuesday of February, September and December, on the third Tuesday of April and the fourth Tuesday of October, and at the Moderator's church on the third Tuesday of June.

Clerk:	**REV. JOHN RUSSELL MA**		**Kilblaan, Gladstone Terrace, Birnam, Dunkeld PH8 0DP**	**01350 728896**
			[E-mail: dunkeldmeigle@churchofscotland.org.uk]	
Depute Clerk:	**REV. ALISON NOTMAN BD**		**The Manse, Dundee Road, Meigle, Blairgowrie PH12 8SB**	**01828 640074**

Aberfeldy (H) linked with Dull and Weem (H) linked with Grantully, Logierait and Strathtay

Vacant *Neil Glover*			The Manse, Taybridge Terrace, Aberfeldy PH15 2BS	

Alyth (H)

Michael J. Erskine MA BD	1985	2012	The Manse, Cambridge Street, Alyth, Blairgowrie PH11 8AW	01828 632238
			[E-mail: MErskine@churchofscotland.org.uk]	

Ardler, Kettins and Meigle

Alison Notman BD		2014	The Manse, Dundee Road, Meigle, Blairgowrie PH12 8SB	01828 640074
			[E-mail: ANotman@churchofscotland.org.uk]	

Bendochy linked with Coupar Angus: Abbey

Vacant			Caddam Road, Coupar Angus, Blairgowrie PH13 9EF	01828 627331

Blair Atholl and Struan linked with Braes of Rannoch linked with Foss and Rannoch (H)

Vacant			The Manse, Blair Atholl, Pitlochry PH18 5SX	01796 481213

Blairgowrie

Harry Mowbray BD CA	2003	2008	The Manse, Upper David Street, Blairgowrie PH10 6HB	01250 872146
			[E-mail: HMowbray@churchofscotland.org.uk]	

Braes of Rannoch linked with Foss and Rannoch (H) See Blair Atholl and Struan

Caputh and Clunie (H) linked with Kinclaven (H)
Peggy Ewart-Roberts BA BD   2003   2011

Cara Beag, Essendy Road, Blairgowrie PH10 6QU
[E-mail: PEwart-Roberts@churchofscotland.org.uk]   01250 876897

Coupar Angus: Abbey See Bendochy
Dull and Weem See Aberfeldy

Dunkeld (H)
R. Fraser Penny BA BD   1984   2001

Cathedral Manse, Dunkeld PH8 0AW
[E-mail: RPenny@churchofscotland.org.uk]   01350 727249

Fortingall and Glenlyon linked with Kenmore and Lawers (H)
Anne J. Brennan BSc BD MTh   1999

The Manse, Balnaskeag, Kenmore, Aberfeldy PH15 2HB
[E-mail: ABrennan@churchofscotland.org.uk]   01887 830218

Foss and Rannoch See Blair Atholl and Struan

Grantully, Logierait and Strathtay See Aberfeldy

Kenmore and Lawers See Fortingall and Glenlyon
Kinclaven See Caputh and Clunie

Kirkmichael, Straloch and Glenshee linked with Rattray (H)
Linda Stewart (Mrs) BD   1996   2012

The Manse, Alyth Road, Rattray, Blairgowrie PH10 7HF
[E-mail: Linda.Stewart@churchofscotland.org.uk]   01250 872462

Pitlochry (H) (01796 472160)
Mary M. Haddow (Mrs) BD   2001   2012

Manse Road, Moulin, Pitlochry PH16 5EP
[E-mail: MHaddow@churchofscotland.org.uk]   01796 472774

Rattray See Kirkmichael, Straloch and Glenshee

Tenandry
Guardianship of the Presbytery

Campbell, Richard S. LTh	1993	2010	(Gargunnock with Kilmadock with Kincardine-in-Menteith)	3 David Farquharson Road, Blairgowrie PH10 6FD [E-mail: revrichards@yahoo.co.uk]	01250 876386
Cassells, Alexander K. MA BD	1961	1997	(Leuchars: St Athernase and Guardbridge)	Alt-Na-Feidh, Bridge of Cally, Blairgowrie PH10 7JL	(Mbl) 07816 043968
Creegan, Christine M. (Mrs) MTh	1993	2005	(Grantully, Logierait and Strathtay)	Lonaig, 28 Lettoch Terrace, Pitlochry PH16 5BA	01796 472422
Duncan, James BTh FSAScot	1980	1995	(Blair Atholl and Struan)	25 Knockard Avenue, Pitlochry PH16 5JE	01796 474096
Ewart, William BSc BD	1972	2010	(Caputh and Clunie with Kinclaven)	Cara Beag, Essendy Road, Blairgowrie PH10 6QU [E-mail: ewe1@btinternet.com]	01250 876897
Knox, John W. MTheol	1992	1997	(Lochgelly: Macainsh)	Heatherlea, Main Street, Ardler, Blairgowrie PH12 8SR	01828 640731
McAlister, D.J.B. MA BD PhD	1951	1989	(North Berwick: Blackadder)	2 Duff Avenue, Moulin, Pitlochry PH16 5EN	01796 473591
McFadzean, Iain MA BD	1989	2010	National Director: Workplace Chaplaincy (Scotland)	2 Lowfield Crescent, Luncarty, Perth PH1 3FG [E-mail: iain.mcfadzean@wpcscotland.co.uk]	01738 827338 (Mbl) 07969 227696
MacRae, Malcolm H. MA PhD	1971	2010	(Kirkmichael, Straloch and Glenshee with Rattray)	10B Victoria Place, Stirling FK8 2QU [E-mail: malcolm.macrae1@btopenworld.com]	01786 465547
MacVicar, Kenneth MBE DFC TD MA	1950	1990	(Kenmore with Lawers with Fortingall and Glenlyon)	Illeray, Kenmore, Aberfeldy PH15 2HE	01887 830514
Nelson, Robert C. BA BD	1980	2010	(Isle of Mull, Kilninian and Kilmore with Salen and Ulva with Tobermory with Torosay and Kinlochspelvie)	St Colme's, Perth Road, Birnam, Dunkeld PH8 0BH [E-mail: rcnelson49@btinternet.com]	01350 727455
Nicol, Robert D.	2013		Ordained Local Minister	Rappla Lodge, Camserney, Aberfeldy PH15 2JF [E-mail: RNicol@churchofscotland.org.uk]	
Ormiston, Hugh C. BSc BD MPhil PhD	1969	2004	(Kirkmichael, Straloch and Glenshee with Rattray)	Cedar Lea, Main Road, Woodside, Blairgowrie PH13 9NP	01828 670539
Oswald, John BSc PhD BD	1997	2011	(Muthill with Trinity Gask and Kinkell)	1 Woodlands Meadow, Rosemount, Blairgowrie PH10 6GZ [E-mail: revdocoz@bigfoot.com]	01250 872598
Ramsay, Malcolm BA LLB DipMin	1986	2011	Overseas service in Nepal	c/o World Mission Council, 121 George Street, Edinburgh EH2 4YN [E-mail: MRamsay@churchofscotland.org.uk]	0131-225 5722
Robertson, Matthew LTh	1968	2002	(Cawdor with Croy and Dalcross)	Inver, Strathtay, Pitlochry PH9 0PG	01887 840780
Russell, John MA	1959	2000	Presbytery Clerk	Kilblaan, Gladstone Terrace, Birnam, Dunkeld PH8 0DP	01350 728896
Shannon, W.G. MA BD	1955	1998	(Pitlochry)	19 Knockard Road, Pitlochry PH16 5HJ	01796 473533
Sloan, Robert BD	1997	2014	(Fauldhouse St Andrew's)	3 Gean Grove, Blairgowrie PH10 6TL	01250 875286
Steele, Grace M.F. MA BTh	2014		Ordained Local Minister	12a Farragon Drive, Aberfeldy PH15 2BQ [E-mail: GSteele@churchofscotland.org.uk]	01887 820025
Tait, Thomas W. BD MBE	1972	1997	(Rattray)	3 Rosemount Park, Blairgowrie PH10 6TZ	01250 874833
Whyte, William B. BD	1973	2003	(Nairn: St Ninian's)	The Old Inn, Park Hill Road, Rattray, Blairgowrie PH10 7DS	01250 874401
Wilson, John M. MA BD	1965	2004	(Altnaharra and Farr)	Berbice, The Terrace, Blair Atholl, Pitlochry PH18 5SZ	01796 481619
Wilson, Mary D. (Mrs) RGN SCM DTM	1990	2004	(Auxiliary Minister)	Berbice, The Terrace, Blair Atholl, Pitlochry PH18 5SZ	01796 481619

(28) PERTH

Meets at 10am on the second Saturday of September, December, March, and June at Kinross and other venues within the bounds.

Clerk:	REV. J. COLIN CASKIE BA BD	
Presbytery Office:	209 High Street, Perth PH1 5PB [E-mail: perth@churchofscotland.org.uk]	**01738 451177**

Aberdalgie (H) and Forteviot (H) linked with Aberuthven and Dunning (H)
James W. Aitchison BD   1993   2015   The Manse, Aberdalgie, Perth PH2 0QD   01738 446771
[E-mail: JAitchison@churchofscotland.org.uk]

Abernethy and Dron and Arngask
Vacant   3 Manse Road, Abernethy, Perth PH2 9JP   01738 850938

Aberuthven and Dunning See Aberdalgie and Forteviot

Almondbank Tibbermore linked with Methven and Logiealmond
Philip W. Patterson BMus BD   1999   2008   The Manse, Pitcairngreen, Perth PH1 3EA   01738 583217
[E-mail: PPatterson@churchofscotland.org.uk]

Ardoch (H) linked with Blackford (H)
Mairi Perkins BA BTh   2012   2016   Manse of Ardoch, Feddoch Road, Braco, Dunblane FK15 5RE   01786 880948
[E-mail: MPerkins@churchofscotland.org.uk]

Auchterarder (H)
Robert D. Barlow   2010   2013   22 Kirkfield Place, Auchterarder PH3 1FP   01764 662399
BA BSc MSc PhD CChem MRSC
[E-mail: RBarlow@churchofscotland.org.uk]

Auchtergaven and Moneydie linked with Redgorton and Stanley
Adrian J. Lough BD   2012   22 King Street, Stanley, Perth PH1 4ND   01738 827952
[E-mail: ALough@churchofscotland.org.uk]

Blackford See Ardoch

Cargill Burrelton linked with Collace
Steven Thomson BSc BD   2001   2016   The Manse, Manse Road, Woodside, Blairgowrie PH13 9NQ   01828 670384
[E-mail: SThomson@churchofscotland.org.uk]

Cleish (H) linked with Fossoway: St Serf's and Devonside
Elisabeth M. Stenhouse BD   2006   2014   Station House, Station Road, Crook of Devon, Kinross KY13 0PG   01577 842128
[E-mail: EStenhouse@churchofscotland.org.uk]

Collace See Cargill Burrelton

Comrie (H) linked with Dundurn (H)
Graham McWilliams BSc BD   2005   The Manse, Strowan Road, Comrie, Crieff PH6 2ES   01764 670076
[E-mail: GMcWilliams@churchofscotland.org.uk]

Crieff (H)
Andrew J. Philip BSc BD   1996   2013   8 Strathearn Terrace, Crieff PH7 3AQ   01764 218976
[E-mail: APhilip@churchofscotland.org.uk]

Dunbarney (H) and Forgandenny
Allan J. Wilson BSc MEd BD   2007   Dunbarney Manse, Manse Road, Bridge of Earn, Perth PH2 9DY   01738 812211
[E-mail: AWilson@churchofscotland.org.uk]
Susan Thorburn MTh   2014   3 Daleally Farm Cottages, St Madoes Road, Errol, Perth PH2 7TJ   01821 642681
(Ordained Local Minister)   [E-mail: SThorburn@churchofscotland.org.uk]

Dundurn See Comrie

Errol (H) linked with Kilspindie and Rait
John Macgregor BD   2001   2016   South Bank, Errol, Perth PH2 7PZ   01821 642279
[E-mail: John.Macgregor@churchofscotland.org.uk]

Fossoway: St Serf's and Devonside See Cleish

Fowlis Wester, Madderty and Monzie linked with Gask (H)
David W. Denniston BD DipMin   1981   2016   Beechview, Abercairney, Crieff PH7 3NF   01764 652116
(Interim Minister)   [E-mail: DDenniston@churchofscotland.org.uk]   07903 926727 (Mbl)

Gask See Fowlis Wester, Madderty and Monzie
Kilspindie and Rait See Errol

Kinross (H) (Office: 01577 862570)
Alan D. Reid MA BD — 1989 2009 — 15 Green Wood, Kinross KY13 8FG [E-mail: AReid@churchofscotland.org.uk] — 01577 862952

Methven and Logiealmond See Almondbank Tibbermore

Muthill (H) linked with Trinity Gask and Kinkell
Klaus O.F. Buwert LLB BD DMin — 1984 2013 — The Manse, Station Road, Muthill, Crieff PH5 2AR [E-mail: klaus@buwert.co.uk] — 01764 681205

Orwell (H) and Portmoak (H) (Office: 01577 862100)
Angus Morrison MA BD PhD — 1979 2011 — 41 Auld Mart Road, Milnathort, Kinross KY13 9FR [E-mail: AMorrison@churchofscotland.org.uk] — 01577 863461

Perth: Craigie and Moncreiffe
Vacant — The Manse, 46 Abbot Street, Perth PH2 0EE — 01738 623748
Robert F. Wilkie — 2011 — 24 Huntingtower Road, Perth PH1 2JS [E-mail: RWilkie@churchofscotland.org.uk] — 01738 628301
(Auxiliary Minister)

Perth: Kinnoull (H)
Graham W. Crawford BSc BD STM — 1991 2016 — 1 Mount Tabor Avenue, Perth PH2 7BT [E-mail: GCrawford@churchofscotland.org.uk] — 01738 626046 / 07817 504042 (Mbl)
Timothy E.G. Fletcher BA FCMA — 1998 — 3 Ardchoille Park, Perth PH2 7TL [E-mail: TFletcher@churchofscotland.org.uk] — 01738 638189 / 07747 013985 (Mbl)
(Auxiliary Minister)

Perth: Letham St Mark's (H) (Office: 01738 446377)
James C. Stewart BD DipMin — 1997 — 35 Rose Crescent, Perth PH1 1NT [E-mail: JStewart@churchofscotland.org.uk] — 01738 624167
Kenneth D. McKay DCS — 11F Balgowan Road, Perth PH1 2JG [E-mail: Kenneth.McKay@churchofscotland.org.uk] — 01738 621169 / 07843 883042 (Mbl)

Perth: North (Office: 01738 622298)
Hugh O'Brien CSS MTheol — 2001 2009 — 127 Glasgow Road, Perth PH2 0LU [E-mail: HObrien@churchofscotland.org.uk] — 01738 625728

Perth: Riverside (Office: 01738 622341)
David R. Rankin MA BD — 2009 2014 — 44 Hay Street, Perth PH1 5HS [E-mail: DRankin@churchofscotland.org.uk] — 07810 008754 (Mbl)

Perth: St John's Kirk of Perth (H) (01738 626159) linked with Perth: St Leonard's-in-the-Fields (H) (01738 632238)

John A.H. Murdoch BA BD DPSS	1979	2016	5 Strathearn Terrace, Perth PH2 0LS [E-mail: JMurdoch@churchofscotland.org.uk]	01738 621709 / 07578 558978 (Mbl)

Perth: St Leonard's-in-the-Fields See Perth: St John's Kirk of Perth

Perth: St Matthew's (Office: 01738 636757; Vestry: 01738 630725)

Scott Burton BD DipMin	1999	2007	23 Kincarrathie Crescent, Perth PH2 7HH [E-mail: SBurton@churchofscotland.org.uk]	01738 626828

Redgorton and Stanley See Auchtergaven and Moneydie

St Madoes and Kinfauns

Marc F. Bircham BD MTh	2000	Glencarse, Perth PH2 7NF [E-mail: MBircham@churchofscotland.org.uk]	01738 860837

Scone and St Martins
Vacant

Alan Livingstone (Ordained Local Minister)	2013	Meadowside, Lawmuir, Methven, Perth PH1 3SZ [E-mail: ALivingstone@churchofscotland.org.uk]	01738 840682

Trinity Gask and Kinkell See Muthill

Ballentine, Ann M. MA BD	1981	2007	(Kirknewton and East Calder)	17 Nellfield Road, Crieff PH7 3DU [E-mail: annmballentine@gmail.com]	01764 652567
Barr, T. Leslie LTh	1969	1997	(Kinross)	8 Fairfield Road, Kelty KY4 0BY [E-mail: leslie_barr@yahoo.com]	01383 839330
Bertram, Thomas A.	1972	1995	(Patna Waterside)	3 Scrimgeours Corner, 29 West High Street, Crieff PH7 4AP	01764 652066
Brown, Elizabeth JP RGN	1996	2007	(Auxiliary Minister)	8 Viewlands Place, Perth PH1 1BS [E-mail: liz_brown@blueyonder.co.uk]	01738 552391
Brown, Marina D. MA BD MTh	2000	2012	(Hawick: St Mary's and Old)	Moneydie School Cottage, Luncarty, Perth PH1 3HZ [E-mail: revmdb1711@btinternet.com]	01738 582163
Buchan, William DipTheol BD	1987	2001	(Kilwinning: Abbey)	34 Bridgewater Avenue, Auchterarder PH3 1DQ [E-mail: billbuchan3@btinternet.com]	01764 660306
Cairns, Evelyn BD	2004	2012	(Chaplain: Rachel House)	15 Talla Park, Kinross KY13 8AB [E-mail: revelyn@btinternet.com]	01577 863990
Caskie, J. Colin BA BD	1977	2012	Presbytery Clerk	13 Anderson Drive, Perth PH1 1JZ [E-mail: jcolincaskie@gmail.com]	01738 445543
Coleman, Sidney H. BA BD MTh	1961	2001	(Glasgow: Merrylea)	'Blaven', 11 Clyde Place, Perth PH2 0EZ [E-mail: sidney.coleman@blueyonder.co.uk]	01738 565072

Craig, Joan H. MTheol	1986	2005	(Orkney: East Mainland)	7 Jedburgh Place, Perth PH1 1SJ [E-mail: joanhcraig@btinternet.com]	01738 580180
Donaldson, Robert B. BSocSc	1953	1997	(Kilchoman with Portnahaven)	11 Strathearn Court, Crieff PH7 3DS	01764 654976
Drummond, Alfred G. BD DMin	1991	2006	Scottish General Secretary: Evangelical Alliance	10 Errochty Court, Perth PH1 2SU [E-mail: frddrmmnd@aol.com]	01738 621305
Fleming, Hamish K. MA	1966	2001	(Banchory Ternan: East)	36 Earnmuir Road, Comrie, Crieff PH6 2EY [E-mail: hamishnan@gmail.com]	01764 679178
Graham, Sydney S. DipYL MPhil BD	1987	2009	(Iona with Kilfinichen and Kilvickeon and the Ross of Mull)	'Aspen', Milton Road, Luncarty, Perth PH1 3ES [E-mail: syd@sydgraham.plus.com]	01738 829350
Gregory, J.C. LTh	1968	1992	(Blantyre: St Andrew's)	2 Southlands Road, Auchterarder PH3 1BA	01764 664594
Gunn, Alexander M. MA BD	1967	2006	(Aberfeldy with Amulree and Strathbraan with Dull and Weem)	'Navarone', 12 Cornhill Road, Perth PH1 1LR [E-mail: sandygunn@btinternet.com]	01738 443216
Halliday, Archibald R. BD MTh	1964	1999	(Duffus, Spynie and Hopeman)	8 Turretbank Drive, Crieff PH7 4LW [E-mail: roberthalliday343@btinternet.com]	01764 656464
Kelly, T. Clifford	1973	1995	(Ferintosh)	20 Whinfield Drive, Kinross KY13 8UB	01577 864946
Lawson, James B. MA BD	1961	2002	(South Uist)	4 Cowden Way, Comrie, Crieff PH6 2NW [E-mail: james.lawson7@btopenworld.com]	01764 679180
Lawson, Ronald G. MA BD	1964	1999	(Greenock: Wellpark Mid Kirk)	6 East Brougham Street, Stanley, Perth PH1 4NJ	01738 828871
Low, J.E. Stewart MA	1957	1997	(Tarbat)	1 Cameron Court, Almond Place, Comrie PH6 2BB	01764 670461
McCarthy, David J. BSc BD	1985	2014	Mission and Discipleship Council	121 George Street, Edinburgh EH2 4YN [E-mail: DMcCarthy@churchofscotland.org.uk]	0131-225 5722
McCormick, Alastair F.	1962	1998	(Creich with Rosehall)	14 Balmanno Park, Bridge of Earn, Perth PH2 9RJ	01738 813588
McCrum, Robert BSc BD	1982	2014	(Ayr: St James')	28 Rose Crescent, Perth PH1 1NT [E-mail: robert.mccrum@virgin.net]	01738 447906
MacDonald, James W. BD	1976	2012	(Crieff)	'Mingulay', 29 Hebridean Gardens, Crieff PH7 3BP [E-mail: rev_up@btinternet.com]	01764 654500
McGregor, William LTh	1987	2003	(Auchtergaven and Moneydie)	'Ard Choille', 7 Taypark Road, Luncarty, Perth PH1 3FE [E-mail: bill.mcgregor7@btinternet.com]	01738 827866
McIntosh, Colin G. MA BD	1976	2013	(Dunblane: Cathedral)	Drumhead Cottage, Drum, Kinross KY13 0PR [E-mail: colinmcintosh4@btinternet.com]	01577 840012
MacMillan, Riada M. BD	1991	1998	(Perth: Craigend Moncreiffe with Rhynd)	73 Muirend Gardens, Perth PH1 1JR	01738 628867
McNaughton, David J.H. BA CA	1976	1995	(Killin and Ardeonaig)	14 Rankine Court, Wormit, Newport-on-Tay DD6 8TA	01738 860867
Main, Douglas M. BD	1986	2014	(Errol with Kilspindie and Rait)	14 Madoch Road, St Madoes, Perth PH2 7TT [E-mail: revdmain@sky.com]	
Malcolm, Alistair BD DPS	1976	2012	(Inverness: Inshes)	11 Kinclaven Gardens, Murthly, Perth PH1 4EX [E-mail: amalcolm067@btinternet.com]	01738 710979
Michie, Margaret		2013	Ordained Local Minister: Loch Leven Parish Grouping	3 Loch Leven Court, Wester Balgedie, Kinross KY13 9NE [E-mail: margaretmichie@btinternet.com]	01592 840602
Millar, Archibald E. DipTh	1965	1991	(Perth: St Stephen's)	7 Maple Place, Perth PH1 1RT	01738 621813
Munro, Gillian BSc BD	1989	2003	Head of Spiritual Care, NHS Tayside	Royal Victoria Hospital, Dundee DD2 1SP	01382 423116
Munro, Patricia BSc DCS			(Deacon)	4 Hewat Place, Perth PH1 2UD [E-mail: patmunrodcs@gmail.com]	01738 443088 (Mbl) 07814 836314

Paton, Iain F. BD FCIS	1980	2006	(Elie with Kilconquhar and Colinsburgh)	Muldoanich, Stirling Street, Blackford, Auchterarder PH4 1QG [E-mail: iain.f.paton@btinternet.com]	01764 682234
Pattison, Kenneth J. MA BD STM	1967	2004	(Kilmuir and Logie Easter)	2 Castle Way, St Madoes, Glencarse, Perth PH2 7NY [E-mail: k_pattison@btinternet.com]	01738 860340
Philip, Elizabeth DCS MA BA PGCSE			Deacon	8 Strathearn Terrace, Crieff PH7 3AQ [E-mail: ephilipstitch@gmail.com]	01764 218976 (Mbl) 07970 767851
Philip, Michael R. BD	1978	2014	(Falkirk: Bainsford)	9 Muir Bank, Scone, Perth PH2 6SZ [E-mail: mrphilip@blueyonder.co.uk]	01738 564533 (Mbl) 07776 011601
Redpath, James G. BD DipPTh	1988	2016	(Auchtermuchty with Edenshead and Strathmiglo)	9 Beveridge Place, Kinross KY13 8QY [E-mail: JRedpath@churchofscotland.org.uk]	(Mbl) 07713 919442
Searle, David C. MA DipTh	1965	2003	(Warden: Rutherford House)	Stonefall Lodge, 30 Abbey Lane, Grange, Errol PH2 7GB [E-mail: dcs@davidsearle-plus.com]	01821 641004
Simpson, James A. BSc BD STM DD	1960	2000	(Dornoch Cathedral)	'Dornoch', Perth Road, Bankfoot, Perth PH1 4ED [E-mail: ja@simpsondornoch.co.uk]	01738 787710
Sloan, Robert P. MA BD	1968	2007	(Braemar and Crathie)	1 Broomhill Avenue, Perth PH1 1EN [E-mail: sloan12@virginmedia.com]	01738 443904
Souter, David I. BD	1996	2015	(Perth: Kinnoull)	Duncairn, 2 Gowrie Farm, Perth PH1 4PP [E-mail: d.souter@blueyonder.co.uk]	
Stenhouse, W. Duncan MA BD	1989	2006	(Dunbarney and Forgandenny)	32 Sandport Gait, Kinross KY13 8FB	01577 866992
Stewart, Anne E. BD CertMin	1998		Prison Chaplain	35 Rose Crescent, Perth PH1 1NT [E-mail: anne.stewart2@sps.pnn.gov.uk]	01738 624167
Stewart, Gordon G. MA	1961	2000	(Perth: St Leonard's-in-the-Fields and Trinity)	'Balnoe', South Street, Rattray, Blairgowrie PH10 7BZ	01250 870626
Stewart, Robin J. MA BD STM	1959	1995	(Orwell with Portmoak)	'Oakbrae', Perth Road, Murthly, Perth PH1 4HF	01738 710220
Thomson, J. Bruce MA BD	1972	2009	(Scone: Old)	47 Elm Street, Errol, Perth PH2 7SQ [E-mail: RevBruceThomson@aol.com]	01821 641039 07850 846404
Thomson, Peter D. MA BD	1968	2004	(Comrie with Dundurn)	34 Queen Street, Perth PH2 0EJ [E-mail: peterthomson208@btinternet.com]	(Mbl) 01738 622418
Wallace, Catherine PGDipC DCS			Deacon	21 Durley Dene Crescent, Bridge of Earn PH2 9RD [E-mail: samesky2407@aol.com]	01738 621709
Wallace, James K. MA BD STM	1988	2015	Scotus Tours	21 Durley Dene Crescent, Bridge of Earn PH2 9RD [E-mail: jkwministry@hotmail.com]	01738 621709
Wylie, Jonathan BSc BD MTh	2000	2015	Chaplain	Strathallan School, Forgandenny, Perth PH2 9EG [E-mail: chaplain@strathallan.co.uk]	01738 815098

PERTH ADDRESSES

Craigie	Abbot Street	Letham St Mark's	Rannoch Road	St John's	St John's Street
Kinnoull	Dundee Rd near Queen's Bridge	Moncreiffe	Glenbruar Crescent	St Leonard's-in-the-Fields	Marshall Place
		North	Mill Street near Kinnoull Street	St Matthew's	Tay Street
		Riverside	Bute Drive		

(29) DUNDEE

Meets at Dundee: The Steeple, Nethergate, on the second Wednesday of February, March, May, September, November and December, and on the fourth Wednesday of June.

Clerk:	REV. JAMES L. WILSON BD CPS	[E-mail: dundee@churchofscotland.org.uk]	01382 459249 (Home) 07885 618659 (Mobile)
Depute Clerk:	REV. JANET P. FOGGIE MA BD PhD	[E-mail: JFoggie@churchofscotland.org.uk]	01382 660152
Presbytery Office:		Whitfield Parish Church, Haddington Crescent, Dundee DD4 0NA	01382 503012

Abernyte linked with Inchture and Kinnaird linked with Longforgan (H)
Marjory A. MacLean LLB BD PhD RNR   1991   2011   The Manse, Longforgan, Dundee DD2 5HB   01382 360238
[E-mail: mmaclean@churchofscotland.org.uk]

Auchterhouse (H) linked with Monikie and Newbigging and Murroes and Tealing (H)
Vacant

Dundee: Balgay (H)
Patricia Ramsay (Mrs) BD   2005   2013   150 City Road, Dundee DD2 2PW   01382 669600 / 07813 189776 (Mbl)
[E-mail: PRamsay@churchofscotland.org.uk]

Dundee: Barnhill St Margaret's (H) (01382 737294) (E-mail: church.office@btconnect.com)
Susan J. Sutherland (Mrs) BD   2009   2 St Margaret's Lane, Barnhill, Dundee DD5 2PQ   01382 779278
[E-mail: SSutherland@churchofscotland.org.uk]

Dundee: Broughty Ferry New Kirk (H)
Catherine E.E. Collins (Mrs) MA BD   1993   2006   New Kirk Manse, 25 Ballinard Gardens, Broughty Ferry, Dundee DD5 1BZ   01382 778874
[E-mail: CCollins@churchofscotland.org.uk]

Dundee: Broughty Ferry St James' (H)
Vacant   2 Ferry Road, Monifieth, Dundee DD5 4NT   01382 534468

Dundee: Broughty Ferry St Luke's and Queen Street (01382 732094)
C. Graham D. Taylor BSc BD FIAB   2001   22 Albert Road, Broughty Ferry, Dundee DD5 1AZ   01382 779212
[E-mail: CTaylor@churchofscotland.org.uk]

Dundee: Broughty Ferry St Stephen's and West (H) linked with Dundee: Dundee (St Mary's) (H) (01382 226271)
Keith F. Hall MA BD   1980   1994   33 Strathern Road, West Ferry, Dundee DD5 1PP   01382 778808
[E-mail: KHall@churchofscotland.org.uk]

Dundee: Camperdown (H) (01382 623958)
Vacant   Camperdown Manse, Myrekirk Road, Dundee DD2 4SF

Dundee: Chalmers-Ardler (H)
Kenneth D. Stott MA BD   1989   1997   The Manse, Turnberry Avenue, Dundee DD2 3TP   01382 827439
[E-mail: KStott@churchofscotland.org.uk]

Dundee: Coldside
Anthony P. Thornthwaite MTh   1995   2011   9 Abercorn Street, Dundee DD4 7HY   01382 458314
[E-mail: AThornthwaite@churchofscotland.org.uk]

Dundee: Craigiebank (H) (01382 731173) linked with Dundee: Douglas and Mid Craigie
Edith F. McMillan (Mrs) MA BD   1981   1999   19 Americanmuir Road, Dundee DD3 9AA   01382 812423
[E-mail: EMcMillan@churchofscotland.org.uk]

Dundee: Douglas and Mid Craigie See Dundee: Craigiebank

Dundee: Downfield Mains (H) (01382 810624/812166)
Nathan S. McConnell BS MA ThM   2005   2016   9 Elgin Street, Dundee DD3 8NL   01382 690196
[E-mail: NMcConnell@churchofscotland.org.uk]

Dundee: Dundee (St Mary's) See Dundee: Broughty Ferry St Stephen's and West

Dundee: Fintry Parish Church
Colin M. Brough BSc BD   1998   2002   4 Clive Street, Dundee DD4 7AW   01382 458629
[E-mail: CBrough@churchofscotland.org.uk]

Dundee: Lochee (H)
Vacant   32 Clayhills Drive, Dundee DD2 1SX   01382 561989
Willie Strachan MBA DipY&C   2013   Ladywell House, Lucky Slap, Monikie, Dundee DD5 3QG   01382 370286
(Ordained Local Minister)   [E-mail: WStrachan@churchofscotland.org.uk]

Dundee: Logie and St John's Cross (H) (01382 668700)
David T. Gray BArch BD   2010   2014
7 Hyndford Street, Dundee DD2 1HQ
[E-mail: DGray@churchofscotland.org.uk]
01382 668853

Dundee: Meadowside St Paul's (H) (01382 225420)
Vacant
36 Blackness Avenue, Dundee DD2 1HH
01382 668828

Dundee: Menzieshill
Robert Mallinson BD   2010
The Manse, Charleston Drive, Dundee DD2 4ED
[E-mail: RMallinson@churchofscotland.org.uk]
01382 667446
07595 249089 (Mbl)

Dundee: St Andrew's (H) (01382 224860)
Janet P. Foggie MA BD PhD   2003   2009
39 Tullideph Road, Dundee DD2 2JD
[E-mail: JFoggie@churchofscotland.org.uk]
01382 660152

Dundee: St David's High Kirk (H)
Marion J. Paton (Miss) MA BMus BD   1991   2007
6 Adelaide Place, Dundee DD3 6LF
[E-mail: MPaton@churchofscotland.org.uk]
01382 322955

Dundee: The Steeple (H) (01382 200031)
Robert A. Calvert BSc BD DMin   1983   2014
128 Arbroath Road, Dundee DD4 7HR
[E-mail: RCalvert@churchofscotland.org.uk]
01382 522837
07532 029343 (Mbl)

Dundee: Stobswell (H) (01382 461397)
William McLaren MA BD   1990   2007
23 Shamrock Street, Dundee DD4 7AH
[E-mail: WMcLaren@churchofscotland.org.uk]
01382 459119

Dundee: Strathmartine (H) (01382 825817)
Stewart McMillan BD   1983   1990
19 Americanmuir Road, Dundee DD3 9AA
[E-mail: SMcMillan@churchofscotland.org.uk]
01382 812423

Dundee: Trinity (H)
Vacant
65 Clepington Road, Dundee DD4 7BQ
01382 458764

Dundee: West
Vacant

Dundee: Whitfield (H) (01382 503012)
James L. Wilson BD CPS   1986   2001   53 Old Craigie Road, Dundee DD4 7JD
[E-mail: James.Wilson@churchofscotland.org.uk]   01382 459249

Fowlis and Liff linked with Lundie and Muirhead (H)
Donna M. Hays (Mrs) MTheol DipEd DipTMHA   2004   149 Coupar Angus Road, Muirhead of Liff, Dundee DD2 5QN
[E-mail: DHays@churchofscotland.org.uk]   01382 580210

Inchture and Kinnaird See Abernyte

Invergowrie (H)
Robert J. Ramsay LLB NP BD   1986   1997   2 Boniface Place, Invergowrie, Dundee DD2 5DW
[E-mail: RRamsay@churchofscotland.org.uk]   01382 561118

Longforgan See Abernyte
Lundie and Muirhead See Fowlis and Liff

Monifieth (H)
Dorothy U. Anderson (Mrs) LLB DipLP BD   2006   2009   8 Church Street, Monifieth, Dundee DD5 4JP
[E-mail: DAnderson@churchofscotland.org.uk]   01382 532607

Monikie and Newbigging and Murroes and Tealing See Auchterhouse

Allan, Jean (Mrs) DCS   (Deacon)   12C Hindmarsh Avenue, Dundee DD3 7LW
[E-mail: jeannieallan45@googlemail.com]   01382 827299
(Mbl) 07709 959474

Barrett, Leslie M. BD FRICS   1991   2014   (Chaplain: University of Abertay, Dundee)   Dunelm Cottage, Logie, Cupar KY15 4SJ
[E-mail: lesliembarrett@btinternet.com]   01334 870396

Campbell, Gordon MA BD CDipAF DipHSM CMgr MCMI MIHM AssocCIPD AFRIN ARSGS FRGS FSAScot   2001   Auxiliary Minister: Chaplain: University of Dundee   2 Falkland Place, Kingoodie, Invergowrie, Dundee DD2 5DY
[E-mail: g.a.campbell@dundee.ac.uk]   01382 561383

Clark, David M. MA BD   1989   2013   (Dundee: Steeple)   2 Rose Street, St Monans, Anstruther KY10 2BQ
[E-mail: dmclark72@gmail.com]   01333 738034

Collins, David A. BSc BD   1993   2016   (Auchterhouse with Monikie and Newbigging and Murroes and Tealing)   New Kirk Manse, 25 Ballinard Gardens, Broughty Ferry, Dundee DD5 1BZ
[E-mail: revdacollins@btinternet.com]   01382 778874

Craik, Sheila (Mrs) BD   1989   2001   (Dundee: Camperdown)   35 Haldane Terrace, Dundee DD3 0HT   01382 802078

Name	Ord.		Charge	Address	Telephone
Cramb, Erik M. LTh	1973	1989	(Industrial Mission Organiser)	Flat 35, Braehead, Methven Walk, Dundee DD2 3FJ [E-mail: erikcramb@aol.com]	01382 526196
Donald, Robert M. LTh BA	1969	2005	(Kilmodan and Colintraive)	2 Blacklaw Drive, Birkhill, Dundee DD2 5RJ [E-mail: robandmoiradonald@yahoo.co.uk]	01382 581337
Douglas, Fiona C. MBE MA BD PhD	1989	1997	Chaplain: University of Dundee	10 Springfield, Dundee DD1 4JE [E-mail: f.c.douglas@dundee.ac.uk]	01382 384157
Fraser, Donald W. MA	1958	2010	(Monifieth)	1 Blake Avenue, Broughty Ferry, Dundee DD5 3LH [E-mail: fraserdonald37@yahoo.co.uk]	01382 477491 (Mbl) 07531 863316
Galbraith, W. James L. BSc BD MICE	1973	1996	(Kilchrenan and Dalavich with Muckairn)	586 Brook Street, Broughty Ferry, Dundee DD5 2EA	01382 732110
Greaves, Andrew T. BD	1985	2016	(Dundee: West)	Wards of Keithock, Brechin DD9 7PZ	01356 624479
Hawdon, John E. BA MTh AICS	1961	1995	(Dundee: Clepington)	53 Hillside Road, Dundee DD2 1QT	01382 646212
Ingram, J.R.	1954	1978	(Chaplain: RAF)	48 Marlee Road, Broughty Ferry, Dundee DD5 3EX	01382 736400
Jamieson, David B. MA BD STM	1974	2011	(Monifieth)	8A Albert Street, Monifieth, Dundee DD5 4JS	01382 532772
Kay, Elizabeth (Miss) DipYCS	1993	2007	(Auxiliary Minister)	1 Kintail Walk, Inchture, Perth PH14 9RY [E-mail: ekay007@btinternet.com]	01828 686029
Laidlaw, John J. MA	1964	1973	(Adviser in Religious Education)	14 Dalhousie Road, Barnhill, Dundee DD5 2SQ	01382 477458
Laing, David J.H. BD DPS	1976	2014	(Dundee: Trinity)	18 Kerrington Crescent, Barnhill, Dundee DD5 2TN [E-mail: david.laing@live.co.uk]	01382 739586
McLeod, David C. BSc MEng BD	1969	2001	(Dundee: Fairmuir)	6 Carseview Gardens, Dundee DD2 1NE	01382 641371
McMillan, Charles D. LTh	1979	2004	(Elgin: High)	11 Troon Terrace, The Orchard, Ardler, Dundee DD2 3FX	01382 831358
Mair, Michael V.A. MA BD	1967	2007	(Craigiebank with Dundee: Douglas and Mid Craigie)	48 Panmure Street, Monifieth DD5 4EH [E-mail: mvamair@gmail.com]	01382 530538
Martin, Janie (Miss) DCS			(Deacon)	16 Wentworth Road, Ardler, Dundee DD2 8SD [E-mail: janimar@aol.com]	01382 813786
Mitchell, Jack MA BD CTh	1987	1996	(Dundee: Menzieshill)	29 Carrick Gardens, Ayr KA7 2RT	01575 572503
Mowat, Gilbert M. MA	1948	1986	(Dundee: Albany-Butterburn)	Abbeyfield House, 16 Grange Road, Bearsden, Glasgow G61 3PL	01382 581790
Powrie, James E. LTh	1969	1995	(Dundee: Chalmers-Ardler)	3 Kirktonhill Road, Kirriemuir DD8 4HU	01382 520519
Rae, Robert LTh	1968	1983	(Chaplain: Dundee Acute Hospitals)	14 Neddertoun View, Liff, Dundee DD3 5RU	(Mbl) 07952 349884
Reid, R. Gordon BSc BD MIET	1993	2010	(Carriden)	6 Bayview Place, Monifieth, Dundee DD5 4TN [E-mail: GordonReid@aol.com]	01382 522773 (Mbl) 07595 465838
Robertson, James H. BSc BD	1975	2014	(Culloden: The Barn)	'Far End', 35 Mains Terrace, Dundee DD4 7BZ [E-mail: jimrob838@gmail.com]	01382 901212
Robson, George K. LTh DPS BA	1983	2011	(Dundee: Balgay)	11 Ceres Crescent, Broughty Ferry, Dundee DD5 3JN [E-mail: gkrobson@virginmedia.com]	01382 816580 (Mbl) 07899 790466
Rose, Lewis (Mr) DCS			(Deacon)	6 Gauldie Crescent, Dundee DD3 0RR [E-mail: lewis_rose48@yahoo.co.uk]	01382 739595
Scott, James MA BD	1973	2010	(Drumoak-Durris)	3 Blake Place, Broughty Ferry, Dundee DD5 3LQ [E-mail: jimscott73@yahoo.co.uk]	01382 501653
Scoular, Stanley	1963	2000	(Rosyth)	31 Duns Crescent, Dundee DD4 0RY	01382 685539
Strickland, Alexander LTh	1971	2005	(Dairsie with Kemback with Strathkinness)	12 Ballumbie Braes, Dundee DD4 0UN	01382 770198
Taylor Caroline (Mrs)	1995	2014	(Leuchars: St Athernase)	The Old Dairy, 15 Forthill Road, Broughty Ferry, Dundee DD5 3DH [E-mail: caro234@btinternet.com]	

DUNDEE ADDRESSES

Balgay — 200 Lochee Road
Barnhill St Margaret's — 10 Invermark Terrace
Broughty Ferry
  New Kirk — 370 Queen Street
St James' — 5 Fort Street
St Luke's and Queen Street — 5 West Queen Street
St Stephen's and West — 96 Dundee Road
Camperdown — 22 Brownhill Road
Chalmers-Ardler — Turnberry Avenue

Coldside — Isla Street x Main Street
Craigiebank — Craigie Avenue at Greendykes Road
Douglas and Mid Craigie — Balbeggie Place/ Longtown Terrace
Downfield Mains — Haldane Street off Strathmartine Road
Dundee (St Mary's) — Nethergate
Fintry — Fintry Road x Fintry Drive
Lochee — 191 High Street, Lochee
Logie and St John's Cross — Shaftesbury Rd x Blackness Ave

Meadowside St Paul's — 114 Nethergate
Menzieshill — Charleston Drive, Menzieshill
St Andrew's — 2 King Street
St David's High Kirk — 119A Kinghorne Road
Steeple — Nethergate
Stobswell — 170 Albert Street
Strathmartine — 507 Strathmartine Road
Trinity — 73 Crescent Street
West — 130 Perth Road
Whitfield — Haddington Crescent

(30) ANGUS

Meets at Forfar in St Margaret's Church Hall on the first Tuesday of February, March, May, September, November and December, and on the last Tuesday of June.

Clerk: **REV. MICHAEL S. GOSS BD DPS** [E-mail: MGoss@churchofscotland.org.uk]
Depute Clerk: **REV. IAN A. McLEAN BSc BD DMin** [E-mail: IMcLean@churchofscotland.org.uk]
Presbytery Office: **St Margaret's Church, West High Street, Forfar   DD8 1BJ**   **01307 464224**
[E-mail: angus@churchofscotland.org.uk]

Aberlemno (H) linked with Guthrie and Rescobie
Brian Ramsay BD DPS MLitt   1980   1984   The Manse, Guthrie, Forfar DD8 2TP   01241 828243
[E-mail: BRamsay@churchofscotland.org.uk]

Arbirlot linked with Carmyllie
Brian Dingwall BTh CQSW   1999   2016   The Manse, Arbirlot, Arbroath DD11 2NX   01241 879800
[E-mail: brian.d12@btinternet.com]   07906 656847 (Mbl)

Arbroath: Knox's (H) linked with Arbroath: St Vigeans (H)
Nelu I. Balaj BD MA ThD   2010   The Manse, St Vigeans, Arbroath DD11 4RF   01241 873206
[E-mail: NBalaj@churchofscotland.org.uk]   07954 436879 (Mbl)

Arbroath: Old and Abbey (H) (Church office: 01241 877068)
Dolly Purnell BD   2003   2014   51 Cliffburn Road, Arbroath DD11 5BA   01241 872196 (Tel/Fax)
[E-mail: DPurnell@churchofscotland.org.uk]

Arbroath: St Andrew's (H) (E-mail: office@arbroathstandrews.org.uk)
W. Martin Fair BA BD DMin | 1992 | 92 Grampian Gardens, Arbroath DD11 4AQ
[E-mail: MFair@churchofscotland.org.uk]
01241 873238 (Tel/Fax)

Arbroath: St Vigeans See Arbroath: Knox's

Arbroath: West Kirk (H)
Alasdair G. Graham BD DipMin | 1981 1986 | 1 Charles Avenue, Arbroath DD11 2EY
[E-mail: AGraham@churchofscotland.org.uk]
01241 872244

Barry linked with Carnoustie
Michael S. Goss BD DPS | 1991 2003 | 44 Terrace Road, Carnoustie DD7 7AR
[E-mail: MGoss@churchofscotland.org.uk]
Dougal Edwards BTh | 2013 | 25 Mackenzie Street, Carnoustie DD7 6HD
(Ordained Local Minister)
[E-mail: DEdwards@churchofscotland.org.uk]
01241 410194
07787 141567 (Mbl)
01241 852666

Brechin: Cathedral (H) (Cathedral office: 01356 629360) (Website: www.brechincathedral.org.uk)
Roderick J. Grahame BD CPS DMin | 1991 2010 | Chanonry Wynd, Brechin DD9 6JS
[E-mail: RGrahame@churchofscotland.org.uk]
01356 624980

Brechin: Gardner Memorial (H) linked with Farnell
Jane M. Blackley MA BD | 2009 | 15 Caldhame Gardens, Brechin DD9 7JJ
[E-mail: JBlackley@churchofscotland.org.uk]
01356 622034

Carmyllie See Arbirlot
Carnoustie See Barry

Carnoustie: Panbride (H)
Matthew S. Bicket BD | 1989 | 8 Arbroath Road, Carnoustie DD7 6BL
[E-mail: MBicket@churchofscotland.org.uk]
01241 854478 (Tel)
01241 855088 (Fax)

Colliston linked with Friockheim Kinnell linked with Inverkeilor and Lunan (H)
Peter A. Phillips BA | 1995 2004 | The Manse, Inverkeilor, Arbroath DD11 5SA
[E-mail: PPhillips@churchofscotland.org.uk]
01241 830464

Dun and Hillside
Fiona C. Bullock (Mrs) MA LLB BD | 2014 | 4 Manse Road, Hillside, Montrose DD10 9FB
[E-mail: FBullock@churchofscotland.org.uk]
01674 830288

Dunnichen, Letham and Kirkden
Dale London BTh FSAScot — 2011 2013 — 7 Braehead Road, Letham, Forfar DD8 2PG — 01307 818025
[E-mail: DLondon@churchofscotland.org.uk]

Eassie, Nevay and Newtyle
Carleen J. Robertson (Miss) BD — 1992 — 2 Kirkton Road, Newtyle, Blairgowrie PH12 8TS — 01828 650461
[E-mail: CRobertson@churchofscotland.org.uk]

Edzell Lethnot Glenesk (H) linked with Fern Careston Menmuir
Vacant — 19 Lethnot Road, Edzell, Brechin DD9 7TG — 01356 647846

Farnell See Brechin: Gardner Memorial
Fern Careston Menmuir See Edzell Lethnot Glenesk

Forfar: East and Old (H)
Barbara Ann Sweetin BD — 2011 — The Manse, Lour Road, Forfar DD8 2BB — 01307 248228
[E-mail: BSweetin@churchofscotland.org.uk]

Forfar: Lowson Memorial (H)
Karen Fenwick PhD MPhil BSc BD — 2006 — 1 Jamieson Street, Forfar DD8 2HY — 01307 468585
[E-mail: KFenwick@churchofscotland.org.uk]

Forfar: St Margaret's (H) (Church office: 01307 464224)
Margaret J. Hunt (Mrs) MA BD — 2014 — St Margaret's Manse, 15 Potters Park Crescent, Forfar DD8 1HH — 01307 462044
[E-mail: MHunt@churchofscotland.org.uk]

Friockheim Kinnell See Colliston

Glamis (H), Inverarity and Kinnettles
Guardianship of the Presbytery — (See Eassie, Nevay and Newtyle)

Guthrie and Rescobie See Aberlemno

Inverkeilor and Lunan See Colliston

Kirriemuir: St Andrew's (H) linked with Oathlaw Tannadice
John K. Orr BD MTh   2012   26 Quarry Park, Kirriemuir DD8 4DR   01575 572610
[E-mail: JOrr@churchofscotland.org.uk]

Montrose: Old and St Andrew's
Ian A. McLean BSc BD DMin   1981   2008   2 Rosehill Road, Montrose DD10 8ST   01674 672447
[E-mail: IMcLean@churchofscotland.org.uk]

Montrose: South and Ferryden

Oathlaw Tannadice See Kirriemuir: St Andrew's

The Glens and Kirriemuir: Old (H) (Church office: 01575 572819) (Website: www.gkopc.co.uk)
Malcolm I.G. Rooney DPE BEd BD   1993   1999   20 Strathmore Avenue, Kirriemuir DD8 4DJ   01575 573724
                                                                                                07909 993233 (Mbl)
[E-mail: MRooney@churchofscotland.org.uk]
Linda Stevens (Mrs) BSc BD PgDip   2006   17 North Latch Road, Brechin DD9 6LE   01356 623415
(Team Minister)   [E-mail: LStevens@churchofscotland.org.uk]   07701 052552 (Mbl)

The Isla Parishes
Vacant   Balduff House, Kilry, Blairgowrie PH11 8HS   01575 560268

Butters, David	1964 1998	(Turriff: St Ninian's and Forglen)	68A Millgate, Friockheim, Arbroath DD11 4TN	01241 828030
Drysdale, James P.R.	1967 1999	(Brechin: Gardner Memorial)	51 Airlie Street, Brechin DD9 6JX	01356 625201
Duncan, Robert F. MTheol	1986 2001	(Lochgelly: St Andrew's)	25 Rowan Avenue, Kirriemuir DD8 4TB	01575 573973
Gray, Ian	2013	(OLM) Children and Family Worker, Arbroath: Knox's with St Vigeans	The Mallards, 15 Rossie Island Road, Montrose DD10 9NH [E-mail: IGray@churchofscotland.org.uk]	01674 677126
Gough, Ian G. MA BD MTh DMin	1974 2009	(Arbroath: Knox's with Arbroath: St Vigeans)	23 Keptie Road, Arbroath DD11 3ED [E-mail: iangough@btinternet.com]	(Mbl) 07891 838379
Hastie, George I. MA BD	1971 2009	(Mearns Coastal)	23 Borrowfield Crescent, Montrose DD10 9BR	01674 672290
Hodge, William N.T.	1966 1995	(Longside)	19 Craigengar Park, Craigshill, Livingston EH54 5NY	01506 435813
Milton, Eric G. BD	1963 1994	(Blairdaff)	16 Bruce Court, Links Parade, Carnoustie DD7 7JE	01241 854928
Morrice, Alastair M. MA BD	1968 2002	(Rutherglen: Stonelaw)	5 Brechin Road, Kirriemuir DD8 4BX [E-mail: ambishkek@swissmail.org]	01575 574102

Name	Years	Charge	Address	Telephone
Norrie, Graham MA BD	1967 2007	(Forfar: East and Old)	'Novar', 14A Wyllie Street, Forfar DD8 3DN [E-mail: grahamnorrie@hotmail.com]	01307 468152
Reid, Albert B. BD BSc	1966 2001	(Ardler, Kettins and Meigle)	1 Mary Countess Way, Glamis, Forfar DD8 1RF [E-mail: abreid@btinternet.com]	01307 840213
Robertson, George R. LTh	1985 2004	(Udny and Pitmedden)	3 Slateford Gardens, Edzell, Brechin DD9 7SX [E-mail: geomag.robertson@btinternet.com]	01356 647322
Smith, Hamish G.	1965 1993	(Auchterless with Rothienorman)	11A Guthrie Street, Letham, Forfar DD8 2PS	01307 818973
Thomas, Martyn R.H. CEng MIStructE	1987 2002	(Fowlis and Liff with Lundie and Muirhead of Liff)	14 Kirkgait, Letham, Forfar DD8 2XQ [E-mail: martyn.thomas@mypostoffice.co.uk]	01307 818084
Thomas, Shirley A. (Mrs) DipSocSci AMIA (Aux)	2000 2006	(Auxiliary Minister)	14 Kirkgait, Letham, Forfar DD8 2XQ [E-mail: martyn.thomas@mypostoffice.co.uk]	01307 818084
Watt, Alan G.N. MTh CQSW DipCommEd	1996 2009	(Edzell Lethnot Glenesk with Fern Careston Menmuir)	16 Thornton Place, Forfar DD8 1HG [E-mail: watt455@btinternet.com]	01307 461686
Webster, Allan F. MA BD	1978 2008	(Workplace Chaplain)	42 McCulloch Drive, Forfar DD8 2EB [E-mail: allanfwebster@aol.com]	01307 464252 / (Mbl) 07546 276725
Youngson, Peter	1961 1996	(Kirriemuir: St Andrew's)	'Coreen', Woodside, Northmuir, Kirriemuir DD8 4PG	01575 572832

ANGUS ADDRESSES

Arbroath: Knox's	Howard Street	Kirriemuir: Old	High Street
Old and Abbey	West Abbey Street	St Andrew's	Glamis Road
St Andrew's	Hamilton Green		
West Kirk	Keptie Street		
Brechin: Cathedral	Bishops Close	Montrose: Melville South	Castle Street
Gardner Memorial	South Esk Street	Old and St Andrew's	High Street
Carnoustie:	Dundee Street		
Panbride	Arbroath Road		
Forfar: East and Old	East High Street		
Lowson Memorial	Jamieson Street		
St Margaret's	West High Street		

(31) ABERDEEN

Meets on the first Tuesday of February, March, May, September, October, November and December, and on the fourth Tuesday of June. The venue varies.

Clerk:	REV. JOHN A. FERGUSON BD DipMin DMin
Administrator:	MRS CHERYL MARWICK-WATT BA
Treasurer:	MR ALAN MORRISON
Presbytery Office:	Mastrick Church, Greenfern Road, Aberdeen AB16 6TR [E-mail: aberdeen@churchofscotland.org.uk] 01224 698119

Aberdeen: Bridge of Don Oldmachar (01224 709299) (Website: www.oldmacharchurch.org)
David J. Stewart BD MTh DipMin   2000   2012   60 Newburgh Circle, Aberdeen AB22 8QZ   01224 823283
[E-mail: DStewart@churchofscotland.org.uk]

Aberdeen: Craigiebuckler (H) (01224 315649) (Website: www.craigiebuckler.org)
Kenneth L. Petrie MA BD   1984   1999   185 Springfield Road, Aberdeen AB15 8AA   01224 315125
[E-mail: KPetrie@churchofscotland.org.uk]

Aberdeen: Ferryhill (H) (01224 213093) (Website: www.ferryhillparishchurch.org)
J. Peter N. Johnston BSc BD   2001   2013   54 Polmuir Road, Aberdeen AB11 7RT   01224 949192
[E-mail: PJohnston@churchofscotland.org.uk]

Aberdeen: Garthdee (H) linked with Aberdeen: Ruthrieston West (H) (Website: www.ruthriestonwestchurch.org.uk)
Benjamin D.W. Byun BS MDiv MTh PhD   1992   2008   53 Springfield Avenue, Aberdeen AB15 8JJ   01224 312706
[E-mail: BByun@churchofscotland.org.uk]

Aberdeen: High Hilton (H) (01224 494717) (Website: www.highhilton.zyberweb.com)
G. Hutton B. Steel MA BD   1982   2013   24 Rosehill Drive, Aberdeen AB24 4JJ   01224 493552
[E-mail: Hutton.Steel@churchofscotland.org.uk]

Aberdeen: Holburn West (H) (01224 571120) (Website: www.holburnwestchurch.org.uk)
Duncan C. Eddie MA BD   1992   1999   31 Cranford Road, Aberdeen AB10 7NJ   01224 325873
[E-mail: DEddie@churchofscotland.org.uk]

Aberdeen: Mannofield (H) (01224 310087) (E-mail: office@mannofieldchurch.org.uk) (Website: www.mannofieldchurch.org.uk)
Keith T. Blackwood BD DipMin   1997   2007   21 Forest Avenue, Aberdeen AB15 4TU   01224 315748
[E-mail: KBlackwood@churchofscotland.org.uk]

Aberdeen: Mastrick (H) (01224 694121)
Vacant

Aberdeen: Middlefield (H)
Vacant

Aberdeen: Midstocket (01224 319519) (Website: www.midstocketchurch.org.uk)
Sarah E.C. Nicol (Mrs) BSc BD MTh   1985   2013   182 Midstocket Road, Aberdeen AB15 5HS   01224 561358
[E-mail: SNicol@churchofscotland.org.uk]

Aberdeen: Northfield (01224 692332)
Scott C. Guy BD   1989 1998   28 Byron Crescent, Aberdeen AB16 7EX   01224 692332
[E-mail: SGuy@churchofscotland.org.uk]

Aberdeen: Queen Street (01224 643567) (Website: www.queenstreetchurch.org.uk)
Graham D.S. Deans MA BD MTh MLitt DMin 1978 2008   51 Osborne Place, Aberdeen AB25 2BX   01224 646429
[E-mail: GDeans@churchofscotland.org.uk]

Aberdeen: Queen's Cross (H) (01224 644742) (Website: www.queenscrosschurch.org.uk)
Scott M. Rennie MA BD STM 1999 2009   1 St Swithin Street, Aberdeen AB10 6XH   01224 322549
[E-mail: SRennie@churchofscotland.org.uk]

Aberdeen: Rubislaw (H) (01224 645477) (Website: rubislawparishchurchofscotland.org.uk)
Robert L. Smith BS MTh PhD 2000 2013   45 Rubislaw Den South, Aberdeen AB15 4BD   01224 314773
[E-mail: RSmith@churchofscotland.org.uk]

Aberdeen: Ruthrieston West See Aberdeen: Garthdee

Aberdeen: St Columba's Bridge of Don (H) (01224 825653) (Website: http://stcolumbaschurch.org.uk)
Louis Kinsey BD DipMin TD 1991   151 Jesmond Avenue, Aberdeen AB22 8UG   01224 705337
[E-mail: LKinsey@churchofscotland.org.uk]

Aberdeen: St George's Tillydrone (H) (01224 482204) (Website: http://tillydrone.church)
James J.C.M. Weir BD 1991 2003   127 Clifton Road, Aberdeen AB24 4RH   01224 483976
[E-mail: JWeir@churchofscotland.org.uk]

Aberdeen: St John's Church for Deaf People
Mary Whittaker   2011   11 Templand Road, Lhanbryde, Elgin IV30 8BR   (text only) (Mbl) 07810 420106
(Auxiliary Minister)
or contact St Mark's, below.

Aberdeen: St Machar's Cathedral (H) (01224 485988) (Website: www.stmachar.com)
Barry W. Dunsmore MA BD 1982 2015   39 Woodstock Road, Aberdeen AB15 5EX   01224 314596
[E-mail: BDunsmore@churchofscotland.org.uk]

Aberdeen: St Mark's (H) (01224 640672) (Website: www.stmarksaberdeen.org.uk)
Diane L. Hobson (Mrs) BA BD 2002 2010   65 Mile-end Avenue, Aberdeen AB15 5PT   01224 641578
[E-mail: DHobson@churchofscotland.org.uk]

Aberdeen: St Mary's (H) (01224 487227)
Elsie J. Fortune (Mrs) BSc BD   2003   456 King Street, Aberdeen AB24 3DE   01224 633778
[E-mail: EFortune@churchofscotland.org.uk]

Aberdeen: St Nicholas Kincorth, South of (Website: www.southstnicholas.org.uk)
Edward C. McKenna BD DPS   1989   2002   The Manse, Kincorth Circle, Aberdeen AB12 5NX   01224 872820
[E-mail: EMcKenna@churchofscotland.org.uk]

Aberdeen: St Nicholas Uniting, Kirk of (H) (01224 643494) (Website: www.kirk-of-st-nicholas.org.uk)
B. Stephen C. Taylor BA BBS MA MDiv   1984   2005   12 Louisville Avenue, Aberdeen AB15 4TX   01224 314318
[E-mail: BSCTaylor@churchofscotland.org.uk]   01224 649242 (Fax)
St Nicholas Uniting is a Local Ecumenical Project shared with the United Reformed Church

Aberdeen: St Stephen's (H) (01224 624443) (Website: www.st-stephens.co.uk)
Maggie Whyte BD   2010   6 Belvidere Street, Aberdeen AB25 2QS   01224 635694
[E-mail: Maggie.Whyte@churchofscotland.org.uk]

Aberdeen: South Holburn (H) (01224 211730) (Website: www.southholburn.org)
George S. Cowie BSc BD   1991   2006   54 Woodstock Road, Aberdeen AB15 5JF   01224 315042
[E-mail: GCowie@churchofscotland.org.uk]

Aberdeen: Stockethill (Website: www.stockethillchurch.org.uk)
Ian M. Aitken MA BD   1999   52 Ashgrove Road West, Aberdeen AB16 5EE   01224 686929
[E-mail: IAitken@churchofscotland.org.uk]

Aberdeen: Summerhill (H) (Website: www.summerhillchurch.org.uk)
Michael R.R. Shewan MA BD CPS   1985   2010   36 Stronsay Drive, Aberdeen AB15 6JL   01224 324669
[E-mail: MShewan@churchofscotland.org.uk]

Aberdeen: Torry St Fittick's (H) (01224 899183) (Website: www.torrychurch.org.uk)
Edmond Gatima BEng BD MSc MPhil PhD   2013   11 Devanha Gardens East, Aberdeen AB11 7UN   01224 588245
[E-mail: EGatima@churchofscotland.org.uk]

Aberdeen: Woodside (H) (01224 277249) (Website: www.woodsidechurch.co.uk)
Markus Auffermann DipTheol   1999   2006   322 Clifton Road, Aberdeen AB24 4HQ   01224 484562
[E-mail: MAuffermann@churchofscotland.org.uk]

Buckburn Stoneywood (H) (01224 712411) (Website: www.bucksburnstoneywoodchurch.com)
Nigel Parker BD MTh DMin   1994   23 Polo Park, Stoneywood, Aberdeen AB21 9JW   01224 712635
[E-mail: NParker@churchofscotland.org.uk]

Cults (H) (01224 869028) (Website: www.cultsparishchurch.co.uk)
Ewen J. Gilchrist BD DipMin DipComm   1982   2005   1 Cairnlee Terrace, Bieldside, Aberdeen AB15 9AE   01224 861692
[E-mail: EGilchrist@churchofscotland.org.uk]

Dyce (H) (01224 771295) (Website: www.dyceparishchurch.org.uk)
Manson C. Merchant BD CPS   1992   2008   100 Burnside Road, Dyce, Aberdeen AB21 7HA   01224 722380
[E-mail: MMerchant@churchofscotland.org.uk]

Kingswells (Website: www.kingswellschurch.com)
Alisa L. McDonald BA MDiv   2008   2013   Kingswells Manse, Lang Stracht, Aberdeen AB15 8PN   01224 740229
[E-mail: Alisa.McDonald@churchofscotland.org.uk]

Newhills (H) (Tel/Fax: 01224 716161)
Hugh M. Wallace MA BD   1980   2007   Newhills Manse, Bucksburn, Aberdeen AB21 9SS   01224 710318
[E-mail: HWallace@churchofscotland.org.uk]

Peterculter (H) (01224 735845) (Website: http://culterkirk.co.uk)
John A. Ferguson BD DipMin DMin   1988   1999   7 Howie Lane, Peterculter AB14 0LJ   01224 735041
[E-mail: JFerguson@churchofscotland.org.uk]

Cowie, Marian (Mrs) MA BD MTh   1990   2012   (Aberdeen: Midstocket)   54 Woodstock Road, Aberdeen AB15 5JF   01224 315042
[E-mail: mcowieou@aol.com]

Craig, Gordon T. BD DipMin   1988   2012   Chaplain to UK Oil and Gas Industry   c/o Total E and P (UK) plc, Altens Industrial Estate, Crawpeel Road, Aberdeen AB12 3FG   01224 297532
[E-mail: gordon.craig@ukoilandgaschaplaincy.com]

Douglas, Andrew M. MA   1957   1995   (Aberdeen: High Hilton)   219 Countesswells Road, Aberdeen AB15 7RD   01224 311932
Falconer, James B. BD   1982   1991   Hospital Chaplain   3 Brimmond Walk, Westhill AB32 6XH   01224 744621
Garden, Margaret J. (Miss) BD   1993   2009   (Cushnie and Tough)   26 Earns Heugh Circle, Cove Bay, Aberdeen AB12 3PY
[E-mail: revmjgarden@gmail.com]

Goldie, George D. ALCM   1953   1995   (Aberdeen: Greyfriars)   27 Broomhill Avenue, Aberdeen AB10 6JL   01224 322503
Gordon, Laurie Y.   1960   1995   (Aberdeen: John Knox)   1 Alder Drive, Portlethen, Aberdeen AB12 4WA   01224 782703
Graham, A. David M. BA BD   1971   2005   (Aberdeen: Rosemount)   Elmhill House, 27 Shaw Crescent, Aberdeen AB25 3BE   01224 648041
Grainger, Harvey L. LTh   1975   2004   (Kingswells)   13 St Ronan's Crescent, Peterculter, Aberdeen AB14 0RL   01224 739824
[E-mail: harveygrainger@btinternet.com]   (Mbl) 07768 333216

Haddow, Angus H. BSc   1963   1999   (Methlick)   25 Lerwick Road, Aberdeen AB16 6RF   01224 696362

Hamilton, Helen (Miss) BD	1991	2003	(Glasgow: St James' Pollok)	The Cottage, West Tilbouries, Maryculter, Aberdeen AB12 5GD	01224 739632
Hutchison, David S. BSc BD ThM	1991	1999	(Aberdeen: Torry St Fittick's)	The Den of Keithfield, Tarves, Ellon AB41 7NU	01651 851501
Lundie, Ann V. (Miss) DCS			(Deacon)	20 Langdykes Drive, Cove, Aberdeen AB12 3HW [E-mail: ann.lundie@btopenworld.com]	01224 898416
Maciver, Norman MA BD DMin	1976	2006	(Newhills)	4 Mundi Crescent, Newmachar, Aberdeen AB21 0LY [E-mail: norirene@aol.com]	01651 869434
Main, Alan (Prof.) TD MA BD STM PhD DD	1963	2001	(University of Aberdeen)	Kirkfield, Barthol Chapel, Inverurie AB51 8TD [E-mail: amain@talktalk.net]	01651 806773
Montgomerie, Jean B. (Miss) MA BD	1973	2005	(Forfar: St Margaret's)	12 St Ronan's Place, Peterculter, Aberdeen AB14 0QX [E-mail: revjeanb@tiscali.co.uk]	01224 732350
Munro, Flora BD DMin	1993	2015	(Portlethen)	87 Gairn Terrace, Aberdeen AB10 6AY [E-mail: floramunro@aol.com]	(Mbl) 07762 966393
Phillippo, Michael MTh BSc BVetMed MRCVS	2003		(Auxiliary Minister)	25 Deeside Crescent, Aberdeen AB15 7PT [E-mail: phillippo@btinternet.com]	01224 318317
Richardson, Thomas C. LTh ThB	1971	2004	(Cults: West)	19 Kinkell Road, Aberdeen AB15 8HR [E-mail: thomas.richardson7@btinternet.com]	01224 315328
Rodgers, D. Mark BA BD MTh	1987	2003	Head of Spiritual Care, NHS Grampian	63 Cordiner Place, Hilton, Aberdeen AB24 4SB [E-mail: mrodgers@nhs.net]	01224 379135
Sefton, Henry R. MA BD STM PhD	1957	1992	(University of Aberdeen)	25 Albury Place, Aberdeen AB11 6TQ	01224 572305
Sheret, Brian S. MA BD DPhil	1982	2009	(Glasgow: Drumchapel Drumry St Mary's)	59 Airyhall Crescent, Aberdeen AB15 7QS	01224 323032
Somevi, Joseph K. BSc MSc (Oxon) PhD MRICS MRTPI MIEMA CertCRS	2015		Ordained Local Minister	97 Ashwood Road, Bridge of Don, Aberdeen AB22 8QX [E-mail: JSomevi@churchofscotland.org.uk]	01224 826362 (Mbl) 07886 533259
Stewart, James C. MA BD STM FSAScot	1960	2000	(Aberdeen: Kirk of St Nicholas)	54 Murray Terrace, Aberdeen AB11 7SB [E-mail: study@jascstewart.co.uk]	01224 587071
Swinton, John (Prof.) BD PhD	1999		University of Aberdeen	51 Newburgh Circle, Bridge of Don, Aberdeen AB22 8XA [E-mail: j.swinton@abdn.ac.uk]	01224 825637
Torrance, Iain R. (Prof.) TD DPhil DD DTheol LHD FRSE	1982	2012	(President: Princeton Theological Seminary)	25 The Causeway, Duddingston Village, Edinburgh EH15 3QA [E-mail: irt@ptsem.edu]	0131-661 3092
Wilson, Thomas F. BD	1984	1996	Education	55 Allison Close, Cove, Aberdeen AB12 3WG	01224 873501
Youngson, Elizabeth J.B. BD	1996	2015	(Aberdeen: Mastrick)	47 Corse Drive, The Links, Dubford, Aberdeen AB23 8LN [E-mail: elizabeth.youngson@btinternet.com]	(Mbl) 07788 294745

ABERDEEN ADDRESSES

Bridge of Don		Dyce	Victoria Street, Dyce
Oldmachar	Ashwood Park	Ferryhill	Fonthill Road x Polmuir Road
Craigiebuckler	Springfield Road	Garthdee	Ramsay Gardens
Cults	Quarry Road, Cults	High Hilton	Hilton Drive
		Holburn West	Great Western Road
		Kingswells	Old Skene Road, Kingswells
		Mannofield	Great Western Road x Craigton Road
Mastrick	Greenfern Road		
Middlefield	Manor Avenue		
Midstocket	Mid Stocket Road		
New Stockethill			
Northfield	Byron Crescent		
Peterculter	Craigton Crescent		
Queen Street	Queen Street		

Queen's Cross — Albyn Place
Rubislaw — Queen's Gardens
Ruthrieston West — Broomhill Road
St Columba's — Braehead Way, Bridge of Don
St George's — Hayton Road, Tillydrone
St John's for the Deaf — at St Mark's
St Machar's — The Chanonry

St Mark's — Rosemount Viaduct
St Mary's — King Street
St Nicholas Kincorth, South of — Kincorth Circle
St Nicholas Uniting, Kirk of — Union Street
St Stephen's — Powis Place

South Holburn — Holburn Street
Summerhill — Stronsay Drive
Torry St Fittick's — Walker Road
Woodside — Church Street, Woodside

(32) KINCARDINE AND DEESIDE

Meets in various locations as arranged on the first Tuesday of September, October, November, December, March and May, and on the last Tuesday of June at 7pm.

Clerk: REV. HUGH CONKEY BSc BD   39 St Ternans Road, Newtonhill, Stonehaven AB39 3PF   **01569 739297**
[E-mail: kincardinedeeside@churchofscotland.org.uk]

Aberluthnott linked with Laurencekirk (H)
Ronald Gall BSc BD   1985   2001   Aberdeen Road, Laurencekirk AB30 1AJ   01561 378838
[E-mail: RGall@churchofscotland.org.uk]

Aboyne-Dinnet (H) (01339 886989) linked with Cromar (E-mail: aboynedinnet.cos@virgin.net)
Frank Ribbons MA BD DipEd   1985   2011   49 Charlton Crescent, Aboyne AB34 5GN   01339 887267
[E-mail: FRibbons@churchofscotland.org.uk]

Arbuthnott, Bervie and Kinneff
Vacant   10 Kirkburn, Inverbervie, Montrose DD10 0RT   01561 362560

Banchory-Ternan: East (H) (01330 820380) (E-mail: banchoryeastchurchoffice@btconnect.com)
Alan J.S. Murray BSc BD PhD   2003   2013   East Manse, Station Road, Banchory AB31 5YP   01330 822481
[E-mail: AJSMurray@churchofscotland.org.uk]

Banchory-Ternan: West (H)
Antony A. Stephen MA BD   2001   2011   The Manse, 2 Wilson Road, Banchory AB31 5UY   01330 822811
[E-mail: TStephen@churchofscotland.org.uk]

Birse and Feughside
Anita Stutter   2008   2013   The Manse, Finzean, Banchory AB31 6PB   01330 850776
[E-mail: AStutter@churchofscotland.org.uk]

Braemar and Crathie
Kenneth I. Mackenzie DL BD CPS — 1990 2005 — The Manse, Crathie, Ballater AB35 5UL [E-mail: KMacKenzie@churchofscotland.org.uk] — 01339 742208

Cromar See Aboyne-Dinnet

Drumoak (H)-Durris (H)
Jean A. Boyd MSc BSc BA — 2016 — 26 Sunnyside Drive, Drumoak, Banchory AB31 3EW [E-mail: JBoyd@churchofscotland.org.uk] — 01330 811031

Glenmuick (Ballater) (H)
David L.C. Barr — 2014 — The Manse, Craigendarroch Walk, Ballater AB35 5ZB [E-mail: DBarr@churchofscotland.org.uk] — 01339 756111

Laurencekirk See Aberluthnott

Maryculter Trinity (01224 735983) (E-mail: thechurchoffice@tiscali.co.uk)
Melvyn J. Griffiths BTh DipTheol DMin — 1978 2014 — The Manse, Kirkton of Maryculter, Aberdeen AB12 5FS [E-mail: MGriffiths@churchofscotland.org.uk] — 01224 730150

Mearns Coastal
Colin J. Dempster BD CertMin — 1990 2010 — The Manse, Kirkton, St Cyrus, Montrose DD10 0BW [E-mail: CDempster@churchofscotland.org.uk] — 01674 850880

Mid Deeside
Alexander C. Wark MA BD STM — 1982 2012 — The Manse, Torphins, Banchory AB31 4GQ [E-mail: AWark@churchofscotland.org.uk] — 01339 882276

Newtonhill
Hugh Conkey BSc BD — 1987 2001 — 39 St Ternans Road, Newtonhill, Stonehaven AB39 3PF [E-mail: HConkey@churchofscotland.org.uk] — 01569 730143

Portlethen (H) (01224 782883)
Vacant — 18 Rowanbank Road, Portlethen, Aberdeen AB12 4NX — 01224 780211

Stonehaven: Dunnottar (H) linked with Stonehaven: South (H)
Rosslyn P. Duncan BD MTh — 2007 — Dunnottar Manse, Stonehaven AB39 3XL [E-mail: RDuncan@churchofscotland.org.uk] — 01569 762166

Stonehaven: Fetteresso (H) (01569 767689) (E-mail: fetteresso.office@btinternet.com)

Fyfe Blair BA BD DMin   1989 2009   11 South Lodge Drive, Stonehaven AB39 2PN   01569 762876
[E-mail: Fyfe.Blair@churchofscotland.org.uk]

Stonehaven: South See Stonehaven: Dunnottar

West Mearns

Brian D. Smith BD (Hons)   1990 2016   West Mearns Parish Church Manse, Fettercairn,   01561 340203
Laurencekirk AB30 1UE
[E-mail: BSmith@churchofscotland.org.uk]

Broadley, Linda J. (Mrs) LTh DipEd	1996	2013	(Dun and Hillside)	Snaefell, Lochside Road, St Cyrus, Montrose DD10 0DB [E-mail: lindabroadley@btinternet.com]	01674 850141
Brown, J.W.S. BTh	1960	1995	(Cromar)	10 Forestside Road, Banchory AB31 5ZH [E-mail: iainisobel@aol.com]	01330 824353
Cameron, Ann J. (Mrs) CertCS DCE TEFL	2005		Auxiliary Minister	Currently resident in Qatar [E-mail: AnnCameron2@churchofscotland.org.uk]	
Christie, Andrew C. LTh	1975	2000	(Banchory-Devenick and Maryculter/Cookney)	17 Broadstraik Close, Elrick, Aberdeen AB32 6JP [E-mail: jrbbbb@icloud.com]	01224 746888
Forbes, John W.A. BD	1973	1999	(Edzell Lethnot with Fern, Careston and Menmuir with Glenesk)	Little Ennochie Steading, Finzean, Banchory AB31 6LX	01330 850785
Kinninburgh, Elizabeth B.F. (Miss) MA BD	1970	1986	(Birse with Finzean with Strachan)	21 Glen Tanar, Allachburn, Low Road, Aboyne AB34 5GW	01339 886757
Lamb, A. Douglas MA	1964	2002	(Dalry: St Margaret's)	9 Luther Drive, Laurencekirk AB30 1FE [E-mail: lamb.edzell@talk21.com]	01561 376816
Smith, Albert E. BD	1983	2006	(Methlick)	42 Haulkerton Crescent, Laurencekirk AB30 1FB [E-mail: aesmith42@googlemail.com]	01561 376111
Wallace, William F. BDS BD	1968	2008	(Wick: Pulteneytown and Thrumster)	Lachan Cottage, 29 Station Road, Banchory AB31 5XX [E-mail: williamwallace39@talktalk.net]	01330 822259
Watt, William D. LTh	1978	1996	(Aboyne-Dinnet)	2 West Toll Crescent, Aboyne AB34 5GB [E-mail: wdwatt22@tiscali.co.uk]	01339 886943
Wilson, Andrew G.N. MA BD DMin	1977	2012	(Aberdeen: Rubislaw)	Auchintarph, Coull, Tarland, Aboyne AB34 4TT [E-mail: agn.wilson@gmail.com]	01339 880918

(33) GORDON

Meets at various locations on the first Tuesday of February, March, April, May, September, October, November and December, and on the last Tuesday of June.

Clerk: REV. G. EUAN D. GLEN BSc BD   The Manse, 26 St Ninians, Monymusk, Inverurie AB51 7HF   01467 651470
[E-mail: gordon@churchofscotland.org.uk]

Barthol Chapel linked with Tarves
Vacant
8 Murray Avenue, Tarves, Ellon AB41 7LZ
01651 851250

Belhelvie (H)
Paul McKeown BSc PhD BD
2000   2005
Belhelvie Manse, Balmedie, Aberdeen AB23 8YR
[E-mail: PMcKeown@churchofscotland.org.uk]
01358 742227

Blairdaff and Chapel of Garioch
Martyn S. Sanders BA CertEd
2015
The Manse, Chapel of Garioch, Inverurie AB51 5HE
[E-mail: MSanders@churchofscotland.org.uk]
01467 681619
07814 164373 (Mbl)

Cluny (H) linked with Monymusk (H)
G. Euan D. Glen BSc BD
1992
The Manse, 26 St Ninians, Monymusk, Inverurie AB51 7HF
[E-mail: GGlen@churchofscotland.org.uk]
01467 651470

Culsalmond and Rayne linked with Daviot (H)
Mary M. Cranfield MA BD DMin
1989
The Manse, Daviot, Inverurie AB51 0HY
[E-mail: MCranfield@churchofscotland.org.uk]
01467 671241

Cushnie and Tough (R) (H)
Rosemary Legge (Mrs) BSc BD MTh
1992   2010
The Manse, Muir of Fowlis, Alford AB33 8JU
[E-mail: RLegge@churchofscotland.org.uk]
01975 581239

Daviot See Culsalmond and Rayne

Echt linked with Midmar (H)
Elspeth M. McKay (Mrs)
LLB LLM PGCert BD
2014
The Manse, Echt, Westhill AB32 7AB
[E-mail: EMcKay@churchofscotland.org.uk]
01330 860004

Ellon
Alastair J. Bruce BD MTh PGCE
2015
The Manse, 12 Union Street, Ellon AB41 9BA
[E-mail: ABruce@churchofscotland.org.uk]
01358 723787

Fintray Kinellar Keithhall
Vacant
20 Kinmohr Rise, Blackburn, Aberdeen AB21 0LJ
01224 791350

Foveran
Richard M.C. Reid BSc BD MTh — 1991 — 2013
The Manse, Foveran, Ellon AB41 6AP
[E-mail: RReid@churchofscotland.org.uk]
01358 789288

Howe Trinity
John A. Cook MA BD — 1986 — 2000
The Manse, 110 Main Street, Alford AB33 8AD
[E-mail: John.Cook@churchofscotland.org.uk]
01975 562282

Huntly Cairnie Glass
Thomas R. Calder LLB BD WS — 1994
The Manse, Queen Street, Huntly AB54 8EB
[E-mail: TCalder@churchofscotland.org.uk]
01466 792630

Insch-Leslie-Premnay-Oyne (H)
Kay Gauld BD STM PhD — 1999 — 2015
66 Denwell Road, Insch AB52 6LH
[E-mail: KGauld@churchofscotland.org.uk]
01464 820404

Inverurie: St Andrew's (Website: standrewschurchinverurie.org.uk)
Vacant
27 Buchan Drive, Newmachar, Aberdeen AB21 0NR
01651 862281

Inverurie: West
Vacant
West Manse, 1 Westburn Place, Inverurie AB51 5QS
01467 620285

Kemnay
Joshua M. Mikelson — 2008 — 2015
15 Kirkland, Kemnay, Inverurie AB51 5QD
[E-mail: JMikelson@churchofscotland.org.uk]
01467 642219 (Tel/Fax)

Kintore (H)
Neil W. Meyer BD MTh — 2000 — 2014
28 Oakhill Road, Kintore, Inverurie AB51 0FH
[E-mail: NMeyer@churchofscotland.org.uk]
01467 632219

Meldrum and Bourtie
Alison Jaffrey (Mrs) MA BD FSAScot — 1990 — 2010
The Manse, Urquhart Road, Oldmeldrum, Inverurie AB51 0EX
[E-mail: AJaffrey@churchofscotland.org.uk]
01651 872250

Methlick
William A. Stalder BA MDiv MLitt PhD — 2014
The Manse, Manse Road, Methlick, Ellon AB41 7DG
[E-mail: WStalder@churchofscotland.org.uk]
01651 806264

Midmar See Echt
Monymusk See Cluny

New Machar
| Douglas G. McNab BA BD | 1999 | 2010 | The New Manse, Newmachar, Aberdeen AB21 0RD [E-mail: DMcNab@churchofscotland.org.uk] | 01651 862278 |

Noth
| Regine U. Cheyne (Mrs) MA BSc BD | 1988 | 2010 | Manse of Noth, Kennethmont, Huntly AB54 4NP [E-mail: RCheyne@churchofscotland.org.uk] | 01464 831690 |

Skene (H)
| Stella Campbell MA (Oxon) BD | 2012 | The Manse, Manse Road, Kirkton of Skene, Westhill AB32 6LX [E-mail: SCampbell@churchofscotland.org.uk] | 01224 745955 |
| Marion G. Stewart (Miss) DCS | | Kirk Cottage, Kirkton of Skene, Westhill AB32 6XE [E-mail: MStewart@churchofscotland.org.uk] | 01224 743407 |

Strathbogie Drumblade
| Neil I.M. MacGregor BD | 1995 | 49 Deveron Park, Huntly AB54 8UZ [E-mail: NMacGregor@churchofscotland.org.uk] | 01466 792702 |

Tarves See Barthol Chapel

Udny and Pitmedden
| Gillean P. MacLean (Ms) BA BD | 1994 | 2013 | The Manse, Manse Road, Udny Green, Ellon AB41 7RS [E-mail: GMacLean@churchofscotland.org.uk] | 01651 843794 |

Upper Donside (H) (E-mail: upperdonsideparishchurch@btinternet.com)
| Vacant | The Manse, Lumsden, Huntly AB54 4GQ | 01464 861757 |

Craggs, Sheila (Mrs)	2001	2008	(Auxiliary Minister)	7 Morar Court, Ellon AB41 9GG	01358 723055
Craig, Anthony J.D. BD	1987	2009	(Glasgow: Maryhill)	4 Hightown, Collieston, Ellon AB41 8RS [E-mail: craig.glasgow@gmx.net]	01358 751247
Davies, James M. BSc BD	1982	2016	(Interim Minister)	27 Buchan Drive, Newmachar, Aberdeen AB21 0NR [E-mail: daviesjim@btinternet.com]	01651 862281

Dryden, Ian MA DipEd	1988 2001	(New Machar)	16 Glenhome Gardens, Dyce, Aberdeen AB21 7FG [E-mail: ian@idryden.freeserve.co.uk]	01224 722820
Groves, Ian B BD CPS	1989 2016	(Inverurie West)	28 Parkhill Circle, Dyce, Aberdeen AB21 7FN [E-mail: IGroves@churchofscotland.org.uk]	01224 774380
Hawthorn, Daniel MA BD DMin	1965 2004	(Belhelvie)	7 Crimond Drive, Ellon AB41 8BT [E-mail: donhawthorn@compuserve.com]	01358 723981
Jones, Robert A. LTh CA	1966 1997	(Marnoch)	13 Gordon Terrace, Inverurie AB51 4GT	01467 622691
Macalister, Eleanor	1994 2006	(Ellon)	Quarryview, Ythan Bank, Ellon AB41 7TH [E-mail: macal1ster@aol.com]	01358 761402
Mack, John C. JP	1985 2008	(Auxiliary Minister)	The Willows, Auchleven, Insch AB52 6QB	01464 820387
McLeish, Robert S.	1970 2000	(Insch-Leslie-Premnay-Oyne)	19 Western Road, Insch AB52 6JR	01464 820749
Renton, John P. BA LTh	1976 2014	(Kennay)	2 Fettermear Way, Kemnay, Inverurie AB51 5JH [E-mail: j.m.renton@btinternet.com]	01467 642403
Rodger, Matthew A. BD	1978 1999	(Ellon)	15 Meadowlands Drive, Westhill AB32 6EJ	01224 743184
Stoddart, A. Grainger	1975 2001	(Meldrum and Bourtie)	6 Mayfield Gardens, Insch AB52 6XL	01464 821124
Thomson, Iain U. MA BD	1970 2011	(Skene)	4 Keirhill Gardens, Westhill AB32 6AZ [E-mail: iainuthomson@googlemail.com]	01224 746743

(34) BUCHAN

Meets at St Kane's Centre, New Deer, Turriff on the first Tuesday of February, March, May, September, October, November and December, and on the third Tuesday of June.

Clerk:	**REV. SHEILA M. KIRK BA LLB BD**		**The Manse, Old Deer, Peterhead AB42 5JB** [E-mail: buchan@churchofscotland.org.uk]	**01771 623582**

Aberdour linked with Pitsligo
Vacant | | | 19 Summers Road, Rosehearty, Fraserburgh AB43 7HP | 01346 571823

Auchaber United linked with Auchterless
Stephen J. Potts BA | 2012 | | The Manse, Auchterless, Turriff AB53 8BA [E-mail: SPotts@churchofscotland.org.uk] | 01888 511058

Auchterless See Auchaber United

Banff linked with King Edward
David I.W. Locke MA MSc BD   2000   2012   7 Colleonard Road, Banff AB45 1DZ
[E-mail: DLocke@churchofscotland.org.uk]   01261 812107
07776 448301 (Mbl)

Crimond linked with Lonmay
Vacant   The Manse, Crimond, Fraserburgh AB43 8QJ   01346 532431

Cruden (H)
Vacant   The Manse, Hatton, Peterhead AB42 0QQ   01779 841229

Deer (H)
Sheila M. Kirk BA LLB BD   2007   2010   The Manse, Old Deer, Peterhead AB42 5JB
[E-mail: SKirk@churchofscotland.org.uk]   01771 623582

Fraserburgh: Old
Vacant   4 Robbies Road, Fraserburgh AB43 7AF   01346 515332

Fraserburgh: South (H) linked with Inverallochy and Rathen: East
Ronald F. Yule   1982   15 Victoria Street, Fraserburgh AB43 9PJ
[E-mail: RYule@churchofscotland.org.uk]   01346 518244

Fraserburgh: West (H) linked with Rathen: West
Vacant   4 Kirkton Gardens, Fraserburgh AB43 8TU   01346 513303

Fyvie linked with Rothienorman
Robert J. Thorburn BD   1978   2004   The Manse, Fyvie, Turriff AB53 8RD
[E-mail: RThorburn@churchofscotland.org.uk]   01651 891230

Inverallochy and Rathen: East See Fraserburgh: South
King Edward See Banff

Longside
Robert A. Fowlie BD   2007   The Manse, Old Deer, Peterhead AB42 5JB
[E-mail: RFowlie@churchofscotland.org.uk]   01771 622228

Lonmay See Crimond

Macduff
Vacant
10 Ross Street, Macduff AB44 1NS
01261 832316

Marnoch
Alan Macgregor BA BD PhD   1992   2013
Marnoch Manse, 53 South Street, Aberchirder, Huntly AB54 7TS
[E-mail: AMacgregor@churchofscotland.org.uk]
01466 781143

Maud and Savoch linked with New Deer: St Kane's
Vacant
The Manse, New Deer, Turriff AB53 6TD
01771 644216

Monquhitter and New Byth linked with Turriff: St Andrew's
James Cook MA MDiv   1999   2002
St Andrew's Manse, Balmellie Road, Turriff AB53 4SP
[E-mail: JCook@churchofscotland.org.uk]
01888 560304

New Deer: St Kane's See Maud and Savoch

New Pitsligo linked with Strichen and Tyrie
Andrew P. Fothergill BA   2012
Kingsville, Strichen, Fraserburgh AB43 6SQ
[E-mail: AFothergill@churchofscotland.org.uk]
01771 637365
William Stewart   2015
Denend, Strichen, Fraserburgh AB43 6RN
[E-mail: billandjunes@live.co.uk]
01771 637256
(Ordained Local Minister)

Ordiquhill and Cornhill (H) linked with Whitehills
W. Myburgh Verster BA BTh LTh MTh   1981   2011
6 Craigneen Place, Whitehills, Banff AB45 2NE
[E-mail: WVerster@churchofscotland.org.uk]
01261 861317

Peterhead: New
Vacant
1 Hawthorn Road, Peterhead AB42 2DW
(New charge formed by the union of Peterhead: Old and Peterhead: Trinity)

Peterhead: St Andrew's (H)
Vacant
1 Landale Road, Peterhead AB42 1QN
01779 238200

Pitsligo See Aberdour

Portsoy
Vacant
The Manse, 4 Seafield Terrace, Portsoy, Banff AB45 2QB
01261 842272

Rathen: West See Fraserburgh: West
Rothienorman See Fyvie

St Fergus
Jeffrey Tippner BA MDiv MCS PhD   1991   2012   26 Newton Road, St Fergus, Peterhead AB42 3DD   01779 838287
[E-mail: JTippner@churchofscotland.org.uk]

Sandhaven
Vacant

Strichen and Tyrie See New Pitsligo
Turriff: St Andrew's See Monquhitter and New Byth

Turriff: St Ninian's and Forglen (H) (L)
Kevin R. Gruer BSc BA   2011   4 Deveronside Drive, Turriff AB53 4SP   01888 563850
[E-mail: KGruer@churchofscotland]

Whitehills See Ordiquhill and Cornhill

Coutts, Fred MA BD   1973 1989 (Hospital Chaplain)   Ladebank, 1 Manse Place, Hatton, Peterhead AB42 0UQ   01779 841320
[E-mail: fred.coutts@btinternet.com]

Fawkes, G.M. Allan BA BSc JP   1979 2000 (Lonmay with Rathen: West)   3 Northfield Gardens, Hatton, Peterhead AB42 0SW   01779 841814
[E-mail: afawkes@aol.com]

Gehrke, Robert B. BSc BD CEng MIEE   1994 2013 (Blackridge with Harthill: St Andrew's)   140 The Green, Gardenstown, Banff AB45 3BD   01261 839129
[E-mail: bob.gehrke@gmail.com]

McMillan, William J. CA LTh BD   1969 2004 (Sandsting and Aithsting with Walls and Sandness)   7 Ardinn Drive, Turriff AB53 4PR   01888 560727
[E-mail: revbillymcmillan@aol.com]

Macnee, Iain LTh BD MA PhD   1975 2011 (New Pitsligo with Strichen and Tyrie)   Wardend Cottage, Alvah, Banff AB45 3TR   01261 815647
[E-mail: macneeiain4@googlemail.com]

Noble, George S. DipTh   1972 2000 (Carfin with Newarthill)   Craigowan, 3 Main Street, Inverallochy, Fraserburgh AB43 8XX   01346 582749
Ross, David S. MSc PhD BD   1978 2013 (Prison Chaplain Service)   3–5 Abbey Street, Old Deer, Peterhead AB42 5LN   01771 623994
[E-mail: padsross@btinternet.com]

van Sittert, Paul BA BD   1997 2011 Chaplain: Army   4Bn The Royal Regiment of Scotland, Bourlon Barracks, Plumer Road, Catterick Garrison DL9 3AD
[E-mail: padre.pvs@gmail.com]

(35) MORAY

Meets at St Andrew's-Lhanbryd and Urquhart on the first Tuesday of February, March, May, September, October, November and December, and at the Moderator's church on the fourth Tuesday of June.

Clerk:	REV. ALASTAIR H. GRAY MA BD			North Manse, Church Road, Keith AB55 5FX [E-mail: moray@churchofscotland.org.uk]	01542 886840 07944 287777 (Mbl)
Aberlour (H)					
Shuna M. Dicks BSc BD		2010		The Manse, Mary Avenue, Aberlour AB38 9QU [E-mail: SDicks@churchofscotland.org.uk]	01340 871687
Alves and Burghead linked with Kinloss and Findhorn					
Louis C. Bezuidenhout BA MA BD DD	1978	2014		The Manse, 4 Manse Road, Kinloss, Forres IV36 3GH [E-mail: LBezuidenhout@churchofscotland.org.uk]	01309 690474
Bellie and Speymouth					
Vacant				11 The Square, Fochabers IV32 7DG	01343 820256
Birnie and Pluscarden linked with Elgin: High					
Stuart M. Duff BA	1997	2014		The Manse, Daisy Bank, 5 Forteath Avenue, Elgin IV30 1TQ [E-mail: SDuff@churchofscotland.org.uk]	01343 545703
Buckie: North (H) linked with Rathven					
Isabel C. Buchan (Mrs) BSc BD RE(PgCE)	1975	2013		The Manse, 14 St Peter's Road, Buckie AB56 1DL [E-mail: IBuchan@churchofscotland.org.uk]	01542 832118
Buckie: South and West (H) linked with Enzie					
Vacant				Craigendarroch, 14 Cliff Terrace, Buckie AB56 1LX	01542 833775
Cullen and Deskford (Website: www.cullen-deskford-church.org.uk)					
Douglas F. Stevenson BD DipMin	1991	2010		14 Seafield Road, Cullen, Buckie AB56 4AF [E-mail: DStevenson@churchofscotland.org.uk]	01542 841963
Dallas linked with Forres: St Leonard's (H) linked with Rafford					
Donald K. Prentice BSc BD	1989	2010		St Leonard's Manse, Nelson Road, Forres IV36 1DR [E-mail: DPrentice@churchofscotland.org.uk]	01309 672380
Anne Attenburrow BSc MB ChB (Auxiliary Minister)	2006	2013		4 Jock Inksons Brae, Elgin IV30 1QE [E-mail: AAttenburrow@churchofscotland.org.uk]	01343 552330

John A. Morrison BSc BA PGCE   2013   35 Kirkton Place, Elgin IV30 6JR   01343 550199
(Ordained Local Minister)   [E-mail: JMorrison@churchofscotland.org.uk]

Duffus, Spynie and Hopeman (H) (Website: www.duffusparish.co.uk)
Jennifer M. Adams BEng BD   2013   The Manse, Duffus, Elgin IV30 5QP   01343 830276
    [E-mail: JAdams@churchofscotland.org.uk]

Dyke linked with Edinkillie
Vacant   Manse of Dyke, Brodie, Forres IV36 2TD   01309 641239

Edinkillie See Dyke
Elgin: High See Birnie and Pluscarden

Elgin: St Giles' (H) and St Columba's South (01343 551501) (Office: Williamson Hall, Duff Avenue, Elgin IV30 1QS)
Vacant   18 Reidhaven Street, Elgin IV30 1QH   01343 545729

Enzie See Buckie: South and West

Findochty linked with Portknockie
Hilary W. Smith BD DipMin MTh PhD   1999   2014   20 Netherton Terrace, Findochty, Buckie AB56 4QD   01542 833180
    [E-mail: Hilary.Smith@churchofscotland.org.uk]

Forres: St Laurence (H)
Barry J. Boyd LTh DPS   1993   12 Mackenzie Drive, Forres IV36 2JP   01309 672260
    [E-mail: BBoyd@churchofscotland.org.uk]   07778 731018 (Mbl)

Forres: St Leonard's See Dallas

Keith: North, Newmill, Boharm and Rothiemay (H) (01542 886390)
Alastair H. Gray MA BD   1978   2015   North Manse, Church Road, Keith AB55 5BR   01542 886840
    [E-mail: AGray@churchofscotland.org.uk]

Keith: St Rufus, Botriphnie and Grange (H)
Vacant   St Rufus' Manse, Church Road, Keith AB55 5BR   01542 882799

Kinloss and Findhorn See Alves and Burghead

Knockando, Elchies and Archiestown (H) linked with Rothes (Website: www.moraykirk.co.uk)

Robert J.M. Anderson BD FInstLM	1993	2000	The Manse, Rothes, Aberlour AB38 7AF [E-mail: RJMAnderson@churchofscotland.org.uk]	01340 831381

Lossiemouth: St Gerardine's High (H) linked with Lossiemouth: St James

Geoffrey D. McKee BA	1997	2014	The Manse, St Gerardine's Road, Lossiemouth IV31 6RA [E-mail: GMcKee@churchofscotland.org.uk]	01343 208852

Lossiemouth: St James' See Lossiemouth: St Gerardine's High

Mortlach and Cabrach (H)

Vacant	Mortlach Manse, Dufftown, Keith AB55 4AR	01340 820380

Portknockie See Findochty
Rafford See Dallas
Rathven See Buckie: North
Rothes See Knockando, Elchies and Archiestown

St Andrew's-Lhanbryd (H) and Urquhart

Vacant	39 St Andrews Road, Lhanbryde, Elgin IV30 8PU	01343 843765

Bain, Brian LTh	1980	2007	(Gask with Methven and Logiealmond)	Bayview, 13 Stewart Street, Portgordon, Buckie AB56 5QT [E-mail: bricoreen@gmail.com]	01542 831215
Buchan, Alexander MA BD PGCE	1975	1992	(North Ronaldsay with Sanday)	The Manse, 14 St Peter's Road, Buckie AB56 1DL [E-mail: revabuchan@bluebucket.org]	01542 832118
Davidson, A.A.B. MA BD	1960	1997	(Grange with Rothiemay)	11 Sutors Rise, Nairn IV12 5BU	01343 820937
King, Margaret MA DCS			(Deacon)	56 Murrayfield, Fochabers IV32 7EZ [E-mail: margaretrking@tiscali.co.uk]	
Morton, Alasdair J. MA BD DipEd FEIS	1960	2000	(Bowden with Newtown)	16 St Leonard's Road, Forres IV36 1DW [E-mail: alasgilmor@hotmail.co.uk]	01309 671719
Morton, Gillian M. (Mrs) MA BD PGCE	1983	1996	(Hospital Chaplain)	16 St Leonard's Road, Forres IV36 1DW [E-mail: gillianmorton@hotmail.co.uk]	01309 671719
Munro, Sheila BD	1995	2016	RAF Station Chaplain	RAF Lossiemouth, Elgin IV31 6SD [E-mail: sheila.munro78@mod.uk]	01343 817180
Poole, Ann McColl (Mrs) DipEd ACE LTh	1983	2003	(Dyke with Edinkillie)	Kirkside Cottage, Dyke, Forres IV36 2TF	01309 641046
Robertson, Peter BSc BD	1988	1998	(Dallas with Forres: St Leonard's with Rafford)	17 Ferryhill Road, Forres IV36 2GY [E-mail: peterrobertsonforres@talktalk.net]	01309 676769
Rollo, George B. BD	1974	2010	(Elgin: St Giles' and St Columba's South)	'Struan', 13 Meadow View, Hopeman, Elgin IV30 5PL [E-mail: rollos@gmail.com]	01343 835226

Smith, Hugh M.C. LTh	1973	2013	(Mortlach and Cabrach)	6 Concraig Walk, Kingswells, Aberdeen AB15 8DU
				01224 745275
Smith, Morris BD	1988	2013	(Cromdale and Advie with Dulnain Bridge with Grantown-on-Spey)	1 Urquhart Grove, New Elgin IV30 8TB
				01343 545019
				[E-mail: mosmith.themanse@btinternet.com]
Watts, Anthony BD DipTechEd JP	1999	2013	(Glenmuick Ballater)	7 Cumiskie Crescent, Forres IV36 2QB
				[E-mail: tony.watts6@btinternet.com]
Whyte, David LTh	1993	2011	(Boat of Garten, Duthil and Kincardine)	1 Lemanfield Crescent, Garmouth, Fochabers IV32 7LS
				01343 870667
				[E-mail: whytedj@btinternet.com]
Wright, David L. MA BD	1957	1998	(Stornoway: St Columba)	84 Wyvis Drive, Nairn IV12 4TP
				01667 451613

(36) ABERNETHY

Meets at Boat of Garten on the first Tuesday of February, March, May, September, October, November and December, and on the last Tuesday of June.

Clerk: REV JAMES A.I. McEWAN MA BD   Rapness, Station Road, Nethy Bridge PA25 3DN   **01479 821116**
[E-mail: abernethy@churchofscotland.org.uk]

Abernethy (H) linked with Boat of Garten (H), Duthil (H) and Kincardine
Donald K. Walker BD   1979   2013   The Manse, Deshar Road, Boat of Garten PH24 3BN   01479 831252
[E-mail: DWalker@churchofscotland.org.uk]

Alvie and Insh (R) (H) linked with Rothiemurchus and Aviemore (H)
Vacant   The Manse, 8 Dalfaber Park, Aviemore PH22 1QF   01479 810280

Boat of Garten, Duthil and Kincardine See Abernethy

Cromdale (H) and Advie linked with Dulnain Bridge (H) linked with Grantown-on-Spey (H)
Gordon Strang   2014   The Manse, Golf Course Road, Grantown-on-Spey PH26 3HY   01479 872084
[E-mail: GStrang@churchofscotland.org.uk]

Dulnain Bridge See Cromdale and Advie
Grantown-on-Spey See Cromdale and Advie

Kingussie (H)
Alison H. Burnside (Mrs) MA BD   1991   2013   The Manse, 18 Hillside Avenue, Kingussie PH21 1PA   01540 662327
[E-mail: ABurnside@churchofscotland.org.uk]

Laggan (H) linked with Newtonmore: St Bride's (H)

Catherine A. Buchan (Mrs) MA MDiv   2002   2009   The Manse, Fort William Road, Newtonmore PH20 1DG   01540 673238
[E-mail: CBuchan@churchofscotland.org.uk]

Newtonmore: St Bride's See Laggan
Rothiemurchus and Aviemore See Alvie and Insh

Tomintoul (H), Glenlivet and Inveraven

Vacant   The Manse, Tomintoul, Ballindalloch AB37 9HA   01807 580254

Duncanson, Mary (Ms) BTh	2013	Ordained Local Minister: Presbytery Pastoral Support	3 Balmenach Road, Cromdale, Grantown-on-Spey PH26 3LJ [E-mail: MDuncanson@churchofscotland.org.uk]	01479 872165
MacEwan, James A.I. MA BD	1973	2012	(Abernethy with Cromdale and Advie)	Rapness, Station Road, Nethy Bridge PH25 3DN [E-mail: wurrus@hotmail.co.uk]	01479 821116
Ritchie, Christine A.Y. (Mrs) BD DipMin	2002	2012	(Braes of Rannoch with Foss and Rannoch)	25 Beachen Court, Grantown-on-Spey PH26 3JD [E-mail: cayritchie@btinternet.com]	01479 873419
Thomson, Mary Ellen (Mrs)	2013	Ordained Local Minister	Riverside Flat, Gynack Street, Kingussie PH21 1EL [E-mail: Mary.Thomson@churchofscotland.org.uk]	01540 661772
Wallace, Sheila D. (Mrs) DCS BA BD		Deacon	Beannach Cottage, Spey Avenue, Boat of Garten PH24 3BE [E-mail: sheilad.wallace53@gmail.com]	01479 831548 (Mbl) 07733 243046

(37) INVERNESS

Meets at Inverness, in Inverness: Trinity, on the first Tuesday of February, March, May, September, October, November and December, and at the Moderator's church on the fourth Tuesday of June.

Clerk: REV. TREVOR G. HUNT BA BD   **7 Woodville Court, Culduthel Avenue, Inverness IV2 6BX**   **01463 250355**
                                              [E-mail: inverness@churchofscotland.org.uk]   **07753 423333 (Mbl)**

Ardersier (H) linked with Petty

Robert Cleland   1997   2014   The Manse, Ardersier, Inverness IV2 7SX   01667 462224
[E-mail: RCleland@churchofscotland.org.uk]

Auldearn and Dalmore linked with Nairn: St Ninian's (H)

Thomas M. Bryson BD   1997   2015   The Manse, Auldearn, Nairn IV12 5SX   01667 451675
[E-mail: TBryson@churchofscotland.org.uk]

Name	Ordained	Inducted	Address	Telephone
Cawdor (H) linked with Croy and Dalcross (H) Vacant			The Manse, Croy, Inverness IV2 5PH	01667 493217
Croy and Dalcross See Cawdor				
Culloden: The Barn (H) Michael Robertson BA	2014		45 Oakdene Court, Culloden IV2 7XL [E-mail: Mike.Robertson@churchofscotland.org.uk]	01463 795430 07740 984395 (Mbl)
Daviot and Dunlichity linked with Moy, Dalarossie and Tomatin Vacant			The Manse, Daviot, Inverness IV2 5XL	01463 772242
Dores and Boleskine Vacant				
Inverness: Crown (H) (01463 231140) Peter H. Donald MA PhD BD	1991	1998	39 Southside Road, Inverness IV2 4XA [E-mail: PDonald@churchofscotland.org.uk]	01463 230537
Inverness: Dalneigh and Bona (GD) (H) Vacant			9 St Mungo Road, Inverness IV3 5AS	01463 232339
Inverness: East (H) Andrew T.B. McGowan (Prof.) BD STM PhD	1979	2009	2 Victoria Drive, Inverness IV2 3QD [E-mail: A.McGowan@churchofscotland.org.uk]	01463 238770
Inverness: Hilton Duncan A.C. MacPherson LLB BD	1994		66 Culduthel Mains Crescent, Inverness IV2 6RG [E-mail: DMacPherson@churchofscotland.org.uk]	01463 231417
Inverness: Inshes (H) David S. Scott MA BD	1987	2013	48 Redwood Crescent, Milton of Leys, Inverness IV2 6HB [E-mail: David.Scott@churchofscotland.org.uk]	01463 772402
Inverness: Kinmylies (H) Andrew Barrie BD	2013		2 Balnafettack Place, Inverness IV3 8TQ [E-mail: ABarrie@churchofscotland.org.uk]	01463 224307

Inverness: Ness Bank (R) (H)
Fiona E. Smith (Mrs) LLB BD   2010   15 Ballifeary Road, Inverness IV3 5PJ
[E-mail: FSmith@churchofscotland.org.uk]   01463 234653

Inverness: Old High St Stephen's
Peter W. Nimmo BD ThM   1996   2004   24 Damfield Road, Inverness IV2 3HU
[E-mail: PNimmo@churchofscotland.org.uk]   01463 250802

Inverness: St Columba (New Charge Development) (H)
Scott A. McRoberts BD MTh   2012   20 Bramble Close, Inverness IV2 6BS
[E-mail: SMcRoberts@churchofscotland.org.uk]   01463 230308
07535 290092 (Mbl)

Inverness: Trinity (H)
Alistair Murray BD   1984   2004   60 Kenneth Street, Inverness IV3 5PZ
[E-mail: Alistair.Murray@churchofscotland.org.uk]   01463 234756

Kilmorack and Erchless
Ian A. Manson BA BD   1989   2016   'Roselynn', Croyard Road, Beauly IV4 7DJ
[E-mail: IManson@churchofscotland.org.uk]   01463 783824

Kiltarlity linked with Kirkhill
Jonathan W. Humphrey BSc BD PhD   2015   Wardlaw Manse, Wardlaw Road, Kirkhill, Inverness IV5 7NZ
[E-mail: JHumphrey@churchofscotland.org.uk]   01463 831662

Kirkhill See Kiltarlity
Moy, Dalarossie and Tomatin See Daviot and Dunlichity

Nairn: Old (H) (01667 452382)
Alison C. Mehigan BD DPS   2003   2015   15 Chattan Gardens, Nairn IV12 4QP
[E-mail: AMehigan@churchofscotland.org.uk]   01667 453777

Nairn: St Ninian's See Auldearn and Dalmore
Petty See Ardersier

Urquhart and Glenmoriston (H)
Hugh F. Watt BD DPS DMin   1986   1996   Blairbeg, Drumnadrochit, Inverness IV3 6UG
[E-mail: HWatt@churchofscotland.org.uk]   01456 450231

Name	Years	Role	Address / E-mail	Telephone
Archer, Morven (Mrs)	2013	Ordained Local Minister	42 Firthview Drive, Inverness IV3 8QE [E-mail: MArcher@churchofscotland.org.uk]	01463 237840
Black, Archibald T. BSc	1964 1997	(Inverness: Ness Bank)	16 Elm Park, Inverness IV2 4WN	01463 230588
Brown, Derek G. BD DipMin DMin	1989 1994	Lead Chaplain: NHS Highland	Cathedral Manse, Cnoc-an-Lobht, Dornoch IV25 3HN [E-mail: derek.brown1@nhs.net]	01862 810296
Burnside, William A.M. MA BD PgCE	1990 2013	(Stromness)	68 Huntly Street, Inverness IV3 5JN [E-mail: bburnside@btinternet.com]	01463 794634
Buell, F. Bart BA MDiv	1980 1995	(Urquhart and Glenmoriston)	6 Towerhill Place, Cradlehall, Inverness IV2 5FN [E-mail: bartbuell@talktalk.net]	
Campbell, Reginald F.	1979 2015	(Urquhart and Glenmoriston)	12 Alloway Drive, Kirkcaldy KY2 6DX [E-mail: campbell578@talktalk.net]	
Chisholm, Archibald F. MA	1957 1997	(Braes of Rannoch with Foss and Rannoch)	32 Seabank Road, Nairn IV12 4EU	01667 452001 (Home) 01463 711609
Fraser, Jonathan MA(Div) MTh ThM	2012	Associate: Inverness: Hilton	20 Moy Terrace, Inverness IV2 4EL [E-mail: jonathan@hiltonchurch.org.uk]	(Work) 01463 233310
Hunt, Trevor G. BA BD	1986 2011	(Evie with Firth with Rendall)	7 Woodville Court, Culduthel Avenue, Inverness IV2 6BX [E-mail: trevorhunt@gmail.com]	01463 250355 07753 423333 (Mbl)
Jeffrey, Stewart D. BSc BD	1962 1997	(Banff with King Edward)	10 Grigor Drive, Inverness IV2 4LP [E-mail: stewart.jeffrey@talktalk.net]	01463 230085
Livesley, Anthony LTh	1979 1997	(Kiltearn)	87 Beech Avenue, Nairn IV12 4ST [E-mail: tonylivesley@googlemail.com]	01667 455126
Lyon, Andrew LTh	1971 2007	(Fraserburgh West with Rathen West)	20 Barnview, Culloden, Inverness IV2 7EX [E-mail: andrewlyon70@hotmail.co.uk]	01463 559609
Mackenzie, Seoras L. BD	1996 1998	Chaplain: Army	39 Engr Regt (Air Support), Kinloss Barracks, Kinloss, Forres IV36 3XL	
MacQuarrie, Donald A. BSc BD	1979 2012	(Fort William: Duncansburgh MacIntosh with Kilmonivaig)	Birch Cottage, 4 Craigrorie, North Kessock, Inverness IV1 3XH [E-mail: pdmacq@ukgateway.net]	01463 731050
McRoberts, T. Douglas BD CPS FRSA	1975 2014	(Malta)	24 Redwood Avenue, Inverness IV2 6HA [E-mail: doug.mcroberts@btinternet.com]	01463 772594
Mitchell, Joyce (Mrs) DCS	1994	(Deacon)	Sunnybank, Farr, Inverness IV2 6XG [E-mail: joyce@mitchell71.freeserve.co.uk]	01808 521285
Morrison, Hector BSc BD MTh	1981 1994	Principal: Highland Theological College	24 Oak Avenue, Inverness IV2 4NX	01463 238561
Rettie, James A. BTh	1981 1999	(Melness and Eriboll with Tongue)	2 Trantham Drive, Westhill, Inverness IV2 5QT	01463 798896
Ritchie, Bruce BSc BD PhD	1977 2014	(Dingwall: Castle Street)	16 Brinckman Terrace, Westhill, Inverness IV2 5BL [E-mail: brucezomba@hotmail.com]	01463 791389
Robb, Rodney P.T.	1995 2004	(Stirling: St Mark's)	2A Mayfield Road, Inverness IV2 4AE	01463 230831
Robertson, Fergus A. MA BD	1971 2010	(Inverness: Dalneigh and Bona)	16 Druid Temple Way, Inverness IV2 6UQ [E-mail: faavrobertson@yahoo.co.uk]	01463 718462
Stirling, G. Alan S. MA	1960 1999	(Leochel Cushnie and Lynturk with Tough)	97 Lochlann Road, Culloden, Inverness IV2 7HJ	01463 798313
Turner, Fraser K. LTh	1994 2007	(Kiltarlity with Kirkhill)	20 Caulfield Avenue, Inverness IV2 5GA [E-mail: fraseratq@yahoo.co.uk]	01463 794004
Warwick, Ivan C. MA BD TD	1980	Army Chaplain	Ardcruidh Croft, Heights of Dochcarty, Dingwall, IV15 9UF [E-mail: L70rev@btinternet.com]	01349 861464 (Mbl) 07787 535083

				(Tel/Fax) 01667 456397
Waugh, John L. LTh	1973 2002	(Ardclach with Auldearn and Dalmore)	58 Wyvis Drive, Nairn IV12 4TP [E-mail: jwaugh334@btinternet.com]	
Younger, Alastair S. BScEcon ASCC	1969 2008	(Inverness: St Columba High)	33 Duke's View, Slackbuie, Inverness IV2 6BB [E-mail: younger873@btinternet.com]	01463 242873

INVERNESS ADDRESSES

Inverness

Crown	Kingsmills Road x Midmills Road	Hilton	Druid Road x Tomatin Road
Dalneigh and Bona	St Mary's Avenue	Inshes	Inshes Retail Park
East	Academy Street x Margaret Street	Kinmylies	Kinmylies Way
		Ness Bank	Ness Bank x Castle Road
		St Stephen's	Old Edinburgh Road x Southside Road

The Old High	Church Street x Church Lane	
Trinity	Huntly Place x Upper Kessock Street	

Nairn

Old	Academy Street x Seabank Road
St Ninian's	High Street x Queen Street

(38) LOCHABER

Meets at Caol, Fort William, in Kilmallie Church Hall at 6pm, on the first Tuesday of September and December, on the last Tuesday of October and on the fourth Tuesday of March. The June meeting is held at 6pm on the first Tuesday in the church of the incoming Moderator.

Clerk:	**REV DONALD B. McCORKINDALE BD DipMin**	The Manse, 2 The Meadows, Strontian, Acharacle PH36 4HZ [E-mail: lochaber@churchofscotland.org.uk]	01967 4022344
Treasurer: MRS CONNIE ANDERSON		Darach, Duror, PA38 4BS [E-mail : faoconnie@gmail.com]	01631 740334

Acharacle (H) linked with Ardnamurchan

Fiona Ogg (Mrs) BA BD	2012	The Manse, Acharacle PH36 4JU [E-mail: Fiona.Ogg@churchofscotland.org.uk]	01967 431654

Ardgour and Kingairloch linked with Morvern linked with Strontian

Donald G.B. McCorkindale BD DipMin	1992	2011	The Manse, 2 The Meadows, Strontian, Acharacle PH36 4HZ [E-mail: DMcCorkindale@churchofscotland.org.uk]	01967 402234

Ardnamurchan See Acharacle

Duror (H) linked with Glencoe: St Munda's (H) (R)

Alexander C. Stoddart BD	2001	9 Cameron Brae, Kentallen, Duror PA38 4BF [E-mail: AStoddart@churchofscotland.org.uk]	01631 740285

Fort Augustus linked with Glengarry
Vacant
The Manse, Fort Augustus   PH32 4BH — 01320 366210

Fort William: Duncansburgh MacIntosh (H) linked with Kilmonivaig
Richard Baxter MA BD   1997   2016
The Manse, The Parade, Fort William   PH33 6BA
[E-mail: RBaxter@churchofscotland.org.uk] — 01397 702297 / 07958 541418 (Mbl)

Glencoe: St Munda's See Duror
Glengarry See Fort Augustus

Kilmallie
Richard T. Corbett BSc MSc PhD BD   1992   2005
Kilmallie Manse, Corpach, Fort William   PH33 7JS
[E-mail: RCorbett@churchofscotland.org.uk] — 01397 772736

Kilmonivaig See Fort William: Duncansburgh MacIntosh

Kinlochleven (H) linked with Nether Lochaber (H)
Malcolm A. Kinnear MA BD PhD   2010
The Manse, Lochaber Road, Kinlochleven   PH50 4QW
[E-mail: MKinnear@churchofscotland.org.uk] — 01855 831227

Morvern See Ardgour
Nether Lochaber See Kinlochleven

North West Lochaber
Edgar J. Ogston BSc BD   1976   2013
Church of Scotland Manse, Annie's Brae, Mallaig   PH41 4RG
[E-mail: EOgston@churchofscotland.org.uk] — 01687 460042

Strontian See Ardgour

Anderson, David M. MSc FCOptom	1984	2012	(Ordained Local Minister)	'Mirlos', 1 Dumfries Place, Fort William PH33 6UQ [E-mail: David.Anderson@churchofscotland.org.uk] — 01397 702091
Lamb, Alan H.W. BA MTh	1959	2005	(Associate Minister)	Smiddy House, Arisaig PH39 4NH [E-mail: h.a.lamb@handalamb.plus.com] — 01687 450227
Millar, John L. MA BD	1981	1990	(Fort William: Duncansburgh with Kilmonivaig)	Flat 0/1, 12 Chesterfield Gardens, Glasgow G12 0BF [E-mail: johnmillar123@btinternet.com] — 0141-339 4098

Muirhead, Morag (Mrs)	2013	Ordained Local Minister	6 Dumbarton Road, Fort William PH33 6UU [E-mail: MMuirhead@churchofscotland.org.uk]	01397 703643
Rae, Peter C. BSc BD	1968 2000	(Beath and Cowdenbeath: North)	8 Wether Road, Great Cambourne, Cambridgeshire CB23 5DT [E-mail: rae.fairview@btinternet.com]	01954 710079
Varwell, Adrian P.J. BA BD PhD	1983 2011	(Fort Augustus with Glengarry)	19 Enrick Crescent, Kilmore, Drumnadrochit, Inverness IV63 6TP [E-mail: adrian.varwell@btinternet.com]	01456 459352
Winning, A. Ann MA DipEd BD	1984 2006	(Morvern)	'Westering', 13C Carnoch, Glencoe, Ballachulish PH49 4HQ [E-mail: awinning009@btinternet.com]	01855 811929

LOCHABER Communion Sundays Please consult the Presbytery website: www.cofslochaber.co.uk

(39) ROSS

Meets on the first Tuesday of September in the church of the incoming Moderator, and in Dingwall: Castle Street Church on the first Tuesday of October, November, December, February, March and May, and on the last Tuesday of June.

| Clerk: | MR RONALD W. GUNSTONE BSc | 20 Bellfield Road, North Kessock, Inverness IV1 3XU [E-mail: ross@churchofscotland.org.uk] | 01463 731337 |

Alness
Vacant

| Michael J. Macdonald (Auxiliary Minister) | 2004 | 2014 | 27 Darroch Brae, Alness IV17 0SD 73 Firhill, Alness IV17 0RT [E-mail: Michael.Macdonald@churchofscotland.org.uk] | 01349 882238 01349 884268 |

Avoch linked with Fortrose and Rosemarkie

| Alan T. McKean BD CertMin | 1982 | 2010 | 5 Ness Way, Fortrose IV10 8SS [E-mail: AMcKean@churchofscotland.org.uk] | 01381 621433 |

Contin (H) linked with Fodderty and Strathpeffer (H)

| A. Fanus Erasmus MA LTh MTh ThD | 1978 | 2013 | The Manse, Contin, Strathpeffer IV14 9ES [E-mail: FErasmus@churchofscotland.org.uk] | 01997 421028 |

Cromarty linked with Resolis and Urquhart
Vacant

| | | | The Manse, Culbokie, Dingwall IV7 8JN | 01349 877452 |

Dingwall: Castle Street (H)

| Stephen Macdonald BD MTh | 2008 | 2014 | 16 Achany Road, Dingwall IV15 9JB [E-mail: SMacdonald@churchofscotland.org.uk] | 01349 866792 07570 804193 (Mbl) |

Dingwall: St Clement's (H)

Bruce Dempsey BD	1997	2014	8 Castlehill Road, Dingwall IV15 9PB [E-mail: BDempsey@churchofscotland.org.uk]	01349 292055

Fearn Abbey and Nigg linked with Tarbat

Robert G.D.W. Pickles BD MPhil ThD	2003	2015	Church of Scotland Manse, Fearn, Tain IV20 1WN [E-mail: RPickles@churchofscotland.org.uk]	01862 832282

Ferintosh

Andrew F. Graham BTh DPS	2001	2006	Ferintosh Manse, Leanaig Road, Conon Bridge, Dingwall IV7 8BE [E-mail: Andrew.Graham@churchofscotland.org.uk]	01349 861275

Fodderty and Strathpeffer See Contin
Fortrose and Rosemarkie See Avoch

Invergordon

Kenneth Donald MacLeod BD CPS	1989	2000	The Manse, Cromlet Drive, Invergordon IV18 0BA [E-mail: KMacLeod@churchofscotland.org.uk]	01349 852273

Killearnan (H) linked with Knockbain (H)

Susan Cord	2016		Tigh-an-Isein, Croftnacreich, North Kessock, Inverness IV1 3ZE [E-mail: SCord@churchofscotland.org.uk]	01463 731930

Kilmuir and Logie Easter

Fraser M.C. Stewart BSc BD	1980	2011	The Manse, Delny, Invergordon IV18 0NW [E-mail: FStewart@churchofscotland.org.uk]	01862 842280

Kiltearn (H)

Donald A. MacSween BD	1991	1998	The Manse, Swordale Road, Evanton, Dingwall IV16 9UZ [E-mail: DMacSween@churchofscotland.org.uk]	01349 830472

Knockbain See Killearnan

Lochbroom and Ullapool (GD)

Vacant			The New Manse, Garve Road, Ullapool IV26 2SX	01854 613146

Resolis and Urquhart See Cromarty

Rosskeen

Robert Jones BSc BD	1990	Rosskeen Manse, Perrins Road, Alness IV17 0XG [E-mail: RJones@churchofscotland.org.uk]	01349 882265

Tain

Vacant	14 Kingsway Avenue, Tain IV19 1NJ	01862 894140

Tarbat See Fearn Abbey and Nigg

Urray and Kilchrist

Scott Polworth LLB BD	2009	The Manse, Corrie Road, Muir of Ord IV6 7TL [E-mail: SPolworth@churchofscotland.org.uk]	01463 870259

Archer, Nicholas D.C. BA BD	1971	1992	(Dores and Boleskine)	2 Aldie Cottages, Tain IV19 1LZ [E-mail: na.2ac777@btinternet.com]	01862 821494
Bissett, James	2016		Ordained Local Minister	Tigh-an-Isein, Croftnacreich, North Kessock, Inverness IV1 3ZE [E-mail: JBissett@churchofscotland.org.uk]	01463 731930
Dupar, Kenneth W. BA BD PhD	1965	1993	(Christ's College, Aberdeen)	The Old Manse, The Causeway, Cromarty IV11 8XJ	01381 600428
Forsyth, James LTh	1970	2000	(Fearn Abbey with Nigg Chapelhill)	Rhives Lodge, Golspie, Sutherland KW10 6DD	
Horne, Douglas A. BD	1977	2009	(Tain)	151 Holm Farm Road, Culduthel, Inverness IV2 6BF [E-mail: douglas.horne@talktalk.net]	01463 712677
Lincoln, John MPhil BD	1986	2014	(Balquhidder with Killin and Ardeonaig)	59 Obsdale Park, Alness IV17 0TR [E-mail: johnlincoln@minister.com]	01349 882791
Mackinnon, R.M. LTh	1968	1995	(Kilmuir and Logie Easter)	27 Riverford Crescent, Conon Bridge, Dingwall IV7 8HL	01349 866293
MacLennan, Alasdair J. BD DCE	1978	2001	(Resolis and Urquhart)	Airdale, Seaforth Road, Muir of Ord IV6 7TA	01463 870704
Macleod, John MA	1959	1993	(Resolis and Urquhart)	'Benview', 19 Balvaird, Muir of Ord IV6 7RG [E-mail: sheilaandjohn@yahoo.co.uk]	01463 871286
Munro, James A. BA BD DMS	1979	2013	(Port Glasgow: Hamilton Bardrainney)	1 Wyvis Crescent, Conon Bridge, Dingwall IV7 8BZ [E-mail: james781munro@btinternet.com]	01349 865752
Niven, William W. BTh	1982	1995	(Alness)	4 Obsdale Park, Alness IV17 0TP	01349 882427
Scott, David V. BTh	1994	2014	(Fearn Abbey and Nigg with Tarbat)	29 Sunnyside, Culloden Moor, Inverness IV2 5ES	01463 795802
Smith, Russel BD	1994	2013	(Dingwall: St Clement's)	1 School Road, Conon Bridge, Dingwall IV7 8AE [E-mail: russanntwo@btinternet.com]	01349 861011
Tallach, John MA MLitt	1970	2010	(Cromarty)	29 Firthview Drive, Inverness IV3 8NS [E-mail: johntallacl@talktalk.net]	01463 418721

(40) SUTHERLAND

Meets at Lairg on the first Tuesday of March, May, September, November and December, and on the first Tuesday of June at the Moderator's church.

Clerk: REV. STEWART GOUDIE BSc BD

St Andrew's Manse, Tongue, Lairg IV27 4XL
[E-mail: sutherland@churchofscotland.org.uk]

01847 611230 (Tel/Fax)
07957 237757 (Mbl)

Altnaharra and Farr
Vacant

The Manse, Bettyhill, Thurso KW14 7SS

01641 521208

Assynt and Stoer
Vacant

Canisp Road, Lochinver, Lairg IV27 4LH

01571 844342

Clyne (H) linked with Kildonan and Loth Helmsdale (H)
Vacant

Golf Road, Brora KW9 6QS

01408 621239

Creich See Kincardine Croick and Edderton

Dornoch Cathedral (H)
Susan M. Brown (Mrs) BD DipMin   1985   1998

Cathedral Manse, Cnoc-an-Lobht, Dornoch IV25 3HN
[E-mail: Susan.Brown@churchofscotland.org.uk]

01862 810296

Durness and Kinlochbervie
Vacant   1990   1998

Manse Road, Kinlochbervie, Lairg IV27 4RG

01971 521287

Eddrachillis
John MacPherson BSc BD   1993

Church of Scotland Manse, Scourie, Lairg IV27 4TQ
[E-mail: JMacPherson@churchofscotland.org.uk]

01971 502431

Golspie
John B. Sterrett BA BD PhD   2007

The Manse, Fountain Road, Golspie KW10 6TH
[E-mail: JSterret@churchofscotland.org.uk]

01408 633295 (Tel/Fax)

Kildonan and Loth Helmsdale See Clyne

Kincardine Croick and Edderton linked with Creich linked with Rosehall

Anthony M. Jones BD DPS DipTheol CertMin FRSA	1994	2010	The Manse, Ardgay IV24 3BG [E-mail: AJones@churchofscotland.org.uk]	01863 766285
Hilary M. Gardner (Miss) (Auxiliary Minister)	2010	2012	Cayman Lodge, Kincardine Hill, Ardgay IV24 3DJ [E-mail: HGardner@churchofscotland.org.uk]	01863 766107

Lairg (H) linked with Rogart (H)

Vacant	The Manse, Lairg IV27 4EH

Melness and Tongue (H)

Stewart Goudie BSc BD	2010	St Andrew's Manse, Tongue, Lairg IV27 4XL [E-mail: SGoudie@churchofscotland.org.uk]	01847 611230 (Tel/Fax) 07957 237757 (Mbl)

Rogart See Lairg
Rosehall See Kincardine Croick and Edderton

Chambers, John OBE BSc	1972	2009	(Inverness: Ness Bank)	Bannlagan Lodge, 4 Earls Cross Gardens, Dornoch IV25 3NR [E-mail: chambersdornoch@btinternet.com]	01862 811520
Goskirk, J.L. LTh	1968	2010	(Lairg with Rogart)	Rathvilly, Lairgmuir, Lairg IV27 4ED [E-mail: leslie_goskirk@sky.com]	01549 402569
McCree, Ian W. BD	1971	2011	(Clyne with Kildonan and Loth Helmsdale)	Tigh Ardachu, Mosshill, Brora KW9 6NG [E-mail: ian@mccree.f9.co.uk]	01408 621185
Stobo, Mary J. (Mrs)	2013		Ordained Local Minister; Community Healthcare Chaplain	Druim-an-Sgairnich, Ardgay IV24 3BG [E-mail: MStobo@churchofscotland.org.uk]	01863 766868

(41) CAITHNESS

Meets alternately at Wick and Thurso on the first Tuesday of February, March, May, September, November and December, and the third Tuesday of June.

Clerk:	REV. RONALD JOHNSTONE BD	2 Comlifoot Drive, Halkirk KW12 6ZA [E-mail: caithness@churchofscotland.org.uk]	01847 839033

Bower linked with Halkirk Westerdale linked with Watten

Vacant	The Manse, Station Road, Watten, Wick KW1 5YN	01955 621220

Canisbay linked with Dunnet linked with Keiss linked with Olrig
Vacant — The Manse, Canisbay, Wick KW1 4YH — 01955 611756

Dunnet See Canisbay
Hallkirk Westerdale See Bower
Keiss See Canisbay
Olrig See Canisbay

The North Coast Parish
Vacant — Church of Scotland Manse, Reay, Thurso KW14 7RE — 01847 811441

The Parish of Latheron
Vacant — Central Manse, Main Street, Lybster KW3 6BN
[E-mail: parish-of-latheron@btconnect.com] — 01593 721706

Thurso: St Peter's and St Andrew's (H)
David S.M. Malcolm BD   2011   2014 — The Manse, 46 Rose Street, Thurso KW14 8RF
[E-mail: David.Malcolm@churchofscotland.org.uk] — 01847 895186

Thurso: West (H)
Vacant — Thorkel Road, Thurso KW14 7LW — 01847 892663

Watten See Bower

Wick: Pulteneytown (H) and Thrumster
Vacant — The Manse, Coronation Street, Wick KW1 5LS — 01955 603166

Wick: St Fergus
John Nugent   1999   2011 — Mansefield, Miller Avenue, Wick KW1 4DF
[E-mail: JNugent@churchofscotland.org.uk] — 01955 602167 / 07511 503946 (Mbl)

Craw, John DCS   (Deacon) — Liabost, 8 Proudfoot Road, Wick KW1 4PQ
[E-mail: johncraw607@btinternet.com] — 01955 603805 / 07544 761653 (Mbl)

Duncan, Esme (Miss)   2013   Ordained Local Minister — Avalon, Upper Warse, Canisbay, Wick KW1 4YD
[E-mail: EDuncan@churchofscotland.org.uk] — 01955 611455

Johnstone, Ronald BD	1977 2011	(Thurso: West)	2 Comlifoot Drive, Halkirk KW12 6ZA [E-mail: ronaldjohnstone@btinternet.com]	01847 839033
Rennie, Lyall	2013	Ordained Local Minister	Ruachmarra, Lower Warse, Canisbay, Wick KW1 4YB [E-mail: LRennie@churchofscotland.org.uk]	01955 611756
Stewart, Heather (Mrs)	2013	Ordained Local Minister	Burnthill, Thrumster, Wick KW1 5TR [E-mail: Heather.Stewart@churchofscotland.org.uk]	01955 651717 (Work) 01955 603333
Warner, Kenneth BD	1981 2008	(Halkirk and Westerdale)	Kilearnan, Clayock, Halkirk KW12 6UZ [E-mail: wmrkenn@btinternet.com]	01847 831825

CAITHNESS Communion Sundays

Bower	1st Jul, Dec	Keiss	1st May, 3rd Nov
Canisbay	1st Jun, Nov	Latheron	Apr, Jul, Sep, Nov
Dunnet	last May, Nov	North Coast	Mar, Easter, Jun, Sep, Dec
Halkirk Westerdale	Apr, Jul, Oct	Olrig	last May, Nov
		Thurso: St Peter's and St Andrew's	Mar, Jun, Sep, Dec

Watten	West	4th Mar, Jun, Nov
Wick: Pulteneytown and Thrumster		1st Jul, Dec
St Fergus		1st Mar, Jun, Sep, Dec
		Apr, Oct

(42) LOCHCARRON – SKYE

Meets in Kyle on the first Tuesday of September, November, December, February, June, and in conference on the first Saturday in March.

Clerk:	REV. JOHN W. MURRAY LLB BA	1 Totescore, Kilmuir, Portree, Isle of Skye IV51 9YN [E-mail: lochcarronskye@churchofscotland.org.uk]	01470 542297

Applecross, Lochcarron and Torridon (GD)
Vacant
The Manse, Colonel's Road, Lochcarron, Strathcarron IV54 8YG   01520 722829

Bracadale and Duirinish (GD)
Janet Easton-Berry BA (SocSc) BA (Theol)
Duirinish Manse, Dunvegan, Isle of Skye IV55 8WQ   01470 521668
[E-mail: JEaston-Berry@churchofscotland.ork.uk]

Gairloch and Dundonnell
Stuart J. Smith BEng BD MTh   1994 2016   Church of Scotland Manse, The Glebe, Gairloch IV21 2BT   01445 712645 (Tel/Fax)
[E-mail: Stuart.Smith@churchofscotland.org.uk]

Glenelg Kintail and Lochalsh
Vacant

Church of Scotland Manse, Inverinate, Kyle IV40 8HE   01599 511245

New change formed by the union of Glenelg and Kintail and Lochalsh

Kilmuir and Stenscholl (GD)
John W. Murray LLB BA   2003   2015   1 Totescore, Kilmuir, Isle of Skye IV51 9YN   01470 542297
[E-mail: JMurray@churchofscotland.org.uk]

Portree (GD)
Sandor Fazakas BD MTh   1976   2007   Viewfield Road, Portree, Isle of Skye IV51 9ES   01478 611868
[E-mail: SFazakas@churchofscotland.org.uk]

Snizort (H) (GD)
Vacant

The Manse, Kensaleyre, Snizort, Portree, Isle of Skye IV51 9XE   01470 532453

Strath and Sleat (GD)
Rory A.R. MacLeod BA MBA BD DMin   1994   2015   The Manse, 6 Upper Breakish, Isle of Skye IV42 8PY   01471 822416
[E-mail: rorymofg@gmail.com]

Anderson, Janet (Miss) DCS   (Deacon)   Creagard, 31 Lower Breakish, Isle of Skye IV42 8QA   01471 822403
[E-mail: jaskye@hotmail.co.uk]

Beaton, Donald MA BD MTh   1961 2002   (Glenelg and Kintail)   Budhmore Home, Portree, Isle of Skye IV51 9DJ
Kellas, David J. MA BD   1966 2004   (Kilfinan with Kyles)   Buarblach, Glenelg, Kyle IV40 8LA   01599 522257
[E-mail: davidkellas@btinternet.com]   (Mbl) 07909 577764

Macarthur, Allan I. BD   1973 1998   (Applecross, Lochcarron and Torridon)   Flat 9, Lyle Court, 25 Barnton Grove, Edinburgh EH4 6EZ   0131-339 5926
[E-mail: a.macarthur@btinternet.com]

McCulloch, Alen J.R. MA BD   1990 2012   (Chaplain: Royal Navy)   Aros, 6 Gifford Terrace Road, Plymouth PL3 4JE   01752 657290
[E-mail: aviljoen90@hotmail.com]

Mackenzie, Hector M.   2008   Chaplain: Army   HQ Military Corrective Training Centre, Berechurch Hall Camp,
Berechurch Hall Road, Colchester CO2 9NU
[E-mail: mackenziehector@hotmail.com]

Martin, George M. MA BD   1987 2005   (Applecross, Lochcarron and Torridon)   8(1) Buckingham Terrace, Edinburgh EH4 3AA   0131-343 3937
Morrison, Derek   1995 2013   (Gairloch and Dundonnell)   2 Cliffton Place, Poolewe, Achnasheen IV22 2JU   01445 781333
[E-mail: derekmorrison1@aol.com]

LOCHCARRON – SKYE Communion Sundays

Applecross	1st Sep	Glenshiel	1st Jul	Plockton and Kyle	2nd May, 1st Oct
Arnisort	3rd Mar, Sep	Kilmuir	1st Mar, Sep	Portree	Easter, Pentecost, Christmas, 2nd Mar, Aug, 1st Nov
Bracadale	Last Feb	Kintail	3rd Apr, Jul	Sleat	Last May
Broadford	3rd Jan, Easter, 3rd Sep	Kyleakin	Last Sep	Snizort	1st Jan, 4th Mar
Duirinish	4th Jun	Lochalsh and Stromeferry	4th Jan, Jun, Sep, Christmas, Easter	Stenscholl	1st Jun, Dec
Dundonnell	1st Aug	Lochcarron and Shieldaig	Easter; communion held on a revolving basis when there is a fifth Sunday in the month	Strath	4th Jan
Elgol	3rd Jun, Nov			Torridon and Kinlochewe	
Gairloch	2nd Jun, Nov				
Glenelg					

In the Parish of Strath and Sleat, Easter communion is held on a revolving basis.

(43) UIST

Meets on the first Tuesday of February, March, September and November in Lochmaddy, and on the third Tuesday of June in Leverburgh.

| Clerk: | MR WILSON McKINLAY | Heatherburn Cottage, Rhughasnish, Isle of South Uist HS8 5PE [E-mail: uist@churchofscotland.org.uk] | **01870 610393** |

Benbecula (GD) (H) linked with Carinish
| Andrew (Drew) P. Kuzma BA | 2007 | 2016 | Church of Scotland Manse, Griminish, Isle of Benbecula HS7 5QA | 01870 602180 |

Berneray and Lochmaddy (GD) (H)
| Vacant | | | Church of Scotland Manse, Lochmaddy, Isle of North Uist HS6 5AA | 01876 500414 |

Carinish (GD) (H) See Benbecula
| | | | Church of Scotland Manse, Clachan, Locheport, Lochmaddy, Isle of North Uist HS6 5HD | 01876 580219 |

Kilmuir and Paible (GE)
| Vacant | | | Paible, Isle of North Uist HS6 5ED | 01876 510310 |

Manish-Scarista (GD) (H)
| David Donaldson MA BD DMin | 1969 | 2015 | Church of Scotland Manse, Scarista, Isle of Harris HS3 3HX [E-mail: DDonaldson@churchofscotland.org.uk] | 01859 550200 |

Tarbert (GD) (H)
Ian Murdo M. Macdonald DPA BD   2001   2015   The Manse, Manse Road, Tarbert, Isle of Harris HS3 3DF   01859 502231
[E-mail: Ian.MacDonald@churchofscotland.org.uk]

Elliott, Gavin J. MA BD	1976 2015	(Ministries Council)	5a Aird, Isle of Benbecula HS7 5LT [E-mail: gavkondwani@gmail.com]	
Macdonald, Ishabel	2011	Ordained Local Minister	'Cleat Afe Ora', 18 Carinish, Isle of North Uist HS6 5HN [E-mail: Ishie.Macdonald@churchofscotland.org.uk]	01876 580367
MacInnes, David MA BD	1966 1999	(Kilmuir and Paible)	9 Golf View Road, Kinmylies, Inverness IV3 8SZ	01463 717377
MacIver, Norman BD	1976 2011	(Tarbert)	57 Boswell Road, Wester Inshes, Inverness IV2 3EW [E-mail: norman@n-cmaciver.freeserve.co.uk]	
Morrison, Donald John	2001	Auxiliary Minister	22 Kyles, Tarbert, Isle of Harris HS3 3BS [E-mail: DMorrison@churchofscotland.org.uk]	01859 502341
Petrie, Jackie G.	1989 2011	(South Uist)	7B Malaclete, Isle of North Uist HS6 5BX [E-mail: jackiegpetrie@yahoo.com]	01876 560804
Smith, John M.	1956 1992	(Lochmaddy)	Hamersay, Clachan, Locheport, Lochmaddy, Isle of North Uist HS6 5HD	
Smith, Murdo MA BD	1988 2011	(Manish-Scarista)	Aisgeir, 15A Upper Shader, Isle of Lewis HS3 3MX	01876 580332

UIST Communion Sundays

Benbecula	2nd Mar, Sep	Carinish	4th Mar, Aug
Berneray and Lochmaddy	4th Jun, last Oct	Kilmuir and Paible	1st Jun, 3rd Nov
		Manish-Scarista	3rd Apr, 1st Oct
		Tarbert	2nd Mar, 3rd Sep

(44) LEWIS

Meets at Stornoway, in St Columba's Church Hall, on the second Tuesday of February, March, September and November. It also meets if required in April, June and December on dates to be decided.

Clerk: MR JOHN CUNNINGHAM   1 Raven's Lane, Stornoway, Isle of Lewis HS2 0EG   01851 709977
    [E-mail: lewis@churchofscotland.org.uk]   07789 878840 (Mbl)

Barvas (GD) (H)
Vacant   Barvas, Isle of Lewis HS2 0QY   01851 840218

Carloway (GD) (H) (Office: 01851 643211)
Vacant
Church of Scotland Manse, Knock, Carloway, Isle of Lewis HS2 9AU   01851 643255

Cross Ness (GE) (H)
Vacant
Cross Manse, Swainbost, Ness, Isle of Lewis HS2 0TB   01851 810375

Kinloch (GE) (H)
Iain M. Campbell BD   2004   2008
Laxay, Lochs, Isle of Lewis HS2 9LA   01851 830218
[E-mail: ICampbell@churchofscotland.org.uk]

Knock (GE) (H)
Guardianship of the Presbytery

Lochs-Crossbost (GD) (H)
Guardianship of the Presbytery

Lochs-in-Bernera (GD) (H) linked with Uig (GE) (H)
Hugh Maurice Stewart DPA BD   2008
7 Tobson, Great Bernera, Isle of Lewis HS2 9NA   01851 612466
(Temporary Manse)
[E-mail: berneralwuig@btinternet.com]

Stornoway: High (GD) (H)
A. S. Wayne Pearce MA PhD
High Manse, 1 Goathill Road, Stornoway, Isle of Lewis HS1 2NJ   01851 703106
[E-mail: ASWaynePearce@churchofscotland.org.uk]

Stornoway: Martin's Memorial (H) (Church office: 01851 700820)
Thomas MacNeil MA BD   2002   2006
Matheson Road, Stornoway, Isle of Lewis HS1 2LR   01851 704238
[E-mail: tommymacneil@hotmail.com]

Stornoway: St Columba (GD) (H) (Church office: 01851 701546)
William J. Heenan BA MTh   2012
St Columba's Manse, Lewis Street, Stornoway, Isle of Lewis HS1 2JF   01851 705933
[E-mail: WHeenan@churchofscotland.org.uk]   07837 770589 (Mbl)

Uig See Lochs-in-Bernera

Amed, Paul LTh DPS   1992 2015   (Barvas)   6 Scotland Street, Stornoway, Isle of Lewis HS1 2JQ   01851 706450
[E-mail: paulamed56@gmail.com]

Johnstone, Ben MA BD DMin   1973 2013   (Strath and Sleat)   Loch Alainn, 5 Breaclete, Great Bernera, Isle of Lewis HS2 9LT   01851 612445
[E-mail: benonbernera@gmail.com]

Maclean, Donald A. DCS   1975 2006   (Deacon)   8 Upper Barvas, Isle of Lewis HS2 0QX   01851 840454
MacLennan, Donald Angus   (Kinloch)   4 Kestrel Place, Inverness IV2 3YH   01463 243750
[E-mail: maclennankinloch@btinternet.com]   (Mbl) 07799 668270

Macleod, William   1957 2006   (Uig)   54 Lower Barvas, Isle of Lewis HS2 0QY   01851 840217
Shadakshari, T.K. BTh BD MTh   1998 2006   Healthcare Chaplain   23D Benside, Newmarket, Stornoway, Isle of Lewis HS2 0DZ   (Home) 01851 701727
[E-mail: tk.shadakshari@nhs.net]   (Office) 01851 704704
(Mbl) 07403 697138

LEWIS   Communion Sundays

Barvas	3rd Mar, Sep
Carloway	1st Mar, last Sep
Cross Ness	2nd Mar, Oct
Kinloch	3rd Mar, 2nd Jun, 2nd Sep
Knock	3rd Apr, 1st Nov
Lochs-Crossbost	4th Mar, Sep
Lochs-in-Bernera	1st Apr, 2nd Sep
Stornoway: High	3rd Feb, last Aug
Martin's Memorial	3rd Feb, last Aug, 1st Dec, Easter
St Columba	3rd Feb, last Aug
Uig	3rd Jun, 4th Oct

(45) ORKNEY

Normally meets at Kirkwall, in the St Magnus Centre, on the first Wednesday of September, November, February, April, and the third Wednesday of June.

Clerk: VERY REV DAVID W. LUNAN MA BD DUniv DLitt DD   30 Mill Road, Banton, Glasgow G65 0RD   01236 824110
[E-mail: orkney@churchofscotland.org.uk]   07500 050855 (Mbl)
Depute Clerk: MARGARET SUTHERLAND LLB BA   13 Cursiter Crescent, Kirkwall, Orkney KW15 1XN   01856 873747

Birsay, Harray and Sandwick
David G. McNeish MB ChB BSc BD   2015   The Manse, North Biggings Road, Dounby, Orkney KW17 2HZ   01856 771599
[E-mail: DMcNeish@churchofscotland.org.uk]

East Mainland
Wilma A. Johnston MTheol MTh   2006 2014   The Manse, Holm, Orkney KW17 2SB   01856 781772
[E-mail: Wilma.Johnston@churchofscotland.org.uk]

Eday linked with Stronsay: Moncur Memorial (H)
Vacant   The Manse, Stronsay, Orkney KW17 2SB

Evie (H) linked with Firth (H) (01856 761117) linked with Rendall linked with Rousay
Roy Cordukes BSc BD   2014   The Manse, Finstown, Orkney KW17 2EG   01856 761328
                                                           [E-mail: RCordukes@churchofscotland.org.uk]

Firth See Evie

Flotta linked with Hoy and Walls linked with Orphir (H) and Stenness (H)
Vacant   Stenness Manse, Stenness, Stromness, Orkney KW16 3HH

Hoy and Walls See Flotta

Kirkwall: East (H) linked with Shapinsay
Julia Meason MTh   2013   East Church Manse, Thoms Street, Kirkwall, Orkney KW15 1PF   01856 874789
                                                           [E-mail: JMeason@churchofscotland.org.uk]

Kirkwall: St Magnus Cathedral (H)
G. Fraser H. Macnaughton MA BD   1982   2002   Berstane Road, Kirkwall, Orkney KW15 1NA   01856 873312
                                                           [E-mail: FMacnaughton@churchofscotland.org.uk]

North Ronaldsay
Guardianship of the Presbytery

Orphir and Stenness See Flotta

Papa Westray linked with Westray
Iain D. MacDonald BD   1993   The Manse, Hilldavale, Westray, Orkney KW17 2DW   01857 677357 (Tel/Fax)
                                                           [E-mail: IMacDonald@churchofscotland.org.uk]   07710 443780 (Mbl)

Rendall See Evie
Rousay (Church centre: 01856 821271) See Evie

Sanday Vacant

Shapinsay See Kirkwall: East

South Ronaldsay and Burray
Stephen Manners MA BD   1989   2012   St Margaret's Manse, Church Road, St Margaret's Hope, Orkney KW17 2SR
[E-mail: SManners@churchofscotland.org.uk]   01856 831670 / 07747 821458 (Mbl)

Stromness (H)
Vacant   5 Manse Lane, Stromness, Orkney KW16 3AP   01856 850203

Westray See Papa Westray

Name	Ordained	Induction/Retired	Previous charge	Address	Telephone
Brown, R. Graeme BA BD	1961	1998	(Birsay with Rousay)	Bring Deeps, Orphir, Orkney KW17 2LX [E-mail: graeme_sibyl@btinternet.com]	(Tel/Fax) 01856 811707
Clark, Thomas L. BD	1985	2008	(Orphir with Stenness)	7 Headland Rise, Burghead, Elgin IV30 5HA [E-mail: toml.clark@btinternet.com]	01343 830144
Fidler, David G.	2013		Ordained Local Minister	34 Guardhouse Park, Stromness, Orkney KW16 3DP [E-mail: DFidler@churchofscotland.org.uk]	01856 850575 / 07900 386473 (Mbl)
Freeth, June BA MA	2015		Ordained Local Minister	Cumlaquoy, Birsay, Orkney KW17 2ND [E-mail: JFreeth@churchofscotland.org.uk]	01856 721449
Graham, Jennifer D. (Mrs) BA MDiv PhD	2000	2011	(Eday with Stronsay: Moncur Memorial)	Lodge, Stronsay, Orkney KW17 2AN [E-mail: jdgraham67@gmail.com]	01857 616487
Prentice, Martin W.M.	2013		Ordained Local Minister	Cot of Howe, Cairston, Stromness, Orkney KW16 3JU [E-mail: MPrentice@churchofscotland.org.uk]	01856 851139 / 07795 817213 (Mbl)
Tait, Alexander	1967	1995	(Glasgow: St Enoch's Hogganfield)	Ingermas, Evie, Orkney KW17 2PH [E-mail: jen1957@hotmail.co.uk]	01856 751477
Trgavolá, Magdaléna	2013	2015	(Stromness)	[E-mail: trgavola@gmail.com]	01506 650027
Whitson, William S. MA	1959	1999	(Cumbernauld: St Mungo's)	2 Chapman's Brae, Bathgate EH48 4LH [E-mail: william_whitson@tiscali.co.uk]	
Wishart, James BD	1986	2009	(Deer)	Upper Westshore, Burray, Orkney KW17 2TE [E-mail: jwishart06@btinternet.com]	01856 731672

(46) SHETLAND

Meets at Lerwick on the first Tuesday of February, April, June, September, November and December.

Clerk: REV DEBORAH J. DOBBY BD PGCE RGN RSCN | The Manse, Hogalee, East Voe, Scalloway, Shetland ZE1 0UU [E-mail: shetland@churchofscotland.org.uk] | 01595 881184

Burra Isle linked with Tingwall
Deborah J. Dobby (Mrs)
BA BD PGCE RGN RSCN | 2014 | The Manse, 25 Hogalee, East Voe, Scalloway, Shetland ZE1 0UU [E-mail: DDobby@churchofscotland.org.uk] | 01595 881184

Delting linked with Northmavine
Vacant | | The Manse, Grindwell, Brae, Shetland ZE2 9QJ | 01806 522219

Dunrossness and St Ninian's inc. Fair Isle linked with Sandwick, Cunningsburgh and Quarff
Vacant

Lerwick and Bressay
Caroline R. Lockerbie BA MDiv DMin
(Transition Minister) | 2007   2013 | The Manse, 82 St Olaf Street, Lerwick, Shetland ZE1 0ES [E-mail: CLockerbie@churchofscotland.org.uk] | 01595 692125

Nesting and Lunnasting linked with Whalsay and Skerries
Irene A. Charlton (Mrs) BTh | 1994   1997 | The Manse, Marrister, Symbister, Whalsay, Shetland ZE2 9AE [E-mail: ICharlton@churchofscotland.org.uk] | 01806 566767

Northmavine See Delting

Sandsting and Aithsting linked with Walls and Sandness
D. Brian Dobby MA BA | 1999   2014 | The Manse, 25 Hogalee, East Voe, Scalloway, Shetland ZE1 0UU [E-mail: BDobby@churchofscotland.org.uk] | 01595 881184

Sandwick, Cunningsburgh and Quarff See Dunrossness and St Ninian's
Tingwall See Burra Isle

Unst and Fetlar linked with Yell
David Cooper BA MPhil | 1975   2008 | North Isles Manse, Gutcher, Yell, Shetland ZE2 9DF [E-mail: DCooper@churchofscotland.org.uk] | 01957 744258
(David Cooper is a minister of the Methodist Church)

Walls and Sandness See Sandsting and Aithsting
Whalsay and Skerries See Nesting and Lunnasting
Yell See Unst and Fetlar

Greig, Charles H.M. MA BD	1976	2016	(Dunrossness and St Ninian's inc. Fair Isle with Sandwick, Cunningsburgh and Quarff)	6 Hayhoull Place, Bigton, Shetland ZE2 9GA [E-mail: chm.greig@btinternet.com]	01950 422468
Kirkpatrick, Alice H. (Miss) MA BD FSAScot	1987	2000	(Northmavine)	1 Daisy Park, Baltasound, Unst, Shetland ZE2 9EA	02829 558925
Knox, R. Alan MA LTh AInstAM	1965	2004	(Fetlar with Unst with Yell)	27 Killyvalley Road, Garvagh, Co. Londonderry, Northern Ireland BT51 5LX	01806 522604
MacGregor, Robert M. CHIOSH DipOSH RSP	2004	2016	(Auxiliary Minister)	Ola Cottage, Brae, Shetland ZE2 9QS [E-mail: revbobdelting@mypostoffice.co.uk]	
Macintyre, Thomas MA BD	1972	2011	(Sandsting and Aithsting with Walls and Sandness)	Lappideks, South Voxter, Cunningsburgh, Shetland ZE2 9HF [E-mail: the2macs.macintyre@btinternet.com]	01950 477549
Smith, Catherine (Mrs) DCS			(Deacon)	21 Lingaro, Bixter, Shetland ZE2 9NN	01595 810207
Williamson, Magnus J.C.	1982	1999	(Fetlar with Yell)	Creekhaven, Houl Road, Scalloway, Shetland ZE1 0XA	01595 880023

(47) ENGLAND

Meets at London, in Crown Court Church, on the second Tuesday of February, and at St Columba's, Pont Street, on the second Tuesday of June and the second Saturday of October.

Clerk:	REV. ALISTAIR CUMMING MSc CCS FInstLM		64 Prince George's Avenue, London SW20 8BH [E-mail: england@churchofscotland.org.uk]	07534 943986 (Mbl)

Corby: St Andrew's (H)

A. Norman Nicoll BD	2003	2016	43 Hempland Close, Corby, Northants NN18 8LR [E-mail: NNicoll@churchofscotland.org.uk]	01536 746429

Corby: St Ninian's (H) (01536 265245)

Kleber Machado BTh MA MTh	1998	2012	The Manse, 46 Glyndebourne Gardens, Corby, Northants NN18 0PZ [E-mail: KMachado@churchofscotland.org.uk]	01536 669478

Guernsey: St Andrew's in the Grange (H)

Graeme W. Beebee BD	1993	2003	The Manse, Le Villocq, Castel, Guernsey GY5 7SB [E-mail: GBeebee@churchofscotland.org.uk]	01481 257345

Jersey: St Columba's (H)
Vacant
18 Claremont Avenue, St Saviour, Jersey JE2 7SF — 01534 730659

Liverpool: St Andrew's
Guardianship of the Presbytery — 0151-524 1915

London: Crown Court (H) (020 7836 5643)

Philip L. Majcher BD	1982	2007	53 Sidmouth Street, London WC1H 8JX	020 7278 5022
			[E-mail: PMajcher@churchofscotland.org.uk]	

London: St Columba's (H) (020 7584 2321) linked with Newcastle: St Andrew's (H)

C. Angus MacLeod MA BD	1996	2012	29 Hollywood Road, Chelsea, London SW10 9HT	020 7584 2321 (Office)
			[E-mail: Angus.MacLeod@churchofscotland.org.uk]	
Andrea E. Price (Mrs)	1997	2014	St Columba's, Pont Street, London SW1X 0BD	020 7610 6994 (Home)
(Associate Minister)			[E-mail: APrice@churchofscotland.org.uk]	020 7584 2321 (Office)
Dorothy I.M. Lunn	2002	2002	14 Bellerby Drive, Ouston, Co. Durham DH2 1TW	0191-492 0647 (Office)
(Auxiliary Minister)			[E-mail: DLunn@churchofscotland.org.uk]	

Newcastle: St Andrew's See London: St Columba's

Anderson, Andrew F. MA BD	1981	2011	(Edinburgh: Greenside)	58 Reliance Way, Oxford OX4 2FG — 01865 778397
				[E-mail: andrew.relianceway@gmail.com]
Anderson, David P. BSc BD	2002	2007	Army Chaplain	[E-mail: padre.anderson180@mod.uk]
Binks, Mike	2007		Auxiliary Minister	Hollybank, 10 Kingsbrook, Corby NN18 9HY — (Mbl) 07590 507917
				[E-mail: MBinks@churchofscotland.org.uk]
Bowie, A. Glen CBE BA BSc	1954	1984	(Principal Chaplain: RAF)	16 Weir Road, Hemingford Grey, Huntingdon PE18 9EH — 01480 381425
Brown, Scott J. CBE QHC BD	1993	2015	(Chaplain of the Fleet: Royal Navy)	[E-mail: scott3568@gmail.com] — (Mbl) 07769 847876
Cairns, W. Alexander BD	1978	2006	(Corby: St Andrew's)	Kirkton House, Kirkton of Craig, Montrose DD10 9TB — (Mbl) 07808 588045
				[E-mail: sandy.cairns@btinternet.com]
Cameron, R. Neil	1975	1981	(Chaplain: Community)	[E-mail: neilandminacameron@yahoo.co.uk]
Coulter, David G. QHC BA BD MDA PhD CF	1989	1994	Chaplain General, HM Land Forces	8 Ashdown Terrace, Tidworth, Wilts SP9 7SQ — 01980 842175
				[E-mail: padredgcoulter@yahoo.co.uk]
Cumming, Alistair MSc CCS FInstLM	2010		Presbytery Clerk	64 Prince George's Avenue, London SW20 8BH — 020 8540 7365
				[E-mail: ACumming@churchofscotland.org.uk] 07534 943986
Dowswell, James A.M.	1991	2001	(Lerwick and Bressay)	Mill House, High Street, Staplehurst, Tonbridge, Kent TN12 0AU (Mbl) — 01580 891271
				[E-mail: jdowswell@btinternet.com]
Fields, James MA BD STM	1988	1997	School Chaplain	The Bungalow, The Ridgeway, Mill Hill, London NW7 1QX — 020 8201 1397
Francis, James BD PhD	2002	2009	Army Chaplain	37 Millburn Road, Coleraine BT52 1QT — 02870 353869
Lancaster, Craig MA BD	2004	2011	RAF Chaplain	[E-mail: bzn-chaplain4@mod.uk]

Langlands, Cameron H. BD MTh ThM PhD MInstLM	1995	2012	Chaplain South London and Maudsley NHS Foundation Trust	Maudsley Hospital, Denmark Road, London SE5 8EZ	(Mbl) 07989 642544
Lovett, Mairi F. BSc BA DipPS MTh	2005	2013	Hospital Chaplain	Royal Brompton Hospital, Sydney Street, London SW3 6NP [E-mail: m.lovett@rbht.nhs.uk]	020 7352 8121 ext. 4736
Lugton, George L. MA BD	1955	1997	(Guernsey: St Andrew's in the Grange)	6 Clos de Beauvoir, Rue Cohu, Guernsey GY5 7TE 4 rue de Rives, 37160 Abilly, France	(Tel/Fax) 01481 254285
Macfarlane, Peter T. BA LTh	1970	1994	(Chaplain: Army)		
McIndoe, John H. MA BD STM DD	1966	2000	(London: St Columba's with Newcastle: St Andrew's)	5 Dunlin, Westerlands Park, Glasgow G12 0FE [E-mail: johnandeve@mcindoe555.fsnet.co.uk]	0141-579 1366
MacLeod, Rory N. BA BD	1986	1992	Chaplain: Army	21 Engr Regt, Clara Barracks, Chatham Road, Ripon HG4 2RD	
McMahon, John K.S. MA BD	1998	2012	Head of Spiritual and Pastoral Care, West London Mental Health Trust	Broadmoor Hospital, Crowthorne, Berkshire RG45 7EG [E-mail: john.mcmahonrev@wlmht.nhs.uk]	01344 754098
Mather, James BA DipArch MA MBA	2010		Auxiliary Minister: University Chaplain	24 Ellison Road, Barnes, London SW13 0AD [E-mail: JMather@churchofscotland.org.uk]	(Home) 020 8876 6540 (Work) 020 7361 1670 (Mbl) 07836 715655
Middleton, Paul BMus BD ThM PhD	2000		University Lecturer	97B Whipcord Lane, Chester CH1 4DG	
Munro, Alexander W. MA BD	1978		Chaplain and Teacher of Religious Studies	Columba House, 12 Alexandra Road, Southport PR9 0NB [E-mail: revdjt@gmail.com]	01704 543044
Thom, David J. BD DipMin	1999	2015	Army Chaplain		
Trevorrow, James A. LTh	1971	2003	(Glasgow: Cranhill)	12 Test Green, Corby, Northants NN17 2HA [E-mail: jimtrevorrow@compuserve.com]	01536 264018
Walker, R. Forbes BSc BD ThM	1987	2013	School Chaplain	Flat 5, 18 Northside Wandsworth Common, London SW18 2SL [E-mail: revrfw@gmail.com]	020 8870 0953
Wallace, Donald S.	1950	1980	(Chaplain: RAF)	7 Delfield Close, Watford, Herts WD1 3BL	
Ward, Michael J. BSc BD PhD MA PGCE	1983	2009	Training and Development Officer: Presbyterian Church of Wales	Apt 6, Bryn Hedd, Conwy Road, Penmaen-mawr, Gwynedd LL34 6BS [E-mail: revmw@btopenworld.com]	01923 223289 (Mbl) 07765 598816
Wood, Peter J. MA BD	1993		(College Lecturer)	97 Broad Street, Cambourne, Cambridgeshire CB23 6DH [E-mail: pejowood@tiscali.co.uk]	01954 715558

ENGLAND – Church Addresses

Corby:	St Andrew's	Occupation Road
	St Ninian's	Beanfield Avenue
Liverpool:		The Western Rooms, Anglican Cathedral
London:	Crown Court	Crown Court WC2
	St Columba's	Pont Street SW1
Newcastle:		Sandyford Road

(48) PRESBYTERY OF INTERNATIONAL CHARGES

Meets over the weekend of the second Sunday of March and October, hosted by congregations in mainland Europe.

Clerk:	REV. JAMES SHARP	102 Rue des Eaux-Vives, CH-1207 Geneva, Switzerland [E-mail: europe@churchofscotland.org.uk]	0041 22 786 4847
Depute Clerk:	REV. DEREK G. LAWSON	Schiedamse Vest 121, 3012BH, Rotterdam, The Netherlands [E-mail: deputeclerk@europepresbytery.net]	0031 10 412 5709

Amsterdam: English Reformed Church
Lance Stone BD MTh PhD   2014   Jan Willem Brouwersstraat 9, NL-1071 LH Amsterdam, The Netherlands   0031 20 672 2288
[E-mail: minister@ercadam.nl]
Church address: Begijnhof 48, 1012WV Amsterdam

Bermuda: Christ Church, Warwick (H) (001 441 236 1882)
Alistair G. Bennett BSc BD   1978   2016   The Manse, 6 Manse Road, Paget PG 01, Bermuda   001 441 236 0400
Church address: Christ Church, Middle Road, Warwick, Warwick, Bermuda
Mailing address: PO Box WK 130, Warwick WK BX, Bermuda
[E-mail: christchurch@logic.bm; Website: www.christchurch.bm]

Bochum (Associated congregation)
James M. Brown MA BD   1982   Neustrasse 15, D-44787 Bochum, Germany   0049 234 133 65
[E-mail: j.brown56@gmx.de]
Church address: Pauluskircke, Grabenstrasse 9, 44787 Bochum

Brussels St Andrew's (H) (0032 2 649 02 19)
Andrew Gardner BSc BD PhD   1997   2004   23 Square des Nations, B-1000 Brussels, Belgium   0032 2 672 40 56
[E-mail: minister@churchofscotland.be]
Church address: Chaussée de Vieurgat 181, 1050 Brussels
[E-mail: secretary@churchofscotland.be]

Budapest St Columba's (0036 1 373 0725)
Aaron Stevens BA MDiv MACE   2010   Stefánia út 32, H-1143, Budapest, Hungary   (Mbl) 0036 70 615 5394
[E-mail: revastevens@yahoo.co.uk]
Church address: Vörösmarty utca 51, 1064 Budapest

Colombo, Sri Lanka: St Andrew's Scots Kirk (0094 112 323 765) Vacant			73 Galle Road, Colpetty, Colombo 3, Sri Lanka [E-mail: minister@standrewsscotskirk.org]	0094 112 386 774
Costa del Sol Vacant			Avenida Jesus Santos Rein, 24 Edf. Lindamar 4 – 3Q, Fuengirola, 29640 Malaga. Spain Church address: Lux Mundi Ecumenical Centre, Calle Nueva 3, 29460 Fuengirola	0034 951 260 982
Geneva (0041 22 788 08 31) Vacant			6 chemin Taverney, 1218 Geneva, Switzerland [E-mail: cofsg@pingnet.ch] Church address: Auditoire de Calvin, 1 Place de la Taconnerie, Geneva	0041 22 788 08 31
Gibraltar St Andrew's Ewen MacLean BA BD	1995	2009	St Andrew's Manse, 29 Scud Hill, Gibraltar [E-mail: scotskirk@gibraltar.gi] Church address: Governor's Parade, Gibraltar	00350 200 77040
Lausanne: The Scots Kirk (H) Ian J.M. McDonald MA BD	1984	2010	26 Avenue de Rumine, CH-1005 Lausanne, Switzerland [E-mail: minister@scotskirklausanne.ch]	0041 21 323 98 28
Lisbon St Andrew's Vacant			Rua Coelho da Rocha, N°75 - 1° Campa de Ourique, 1350-073 Lisbon, Portugal [E-mail: cofslx@netcabo.pt] Church address: Rua da Arriaga. Lisbon	00351 213 951 165
Malta St Andrew's Scots Church (H) Kim Hurst	2014		La Romagnola, 15 Triq is-Seiqia, Misrah Kola, Attard ATD 1713, Malta [E-mail: minister@saintandrewsmalta.com] Church address: 210 Old Bakery Street, Valletta, Malta	(Tel/Fax) 00356 214 15465
Paris: The Scots Kirk Vacant			10 Rue Thimmonier, F-75009 Paris, France Church address: 17 Rue Bayard, 75009 Paris	0033 1 48 78 47 94

Rome: St Andrew's
Vacant
Via XX Settembre 7, 00187 Rome, Italy　　(Tel) 0039 06 482 7627
　　(Fax) 0039 06 487 4370

Rotterdam: Scots International Church (0031 10 412 4779)
Derek G. Lawson LLB BD　　1998　2016
Church address: Schiedamse Vest 121, 3012BH Rotterdam, The Netherlands
Meeuwenstraat 4A, NL-3071 PE Rotterdam, The Netherlands　0031 10 412 5709
[E-mail: info@scotsintchurch.com]

Trinidad: Greyfriars St Ann's, Port of Spain l/w Arouca and Sangre Grande
Vacant
50 Frederick Street, Port of Spain, Trinidad　001 868 623 6684

Bom, Irene	2008	Ordained Local Minister-worship resourcing	Bergpolderstraat 53A, NL-3038 KB Rotterdam, The Netherlands [E-mail: ibsalem@xs4all.nl]	0031 10 265 1703
Burns, Terry BA MA	2014	(Nicosia Community Church, Cyprus)	63-65 Vyronos, Flat 501, 1096 Nicosia, Cyprus [E-mail: terrance.burns1955@yahoo.com]	00357 22 783 101
Johnston, Colin D. MA BD	1986 2016	Evangelical Theological Seminary Cairo	8 El - Sekka El - Beidah Street, Abassiyya, Cairo 11381, Egypt	
McLay, Neil BA BD	2006 2012	Chaplain: Army	Barker Barracks, Paderborn, BFPO 22	
Pitkeathly, Thomas C. MA CA BD	1984 2004	(Brussels)	77 St Thomas Road, Lythan St. Anne's FY8 1JP [E-mail: tpitkeathly@yahoo.co.uk]	01253 789634
Pot Joost BSc	1992 2004	(Rotterdam – Auxilliary Minister)	[E-mail: joostpot@gmail.com]	
Sharp, James	2005	OLM, Presbytery Clerk	102 Rue des Eaux-Vives, 1207 Geneva, Switzerland [E-mail: jimsharp@bluewin.ch]	0041 22 786 4847

(49) JERUSALEM

Clerk:　JOANNA OAKLEY-LEVSTEIN　　St Andrew's, Galilee, PO Box 104, Tiberias 14100, Israel　**00972 50 5842517**

Jerusalem: St Andrew's
Paraic Reamonn BA BD　1982　2014　St Andrew's Scots Memorial Church, 1 David Remez Street, PO Box 8619, Jerusalem 91086, Israel　00972 2 673 2401
[E-mail: PReamonn@churchofscotland.org.uk]

Tiberias: St Andrew's
Katharine S. Reynolds BA MSc BD MLitt　2012　2015　St Andrew's, Galilee, 1 Gdud Barak Street, PO Box 104, Tiberias 14100, Israel　00972 4 671 0759
(Scottish Episcopal Church)　[E-mail: kreynolds@churchofscotland.org.uk]

SECTION 6

Additional Lists of Personnel

		Page
A	Ordained Local Ministers	242
	Ordained Local Ministers (Retired List)	243
B	Auxiliary Ministers	244
	Auxiliary Ministers (Retired List)	245
C	The Diaconate	246
	The Diaconate (Retired List)	247
	The Diaconate (Supplementary List)	249
D	Ministers Not in Presbyteries (Practising Certificate)	249
E	Ministers Not in Presbyteries (Without Certificate)	254
F	Chaplains, Health and Social Care	257
G	Chaplains to HM Forces	260
H	Readers	262
I	Ministries Development Staff	277
J	Overseas Locations	280
K	Overseas Resigned and Retired Mission Partners	281
L	Chaplains, Full-time Workplace	281
M	Chaplains, Prison	282
N	Chaplains, University	282
O	Representatives on Council Education Committees	282
P	Retired Lay Agents	282
Q	Ministers Ordained for Sixty Years and Upwards	282
R	Deceased Ministers	283

LIST A – ORDAINED LOCAL MINISTERS

Further information, including E-mail addresses, may be found under the presbytery (Section 5) to which an OLM belongs, its number recorded in the final column.

NAME	ORD	ADDRESS	TEL	PR
Allardice, Michael MA MPhil PGCertTHE FHEA	2014	20 Parbroath Road, Glenrothes KY7 4TH	01592 772280	25
Archer, Morven (Mrs)	2013	42 Firthview Drive, Inverness IV3 8QE	01463 237840	37
Bellis, Pamela A. BA	2014	Maughold, Low Killantrae, Port William, Newton Stewart DG8 9QR	01988 700590	9
Bissett, James	2016	Tigh-an-Isein, Croftnacreich, North Kessock, Inverness IV1 3ZE	01463 731930	39
Black, Sandra (Mrs)	2013	5 Doon Place, Troon KA10 7EQ	01292 220075	10
Bom, Irene	2008	Bergpolderstraat 53A, NL-3038 KB Rotterdam, The Netherlands	0031 10 265 1703	48
Breingan, Mhairi	2011	6 Park Road, Inchinnan, Renfrew PA4 4QJ	0141-812 1425	14
Brown, Kathryn (Mrs)	2014	1 Callendar Park Walk, Callendar Grange, Falkirk FK1 1TA	01324 617352	22
Crossan, William	2014	Gowanbank, Kilkerran Road, Campbeltown PA28 6JL	01586 553453	19
Dee, Oonagh	2014	'Kendoon', Merse Way, Kippford, Dalbeattie DG5 4LL	01556 620001	8
Dempster, Eric T. MBA	2016	Annanside, Wamphray, Moffat DG10 9LZ	01576 470496	7
Don, Andrew MBA	2006	5 Eskdale Court, Penicuik EH26 8HT	01968 675766	3
Duncan, Esme (Miss)	2013	Avalon, Upper Warse, Canisbay, Wick KW1 4YD	01955 611455	41
Duncanson, Mary (Ms)	2013	3 Balmenach Road, Cromdale, Grantown-on-Spey PH26 3LJ	01479 872165	36
Edwards, Dougal BTh	2013	25 Mackenzie Street, Carnoustie DD7 6HD	01241 852666	30
Fidler, David G.	2013	48 Priory Close, Louth LN11 9AS	01507 609806	47
Finnie, Bill H. BA PgDipSW CertCRS	2015	27 Hallside Crescent, Cambuslang, Glasgow G72 7DY	07518 357138 (Mbl)	16
Freeth, June	2015	Cumlaquoy, Birsay, Orkney KW17 2ND	01856 721449	45
Fulcher, Christine	2012	St Blaan's Manse, Southend, Campbeltown PA28 6RQ	01586 830504	19
Geddes, Elizabeth (Mrs)	2013	9 Shillingworth Place, Bridge of Weir PA11 3DY	01505 612639	14
Gray, Ian	2013	'The Mallards', 15 Rossie Island Road, Montrose DD10 9NH	01674 677126	30
Grieve, Leslie E.T.	2014	23 Hertford Avenue, Kelvindale, Glasgow G12 0LG	07813 255052 (Mbl)	16
Hardman Moore, Susan (Prof.) BA PGCE MA PhD	2013	c/o New College, Mound Place, Edinburgh EH1 2LX	0131-650 8908	1
Harrison, Frederick	2013	33 Castle Avenue, Gorebridge EH23 4TH	01875 820908	3
Harvey, Joyce (Mrs)	2013	4A Allanfield Place, Newton Stewart DG8 6BS	01671 403693	9
Hickman, Mandy R. RGN	2013	Lagnaleon, 4 Wilson Street, Largs KA30 9AQ	01475 675347	12
Hughes, Barry MA	2011	Dunslair, Cardrona Way, Cardrona, Peebles EH45 9LD	01896 831197	4
Johnston, June E. BSc MEd BD	2013	Tarmachan, Main Street, Killin FK21 8TN	07754 448889 (Mbl)	23
Livingstone, Alan	2013	Meadowside, Lawmuir, Methven, Perth PH1 3SZ	01738 840682	28
McCutcheon, John	2014	Flat 2/6 Parkview, Milton Brae, Milton, Dumbarton G82 2TT	01389 739034	18
Macdonald, Ishabel	2011	'Cleat Afe Ora', 18 Carinish, Isle of North Uist HS6 5HN	01876 580367	43
MacDonald, Monica (Mrs)	2014	32 Reilly Gardens, High Bonnybridge, Bonnybridge FK4 2BB	01324 874807	22
Mack, Lynne (Mrs)	2013	36 Middleton, Menstrie FK11 7HD	01259 761465	23
McLaughlin, Cathie H. (Mrs)	2012	8 Lamlash Place, Glasgow G33 3XH	0141-774 2483	16
MacLeod, Iain A.	2014	6 Hallydown Drive, Glasgow G13 1UF	07795 014889 (Mbl)	16
McLeod, Tom	2014	3 Martnaham Drive, Coylton KA6 6JE	01292 570100	10

Name	Year	Address	Phone	No.
Mathers, Alexena (Sandra)	2015	10 Ercall, Brightons, Falkirk FK2 0RS	01324 872253	22
Maxwell, David	2014	248 Old Castle Road, Glasgow G44 5EZ	0141-569 6379	16
Michie, Margaret (Mrs)	2013	3 Loch Leven Court, Wester Balgedie, Kinross KY13 9NE	01592 840602	28
Morrison, John A. BSc BA PGCE	2013	35 Kirkton Place, Elgin IV30 6JR	01343 550199	35
Muirhead, Morag Y. (Mrs)	2013	6 Dunbarton Road, Fort William PH33 6UU	01397 703643	38
Murphy, Jim	2014	10 Hillview Crescent, Bellshill ML4 1N	01698 740189	17
Nicol, Robert D.	2013	3 Castlegreen Road, Thurso KW14 7DN		41
Noonan, Pam (Mrs)	2013			
Nutter, Margaret A.E.	2014	Kilmorich, 14 Balloch Road, Balloch, Alexandria G83 8SR	01389 754505	18
Perkins, Mairi (Mrs)	2012	Ashlea, Cuil Road, Duror, Appin PA38 3DA (Work)	01631 740313	38
Prentice, Martin W.M.	2013	Cott of Howe, Cairston, Stromness, Orkney KW16 3JU	01856 851139	45
Rennie, Lyall	2013	Ruachmarra, Lower Warse, Canisbay, Wick KW1 4YB	01955 611756	41
Robertson, Ishbel A.R. MA BD	2013	Oakdene, 81 Bonhill Road, Dumbarton G82 2DU	01389 763436	18
Sarle, Andrew BSc BD	2013	114 High Station Road, Falkirk FK1 5LN	01324 621648	22
Sharp, James	2005	102 Rue des Eaux-Vives, CH-1207 Geneva, Switzerland	0041 22 786 4847	48
Somevi, Joseph K. BSc MSc (Oxon) PhD MRICS MRTPI MIEMA CertCRS	2015	97 Ashwood Road, Bridge of Don, Aberdeen AB22 8QX	01224 826362	31
Steele, Grace M.F. MA	2014	12a Farragon Drive, Aberfeldy PH15 2BQ	01887 820025	27
Stevenson, Stuart	2011	143 Springfield Park, Johnstone PA5 8JT	0141-886 2131	14
Stewart, Heather (Mrs)	2013	Burnthill, Thrumster, Wick KW1 5TR	01955 651717	41
Stewart, William	2015	Denend, Strichen, Fraserburgh AB43 6RN	01771 637256	34
Stobo, Mary J. (Mrs)	2013	Druim-an-Sgairnich, Ardgay IV24 3BG	01863 766868	40
Strachan, Pamela D. (Lady) MA (Cantab)	2015	Glenhighton, Broughton, Biggar ML12 6JF	01899 830423	4
Strachan, Willie MBA DipY&C	2014	Ladywell House, Lucky Slap, Monikie, Dundee DD5 3QG	01382 370286	29
Stuart, Alex P.	2014	107 Baldorran Crescent, Cumbernauld, Glasgow G68 9EX	01236 727710	16
Sturrock, Roger D. (Prof.) BD MD FCRP	2014	36 Thomson Drive, Bearsden, Glasgow G61 3PA	0141-942 7412	16
Thomson, Mary Ellen (Mrs)	2013	Riverside Flat, Gynack Street, Kingussie PH21 1EL	01540 661772	36
Thorburn, Susan (Mrs) MTh	2014	3 Daleally Cottages, St Madoes Road, Errol, Perth PH2 7JH	01821 642681	28
Tweedie, Fiona BSc PhD	2011	121 George Street, Edinburgh EH2 4YN	0131-225 5722	1
Wallace, Mhairi (Mrs)	2013	5 Dee Road, Kirkcudbright DG6 4HQ (Mbl)	07701 375064	8
Watson, Michael D.	2013	47 Crichton Terrace, Pathhead EH37 5QZ	01875 320043	3
Watt, Kim	2015	Reddans Park Gate, The Crescent, Stewarton, Kilmarnock KA3 5AY	01560 482267	11

ORDAINED LOCAL MINISTERS (Retired List)

Name	Year	Address	Phone	No.
Anderson, David M. MSc FCOptom	1984	'Mirlos', 1 Dumfries Place, Fort William PH33 6UQ	01397 702091	38
McAllister, Anne C. (Mrs) BSc DipEd CCS	2013	39 Bowes Rigg, Stewarton, Kilmarnock KA3 5EN	01560 483191	11

LIST B – AUXILIARY MINISTERS

Further information, including E-mail addresses, may be found under the presbytery (Section 5) to which an Auxiliary Minister belongs, as recorded in the final column.

NAME	ORD	ADDRESS	TEL	PR
Attenburrow, Anne BSc MB ChB	2006	4 Jock Inksons Brae, Elgin IV30 1QE	01343 552330	35
Binks, Mike	2007	Hollybank, 12 Kingsbrook, Corby NN18 9HY	(Mbl) 07590 507917	47
Buck, Maxine	2007	Brownlee House, Mauldslie Road, Carluke ML8 5HW	01555 759063	17
Cameron, Ann J. (Mrs) CertCS DCE TEFL	2005	Currently resident in Qatar		32
Campbell, Gordon A. MA BD CDipAF DipHSM CMer MCMI MIHM AssocCIPD AFRIN ARSGS FRGS FSAScot	2001	2 Falkland Place, Kingoodie, Invergowrie, Dundee DD2 5DY	01382 561383	29
Dick, Roddy S.	2010	27 Easter Crescent, Wishaw ML2 8XB	01698 383453	17
Fletcher, Timothy E.G. BA FCMA	1998	3 Ardchoille Park, Perth PH2 7TL	01738 638189	28
Forrest, Kenneth P. CBE BSc PhD	2006	5 Carruth Road, Bridge of Weir PA11 3HQ	01505 612651	14
Gardner, Hilary M. (Miss)	2010	Cayman Lodge, Kincardine Hill, Ardgay IV24 3DJ	01863 766107	40
Griffiths, Ruth I. (Mrs)	2004	Kirkwood, Mathieson Lane, Innellan, Dunoon PA23 7TA	01369 830145	19
Hood, Catriona A.	2006	'Elyside', Dalintober, Campbeltown PA28 6EB	01586 551490	19
Howie, Marion L.K. (Mrs) MA ARCS	1992	51 High Road, Stevenston KA20 3DY	01294 466571	12
Jackson, Nancy	2009	35 Auchentrae Crescent, Ayr KA7 4BD	01292 262034	10
Kemp, Tina MA	2005	12 Oaktree Gardens, Dumbarton G82 1EU	01389 730477	18
Landale, William S.	2005	Green Hope Guest House, Green Hope, Duns TD11 3SG	01361 890242	5
Lunn, Dorothy	2002	14 Bellerby Drive, Ouston, Co. Durham DH2 1TW	0191-492 0647	47
Macdonald, Michael	2004	73 Firhill, Alness IV17 0RT	01349 884268	39
MacDougall, Lorna I. (Miss) MA DipGC BD	2003	11 Range View, Cleghorn, Carstairs, Lanark ML11 8TF	01555 871258	13
Manson, Eileen (Mrs) DipCE	1994	1 Cambridge Avenue, Gourock PA19 1XT	01475 632401	14
Mather, James BA DipArch MA MBA	2010	24 Ellison Road, Barnes, London SW13 0AD	020 8876 6540	47
Moore, Douglas T.	2003	9 Milton Avenue, Prestwick KA9 1PU	01292 671352	10
Morrison, Donald John	2001	22 Kyles, Tarbert, Isle of Harris HS3 3BS	01859 502341	43
O'Donnell, Barbara BD PGSE	2007	Ashbank, 258 Main Street, Alexandria G83 0NU	01389 752356	18
Paterson, Andrew E. JP	1994	6 The Willows, Kelty KY4 0FQ	01383 830998	24
Perry, Marion (Mrs)	2009	17a Tarbolton Road, Cumbernauld, Glasgow G67 2AJ	01236 898519	22
Riddell, Thomas S. BSc CEng FIChemE	1993	4 The Maltings, Linlithgow EH49 6DS	01506 843251	2
Robson, Brenda PhD	2005	2 Baird Road, Ratho, Newbridge EH28 8RA	0131-333 2746	2
Shearer, Anne F. BA DipEd	2010	10 Colsnaur, Menstrie FK11 7HG	01259 769176	23
Sutherland, David A.	2001	3/1, 145 Broomhill Drive, Glasgow G11 7ND	0141-357 2058	16
Vivers, Katherine A.	2004	Blacket House, Eaglesfield, Lockerbie DG11 3AA	01461 500412	7

NAME	ORD	ADDRESS	TEL	PR
Walker, Linda	2008	18 Valeview Terrace, Glasgow G42 9LA	0141-649 1340	16
Wandrum, David C.	1993	5 Cawder View, Carrickstone Meadows, Cumbernauld, Glasgow G68 0BN		22
Whittaker, Mary	2011	11 Templand Road, Lhanbryde, Elgin IV30 8BR (text only) (Mbl)	01236 723288 07810 420106	35
Wilkie, Robert F.	2011	24 Huntingtower Road, Perth PH1 2JS	01738 628301	28

AUXILIARY MINISTERS (Retired List)

NAME	ORD	ADDRESS	TEL	PR
Birch, James PgDip FRSA FIOC	2001	1 Kirkhill Grove, Cambuslang, Glasgow G72 8EH	0141-583 1722	16
Brown, Elizabeth (Mrs) JP RGN	1996	8 Viewlands Place, Perth PH1 1BS	01738 552391	28
Cloggie, June (Mrs)	1997	11A Tulipan Crescent, Callander FK17 8AR	01877 331021	23
Craggs, Sheila (Mrs)	2001	7 Morar Court, Ellon AB41 9GG	01358 723055	33
Ferguson, Archibald M. MSc PhD CEng FRINA	1989	The Whins, 2 Barrowfield, Station Road, Cardross, Dumbarton G82 5NL	01389 841517	18
Harrison, Cameron	2006	Woodfield House, Priormuir, St Andrews KY16 8LP	01334 478067	26
Jenkinson, John J. JP LTCL ALCM DipEd DipSen	1991	8 Rosehall Terrace, Falkirk FK1 1PY	01324 625498	22
Kay, Elizabeth (Miss) DipYCS	1993	1 Kintail Walk, Inchture, Perth PH14 9RY	01828 686029	29
McAlpine, John BSc	1988	Braeside, 201 Bonkle Road, Newmains, Wishaw ML2 9AA	01698 384610	17
MacDonald, Kenneth MA BA	2001	5 Henderland Road, Bearsden, Glasgow G61 1AH	0141-943 1103	16
MacFadyen, Anne M. (Mrs) BSc BD FSAScot	1995	295 Mearns Road, Glasgow G77 5LT	0141-639 3605	16
MacGregor, Robert M. CMIOSH DipOSH RSP	2004	Olna Cottage, Brae, Shetland ZE2 9QS	01806 522604	46
Mack, Elizabeth A. (Miss) DipPEd	1994	24 Roberts Crescent, Dumfries DG2 7RS	01387 264847	8
Mack, John C. JP	1985	The Willows, Auchleven, Insch AB52 6QB	01464 820387	33
Mailer, Colin	1996	Innis Chonain, Back Row, Polmont, Falkirk FK2 0RD	01324 712401	22
Munro, Mary (Mrs) BA	1993	14 Auchneel Crescent, Stranraer DG9 0JH	01776 702305	9
Paterson, Maureen (Mrs) BSc	1992	91 Dalmahoy Crescent, Kirkcaldy KY2 6TA	01592 262300	25
Phillippo, Michael MTh BSc BVetMed MRCVS	2003	25 Deeside Crescent, Aberdeen AB15 7PT	01224 318317	31
Pot, Joost BSc	1992	[E-mail: joostpot@gmail.com]		48
Ramage, Alastair E. MA BA ADB CertEd	1996	16 Claremont Gardens, Milngavie, Glasgow G62 6PG	0141-956 2897	18
Shaw, Catherine A.M. MA	1998	40 Merrygreen Place, Stewarton, Kilmarnock KA3 5EP	01560 483352	11
Thomas, Shirley A. (Mrs) DipSocSci AMIA	2000	14 Kirkgait, Letham, Forfar DD8 2XQ	01307 818084	30
Wilson, Mary D. (Mrs) RGN SCM DTM	1990	Berbice, The Terrace, Bridge of Tilt, Blair Atholl, Pitlochry PH18 5SZ	01796 481619	27
Zambonini, James LIADip	1997	100 Old Manse Road, Netherton, Wishaw ML2 0EP	01698 350889	17

LIST C – THE DIACONATE

Fuller information, including E-mail addresses, may be found under the presbytery (Section 5) to which a Deacon belongs, whose number is recorded in the final column.

NAME	COM	APP	ADDRESS	TEL	PRES
Beck, Isobel DCS	2014	2014	16 Patrick Avenue, Stevenston KA20 4AW	(Mbl) 07919 193425	16
Blair, Fiona (Miss) DCS	1994	2010	Mure Church Manse, 9 West Road, Irvine KA12 8RE	(Mbl) 07977 235168	12
Buchanan, Marion (Mrs) MA DCS	1983	2006	16 Almond Drive, East Kilbride, Glasgow G74 2HX	(Mbl) 07999 889817	16
Brydson, Angela (Mrs) DCS	2015		52 Victoria Park, Lockerbie DG11 2AY	(Mbl) 07543 796820	7
Cathcart, John Paul (Mr) DCS	2000		9 Glen More, East Kilbride, Glasgow G74 2AP	01355 243970	16
Corrie, Margaret (Miss) DCS	1989	2013	44 Sunnyside Street, Camelon, Falkirk FK1 4BH	(Mbl) 07955 633969	2
Crawford, Morag (Miss) MSc DCS	1977	1998	118 Wester Drylaw Place, Edinburgh EH4 2TG	0131-332 2253	24
Crocker, Liz (Mrs) DipComEd DCS	1985	2003	77C Craigcrook Road, Edinburgh EH4 3PH	(Tel/Fax) 0131-332 0227	1
Cunningham, Ian (Mr) DCS	1994	2002	110 Nelson Terrace, Keith AB55 5FD		35
Cuthbertson, Valerie (Miss) DipTMus DCS	2003		105 Bellshill Road, Motherwell ML1 3SJ	01698 259001	22
Deans, Raymond (Mr) DCS	1994	2003	60 Ardmory Road, Rothesay, Isle of Bute PA20 0PG [E-mail: r.deans93@btinternet.com]	01700 504893	19
Evans, Mark (Mr) BSc MSc DCS	1988	2006	13 Easter Drylaw Drive, Edinburgh EH4 2QA	0131-343 3089	1
Gargrave, Mary (Mrs) DCS	1989	2002	12 Parkholm Quad, Glasgow G63 7ZH	0141-880 5532	16
Getliffe, Dot (Mrs) DCS BA BD DipEd	2006	2013	3 Woodview Terrace, Hamilton ML3 9DP	01698 423504	16
Hamilton, James (Mr) DCS	1997	2000	6 Beckfield Gate, Glasgow G33 1SW	0141-558 3195	16
Hamilton, Karen (Mrs) DCS	1995	2009	6 Beckfield Gate, Glasgow G33 1SW	0141-558 3195	16
Love, Joanna (Ms) BSc DCS	1992	2009	92 Everard Drive, Glasgow G21 1XQ	0141-772 0149	16
Lyall, Ann (Miss) DCS	1980	2016	The Manse, 2 Lanark Road, Kirkmuirhill, Lanark ML11 9RB	01555 892409	13
MacDonald, Anne (Miss) BA DCS	1980	2002	502 Castle Gait, Paisley PA1 2PA	0141-840 1875	16
McIntosh, Kay (Mrs) DCS	2008	2013	4 Jacklin Green, Livingston EH54 8PZ	01506 440543	2
McKay, Kenneth D. (Mr) DCS	1996	1998	11F Balgowan Road, Letham, Perth PH1 2JG	01738 621169	28
McLelan, Margaret DCS	1986	2014	18 Broom Road East, Newton Mearns, Glasgow G77 5SD	0141-639 6853	16
McPheat, Elspeth (Miss) DCS	1985	2001	11/5 New Orchardfield, Edinburgh EH6 5ET	0131-554 4143	1
Nicholson, David (Mr) DCS	1994	1993	2D Doonside. Kildrum, Cumbernauld, Glasgow G67 2HX	01236 732260	22
Ogilvie, Colin (Mr) BA DCS	1998		21 Neilsland Drive, Motherwell ML1 3DZ [E-mail: colinogilvie2@gmail.com]	01698 321836	
Pennykid, Gordon J. BD DCS	2015		8 Glenfield, Livingston EH54 7BG	(Mbl) 07837 287804	2
Philip, Elizabeth (Mrs) DCS MA BA PGCSE	2007		8 Strathearn Terrace, Crieff PH7 3AQ	(Mbl) 07747 652652 01764 218976	28
Porter, Jean (Mrs) BD DCS	2006	2008	St Mark's Church, Drip Road, Stirling FK8 1RE	(Mbl) 07729 316321	23
Robertson, Pauline (Mrs) DCS BA CertTheol	2003	2006	6 Ashville Terrace, Edinburgh EH6 8DD	0131-554 6564	1

NAME			ADDRESS	TEL	PRES
Stewart, Marion G. (Miss) DCS	1991	1994	Kirk Cottage, Kirkton of Skene, Westhill, Skene AB32 6XE	01224 743407	33
Thomson, Jacqueline (Mrs) MTh DCS	2004	2004	16 Aitken Place, Coaltown of Wemyss, Kirkcaldy KY1 4PA	01592 653995	25
Urquhart, Barbara (Mrs) DCS	1986	2006	9 Standalane, Kilmaurs, Kilmarnock KA3 2NB	01563 538289	11
Wallace, Catherine (Mrs) PGDipC DCS	1987		21 Durley Dene Crescent, Bridge of Earn PH2 9RD	01738 621709	28
Wallace, Sheila (Mrs) DCS BA BD	2009	2011	Beannach Cottage, Spey Avenue, Boat of Garten PH24 3BE	01479 831548	36
Wilson, Glenda (Mrs) DCS	1990	2006	5 Allan Terrace, Sandbank, Dunoon PA23 8PR	01369 704168	19
Wright, Lynda (Miss) BEd DCS	1979	1992	1a Broomhill Avenue, Burntisland KY3 0BP	(Mbl) 07835 303395	25

THE DIACONATE (Retired List)

Fuller contact details are found in the presbytery, indicated by its number in the last column, in which the retired deacon has a seat. Where a retired deacon does not have a seat on presbytery, full contact details are given here.

NAME	COM	ADDRESS	TEL	PRES
Allan, Jean (Mrs) DCS	1989	12C Hindmarsh Avenue, Dundee DD3 7LW	01382 827299	29
Anderson, Janet (Miss) DCS	1979	Creagard, 31 Lower Breakish, Isle of Skye IV42 8QA	01471 822403	42
Bayes, Muriel C. (Mrs) DCS	1963	Flat 6, Carleton Court, 10 Fenwick Road, Glasgow G46 4AN	0141-633 0865	16
Beaton, Margaret (Miss) DCS	1989	64 Gardenside Grove, Carmyle, Glasgow G32 8EZ	0141-646 2297	16
Bell, Sandra (Mrs) DCS	2001	62 Loganswell Road, Thornliebank, Glasgow G46 8AX	0141-638 5884	
Black, Linda (Miss) BSc DCS	1993	148 Rowan Road, Abronhill, Cumbernauld, Glasgow G67 3DA	01236 786265	22
Buchanan, John (Mr) DCS	2010	19 Gillespie Crescent, Edinburgh EH10 4HZ	0131-229 0794	
Burns, Marjory (Mrs) DCS	1997	22 Kirklee Road, Mossend, Bellshill ML4 2QN [E-mail: mburns8070@aol.co.uk]	01698 292685 (Mbl) 07792 843922	3
Cameron, Margaret (Miss) DCS	1961	2 Rowans Gate, Paisley PA2 6RD	0141-840 2479	14
Craw, John (Mr) DCS	1998	Liabost, 8 Proudfoot Road, Wick KW1 4PQ	01955 603805	41
Drummond, Rhoda (Miss) DCS	1960	Flat K, 23 Grange Loan, Edinburgh EH9 2ER	0131-668 3631	1
Dunnett, Linda (Mrs) BA DCS	1976	9 Tulipan Crescent, Callander FK17 8AR	01877 339640	23
Erskine, Morag (Miss) DCS	1979	111 Mains Drive, Park Mains, Erskine PA8 7JJ	0141-812 6096	14
Forrest, Janice (Mrs)	1990	4/1, 7 Blochairm Place, Glasgow G21 2EB	0141-552 1132	
Gordon, Fiona S. (Mrs) MA DCS	1958	Machrie, 3 Cupar Road, Cuparmuir, Cupar KY15 5RH [E-mail: machrie@madasafish.com]	01334 652341	
Gordon, Margaret (Mrs) DCS	1998	92 Lanark Road West, Currie EH14 5LA	0131-449 2554	1
Gray, Catherine (Miss) DCS	1969	10C Eastern View, Gourock PA19 1RJ [E-mail: gray_catherine2@sky.com]	01475 637479	
Gray, Christine M. (Mrs) DCS	1969	11 Woodside Avenue, Thornliebank, Glasgow G46 7HR	0141-571 1008	16
Gray, Greta (Miss) DCS	1992	67 Crags Avenue, Paisley PA2 6SG	0141-884 6178	14
Hughes, Helen (Miss) DCS	1977	2/2, 43 Burnbank Terrace, Glasgow G20 6UQ	0141-333 9459	16

Name	Year	Address	Phone	
Hutchison, Alan E.W. (Mr) DCS	1988	132 Lochbridge Road, North Berwick EH39 4DR	01620 894077	3
Johnston, Mary (Miss) DCS	1988	19 Lounsdale Drive, Paisley PA2 9ED	0141-849 1615	14
King, Chris (Mrs) DCS	2002	28 Kilnford Drive, Dundonald, Kilmarnock KA2 9ET [E-mail: chrisking99@tiscali.co.uk]	01563 851197	
King, Margaret MA DCS	2002	56 Murrayfield, Fochabers IV32 7EZ	01343 820937	35
Lundie, Ann V. (Miss) DCS	1972	20 Langdykes Drive, Cove, Aberdeen AB12 3HW	01224 898416	31
McBain, Margaret (Miss) DCS	1974	33 Quarry Road, Paisley PA2 7RD	0141-884 2920	14
McCully, M. Isobel (Miss) DCS	1974	10 Broadstone Avenue, Port Glasgow PA14 5BB	01475 742240	14
MacKinnon, Ronald M. (Mr) DCS	1996	12 Mossywood Court, McGregor Avenue, Airdrie ML6 7DY	01236 763389	22
MacLean, Donald A. (Mr) DCS	1988	8 Upper Barvas, Isle of Lewis HS2 0QX	01851 840454	44
McNaughton, Janette (Miss) DCS	1982	4 Dunellan Avenue, Moodiesburn, Glasgow G69 0GB	01236 870180	
MacPherson, James B. (Mr) DCS	1988	0/1, 104 Cartside Street, Glasgow G42 9TQ	0141-616 6468	16
MacQuien, Duncan (Mr) DCS	1988	35 Criffel Road, Mount Vernon, Glasgow G32 9JE	0141-575 1137	
Martin, Janie (Miss) DCS	1979	16 Wentworth Road, Dundee DD2 3SD	01382 813786	29
Merrilees, Ann (Miss) DCS	1994	23 Cuthill Brae, Willow Wood Residential Park, West Calder EH55 8QE	01501 762909	2
Miller, Elsie M. (Miss) DCS	1974	30 Swinton Avenue, Rowanbank, Baillieston, Glasgow G69 6JR	0141-771 0857	22
Mitchell, Joyce (Mrs) DCS	1994	Sunnybank, Farr, Inverness IV2 6XG	01808 521285	37
Morrison, Jean (Dr) DCS	1964	9 The Courtyard, Inchmarlo, Banchory AB31 4AZ [E-mail: morrison.jc612@btinternet.com]	01330 824426	
Moyes, Sheila (Miss) DCS	1957	158 Pilton Avenue, Edinburgh EH5 2JZ	0131-551 1731	1
Mulligan, Anne MA DCS	1974	27A Craigour Avenue, Edinburgh EH17 7NH	0131-664 3426	1
Munro, Patricia (Ms) BSc DCS	1986	4 Hewat Place, Perth PH1 2UD	01738 443088	28
Nicol, Joyce (Mrs) BA DCS	1974	93 Brisbane Street, Greenock PA16 8NY	01475 723235	14
Palmer, Christine (Ms) DCS	2003	Flat 4, Carissima Court, 99 Elmer Road, Elmer, Bognor Regis PO22 6LH	01243 858641	
Rennie, Agnes M. (Miss) DCS	1974	3/1 Cragmillar Court, Edinburgh EH16 4AD	0131-661 8475	1
Rose, Lewis (Mr) DCS	1993	6 Gauldie Crescent, Dundee DD3 0RR	01382 816580	29
Ross, Duncan (Mr) DCS	1996	1 John Neilson Avenue, Paisley PA1 2SX	0141-887 2801	14
Smith, Catherine (Mrs) DCS	1964	21 Lingaro, Bixter, Shetland ZE2 9NN	01595 810207	
Steele, Marilynn J. (Mrs) BD DCS	1999	2 Northfield Gardens, Prestonpans EH32 9LQ	01875 811497	1
Steven, Gordon R. BD DCS	1997	51 Nantwich Drive, Edinburgh EH7 6RB	0131-669 2054	3
Stuart, Anne (Miss) DCS	1966	1 Murrell Terrace, Aberdour, Burntisland KY3 0XH	01383 860049	24
Tait, Agnes (Mrs) DCS	1995	10 Carnoustie Crescent, Greenhills, East Kilbride, Glasgow G75 8TE	01355 243095	
Teague, Yvonne (Mrs) DCS	1965	46 Craigcrook Avenue, Edinburgh EH4 3PX	0131-336 3113	
Thom, Helen (Miss) BA DipEd MA DCS	1959	84 Great King Street, Edinburgh EH3 6QU	0131-556 5687	1
Thomson, Phyllis (Miss) DCS	2003	63 Caroline Park, Mid Calder, Livingston EH53 0SJ	01506 883207	2
Trimble, Robert DCS	1988	5 Templar Rise, Livingston EH54 6PJ	01506 412504	2
Webster, Elspeth H. (Miss) DCS	1950	82 Broomhill Avenue, Burntisland KY3 0BP	01592 873616	
Wilson, Muriel (Miss) MA BD DCS	1997	28 Bellevue Crescent, Ayr KA7 2DR [E-mail: muriel.wilson4@btinternet.com]	01292 264939	
Wishart, William (Mr) DCS	1994	1 Brunstane Road North, Edinburgh EH15 2DL	(Mbl) 07846 555654	1

THE DIACONATE (Supplementary List)

Carson, Christine (Miss) MA DCS	2006	36 Upper Wellhead, Limekilns, Dunfermline KY11 3JQ	01383 873131
Gilroy, Lorraine (Mrs) DCS	1988	5 Bluebell Drive, Bedworth CV12 0GE	02476 366031
Guthrie, Jennifer M. (Miss) DCS		14 Eskview Terrace, Ferryden, Montrose DD10 9RD	01674 674413
Harris, Judith (Mrs) DCS	1993	243 Western Avenue, Sandfields, Port Talbot, West Glamorgan SA12 7NF	01639 884855
Hood, Katrina (Mrs) DCS	1988	67C Farquhar Road, Edgbaston, Birmingham B18 2QP	
Hudson, Sandra (Mrs) DCS	1982	10 Albany Drive, Rutherglen, Glasgow G73 3QN	
Muir, Alison M. (Mrs) DCS	1969	77 Arthur Street, Dunfermline KY12 0JJ	
Ramsden, Christine (Miss) DCS	1978	2 Wykeham Close, Bassett, Southampton SO16 7LZ	01828 628251
Walker, Wikje (Mrs) DCS	1970	24 Brodie's Yard, Queen Street, Coupar Angus PH13 9RA	

LIST D – MINISTERS WHO HOLD PRACTISING CERTIFICATES (in accordance with Act II (2000), but who are not members of a Presbytery)

NAME	ORD	ADDRESS	TEL	PRES
Adamson, Hugh M. BD	1976	38F Maybole Road, Ayr KA7 4SF [E-mail: hmadamson768@btinternet.com]	01292 440958	10
Aitken, Ewan R. BA BD	1992	159 Restalrig Avenue, Edinburgh EH7 6PJ	0131-467 1660	1
Alexander, William M. BD	1971	110 Fairview Circle, Danestone, Aberdeen AB22 8YR	01224 703752	31
Anderson, David MA BD	1975	Rowan Cottage, Aberlour Gardens, Aberlour AB38 9LD	01340 871906	35
Anderson, Kenneth G. MA BD	1967	8 School Road, Arbroath DD11 2LT	01241 874825	30
Anderson, Susan M. (Mrs) BD	1997	32 Murrayfield, Bishopbriggs, Glasgow G64 3DS [E-mail: susanbriggs32@gmail.com]	0141-772 6338	16
Auld, A. Graeme (Prof.) MA BD PhD DLitt FSAScot FRSE	1973	Nether Swanshiel, Hobkirk, Bonchester Bridge, Hawick TD9 8JU [E-mail: a.g.auld@ed.ac.uk]		
Barclay, Neil W. BSc BEd BD	1986	4 Gibsongray Street, Falkirk FK2 7LN	01324 874681	22
Bardgett, Frank D. MA BD PhD	1987	Tigh an Iasgair, Street of Kincardine, Boat of Garten PH24 3BY [E-mail: tigh@bardgett.plus.com]	01479 831751	36
Bartholomew, Julia (Mrs) BSc BD	2002	Kippenhill, Dunning, Perth PH2 0RA	01764 684929	28
Beattie, Warren R. BSc BD MSc PhD	1991	Director for Mission Research, OMF International, 2 Cluny Road, Singapore 259570 [E-mail: beattiewarren@omf.net]	0065 6319 4550	1
Biddle, Lindsay (Ms)	1991	30 Ralston Avenue, Glasgow G52 3NA [E-mail: lindsaybiddle@hotmail.com]	0141-883 7405	
Birrell, John M. MA LLB BD	1974	'Hiddlehame', 5 Hewat Place, Perth PH1 2UD [E-mail: john.birrell@nhs.net]	01738 443335	28
Bjarnason, Sven S. CandTheol	1975	14 Edward Street, Dunfermline KY12 0JW [E-mail: sven@bjarnason.org.uk]	01383 724625	36

Name	Year	Address / E-mail	Phone	No.
Black, James S. BD DPS	1976	7 Breck Terrace, Penicuik EH26 0RJ [E-mail: jsb.black@btopenworld.com]	01968 677559	3
Boyd, Ian R. MA BD PhD	1989	33 Castleton Drive, Newton Mearns, Glasgow G77 3LE		26
Brady, Lynn BD DipMin	1996	[E-mail: LBrady@churchofscotland.org.uk]		16
Bradley, Andrew W. BD	1975	Flat 1/1, 38 Cairnhill View, Bearsden, Glasgow G61 1RP	0141-931 5344	31
Brown, Robert F. MA BD ThM	1971	55 Hilton Drive, Aberdeen AB24 4NJ [E-mail: Bjacob546@aol.com]	01224 491451	
Caie, Albert LTh	1983	34 Ringwell Gardens, Stonehouse, Larkhall ML9 3QW	01698 792187	17
Coogan, J. Melvyn LTh	1992	19 Glen Grove, Largs KA30 8QQ		12
Cowie, James M. BD	1977	The Blue House, 24 Cowdrait, Burnmouth, Eyemouth TD14 5SW [E-mail: jimcowie@europe.com]	01890 781394	
Cowieson, Roy J. BD	1979	2160-15 Hawk Drive, Courtenay, BC V9N 9B2, Canada [E-mail: arjay1232@gmail.com]		13
Craig, Ronald A.S. BAcc BD	1983	29 Third Avenue, Auchinloch, Kirkintilloch, Glasgow G66 5EB [E-mail: rascraig@ntlworld.com]	0141-573 9220	16
Currie, David E.P. BSc BD	1983	49 Craigmill Gardens, Carnoustie DD7 6HX [E-mail: davidson900@btinternet.com]	01241 854566	30
Davidson, John F. BSc DipEdTech	1970	The Manse, Main Street, Kippen FK8 3DN	01786 871249	33
Davidson, Mark R. MA BD STM PhD RN	2005	[E-mail: mark.davidson122@mod.uk]		31
Dick, John H.A. MA MSc BD	1982	18 Fairfield Road, Kelty KY4 0BY	01506 237597	2
Dickson, Graham T. MA BD	1985	43 Hope Park Gardens, Bathgate EH48 2QT [E-mail: gtd194@googlemail.com]		
Donaldson, Colin V.	1982	3A Playfair Terrace, St Andrews KY16 9HX	01334 472889	3
Drake, Wendy F. (Mrs) BD	1978	21 William Black Place, South Queensferry EH30 9QR [E-mail: revwdrake@hotmail.co.uk]	0131-331 1520	1
Drummond, Norman W. (Prof.) CBE MA BD DUniv FRSE	1976	c/o Columba 1400 Ltd, Staffin, Isle of Skye IV51 9JY	01478 611400	42
Ellis, David W. GIMechE GIProdE	1962	4 Wester Tarsappie, Rhynd Road, Perth PH2 8PT	01738 449618	16
Espie, Howard	2011	1 Sprucebank Avenue, Langbank, Port Glasgow PA14 6YX [E-mail: howardespie.me.com]	01475 540391	1
Fairful, John BD	1994	12 Forth Road, Bearsden, Glasgow G61 1JT	01856 811353	45
Ferguson, Ronald MA BD ThM DUniv	1972	Vinbreck, Orphir, Orkney KW17 2RE [E-mail: ronbluebrazil@aol.com]		
Forbes, John W.A. BD	1973	Little Ennochie Steading, Finzean, Banchory AB31 6LX [E-mail: jrbbbb@icloud.com]	01330 850785	32
Fowler, Richard C.A. BSc MSc BD	1978	4 Gardentown, Whalsay, Shetland ZE2 9AB	01806 566538	46
Fraser, Ian M. MA BD PhD	1946	Ferndale, Gargunnock, Stirling FK8 3BW	01786 860612	23
Frew, John M. MA BD	1946	17 The Furrows, Walton-on-Thames KT12 3JQ		16
Gammack, George BD	1985	13A Hill Street, Broughty Ferry, Dundee DD5 2JP	01382 778636	29
Gardner, Bruce K. MA BD PhD	1988	21 Hopetown Crescent, Bucksburn, Aberdeen AB21 9QY [E-mail: drbrucegardner@aol.com]	(Mbl) 07891 186724	31
Gauld, Beverly G.D.D. MA BD	1972	7 Rowan View, Lanark ML11 9FQ	01555 665765	13
Gillies, Janet E. BD	1998	18 McIntyre Lane, Macmerry, Tranent EH33 1QL	01875 824607	3
Gordon, Elinor J. (Miss) BD	1988	6 Balgibbon Drive, Callander FK17 8EU	01877 331049	22
Grainger, Alison J. BD	1995	2 Hareburn Avenue, Avonbridge, Falkirk FK1 2NR [E-mail: revajgrainger@btinternet.com]	01324 861632	2

Name & Qualifications	Year	Address / E-mail	Telephone	No.
Grubb, George D.W. BA BD BPhil DMin	1962	10 Wellhead Close, South Queensferry EH30 9WA	0131-331 2072	1
Harper, Anne J.M. (Miss) BD STM MTh CertSocPsych	1979	122 Greenock Road, Bishopton PA7 5AS	01505 862466	16
Haslett, Howard J. BA BD	1972	26 The Maltings, Haddington EH41 4EF [E-mail: howard.haslett@btinternet.com]	01620 820292	3
Hendrie, Yvonne (Mrs) MA BD	1995	The Manse, 16 McAdam Way, Maybole KA19 8FD	01655 883710	10
Hibbert, Frederick W. BD	1986	4 Cemydd Terrace, Senghemydd, Caerphilly, Mid Glamorgan CF83 4HL	02920 831653	47
Homewood, Ivor Maxwell MSc BD	1997	An der Fließwiese 26, D-14052 Berlin, Germany [E-mail: maxhomewood@me.com]	0049 30 3048722	48
Hutcheson, Norman M. MA BD	1973	66 Maxwell Park, Dalbeattie DG5 4LS [E-mail: norman.hutcheson@gmail.com]		8
Hutchison, Alison M. (Mrs) BD DipMin	1988	Ashfield, Drumoak, Banchory AB31 5AG [E-mail: amhutch62@aol.com]	01330 811309	31
Jamieson, Esther M.M. (Mrs) BD	1984	1 Redburn, Bayview, Stornoway, Isle of Lewis HS1 2UU [E-mail: ianandejamieson@btinternet.com]	01851 704789	44
Jenkinson, John J. JP LTCL ALCM DipEd DipSen	1991	8 Rosehall Terrace, Falkirk FK1 1PY	01324 625498	22
Kelly, Ewan R. MB ChB BD PhD	1994	2/1, 117 Novar Drive, Glasgow G12 9 SZ [E-mail: ewanrkelly@outlook.com]	0141 357 2599	8
Kenny, Celia G. BA MTh MPhil PhD	1995	37 Grosvenor Road, Rathgar, Dublin 6, Ireland [E-mail: cgkenny@tcd.ie]		5
Kerr, Hugh F. MA BD	1968	134C Great Western Road, Aberdeen AB10 6QE	01224 580091	31
Lamont, Stewart J. BSc BD	1972	13/1 Grosvenor Crescent, Edinburgh EH12 5EL [E-mail: lamontsj@gmail.com]	(Mbl) 07557 532012	30
Lawrie, Robert M. BD MSc DipMin LLCM(TD) MCMI	1994	18/1 John's Place, Edinburgh EH6 7EN [E-mail: robert.lawrie@ed.ac.uk]	0131-554 9765	1
Ledgard, J. Christopher BA	1969	Streonshalh, 8 David Hume View, Chirnside, Duns TD11 3SX [E-mail: ledgard07@btinternet.com]	01890 817124	5
Leishman, James S. LTh BD MA	1969	11 Hunter Avenue, Heathhall, Dumfries DG1 3UX	01387 249241	8
Liddiard, F.G.B. MA	1957	34 Trinity Fields Crescent, Brechin DD9 6YF	01356 622966	30
Lindsay, W. Douglas BD CPS	1978	3 Drummond Place, Calderwood, East Kilbride, Glasgow G74 3AD	01355 234169	16
Lithgow, Anne R. (Mrs) MA BD	1992	13 Cameron Park, Edinburgh EH16 5JY [E-mail: anne.lithgow@btinternet.com]		3
Logan, Thomas M. LTh	1971	3 Duncan Court, Kilmarnock KA3 7TF	01563 524398	11
Lyall, David BSc BD STM PhD	1965	16 Brian Crescent, Tunbridge Wells, Kent TN4 0AP [E-mail: lyall3@gmail.com]	01892 670323	47
McAdam, David J. BSc BD (Assoc)	1990	12 Dunellan Crescent, Moodiesburn, Glasgow G69 0GA [E-mail: dmca29@hotmail.co.uk]	01236 870472	16
McDonald, Alan D. LLB BD MTh DLitt DD	1979	34 Gordon's Lane, Cromarty IV11 8XN [E-mail: alan.d.mcdonald@talk21.com]	01381 600954	
McDonald, Ross J.	1998	HMS *Dalriada*, Navy Buildings, Eldon Street, Greenock PA16 7SL [E-mail: rossjmcdonald@tiscali.com]	0141-883 7545 (Mbl) 07952 558767	16
McFadyen, Gavin BEng BD	2006	20 Tennyson Avenue, Bridlington YO15 2EP [E-mail: mcfadyen.gavin@gmail.com]	01262 608659 (Mbl) 07503 971068	18
McGillivray, A. Gordon MA BD STM	1951	36 Larchfield Neuk, Balerno EH14 7NL		1

Name	Ord.	Address / E-mail	Tel	Cong.
Maciver, Iain BD	2007	5 MacLeod Road, Stornoway, Isle of Lewis HS1 2HJ [E-mail: iain.maciver@hebrides.net]		44
MacKay, Alan H. BD	1974	Flat 1/1, 18 Newburgh Street, Glasgow G43 2XR [E-mail: alanhmackay@aol.com]	0141-632 0527	
McKay, Johnston R. MA BA PhD	1969	15 Montgomerie Avenue, Fairlie, Largs KA29 0EE [E-mail: johnston.mckay@btopenworld.com]	01475 568802	16
McKay, Margaret MA BD MTh	1991	19 Richmond Road, Huntly AB54 8BH [E-mail: elricksmithy@yahoo.co.uk]	01466 793937	34
McKean, Martin J. BD DipMin	1984	56 Kingsknowe Drive, Edinburgh EH14 2JX	0131-466 1157	1
Mackenzie, A. Cameron MA	1955	Hedgerow, 5 Shiels Avenue, Freuchie, Cupar KY15 7JD	01337 857763	26
McLachlan, Fergus C. BD	1982	46 Queen Square, Glasgow G41 2AZ	0141-423 3830	16
McLean, Gordon LTh	1972	Beinn Dhorain, Kinnettas Square, Strathpeffer IV14 9BD [E-mail: gmaclean@hotmail.co.uk]	01997 421380	39
MacPherson, Gordon C.	1963	203 Capelrig Road, Patterton, Newton Mearns, Glasgow G77 6ND	0141-616 2107	16
McPherson, William BD DipEd	1993	83 Laburnum Avenue, Port Seton, Prestonpans EH32 0UD	01875 812252	22
McWilliam, Thomas M. MA BD	1964	Flat 3, 13 Culduthel Road, Inverness IV2 4AG [E-mail: tommcwilliam@btconnect.com]	01463 718981	39
Mailer, Colin	1996	Innis Chonain, Back Row, Polmont, Falkirk FK2 0RD	01324 712401	22
Main, Arthur W.A. BD	1954	13/3 Eildon Terrace, Edinburgh EH3 5NL	0131-556 1344	16
Masson, John D. MA BD PhD BSc	1984	2 Beechgrove, Craw Hall, Brampton CA8 1TS [E-mail: jmasson96@btinternet.com]		7
Melville, David D. BD	1989	28 Porterfield, Comrie, Dunfermline KY12 9HJ	01383 850075	24
Millar, Peter W. MA BD PhD	1971	6/5 Etrickdale Place, Edinburgh EH3 5JN [E-mail: ionacottage@hotmail.com]	0131-557 0517	1
Minto, Joan E. (Mrs) MA BD	1993	139/1 New Street, Musselburgh EH21 6DH	0131-665 6736	3
Moodie, Alastair R. MA BD	1978	4 Burnbrae Road, Auchinloch, Glasgow G66 5DQ		16
Morton, Andrew Q. MA BSc BD FRSE	1949	Sunnyside, 4A Manse Street, Aberdour, Burntisland KY3 0TY		18
Muckart, Graeme W.M. MTh MSc FSAScot	1983	Kildale, Clashmore, Dornoch IV25 3RG [E-mail: gw2m.kildale@gmail.com]	01862 881715	40
Muir, Eleanor D. (Miss) MTheol DipPTheol	1986	[E-mail: eleanordmuir@tiscali.co.uk]		28
Muir, Margaret A. (Miss) MA LLB BD	1989	59/4 South Beechwood, Edinburgh EH12 5YS	0131-313 3240	13
Murray, George M. MTh	1995	6 Mayfield, Lesmahagow ML11 0FH [E-mail: george.murray7@gmail.com]	01555 895216	
Neilson, Rodger BSc BD	1972	4 Waulkmill Steading, Charlestown, Dunfermline KY12 8ZS	01383 873336	34
Newell, Alison M. (Mrs) BD	1986	1A Inverleith Terrace, Edinburgh EH3 5NS [E-mail: alinewell@aol.com]	0131-556 3505	1
Newell, J. Philip MA BD PhD	1982	1A Inverleith Terrace, Edinburgh EH3 5NS	0131-556 3505	1
Newlands, George M. (Prof.) MA BD PhD DLitt FRSA FRSE	1970	12 Jamaica Street North Lane, Edinburgh EH3 6HQ		16
Nicolson, John Murdo	1997	731 16th Street North, Lethbridge, Alberta, Canada T1H 3B3		42
Notman, John R. BSc BD	1990	5 Dovecote Road, Bromsgrove, Worcs B61 7BN		47
Ostler, John H. MA LTh	1975	5 Osborne Terrace, Port Seton, Prestonpans EH32 0BZ	01875 814358	3

Name	Year	Address / E-mail	Telephone	
Owen, Catherine W. MTh	1984	10 Waverley Park, Kirkintilloch, Glasgow G66 2BP	0141-776 0407	16
Paterson, Andrew E. JP	1994	6 The Willows, Kelty KY4 0FQ	01383 830998	24
Penman, Iain D. BD	1977	33/5 Carnbee Avenue, Edinburgh EH16 6GA [E-mail: iainpenmanklm@aol.com]	0131-664 0673 (Mbl) 07931 993427	1
Petrie, Ian D. MA BD	1970	27/111 West Savile Terrace, Edinburgh EH9 3DR [E-mail: idp-77@hotmail.com]	0131-237 2857	26
Pieterse, Ben BA BTh LTh	2001	15 Bakeoven Close, Seaforth Sound, Simon's Town 7975, South Africa		25
Provan, Iain W. MA BA PhD	1991	Regent College, 5800 University Boulevard, Vancouver BC V6T 2E4, Canada	001 604 224 3245	1
Risby, Lesley P. (Mrs) BD	1994	Tigh an Achaidh, 21 Fernoch Crescent, Lochgilphead PA31 8AE [E-mail: mrsrisby@hotmail.com]	01546 600464	19
Rosener, Alexandra M (Mrs)	2007	Lüttinglehm 3, 41352 Korschenbroich, Germany	0049 2182 833 9535	25
Roy, Alistair A. MA BD	1955	1 Broaddykes Close, Kingswells, Aberdeen AB15 8UF	01224 743310	31
Salters, Robert B. MA BD PhD	1966	Vine Cottage, 119 South Street, St Andrews KY16 9UH	01334 473198	
Saunders, Keith BD	1983	Western Infirmary, Dumbarton Road, Glasgow G11 6NT	0141-211 2000	16
Sawers, Hugh BA	1968	2 Rosemount Meadows, Castlepark, Bothwell, Glasgow G71 8EL	01698 853960	17
Scotland, Ronald J. BD	1993	7A Rose Avenue, Elgin IV30 1NX [E-mail: ronnieandjill@thescotlands.co.uk]	01343 543086	35
Scouller, Hugh BSc BD	1985	11 Kirk View, Haddington EH41 4AN [E-mail: h.scouller@btinternet.com]		3
Shanks, Norman J. MA BD DD	1983	1 Marchmont Terrace, Glasgow G12 9LT [E-mail: rufuski@btinternet.com]	0141-339 4421	16
Shaw, D.W.D. BA BD LLB WS DD	1960	4/13 Succoth Court, Edinburgh EH12 6BZ	0131-337 2130	26
Smith, Ronald W. BA BEd BD	1979	1F1, 2 Middlefield, Edinburgh EH7 4PF	0131-553 1174 (Mbl) 07900 896954	23
Stewart, Margaret L. (Mrs) BSc MB ChB BD	1985	28 Inch Crescent, Bathgate EH48 1EU [E-mail: famstewart@ormail.co.uk]	01506 653428	2
Stewart, Una B. (Ms) BD DipEd	1995	10 Inch Park, Kelso TD5 7BQ [E-mail: rev.ubs@virgin.net]	01573 219231	13
Storrar, William F. (Prof.) MA BD PhD	1984	Director, Center of Theological Inquiry, 50 Stockton Street, Princeton, NJ 08540, USA		1
Strachan, Alexander E. MA BD	1974	2 Leafield Road, Dumfries DG1 2DS [E-mail: aestrachan@aol.com]	01387 279460	8
Strachan, David G. BD DPS	1978	1 Deeside Park, Aberdeen AB15 7PQ	01224 324101	31
Strachan, Ian M. MA BD	1959	'Cardenwell', Glen Drive, Dyce, Aberdeen AB21 7EN	01224 772028	31
Tamas, Bertalan		Pozsonyi út 34, Budapest H-1137, Hungary [E-mail: bertalantamas@hotmail.com]	0036 1 239 6315 (Mbl) 0036 30 638 6647	48
Taylor, Ian BSc MA LTh DipEd	1983	Lundie Cottage, Arncroach, Anstruther KY10 2RN	01333 720222	26
Taylor, Jane C. BD DipMin	1990	1/2 72 St Vincent Crescent, Glasgow G3 8NQ [E-mail: jane.c.taylor@btinternet.com]	0141-204 3022	16
Thomas, W. Colville ChLJ BTh BPhil DPS DSc	1964	11 Muirfield Crescent, Gullane EH31 2HN	01620 842415	3
Thrower, Charles B. BSc	1965	Grange House, Wester Grangemuir, Pittenweem, Anstruther KY10 2RB [E-mail: charlesandsteph@btinternet.com]	01333 312631	26
Tollick, Frank BSc DipEd	1958	3 Bellhouse Road, Aberdour, Burntisland KY3 0TL	01383 860559	24
Turnbull, John LTh	1994	4 Rathmor Road, Biggar ML12 6QG	01899 221502	13

NAME	ORD	ADDRESS	TEL	PRES
Turnbull, Julian S. BSc BD MSc CEng MBCS	1980	39 Suthern Yett, Prestonpans EH32 9GL [E-mail: jules@turnbull25.plus.com]	01875 818305	3
Watson, John M. LTh	1989	20 Greystone Place, Newtonhill, Stonehaven AB39 3UL [E-mail: watson-john18@sky.com]	01569 730604 (Mbl) 07733 334380	31
Weatherhead, James L. CBE MA LLB DD	1960	29/1 Castle Terrace, Edinburgh EH1 2EL	0131-228 2871	30
Webster, Brian G. BSc BD CEng MIET	1998	3/1 Cloch Court, 57 Albert Road, Gourock PA19 1NJ [E-mail: revwebby@aol.com]	01475 638332	23
Whitton, John P.	1977	115 Sycamore Road, Farnborough, Hants GU14 6RE	01252 674488	47
Whyte, Ron C. BD CPS	1990	13 Hillside Avenue, Kingussie PH21 1PA [E-mail: ron4xst@btinternet.com]	01540 661101 (Mbl) 07979 026973	36
Wilkie, James L. MA BD	1959	7 Comely Bank Avenue, Edinburgh EH4 1EW [E-mail: jl.wilkie@btinternet.com]	0131-343 1552	1
Wood, James L.K.	1967	1 Glen Drive, Dyce, Aberdeen AB21 7EN	01224 722543	31
Young, Evelyn (Mrs) BSc BD	1984	2 Priestden Place, St Andrews KY16 8DP	01334 479662	26

LIST E – MINISTERS WHO ARE NOT MEMBERS OF A PRESBYTERY AND WHO DO NOT CURRENTLY HOLD A PRACTISING CERTIFICATE (in terms of Act II (2000))

NAME	ORD	ADDRESS	TEL	PRES
Beck, John C. BD	1975	31 The Woodlands, Stirling FK8 2LB	01738 443335	35
Birrell, Isobel (Mrs) BD	1994	'Hiddlehame', 5 Hewat Place, Perth PH1 2UD [E-mail: isobel@ibmail.org.uk]	07540 797945 (Mbl)	17
Black, W. Graham MA BD	1983	72 Linksview, Linksfield Road, Aberdeen AB24 5RG [E-mail: graham.black@virgin.net]	01224 492491	31
Bonar, Alexander F. LTh LRIC	1988	7 Westbank Court, Westbank Terrace, Macmerry, Tranent EH33 1QS [E-mail: sandybonar@tiscali.co.uk]	01875 615165	3
Breakey, Judith (Ms) LizTheol MTh DipEd	2010	[E-mail: judith.breakey@gmail.com]		16
Brown, Alastair BD	1986	52 Henderson Drive, Kintore, Inverurie AB51 0FB	01467 632787	32
Brown, Joseph MA	1954	The Orchard, Hermitage Lane, Shedden Park Road, Kelso TD5 7AN	01573 223481	6
Burgess, Paul C.J. MA	1968	Springvale, Halket Road, Lugton, Kilmarnock KA3 4EE [E-mail: paulandcathie@gmail.com]	01505 850254	2
Campbell, J. Ewen R. MA BD	1967	85/15 High Street, North Berwick EH39 4HD	01620 894839	25
Christie, James LTh	1993	20 Wester Inshes Crescent, Inverness IV2 5HL		
Cooper, George MA BD	1943	8 Leighton Square, Alyth, Blairgowrie PH11 8AQ	01828 633746	1
Craig, Eric MA BD BA	1959	5 West Relugas Road, Edinburgh EH9 2PW	0131-667 8210	1
Craig, Gordon W. MBE MA BD	1972	1 Beley Bridge, Dunino, St Andrews KY16 8LT	01334 880285	26
Crawford, Michael S.M. LTh	1966	Brownside of Strichen, New Pitsligo, Fraserburgh AB43 6NY		31
Cullen, William T. BA LTh	1984	6 Laurel Wynd, Cambuslang, Glasgow G72 7BA	0141-641 4337	17

Name		Address	Tel	No.
Cumming, David P.L.	MA	1957	Shillong, Tarbat Ness Road, Portmahomack, Tain IV20 1YA	01862 871794	19
Currie, Gordon C.M.	MA BD	1975	43 Deanburn Park, Linlithgow EH49 6HA	01506 842759	2
Davies, Gareth W.	BA BD	1979	Pitadro House, Fordell Gardens, Dunfermline KY11 7EY	01383 417634	24
Dean, Roger A.F.	LTh	1983	0/2, 20 Ballogie Road, Glasgow G44 4TA [E-mail: roger.dean4@btopenworld.com]		16
Dick, James S.	MA BTh	1988	8 Malthouse Drive, Belper DE56 1RU [E-mail: jim.s.dick@gmail.com]		
Dodman, R.		1983	13 Acredales, Haddington EH41 4NT	01620 825999	9
Dutton, David W.	BA	1973	[E-mail: duttondw@gmail.com]		
Finlay, Quintin	BA BD	1975	Ivy Cottage, Greenlees Farm, Kelso TD5 8BT	(Mbl) 07901 981171	6
Flockhart, D. Ross	OBE BA BD DUniv	1956	Longwood, Humbie EH36 5PN [E-mail: rossflock@btinternet.com]	01875 833208	3
Foggitt, Eric W.	MA BSc BD	1991	Christiaan de Wet Straat 1/2, 1091 NG Amsterdam, The Netherlands [E-mail: ericleric3@btinternet.com]		1
Forrester, Duncan B. (Prof.)	MA BD DPhil DD FRSE	1962	25 Kingsburgh Road, Edinburgh EH12 6DZ [E-mail: dbforrester@rosskeen.org.uk]	0131-337 5646	1
Frizzell, R. Stewart	BD	1961	98 Boswell Road, Inverness IV2 3EW		
Gardner, Frank J.	MA	1966	1 Levanne Place, Gourock PA16 1AX [E-mail: fjg@clyde-mail.co.uk]	01475 630187	14
Gow, Neil	BSc MEd BD	1996	Hillhead Lodge, Portknockie, Buckie AB56 4PB [E-mail: n.gow334@btinternet.com]	01542 840625	35
Hamilton, David S.M.	MA BD STM	1958	63 Pendreich Avenue, Bonnyrigg EH19 2EE [E-mail: dandmhamilton@gmail.com]	0131-654 2604	47
Homewood, I.M.	MSc BD	1997	Ander Fließwiese 26, D-14052 Berlin, Germany [E-mail: maxhomewood@me.com]		48
Howie, William	MA BD STM	1964	26 Morgan Road, Aberdeen AB16 5JY	01224 483669	31
Huie, David F.	MA BD	1962	17 St Mary's Mead, Witney OX28 4EZ	01993 778310	48
Hurst, Frederick R.	MA	1965	Flat 6, 21 Bulldale Place, Glasgow G14 0NE	0141-959 2604	40
Inglis, Donald B.C.	MA MEd BD	1975	39 Thomson Drive, Bearsden, Glasgow G61 3PA	0141-942 1387	18
Johnstone, William (Prof.)	MA BD	1963	9/5 Mount Alvernia, Edinburgh EH16 6AW	0131-664 3140	31
Logan, Robert J.V.	MA BD	1962	Lindores, 1 Murray Place, Smithton, Inverness, IV2 7PX [E-mail: rjvlogan@btinternet.com]	01463 790226	
Lynn, Joyce (Mrs)	MIPM BD	1995	Flat 8, 131 St Vincent Street, Broughty Ferry, Dundee DD5 2DA	01382 690556	29
Macaskill, Donald	MA BD PhD	1994			16
McClenaghan, L. Paul	BA	1973	4 Glendale Gardens, Randalstown, Co. Antrim BT41 3EJ [E-mail: paul.mcclenaghan@gmail.com]	02894 478545	34
McCreadie, David W.		1961	23 Willoughby Place, Callander PH17 8DG	01877 330785	23
Macdonald, Murdo C.	MA BD	2002	36 Graham Court, Blackburn, Bathgate EH47 7BT [E-mail: murdocmacdonald@gmail.com]	(Mbl) 07714 016805	2
Macfarlane, Alwyn J.C.	MA	1951	Flat 12, Homeburn House, 177 Fenwick Road, Giffnock, Glasgow G46 6JD	0141-620 3235	1
Macfarlane, Thomas G.	BSc PhD BD	1956			14
McGill, Sandi (Ms)	BD	2002	12 Elphinstone Court, Lochwinnoch Road, Kilmacolm PA13 4DW [E-mail: sandimac376@gmail.com]	01505 874962	2
McGill, Thomas W.		1972	Flat 75, J M Barry House, George Street, Dumfries DG1 1EA		9
McKenzie, Mary O. (Miss)		1976	4 Dunellan Avenue, Moodiesburn, Glasgow G69 0GB	01236 870180	16
McKenzie, W.M.		1958	41 Kingholm Drive, Dumfries DG1 4SR		8
Mackie, John F.	BD	1979	1A Halls Close, Weldon, Corby, Northants NN17 3HH		40

Name	Year	Address	Phone	No.
Mackinnon, Thomas J.R. LTh DipMin	1996	4 Flashadder, Arnisort, Portree, Isle of Skye IV51 9PT	01470 582377	39
McLean, John MA BD	1967	16 Eastside Drive, Westhill AB32 6QN	01224 747701	33
Miller, Irene B. (Mrs) MA BD	1984	5 Braeside Park, Aberfeldy PH15 2DT	01887 829396	27
Murray, Douglas R. MA BD	1965	32 Forth Park, Bridge of Allan, Stirling FK9 5NT [E-mail: d-smurray@supanet.com]	01786 831081	23
O'Leary, Thomas BD	1983	1 Carter's Place, Irvine KA12 0BU	01294 313274	11
Oliver, Gordon BD	1979	129 Knockomie Drive, Forres IV36 2HE	01309 672667	41
Osbeck, John R. BD	1979	15 Deeside Crescent, Aberdeen AB15 7PT	01224 315595	31
Park, Christopher BSc BD	1977	65 Moubray Road, Dalgety Bay, Dunfermline KY11 9JP [E-mail: chrispark8649@hotmail.com]	01383 821111	24
Patterson, James BSc BD	2003	c/o 9 Oakview, Balmedie, Aberdeen AB23 8SR		1
Peacock, Heather M. BSc PhD BD	2009	9 Frankscroft, Peebles EH45 9DX [E-mail: hmpeacock@btinternet.com]		32
Petrie, Ian D. MA BD	1970	136 Colinton Mains Drive, Edinburgh EH13 9BN	0131-366 0520	29
Pryce, Stuart F.A.	1963	36 Forth Park, Bridge of Allan, Stirling FK9 5NT	01786 831026	23
Purves, John P.S. MBE BSc BD	1978	37 Hollywood, Largs KA30 8SR	01475 676180	48
Ramsay, Alan MA	1967	12 Riverside Grove, Lochyside, Fort William PH33 7RD	01397 702054	38
Reid, Janette G. (Miss) BD	1991	c/o Glasgow Presbytery Office, 260 Bath Street, Glasgow G2 4JP		16
Ritchie, Garden W.M.	1961	23 Croft Road, Kelso TD5 7EP	01573 224419	6
Robertson, John M. BSc BD	1975	8 North Green Drive, The Wilderness, Airth, Falkirk FK2 8RA	01324 832244	16
Robertson, Thomas G.M. LTh	1971	23 Muirend Avenue, Perth PH1 1JL	01738 624432	28
Roy, James A. MA BD	1965	'Beechwood', 7 Northview Terrace, Wormit, Newport-on-Tay DD6 8PP [E-mail: jim.roy@dundeepresbytery.org.uk]	01382 543578	29
Duncan Shaw of Chapelverna Bundesverdienstkreuz PhD ThDr Drhc	1951	4 Sydney Terrace, Edinburgh EH7 6SL		19
Shaw, Duncan LTh CPS	1984	73 Woodside Drive, Forres IV36 0UF		
Smith, Ralph C.P. MA STM	1960	2A Waverley Road, Eskbank, Dalkeith EH22 3DJ [E-mail: rcpsmith@waitrose.com]	0131-663 1234	1
Spowart, Mary G. (Mrs) BD	1978	Aldersyde, St Abbs Road, Coldingham, Eyemouth TD14 5NR	01890 771697	26
Stone, W. Vernon MA BD	1949	36 Woodrow Court, Port Glasgow Road, Kilmacolm PA13 4QA [E-mail: stone@kilmacolm.fsnet.co.uk]	01505 872644	14
Sutcliffe, Clare B. BSc BD	2000	4 Dalmailing Avenue, Dreghorn, Irvine KA11 4HX		11
Taylor, David J. MA BD	1982	32 Croft an Righ, Inverkeithing KY11 1PF	01383 413227	24
Thomson, Alexander BSc BD MPhil PhD	1973	4 Munro Street, Dornoch IV25 3RA [E-mail: alexander.thomsonf@btinternet.com]	01862 811650	40
Thomson, Gilbert L. BA	1965	3 Fortharfield, Freuchie, Cupar KY15 7JJ	01337 857431	25
Thorne, Leslie W. BA LTh	1987	c/o McKellar, 24 Arranview Street, Chapelhall, Airdrie ML6 8XN		17
Watson, James B. BSc	1968	3 Royal Terrace, Hutton, Berwick-upon-Tweed TD15 1TP [E-mail: jimwatson007@hotmail.com]	01289 386282	5
Webster, John G. BSc	1964	Plane Tree, King's Cross, Brodick, Isle of Arran KA27 8RG	01770 700747	16
Wedderburn, A.J.M. (Prof.) MA BA PhD	1975	Therese-Danner-Platz 3, D-80636 Munich, Germany [E-mail: ajmw42@gmx.de]	0049 89 1200 3726	
Weir, Mary K. BD PhD	1968	1249 Millar Road RRI, SITEH-46, BC V0N 1G0, Canada	001 604 947 0636	1

Westmarland, Colin A.   1971   PO Box 5, Cospicua, CSPOI, Malta   00356 216 923552   48
Wilkie, George D. OBE BL   1948   2/37 Barnton Avenue West, Edinburgh EH4 6EB   0131-339 3973   1
Wilkie, William E. LTh   1978   32 Broomfield Park, Portlethen, Aberdeen AB12 4XT   01224 782052   31
Wilson, M.   1988   37 King's Avenue, Longniddry EH32 0QN

LIST F – HEALTH AND SOCIAL CARE CHAPLAINS (NHS)

LOTHIAN

Lead Chaplain   Caroline Applegath
                           [E-mail: carrie.applegath@nhslothian.scot.nhs.uk]

Spiritual Care Office: 0131-242 1990

The Royal Infirmary of Edinburgh
51 Little France Crescent, Edinburgh EH16 4SA (0131-536 1000)

Full details of chaplains and contacts in all hospitals: www.nhslothian.scot.nhs.uk > Services > Health Services A-Z > Spiritual Care

BORDERS

Head of Spiritual Care   Rev Robert P. Devenny   Chaplaincy Centre, Borders General Hospital, Melrose TD6 9BS 01896 826564
                                                           [E-mail. bob.devenny@borders.scot.nhs.uk]

Further information: www.nhsborders.scot.nhs.uk > Patients and Visitors > Our services > Chaplaincy Centre

DUMFRIES AND GALLOWAY

Chaplaincy Service   Macmillan Wing, Dumfries and Galloway Royal
                                Infirmary, Bankend Road, Dumfries DG1 4AP   01387 241625

Further information: www.nhsdg.scot.nhs.uk > Focus on > Search > Chaplaincy

AYRSHIRE AND ARRAN

Service Lead for Chaplaincy and Staff Care   Rev. Judith A. Huggett   Crosshouse Hospital, Kilmarnock KA2 0BE 01563 577301
                                                                                [E-mail: judith.huggett@aaaht.scotnhs.uk]

Further information: www.nhsaaa.net > Services A-Z > Chaplaincy service

LANARKSHIRE

Head of Spiritual Care	Vacant		
Chaplaincy Office		Law House, Airdrie Road, Carluke ML8 5EP	01698 377637
		Law House, Airdrie Road, Carluke ML8 5EP	01698 377637

Further information: www.nhslanarkshire.org.uk > Our services A-Z > Palliative care > Palliative care support > Spiritual care

GREATER GLASGOW AND CLYDE

Head of Chaplaincy and Spiritual Care   Rev. Blair Robertson   The Sanctuary, Queen Elizabeth University Hospital,   0141-201 2156
Govan Road, Glasgow G51 4TF
[E-mail: blair.robertson@ggc.scot.nhs.uk]

Further information: www.nhsggc.org.uk > Services > Spiritual Care

FORTH VALLEY

Head of Spiritual Care   Rev. Margery Collin   Forth Valley Royal Hospital, Larbert FK5 4WR   01324 566072
[E-mail: margery.collin@nhs.net]   (Mbl) 07824 460882

Further information: www.nhsforthvalley.com > Services > Spiritual Care

FIFE

Head of Spiritual Care   Mr Mark Evans DCS   Department of Spiritual Care, Queen Margaret Hospital,   01383 674136
Whitefield Road, Dunfermline KY12 0SU
[E-mail: mark.evans59@nhs.net]

Victoria Hospital, Kirkcaldy	Chaplain's Office		01592 648158
Queen Margaret Hospital, Dunfermline	Chaplain's Office		01383 674136
Community Chaplaincy Listening (Scotland): National Coordinator	Miss Lynda Wright DCS	[E-mail: lynda.wright1@nhs.net]	(Mbl) 07835 303395

Further information: www.nhsfife.org > Your Health > Support Services > Spiritual Care

TAYSIDE

Head of Spiritual Care   Rev. Gillian Munro   The Wellbeing Centre, Royal Victoria Hospital,   01382 423110
Dundee DD2 1SP
[E-mail: lynne.downie@nhs.net]

Further information: www.nhstayside.scot.nhs.uk > Your Health/Wellbeing > Our Services A-Z > Spiritual Care

GRAMPIAN

Lead Chaplain — Rev. Mark Rodgers — Chaplains' Office, Aberdeen Royal Infirmary, Foresterhill, Aberdeen AB25 2ZN
[E-mail: mrodgers@nhs.net] — 01224 553166

Further information: www.nhsgrampian.co.uk > Home > Local Services and Clinics > Spiritual Care

HIGHLAND

Lead Chaplain — Rev. Dr Derek Brown — Raigmore Hospital, Old Perth Road, Inverness IV2 3UJ
[E-mail: derek.brown1@nhs.net] — 01463 704463

Community Healthcare Chaplain — Rev. Mary Stobo — Druim-an-Sgairnich, Ardgay IV24 3BG — 01863 766868
(East Sutherland)

Further information: www.nhshighland.scot.nhs.uk > Services > All Services A-Z > NHS Chaplaincy

WESTERN ISLES HEALTH BOARD

Lead Chaplain — Rev T. K. Shadakshari — 23D Benside, Newmarket, Stornoway, Isle of Lewis HS2 0DZ
[E-mail: tk.shadakshari@nhs.net]

(Home) 01851 701727
(Office) 01851 704704
(Mbl) 07403 697138

NHS SCOTLAND

Programme Director for Health & Social Care Chaplaincy & Spiritual Care
Rev Sheila Mitchell — NHS Education for Scotland, 3rd Floor, 2 Central Quay, 89 Hydepark Street, Glasgow G3 8BW
[E-mail: sheila.mitchell@nes.scot.nhs.uk] — (Mbl) 07769 367615

LIST G – CHAPLAINS TO HM FORCES

The three columns give dates of ordination and commissioning, and branch where the chaplain is serving: Royal Navy, Army, Royal Air Force, Royal Naval Reserve, Army Reserve, Army Cadet Force, or where the person named is an Officiating Chaplain to the Military.

NAME	ORD	COM	BCH	ADDRESS
Anderson, David P. BSc BD	2002	2007	A	HQ 102 LOG Bde, Prince William of Gloucester Barracks, Grantham NG31 7TG
Begg, Richard MA BD	2008			
Berry, Geoff T. BD BSc	2009	2012	A	JSSU Cyprus, Mercury Barracks, Ayios Nikolaos, BFPO 59
Blackwood, Keith T. BD DipMin	1997		ACF	Shetland Independent Battery, ACF, TA Centre, Fort Charlotte, Lerwick, Shetland ZE1 0JN
Blakey, Stephen A. BSc BD	1977	1977	AR	6 Bn The Royal Regiment of Scotland, Walcheran Barracks, 122 Hotspur Street, Glasgow G20 8LQ
Blakey, Stephen A. BSc BD	1977	1977	ACF	Lothian & Borders Bn ACF, Drumshoreland House, Broxburn EH52 5PF
Blakey, Stephen B. BSc BD	1977		OCM	HQ 51 Infantry Brigade & 2 SCOTS, Glencorse Barracks, Penicuik EH26 0QH
Bryson, Thomas M. BD	1997		ACF	2 Bn The Highlanders, ACF, Cadet Training Centre, Rocksley Drive, Boddam, Peterhead AB42 3BA
Bryson, Thomas M. BD	1997		OCM	51 Infantry Brigade, Forthside, Stirling FK7 7RR
Campbell, Karen K. BD MTh DMin	1997		OCM	Personnel Recovery Centre, Edinburgh
Cobain, Alan R. BD	2000		AR	71 Engineer Regiment, RAF Leuchars, Fife KY16 0JX
Connolly, Daniel BD DipTheol DipMin	1983		AR	Scottish and North Irish Yeomanry, Redford Barracks, Colinton Road, Edinburgh EH13 0PP
Coulter, David G. QHC BA BD MDA PhD	1989	1994	A	Chaplain General, MoD Chaplains (Army), HQ Land Forces, 2nd Floor Zone 6, Ramillies Building, Marlborough Lines, Andover, Hants SP11 8HJ
Dalton, Mark BD DipMin RN	2002	2012	RN	HM Naval Base Clyde, Faslane, Helensburgh G84 8HL
Davidson, Mark R. MA BD STM PhD RN	2005	2009	RN	Naval Chaplaincy Service, NCHQ, Whale Island, Portsmouth PO2 8BY
Dicks, Shuna M. BSc BD	2010		ACF	2 Bn The Highlanders, ACF, Cadet Training Centre, Rocksley Drive, Boddam, Peterhead AB42 3BA
Frail, Nicola BLE MBA MDiv	2000		A	32 Engineer Regiment, Marne Barracks, Catterick Garrison, DL10 7NP
Francis, James BD PhD	2002		A	MoD Chaplains (Army), HQ Land Forces, 2nd Floor Zone 6, Ramillies Building, Marlborough Lines, Andover SP11 8HJ
Gardner, Neil N. MA BD RNR	1991		OCM	Edinburgh Universities Officers' Training Corps
Gardner, Neil N. MA BD RNR	1991	2015	A	Royal Scots Dragoon Guards, Leuchars Station, Leuchars KY16 0JX
Goodison, Michael J. BSc BD	2013		RNR	Honorary Chaplain, Royal Navy
Kellock, Chris N. MA BD	1998	2012	A	1 Bn Royal Regiment of Fusiliers, Mooltan Barracks, Tidworth SP9 7SJ
Kennon, Stanley BA BD RN	1992	2000	RN	Britannia Royal Naval College, Dartmouth TO6 0HJ
Kinsey, Louis BD DipMin TD	1991		AR	205 (Scottish) Field Hospital (V), Graham House, Whitefield Road, Glasgow G51 6JU
Lancaster, Craig MA BD	2004	2011	RAF	RAF Brize Norton, Carterton OX18 3LX
McCulloch, Alen J.R. MA BD	1990		ACF	Cornwall ACF, 7 Castle Canyke Road, Bodmin PL31 1DX
McDonald, Roderick I.T. BD CertMin	1992		ACF	West Lowland Bn, ACF, Fusilier House, Seaforth Road, Ayr KA8 9HX

MacKay, Stewart A.	2009	2009	A	3 Bn Black Watch, Royal Regiment of Scotland, Fort George, Ardersier, Inverness IV1 2TD
Mackenzie, Cameron BD	1997	2011	ACF	Lothian and Borders Bn, ACF, Drumshoreland House, Broxburn EH52 5PF
Mackenzie, Hector M.	2008	2008	A	HQ Military Corrective Training Centre, Berechurch Hall Camp, Berechurch Hall Road, Colchester CO2 9NU
Mackenzie, Seoras L. BD	1996	1998	A	39 Engr Regt (Air Support), Kinloss Barracks, Kinloss, Forres IV36 3XL
McLaren, William MA BD	1990		ACF	Angus and Dundee Bn, ACF, Barry Buddon, Carnoustie DD7 7RY
McLaren, William MA BD	1990		OCM	225 GS Med Regt (V), Oliver Barracks, Dalkeith Road, Dundee DD4 7DL
McLay, Neil BA BD	2006	2012	A	1 Bn Princess of Wales's Royal Regiment, Barker Barracks, Sennelager, Paderborn BFPO 22
MacLean, Marjory A. LLB BD PhD RNR	1991		RNR	HMS Scotia, MoD Caledonia, Hilton Road, Rosyth, Dunfermline KY11 2XH
MacLeod, Rory N. MA BD	1986	1992	A	21 Engineer Regt, Claro Barracks, Chatham Road, Ripon HG4 2RD
MacPherson, Duncan J. BSc BD	1993	2002	A	Army Personnel Centre, MP413, Kentigern House, 65 Brown Street, Glasgow G2 8EX
Mathieson, Angus R. MA BD	1988		OCM	Edinburgh Garrison & the Personnel Recovery Unit (PRU)
Milliken, Jamie BD	2005		RNR	HMS *Dalriada*, Govan, Glasgow G51 3JH
Munro, Sheila BD	1995	2003	RAF	Station Chaplain, RAF Lossiemouth, Elgin IV31 6SD
Prentice, Donald K. BSc BD	1989		OCM	205 (Scottish) Field Hospital (V), Graham House, Whitefield Road, Glasgow G51 6JU
Rankin, Lisa-Jane BD CPS	2003		OCM	2 Bn Royal Regiment of Scotland, Glencorse Barracks, Penicuik EH26 0QH
Rowe, Christopher J. BA BD	2008	2008	AR	32 (Scottish) Signal Regiment, 21 Jardine Street, Glasgow G20 6JU
Selemani, Ecilo LTh MTh	1993	2011	ACF	Glasgow and Lanark Bn, ACF, Gilbertfield Road, Cambuslang, Glasgow G72 8YP
Selemani, Ecilo LTh MTh	1993	2011	OCM	51 Infantry Brigade, Forthside, Stirling FK7 7RR
Shackleton, Scott J.S. QCVS BA RN BD PhD HQ Cdo Bde RM	1993	2010	RN	Chaplain headquarters, 3 Commando Brigade, RMB Stonehouse, Dumford Street, Plymouth PL1 3QS
Stewart, Fraser M.C. BSc BD	1980	1980	ACF	1 Bn The Highlanders, ACF, Gordonville Road, Inverness IV2 4SU
Stewart, Fraser M.C. BSc BD	1980	1980	OCM	51 Infantry Brigade, Forthside, Stirling FK7 7RR
Taylor, Gayle J.A. MA BD	1999	1999	OCM	3 Bn The Rifles, Redford Barracks, Colinton Road, Edinburgh EH13 0PP
Thom, David J. BD DipMin	1999		A	1 Bn Scots Guards, Mons Barracks, Prince's Avenue, Aldershot GU11 2LF
van Sittert, Paul BA BD	1997	2015	A	4 Bn The Royal Regiment of Scotland, Bourlon Barracks, Plumer Road, Catterick Garrison DL9 3AD
Warwick, Ivan C. MA BD TD	1980		ACF	1 Bn The Highlanders, ACF, Gordonville Road, Inverness IV2 4SU
Warwick, Ivan C. MA BD TD	1980		ACF	Orkney Independent Battery, ACF, Territorial Army Centre, Weyland Park, Kirkwall KW1 5LP
Warwick, Ivan C. MA BD TD	1980		OCM	Fort George and Cameron Barracks, Inverness
Wilson, Fiona A. BD	2008	2011	ACF	West Lowland Battalion, ACF, Fusilier House, Seaforth Road, Ayr KA8 9HX

LIST H – READERS

1. EDINBURGH

Brown, Ivan
4 St Cuthberts Court, Edinburgh EH13 0LG
[E-mail: j.ivanb@btinternet.com]
0131-441 1245
(Mbl) 07730 702860

Christie, Gillian L. (Mrs)
32 Allan Park Road, Edinburgh EH14 1LJ
[E-mail: mrsglchristie@aol.com]
0131-443 4472
(Mbl) 07914 883354

Davies, Ruth (Ms) (attached to Liberton)
4 Hawkhead Grove, Edinburgh EH16 6LS
[E-mail: ruth@mdavies.me.uk]
0131-664 3608

Farrant, Yvonne (Ms)
Flat 7, 14 Duddingston Mills, Edinburgh EH8 7NF
[E-mail: yvonne.farrant@crossreach.org.uk]
0131-661 0672
(Mbl) 07747 766405

Farrell, William J.
50 Ulster Crescent, Edinburgh EH8 7JS
[E-mail: w.farrell154@btinternet.com]
0131-661 1026

Farrow, Edmund
14 Brunswick Terrace, Edinburgh EH7 5PG
[E-mail: edmundfarrow@blueyonder.co.uk]
0131-558 8210

Johnston, Alan
8/19 Constitution Street, Edinburgh EH6 7BT
[E-mail: alanacj@cairnassoc.wanadoo.co.uk]
0131-554 1326
(Mbl) 07901 510819

Kerrigan, Herbert A. (Prof.) MA LLB QC
Airdene, 20 Edinburgh Road, Dalkeith EH22 1JY
[E-mail: kerrigan@kerriganqc.com]
0131-660 3007
07725 953772

McKenzie, Janet (Mrs)
80C Colinton Road, Edinburgh EH14 1DD
[E-mail: jintymck@talktalk.net]
(Mbl) 0131-444 2054

McPherson, Alistair
77 Bonaly Wester, Edinburgh EH13 0RQ
[E-mail: amjhmcpherson@blueyonder.co.uk]
0131-478 5384

Pearce, Martin
4 Corbiehill Avenue, Edinburgh EH4 5DR
[E-mail: martin.j.pearce@blueyonder.co.uk]
0131-336 4864
(Mbl) 07801 717222

Sheriffs, Irene (Mrs)
22/2 West Mill Bank, Edinburgh EH13 0QT
[E-mail: reenie.sherriffs@blueyonder.co.uk]
0131-466 9530

Tew, Helen (Mrs)
318 Lanark Road, Edinburgh EH14 2LJ
[E-mail: helentew9@gmail.com]
0131-478 1268
(Mbl) 07986 170802

Wyllie, Anne (Miss)
2F3, 46 Jordan Lane, Edinburgh EH10 4QX
[E-mail: anne.wyllie@tiscali.co.uk]
0131-447 9035

2. WEST LOTHIAN

Coyle, Charlotte (Mrs)
28 The Avenue, Whitburn EH47 0DA
[E-mail: paulcharlotte@talktalk.net]
01501 740687

Elliott, Sarah (Miss)
105 Seafield Rows, Seafield, Bathgate EH47 7AW
[E-mail: sarah.elliott6@btopenworld.com]
01506 654950

Galloway, Brenda (Dr)
Lochend, 58 St Ninians Road, Linlithgow EH49 7BN
[E-mail: bhgallo@yahoo.co.uk]
01506 842028

Holden, Louise (Mrs)
Am Batnach, Easter Breich, West Calder EH55 8PP
[E-mail: louise.holden@btinternet.com]
01506 873030

Middleton, Alex — 19 Cramond Place, Dalgety Bay KY11 9LS
[E-mail: alex.middleton@btinternet.com] — 01383 820800

Orr, Elizabeth (Mrs) — 64a Marjoribanks Street, Bathgate EH48 1AL
[E-mail: liz-orr@hotmail.co.uk] — 01506 653116

Paxton, James — 5 Main Street, Longridge, Bathgate EH47 8AE
[E-mail: jim_paxton@btinternet.com] — 01501 772192

Salmon, Jeanie (Mrs) — 81 Croftfoot Drive, Fauldhouse, Bathgate EH47 9EH
[E-mail: jeaniesalmon@aol.com] — (Work) 01501 772468 / 01501 828509

Scoular, Iain W. — 15 Bonnyside Road, Bonnybridge FK4 2AD
[E-mail: iain@iwsconsultants.com] — 01324 812395 / (Mbl) 07717 131596

Wilkie, David — 53 Goschen Place, Broxburn EH52 5JH
[E-mail: david-fmu_09@tiscali.co.uk] — 01506 854777

3. LOTHIAN

Evans, W. John IEng MIIE(Elec) — Waterlily Cottage, 10 Fenton Steading, North Berwick EH39 5AF
[E-mail: jevans7is@hotmail.com] — 01620 842990

Hogg, David MA — 82 Eskhill, Penicuik EH26 8DQ
[E-mail: hogg-d2@sky.com] — 01968 676350 / (Mbl) 07821 693946

Millan, Mary (Mrs) — 33 Polton Vale, Loanhead EH20 9DF
[E-mail: marymillan@fsmail.net] — 0131-440 1624 / (Mbl) 07814 466104

Trevor, A. Hugh MA MTh — 29A Fidra Road, North Berwick EH39 4NE
[E-mail: htrevor@talktalk.net] — 01620 894924

Yeoman, Edward T.N. FSAScot — 75 Newhailes Crescent, Musselburgh EH21 6EF
[E-mail: edwardyeoman6@aol.com] — 0131-653 2291 / (Mbl) 07896 517666

4. MELROSE AND PEEBLES

Cashman, Margaret D. (Mrs) — 38 Abbotsford Road, Galashiels TD1 3HR
[E-mail: mcashman@tiscali.co.uk] — 01896 752711

Selkirk, Frances (Mrs) — 2 The Glebe, Ashkirk, Selkirk TD7 4PJ
[E-mail: f.selkirk@btinternet.com] — 01750 32204

5. DUNS

Landale, Alison (Mrs) — Green Hope Guest House, Ellemford, Duns TD11 3SG
[E-mail: alison@greenhope.co.uk] — 01361 890242

Taylor, Christine (Mrs) — Rowardennan, Main Street, Gavinton, Duns TD11 3QT
[E-mail: christine2751@btinternet.com] — 01361 882994

6. JEDBURGH

Findlay, Elizabeth (Mrs) — 2 Hendersons Court, Kelso TD5 7BG
[E-mail: elizabeth@findlay8124.fsworld.co.uk] — 01573 226641

Knox, Dagmar (Mrs) — 3 Stichill Road, Ednam, Kelso TD5 7QQ
[E-mail: dagmar.knox.riding@btinternet.com] — 01573 224883

7. ANNANDALE AND ESKDALE

Boncey, David — Redbrae, Beattock, Moffat DG10 9RF
[E-mail: david.boncey613@btinternet.com] — 01683 300613

Brown, Martin J. — Lochhouse Farm, Beattock, Moffat DG10 9SG
[E-mail: martin@lochhousefarm.com] — 01683 300451

Brown, S. Jeffrey BA — Skara Brae, 8 Ballplay Road, Moffat DG10 9JU
[E-mail: sjbrown@btinternet.com] — 01683 220475

Chisholm, Dennis A.G. MA BSc — Moss-side, Hightae, Lockerbie DG11 1JR
[E-mail: dchis@talktalk.net] — 01387 811803

Dodds, Alan — Trinco, Battlehill, Annan DG12 6SN
[E-mail: alanandjen46@talktalk.net] — 01461 201235

Jackson, Susan (Mrs) — 48 Springbells Road, Annan DG12 6LQ
[E-mail: peter-jackson24@sky.com] — 01461 204159

Morton, Andrew A. BSc — 19 Sherwood Park, Lockerbie DG11 2DX
[E-mail: andrew.a.morton@btinternet.com]
[E-mail: andrew_morton@mac.com] — 01576 203164

Saville, Hilda A. (Mrs) — 32 Crosslaw Burn, Moffat DG10 9LP
[E-mail: saville.c@sky.com] — 01683 222854

8. DUMFRIES AND KIRKCUDBRIGHT

Corson, Gwen (Mrs) — 7 Sunnybrae, Borgue, Kirkcudbright DG6 4SJ — 01557 870328

Matheson, David — 44 Auchenkeld Avenue, Heathhall, Dumfries DG1 3QY

Ogilvie, D. Wilson MA FSAScot — Lingerwood, 2 Nelson Street, Dumfries DG2 9AY — 01387 264267

Paterson, Ronald M. (Dr) — Mirkwood, Ringford, Castle Douglas DG7 2AL
[E-mail: mirkwoodtyke@aol.com] — 01557 820202

Smith, Nicola (Mrs) — Brightwater Lodge, Kelton, Castle Douglas DG7 1SZ
[E-mail: nickysasmith@btinternet.com] — 01556 680453

9. WIGTOWN AND STRANRAER

McQuistan, Robert — Old Schoolhouse, Carsluith, Newton Stewart DG8 7DT
[E-mail: mcquistan@mcquistan.plus.com] — 01671 820327

Williams, Roy — 120 Belmont Road, Stranraer DG9 7BG
[E-mail: roywilliams84@hotmail.com] — 01776 705762

10. AYR

Anderson, James (Dr)
BVMS PhD DVM FRCPath FIBiol MRCVS — 67 Henrietta Street, Girvan KA26 9AN
[E-mail: jc.anderson@tesco.net] — 01465 710059
(Mbl) 07952 512720

Gowans, James — 2 Cochrane Avenue, Dundonald, Kilmarnock KA2 9EJ
[E-mail: jim@luker42.freeserve.co.uk]
01563 850904   (Mbl) 07985 916814

Jamieson, Ian A. — 2 Whinfield Avenue, Prestwick KA9 2BH
[E-mail: ian@jamieson4189.freeserve.co.uk]
01242 476898

Morrison, James — 27 Monkton Road, Prestwick KA9 1AP
[E-mail: jim.morrison@talktalk.net]
01292 479313   (Mbl) 07773 287852

Murphy, Ian — 56 Lamont Crescent, Netherthird, Cumnock KA18 3DU
[E-mail: ianm_cumnock@yahoo.co.uk]
01290 423675

Riome, Elizabeth (Mrs) — Monkwood Mains, Minishant, Maybole KA19 8EY
[E-mail: aj.riome@btinternet.com]
01292 443440

Stewart, Christine (Mrs) — 52 Kilnford Drive, Dundonald KA2 9ET
[E-mail: christistewart@btinternet.com]
01563 850486

11. IRVINE AND KILMARNOCK

Bircham, James F. — 8 Holmlea Place, Kilmarnock KA1 1UU
[E-mail:james.bircham@sky.com]
01563 532287

Cooper, Fraser — 5 Balgray Way, Irvine KA11 1RP
[E-mail: frasercooper@wightcablenorth.net]
01294 211235

Crosbie, Shona (Mrs) — 4 Campbell Street, Darvel KA17 0DA
[E-mail: fawltytowersdarvel@yahoo.co.uk]
01560 322229

Dempster, Ann (Mrs) — 20 Graham Place, Kilmarnock KA3 7JN
[E-mail: ademp99320@aol.com]
(Work) 01563 529361   01563 534080   (Mbl) 07729 152945   01563 540009

Gillespie, Janice (Miss) — 12 Jeffrey Street, Kilmarnock KA1 4EB
[E-mail: janice.gillespie@tiscali.co.uk]
01563 534431

Hamilton, Margaret A. (Mrs) — 59 South Hamilton Street, Kilmarnock KA1 2DT
[E-mail: tomhnltn@sky.com]
01563 534065

Jamieson, John H. BSc DEP AFBPSS — 22 Moorfield Avenue, Kilmarnock KA1 1TS
[E-mail: johnhjamieson@tiscali.co.uk]

McGeever, Gerard — 23 Kinloch Avenue, Stewarton, Kilmarnock KA3 3HQ
[E-mail: gerard@gmcgeever.freeserve.co.uk]
(Work) 01560 484331   0141-847 5717   01563 538475

MacLean, Donald — 1 Four Acres Drive, Kilmaurs, Kilmarnock KA3 2ND
[E-mail: donannmac@yahoo.co.uk]
01563 535305

Mills, Catherine (Mrs) — 59 Crossdene Road, Crosshouse, Kilmarnock KA2 0JU
[E-mail: cfmills5lib@hotmail.com]
01563 539377

Raleigh, Gavin — 21 Landsborough Drive, Kilmarnock KA3 1RY
[E-mail: gavin.raleigh@lineone.net]

Robertson, William — 1 Archers Avenue, Irvine KA11 2GB
[E-mail: willie.robert@yahoo.co.uk]
01294 203577

Whitelaw, David — 9 Kirkhill, Kilwinning KA13 6NB
[E-mail: whitelawfam@talktalk.net]
01294 551695

12. ARDROSSAN

Barclay, Elizabeth (Mrs)
2 Jacks Road, Saltcoats KA21 5NT
[E-mail: mfiz98@dsl.pipex.com]
01294 471855

Clarke, Elizabeth (Mrs)
Swallowbrae, Torbeg, Isle of Arran KA27 8HE
[E-mail: lizahclarke@gmail.com]
01770 860219
(Mbl) 07780 574367

Currie, Archie BD
55 Central Avenue, Kilbirnie KA25 6JP
[E-mail: archiecurrie@yahoo.co.uk]
01505 681474
(Mbl) 07881 452115

Hunter, Jean C.Q. (Mrs) BD
Church of Scotland Manse, Shiskine, Isle of Arran KA27 3EP
[E-mail: j.hunter744@btinternet.com]
01770 860380

McCool, Robert
17 McGregor Avenue, Stevenston KA20 4BA
01294 466548

Mackay, Brenda H. (Mrs)
19 Eglinton Square, Ardrossan KA22 8LN
[E-mail: bremac82@aol.com]
01294 464491

Macleod, Sharon (Mrs)
Creag Dhubh, Golf Course Road, Whiting Bay, Isle of Arran KA27 8QT
[E-mail: macleodsharon@hotmail.com]
01770 700353

Nimmo, Margaret (Mrs)
12 Muirfield Place, Kilwinning KA13 6NL
[E-mail: margtmcmn@aol.com]
01294 553718
(Work) 01292 220336

Ross, Magnus BA MEd
39 Beachway, Largs KA30 8QH
[E-mail: m.b.ross@btinternet.com]
01475 689572

13. LANARK

Grant, Alan
25 Moss-side Avenue, Carluke ML8 5UG
[E-mail: amgrant25@aol.com]
01555 771419

Love, William
30 Barmore Avenue, Carluke ML8 4PE
[E-mail: janbill30@tiscali.co.uk]
01555 751243

14. GREENOCK AND PAISLEY

Banks, Russell
18 Aboyne Drive, Paisley PA2 7SJ
[E-mail: margaret.banks2@ntlworld.com]
0141-884 6925

Bird, Mary Jane

Boag, Jennifer (Miss)
11 Madeira Street, Greenock PA16 7UJ
[E-mail: jenniferboag@hotmail.com]
01475 720125

Campbell, Tom BA DipCPC
3 Grahamston Place, Paisley PA2 7BY
[E-mail: tomcam38@googlemail.com]
0141-840 2273

Davey, Charles L.
16 Divert Road, Gourock PA19 1DT
[E-mail: charles.davey@talktalk.net]
01475 631544

Glenny, John C.
49 Cloch Road, Gourock PA19 1AT
[E-mail: jacklizg@aol.com]
01475 636415

Hood, Eleanor (Mrs)
12 Clochoderick Avenue, Kilbarchan, Johnstone PA10 2AY
[E-mail: eleanor.hood.kilbarchan@ntlworld.com]
01505 704208

MacDonald, Christine (Ms)
33 Collier Street, Johnstone PA5 8AG
[E-mail: christine.macdonald10@ntlworld.com]
01505 355779

McFarlan, Elizabeth (Miss)
20 Fauldswood Crescent, Paisley PA2 9PA
[E-mail: elizabeth.mcfarlan@ntlworld.com]
01505 358411

McHugh, Jack
'Earlshaugh', Earl Place, Bridge of Weir PA11 3HA
[E-mail: jackmchugh@tiscali.co.uk]
01505 612789

Marshall, Leon M.
'Glenisla', Gryffe Road, Kilmacolm PA13 4BA
[E-mail: lm@stevenson-kyles.co.uk]
01505 872417

Maxwell, Sandra A. (Mrs) BD
2 Grants Avenue, Paisley PA2 6AZ
[E-mail: sandra1.maxwell@virgin.net]
0141-884 3710

Orry, Geoff
'Rhu Eilan', 4 Seaforth Crescent, Barrhead, Glasgow G78 1PL
[E-mail: geoff.orry@googlemail.com]
0141-881 9748

Rankin, Kenneth
20 Bruntsfield Gardens, Glasgow G53 7QJ
0141-880 7474

16. GLASGOW

Birchall, Edwin

Bremner, David
Greenhill Lodge, 1 Old Humbie Road, Glasgow G77 5DF
[E-mail: david.bremner@tiscali.co.uk]
0141-639 1742

Campbell, Jack T. BD BEd
40 Kenmure Avenue, Bishopbriggs, Glasgow G64 2DE
[E-mail: jack.campbell@ntlworld.com]
0141-563 5837

Dickson, Hector M.K.
'Gwito', 61 Whitton Drive, Giffnock, Glasgow G46 6EF
[E-mail: hectordickson@hotmail.com]
0141-637 0080

Fullarton, Andrew

Grant, George
8 Erskine Street, Stirling FK7 0QN
[E-mail: georgegrant@gmail.com]
0141-883 9518
01786 609594
(Mbl) 07921 168057

Grieve, Leslie
23 Hertford Avenue, Glasgow G12 0LG
[E-mail: leslie.grieve@gmail.com]
0141-576 1376

Horner, David J.
20 Ledi Road, Glasgow G43 2AJ
[E-mail: djhorner@binternet.com]
0141-637 7369

Hunt, Roland BSc PhD CertEd
4 Flora Gardens, Bishopbriggs, Glasgow G64 1DS
[E-mail: roland.hunt@ntlworld.com]
0141-563 3257
0141-563 3257
0141-429 6733
(Evenings and weekends)

Joansson, Tordur
1/2, 18 Eglinton Court, Glasgow G5 9NE
[E-mail: to41jo@yahoo.co.uk]
0141-621 1809

Kilpatrick, Mrs Joan
39 Brent Road, Regent's Park, Glasgow G46 8JG
[E-mail: je-kilpatrick@sky.com]
0141-643 9730

McChlery, Stuart
62 Grenville Drive, Cambuslang, Glasgow G72 8DP
[E-mail: s.mcchlery@gcu.ac.uk]

McColl, John
2FL, 53 Aberfoyle Street, Glasgow G31 3RP
[E-mail: solfolly11@gmail.com]
0141-554 9881
(Mbl) 07757 303195
0141-954 5540

McFarlane, Robert
25 Avenel Road, Glasgow G13 2PB
[E-mail: robertmcfrln@yahoo.co.uk]

McInally, Gordon
10 Melville Gardens, Bishopbriggs, Glasgow G64 3DF
[E-mail: gmcinally@sky.com]
0141-563 2685

Mackenzie, Norman	Flat 3/2, 41 Kilmailing Road, Glasgow G44 5UH [E-mail: mackenzie799@btinternet.com]	(Mbl) 07780 733710
MacLeod, John	2 Shuna Place, Newton Mearns, Glasgow G77 6TN [E-mail: jmacleod2@sky.com]	0141-639 6862
Millar, Kathleen (Mrs)	9 Glenbank Court, Thornliebank, Glasgow G46 7EJ [E-mail: kathleen.millar@tesco.net]	0141-638 6250 (Mbl) 07793 203045
Montgomery, Hamish	13 Avon Avenue, Bearsden, Glasgow G61 2PS	0141-942 3640
Nairne, Elizabeth	229 Southbrae Drive, Glasgow G13 1TT	0141-959 5066
Nicolson, John	2 Lindsaybeg Court, Chryston, Glasgow G69 9DD [E-mail: john.c.nicolson@btinternet.com]	0141-779 2447
Phillips, John B.	2/3, 30 Handel Place, Glasgow G5 0TP [E-mail: johnphillips@fish.co.uk]	0141-429 7716
Robertson, Adam	423 Amulree Street, Glasgow G32 7SS	0141-573 6662
Roy, Mrs Shona	81 Busby Road, Clarkston, Glasgow G76 8BD [E-mail: theroyfamily@yahoo.co.uk]	0141-644 3713
Smith, Ann	52 Robslee Road, Thornliebank, Glasgow G46 7BX	0141-621 0638
Stead, Mrs Mary	9A Carrick Drive, Mount Vernon, Glasgow G32 0RW [E-mail: maystead@hotmail.co.uk]	0141-764 1016
Stewart, James	45 Airthrey Avenue, Glasgow G14 9LY [E-mail: jmstewart325@btinternet.com]	0141-959 5814
Tindall, Margaret (Mrs)	23 Ashcroft Avenue, Lennoxtown, Glasgow G65 7EN [E-mail: margarettindall@aol.com]	01360 310911
Wilson, George A.	46 Maxwell Drive, Garrowhill, Baillieston, Glasgow G69 6LS [E-mail: healthandsafety@talk21.com]	0141-771 3862

17. HAMILTON

Allan, Angus J.	Blackburn Mill, Chapelton, Strathaven ML10 6RR [E-mail: angus.allan@hotmail.com]	01357 528548
Beattie, Richard	4 Bent Road, Hamilton ML3 6QB [E-mail: richardbeattie1958@hotmail.com]	01698 420086
Bell, Sheena	2 Langdale, East Kilbride, Glasgow G74 4RP [E-mail: belljsheena@hotmail.co.uk]	01355 248217
Chirnside, Peter	141 Kyle Park Drive, Uddingston, Glasgow G71 7DB	01698 813769
Codona, Joy (Mrs)	Dykehead Farm, 300 Dykehead Road, Airdrie ML6 7SR [E-mail: jcodona772@btinternet.com]	01236 767063 (Mbl) 07810 770609
Hastings, William Paul	186 Glen More, East Kilbride, Glasgow G74 2AN [E-mail: wphastings@hotmail.co.uk]	01355 521228
Hislop, Eric	1 Castlegait, Strathaven ML10 6FF [E-mail: eric.hislop@tiscali.co.uk]	01357 520003
Jardine, Lynette	32 Powburn Crescent, Uddingston, Glasgow G71 7SS [E-mail: lpjardine@blueyonder.co.uk]	01698 812404

Keir, Dickson — 46 Brackenhill Drive, Hamilton ML3 8AY
[E-mail: dickson.keir@btinternet.com] — 01698 457351

McCleary, Isaac — 719 Coatbridge Road, Baillieston, Glasgow G69 7PH — 01236 421073
Preston, J. Steven — 24 Glen Prosen, East Kilbride, Glasgow G74 3TA — 01355 237359
[E-mail: steven.preston1@btinternet.com]

Robertson, Rowan — 68 Townhead Road, Coatbridge ML5 2HU — 01236 425703
Stevenson, Thomas — 34 Castle Wynd, Quarter, Hamilton ML3 7XD — 01698 282263
White, Ian T. — 21 Muirhead, Stonehouse, Larkhall ML9 3HG — 01698 792772
[E-mail: iantwhite@aol.com]

18. DUMBARTON
Foster, Peter — Flat 3 Templeton, 51 John Street, Helensburgh G84 8XN — 01436 678226
[E-mail: peterfostera39@btinternet.com]

Galbraith, Iain B. MA MPhil MTh ThD FTCL — Beechwood, Overton Road, Alexandria G83 0LJ — 01389 753563
[E-mail: iainbg@icloud.com]

Giles, Donald (Dr) — Levern House, Stuckenduff, Shandon, Helensburgh G84 8NW — 01436 820565
[E-mail: don.giles@btopenworld.com]

Harold, Sandy — The Laurels, Risk Street, Clydebank G81 3LW — 0141-952 3673
[E-mail: harold996@btinternet.com]

Hart, R.J.M. BSc — 7 Kidston Drive, Helensburgh G84 8QA — 01436 672039
[E-mail: rjm7k@yahoo.com]

Morgan, Richard — Annandale, School Road, Rhu, Helensburgh G84 8RS — 01436 821269
[E-mail: themorgans@hotmail.co.uk]

Rettie, Sara (Mrs) — 86 Dennistoun Crescent, Helensburgh G84 7JF — 01436 677984
[E-mail: sarajayne.rettie@btinternet.com]

19. ARGYLL
Alexander, John — 11 Cullipool Village, Isle of Luing, Oban PA34 4UB — 01852 314242
[E-mail: jandjalex@gmail.com]

Allan, Douglas — 1 Camplen Court, Rothesay PA20 0NL
[E-mail:douglasallan94@btinternet.com]

Binner, Aileen (Mrs) — 'Ailand', North Connel, Oban PA37 1QX — 01631 710264
[E-mail: binners@ailand.plus.com]

Logue, David — 3 Braeface, Tayvallich, Lochgilphead PA31 8PN — 01546 870647
[E-mail: david@loguenet.co.uk]

Macdonald, Duncan N. BD MBA — Clachacharra, Taynuilt PA35 1JE — 01866 822651
[E-mail: duncan@dnmacdonald.co.uk] — (Mbl) 07801 439795

MacKellar, Janet BSc — Laurel Bank, 23 George Street, Dunoon PA23 8JT — 01369 705549
[E-mail: jkmackellar@aol.com]

McLellan, James A. — West Drimvore, Lochgilphead PA31 8SU — 01546 606403
[E-mail: james.mclellan8@btinternet.com]

Mills, Peter A.
Northton, Ganavan, Oban PA34 5TU
[E-mail: peter@peteramills.com]

Morrison, John L.
Tigh na Barnashaig, Tayvallich, Lochgilphead PA31 8PN
[E-mail: jolomo@thejolomostudio.com]
01546 870637

Ramsay, Mathew M.
Portnastorm, Carradale, Campbeltown PA28 6SB
[E-mail: kintyre@fishermensmission.org.uk]
01583 431381

Scouller, Alastair
15 Allanwater Appartments, Bridge of Allan, Stirling FK9 4DZ
[E-mail: scouller@globalnet.co.uk]
01786 832496

Sinclair, Margaret (Ms)
2 Quarry Place, Furnace, Inveraray PA32 8XW
[E-mail: margaret_sinclair@btinternet.com]
01499 500633

Stather, Angela (Ms)
1 Dunlossit Cottages, Port Askaig, Isle of Islay PA46 7RB
[E-mail: angstat@btinternet.com]
01496 840726

Thornhill, Christopher R.
4 Ardfern Cottages, Ardfern, Lochgilphead PA31 8QN
[E-mail: c.thornhill@btinternet.com]
01852 300011

Waddell, Martin
Fasgadh, Clachan Seil, Oban PA34 4TJ
[E-mail: waddell715@btinternet.com]
01852 300395

Zielinski, Jenneffer C. (Mrs)
26 Cromwell Street, Dunoon PA23 7AX
[E-mail: jennefferzielinski@gmail.com]
01369 706136

22. FALKIRK

Duncan, Lorna M. (Mrs) BA
Richmond, 28 Solway Drive, Head of Muir, Denny FK6 5NS
[E-mail: ell.dee@blueyonder.co.uk]
01324 813020

Mathers, Sandra (Mrs)
10 Ercall Road, Brightons, Falkirk FK2 0RS
[E-mail: alexena@btinternet.com]
01324 872253

McMillan, Isabelle (Mrs)
Treetops, 17 Castle Avenue, Airth FK2 8GA
[E-mail: arthur.stewart1@btinternet.com]
(Mbl) 07896 433314

Stewart, Arthur MA
51 Bonnymuir Crescent, Bonnybridge FK4 1GD
01324 812667

Struthers, Ivar B.
7 McVean Place, Bonnybridge FK4 1QZ
[E-mail: ivar.struthers@btinternet.com]
01324 841145
(Mbl) 07921 778208

23. STIRLING

Durie, Alastair (Dr)
25 Forth Place, Stirling FK8 1UD
[E-mail: acdurie@btinternet.com]
01786 451029

Grier, Hunter
17 Station Road, Bannockburn, Stirling FK7 8LG
[E-mail: hunter@xaltmail.com]
01786 815192

Tilly, Patricia (Mrs)
25 Meiklejohn Street, Stirling FK9 5HQ
[E-mail: Trishatilly@aol.com]
01786 446401
(Mbl) 07428 559554

Weir, Andrew (Dr)
16 The Oaks, Killearn, Glasgow G63 9SF
[E-mail: andrewweir@btinternet.com]
01360 550779
(Mbl) 07534 506075

24. DUNFERMLINE

Brown, Gordon — Nowell, Fossoway, Kinross KY13 0UW [E-mail: brown.nowell@hotmail.co.uk] — 01577 840248

Conway, Bernard — 4 Centre Street, Kelty KY4 0EQ — 01383 830442

Grant, Allan — 6 Normandy Place, Rosyth KY11 2HJ [E-mail: allan75@btinternet.com] — 01383 428760

McCafferty, Joyce (Mrs) — 53 Foulford Street, Cowdenbeath KY4 9AS — 01383 515775

McDonald, Elizabeth (Mrs) — Parleyhill, Culross, Dunfermline KY12 8JD — 01383 880231

Meiklejohn, Barry — 40 Lilac Grove, Dunfermline KY11 8AP [E-mail: barry.meiklejohn@btinternet.com] — 01383 731550

Mitchell, Ian G. QC — 17 Carlingnose Point, North Queensferry, Inverkeithing KY11 1ER [E-mail: igmitchell@easynet.co.uk] — 01383 416240

25. KIRKCALDY

Biernat, Ian — 2 Formonthills Road, Glenrothes KY6 3EF [E-mail: ian.biernat@btinternet.com] — 01592 655565

26. ST ANDREWS

Elder, Morag Anne (Ms) — 5 Provost Road, Tayport DD6 9JE [E-mail: benuardin@tiscali.co.uk] — 01382 552218

Grant, Allan — 6 Normandy Place, Rosyth KY11 2HJ [E-mail: allan75@talktalk.net] — 01383 428760

King, C.M. (Mrs) — 8 Bankwell Road, Anstruther KY10 3DA — 01333 310017

Porteous, Brian — Kirkdene, Westfield Road, Cupar KY15 5DS [E-mail: brian@porteousleisure.co.uk] — 01334 653561

Smith, Elspeth (Mrs) — Glentarkie Cottage, Glentarkie, Strathmiglo, Cupar KY14 7RU [E-mail: elspeth.smith@btopenworld.com] — 01337 860824

27. DUNKELD AND MEIGLE

Howat, David — Lilybank Cottage, Newton Street, Blairgowrie PH10 6HZ [E-mail: david@thehowats.net] — 01250 874715

Theaker, Phillip — 5 Altamount Road, Blairgowrie PH10 6QL [E-mail: ptheaker@talktalk.net] — 01250 871162

28. PERTH

Archibald, Michael — Wychwood, Culdeesland Road, Methven, Perth PH1 3QE [E-mail: michael.archibald@gmail.com] — 01738 840995

Begg, James — 8 Park Village, Turretbank Road, Crieff PH7 4JN [E-mail: Bjimmy37@aol.com] — 01764 655907

Benneworth, Michael — 7 Hamilton Place, Perth PH1 1BB [E-mail: mbenneworth@hotmail.com] — 01738 628093

Davidson, Andrew — 95 Needless Road, Perth PH2 0LD [E-mail: a.r.davidson.91@cantab.net] — 01738 620839

Laing, John — 10 Graybank Road, Perth PH2 0GZ [E-mail: johnandmarylaing@hotmail.co.uk] — 01738 623888

Ogilvie, Brian — 67 Whitecraigs, Kinnesswood, Kinross KY13 9JN [E-mail: brianj.ogilvie1@btopenworld.com] — (Mbl) 01592 840823 / 07815 759864

Stewart, Anne — Ballcraine, Murthly Road, Stanley, Perth PH1 4PN [E-mail: anne.stewart13@btinternet.com] — 01738 828637

Yellowlees, Deirdre (Mrs) — Ringmill House, Gannochy Farm, Perth PH2 7JH [E-mail: d.yellowlees@btinternet.com] — 01738 633773 / (Mbl) 07920 805399

29. DUNDEE

Brown, Isobel (Mrs) — 10 School Wynd, Muirhead, Dundee DD2 5LW [E-mail: isobel73@btinternet.com] — 01382 580545

Brown, Janet (Miss) — G2, 6 Baxter Park Terrace, Dundee DD4 6NL [E-mail: j.herries.brown@blueyonder.co.uk] — 01382 453066

Sharp, Gordon — 6 Kelso Street, Dundee DD2 1SJ — 01382 643002 / 01382 630355

Xenophontos-Hellen, Tim — Aspro Spiti, 23 Ancrum Drive, Dundee DD2 2JG [E-mail: tim.xsf@btinternet.com] — (Work) 01382 567756

30. ANGUS

Beedie, Alexander W. — 62 Newton Crescent, Arbroath DD11 3JZ [E-mail: bill.beedie@hotmail.co.uk] — 01241 875001

Davidson, Peter I. — 24 Kinnaird Place, Brechin DD9 7HF [E-mail: mail@idavidson.co.uk]

Gray, Linda (Mrs) — 8 Inchgarth Street, Forfar DD8 3LY [E-mail: lindamgray@sky.com] — 01307 464039

Nicoll, Douglas — 16 New Road, Forfar DD8 2AE — 01307 463264

Walker, Eric — 12 Orchard Brae, Kirriemuir DD8 4JY — 01575 572082

Walker, Pat — 12 Orchard Brae, Kirriemuir DD8 4JY — 01575 572082

31. ABERDEEN

Cooper, Gordon — 4 Springfield Place, Aberdeen AB15 7SF [E-mail: ga_cooper@hotmail.co.uk] — 01224 316667

Gray, Peter (Prof.) — 165 Countesswells Road, Aberdeen AB15 7RA [E-mail: pmdgray@bcs.org.uk] — 01224 318172

32. KINCARDINE AND DEESIDE

Bell, Robert — 27 Mearns Drive, Stonehaven AB39 2DZ [E-mail: r.bell282@btinternet.com] — (Mbl) 01569 767173 / 07733 014826

Broere, Teresa (Mrs)	3 Balnastraid Cottages, Dinnet, Aboyne AB34 5NE [E-mail: broere@btinternet.com]	01339 880058
Coles, Stephen	43 Mearns Walk, Laurencekirk AB30 1FA [E-mail: steve@sbcco.com]	01561 378400
McCafferty, W. John	Lynwood, Cammachmore, Stonehaven AB39 3NR [E-mail: wjmccafferty@yahoo.co.uk]	01569 730281
McLuckie, John	7 Monaltrie Close, Ballater AB35 5PT [E-mail: johnemcluckie@btinternet.com]	01339 755489
Middleton, Robin B. (Capt.)	7 St Ternan's Road, Newtonhill, Stonehaven AB39 3PF [E-mail: robbiemiddleton7@hotmail.co.uk]	01569 730852
Platt, David	2 St Michael's Road, Newtonhill, Stonehaven AB39 3RW [E-mail: daveplatt01@btinternet.com]	01569 730465
Simpson, Elizabeth (Mrs)	Connemara, 33 Golf Road, Ballater AB35 5RS [E-mail: connemara33@yahoo.com]	01339 755597

33. GORDON

Bichard, Susanna (Mrs)	Beechlee, Haddo Lane, Tarves, Ellon AB41 7JZ [E-mail: smbichard@aol.com]	01651 851345
Doak, Alan B.	17 Chievres Place, Ellon AB41 9WH [E-mail: alanbdoak@aol.com]	01358 721819
Findlay, Patricia (Mrs)	Douglas View, Tullynessle, Alford AB33 8QR [E-mail: p.a.findlay@btopenworld.com]	01975 562379
Mitchell, Jean (Mrs)	6 Cowgate, Oldmeldrum, Inverurie AB51 0EN [E-mail: j.g.mitchell@btinternet.com]	01651 872745
Robb, Margaret (Mrs)	Chrislouan, Keithhall, Inverurie AB51 0LN [E-mail: Robbminister1@aol.com]	01651 882310
Robertson, James Y. MA	1 Nicol Road, Kintore, Inverurie AB51 0QA [E-mail: j.robertson833@btinternet.com]	01467 633001

34. BUCHAN

Armitage, Rosaline (Mrs)	Whitecairn, Blackhills, Peterhead AB42 3LR [E-mail: r.r.armitage@btinternet.com]	01779 477267
Barker, Tim	South Silverford Croft, Longmanhill, Banff AB45 3SB [E-mail: tbarker05@aol.com]	01261 851839
Brown, Lillian (Mrs)	45 Main Street, Aberchirder, Huntly AB54 7ST	01466 780330
Forsyth, Alicia (Mrs)	Rothie Inn Farm, Forgue Road, Rothienorman, Inverurie AB51 8YH [E-mail: a.forsyth@btinternet.com]	01651 821359
Givan, James	Zimra, Longmanhill, Banff AB45 3RP [E-mail: jim.givan@btinternet.com]	01261 833318 (Mbl) 07753 458864
Grant, Margaret (Mrs)	22 Elphin Street, New Aberdour, Fraserburgh AB43 6LH [E-mail: margaret@wilmar.demon.co.uk]	01346 561341

Higgins, Scott — St Ninian's, Manse Terrace, Turriff AB53 4BA — 01888 569103
[E-mail: mhairiandscott@btinternet.com]

Lumsden, Vera (Mrs) — 8 Queen's Crescent, Portsoy, Banff AB45 2PX — 01261 842712
[E-mail: ivsd@lumsden77.freeserve.co.uk]

McColl, John — East Cairnchina, Lonmay, Fraserburgh AB43 8RH — 01346 532558 (Mbl) 07757 303195
[E-mail: solfolly11@gmail.com]

MacLeod, Ali (Ms) — 11 Pitfour Crescent, Fetterangus, Peterhead AB42 4EL — 01771 622992 (Mbl) 07821 670705
[E-mail: aliowl@hotmail.com]

Macnee, Anthea (Mrs) — Wardend Cottage, Alvah, Banff AB45 3TR — 01261 815647
[E-mail: macneeiain4@googlemail.com]

Mair, Dorothy L.T. (Miss) — Flat F, 15 The Quay, Newburgh, Ellon AB41 6DA — 01358 788832 (Mbl) 07505 051305
[E-mail: dorothymair2@aol.com]

Noble, John M. — 44 Henderson Park, Peterhead AB42 2WR — 01779 472522
[E-mail: john_m_noble@hotmail.co.uk]

Ogston, Norman — Rowandale, 6 Rectory Road, Turriff AB53 4SU — 01888 560342
[E-mail: norman.ogston@gmail.com]

Simpson, Andrew C. — 10 Wood Street, Banff AB45 1JX — 01261 812538
[E-mail: andy.louise1@btinternet.com]

Smith, Ian M.G. — 2 Hill Street, Cruden Bay, Peterhead AB42 0HF — 01779 812698
Sneddon, Richard — 100 West Road, Peterhead AB42 2AQ — 01779 480803
[E-mail: richard.sneddon@btinternet.com]

Taylor, Elaine (Mrs) — 101 Cairntrodlie, Peterhead AB42 2AY — 01779 472978
[E-mail: elaine.taylor60@btinternet.com]

35. MORAY
Forbes, Jean (Mrs) — Greenmoss, Drybridge, Buckie AB56 2JB — 01542 831646 (Mbl) 07974 760337
[E-mail: dancingfeet@tinyworld.co.uk]

36. ABERNETHY
Bardgett, Alison (Mrs) — Tigh an Iasgair, Street of Kincardine, Boat of Garten PH24 3BY — 01479 831751
[E-mail: tigh@bardgett.plus.com]

37. INVERNESS
Appleby, Jonathan — 91 Cradlehall Park, Inverness IV2 5DB — 01463 791470
[E-mail: jon.wyvis@gmail.com]

Cazaly, Leonard — 9 Moray Park Gardens, Culloden, Inverness IV2 7FY — 01463 794469
[E-mail: len_cazaly@lineone.net]

Cook, Arnett D. — 66 Millerton Avenue, Inverness IV3 8RY — 01463 224795
[E-mail: arnett.cook@btinternet.com]

Dennis, Barry — 50 Holm Park, Inverness IV2 4XU — 01463 225883 (Work) 01463 663448
[E-mail: barry.dennis@tiscali.co.uk]

Innes, Derek — Allanswell, Cawdor Road, Auldearn, Nairn IV12 5TQ
[E-mail: dereklinnes@btinternet.com]
01463 230321

MacInnes, Ailsa (Mrs) — Kilmartin, 17 Southside Road, Inverness IV2 3BG
[E-mail: ailsa.macinnes@btopenworld.com]
(Mbl) 07704 485055

Robertson, Hendry — Park House, 51 Glenurquhart Road, Inverness IV3 5PB
[E-mail: hendry.robertson@connectfree.co.uk]
01463 231858
(Mbl) 07929 766102

Robertson, Stewart J.H. — 21 Towerhill Drive, Cradlehall, Inverness IV2 5FD
01463 793144

Roden, Vivian (Mrs) — 15 Old Mill Road, Tomatin, Inverness IV13 7YW
[E-mail: vroden@btinternet.com]
01808 511355
(Mbl) 07887 704915

Todd, Iain — 9 Leanach Gardens, Inverness IV2 5DD
[E-mail: itoddyo@aol.com]
01463 791161

38. LOCHABER

Chalkley, Andrew BSc — 41 Hillside Road, Campbeltown PA28 6NE
[E-mail: andrewjoan@googlemail.com]
01687 460042

Ogston, Jean (Mrs) — Church of Scotland Manse, Annie's Brae, Mallaig PH41 4RG
[E-mail: jeanogston@googlemail.com]

Walker, Eric — Tigh a' Chlamn, Inverroy, Roy Bridge PH31 4AQ
[E-mail: line15@btinternet.com]
01397 712028

Walker, Pat (Mrs) — Tigh a' Chlamn, Inverroy, Roy Bridge PH31 4AQ
[E-mail: pat.line15@btinternet.com]
01397 712028

39. ROSS

Finlayson, Michael R. — Amberlea, Glenskiach, Evanton, Dingwall IV16 9UU
[E-mail: finlayson935@btinternet.com]
01349 830598

Greer, Kathleen (Mrs) MEd — 17 Duthac Wynd, Tain IV19 1LP
[E-mail: greer2@talktalk.net]
01862 892065

Gunstone, Ronald W. — 20 Bellfield Road, North Kessock, Inverness IV1 3XU
[E-mail: ronald.gunstone@virgin.net]
01463 731337
(Mbl) 07974 443948

Jamieson, Patricia A. (Mrs) — 9 Craig Avenue, Tain IV19 1JP
[E-mail: hapjjam179@yahoo.co.uk]
01862 893154

McAlpine, James — 5 Cromlet Park, Invergordon IV18 0RN
[E-mail: jmca1@tinyworld.co.uk]
01349 852801

McCreadie, Frederick — 7 Castle Gardens, Dingwall IV15 9HY
[E-mail: fredmccreadie@tesco.net]
01349 862171

Munro, Irene (Mrs) — 1 Wyvis Crescent, Conon Bridge, Dingwall IV15 9HY
[E-mail: irenemunro@rocketmail.com]
01349 865752

Riddell, Keith — 2 Station Cottages, Fearn, Tain IV20 1RR
[E-mail: keithriddell@hotmail.co.uk]
01862 832867
(Mbl) 07719 645995

40. SUTHERLAND

Baxter, A. Rosie (Dr) — Daylesford, Invershin, Lairg IV27 4ET
[E-mail: drrosiereid@yahoo.co.uk]   01549 421326   (Mbl) 07748 761694

Roberts, Irene (Mrs) — Flat 4, Harbour Buildings, Main Street, Portmahomack, Tain IV20 1YG
[E-mail: ireneroberts43@hotmail.com]   01862 871166   (Mbl) 07854 436854

Weidner, Karl — 6 St Vincent Road, Tain IV19 1JR
[E-mail: kweidner@btinternet.com]   01862 894202

41. CAITHNESS

MacDonald, Dr Morag — Orkney View, Portskerra, Melvich KW14 7YL
[E-mail: liliasmacdonald@btinternet.com]   01641 531281

42. LOCHCARRON – SKYE

Lamont, John H. BD — 6 Tigh na Filine, Aultbea, Achnasheen IV22 2JE
[E-mail: jhlamont@btinternet.com]   (Mbl) 07714 720753

MacRae, Donald E. — Nethania, 52 Strath, Gairloch IV21 2DB
[E-mail: Dmgair@aol.com]   01445 712235

Ross, R. Ian — St Conal's, Inverinate, Kyle IV40 8HB   01599 511371

43. UIST

Browning, Margaret (Miss) — 1 Middlequarter, Sollas, Lochmaddy, Isle of North Uist HS6 5BU
[E-mail: margaretckb@tiscali.co.uk]   01876 560392

Lines, Charles M.D. — Flat 1/02, 8 Queen Margaret Road, Glasgow G20 6DP

MacAulay, John — Fernhaven, 1 Flodabay, Isle of Harris HS3 3HA   01859 530340

MacNab, Ann (Mrs) — Druim Skilivat, Scolpaig, Lochmaddy, Isle of North Uist HS6 5DH
[E-mail: annabhan@hotmail.com]   01876 510701

44. LEWIS

Macleod, Donald — 14 Balmerino Drive, Stornoway, Isle of Lewis HS1 2TD
[E-mail: donaldmacleod25@btinternet.com]   01851 704516

Macmillan, Iain — 34 Scotland Street, Stornoway, Isle of Lewis HS1 2JR
[E-mail: macmillan@brocair.fsnet.co.uk]   01851 704826   07775 027987

Murray, Angus — 4 Ceann Chilleagraidh, Stornoway, Isle of Lewis HS1 2UJ
[E-mail: angydmurray@btinternet.com]   (Mbl) 01851 703550

45. ORKNEY

Dicken, Marion (Mrs) — 6 Claymore Brae, Kirkwall, Orkney KW15 1UQ
[E-mail: mj44@hotmail.co.uk]   01856 879509

Robertson, Johan (Mrs) — Old Manse, Eday, Orkney KW17 2AA   01857 622251

46. SHETLAND

Greig, Diane (Mrs) MA — 6 Hayhoull Place, Bigton, Shetland ZE2 9GA
[E-mail: mrschm.greig@btinternet.com] — 01950 422468

Harrison, Christine (Mrs) BA — Gerdavatn, Baltasound, Unst, Shetland ZE2 9DY
[E-mail: chris4242@btinternet.com] — 01957 711578

Smith, M. Beryl (Mrs) DCE MSc — Vakterlee, Cumliewick, Sandwick, Shetland ZE2 9HH
[E-mail: beryl@brooniestaing.co.uk] — 01950 431280

47. ENGLAND

Houghton, Mark (Dr) — Kentcliffe, Charney Road, Grange-over-Sands, Cumbria LA11 6BP
[E-mail: mark@chaplain.me.uk] — 01539 525048

Menzies, Rena (Mrs) — 49 Elizabeth Avenue, St Brelade's, Jersey JE3 8GR
[E-mail: menzfamily@jerseymail.co.uk] — (Work) 01629 813505 / 01534 741095

Milligan, Elaine (Mrs) — 16 Surrey Close, Corby, Northants NN17 2TG
[E-mail: elainemilligan@ntlworld.com] — 01536 205259

Munro, William — 35 Stour Road, Corby, Northants NN17 2HX — 01536 504864

48. INTERNATIONAL CHARGES

Ross, David — Urb. El Campanario, EDF Granada, Esc. 14, Baja B, Ctra Cadiz N-340, Km 168, 29680 Estepona, Malaga, Spain
[E-mail: rosselcampanario@yahoo.co.uk] — (Tel/Fax) 0034 952 88 26 34

49. JERUSALEM

Oakley-Levstein, Joanna (Mrs) BA — Mevo Hamma, 12934, Israel
[E-mail: j.oak.lev@gmail.com] — 00972 50584 2517

ASSOCIATE (Ireland)

Binnie, Jean (Miss) — 2 Ailesbury Lawn, Dundrum, Dublin 16, Ireland
[E-mail: jeanbinnie@eircom.net] — 00353 1 298 7229

LIST I – MINISTRIES DEVELOPMENT STAFF

Ministries Development Staff support local congregations, parish groupings and presbyteries in a wide variety of ways, bringing expertise or experience to pastoral work, development, and outreach in congregation and community. Some of these may be ministers and deacons undertaking specialist roles; these are not listed below but are found in Section 5 (Presbyteries), with deacons also in List C of the present section.

NAME	APPOINTMENT AND PRESBYTERY	CONTACT
Adam, Pamela BD	Ellon (Gordon)	pbaker@churchofscotland.org.uk
Amanaland, John	Aberdeen: Garthdee l/w Ruthrieston West (Aberdeen)	jamanaland@churchofscotland.org.uk
Archer, Janice	Cumbernauld: Kildrum – Admin Support Worker (Falkirk)	
Baird, Janette Y.	Glasgow: St Andrew and St Nicholas – Community Development (Glasgow)	JBaird@churchofscotland.org.uk
Baker, Paula (Mrs)	Birnie and Pluscarden l/w Elgin: High – Parish Assistant (Moray)	PBaker@churchofscotland.org.uk
Berry, Gavin R.	Arbroath Old and Abbey – Parish Assistant (Angus)	GBerry@churchofscotland.org.uk
Bloomfield, Frances (Rev)	Glasgow: St Christopher's Priesthill and Nitshill (Glasgow)	FBloomfield@churchofscotland.org.uk
Binnie, Michelle	Possilpark (Glasgow)	MBinnie@churchofscotland.org.uk
Boland, Susan (Mrs) DipHE(Theol)	Cumbernauld: Abronhill (Falkirk)	SBoland@churchofscotland.org.uk
Boyle, Deborah	Glasgow: Ruchill Kelvinside – Children and Family Outreach (Glasgow)	
Broere, Paula	Aberdeen: Mastrick – Parish Assistant (Aberdeen)	PBroere@churchofscotland.org.uk
Brown, Kenneth	Livingston United – Church and Community Worker (West Lothian)	Kenneth.Brown@churchofscotland.org.uk
Bruce, Stuart	Glasgow: Queen's Park Govanhill – Parish Assistant (Glasgow)	
Burton, Rebecca A.	Presbytery Youth and Children's Worker (Argyll)	Rburton@churchofscotland.org.uk
Campbell, Alasdair D. BA	Anan and Gretna churches – Parish Assistant (Annandale and Eskdale)	Alasdair.Campbell@churchofscotland.org.uk
Campbell, Iain	Glasgow: Pollokshaws – Congregation and Parish Transition Worker (Glasgow)	ICampbell@churchofscotland.org.uk
Campbell, Julie	Drumchapel: St Andrew's (Glasgow)	0141-944 3758
Campbell, Neil MA	Dundee: Craigiebank l/w Douglas and Mid Craigie – Youth and Young Adult Development Worker (Dundee)	Neil.Campbell@churchofscotland.org.uk
Craig, Iona S.	Glasgow: Maryhill – Volunteer Development Worker (Glasgow)	ICraig@churchofscotland.org.uk
Crawford, Fiona	Presbytery Strategy Officer (Glasgow)	FCrawford@churchofscotland.org.uk
Crossan, Morag BA	Dalmellington l/w Patna Waterside – Youth and Childen's Worker (Ayr)	MCrossan@churchofscotland.org.uk
Crumlin, Melodie BA PGMgt DipBusMgt	PEEK (Possibilities for Each and Every Kid) – Project Development Manager (Glasgow)	MCrumlin@churchofscotland.org.uk
Currie, Archie	Ardrossan Park – Outreach and Family Worker (Ardrossan)	archie.currie@churchofscotland.org.uk
Douglas, Ian	Motherwell Crosshill l/w St Margaret's – Parish Assistant (Hamilton)	IDouglas@churchofscotland.org.uk
Duncan, Emma	Montrose churches (Angus)	WMacDonald@churchofscotland.org.uk
Dungavel, Marie Claire	Dumbarton: Riverside l/w West, Development Worker (Dumbarton)	01389 742551
Finch, John BA	Gorbals Parish Church – Community Development Worker (Glasgow)	jfinch@churchofscotland.org.uk
Gray, Ian	Arbroath: Knox's l/w St Vigeans – Children and Family Worker (Angus)	IGray@churchofscotland.org.uk
Gunn, Philip BSc	Aberdeen: Mannofield – Parish Assistant (Aberdeen)	PGunn@churchofscotland.org.uk
Haringman, Paul MSc	Culloden: The Barn – Community Worker (Inverness)	Paul.Haringman@churchofscotland.org.uk
Harper, Kirsty BA	Edinburgh: Granton (Edinburgh)	KHarper@churchofscotland.org.uk
Hislop, Donna	Youth Worker (Annandale and Eskdale)	DHislop@churchofscotland.org.uk

Hunter, Jean	Brodick and linked parishes – Parish Assistant (Ardrossan)	JHunter@churchofscotland.org.uk
Hutchison, John BA	Rothes Trinity Parish Grouping (Kirkcaldy)	JHutchison@churchofscotland.org.uk
Hyndman, Graham	Church House, Bridgeton – Youth Worker (Glasgow)	GHyndman@churchofscotland.org.uk
Johnston, Ashley L.	Abercorn with Pardovan, Kinscavil and Winchburgh – Family Development Worker (West Lothian)	AJohnston@churchofscotland.org.uk
Keenan, Deborah	Glasgow: Easterhouse St George's and St Peter's (Glasgow)	DKeenan@churchofscotland.org.uk
Kennedy, Sarah	Kilmarnock New Laigh l/w Onthank – Community Development (Irvine/Kilmarnock)	SKennedy@churchofscotland.org.uk
Kerr, Fiona A.	Dalgety Bay – Parish Assistant (Dunfermline)	FKerr@churchofscotland.org.uk
Knights, Chris (Rev Dr)	Musselburgh churches (Lothian)	revchrisknights@gmail.com
Lightbody, Philip (Rev)	Credo Centre – Mission Development (Aberdeen)	PLightbody@churchofscotland.org.uk
Lynch, David J.	Inverness: Trinity – Children's and Family Worker (Inverness)	DLynch@churchofscotland.org.uk
McDougall, Hilary N.	Presbytery Congregational Facilitator (Glasgow)	HMacDougall@churchofscotland.org.uk
McDowell, Bonnie J.	Alloa: Ludgate and Alloa: St Mungo's – Community Development (Stirling)	BMcDowell@churchofscotland.org.uk
McGreechin, Anne	Glasgow: Cranhill, Ruchazie and Garthamlock and Craigend East Parish Grouping (Glasgow)	AMcGreechin@churchofscotland.org.uk
McIlreavy, Gillian M.	Glasgow: Govan and Linthouse (Glasgow)	GMcIlreavy@churchofscotland.org.uk
McKay, Angus	Glasgow Lodging House Mission (Glasgow)	AMcKay@churchofscotland.org.uk
McLaren, Gordon G.	Thurso: St Peter's and St. Andrew's – Pastoral Assistant (Caithness)	GMcLaren@churchofscotland.org.uk
MacLeod, Penny	Glasgow: Queen's Park Govanhill – Community Research Worker (Glasgow)	0141-423 3654
McQuaid, Ruth Clements	Glasgow: Castlemilk – Community Arts Worker (Glasgow)	0141-634 1480
Middlemass, Deborah	Tranent Cluster (Lothian)	DMiddlemass@churchofscotland.org.uk
Mikelson, (Rev) Heather	Presbytery Mission Development Worker (Gordon)	HMikelson@churchofscotland.org.uk
Miller, Susan	Glasgow: Shettleston New – Youth and Children's Worker (Glasgow)	0141-778 0857
Moodie, David Parish	Assistant, Granton (Edinburgh)	DMoodie@churchofscotland.org.uk
Morrison, Iain J.	Glasgow: Colston Milton – Community Arts Worker	IMorrison@churchofscotland.org.uk
Orr, Gillian	Presbytery Youth Worker (Abernethy)	GOrr@churchofscotland.org.uk
Philip, Darrren BSc	Livingston United – Youth and Children's Worker (West Lothian)	DPhilip@churchofscotland.org.uk
Pringle, Iona	Kennoway St Kenneth's – Pastoral Assistant (Kirkcaldy)	Ipringle@churchofscotland.org.uk
Pryde, Erica	Newbattle Parish Church – Mission and Outreach Co-ordinator (Lothian)	EPryde@churchofscotland.org.uk
Reynolds, Jessica	Inverness Trinity – Children's and Family Worker (Inverness)	07445 491132
Robertson, Douglas S. BEng BA MTh	Kaimes Lockhart Memorial – Team Leader, Project Worker (Edinburgh)	Douglas.Robertson@churchofscotland.org.uk
Robertson, Douglas J.	Baillieston – Children, Young People and Family Worker (Glasgow)	DJRobertson@churchofscotland.org.uk

Safrany, Zoltan (Rev.)	Bathgate: St John's – Parish Development Worker (West Lothian)	ZSafrany@churchofscotland.org.uk
Smith, David J.	Dundee: Lochee – Children and Young Persons Development Worker (Dundee)	DJSmith@churchofscotland.org.uk
Smith, Rebecca	Edinburgh: Richmond Craigmillar – Community Project Worker (Edinburgh)	Rebecca.Smith@churchofscotland.org.uk
Stark, Alastair BA	Glenrothes and Leslie: Youth and Children's Worker (Kirkcaldy)	AStark@churchofscotland.org.uk
Stark, Jennifer MA MATheol	Glenrothes and Leslie – Families and Projects (Kirkcaldy)	JStark@churchofscotland.org.uk
Stigant, Victoria J.	Presbytery Youth Work Facilitator (Gordon)	VStigant@churchofscotland.org.uk
Taylor, Valerie AssocCIPD PGDip	Aberdeen: Torry St Fittick's – Ministry Assistant (Aberdeen)	VTaylor@churchofscotland.org.uk
Temple, Tracy	Dumfries Northwest – Parish Assistant (Dumfries and Kirkcudbright)	TTemple@churchofscotland.org.uk
Thomas, Jay MA BA	Glasgow: St James' (Pollok) (Glasgow)	JThomas@churchofscotland.org.uk
Usher, Eileen	Glasgow: Cranhill, Ruchazie, Garthamlock and Craigend East Parish Grouping (Glasgow)	EUsher@churchofscotland.org.uk
Wellstood, Keith A. PGDip MICG	Perth: Riverside – Community Worker (Perth)	KWellstood@churchofscotland.org.uk
Wilson, Jeanette L.	Parish Assistant (Annandale and Eskdale, Dumfries and Kircudbright)	jlisa@tiscali.co.uk
Wilson, John K.	Presbytery Youth and Children's Worker (Argyll)	
Willis, Mags	Dundee: Chalmers-Ardler (Dundee)	mwillis@churchofscotland.org.uk
Young, Neil J.	Glasgow: St Paul's – Youth Worker (Glasgow)	NYoung@churchofscotland.org.uk

LIST J – OVERSEAS LOCATIONS

AFRICA
MALAWI

Church of Central Africa Presbyterian
Synod of Blantyre

Dr Ruth Shakespeare (2011)   Mulanje Mission Hospital, PO Box 45, Mulanje, Malawi [E-mail: shakespeareruth@gmail.com]   (Tel) 00265 9922 61569 (Fax) 00265 1 467 022

Synod of Livingstonia   CCAP Girls' Secondary School, PO Box 2, Ekwendeni, Malawi   (Tel) 00265 1929 1932

Synod of Nkhoma

Dr David Morton (2009)   Nkhoma Hospital, PO Box 48. Nkhoma, Malawi [E-mail: kuluva2@gmail.com]   (Tel) 00265 9940 74022

ZAMBIA   **United Church of Zambia**

Mr Keith and Mrs Ida Waddell   UCZ Synod, Nationalist Road at Burma Road,
P.O. Box 50122, 15101 Ridgeway,
Lusaka, Zambia
[E-mail: keithida2014@gmail.com]   (Tel) 00260 964 761 039

Ms Jenny Featherstone
(Ecum) (2007)   c/o Chodort Training Centre, PO Box 630451,
Choma, Zambia
[E-mail: jenny.featherstone@googlemail.com]   (Tel) 00260 979 703 130

ASIA
NEPAL

Mr Joel Githinji (2010)   c/o United Mission to Nepal, PO Box 126, Kathmandu, Nepal
(Tel: 00 977 1 4228 118)
[E-mail: joelkavari2003@gmail.com]

Mr Joel Hasvenstein and Mrs Fiona Hasvenstein (2015)   Address and telephone as above

For European, Middle Eastern and other locations, see the Presbyteries of International Charges and Jerusalem (Section 5; 48 and 49, above)

LIST K – OVERSEAS RESIGNED AND RETIRED MISSION PARTNERS (ten or more years' service)

For a full list see: www.churchofscotland.org.uk > Resouces > Yearbook > Section 6-K

LIST L – FULL-TIME WORKPLACE CHAPLAINS

CHIEF EXECUTIVE OFFICER   Rev. Iain McFadzean   iain.mcfadzean@wpcscotland.co.uk   (Mbl) 07969 227696
For a full list of Regional Organisers, Team Leaders and Chaplaincy Locations see: www.churchofscotland.org.uk > Resouces > Yearbook > Section 6-L

LIST M – PRISON CHAPLAINS

ADVISER TO SCOTTISH PRISON SERVICE   Rev. William R. Taylor   SPS HQ, Calton House, 5 Redheughs Rigg, South Gyle,   0131-244 8640
(NATIONAL)   Edinburgh EH12 9DQ
                                                                   [E-mail: bill.taylor@sps.pnn.gov.uk]

For a list of Prisons and Chaplains see: www.churchofscotland.org.uk > Resouces > Yearbook > Section 6-M

LIST N – UNIVERSITY CHAPLAINS

For a list of Universities and Chaplains see: www.churchofscotland.org.uk > Resouces > Yearbook > Section 6-N

LIST O – REPRESENTATIVES ON COUNCIL EDUCATION COMMITTEES

For a full list see: www.churchofscotland.org.uk > Resouces > Yearbook > Section 6-O

LIST P – RETIRED LAY AGENTS

See further: www.churchofscotland.org.uk > Resouces > Yearbook > Section 6-P

LIST Q – MINISTERS ORDAINED FOR SIXTY YEARS AND UPWARDS

For a full list see: www.churchofscotland.org.uk > Resouces > Yearbook > Section 6-Q

LIST R – DECEASED MINISTERS

The Editor has been made aware of the following ministers who have died since the publication of the previous volume of the *Year Book*.

Allison, May McGill	(Glasgow: Househillwood St Christopher's)
Anderson, John Ferguson	(Aberdeen: Mannofield)
Barr, Alexander Craib	(Glasgow: St Nicholas' Cardonald)
Barr, George Kidd	(Uddingston: Viewpark)
Beattie, Walter Gordon	(Arbroath: Old and Abbey)
Brodie, James McNaughton	(Hurlford)
Brown, James	(Abercorn l/w Dalmeny)
Brown, Harry James	(Dundee: Menzieshill)
Craig, William	(Cambusbarron: The Bruce Memorial)
Cumming, David Patrick Low	(Kilmodan and Colintraive)
Dick, Roddy S.	(Auxiliary Minister)
Dundas, Thomas Borland Shearer	(West Kirk of Calder)
Forbes, Iain Macdonald	(Aberdeen: Beechgrove)
Fraser, James Pringle	(Strathaven: Avendale Old and Drumclog)
Glass, Alexander	(Auxiliary Minister)
Greig, James Carruthers Gorrie	(Paisley: St Matthew's)
Hamill, Robert	(Castle Douglas St Ringan's)
Hay, William John Robertson	(Buchanan l/w Drymen)
Hegarty, John Davidson	(Buckie South and West l/w Enzie)
Helon, George Graham	(Barr l/w Dailly)
Herkes, Moira	(Abernethy and Dron and Arngask)
Heriot, Charles Rattray	(Brightons)
Holland, John Crindle	(Strone and Ardentinny)
Hosie, James	(Ardrishaig lw South Knapdale)
Jackson, John Andrew	(Cleland)
Johnston, Robert	(Aberluthnott l/w Laurencekirk)
Keddie, David Allan	(Glasgow: Linthouse St Kenneth's)
Kelly, Isobel Jean Mollins	(Greenock St Margaret's)
Kincaid, James	(Fintray l/w Keithhall l/w Kinellar)
Liddell, Margaret	(Contin)
McDonald, Alexander	(Department of Ministry)
Macdonald, Ian Uidhist	(Tarbolton)
McDonald, William James Gilmour	(Edinburgh: Mayfield)
McGlynn, Moyna	(Glasgow: Govan and Linthouse)
MacKenzie, Donald W	(Auchterarder Barony)
MacLean, Andrew Thomas	(Langbank l/w Port Glasgow St Andrew's)

Mair, John	(Crimond l/w St Fergus)
Morton, Andrew Reyburn	(Board of World Mission and Unity)
Murdoch, William M	(Craigrownie l/w Rosneath St Modan's)
Page, Ruth	(University of Edinburgh)
Patterson, Andrew R M	(Portobello Old)
Reid, William McEwin	(Paris)
Perry, Joseph Baldwin	(Farnell)
Rogers, James Murdoch	(Gibraltar St Andrew's l/w Costa del Sol)
Scott, Allan Davidson	(Culsalmond l/w Daviot l/w Rayne)
Shirra, James	(St Martins l/w Scone: New)
Silcox, John Richard	(Blantyre Old)
Simpson, Neil Alexander	(Glasgow: Yoker Old l/w Yoker St Matthew's)
Sutherland, Elizabeth Wylie	(Balornock North l/w Barmulloch)
Thane, Markus	(Cumbrae l/w Largs St John's)
Thomson, James Mercier	(Elgin St Giles' and St Columba's South (Assoc.))
Wilkie, James Ross	(Penpont Keir and Tynron)

SECTION 7

Legal Names and Scottish Charity Numbers for Individual Congregations

(All congregations in Scotland, and congregations furth of Scotland which are registered with OSCR, the Office of the Scottish Charity Regulator)

For a complete list of legal names see:
www.churchofscotland.org.uk > Resources > Yearbook > Section 7

Further information

All documents, as defined in the Charities References in Documents (Scotland) Regulations 2007, must specify the Charity Number, Legal Name of the congregation, any other name by which the congregation is commonly known and the fact that it is a Charity. For more information, please refer to the Law Department circular on the Regulations on the Church of Scotland website.

www.churchofscotland.org.uk > Resources > Subjects > Law Department Circulars > 'Charity Law'

SECTION 8

Church Buildings: Ordnance Survey National Grid References

Please go to: www.churchofscotland.org.uk > Resources > Yearbook > Section 8

SECTION 9

A
Discontinued Parish
and Congregational Names

The purpose of this list, compiled by Roy Pinkerton, is to assist those who are trying to identify the present-day successor of some former parish or congregation whose name is now wholly out of use and which can therefore no longer be easily traced.

Where the former name has not disappeared completely, and the whereabouts of the former parish or congregation may therefore be easily established by reference to the name of some existing parish, the former name has not been included in this list.

Present-day names, in the right-hand column of the list, may be found in the 'Index of Parishes and Places' in the print edition of the Year Book.

The list, with explanatory notes, may be found at:

www.churchofscotland.org.uk/Resources/Yearbook > Section 9

B
Recent Readjustment and Other
Congregational Changes

This is a list, also compiled by Roy Pinkerton, of parish adjustments made by presbyteries since mid-2014.

(see following pages)

B. READJUSTMENT AND OTHER CONGREGATIONAL CHANGES

The following list incorporates all instances of readjustment (i.e. union, linkage and dissolution) and certain other congregational changes, such as a change of name, which have taken place over the last two years (i.e. since the publication of the 2014–15 Year Book).

Edinburgh	**Edinburgh: Albany Deaf Church of Edinburgh** now a Mission Initiative of **Edinburgh: St Andrew's and St George's West**
	Edinburgh: Craigentinny St Christopher's and **Edinburgh: New Restalrig** united as **Edinburgh: Willowbrae**
	Edinburgh: Gorgie Dalry and **Edinburgh: Stenhouse St Aidan's** united as **Edinburgh: Gorgie Dalry Stenhouse**
	Edinburgh: Kaimes Lockhart Memorial renamed **Edinburgh: Gracemount**
West Lothian	**Livingston Ecumenical Parish** renamed **Livingston United Parish**
Lothian	**Bolton and Saltoun** and **Yester** united as **Yester, Bolton and Saltoun**
Duns	**Ayton and Burnmouth, Foulden and Mordington** and **Grantshouse and Houndwood and Reston** united as **Ayton and District Churches**
	Bonkyl and Edrom, Duns and **Langton and Lammermuir Kirk** united as **Duns and District Parishes**
	Coldstream, Ladykirk and Whitsome and **Swinton** united as **Coldstream and District Parishes**
	Eccles and **Leitholm** united as **Eccles and Leitholm**
	Fogo and Swinton linked with **Ladykirk and Whitsome** linked with **Leitholm**: linkage severed
	Fogo and **Swinton**: union dissolved
Jedburgh	**Kelso Country Churches** linked with **Kelso: Old and Sprouston**: linkage severed
	Kelso Country Churches linked with **Oxnam**
Annandale and Eskdale	**Dalton** and **Hightae** united as **Dalton and Hightae**
Dumfries and Kirkcudbright	**Balmaghie** linked with **Tarff and Twynholm**: linkage severed
	Balmaghie and **Crossmichael and Parton** united as **Crossmichael, Parton and Balmaghie**
	Borgue and **Gatehouse of Fleet** united as **Gatehouse and Borgue**
	Closeburn linked with **Kirkmahoe**

	Gatehouse and Borgue linked with **Tarff and Twynholm**
Wigtown and Stranraer	**Kirkinner** linked with **Mochrum** linked with **Sorbie**
	New Luce and **Old Luce** united as **Luce Valley**
Ayr	**Craigie Symington** linked with **Prestwick: South**
Ardrossan	**Fairlie** linked with **Largs: St Columba's**
Lanark	**The United Church of Carstairs and Carstairs Junction** renamed **Carstairs**
Greenock and Paisley	**Kilbarchan: East** and **Kilbarchan: West** united as **Kilbarchan**
	Paisley: St James dissolved
Glasgow	**Glasgow: Easterhouse St George's and St Peter's** and **Glasgow: Lochwood** united as **Glasgow: Easterhouse**
	Glasgow: High Carntyne and **Glasgow: South Carntyne** united as **Glasgow: Carntyne**
	Glasgow: Penilee St Andrew and **Glasgow: St Nicholas' Cardonald** united as **Glasgow: St Andrew and St Nicholas**
	Glasgow: Shettleston Old and **Glasgow: Victoria Tollcross** united as **Glasgow: Causeway, Tollcross**
Hamilton	**Airdrie: Broomknoll** and **Airdrie: Flowerhill** united as **Airdrie: Cairnlea**
	Airdrie: Cairnlea linked with **Calderbank**
	Airdrie: High linked with **Caldercruix and Longriggend**
	Blantyre: Livingstone Memorial linked with **Blantyre: St Andrew's**
	Chapelhall linked with **Kirk o' Shotts**
	Cleland linked with **Wishaw: St Mark's**
	Coatbridge: Blairhill Dundyvan linked with **Coatbridge: Middle**
	Hamilton: Gilmour and Whitehill linked with **Hamilton: West**
Dumbarton	**Helensburgh: Park** and **Helensburgh: St Andrew's Kirk** united as **Helensburgh**
Argyll	**Skipness** linked with **Tarbert, Loch Fyne and Kilberry**
Falkirk	**Denny: Old** linked with **Haggs**
St Andrews	**Boarhills and Dunino** linked with **St Andrews: Holy Trinity**
	Creich, Flisk and Kimany linked with **Monimail**: linkage severed
	Cupar: Old and St Michael of Tarvit linked with **Monimail**

Dunkeld and Meigle	**Amulree and Strathbraan** united with **Dunkeld** as **Dunkeld**
	Blair Atholl and Struan linked with **Tenandry**: linkage severed
	Blair Atholl and Struan linked with **Braes of Rannoch** linked with **Foss and Rannoch**
Angus	**Inchbrayock** and **Montrose: Melville South** united as **Montrose: South and Ferryden**
Aberdeen	**Aberdeen: Cove** (New Charge Development) dissolved
Kincardine and Deeside	**Banchory-Devenick and Maryculter/Cookney** renamed **Maryculter Trinity**
Buchan	**Gardenstown** dissolved
	Peterhead: Old and **Peterhead: Trinity** united as **Peterhead: New**
Moray	**Bellie** and **Speymouth** united as **Bellie and Speymouth**
	Lossiemouth: St Gerardine's High linked with **Lossiemouth: St James**
Lochcarron-Skye	**Glenelg and Kintail** and **Lochalsh** united as **Glenelg, Kintail and Lochalsh**
Uist	**Benbecula** linked with **Carinish**
Orkney	**North Ronaldsay** linked with **Sanday**: linkage severed
Shetland	**Fetlar** and **Unst** united as **Unst and Fetlar**

SECTION 10

Congregational
Statistics
2015

Compiled by Sandy Gemmill

CHURCH OF SCOTLAND
Comparative Statistics: 1975–2015

	2015	2005	1995	1985	1975
Communicants	363,597	520,940	698,552	870,527	1,041,772
Elders	30,301	41,218	46,010	47,485	49,430

NOTES ON CONGREGATIONAL STATISTICS

Com   Number of communicants at 31 December 2015.

Eld   Number of elders at 31 December 2015.

G   Membership of the Guild including Young Woman's Group and others as recorded on the 2015 annual return submitted to the Guild Office.

In 15   Ordinary General Income for 2015. Ordinary General Income consists of members' offerings, contributions from congregational organisations, regular fund-raising events, income from investments, deposits and so on. This figure does not include extraordinary or special income, or income from special collections and fund-raising for other charities.

M&M   Final amount allocated to congregations after allowing for Presbytery-approved amendments up to 31 December 2015, but before deducting stipend endowments and normal allowances given for stipend purposes in a vacancy.

–18   This figure shows 'the number of children and young people aged 17 years and under who are involved in the life of the congregation'.

(NB: Figures may not be available for new charges created or for congregations which have entered into readjustment late in 2015 or during 2016. Figures might also not be available for congregations which failed to submit the appropriate schedule.)

Congregation	Com	Eld	G	In 15	M&M	–18
1. Edinburgh						
Albany Deaf Church of Edinburgh	71	-	-	-	-	-
Balerno	574	73	34	131,472	71,538	54
Barclay Viewforth	326	30	-	161,015	119,717	50
Blackhall St Columba's	722	68	29	188,115	106,479	35
Bristo Memorial Craigmillar	59	7	-	61,007	30,752	45
Broughton St Mary's	196	27	-	58,067	49,176	29
Canongate	360	35	-	105,030	74,466	15
Carrick Knowe	369	50	61	58,074	39,054	309
Colinton	870	58	-	190,979	120,878	100
Corstorphine: Craigsbank	475	27	-	107,853	62,398	77
Corstorphine: Old	413	42	50	117,330	71,966	75
Corstorphine: St Anne's	353	55	63	112,002	59,837	28
Corstorphine: St Ninian's	722	83	60	179,183	94,386	55
Craigentinny St Christopher's	86	10	-	24,812	23,211	-
Craiglockhart	434	48	31	156,717	100,104	40
Craigmillar Park	211	17	24	81,412	48,565	2
Cramond	1,025	92	-	265,407	151,373	84
Currie	515	34	68	154,795	89,172	105
Dalmeny	94	12	-	28,653	20,359	6
Queensferry	528	43	50	123,123	65,091	160
Davidson's Mains	473	75	39	208,020	115,069	80
Dean	130	19	-	61,147	37,439	5
Drylaw	96	18	-	20,054	11,330	5
Duddingston	456	39	31	118,282	70,029	220
Fairmilehead	545	58	30	107,966	72,573	68
Gorgie Dalry	205	21	-	87,260	60,255	27
Granton	197	17	-	51,477	21,204	34
Greenbank	729	76	33	269,225	141,747	73
Greenside	136	31	-	-	29,988	-
Greyfriars Kirk	299	38	-	228,829	95,757	22
High (St Giles')	489	33	-	279,881	177,089	16
Holyrood Abbey	34	1	-	-	82,688	-
Holy Trinity	225	29	-	191,672	89,562	95
Inverleith St Serf's	366	38	22	110,657	86,186	33
Juniper Green	318	27	-	99,451	65,047	40
Kaimes Lockhart Memorial	45	5	-	24,046	1,635	-
Liberton	717	73	46	209,858	119,802	83
Kirkliston	240	31	49	94,791	61,100	37
Leith: North	223	25	-	87,494	50,311	47
Leith: St Andrew's	206	24	-	87,706	52,721	20
Leith: South	355	64	-	149,783	83,020	93
Leith: Wardie	519	52	40	175,281	85,588	113
Liberton Northfield	182	10	19	44,659	34,219	53
London Road	174	27	25	72,050	39,294	9
Marchmont St Giles'	227	33	25	91,314	73,195	66
Mayfield Salisbury	526	51	-	262,665	132,096	35
Morningside	437	60	17	198,640	118,449	91
Morningside United	141	15	-	68,008	-	8

Congregation	Com	Eld	G	In 15	M&M	–18
Murrayfield	526	47	-	159,064	85,672	74
Newhaven	158	16	32	120,253	47,539	123
New Restalrig	67	5	-	38,327	31,723	-
Old Kirk and Muihouse	104	15	-	39,772	15,179	17
Palmerston Place	385	39	-	167,817	100,458	100
Pilrig St Paul's	228	18	24	42,746	31,189	3
Polwarth	190	22	14	93,483	56,774	19
Portobello and Joppa	898	78	90	223,006	159,232	183
Priestfield	120	20	20	84,510	40,180	48
Ratho	192	18	-	46,460	25,553	9
Reid Memorial	295	18	-	92,990	64,263	38
Richmond Craigmillar	91	12	-	27,228	5,387	12
St Andrew's and St George's West	304	45	-	285,809	162,381	64
St Andrew's Clermiston	213	13	-	-	34,176	14
St Catherine's Argyle	108	5	-	59,452	96,185	6
St Cuthbert's	316	49	-	145,566	91,315	15
St David's Broomhouse	127	12	-	32,443	15,880	23
St John's Colinton Mains	232	19	-	54,883	44,881	55
St Margaret's	250	32	18	51,054	32,068	28
St Martin's	90	12	-	21,709	3,778	8
St Michael's	337	27	32	65,034	52,046	13
St Nicholas' Sighthill	347	30	14	45,296	23,358	19
St Stephen's Comely Bank	196	10	-	13,344	82,081	25
Slateford Longstone	214	15	37	48,368	27,384	30
Stenhouse St Aidan's	60	6	-	19,018	16,752	2
Stockbridge	194	21	-	87,698	57,449	14
Tron Kirk (Gilmerton and Moredun)	91	10	-	-	6,661	138

2. West Lothian

Abercorn	66	9	-	14,393	10,642	-
Pardovan, Kingscavil and Winchburgh	268	27	11	65,106	42,781	207
Armadale	522	43	33	83,773	45,432	201
Avonbridge	79	7	-	13,905	6,842	5
Torphichen	233	14	-	-	32,399	15
Bathgate: Boghall	242	28	23	88,666	46,826	176
Bathgate: High	489	35	31	87,635	62,209	60
Bathgate: St John's	351	26	35	66,463	39,643	118
Blackburn and Seafield	398	30	-	78,903	43,868	80
Blackridge	69	5	-	22,795	10,346	-
Harthill: St Andrew's	181	8	28	57,935	33,935	81
Breich Valley	174	11	25	32,543	22,640	12
Broxburn	352	33	44	72,794	44,643	157
Fauldhouse: St Andrew's	183	13	-	54,189	34,030	12
Kirknewton and East Calder	338	34	26	109,901	68,630	74
Kirk of Calder	538	42	23	83,956	48,625	66
Linlithgow: St Michael's	1,327	112	54	311,416	172,203	169
Linlithgow: St Ninian's Craigmailen	412	40	54	74,606	44,023	83
Livingston United	310	25	-	-6,573	-	167
Livingston: Old	343	39	22	87,924	55,373	40
Polbeth Harwood	172	19	-	32,192	16,677	7

Congregation	Com	Eld	G	In 15	M&M	–18
West Kirk of Calder	249	18	14	57,517	42,529	24
Strathbrock	286	30	20	99,903	69,697	75
Uphall South	204	25	-	61,757	34,608	25
Whitburn: Brucefield	225	19	19	87,056	49,017	130
Whitburn: South	354	27	30	73,188	48,198	97

3. Lothian

Aberlady	201	21	-	37,389	20,285	6
Gullane	359	28	23	55,424	37,123	20
Athelstaneford	205	14	-	26,420	17,074	12
Whitekirk and Tyninghame	134	14	-	-	22,139	15
Belhaven	630	46	61	84,282	50,326	36
Spott	103	7	-	20,542	9,008	4
Bilston	89	3	13	12,125	4,680	2
Glencorse	298	13	20	-	15,137	5
Roslin	228	8	-	26,868	16,778	6
Bonnyrigg	648	60	41	102,740	67,859	20
Cockenzie and Port Seton: Chalmers M'rl	188	29	30	-	51,814	88
Cockenzie and Port Seton: Old	235	22	24	-1,590	32,213	20
Cockpen and Carrington	200	23	39	29,972	20,035	38
Lasswade and Rosewell	280	19	-	28,478	23,078	8
Dalkeith: St John's and King's Park	463	35	25	118,433	61,757	65
Dalkeith: St Nicholas' Buccleuch	365	20	-	66,037	36,278	9
Dirleton	224	17	-	-	33,714	16
North Berwick: Abbey	274	30	37	90,085	53,543	12
Dunbar	381	23	25	109,089	70,682	81
Dunglass	286	13	-	30,627	21,469	-
Garvald and Morham	41	10	-	-	7,315	14
Haddington: West	220	21	31	54,967	40,637	22
Gladsmuir	176	12	-	-	16,212	25
Longniddry	348	43	39	76,608	48,128	38
Gorebridge	117	11	-	118,403	58,493	98
Haddington: St Mary's	514	42	-	-	57,310	69
Howgate	40	6	-	22,748	10,397	8
Penicuik: South	104	11	-	-	42,567	20
Humbie	69	8	-	-	13,519	12
Yester, Bolton and Saltoun	288	28	-	43,145	34,750	44
Loanhead	304	24	28	-	30,551	42
Musselburgh: Northesk	316	26	38	-	40,658	73
Musselburgh: St Andrew's High	292	27	22	78,826	41,064	-
Musselburgh: St Clement's & St Ninian's	205	13	-	21,143	18,629	-
Musselburgh: St Michael's Inveresk	376	41	-	83,007	50,104	12
Newbattle	391	35	18	82,731	50,446	235
Newton	112	3	-	21,472	13,356	15
North Berwick: St Andrew Blackadder	614	36	29	160,744	84,695	95
Ormiston	152	11	24	44,097	24,225	21
Pencaitland	166	5	-	-	29,651	19
Penicuik: North	439	38	-	75,965	47,844	62
Penicuik: St Mungo's	328	20	18	62,188	43,690	7
Prestonpans: Prestongrange	263	23	16	54,524	34,841	17

Congregation	Com	Eld	G	In 15	M&M	–18
Tranent	233	13	30	54,494	32,973	21
Traprain	425	31	36	77,409	48,678	48
Tyne Valley Parish	315	23	-	76,341	53,000	40

4. Melrose and Peebles

Ashkirk	37	5	-	9,807	5,313	1
Selkirk	460	19	-	65,761	43,341	29
Bowden and Melrose	876	67	33	116,421	76,625	45
Broughton, Glenholm and Kilbucho	143	10	26	18,557	11,263	-
Skirling	62	5	-	8,265	5,569	-
Stobo and Drumelzier	87	8	-	21,120	11,791	3
Tweedsmuir	-	-	-	5,969	5,207	-
Caddonfoot	-	-	-	18,686	10,159	-
Galashiels: Trinity	436	-	34	61,713	46,214	-
Carlops	50	13	-	23,334	9,714	30
Kirkurd and Newlands	90	-	13	19,434	15,850	-
West Linton: St Andrew's	216	-	-	37,941	23,546	-
Channelkirk & Lauder	412	-	23	-	44,668	-
Earlston	383	23	10	45,568	33,401	48
Eddleston	106	5	6	-	8,835	11
Peebles: Old	485	-	-	-	66,932	-
Ettrick and Yarrow	187	18	-	41,149	33,046	12
Galashiels: Old and St Paul's	260	26	28	69,698	40,250	19
Galashiels: St John's	200	-	-	39,764	27,987	-
Innerleithen, Traquair and Walkerburn	370	28	37	56,316	37,343	30
Lyne and Manor	107	7	-	32,524	18,032	9
Peebles: St Andrew's Leckie	561	-	-	111,476	62,001	-
Maxton and Mertoun	122	11	-	12,826	10,779	6
Newtown	133	10	-	17,414	8,848	1
St Boswells	192	24	24	32,288	22,422	4
Stow: St Mary of Wedale and Heriot	182	12	-	34,275	23,055	10

5. Duns

Ayton and Burnmouth	154	9	-	-	12,742	6
Foulden and Mordington	68	4	-	5,215	6,766	-
Grantshouse and Houndwood and Reston	90	6	10	10,405	10,504	3
Berwick-upon-Tweed: St Andrew's						
Wallace Green & Lowick	324	20	23	-	31,770	23
Chirnside	87	9	16	15,254	13,447	-
Hutton and Fishwick and Paxton	64	6	10	16,141	11,329	1
Coldingham and St Abb's	74	11	-	37,586	24,664	20
Eyemouth	127	19	29	37,973	19,278	45
Coldstream	341	28	-	46,184	31,293	24
Eccles	77	11	16	12,428	8,323	2
Duns	-	-	38	67,499	39,247	-
Langton and Lammermuir Kirk	129	10	20	31,511	30,954	-
Fogo and Swinton	55	6	-	9,148	9,778	2
Ladykirk and Whitsome	-	-	-	-	13,203	-
Leitholm	70	7	-	11,673	6,614	-
Gordon: St Michael's	63	7	-	8,009	6,124	4

Congregation	Com	Eld	G	In 15	M&M	–18
Greenlaw	92	7	10	18,937	11,921	-
Legerwood	60	6	-	12,219	5,376	5
Westruther	40	7	14	7,695	4,506	32

6. Jedburgh

Ale and Teviot United	410	27	20	45,011	38,413	14
Cavers and Kirkton	118	8	-	11,135	9,628	-
Hawick: Trinity	731	28	50	56,906	30,572	60
Cheviot Churches	352	23	30	73,405	54,270	50
Hawick: Burnfoot	87	14	10	25,922	19,171	101
Hawick: St Mary's and Old	412	20	21	37,901	29,267	-
Hawick: Teviot and Roberton	284	8	8	47,734	35,817	26
Hawick: Wilton	348	25	-	43,911	32,552	36
Teviothead	71	5	-	4,630	3,793	5
Hobkirk and Southdean	162	13	16	11,634	17,156	12
Ruberslaw	252	19	12	37,342	23,663	12
Jedburgh: Old and Trinity	641	17	31	72,440	51,211	-
Kelso Country Churches	209	15	19	31,116	33,391	15
Kelso: Old and Sprouston	482	30	-	56,501	35,661	8
Kelso: North and Ednam	978	67	30	138,226	88,983	9
Oxnam	125	13	-	14,222	6,684	6

7. Annandale and Eskdale

Annan: Old	365	46	39	64,656	42,487	20
Dornock	110	10	-	-	6,407	-
Annan: St Andrew's	619	45	59	66,030	36,916	85
Brydekirk	54	4	-	9,088	4,788	-
Applegarth, Sibbaldbie and Johnstone	127	8	8	9,904	9,138	-
Lochmaben	259	20	42	61,049	35,378	6
Canonbie United	94	15	-	35,091	-	21
Liddesdale	112	7	22	27,943	23,474	5
Dalton	104	7	-	16,643	6,999	3
Hightae	80	3	-	-	6,058	-
St Mungo	85	10	13	16,254	8,952	-
Gretna: Old, Gretna: St Andrew's Half Morton & Kirkpatrick Fleming	317	29	27	-	38,458	70
Hoddom, Kirtle-Eaglesfield and Middlebie	214	20	23	30,801	21,163	28
Kirkpatrick Juxta	105	6	-	10,771	7,194	1
Moffat: St Andrew's	358	32	24	71,118	44,369	70
Wamphray	55	6	-	8,898	4,024	8
Langholm Eskdalemuir Ewes and Westerkirk	450	27	15	84,856	40,724	35
Lockerbie: Dryfesdale, Hutton and Corrie	730	42	28	80,405	43,369	19
The Border Kirk	312	45	34	62,437	38,710	35
Tundergarth	32	7	-	10,932	4,944	-

8. Dumfries and Kirkcudbright

Balmaclellan and Kells	62	6	12	15,671	15,056	7
Carsphairn	92	11	-	12,924	6,449	6
Dalry	78	12	16	29,578	10,900	1
Caerlaverock	106	7	-	11,376	6,952	2

Congregation	Com	Eld	G	In 15	M&M	–18
Dumfries: St Mary's-Greyfriars	414	31	33	70,143	43,780	6
Castle Douglas	371	22	11	83,242	39,234	10
The Bengairn Parishes	-	-	-	29,235	24,393	-
Closeburn	187	13	-	-	16,717	21
Colvend, Southwick and Kirkbean	224	17	30	88,340	55,054	-
Corsock and Kirkpatrick Durham	87	13	10	24,065	14,603	11
Crossmichael, Parton and Balmaghie	209	11	17	20,347	25,166	-
Cummertrees, Mouswald and Ruthwell	192	21	-	15,046	19,348	-
Dalbeattie and Kirkgunzeon	-	-	53	56,167	36,306	-
Urr	182	10	-	-	12,691	-
Dumfries: Maxwelltown West	589	43	36	87,469	61,521	118
Dumfries: Northwest	360	14	-	35,860	27,227	9
Dumfries: St George's	509	45	36	127,616	70,180	70
Dumfries: St Michael's and South	746	44	28	100,305	58,027	113
Dumfries: Troqueer	261	21	22	95,031	58,366	68
Dunscore	197	19	8	30,331	26,551	-
Glencairn and Moniaive	166	14	-	39,673	25,275	8
Durisdeer	149	6	-	22,663	11,281	9
Penpont, Keir and Tynron	158	10	-	-	17,480	10
Thornhill	142	10	10	28,380	25,806	-
Gatehouse and Borgue	294	20	15	53,196	31,956	10
Tarff and Twynholm	140	13	24	21,797	18,307	30
Irongray, Lochrutton and Terregles	203	24	-	-	22,679	-
Kirkconnel	258	16	-	-	23,941	5
Kirkcudbright	510	24	-	-	54,383	50
Kirkmahoe	292	14	13	24,159	19,524	-
Kirkmichael, Tinwald & Torthorwald	427	38	27	55,113	42,734	10
Lochend and New Abbey	200	16	11	29,155	15,919	-
Sanquhar: St Bride's	397	24	15	44,463	26,862	37
9. Wigtown and Stranraer						
Ervie Kirkcolm	181	12	-	21,458	14,558	12
Leswalt	267	18	-	31,739	16,404	5
Glasserton and Isle of Whithorn	100	6	-	-	8,356	-
Whithorn: St Ninian's Priory	309	9	22	-500	27,411	24
Inch	218	-	8	18,674	14,995	56
Portpatrick	216	9	23	-	15,579	-
Stranraer: Trinty	523	42	39	84,872	71,113	51
Kirkcowan	114	9	-	35,587	19,708	10
Wigtown	161	14	10	33,816	23,023	40
Kirkinner	128	8	10	15,729	8,961	-
Mochrum	244	17	27	25,580	18,345	30
Sorbie	115	10	-	-	11,872	-
Kirkmabreck	128	12	22	18,081	11,570	-
Monigaff	233	16	-	32,034	22,294	22
Kirkmaiden	209	22	-	27,732	23,230	24
Stoneykirk	298	20	15	-	28,248	6
New Luce	86	6	-	7,657	6,610	-
Old Luce	110	16	27	40,948	25,303	23

Congregation	Com	Eld	G	In 15	M&M	–18
Penninghame	409	17	19	-	52,096	24
Stranraer: High Kirk	543	37	29	77,162	51,282	166

10. Ayr

Congregation	Com	Eld	G	In 15	M&M	–18
Alloway	1,144	-	-	219,068	119,095	-
Annbank	263	17	15	31,261	22,694	-
Tarbolton	448	28	22	57,262	35,418	14
Auchinleck	327	16	20	-	29,009	22
Catrine	112	11	18	23,822	16,321	-
Ayr: Auld Kirk of Ayr	504	60	35	78,089	53,152	-
Ayr: Castlehill	597	-	49	100,135	65,197	-
Ayr: Newton Wallacetown	390	47	52	117,341	73,843	33
Ayr: St Andrew's	312	-	12	89,453	45,584	-
Ayr: St Columba	1,306	116	92	299,571	138,022	80
Ayr: St James'	397	-	38	76,716	45,355	-
Ayr: St Leonard's	513	-	31	79,057	46,323	-
Dalrymple	126	-	-	25,822	16,105	-
Ayr: St Quivox	233	23	13	42,387	34,903	7
Ballantrae	241	-	21	39,534	25,262	-
St Colmon (Arnsheen Barrhill and Colmonell)	226	-	-	20,070	17,045	-
Barr	66	-	-	1,646	3,085	-
Dailly	129	8	-	12,555	11,023	-
Girvan: South	308	-	27	34,110	22,917	-
Coylton	323	-	-	40,076	26,920	-
Drongan: The Schaw Kirk	186	-	16	31,618	23,208	-
Craigie and Symington	-	-	22	54,226	43,010	-
Prestwick: South	292	36	27	89,755	56,882	85
Crosshill	173	-	20	14,138	10,494	-
Maybole	324	29	24	73,574	41,768	10
Dalmellington	214	-	-	33,679	28,822	-
Patna: Waterside	135	-	-	24,892	15,919	-
Dundonald	456	46	50	-	52,860	97
Fisherton	106	9	-	10,359	8,092	-
Kirkoswald	212	13	20	31,415	18,354	5
Girvan: North (Old and St Andrew's)	662	-	-	71,073	42,867	-
Kirkmichael	208	16	20	22,223	15,078	5
Straiton: St Cuthbert's	169	9	14	22,941	13,484	10
Lugar	159	-	16	19,259	9,523	-
Old Cumnock: Old	350	-	31	64,253	46,434	-
Mauchline	435	-	39	71,308	54,208	-
Sorn	144	-	14	22,137	13,487	-
Monkton and Prestwick: North	313	29	38	-	59,674	18
Muirkirk	181	-	-	20,593	13,517	-
Old Cumnock: Trinity	328	17	35	51,851	39,173	21
New Cumnock	469	32	29	85,683	51,003	122
Ochiltree	240	20	19	31,927	23,322	22
Stair	213	14	17	31,855	25,693	20
Prestwick: Kingcase	651	-	71	121,021	82,178	-
Prestwick: St Nicholas'	600	73	55	118,244	74,912	170

Congregation	Com	Eld	G	In 15	M&M	–18
Troon: Old	922	60	-	131,628	81,854	160
Troon: Portland	515	44	29	135,793	77,190	15
Troon: St Meddan's	768	86	43	156,292	101,571	107

11. Irvine and Kilmarnock

Caldwell	223	16	-	68,786	40,610	7
Dunlop	387	37	26	84,523	39,427	42
Crosshouse	280	34	16	55,498	37,055	70
Darvel	330	27	35	57,064	29,320	45
Dreghorn and Springside	470	44	29	84,489	51,402	42
Fenwick	323	27	30	60,820	35,809	30
Galston	617	57	58	98,437	66,458	44
Hurlford	337	26	28	68,870	42,227	8
Irvine: Fullarton	354	43	50	98,148	62,149	149
Irvine: Girdle Toll	156	16	20	-	20,349	109
Irvine: Mure	302	29	19	69,717	42,575	34
Irvine: Old	384	23	16	-	50,878	8
Irvine: Relief Bourtreehill	224	23	28	61,292	26,590	10
Irvine: St Andrew's	266	14	32	62,632	34,866	30
Kilmarnock: Kay Park	527	73	32	-7,159	85,324	24
Kilmarnock: New Laigh Kirk	847	77	60	199,793	124,536	156
Kilmarnock: Riccarton	236	26	20	67,923	43,594	56
Kilmarnock: St Andrew's & St Marnock's	818	96	36	175,952	103,601	445
Kilmarnock: St John's Onthank	251	22	20	-	32,216	75
Kilmarnock: St Kentigern's	278	23	-	50,859	36,028	84
Kilmarnock: South	255	7	23	37,777	28,840	26
Kilmaurs: St Maur's Glencairn	294	15	25	51,176	31,151	-
Newmilns: Loudoun	181	12	-	39,805	38,964	2
Stewarton: John Knox	267	22	24	100,699	53,492	50
Stewarton: St Columba's	409	38	44	75,414	50,643	113

12. Ardrossan

Ardrossan: Park	391	25	44	71,201	44,278	18
Ardrossan and Saltcoats Kirkgate	254	40	29	74,902	56,664	5
Beith	747	57	24	109,869	63,415	31
Brodick	130	17	-	54,568	32,108	88
Corrie	41	4	-	21,226	10,014	-
Lochranza and Pirnmill	67	13	10	25,810	11,852	4
Shiskine	69	11	10	31,125	21,037	11
Cumbrae	232	25	47	47,063	36,561	57
Largs: St John's	704	45	52	148,598	77,503	26
Dalry: St Margaret's	519	57	33	-	85,028	90
Dalry: Trinity	185	16	-	82,994	50,036	174
Fairlie	237	25	43	-	48,485	11
Largs: St Columba's	359	35	62	92,055	60,337	22
Kilbirnie: Auld Kirk	308	34	-	62,366	40,148	14
Kilbirnie: St Columba's	523	32	-	62,988	37,005	75
Kilmory	34	7	-	12,134	7,406	-
Lamlash	96	13	26	40,017	20,361	10
Kilwinning: Mansefield Trinity	205	15	30	54,806	29,777	63

Congregation	Com	Eld	G	In 15	M&M	–18
Kilwinning: Old	563	51	44	113,835	66,273	23
Largs: Clark Memorial	743	84	65	139,113	82,281	35
Saltcoats: North	278	24	21	59,238	27,579	40
Saltcoats: St Cuthbert's	264	32	15	84,924	49,916	149
Stevenston: Ardeer	246	32	26	40,888	29,349	159
Stevenston: Livingstone	266	33	27	53,139	34,305	12
Stevenston: High	237	19	20	90,225	54,704	37
West Kilbride	449	46	27	114,331	75,578	31
Whiting Bay and Kildonan	88	10	-	42,847	26,695	6

13. Lanark

Congregation	Com	Eld	G	In 15	M&M	–18
Biggar	542	25	32	-	55,134	25
Black Mount	64	6	15	-	10,285	-
Cairngryffe	155	14	11	25,635	20,941	17
Libberton and Quothquan	84	13	-	15,740	8,007	16
Symington	185	19	22	37,778	22,053	7
Carluke: Kirkton	751	51	29	132,189	70,876	355
Carluke: St Andrew's	200	13	18	51,448	32,646	27
Carluke: St John's	617	43	30	82,776	57,078	74
Carnwath	130	11	17	-	21,441	-
Carstairs	190	19	18	39,820	31,993	116
Coalburn	119	8	15	17,992	11,996	12
Lesmahagow: Old	375	21	12	79,130	54,331	27
Crossford	163	6	-	35,854	17,733	70
Kirkfieldbank	77	6	-	16,635	9,087	-
Forth: St Paul's	336	24	40	71,493	35,896	80
Kirkmuirhill	142	5	44	66,555	68,019	24
Lanark: Greyfriars	541	49	32	95,673	54,063	178
Lanark: St Nicholas'	495	41	23	99,111	64,395	58
Law	177	9	-	-180	32,181	116
Lesmahagow: Abbeygreen	173	16	-	62,528	53,054	165
The Douglas Valley Church	304	24	32	54,668	36,503	5
Upper Clyde	201	14	21	30,316	21,284	13

14. Greenock and Paisley

Congregation	Com	Eld	G	In 15	M&M	–18
Barrhead: Bourock	440	41	40	92,503	57,225	253
Barrhead: St Andrew's	437	45	40	141,236	90,879	218
Bishopton	607	45	-	106,550	56,908	58
Bridge of Weir: Freeland	390	53	-	-	80,739	74
Bridge of Weir: St Machar's Ranfurly	345	33	32	93,834	61,355	105
Elderslie Kirk	450	45	50	99,324	71,636	159
Erskine	346	33	44	101,174	62,978	257
Gourock: Old Gourock and Ashton	661	56	27	-	73,271	224
Gourock: St John's	442	65	14	121,018	74,434	306
Greenock: East End	56	-	-	10,538	3,234	-
Greenock: Mount Kirk	310	-	-	58,380	42,665	-
Greenock: Lyle Kirk	768	51	21	-	97,644	111
Greenock: St Margaret's	159	29	-	39,266	16,493	18
Greenock: St Ninian's	229	17	-	-	17,818	44
Greenock: Wellpark Mid Kirk	503	51	12	-	67,902	80

Congregation	Com	Eld	G	In 15	M&M	–18
Greenock: Westburn	647	92	30	129,679	80,975	106
Houston and Killellan	663	62	70	147,426	88,467	160
Howwood	147	10	20	45,641	28,472	14
Lochwinnoch	96	12	-	39,535	27,087	156
Inchinnan	309	27	25	-	42,664	64
Inverkip	300	32	28	90,672	38,455	45
Skelmorlie and Wemyss Bay	259	39	-	85,040	54,981	12
Johnstone: High	228	32	32	92,128	61,770	152
Johnstone: St Andrew's Trinity	208	28	22	41,956	30,327	78
Johnstone: St Paul's	393	60	-	77,497	48,189	139
Kilbarchan: East	336	38	26	72,424	45,386	48
Kilbarchan: West	354	35	-	-	59,759	20
Kilmacolm: Old	406	43	-	138,228	73,935	20
Kilmacolm: St Columba	171	15	-	90,546	58,762	4
Langbank	135	13	-	37,002	22,318	16
Port Glasgow: St Andrew's	458	63	31	83,435	49,387	310
Linwood	204	17	19	46,096	36,127	12
Neilston	477	40	16	113,937	67,291	126
Paisley: Abbey	700	42	-	147,779	101,916	98
Paisley: Glenburn	229	18	-	50,206	30,458	10
Paisley: Lylesland	305	46	20	94,677	60,328	34
Paisley: Martyrs' Sandyford	477	61	26	115,127	78,584	125
Paisley: Oakshaw Trinity	434	61	34	-	-	31
Paisley: St Columba Foxbar	156	20	-	29,881	22,270	-
Paisley: St James'	192	27	-	64,906	43,026	50
Paisley: St Luke's	192	26	-	45,686	35,496	13
Paisley: St Mark's Oldhall	461	53	60	114,150	69,138	31
Paisley: St Ninian's Ferguslie	56	-	-	-	4,000	-
Paisley: Sherwood Greenlaw	570	74	32	129,106	68,925	166
Paisley: Stow Brae Kirk	345	73	50	117,693	60,490	21
Paisley: Wallneuk North	375	32	-	62,034	42,842	15
Port Glasgow: Hamilton Bardrainney	236	16	14	40,030	24,374	15
Port Glasgow: St Martin's	147	10	-	-	15,049	11
Renfrew: North	674	64	32	113,481	70,509	185
Renfrew: Trinity	358	32	43	92,726	61,360	18

16. Glasgow

Banton	64	10	-	14,059	4,718	8
Twechar	70	11	-	22,414	9,832	13
Bishopbriggs: Kenmure	263	19	29	95,683	63,666	110
Bishopbriggs: Springfield Cambridge	623	43	86	123,463	79,639	128
Broom	522	52	30	123,355	88,880	423
Burnside Blairbeth	573	42	98	261,146	145,707	292
Busby	227	33	29	79,667	46,148	35
Cadder	646	76	46	-	95,551	121
Cambuslang: Flemington Hallside	298	26	20	61,528	34,777	133
Cambuslang Parish Church	653	-	40	128,828	86,498	161
Campsie	148	-	21	51,556	36,552	-
Chryston	594	27	16	192,889	114,929	76
Eaglesham	518	45	45	144,067	88,364	170

Congregation	Com	Eld	G	In 15	M&M	–18
Fernhill and Cathkin	251	24	19	54,695	35,147	110
Gartcosh	140	13	-	29,147	11,777	78
Glenboig	112	9	11	15,947	7,486	9
Giffnock: Orchardhill	418	46	19	150,492	81,718	230
Giffnock: South	609	74	38	150,983	104,183	32
Giffnock: The Park	252	-	-	70,508	41,918	-
Greenbank	860	74	69	242,490	124,789	240
Kilsyth: Anderson	300	22	60	70,176	46,149	112
Kilsyth: Burns and Old	371	28	45	80,513	50,293	63
Kirkintilloch: Hillhead	70	2	14	13,547	8,404	24
Kirkintilloch: St Columba's	437	-	31	88,433	56,935	-
Kirkintilloch: St David's Memorial Park	558	19	35	84,274	54,434	84
Kirkintilloch: St Mary's	705	-	33	-	78,316	-
Lenzie: Old	427	42	-	106,306	72,652	14
Lenzie: Union	590	59	78	190,453	105,890	270
Maxwell Mearns Castle	257	28	-	170,275	94,234	321
Mearns	722	44	-	-	115,887	46
Milton of Campsie	317	31	43	70,645	44,160	106
Netherlee	610	59	33	199,692	118,229	252
Newton Mearns	392	33	26	121,729	67,496	110
Rutherglen: Old	292	29	-	63,624	38,573	25
Rutherglen: Stonelaw	307	41	-	150,210	83,746	70
Rutherglen: West and Wardlawhill	463	-	53	78,776	56,193	-
Stamperland	342	33	23	80,547	44,730	82
Stepps	278	24	-	57,466	33,844	120
Thornliebank	115	10	28	46,873	27,728	8
Torrance	317	18	-	100,295	60,411	150
Williamwood	415	66	36	-	68,580	106
Glasgow: Anderston Kelvingrove	50	7	8	-	20,803	-
Glasgow: Baillieston Mure Memorial	360	37	76	89,229	59,890	185
Glasgow: Baillieston St Andrew's	263	23	36	-	40,897	145
Glasgow: Balshagray Victoria Park	147	26	19	107,101	61,791	35
Glasgow: Barlanark Greyfriars	90	16	12	-	21,101	207
Glasgow: Blawarthill	167	23	24	-	15,065	64
Glasgow: Bridgeton St Francis in the East	77	15	13	36,623	21,124	5
Glasgow: Broomhill	394	57	50	133,389	84,918	182
Glasgow: Hyndland	225	39	22	96,860	57,089	10
Glasgow: Calton Parkhead	84	-	-	14,513	6,291	-
Glasgow: Cardonald	347	36	50	112,160	70,697	113
Glasgow: Carmunnock	289	23	24	45,361	32,152	44
Glasgow: Carmyle	88	5	16	24,385	9,871	27
Glasgow: Kenmuir Mount Vernon	122	-	24	67,779	34,439	-
Glasgow: Carnwadric	146	16	-	-	21,957	25
Glasgow: Castlemilk	136	20	11	31,171	18,232	14
Glasgow: Cathcart Old	252	40	27	86,707	62,022	185
Glasgow: Cathcart Trinity	429	58	56	205,005	115,629	130
Glasgow: Cathedral (High or St Mungo's)	398	46	-	91,911	69,137	14
Glasgow: Clincarthill	241	33	29	-	67,766	109
Glasgow: Colston Milton	58	-	-	14,855	10,335	-
Glasgow: Colston Wellpark	94	12	-	27,101	14,164	43

Congregation	Com	Eld	G	In 15	M&M	–18
Glasgow: Cranhill	43	8	-	-	2,484	113
Glasgow: Croftfoot	262	33	43	-	48,130	82
Glasgow: Dennistoun New	173	34	16	83,118	60,848	90
Glasgow: Drumchapel St Andrew's	176	-	-	40,910	42,505	-
Glasgow: Drumchapel St Mark's	71	-	-	16,468	1,117	-
Glasgow: Easterhouse	57	7	8	-	6,046	113
Glasgow: Eastwood	212	41	20	94,927	60,926	110
Glasgow: Gairbraid	119	13	17	33,199	20,834	3
Glasgow: Gallowgate	50	-	-	32,130	11,993	-
Glasgow: Garthamlock and Craigend East	56	13	-	-	2,682	86
Glasgow: Gorbals	93	16	-	27,050	18,897	13
Glasgow: Govan and Linthouse	190	48	47	-	54,938	294
Glasgow: High Carntyne	254	22	39	58,360	36,771	83
Glasgow: Hillington Park	272	32	35	70,855	44,566	110
Glasgow: Ibrox	127	20	18	-	33,382	47
Glasgow: John Ross Memorial (For Deaf People)	53	4	-	-	-	-
Glasgow: Jordanhill	382	64	25	168,648	104,937	42
Glasgow: Kelvinbridge	89	29	10	38,416	38,963	50
Glasgow: Kelvinside Hillhead	152	21	-	-	48,220	98
Glasgow: King's Park	577	60	44	144,599	89,273	110
Glasgow: Kinning Park	130	11	-	33,849	23,871	-
Glasgow: Knightswood St Margaret's	188	24	26	47,983	30,303	7
Glasgow: Langside	204	51	19	93,168	52,630	110
Glasgow: Maryhill	143	14	10	-	24,267	94
Glasgow: Merrylea	287	58	26	75,895	48,127	64
Glasgow: Mosspark	107	24	35	47,734	32,120	49
Glasgow: Newlands South	457	56	18	143,612	92,310	37
Glasgow: Partick South	135	20	-	45,996	43,359	25
Glasgow: Partick Trinity	167	-	-	-	55,016	-
Glasgow: Pollokshaws	115	21	-	44,255	24,343	27
Glasgow: Pollokshields	174	27	22	-	57,073	70
Glasgow: Possilpark	104	18	12	26,776	18,173	49
Glasgow: Queen's Park Govanhill	253	44	35	106,878	65,976	20
Glasgow: Renfield St Stephen's	141	21	24	-	45,533	16
Glasgow: Robroyston	42	-	-	32,224	3,000	-
Glasgow: Ruchazie	26	8	-	7,021	2,457	129
Glasgow: Ruchill Kelvinside	77	21	-	36,010	43,642	45
Glasgow: St Andrew and St Nicholas	342	-	9	87,403	57,377	-
Glasgow: St Andrew's East	70	-	14	32,932	23,114	-
Glasgow: St Christopher's Priesthill and Nitshill	220	-	-	36,472	32,497	-
Glasgow: St Columba	134	11	11	-	16,053	18
Glasgow: St David's Knightswood	231	19	24	79,251	56,776	28
Glasgow: St Enoch's Hogganfield	123	14	26	38,338	27,741	5
Glasgow: St George's Tron	380	-	-	4,332	1,315	-
Glasgow: St James' (Pollok)	157	23	30	49,909	28,901	93
Glasgow: St John's Renfield	299	47	-	138,368	87,416	87
Glasgow: St Margaret's Tollcross Park	131	-	-	-	10,294	-
Glasgow: St Paul's	57	5	-	-	4,248	9
Glasgow: St Rollox	75	7	-	40,486	23,936	25

Congregation	Com	Eld	G	In 15	M&M	–18
Glasgow: Sandyford Henderson Memorial	201	22	14	162,919	106,334	20
Glasgow: Sandyhills	272	-	46	73,736	48,831	-
Glasgow: Scotstoun	127	-	-	55,470	40,917	-
Glasgow: Shawlands	220	22	27	69,229	55,855	33
Glasgow: South Shawlands	147	22	-	58,113	44,632	80
Glasgow: Sherbrooke St Gilbert's	252	41	-	140,741	86,834	-
Glasgow: Shettleston New	209	31	24	80,860	50,208	81
Glasgow: Shettleston Old	209	26	20	61,635	34,406	60
Glasgow: South Carntyne	46	6	-	-	16,324	39
Glasgow: Springburn	204	31	18	-	38,746	70
Glasgow: Temple Anniesland	280	22	40	94,152	60,855	100
Glasgow: Toryglen	96	9	-	17,469	8,755	7
Glasgow: Trinity Possil and Henry Drummond	64	6	-	55,171	36,747	2
Glasgow: Tron St Mary's	103	16	-	40,729	27,740	55
Glasgow: Victoria Tollcross	83	-	20	29,076	14,716	-
Glasgow: Wallacewell	126	-	-	-	1,293	-
Glasgow: Wellington	174	32	-	72,921	79,419	22
Glasgow: Whiteinch	56	6	-	-	35,814	66
Glasgow: Yoker	94	-	-	27,833	17,809	-

17. Hamilton

Airdrie: Broomknoll	213	23	29	-	29,083	70
Calderbank	111	9	11	21,013	12,468	-
Airdrie: Clarkston	346	37	26	74,358	42,903	135
Airdrie: Flowerhill	538	33	-	-	70,888	14
Airdrie: High	293	32	-	73,030	40,865	142
Airdrie: Jackson	341	51	17	90,552	52,334	196
Airdrie: New Monkland	286	30	18	69,689	35,600	135
Greengairs	124	9	-	22,808	13,717	7
Airdrie: St Columba's	218	11	-	18,407	11,213	-
Airdrie: The New Wellwynd	743	84	-	163,156	83,984	-
Bargeddie	85	7	-	67,896	39,543	5
Bellshill: Central	-1	29	23	53,856	35,910	-
Bellshill: West	476	38	24	64,084	45,479	21
Blantyre: Livingstone Memorial	207	21	18	59,775	33,110	200
Blantyre: Old	263	13	27	-	42,235	45
Blantyre: St Andrew's	192	21	-	53,923	34,808	16
Bothwell	486	55	29	123,752	64,304	124
Caldercruix and Longriggend	187	10	-	51,434	33,035	54
Chapelhall	214	23	33	42,405	27,151	55
Chapelton	156	17	18	27,557	15,704	34
Strathaven: Rankin	526	57	27	110,982	51,450	190
Cleland	164	10	-	27,450	17,217	14
Wishaw: St Mark's	312	26	46	68,535	45,990	113
Coatbridge: Blairhill Dundyvan	257	22	22	51,524	36,196	108
Coatbridge: Middle	323	35	38	49,353	37,849	147
Coatbridge: Calder	336	22	26	53,022	31,876	7
Coatbridge: Old Monkland	111	21	21	47,064	31,850	-
Coatbridge: New St Andrew's	707	78	24	132,202	69,120	222

Congregation	Com	Eld	G	In 15	M&M	–18
Coatbridge: Townhead	124	18	-	33,425	27,227	77
Dalserf	207	17	29	69,897	55,680	51
East Kilbride: Claremont	415	59	-	132,695	74,527	180
East Kilbride: Greenhills	175	12	20	-	18,673	12
East Kilbride: Moncrieff	631	66	50	125,418	69,850	196
East Kilbride: Mossneuk	255	12	-	29,784	20,113	65
East Kilbride: Old	686	64	38	130,046	71,013	98
East Kilbride: South	268	32	22	-	52,156	98
East Kilbride: Stewartfield	19	3	-	16,401	6,000	5
East Kilbride: West	350	31	38	56,118	45,552	100
East Kilbride: Westwood	491	35	-	82,472	52,157	41
Glasford	121	7	16	27,649	10,844	-
Strathaven: East	293	32	36	67,337	38,984	32
Hamilton: Cadzow	420	56	49	124,569	79,743	117
Hamilton: Gilmour and Whitehill	142	24	-	32,333	38,537	76
Hamilton: West	257	27	-	66,668	43,779	21
Hamilton: Hillhouse	372	43	-	76,380	54,660	183
Hamilton: Old	525	77	26	-	91,319	63
Hamilton: St John's	516	56	60	-	67,907	250
Hamilton: South	197	26	24	59,419	38,657	20
Quarter	93	13	18	26,051	15,629	6
Hamilton: Trinity	294	25	-	59,309	35,827	66
Holytown	172	18	28	49,911	29,158	82
New Stevenston: Wrangholm Kirk	95	12	18	37,792	24,237	9
Kirk o' Shotts	165	9	10	25,187	19,216	15
Larkhall: Chalmers	108	11	24	31,646	18,447	54
Larkhall: St Machan's	407	60	45	-	64,379	75
Larkhall: Trinity	176	18	26	49,558	36,949	148
Motherwell: Crosshill	345	56	55	99,976	55,430	85
Motherwell: St Margaret's	358	15	11	42,384	25,075	85
Motherwell: Dalziel St Andrew's	497	54	34	-	78,680	240
Motherwell: North	122	18	30	50,827	34,495	166
Motherwell: St Mary's	724	96	70	142,282	80,615	290
Motherwell: South	382	59	53	97,364	71,781	30
Newarthill and Carfin	363	30	21	83,217	37,027	134
Newmains: Bonkle	122	18	-	34,676	20,977	13
Newmains: Coltness Memorial	192	20	15	-	33,688	87
Overtown	260	30	52	43,367	28,097	130
Shotts: Calderhead Erskine	449	34	23	92,979	53,144	13
Stonehouse: St Ninian's	403	46	30	-	-	25
Strathaven: Avendale Old and Drumclog	621	56	51	131,646	78,175	33
Uddingston: Burnhead	260	22	8	-	27,240	28
Uddingston: Old	528	54	45	133,304	75,327	85
Uddingston: Viewpark	425	71	28	106,754	58,738	35
Wishaw: Cambusnethan North	440	35	-	78,091	46,708	101
Wishaw: Cambusnethan Old & Morningside	400	37	24	83,758	54,164	216
Wishaw: Craigneuk and Belhaven	145	28	18	42,767	34,462	10
Wishaw: Old	205	29	-	41,346	25,693	60
Wishaw: South Wishaw	438	-	36	89,623	53,515	-

Congregation	Com	Eld	G	In 15	M&M	–18
18. Dumbarton						
Alexandria	275	35	19	75,973	47,546	32
Arrochar	66	14	9	-	13,708	3
Luss	101	-	20	53,180	24,386	-
Baldernock	179	19	-	38,768	23,341	16
Bearsden: Baljaffray	355	29	43	79,354	47,646	80
Bearsden: Cross	793	90	29	170,375	102,518	54
Bearsden: Killermont	628	56	48	175,011	87,669	65
Bearsden: New Kilpatrick	1,384	120	110	315,430	161,497	45
Bearsden: Westerton Fairlie Memorial	363	42	54	88,867	54,045	33
Bonhill	835	-	-	61,953	48,052	-
Renton: Trinity	245	-	-	-	20,947	-
Cardross	379	227	29	82,230	50,796	20
Clydebank: Abbotsford	140	15	-	43,820	30,025	35
Dalmuir: Barclay	188	15	-	42,536	27,682	26
Clydebank: Faifley	177	18	36	43,267	26,314	20
Clydebank: Kilbowie St Andrew's	262	21	17	46,632	30,425	125
Clydebank: Radnor Park	144	24	20	46,166	29,152	2
Clydebank: St Cuthbert's	115	11	16	14,443	10,305	1
Duntocher	215	26	44	39,283	30,934	1
Craigrownie	149	19	23	37,784	28,616	2
Garelochhead	171	15	-	-	38,801	45
Rosneath: St Modan's	112	12	10	23,431	16,901	3
Dumbarton: Riverside	494	60	52	110,630	70,292	233
Dumbarton: West Kirk	274	26	-	-	28,331	100
Dumbarton: St Andrew's	106	22	-	32,823	17,528	-
Old Kilpatrick Bowling	240	21	20	48,421	39,574	85
Helensburgh	1,122	113	68	220,619	166,402	35
Rhu and Shandon	271	21	33	59,801	40,395	18
Jamestown	188	21	18	-	29,292	7
Kilmaronock Gartocharn	214	12	-	30,624	18,339	8
Milngavie: Cairns	371	40	-	155,009	81,048	20
Milngavie: St Luke's	371	23	30	82,241	48,047	32
Milngavie: St Paul's	887	86	89	211,609	116,768	162
19 Argyll						
Appin	100	12	24	31,124	13,304	12
Lismore	42	6	12	12,528	8,946	11
Ardchattan	104	9	-	30,010	15,561	31
Ardrishaig	127	19	29	34,849	22,113	-
South Knapdale	34	6	-	-	4,844	-
Barra	44	3	-	-	9,418	40
South Uist	51	10	-	22,648	12,061	8
Campbeltown: Highland	383	31	-	47,144	35,677	11
Campbeltown: Lorne and Lowland	766	54	35	94,094	52,662	85
Coll	14	3	-	5,632	1,748	-
Connel	118	19	11	49,857	28,355	12
Colonsay and Oronsay	13	2	-	-	6,749	-
Craignish	47	10	-	13,971	5,267	2

Congregation	Com	Eld	G	In 15	M&M	–18
Kilbrandon and Kilchattan	93	17	-	-	18,929	17
Kilninver and Kilmelford	60	6	-	-	8,938	12
Cumlodden, Lochfyneside and Lochgair	85	12	12	23,242	15,878	-
Glenaray and Inveraray	101	18	-	30,154	19,185	1
Dunoon: St John's	173	23	39	46,678	29,933	4
Kirn	277	28	-	45,333	42,066	15
Sandbank	92	6	-	-	7,639	-
Dunoon: The High Kirk	306	30	37	-	44,354	38
Innellan	54	7	-	17,381	11,945	2
Toward	62	11	-	20,414	12,613	11
Gigha and Cara	33	7	-	8,993	6,006	9
Kilcalmonell	45	11	14	13,318	4,592	3
Killean and Kilchenzie	124	13	17	25,639	16,622	30
Glassary, Kilmartin and Ford	96	12	-	-	15,836	15
North Knapdale	53	8	-	27,651	20,356	8
Glenorchy and Innishael	58	6	-	-	5,439	-
Strathfillan	45	-	-	7,070	6,851	-
Iona	15	6	-	-	7,226	3
Kilfinichen & Kilvickeon & the Ross of Mull	34	5	-	11,885	6,239	-
Jura	24	5	-	5,670	5,212	-
Kilarrow	46	11	-	31,592	17,033	10
Kildalton and Oa	88	15	-	-	25,170	15
Kilchoman	76	6	-	15,678	16,798	14
Kilmeny	30	5	-	12,569	6,844	-
Portnahaven	26	5	12	19,613	3,162	4
Kilchrenan and Dalavich	23	7	8	13,958	9,524	-
Muckairn	129	18	7	37,602	18,141	-
Kilfinan	29	5	-	7,902	3,363	-
Kilmodan and Colintraive	77	-	-	18,233	13,836	-
Kyles	103	17	19	30,894	19,886	4
Kilmore and Oban	481	50	26	78,900	62,517	35
Kilmun (St Munn's)	71	6	15	15,985	12,066	-
Strone and Ardentinny	106	13	17	39,074	22,996	7
Kilninian and Kilmore	26	5	-	11,265	4,108	-
Salen and Ulva	30	4	-	-	6,405	20
Tobermory	54	12	-	25,507	17,124	8
Torosay and Kinlochspelvie	23	3	-	-	4,077	1
Lochgilphead	216	12	20	29,315	20,228	43
Lochgoilhead and Kilmorich	59	9	-	21,172	17,297	7
Strachur and Strachlachlan	115	12	17	25,286	22,270	1
Rothesay: Trinity	358	42	28	61,358	41,720	44
Saddell and Carradale	192	15	21	37,714	20,399	23
Southend	226	12	13	30,765	20,223	16
Skipness	17	4	-	10,182	3,930	-
Tarbert, Loch Fyne and Kilberry	114	17	23	-	26,006	3
The United Church of Bute	510	32	44	-	50,775	23
Tiree	79	11	18	-	16,365	2

Congregation	Com	Eld	G	In 15	M&M	–18
22. Falkirk						
Airth	150	7	18	-	27,935	45
Blackbraes and Shieldhill	168	23	20	31,973	18,240	8
Muiravonside	189	23	-	42,394	26,344	4
Bo'ness: Old	336	23	7	55,130	41,204	30
Bo'ness: St Andrew's	499	21	-	104,569	56,575	70
Bonnybridge: St Helen's	326	14	-	61,264	37,346	6
Bothkennar and Carronshore	213	20	-	34,759	21,661	14
Brightons	623	39	59	-	80,915	218
Carriden	400	42	25	61,921	41,135	4
Cumbernauld: Abronhill	207	16	25	63,335	43,519	119
Cumbernauld: Condorrat	311	24	38	67,469	44,835	105
Cumbernauld: Kildrum	268	29	-	66,759	38,412	3
Cumbernauld: Old	312	46	-	-	50,557	84
Cumbernauld: St Mungo's	179	35	-	41,425	29,089	20
Denny: Old	343	42	27	61,348	46,218	50
Haggs	242	24	16	39,821	24,931	53
Denny: Westpark	470	35	36	87,885	60,902	120
Dunipace	336	26	-	55,858	36,351	70
Falkirk: Bainsford	128	12	-	-	24,394	100
Falkirk: St James'	229	33	-	33,527	22,062	-
Falkirk: Camelon	289	20	-	100,595	49,476	110
Falkirk: Grahamston United	318	46	30	-	-	44
Falkirk: Laurieston	211	20	24	38,670	26,392	8
Redding and Westquarter	153	13	22	26,030	17,755	-
Falkirk: St Andrew's West	432	32	-	85,086	58,128	40
Falkirk: Trinity	-	-	14	176,195	101,335	-
Grangemouth: Abbotsgrange	368	52	26	65,523	49,736	83
Grangemouth: Kirk of the Holy Rood	364	37	-	54,869	36,559	33
Grangemouth: Zetland	729	69	66	112,190	73,165	165
Larbert: East	630	53	50	125,865	73,283	109
Larbert: Old	314	22	-	79,861	61,202	112
Larbert: West	366	35	35	80,908	45,406	130
Polmont: Old	349	27	49	102,107	55,069	60
Slamannan	209	8	-	-	19,345	6
Stenhouse and Carron	355	31	16	-	45,942	10
23. Stirling						
Aberfoyle	93	7	20	26,212	14,001	10
Port of Menteith	56	7	-	14,014	6,605	-
Alloa: Ludgate	300	20	19	76,185	48,145	12
Alloa: St Mungo's	334	44	50	73,682	50,542	20
Alva	472	52	22	76,859	46,811	111
Balfron	139	19	16	52,051	29,754	32
Fintry	107	10	18	23,211	15,802	6
Balquhidder	56	2	-	11,315	15,281	1
Killin and Ardeonaig	85	6	6	20,800	13,455	5
Bannockburn: Allan	371	34	-	56,545	35,947	-
Bannockburn: Ladywell	388	15	-	29,996	17,782	11

Congregation	Com	Eld	G	In 15	M&M	–18
Bridge of Allan	704	51	68	128,464	81,463	42
Buchanan	97	8	-	41,588	9,143	8
Drymen	257	24	-	70,963	41,630	27
Buchlyvie	204	12	15	25,748	20,178	20
Gartmore	70	13	-	19,035	14,703	5
Callander	541	23	26	104,320	72,534	60
Cambusbarron: The Bruce Memorial	299	21	-	75,018	33,170	31
Clackmannan	398	22	31	75,988	51,645	55
Cowie and Plean	181	8	6	21,476	12,819	1
Fallin	244	7	-	39,313	20,358	65
Dollar	243	28	61	94,001	57,453	15
Glendevon	44	-	-	5,739	3,223	-
Muckhart	112	7	-	21,329	14,633	7
Dunblane: Cathedral	816	76	58	221,283	123,985	293
Dunblane: St Blane's	310	35	37	103,453	62,244	130
Lecropt	155	16	-	44,818	28,927	12
Gargunnock	137	9	-	27,155	19,784	20
Kilmadock	94	-	-	17,499	12,442	-
Kincardine-in-Menteith	79	6	-	17,275	11,053	8
Killearn	376	25	39	95,650	61,053	70
Kippen	201	17	19	30,090	19,704	-
Norrieston	103	10	9	19,841	14,338	1
Logie	523	61	33	100,644	61,972	18
Menstrie	355	19	21	68,554	44,066	71
Sauchie and Coalsnaughton	450	28	18	54,318	36,960	9
Stirling: Allan Park South	172	27	-	53,027	24,958	99
Stirling: Church of The Holy Rude	145	21	-	-	27,968	8
Stirling: Viewfield Erskine	269	21	28	45,169	25,221	8
Stirling: North	335	25	24	89,924	55,299	41
Stirling: St Columba's	470	53	-	113,445	61,923	80
Stirling: St Mark's	191	12	-	28,885	19,971	32
Stirling: St Ninian's Old	639	60	-	94,593	57,176	55
Strathblane	188	17	45	78,066	45,284	80
Tillicoultry	597	67	39	95,126	59,402	86
Tullibody: St Serf's	346	17	25	51,782	34,844	60

24. Dunfermline

Aberdour: St Fillan's	363	19	-	73,914	46,278	10
Beath and Cowdenbeath: North	208	25	14	59,985	38,539	31
Cairneyhill	111	19	-	29,081	15,880	10
Limekilns	243	43	-	76,012	42,419	8
Carnock and Oakley	175	21	23	58,453	33,873	36
Saline and Blairingone	151	14	15	-	26,984	27
Cowdenbeath: Trinity	302	28	14	71,383	41,205	17
Culross and Torryburn	91	12	-	54,010	34,666	24
Dalgety	511	49	25	138,048	69,661	131
Dunfermline: Abbey	658	69	-	137,123	82,359	160
Dunfermline: East	67	-	-	42,837	8,936	75
Dunfermline: Gillespie Memorial	222	28	17	45,940	49,862	17
Dunfermline: North	158	14	-	32,230	23,175	5

Congregation	Com	Eld	G	In 15	M&M	–18
Dunfermline: St Andrew's Erskine	182	23	12	52,919	27,365	15
Dunfermline: St Leonard's	319	26	32	94,323	44,188	59
Dunfermline: St Margaret's	238	31	19	75,193	51,227	47
Dunfermline: St Ninian's	173	23	23	-	29,829	54
Dunfermline: Townhill and Kingseat	323	25	30	68,146	44,458	16
Inverkeithing	317	27	-	61,634	42,330	63
North Queensferry	53	7	-	17,726	9,432	3
Kelty	269	27	55	98,064	45,144	33
Lochgelly and Benarty: St Serf's	395	40	-	59,574	44,744	22
Rosyth	217	26	-	38,834	23,502	50
Tulliallan and Kincardine	285	21	40	67,937	33,535	70

25. Kirkcaldy

Congregation	Com	Eld	G	In 15	M&M	–18
Auchterderran Kinglassie	311	29	14	53,362	29,951	10
Auchtertool	64	6	-	9,233	6,147	6
Kirkcaldy: Linktown	242	31	32	57,819	38,431	40
Buckhaven and Wemyss	246	23	30	51,531	34,113	8
Burntisland	305	36	16	-	45,404	42
Dysart: St Clair	456	29	18	55,696	36,776	70
Glenrothes: Christ's Kirk	201	18	40	44,993	25,331	9
Glenrothes: St Columba's	450	39	-	62,367	29,403	71
Glenrothes: St Margaret's	301	30	37	61,038	39,437	70
Glenrothes: St Ninian's	237	37	15	71,669	43,316	47
Kennoway, Windygates and						
Balgonie St Kenneth's	628	48	66	92,021	59,559	30
Kinghorn	308	19	-	75,148	43,244	14
Kirkcaldy: Abbotshall	485	43	-	85,570	46,947	15
Kirkcaldy: Bennochy	445	40	43	85,785	58,026	8
Kirkcaldy: Pathhead	348	35	42	74,599	44,908	160
Kirkcaldy: St Bryce Kirk	346	32	25	79,219	80,420	44
Kirkcaldy: Templehall	167	11	14	38,539	26,675	-
Kirkcaldy: Torbain	229	33	12	47,290	26,236	69
Leslie: Trinity	173	16	17	26,442	21,874	4
Leven	471	33	39	107,213	70,830	8
Markinch and Thornton	604	45	-	84,965	60,930	10
Methil: Wellesley	308	25	18	51,483	21,642	119
Methilhill and Denbeath	198	17	37	29,817	21,935	14

26. St Andrews

Congregation	Com	Eld	G	In 15	M&M	–18
Abdie and Dunbog	158	16	-	20,325	15,051	17
Newburgh	229	-	-	19,462	16,055	-
Anstruther	202	21	-	39,569	26,795	30
Cellardyke	245	20	39	47,358	30,644	38
Kilrenny	118	14	-	29,646	19,582	10
Auchtermuchty	268	-	14	43,617	24,858	-
Edenshead and Strathmiglo	162	-	-	-	11,276	-
Balmerino	121	-	10	23,082	15,443	-
Wormit	213	16	33	39,906	25,610	35
Boarhills and Dunino	137	8	-	19,812	16,484	-
St Andrews: Holy Trinity	342	32	41	118,170	85,129	45

Congregation	Com	Eld	G	In 15	M&M	–18
Cameron	93	14	14	20,044	11,927	14
St Andrews: St Leonard's	567	46	29	134,398	77,028	25
Carnbee	89	15	20	15,966	11,816	1
Pittenweem	243	14	14	21,188	17,222	3
Ceres, Kemback and Springfield	386	35	24	52,663	68,954	30
Crail	352	22	39	53,032	34,116	10
Kingsbarns	67	10	-	18,369	10,345	-
Creich, Flisk and Kilmany	105	-	11	21,887	16,149	-
Cupar: Old and St Michael of Tarvit	562	32	20	127,196	82,019	53
Monimail	97	14	-	16,136	16,769	4
Cupar: St John's and Dairsie United	680	50	39	-	67,631	13
Elie Kilconquhar and Colinsburgh	325	30	78	82,010	61,142	29
Falkland	135	18	-	-	19,557	5
Freuchie	134	18	14	23,311	12,314	-
Howe of Fife	290	21	-	59,359	30,797	20
Largo and Newburn	268	17	-	57,009	34,616	12
Largo: St David's	128	8	36	33,447	22,247	5
Largoward	72	7	-	9,863	5,833	10
St Monans	262	14	31	67,283	43,026	20
Leuchars: St Athernase	301	25	30	49,324	40,682	5
Newport-on-Tay	377	-	-	71,475	47,670	-
St Andrews: Hope Park and Martyrs'	597	55	26	172,247	84,123	10
Strathkinness	90	11	-	17,408	11,444	-
Tayport	330	17	20	40,647	39,493	8

27. Dunkeld and Meigle

Congregation	Com	Eld	G	In 15	M&M	–18
Aberfeldy	176	9	-	-	27,163	111
Dull and Weem	106	15	14	27,290	15,325	6
Alyth	666	34	26	92,817	45,380	12
Ardler, Kettins and Meigle	395	21	34	47,350	34,884	22
Bendochy	83	12	-	25,073	15,803	2
Coupar Angus: Abbey	291	16	-	-	26,222	85
Blair Atholl and Struan	124	16	12	17,158	18,372	-
Tenandry	52	7	-	21,630	15,985	-
Blairgowrie	862	42	36	116,100	72,842	104
Braes of Rannoch	26	6	-	12,387	8,994	-
Foss and Rannoch	88	9	12	12,146	12,561	12
Caputh and Clunie	150	18	17	23,532	16,875	-
Kinclaven	140	15	15	21,525	16,050	-
Dunkeld	-	-	13	89,834	64,225	-
Fortingall and Glenlyon	47	10	-	16,826	12,984	4
Kenmore and Lawers	63	7	25	-	23,667	11
Grantully, Logierait and Strathtay	133	10	6	28,924	29,798	2
Kirkmichael, Straloch and Glenshee	101	5	-	12,032	12,302	6
Rattray	349	17	16	38,406	19,604	11
Pitlochry	365	31	25	83,728	58,704	40

28. Perth

Congregation	Com	Eld	G	In 15	M&M	–18
Aberdalgie and Forteviot	177	13	-	26,923	28,510	15
Aberuthven and Dunning	197	11	-	44,756	28,510	44

Congregation	Com	Eld	G	In 15	M&M	–18
Abernethy & Dron & Arngask	294	25	24	36,448	35,746	19
Almondbank Tibbermore	273	-	30	-	26,696	-
Methven and Logiealmond	256	16	15	21,535	22,681	-
Ardoch	176	16	27	40,815	14,734	26
Blackford	110	-	-	29,207	8,968	-
Auchterarder	575	29	45	101,235	65,800	52
Auchtergaven and Moneydie	497	-	31	-	43,501	-
Redgorton and Stanley	336	18	39	43,754	28,872	21
Cargill Burrelton	254	21	20	32,032	21,960	8
Collace	111	10	14	15,365	9,839	5
Cleish	211	13	19	48,522	29,142	9
Fossoway St Serf's and Devonside	219	17	-	45,756	29,658	15
Comrie	410	29	20	100,118	62,946	22
Dundurn	53	8	-	17,947	10,576	-
Crieff	689	53	33	96,317	66,333	18
Dunbarney and Forgandenny	548	31	12	84,833	51,326	19
Errol	264	22	19	42,118	30,209	5
Kilspindie and Rait	64	6	-	11,250	7,991	-
Fowlis Wester, Madderty & Monzie	284	22	13	41,552	32,594	30
Gask	84	9	12	19,756	20,217	-
Kinross	660	36	40	143,554	62,619	164
Muthill	259	22	16	41,589	28,646	17
Trinity Gask and Kinkell	53	-	-	11,108	5,288	-
Orwell and Portmoak	437	36	39	74,748	46,504	19
Perth: Craigie and Moncrieffe	627	44	40	-	56,052	88
Perth: Kinnoull	405	36	23	70,298	48,081	42
Perth: Letham St Mark's	490	9	20	112,707	68,789	70
Perth: North	1,005	56	38	210,972	123,517	94
Perth: Riverside	59	-	-	40,483	17,459	-
Perth: St John's Kirk of Perth	465	31	-	95,307	61,742	-
Perth: St Leonard's-in-the-Fields	442	38	-	79,127	54,996	6
Perth: St Matthew's	763	23	19	96,454	64,817	160
St Madoes and Kinfauns	284	29	18	58,189	36,493	58
Scone and St Martins	-	-	52	114,778	77,680	-

29. Dundee

Abernyte	89	11	-	18,279	13,338	10
Inchture and Kinnaird	165	25	-	36,742	23,642	8
Longforgan	178	21	23	-	27,493	15
Auchterhouse	140	13	15	25,475	17,902	12
Monikie & Newbigging and Murroes & Tealing	461	25	11	53,244	36,760	31
Dundee: Balgay	356	31	24	66,497	45,086	16
Dundee: Barnhill St Margaret's	740	52	66	170,537	94,474	70
Dundee: Broughty Ferry New Kirk	710	50	48	110,718	65,108	16
Dundee: Broughty Ferry St James'	135	6	12	28,145	36,051	84
Dundee: Broughty Ferry St Luke's and Queen Street	400	47	29	75,241	48,917	17
Dundee: Broughty Ferry St Stephen's and West	313	24	-	-	30,124	18

Congregation	Com	Eld	G	In 15	M&M	–18
Dundee: Dundee (St Mary's)	532	43	21	108,884	62,342	10
Dundee: Camperdown	134	10	11	-	18,806	8
Dundee: Chalmers Ardler	205	20	32	84,448	52,983	78
Dundee: Coldside	263	21	-	55,955	33,871	49
Dundee: Craigiebank	171	12	-	33,623	23,427	85
Dundee: Douglas and Mid Craigie	122	10	16	20,684	19,635	45
Dundee: Downfield Mains	380	30	30	87,124	57,297	25
Dundee: Fintry Parish Church	92	7	-	50,371	34,801	27
Dundee: Lochee	498	33	27	79,889	44,847	204
Dundee: Logie and St John's Cross	195	10	21	81,639	66,060	14
Dundee: Meadowside St Paul's	480	22	21	85,657	33,552	28
Dundee: Menzieshill	258	14	-	46,949	27,079	140
Dundee: St Andrew's	453	51	30	121,622	69,569	23
Dundee: St David's High Kirk	257	45	24	-	34,444	36
Dundee: Steeple	205	29	-	119,865	72,075	15
Dundee: Stobswell	417	39	-	64,912	42,794	1
Dundee: Strathmartine	247	24	28	-	32,127	5
Dundee: Trinity	440	36	28	-	33,320	58
Dundee: West	290	27	24	77,904	50,369	-
Dundee: Whitfield	43	7	-	-	6,550	66
Fowlis and Liff	148	13	12	27,937	26,685	43
Lundie and Muirhead	307	29	-	48,013	25,666	53
Invergowrie	390	57	41	68,230	41,672	-
Monifieth	1,093	59	52	173,950	81,462	108

30. Angus

Congregation	Com	Eld	G	In 15	M&M	–18
Aberlemno	200	11	-	26,485	12,898	10
Guthrie and Rescobie	222	10	12	24,952	12,926	13
Arbirlot	154	10	-	-	18,744	1
Carmyllie	119	12	-	-	19,739	-
Arbroath: Knox's	292	17	24	42,638	26,428	3
Arbroath: St Vigeans	503	37	23	70,656	43,948	70
Arbroath: Old and Abbey	490	42	23	98,855	70,099	30
Arbroath: St Andrew's	586	47	40	168,617	93,023	100
Arbroath: West Kirk	740	77	45	93,551	59,051	36
Barry	201	8	11	28,845	16,820	4
Carnoustie	330	23	24	67,247	45,184	13
Brechin: Cathedral	499	34	12	-	52,408	30
Brechin: Gardner Memorial	477	23	-	47,744	39,280	25
Farnell	112	12	-	7,392	10,085	11
Carnoustie: Panbride	659	33	-	67,440	41,414	42
Colliston	170	7	10	-	11,786	2
Friockheim Kinnell	138	11	22	19,793	12,383	1
Inverkeilor and Lunan	118	7	21	18,832	16,237	6
Dun and Hillside	408	45	43	-	41,822	200
Dunnichen, Letham and Kirkden	258	15	24	42,189	23,375	2
Eassie, Nevay and Newtyle	210	16	22	28,570	23,209	25
Edzell Lethnot Glenesk	337	24	28	35,594	35,041	12
Fern Careston Menmuir	103	7	-	14,197	15,055	15

Congregation	Com	Eld	G	In 15	M&M	-18
Forfar: East and Old	802	58	44	124,159	64,483	27
Forfar: Lowson Memorial	873	36	31	99,867	60,637	226
Forfar: St Margaret's	491	27	17	80,414	48,380	97
Glamis, Inverarity and Kinettles	367	26	-	52,372	42,119	15
Inchbrayock	170	7	-	26,596	25,119	16
Montrose: Melville South	258	14	-	-	21,761	4
Kirriemuir: St Andrew's	277	21	29	45,405	35,379	20
Oathlaw Tannadice	129	9	-	18,440	17,563	10
Montrose: Old and St Andrew's	676	46	27	84,071	63,701	30
The Glens and Kirriemuir Old	975	68	43	-	75,662	1,000
The Isla Parishes	140	23	10	36,419	31,598	8

31. Aberdeen

Congregation	Com	Eld	G	In 15	M&M	-18
Aberdeen: Bridge of Don Oldmachar	185	9	-	57,147	39,836	11
Aberdeen: Cove	55	6	-	25,047	7,000	17
Aberdeen: Craigiebuckler	765	72	39	-	72,306	90
Aberdeen: Ferryhill	346	47	25	80,754	55,601	85
Aberdeen: Garthdee	202	15	8	-	20,098	43
Aberdeen: Ruthrieston West	331	31	15	60,895	46,421	6
Aberdeen: High Hilton	334	25	27	56,999	30,800	48
Aberdeen: Holburn West	409	39	27	111,408	66,969	23
Aberdeen: Mannofield	1,049	112	38	158,353	97,611	170
Aberdeen: Mastrick	240	15	10	41,892	32,520	30
Aberdeen: Middlefield	111	7	-	14,926	2,473	7
Aberdeen: Midstocket	477	48	39	96,960	76,402	32
Aberdeen: Northfield	156	12	15	28,960	15,508	1
Aberdeen: Queen Street	378	37	33	78,633	62,736	54
Aberdeen: Queen's Cross	418	43	24	187,766	92,271	140
Aberdeen: Rubislaw	451	61	35	143,525	89,128	32
Aberdeen: St Columba's Bridge of Don	247	13	-	-	53,258	60
Aberdeen: St George's Tillydrone	94	10	-	15,173	8,681	3
Aberdeen: St John's Church for Deaf People	90	1	-	-	-	-
Aberdeen: St Machar's Cathedral	517	39	-	160,216	69,132	18
Aberdeen: St Mark's	326	36	31	103,298	63,011	30
Aberdeen: St Mary's	323	33	-	71,889	39,294	60
Aberdeen: St Nicholas Kincorth, South of	322	30	30	69,182	44,409	58
Aberdeen: St Nicholas Uniting, Kirk of	347	33	15	-	-	6
Aberdeen: St Stephen's	163	21	12	-	44,595	35
Aberdeen: South Holburn	489	50	40	90,389	66,137	11
Aberdeen: Stockethill	91	7	-	27,405	14,993	19
Aberdeen: Summerhill	131	19	-	30,120	21,551	5
Aberdeen: Torry St Fittick's	336	19	23	63,991	41,629	1
Aberdeen: Woodside	259	34	27	42,425	32,324	60
Bucksburn: Stoneywood	403	24	7	35,107	28,456	-
Cults	748	70	47	157,392	93,837	28
Dyce	969	49	29	-	54,815	235
Kingswells	337	22	24	57,415	32,840	10
Newhills	408	35	40	-	73,921	60
Peterculter	577	49	-	107,115	67,961	237

Congregation	Com	Eld	G	In 15	M&M	–18
32. Kincardine and Deeside						
Aberluthnott	182	8	11	14,195	11,434	3
Laurencekirk	392	9	30	33,669	21,609	7
Aboyne and Dinnet	315	7	30	45,716	32,033	45
Cromar	217	13	-	27,648	25,490	-
Arbuthnott, Bervie and Kinneff	670	-	29	77,650	49,877	-
Banchory-Ternan East	566	31	28	115,695	67,583	165
Banchory-Ternan West	579	27	28	135,246	71,097	90
Birse and Feughside	225	17	15	36,465	32,295	35
Braemar and Crathie	203	30	11	64,273	42,120	37
Drumoak – Durris	380	19	-	55,264	42,522	48
Glenmuick (Ballater)	264	20	29	39,569	26,294	14
Maryculter Trinity	147	15	9	37,619	23,571	60
Mearns Coastal	249	10	8	27,167	19,638	15
Mid Deeside	617	42	23	63,989	50,656	9
Newtonhill	254	11	14	28,844	20,671	73
Portlethen	298	18	-	58,868	45,828	40
Stonehaven: Dunnottar	578	27	24	67,790	52,889	12
Stonehaven: South	245	13	-	-	24,599	9
Stonehaven: Fetteresso	784	38	25	-	107,936	-
West Mearns	461	15	31	54,728	36,671	8
33. Gordon						
Barthol Chapel	78	10	10	-	4,962	18
Tarves	266	18	33	44,515	25,096	88
Belhelvie	364	34	18	93,559	50,956	68
Blairdaff and Chapel of Garioch	357	30	11	34,103	28,060	10
Cluny	189	10	-	31,546	18,916	21
Monymusk	106	5	-	24,067	12,501	31
Culsalmond and Rayne	168	8	-	13,436	9,809	20
Daviot	141	8	-	12,804	9,868	17
Cushnie and Tough	256	13	9	27,146	19,555	1
Echt	176	11	-	26,861	16,035	10
Midmar	122	7	-	18,705	8,908	3
Ellon	1,426	87	-	177,787	103,010	164
Fintray Kinellar Keithhall	168	13	14	-	25,802	3
Foveran	307	12	-	62,319	32,405	21
Howe Trinity	520	24	24	80,335	45,448	22
Huntly: Cairnie Glass	616	9	16	-	38,049	3
Insch-Leslie-Premnay-Oyne	332	27	16	34,222	25,425	12
Inverurie: St Andrew's	936	32	-	74,451	68,122	9
Inverurie: West	646	45	26	108,295	56,813	18
Kemnay	491	39	-	70,364	49,034	130
Kintore	680	48	-	79,481	60,092	16
Meldrum and Bourtie	419	29	31	68,446	48,049	24
Methlick	345	26	21	66,227	35,439	20
New Machar	418	19	14	63,981	51,660	35
Noth	240	10	-	23,103	21,713	2
Skene	1,219	76	55	147,151	87,728	163
Strathbogie Drumblade	503	33	34	61,619	46,956	50

Congregation	Com	Eld	G	In 15	M&M	–18
Udny and Pitmedden	253	30	18	69,354	43,665	55
Upper Donside	358	22	-	37,685	28,845	14

34. Buchan

Congregation	Com	Eld	G	In 15	M&M	–18
Aberdour	107	8	11	11,401	8,420	-
Pitsligo	80	10	-	-	12,524	-
Auchaber United	145	12	9	15,472	13,489	3
Auchterless	183	18	11	23,911	16,368	10
Banff	576	32	15	74,746	48,151	148
King Edward	140	16	12	20,474	11,814	9
Crimond	173	8	-	26,333	14,492	15
Lonmay	108	12	12	17,067	9,756	-
Cruden	386	25	23	-	34,872	28
Deer	686	22	24	55,928	41,317	10
Fraserburgh: Old	517	56	62	108,211	76,849	154
Fraserburgh: South	268	18	-	-	32,153	5
Inverallochy and Rathen: East	81	8	-	19,820	8,278	13
Fraserburgh: West	481	49	-	68,228	47,770	116
Rathen: West	98	7	-	14,244	6,174	16
Fyvie	221	16	14	-	25,266	-
Rothienorman	121	8	8	15,562	8,397	20
Longside	470	27	-	59,935	39,066	63
Macduff	619	26	33	99,601	54,419	104
Marnoch	381	-	14	35,985	22,824	-
Maud and Savoch	181	12	-	25,846	18,182	-
New Deer: St Kane's	344	-	17	44,261	38,284	-
Monquhitter and New Byth	297	20	11	21,740	22,217	2
Turriff: St Andrew's	542	30	15	-	30,489	95
New Pitsligo	262	5	-	25,412	17,311	25
Strichen and Tyrie	449	16	26	48,542	32,230	20
Ordiquihill and Cornhill	136	9	13	-	7,660	25
Whitehills	273	19	20	42,399	28,530	8
Peterhead: Old	369	23	26	60,652	38,502	41
Peterhead: St Andrew's	447	31	20	51,030	37,436	24
Peterhead: Trinity	264	15	21	90,505	61,108	-
Portsoy	305	14	27	42,759	27,154	-
St Fergus	165	10	10	17,838	8,536	4
Sandhaven	68	6	-	6,878	3,497	35
Turriff: St Ninian's and Forglen	742	23	18	75,957	48,998	25

35. Moray

Congregation	Com	Eld	G	In 15	M&M	–18
Aberlour	288	18	25	54,786	32,331	28
Alves and Burghead	145	14	40	43,513	20,602	10
Kinloss and Findhorn	91	-	12	27,419	19,008	-
Bellie and Speymouth	347	26	50	64,750	48,872	-
Birnie and Pluscarden	251	24	23	-	32,141	1
Elgin: High	442	40	-	72,447	43,525	37
Buckie: North	380	29	52	60,949	39,002	13
Rathven	77	15	19	15,348	18,242	5
Buckie: South and West	230	-	34	-	28,177	-

Congregation	Com	Eld	G	In 15	M&M	–18
Enzie	68	-	9	8,598	10,218	-
Cullen and Deskford	286	23	22	-	40,742	-
Dallas	47	-	10	13,776	8,427	-
Forres: St Leonard's	175	9	32	50,984	30,987	30
Rafford	58	6	-	14,193	8,873	22
Duffus, Spynie and Hopeman	230	31	13	57,551	30,308	45
Dyke	115	11	11	28,531	17,794	12
Edinkillie	77	9	-	15,642	14,728	8
Elgin: St Giles' & St Columba's South	435	-	42	119,051	79,622	-
Findochty	44	8	11	-	9,660	4
Portknockie	60	9	14	21,967	10,925	33
Forres: St Laurence	388	-	25	75,001	52,302	-
Keith: North, Newmill, Boharm and Rothiemay	503	37	27	44,522	76,962	25
Keith: St Rufus, Botriphnie and Grange	943	-	34	-	63,473	-
Knockando, Elchies and Archiestown	230	15	10	41,668	27,727	7
Rothes	295	17	12	40,035	27,178	12
Lossiemouth: St Gerardine's High	254	11	28	54,130	33,039	1
Lossiemouth: St James'	293	18	33	54,879	33,713	6
Mortlach and Cabrach	313	13	13	26,650	24,265	-
St Andrew's-Lhanbryd and Urquhart	372	-	30	64,110	46,252	-

36. Abernethy

Abernethy	146	-	-	46,946	25,194	-
Boat of Garten, Duthil and Kincardine	140	-	33	38,513	19,345	-
Alvie and Insh	70	-	-	31,888	18,091	-
Rothiemurchus and Aviemore	-	-	-	13,590	9,908	-
Cromdale and Advie	60	-	-	16,888	15,872	-
Dulnain Bridge	34	-	-	13,282	8,773	-
Grantown-on-Spey	160	-	13	45,262	26,863	-
Kingussie	93	-	-	22,873	18,745	-
Laggan	37	-	-	19,928	9,313	-
Newtonmore	79	-	-	33,119	17,622	-
Tomintoul, Glenlivet and Inveraven	138	-	-	21,060	16,900	-

37. Inverness

Ardersier	52	7	-	41,253	10,442	24
Petty	68	-	12	18,817	9,857	-
Auldearn and Dalmore	56	-	-	11,103	8,214	-
Nairn: St Ninian's	184	13	29	45,519	27,300	9
Cawdor	149	-	-	29,567	20,175	-
Croy and Dalcross	56	-	13	17,292	9,550	-
Culloden: The Barn	232	18	23	96,013	55,895	115
Daviot and Dunlichity	59	-	8	17,634	11,149	-
Moy, Dalarossie and Tomatin	27	3	10	8,894	8,548	12
Dores and Boleskine	70	8	-	14,676	10,221	-
Inverness: Crown	549	73	38	137,929	82,020	110
Inverness: Dalneigh and Bona	179	20	17	59,357	52,722	60
Inverness: East	241	25	-	105,411	75,335	101

Congregation	Com	Eld	G	In 15	M&M	−18
Inverness: Hilton	241	11	-	73,205	56,742	52
Inverness: Inshes	232	18	-	-	80,507	125
Inverness: Kinmylies	82	9	-	41,052	29,135	65
Inverness: Ness Bank	640	65	31	142,881	81,225	75
Inverness: Old High St Stephen's	413	33	-	115,715	76,592	20
Inverness: St Columba	47	-	-	53,626	4,000	-
Inverness: Trinity	213	28	18	74,979	49,840	34
Kilmorack and Erchless	7	9	15	37,785	34,446	14
Kiltarlity	44	5	-	22,278	13,045	10
Kirkhill	109	8	11	19,340	10,283	9
Nairn: Old	517	-	20	107,326	64,766	-
Urquhart and Glenmoriston	110	6	-	56,173	35,366	30

38. Lochaber

Congregation	Com	Eld	G	In 15	M&M	−18
Acharacle	37	5	-	19,696	10,139	22
Ardnamurchan	15	5	-	10,265	5,206	8
Ardgour and Kingairloch	49	6	18	12,439	7,689	10
Morvern	40	5	9	12,674	7,656	15
Strontian	25	4	-	6,361	4,978	-
Duror	33	6	13	11,977	7,158	-
Glencoe: St Munda's	39	8	-	15,221	8,652	-
Fort Augustus	68	10	6	20,794	14,758	30
Glengarry	29	5	11	15,648	7,899	12
Fort William: Duncansburgh MacIntosh	358	24	24	-	59,904	60
Kilmonivaig	63	6	14	25,356	17,518	12
Kilmallie	103	13	22	31,113	25,516	18
Kinlochleven	50	7	15	21,390	11,906	4
Nether Lochaber	45	9	-	18,565	12,711	3
North West Lochaber	87	14	17	31,537	19,360	15

39. Ross

Congregation	Com	Eld	G	In 15	M&M	−18
Alness	75	10	-	27,722	19,464	17
Avoch	17	4	-	16,013	9,791	8
Fortrose and Rosemarkie	73	5	-	34,915	28,917	4
Contin	49	13	-	15,026	15,213	-
Fodderty and Strathpeffer	93	18	-	29,691	16,670	18
Cromarty	38	5	-	13,666	4,158	2
Resolis and Urquhart	75	7	-	35,870	24,010	12
Dingwall: Castle Street	143	19	20	51,402	31,469	28
Dingwall: St Clement's	191	26	14	69,642	32,418	14
Fearn Abbey and Nigg	53	7	-	-	16,546	-
Tarbat	42	8	-	18,376	9,530	2
Ferintosh	136	23	13	52,482	32,129	14
Invergordon	131	10	-	53,862	34,607	30
Killearnan	114	17	-	26,128	34,402	5
Knockbain	46	8	-	-	14,672	-
Kilmuir and Logie Easter	74	9	20	37,951	23,502	7
Kiltearn	61	8	-	33,144	19,596	8
Lochbroom and Ullapool	37	6	-	29,388	19,804	10

Congregation	Com	Eld	G	In 15	M&M	–18
Rosskeen	119	15	20	57,787	38,152	51
Tain	99	7	18	53,623	30,970	10
Urray and Kilchrist	77	13	-	51,320	29,194	64

40. Sutherland

Altnaharra and Farr	22	1	-	-	8,011	-
Assynt and Stoer	13	4	-	18,484	6,564	-
Clyne	59	15	-	-	18,385	2
Kildonan and Loth Helmsdale	30	4	-	13,474	7,711	6
Creich	15	6	-	13,769	14,700	4
Kincardine Croick and Edderton	43	9	-	23,001	16,332	10
Rosehall	18	3	-	13,994	6,387	5
Dornoch: Cathedral	325	33	47	-	71,441	55
Durness and Kinlochbervie	17	1	-	19,098	12,999	-
Eddrachillis	8	2	-	13,889	8,238	2
Golspie	69	15	12	-	30,609	49
Lairg	30	2	12	-	14,519	-
Rogart	13	3	-	-	10,499	-
Melness and Tongue	43	6	-	-	14,477	7

41. Caithness

Bower	36	-	6	-	8,012	-
Halkirk Westerdale	46	6	10	11,714	11,692	-
Watten	40	-	-	11,390	9,172	-
Canisbay	45	-	14	-	9,110	-
Dunnet	18	-	5	6,908	4,806	-
Keiss	27	-	9	9,362	4,955	-
Olrig	51	-	4	6,573	4,776	-
The North Coast Parish	54	-	21	21,720	15,418	-
The Parish of Latheron	64	13	9	22,703	17,875	25
Thurso: St Peter's and St Andrew's	192	-	27	70,505	34,221	-
Thurso: West	218	-	22	57,096	31,024	-
Wick: Pultneytown and Thrumster	240	-	28	-	38,513	-
Wick: St Fergus	259	-	26	53,267	41,913	-

42. Lochcarron-Skye

Applecross, Lochcarron and Torridon	70	6	17	35,327	37,082	10
Bracadale and Duirinish	54	8	8	33,305	23,049	1
Gairloch and Dundonnell	71	-	-	62,669	42,669	-
Glenelg Kintail and Lochalsh	98	9	10	-	40,854	9
Kilmuir and Stenscholl	47	5	-	29,229	21,670	15
Portree	93	12	-	65,692	37,735	19
Snizort	34	3	-	29,042	23,146	2
Strath and Sleat	127	5	17	91,489	62,421	46

43. Uist

Benbecula	60	10	9	33,416	24,551	48
Carinish	78	11	13	46,268	28,020	6
Berneray and Lochmaddy	45	3	9	17,274	19,308	1

Congregation	Com	Eld	G	In 15	M&M	–18
Kilmuir and Paible	28	4	-	26,732	19,776	11
Manish-Scarista	30	3	-	32,606	24,988	11
Tarbert	71	7	-	73,530	44,434	21
44. Lewis						
Barvas	75	10	-	57,780	49,563	26
Carloway	44	2	-	23,583	23,330	22
Cross Ness	60	4	-	44,528	33,282	61
Kinloch	35	4	-	33,989	25,635	16
Knock	50	4	-	29,098	21,913	8
Lochs-Crossbost	11	1	-	20,154	16,067	7
Lochs-in-Bernera	25	3	-	20,331	12,327	10
Uig	24	3	-	21,383	16,525	2
Stornoway: High	83	3	-	-	72,280	20
Stornoway: Martin's Memorial	285	10	-	214,934	60,468	80
Stornoway: St Columba	132	9	35	93,988	53,164	180
45. Orkney						
Birsay, Harray and Sandwick	306	25	33	34,962	26,466	35
East Mainland	225	20	15	28,225	18,527	16
Eday	8	1	-	3,431	1,776	6
Stronsay: Moncur Memorial	70	7	-	14,155	9,017	8
Evie	23	4	-	7,347	8,875	-
Firth	93	7	-	24,499	16,249	43
Rendall	46	5	-	13,899	6,231	27
Rousay	14	2	-	1,916	3,402	-
Flotta	25	7	-	5,459	2,659	-
Hoy and Walls	53	10	13	7,988	3,323	8
Orphir and Stenness	175	12	16	21,414	14,887	8
Kirkwall: East	356	22	30	68,013	43,347	21
Shapinsay	40	8	-	8,085	5,314	12
Kirkwall: St Magnus Cathedral	540	41	25	76,484	41,779	-
North Ronaldsay	8	-	-	-	1,419	-
Sanday	52	4	9	8,830	7,336	-
Papa Westray	8	-	-	11,568	3,548	5
Westray	73	17	27	26,276	20,848	35
South Ronaldsay and Burray	136	11	16	17,807	10,844	12
Stromness	296	26	21	48,118	25,635	25
46. Shetland						
Burra Isle	33	6	12	11,565	5,292	13
Tingwall	120	14	12	35,238	19,911	-
Delting	68	6	13	-	11,154	14
Northmavine	64	8	-	8,363	7,081	9
Dunrossness and St Ninian's	39	11	-	13,048	13,142	9
Sandwick, Cunningsburgh & Quarff	74	7	7	25,731	14,167	13
Lerwick and Bressay	339	28	9	80,547	49,336	37
Nesting and Lunnasting	30	6	13	6,543	5,301	-
Whalsay and Skerries	180	14	15	-	15,206	17

Congregation	Com	Eld	G	In 15	M&M	–18
Sandsting and Aithsting	39	9	-	7,789	4,521	15
Walls and Sandness	31	12	-	7,509	5,136	1
Unst and Fetlar	123	9	20	22,730	11,212	-
Yell	47	10	14	-	7,743	-

47. England

Corby: St Andrew's	239	12	37	41,957	31,493	2
Corby: St Ninian's	181	13	-	45,188	30,227	-
Guernsey: St Andrew's in the Grange	186	19	-	70,486	43,007	25
Jersey: St Columba's	107	17	-	55,540	42,322	-
Liverpool: St Andrew's	24	4	-	24,924	12,258	1
London: Crown Court	226	31	5	-	59,904	14
London: St Columba's	895	53	-	354,755	194,283	27
Newcastle: St Andrew's	101	17	-	-	8,091	6

INDEX OF ADVERTISERS

CARE HOMES
Erskine Hospital ix

CHAPLAINCY
RAF viii

CHURCH BUILDING
Balmore Specialist xviii
Church Lighting xiv
Thomas Robinson xix
Scotia UK x

CHURCH FURNITURE
Fullers xiii
Hayes & Finch xi

CLERICAL TAILORS
J & M Sewing Service xiv
Wippell's xvi

MUSICAL SUPPLIES
Harrison & Harrison xviii
Viscount Classical Organs i

PRINTERS AND STATIONERS
Donation Envelopes ii
Warners Midlands xvii

PUBLISHERS AND BOOKSELLERS
FM Bookshops v
Life and Work .... IFC
Saint Andrew Press 345–7

SOCIAL WORKS
Alcohol Abstainers .... OBC
Christian Aid iv
Craft Worx ii
Housing and Loan Fund vi
MAF .... IBC
Mercy Ships xii
Stewardship Dept xv

STAINED GLASS
Artisan Stained Glass iii
Rainbow Glass vii

INDEX OF MINISTERS

NOTE: Ministers who are members of a Presbytery are designated 'A' if holding a parochial appointment in that Presbytery, or 'B' if otherwise qualifying for membership. 'A-1, A-2' etc. indicate the numerical order of congregations in the Presbyteries of Edinburgh, Glasgow, and Hamilton.

Also included are ministers listed in Section 6:
  (1) Ministers who have resigned their seat in Presbytery and hold a Practising Certificate (List 6-D)
  (2) Ministers who have resigned their seat in Presbytery but who do not hold a Practising Certificate (List 6-E)
  (3) Ministers serving overseas (List 6-J) – see also Presbyteries 48 and 49
  (4) Ordained Local Ministers and Auxiliary Ministers, who are listed both in Presbyteries and in List 6-A and List 6-B respectively
  (5) Ministers who have died since the publication of the last *Year Book* (List 6-R)

NB *For a list of the Diaconate, see List 6-C.*

Abeledo, B.J.A.	Edinburgh 1A-4	Anderson, K.G.	List 6-D	Barr, J.	Stirling 23B
Abernethy, W.	Edinburgh 1B	Anderson, R.A.	West Lothian 2A	Barr, T.L.	Perth 28B
Acklam, C.R.	Argyll 19A	Anderson, R.J.M.	Moray 35A	Barrett, L.M.	Dundee 29B
Adams, D.G.	Kirkcaldy 25B	Anderson, R.S.	Edinburgh 1B	Barrie, A.	Inverness 37A
Adams, J.M.	Moray 35A	Anderson, S.M.	List 6-D	Barrie, A.P.	Hamilton 17B
Adamson, H.M.	List 6-D	Anderson. J.F.	List 6-R	Barrie, D.	Stirling 23A
Adamson, R.A.	Ardrossan 12A	Andrews, J.E.	Lothian 3B	Barrington, C.W.H.	Edinburgh 1B
Addis, R.A.	Edinburgh 1 A-1	Annand, J.M.	Annandale/Eskdale 7B	Barron, J.L.	St Andrews 26B
Ahmed, P.	Lewis 44B	Archer, M.	Inverness 37B	Bartholomew, D.S.	
Aitchison, J.W.	Perth 28A	Archer, N.	Ross 39B		Dumfries/Kirkcudbright 8A
Aitken, A.R.	Edinburgh 1B	Armitage, W.L.	Edinburgh 1B	Bartholomew, J.	List 6-D
Aitken, E.D.	Stirling 23B	Armstrong, G.B.	Greenock/Paisley 14A	Baxendale, G.M.	Hamilton 17B
Aitken, E.R.	List 6-D	Armstrong, W.R.	Greenock/Paisley 14B	Baxter, R.	Lochaber 38A
Aitken, F.R.	Ayr 10A	Arnott, A.D.K.	Melrose/Peebles 4B	Bayne, A.L.	Lothian 3B
Aitken, I.M.	Aberdeen 31A	Ashley-Emery, S.	Edinburgh 1 A-49	Beaton, D.	Lochcarron/Skye 42B
Aitken, J.D.	Edinburgh 1 A-67	Astles, G.D.	Jedburgh 6A	Beattie, C.J.	Glasgow 16A-16
Aitken, P.W.I.	Wigtown/Stranraer 9B	Atkins, Y.E.S.	Lothian 3A	Beattie, W.G.	List 6-R
Albon, D.A.	Ayr 10A	Atkinson, G.T.	Glasgow 16A-116	Beattie, W.R.	List 6-D
Alexander, D.N.	Greenock/Paisley 14B	Attenburrow, A.	Moray 35A	Beautyman, P.H.	Argyll 19B
Alexander, E.J.	Glasgow 16B	Auffermann, M.	Aberdeen 31A	Beck, J.C.	List 6-E
Alexander, H.J.R.	Edinburgh 1 A-30	Auld, A.G.	List 6-D	Beckett, D.M.	Edinburgh 1B
Alexander, I.W.	Edinburgh 1B	Austin, G.	Hamilton 17A-19	Beebee, G.W.	England 47A
Alexander, J.S.	St Andrews 26B			Begg, R.	Stirling 23B
Alexander, W.M.	List 6-D	Bain, B.	Moray 35B	Bell, D.W.	Argyll 19B
Allan, R.S.T.	Falkirk 22A	Baird, K.S.	Edinburgh 1B	Bell, G.K.	Glasgow 16A-55
Allardyce, M.	Kirkcaldy 25A	Baker, C.M.	Wigtown/Stranraer 9B	Bell, I.W.	Greenock/Paisley 14B
Allen, M.A.W.	Glasgow 16B	Balaj, N.I.	Angus 30A	Bell, J.L.	Glasgow 16B
Allen, V.L.	Stirling 23B	Ballentine, A.M.	Perth 28B	Bell, M.	Greenock/Paisley 14B
Allison, A.	St Andrews 26A	Barber, P.I.	Edinburgh 1 A-24	Bellis, P.A.	Wigtown/Stranraer 9B
Allison, M.M.	List 6-R	Barclay, I.C.	Argyll 19A	Bennett, A.G.	Int. Charges 48A
Allison, R.N.	Greenock/Paisley 14A	Barclay, N.W.	List 6-D	Bennett, D.K.P.	
Almond, D.M.	Dunfermline 24B	Barclay, S.G.	Glasgow 16A-15		Dumfries/Kirkcudbright 8B
Alston, C.M.	Dunfermline 24A	Bardgett, F.D.	List 6-D	Benzie, I.W.	Irvine/Kilmarnock 11A
Alston, W.G.	Glasgow 16B	Barge, N.L.	Glasgow 16A-39	Berry, G.T.	Lothian 3B
Anderson, A.F.	England 47B	Barlow, R.D.	Perth 28A	Bertram, T.A.	Perth 28B
Anderson, D.	List 6-D	Barr, A.C.	List 6-R	Beveridge, S.E.P.	
Anderson, D.M.	Lochaber 38B	Barr, D.L.C.	Kincardine/Deeside 32A		Annandale/Eskdale 7B
Anderson, D.P.	England 47B	Barr, G.K.	List 6-R	Bezuidenhout, L.C.	Moray 35A
Anderson, D.U.	Dundee 29A	Barr, G.R.	Edinburgh 1 A-16	Bezuidenhout, W.J.	Glasgow 16A-46

Bicket, M.S. — Angus 30A
Biddle, L. — List 6-D
Billes, R.H. — Edinburgh 1 A-9
Binks, M. — England 47B
Birch, J. — Glasgow 16B
Bircham, M.F. — Perth 28A
Birrell, G.N. — List 6-D
Birrell, I. — List 6-E
Birse, G.S. — Ayr 10B
Birss, A.D. — Greenock/Paisley 14A
Bissett, J. — Ross 39B
Bjarnason, S.S. — List 6-D
Black, A.G. — Lothian 3B
Black, A.R. — Irvine/Kilmarnock 11A
Black, A.T. — Inverness 37B
Black, D.R. — Glasgow 16A-96
Black, D.W. — West Lothian 2B
Black, G.S. — List 6-D
Black, G.W.G. — Hamilton 17A-51
Black, I.W. — Falkirk 22B
Black, J.M.K. — Greenock/Paisley 14B
Black, S. — Ayr 10B
Black, S. — Greenock/Paisley 14A
Black, W.B. — Glasgow 16B
Black, W.G. — List 6-E
Blackley, J.M. — Angus 30A
Blackman, I.R. — Hamilton 17A-41
Blackwood, K.T. — Aberdeen 31A
Blair, F. — Kincardine/Deeside 32A
Blakey, R.S. — Edinburgh 1B
Blakey, S.A. — Duns 5A
Blount, A.S. — Glasgow 16B
Blount, G.K. — Glasgow 16B
Bluett, P. — Edinburgh 1 A-48
Blyth, J.G.S. — Ayr 10B
Boag, J.A.S. — Glasgow 16A-4
Bogle, A.O. — Falkirk 22A
Bogle, T.C. — Ayr 10B
Bom, I. — Int. Charges 48B
Bonar, A.F. — List 6-E
Bond, M.S. — Dumfries/Kirkcudbright 8A
Boonzaaier, J. — West Lothian 2A
Booth, F.M. — Dumbarton 18B
Booth, J. — Edinburgh 1B
Borthwick, K.S. — Edinburgh 1B
Boswell, G.R. — Dunfermline 24A
Bowie, A.G. — England 47B
Bowie, A.M. — Melrose/Peebles 4B
Boyd, B.J. — Moray 35A
Boyd, I.R. — List 6-D
Boyd, J.A. — Kincardine/Deeside 32A
Boyd, K.M. — Edinburgh 1B
Boyd, R.M.H. — Stirling 23B
Boyd, S. — Glasgow 16A-84
Boyes, A.M. — Hamilton 17A-48
Boyle, E. — Wigtown/Stranraer 9A
Boyle, R.P. — Dunfermline 24B
Bradley, A.W. — List 6-D
Bradley, I.C. — St Andrews 26B
Bradwell, A.S. — Lothian 3A
Brady, I.D. — Edinburgh 1B
Brady, L. — St Andrews 26B
Brain, I.J. — Glasgow 16B
Breakey, J. — List 6-E
Breingan, M. — Greenock/Paisley 14B
Brennan, A.J. — Dunkeld/Meigle 27A
Brewster, J. — Hamilton 17A-28
Brice, D.G. — Glasgow 16B
Bristow, W.H.G. — Argyll 19B
Britchfield, A.E.P. — Stirling 23A
Broadley, L.J. — Kincardine/Deeside 32B
Brockie, C.G.F. — Irvine/Kilmarnock 11B

Brodie, J.M. — List 6-R
Brook, S.A. — Edinburgh 1B
Brookes, R.E. — Argyll 19A
Brough, C.M. — Dundee 29A
Brown, A. — List 6-E
Brown, A.B. — Hamilton 17A-63
Brown, D.G. — Inverness 37B
Brown, E. — Perth 28B
Brown, H.J. — List 6-R
Brown, H.T. — Irvine/Kilmarnock 11A
Brown, J. — List 6-E
Brown, J. — List 6-R
Brown, J.H. — Stirling 23B
Brown, J.M. — Ayr 10B
Brown, J.M. — Int. Charges 48A
Brown, J.W.S. — Kincardine/Deeside 32B
Brown, K. — Falkirk 22A
Brown, M.D. — Perth 28B
Brown, P. — Dunfermline 24B
Brown, R.F. — List 6-D
Brown, R.G. — Orkney 45B
Brown, R.H. — Lothian 3B
Brown, S.A. — Glasgow 16A-56
Brown, S.J. — England 47B
Brown, S.M. — Sutherland 40A
Brown, T.J. — Falkirk 22B
Brown, W. — Lothian 3B
Brown, W.D. — Edinburgh 1B
Brown, W.D. — Edinburgh 1B
Browning, D. — Edinburgh 1 A-45
Bruce, A.J. — Gordon 33A
Brunger, L.N. — Hamilton 17A-68
Bryden, W.A. — Glasgow 16B
Bryson, T.M. — Inverness 37A
Buchan, A. — Moray 35B
Buchan, C.A. — Abernethy 36A
Buchan, I.C. — Moray 35A
Buchan, W. — Perth 28B
Buchanan, F.C. — Dumbarton 18A
Buchanan, N. — Hamilton 17A-29
Buck, M. — Hamilton 17B
Buckley, R.G. — Glasgow 16A-125
Buell, F.B. — Inverness 37B
Bull, A.W. — Glasgow 16B
Bullock, F.C. — Angus 30A
Burgess, P.C.J. — List 6-E
Burns, J.H. — Wigtown/Stranraer 9A
Burns, T. — Int. Charges 48B
Burnside, A.H. — Abernethy 36A
Burnside, W.A.M. — Inverness 37B
Burt, D.W.G. — Greenock/Paisley 14A
Burt, T. — Lothian 3B
Burton, S. — Perth 28A
Butters, D. — Angus 30B
Buwert, K.O.F. — Perth 28A
Byers, M.C. — Annandale/Eskdale 7B
Byun, B.D.W. — Aberdeen 31A

Caie, A. — List 6-D
Cairns, A.B. — Wigtown/Stranraer 9B
Cairns, E. — Perth 28B
Cairns, J.B. — Lothian 3B
Cairns, W.A. — England 47B
Cairns, W.R.C. — Kirkcaldy 25A
Calder, B. — Glasgow 16A-24
Calder, T.R. — Gordon 33A
Caldwell, G.J. — Stirling 23A
Calvert, R.A. — Dundee 29A
Cameron, A.J. — Kincardine/Deeside 32B
Cameron, C.M. — Greenock/Paisley 14A
Cameron, D.C. — Edinburgh 1 A-18
Cameron, D.J.R. — Argyll 19A

Cameron, D.S. — Irvine/Kilmarnock 11A
Cameron, G.G. — Edinburgh 1B
Cameron, I. — West Lothian 2B
Cameron, J.U. — St Andrews 26B
Cameron, J.W.M. — Edinburgh 1B
Cameron, M.S. — Ardrossan 12A
Cameron, R. — Glasgow 16A-117
Cameron, R.N. — England 47B
Campbell, A.B. — Stirling 23A
Campbell, A.I. — Glasgow 16B
Campbell, D. — Dumfries/Kirkcudbright 8A
Campbell, D. — Greenock/Paisley 14A
Campbell, F. — Jedburgh 6A
Campbell, G. — Dundee 29B
Campbell, I.M. — Lewis 44A
Campbell, J. — Glasgow 16B
Campbell, J.A. — Irvine/Kilmarnock 11B
Campbell, J.E.R. — List 6-E
Campbell, J.W. — St Andrews 26A
Campbell, K.K. — Edinburgh 1 A-43
Campbell, M.M. — Falkirk 22A
Campbell, N.G. — Dumfries/Kirkcudbright 8A
Campbell, R.D.M. — Argyll 19A
Campbell, R.F. — Inverness 37B
Campbell, R.S. — Dunkeld/Meigle 27B
Campbell, S. — Gordon 33A
Campbell-Jack, W.C. — Falkirk 22B
Cant, T.M. — Irvine/Kilmarnock 11B
Carmichael, D.J.M. — Glasgow 16A-27
Carmichael, D.S. — Lanark 13A
Carruth, P.A. — Glasgow 16A-54
Carruthers, D. — Argyll 19A
Carswell, J.W. — Hamilton 17A-38
Cartlidge, G.R.G. — Glasgow 16B
Cartwright, A.C.D. — Duns 5B
Casey, B.M. — Glasgow 16A-122
Cashman, P.H. — Melrose/Peebles 4B
Caskie, J.C. — Perth 28B
Cassells, A.K. — Dunkeld/Meigle 27B
Cathcart, I.A. — Lothian 3A
Cha, S.Y. — Stirling 23A
Chalmers, G.A. — Falkirk 22B
Chalmers, J.P. — Dunfermline 24B
Chalmers, M. — Edinburgh 1B
Chambers, J. — Sutherland 40B
Charlton, I.A. — Shetland 46A
Cherry, A.J. — Greenock/Paisley 14B
Chestnut, A. — Greenock/Paisley 14B
Cheyne, R.U. — Gordon 33A
Chisholm, A.F. — Inverness 37B
Christie, A.A. — St Andrews 26A
Christie, A.C. — Kincardine/Deeside 32B
Christie, H.F. — Falkirk 22B
Christie, J. — List 6-E
Christie, J.C. — Dumbarton 18B
Christie, R.S. — Irvine/Kilmarnock 11B
Clancy, P.J. — Ayr 10A
Clark, C.M. — Edinburgh 1B
Clark, D.M. — Dundee 29B
Clark, D.W. — Dumbarton 18B
Clark, D.W. — Glasgow 16B
Clark, M. — Melrose/Peebles 4A
Clark, T.L. — Orkney 45B
Clarkson, D. — Ayr 10A
Clegg, O.M.H. — Edinburgh 1 A-32
Cleland, R. — Inverness 37A
Clelland, E. — Lanark 13B
Clinkenbeard, W.W. — Edinburgh 1B
Clipston, S.F. — Ayr 10A
Cloggie, J. — Stirling 23B

Cobain, A.R.	Lothian 3A	Currie, M.F.	Hamilton 17A-6	Douglas, C.R.	Edinburgh 1B
Cochrane, J.P.N.	Stirling 23B	Currie, R.D.	Hamilton 17B	Douglas, F.C.	Dundee 29B
Coleman, S.H.	Perth 28B	Cuthbert, H.E.	Ayr 10A	Douglas, P.C.	St Andrews 26B
Collard, J.K.	Hamilton 17A-20	Cuthbertson, M.	Glasgow 16A-43	Dowswell, J.A.M.	England 47B
Collins, C.E.E.	Dundee 29A	Cuthell, T.C.	Edinburgh 1B	Doyle, D.W.	Hamilton 17B
Collins, D.A.	Dundee 29B	Cutler, J.S.H.	Melrose/Peebles 4B	Doyle, I.B.	Edinburgh 1B
Collins, M.	Kirkcaldy 25B			Drake, W.F.	List 6-D
Coltart, I.O.	Lothian 3B	Dailly, J.R.	Ardrossan 12B	Drummond, A.G.	Perth 28B
Colvin, S.E.F.	Hamilton 17B	Dalton, M.	Dumbarton 18B	Drummond, J.W.	Glasgow 16B
Combe, N.R.	Jedburgh 6B	Darroch, R.J.G.	West Lothian 2B	Drummond, N.W.	List 6-D
Conkey, H.	Kincardine/Deeside 32A	Davidge, A.E.S.	Glasgow 16A-50	Dryden, I.	Gordon 33B
Connolly, D.	St Andrews 26B	Davidge, P.L.V.	Glasgow 16A-72	Drysdale, J.H.	Ardrossan 12B
Connolly, J.	St Andrews 26A	Davidson Kelly, T.		Drysdale, J.P.R.	Angus 30B
Cook, A.W.	Greenock/Paisley 14A		Irvine/Kilmarnock 11B	Du Plessis, J.J.H.	
Cook, H.	Stirling 23B	Davidson, A.	Hamilton 17B		Dumfries/Kirkcudbright 8A
Cook, J.	Buchan 34A	Davidson, A.A.B.	Moray 35B	Duff, S.M.	Moray 35A
Cook, J.	Edinburgh 1B	Davidson, D.H.	Edinburgh 1B	Duff, T.M.F.	Glasgow 16B
Cook, J.A.	Gordon 33A	Davidson, E.L.	Stirling 23A	Duff, V.J.	Glasgow 16A-118
Cook, J.S.	Hamilton 17B	Davidson, I.M.P.	Edinburgh 1B	Duffin, G.L.	Lothian 3A
Cooper, D.	Shetland 46A	Davidson, J.	Irvine/Kilmarnock 11B	Dunbar, L.J.	Melrose/Peebles 4A
Cooper, G.	List 6-E	Davidson, J.F.	List 6-D	Duncan, A.S.	Glasgow 16A-109
Corbett, R.T.	Lochaber 38A	Davidson, M.R.	List 6-D	Duncan, C.A.	Melrose/Peebles 4B
Cord, S.	Ross 39A	Davidson, S.	Stirling 23A	Duncan, E.	Caithness 41B
Cordukes, R.	Orkney 45A	Davies, G.W.	List 6-E	Duncan, J.	Dunkeld/Meigle 27B
Cougan, G.M.	List 6-D	Davies, J.M.	Gordon 33B	Duncan, J.C.	St Andrews 26A
Coull, M.C.	Greenock/Paisley 14A	Dawson, M.A.	Annandale/Eskdale 7B	Duncan, M.M.	
Coulter, D.G.	England 47B	Dawson, M.S.	Edinburgh 1B		Dumfries/Kirkcudbright 8A
Coutts, F.	Buchan 34B	De Beer, K.M.	Hamilton 17A-9	Duncan, R.F.	Angus 30B
Cowan, J.S.A.	Greenock/Paisley 14A	De Groot, J.	Glasgow 16A-115	Duncan, R.P.	Kincardine/Deeside 32A
Cowell, S.G.	Lanark 13B	De Jager, L.	Edinburgh 1 A-53	Duncanson, M.	Abernethy 36B
Cowie, G.S.	Aberdeen 31A	Dean, R.A.F.	List 6-R	Dundas, T.B.S.	List 6-R
Cowie, J.A.	Edinburgh 1 A-71	Deans, G.D.S.	Aberdeen 31A	Dunleavy, S.	West Lothian 2B
Cowie, J.M.	List 6-D	Dee, O.	Dumfries/Kirkcudbright 8A	Dunlop, A.J.	Argyll 19B
Cowie, M.	Aberdeen 31B	Dempsey, B.	Ross 39A	Dunn, W.I.C.	Edinburgh 1B
Cowieson, R.J.	List 6-D	Dempster, C.J.	Kincardine/Deeside 32A	Dunn, W.S.	Hamilton 17B
Cowper, A.	Stirling 23A	Dempster, E.T.	Annandale/Eskdale 7A	Dunnett, A.L.	Stirling 23B
Craggs, S.	Gordon 33B	Denniston, D.W.	Perth 28A	Dunphy, R.	West Lothian 2B
Craig, A.J.D.	Gordon 33B	Denniston, J.M.	Glasgow 16A-10	Dunsmore, B.W.	Aberdeen 31A
Craig, E.	List 6-E	Derrick, O.	Greenock/Paisley 14A	Dupar, K.W.	Ross 39B
Craig, G.T.	Aberdeen 31B	Devenny, R.P.	Melrose/Peebles 4B	Durno, R.C.	Glasgow 16A-79
Craig, G.W.	List 6-E	Dewar, J.S.	Edinburgh 1 A-34	Durno, R.C.	Irvine/Kilmarnock 11A
Craig, J.H.	Perth 28B	Dick, A.B.	Lothian 3B	Dutch, M.M.	Glasgow 16B
Craig, R.	Greenock/Paisley 14A	Dick, J.H.A.	List 6-D	Dutton, D.W.	List 6-E
Craig, R.A.S.	List 6-D	Dick, J.R.	Melrose/Peebles 4B		
Craig, W.	List 6-R	Dick, J.S.	List 6-E	Earl, J.	Jedburgh 6B
Craik, S.	Dundee 29B	Dick, R.S.	List 6-R	Earnshaw, P.	St Andrews 26B
Cramb, E.M.	Dundee 29B	Dickie, M.M.	Ayr 10B	Easton, D.J.C.	Lanark 13B
Cranfield, E.F.	Kirkcaldy 25A	Dicks, S.M.	Moray 35A	Easton, L.C.	Greenock/Paisley 14B
Cranfield, M.N.	Gordon 33A	Dickson, G.T.	List 6-D	Easton-Berry, J.	Lochcarron/Skye 42A
Cranston, R.D.	Greenock/Paisley 14A	Dilbey, M.D.	Edinburgh 1B	Eddie, D.C.	Aberdeen 31A
Crawford, G.W.	Perth 28A	Dillon, A.J.	Annandale/Eskdale 7A	Edwards, D.	Angus 30A
Crawford, M.	List 6-E	Dingwall, B.	Angus 30A	Elliott, G.J.	Uist 43A
Creegan, C.M.	Dunkeld/Meigle 27B	Dobby, D.B.	Shetland 46A	Elliott, K.C.	Ayr 10A
Crichton, J.	Ayr 10A	Dobby, D.J.	Shetland 46A	Ellis, D.W.	List 6-D
Cringles, G.G.	Argyll 19A	Dobie, R.J.W.	Melrose/Peebles 4B	Elston, I.J.	Kirkcaldy 25A
Crombie, W.D.	Dumbarton 18B	Dodd, M.E.	Melrose/Peebles 4B	Elston, P.K.	Kirkcaldy 25B
Crossan, W.	Argyll 19B	Dodman, R.	List 6-E	Embleton, B.M.	Edinburgh 1B
Crosthwaite, M.D.	Falkirk 22A	Don, A.	Lothian 3A	Embleton, S.R.	Edinburgh 1B
Cruickshank, N.	Ardrossan 12B	Donaghy, L.G.	Dumbarton 18B	Erasmus, A.F.	Ross 39A
Crumlish, E.A.	Ayr 10B	Donald, A.C.	Kirkcaldy 25A	Erskine, C.	Kirkcaldy 25A
Cubie, J.P.	Greenock/Paisley 14B	Donald, A.P.	Edinburgh 1B	Erskine, M.J.	Dunkeld/Meigle 27A
Cullen, W.T.	List 6-E	Donald, K.W.	Lothian 3A	Espie, H.	List 6-D
Cumming, A.	England 47B	Donald, P.H.	Inverness 37A	Evans-Boiten, J.H.G.	Lothian 3A
Cumming, D.P.L.	List 6-R	Donald, R.M.	Dundee 29B	Eve, J.C.	Glasgow 16A-6
Cunningham, A.	Glasgow 16B	Donaldson, C.V.	List 6-D	Ewart, W.	Dunkeld/Meigle 27B
Cunningham, I.D.	Lanark 13A	Donaldson, D.	Uist 43A	Ewart-Roberts, P.	Dunkeld/Meigle 27A
Cunningham, J.S.A.	Glasgow 16B	Donaldson, G.M.	Hamilton 17B		
Curran, E.M.	Edinburgh 1B	Donaldson, R.B.	Perth 28B	Fair, W.M.	Angus 30A
Currie, A.I.	Wigtown/Stranraer 9A	Dougall, E.G.	Edinburgh 1B	Fairful, J.	List 6-D
Currie, D.E.P.	List 6-D	Dougall, N.J.	Lothian 3A	Fairlie, G.	St Andrews 26B
Currie, G.C.M.	List 6-E	Douglas, A.B.	Edinburgh 1B	Falconer, A.D.	Ardrossan 12B
Currie, I.S.	Ardrossan 12B	Douglas, A.M.	Aberdeen 31B	Falconer, J.B.	Aberdeen 31B

Faris, J.M.	Melrose/Peebles 4A
Farmes, S.	Wigtown/Stranraer 9A
Farquhar, W.E.	Dunfermline 24B
Farquharson, G.	Edinburgh 1B
Farrington, A.	Glasgow 16B
Faulds, N.L.	Edinburgh 1B
Fawkes, G.M.A.	Buchan 34B
Fazakas, S.	Lochcarron/Skye 42A
Fenwick, K.	Angus 30A
Ferguson, A.M.	Dumbarton 18B
Ferguson, D.J.	Kirkcaldy 25B
Ferguson, J.A.	Aberdeen 31A
Ferguson, J.B.	Glasgow 16B
Ferguson, R.	List 6-D
Ferguson, W.B.	Glasgow 16B
Fergusson, D.A.S.	Edinburgh 1B
Fiddes, G.F.	Ayr 10A
Fidler, D.G.	Orkney 45B
Fields, J.	England 47B
Finch, G.S.	Dumfries/Kirkcudbright 8B
Findlay, H.J.W.	Lanark 13B
Findlay, Q.	List 6-E
Finlay, W.P.	Ardrossan 12B
Finnie, B.H.	Glasgow 16A-22
Finnie, C.J.	Jedburgh 6A
Fisk, E.A.	Dunfermline 24A
Fleming, A.F.	Glasgow 16B
Fleming, H.K.	Perth 28B
Fleming, J.C.	Greenock/Paisley 14A
Fletcher, G,G,	Glasgow 16A-52
Fletcher, S.G.	Lothian 3A
Fletcher, T.E.G.	Perth 28A
Flockhart, D.R.	List 6-E
Foggie, A.P.	Dundee 29A
Foggitt, E.W.	List 6-E
Forbes, I.M.	List 6-R
Forbes, J.W.A.	List 6-E
Ford, A.A.	Ardrossan 12B
Ford, C.H.M.	Edinburgh 1 A-65
Forrest, A.B.	Argyll 19B
Forrest, K.P.	Greenock/Paisley 14B
Forrest, M.R.	Glasgow 16B
Forrester, D.D.	List 6-E
Forrester, I.L.	Kirkcaldy 25B
Forsyth, A.R.	Kirkcaldy 25B
Forsyth, J.	Ross 39B
Forsyth, S.	Glasgow 16B
Fortune, E.J.	Aberdeen 31A
Foster, J.G.	Edinburgh 1 A-33
Foster, M.M.	Edinburgh 1 A-51
Foster-Fulton, S.	Stirling 23B
Fothergill, A.P.	Buchan 34A
Fowler, A.J.R.	Kirkcaldy 25A
Fowler, R.C.A.	List 6-E
Fowlie, R.A.	Buchan 34A
Frail, N.R.	Lothian 3B
Francis, J.	England 47B
Frank, D.L.	Glasgow 16A-127
Fraser, A.G.	St Andrews 26B
Fraser, A.M.	Glasgow 16A-86
Fraser, D.W.	Dundee 29B
Fraser, I.C.	Greenock/Paisley 14B
Fraser, I.M.	List 6-D
Fraser, J.	Inverness 37B
Fraser, J.P.	List 6-R
Fraser, J.W.	Lothian 3B
Fraser, S.A.	Edinburgh 1B
Frater, A.	Dumbarton 18A
Frazer, R.E.	Edinburgh 1 A-29
Freeth, J.	Orkney 45B
Frew, J.M.	List 6-D
Frew, M.W.	Edinburgh 1 A-70
Frew, R.	Kirkcaldy 25A
Frizzell, R.S.	List 6-E
Froude, J.K.	Kirkcaldy 25A
Fucella, M.	Lanark 13A
Fulcher, C.P.	Argyll 19A
Fulcher, S.	Argyll 19A
Fulton, R.S.M.	Stirling 23A
Gaddes, Donald R.	Duns 5B
Galbraith, C.	West Lothian 2A
Galbraith, D.D.	Kirkcaldy 25B
Galbraith, N.W.	Glasgow 16A-57
Galbraith, W.J.L.	Dundee 29B
Gale, R.A.A.	Duns 5B
Gall, R.	Kincardine/Deeside 32A
Gallacher, J.W.	Falkirk 22A
Galloway, I.F.	Glasgow 16A-74
Galloway, K.	Glasgow 16B
Galloway, R.W.C.	St Andrews 26B
Gammack, G.	List 6-D
Garden, M.J.	Aberdeen 31B
Gardner, A.	Int. Charges 48A
Gardner, B.K.	List 6-D
Gardner, F.J.	List 6-E
Gardner, F.M.E.	Glasgow 16A-123
Gardner, H.M.	Sutherland 40A
Gardner, J.V.	Edinburgh 1B
Gardner N.N.	Edinburgh 1 A-7
Gardner, P.M.	Glasgow 16A-99
Gargrave, M.R.	Glasgow 16A-38
Garrett, M.	Ayr 10A
Garrity, T.A.W.	Irvine/Kilmarnock 11B
Gaston, A.R.C.	Stirling 23B
Gatherer, J.F.	Dumfries/Kirkcudbright 8A
Gatima, E.	Aberdeen 31A
Gatt, D.W.	Kirkcaldy 25B
Gauld, B.	List 6-D
Gauld, K.	Gordon 33A
Gay, D.C.	Glasgow 16B
Geddes, A.J.	Ayr 10B
Geddes, E.	Greenock/Paisley 14B
Gehrke, R.B.	Buchan 34B
Gemmell, D.R.	Ayr 10A
Gemmell, J.	Glasgow 16A-2
Gerbrandy-Baird, P.S.	Dunfermline 24A
Gibb, J.D.M.	Annandale/Eskdale 7B
Gibson, A.W.	Hamilton 17A-56
Gibson, E.A.	Argyll 19B
Gibson, F.S.	Argyll 19B
Gibson, H.M.	Glasgow 16B
Gibson, I.	Kirkcaldy 25B
Gibson, J.M.	Hamilton 17A-13
Gilchrist, E.J.	Aberdeen 31A
Gilchrist, K.	Hamilton 17A-4
Gill, P.G.	Greenock/Paisley 14A
Gillan, D.S.	West Lothian 2A
Gillespie, I.C.	Stirling 23B
Gillies, J.E.	List 6-D
Gillon, C. B.	Irvine/Kilmarnock 11B
Gillon, D.R.M.	Greenock/Paisley 14A
Gilmour, I.Y.	Edinburgh 1 A-59
Gilmour, W.M.	Stirling 23B
Gisbey, J.E.	Kirkcaldy 25B
Glass, A.	List 6-R
Glen, G.E.D.	Gordon 33A
Glencross, W.M.	Ayr 10B
Glover, N.M.	Glasgow 16A-8
Glover, R.L.	Lothian 3B
Godfrey, L.	Irvine/Kilmarnock 11B
Gohar, A.	Falkirk 22A
Goldie, C.M.	Dumbarton 18A
Goldie, G.D.	Aberdeen 31B
Goncalves, D.P.	Edinburgh 1 A-5
Goodison, M.J.	Stirling 23B
Gordon, A.B.	Hamilton 17B
Gordon, D.C.	Ardrossan 12B
Gordon, E.J.	List 6-D
Gordon, I.D.	Kirkcaldy 25B
Gordon, L.Y.	Aberdeen 31B
Gordon, P.	Greenock/Paisley 14A
Gordon, P.M.	St Andrews 26B
Gordon, T.	Edinburgh 1B
Goring, I.M.	Stirling 23B
Goskirk, J.L.	Sutherland 40B
Goss, A.J.	Argyll 19B
Goss, M.S.	Angus 30A
Goudie, S.	Sutherland 40A
Gough, I.G.	Angus 30B
Gow, N.	List 6-E
Graham, A.D.M.	Aberdeen 31B
Graham, A.F.	Ross 39A
Graham, A.G.	Angus 30A
Graham, D.J.	Lothian 3A
Graham, J.D.	Orkney 45B
Graham, K.E.	Edinburgh 1 A-47
Graham, R.E.	Glasgow 16A-126
Graham, S.S.	Perth 28B
Graham, W.P.	Edinburgh 1B
Grahame, R.J.	Angus 30A
Grainger, A.J.	List 6-D
Grainger, H.L.	Aberdeen 31B
Granger, D.A.	Ardrossan 12A
Grant, D.I.M.	Glasgow 16B
Grant, J.G.	Ayr 10B
Grant, N.M.	Dunfermline 24A
Grant, P.G.R.	Hamilton 17B
Gray, A.H.	Moray 35A
Gray, C.M.	Glasgow 16B
Gray, D.T.	Dundee 29A
Gray, I.	Angus 30B
Gray, K.N.	Greenock/Paisley 14A
Gray, W.	Argyll 19B
Greaves, A.T.	Dundee 29B
Green, A.H.	Glasgow 16B
Greenshields, I.M.	Dunfermline 24A
Greer, A.D.C.	Dumfries/Kirkcudbright 8B
Gregory, J.C.	Perth 28B
Gregson, E.M.	Glasgow 16B
Greig, A.	Dunfermline 24A
Greig, C.H.M.	Shetland 46B
Greig, J.C.G.	List 6-R
Greig, R.G.	West Lothian 2A
Grier, J.	Hamilton 17B
Grieve, L.	Glasgow 16A-63
Griffiths, M.J.	Kincardine/Deeside 32A
Griffiths, R.I.	Argyll 19A
Griggs, J.J.	Edinburgh 1 A-12
Groenewald, A.	West Lothian 2A
Groenewald, J.	West Lothian 2A
Groves, I.	Gordon 33B
Grubb, G.D.W.	List 6-D
Gruer, K.R.	Buchan 34A
Gunn, A.M.	Perth 28B
Gunn. F.D.	Hamilton 17A-2
Guthrie, J.A.	Ayr 10B
Guy, S.C.	Aberdeen 31A
Haddow, A.	Duns 5A
Haddow, A.H.	Aberdeen 31B
Haddow, M.M.	Dunkeld/Meigle 27A
Haley, D.	Glasgow 16B

Hall, K.F.   Dundee 29A
Hall, W.M.   Irvine/Kilmarnock 11B
Halley, R.D.   Lothian 3A
Halliday, A.R.   Perth 28B
Hamill, R.   List 6-R
Hamilton, A.J.   Dumbarton 18A
Hamilton, D.G.   Dumbarton 18A
Hamilton, D.S.M.   List 6-E
Hamilton, H.   Aberdeen 31B
Hamilton, I.W.F.   St Andrews 26B
Hamilton, R.A.   Hamilton 17A-7
Hamilton, R.G.   Dumbarton 18A
Hamilton, W.D.   Greenock/Paisley 14B
Hammond, R.J.   Dumfries/Kirkcudbright 8B
Hannah, W.   Ayr 10B
Harbison, D.J.H.   Ardrossan 12B
Harbison, K.E.   Greenock/Paisley 14A
Hardie, H.W.   Melrose/Peebles 4B
Hardie, R.K.   Falkirk 22B
Hardman Moore, S.   Edinburgh 1B
Hare, M.M.W.   Irvine/Kilmarnock 11B
Harkness, J.   Edinburgh 1B
Harley, E.   Melrose/Peebles 4A
Harper, A.J.M.   List 6-D
Harper, D.J.   Stirling 23A
Harper, D.L.   Ayr 10B
Harris, J.W.F.   Dumbarton 18B
Harrison, C.   St Andrews 26B
Harrison, F.   Lothian 3A
Harvey, J.   Wigtown/Stranraer 9B
Harvey, P.R.   Annandale/Eskdale 7B
Harvey, W.J.   Glasgow 16B
Haslett, H.J.   List 6-D
Hastie, G.I.   Angus 30B
Haston, C.B.   Annandale/Eskdale 7A
Hawdon, J.E.   Dundee 29B
Hawthorn, D.   Gordon 33B
Hay, J.W.   Edinburgh 1 A-54
Hay, W.J.R.   List 6-R
Hays, D.M.   Dundee 29A
Hazlett, W.I.P.   Glasgow 16B
Hebenton, D.J.   Ardrossan 12B
Heenan, W.J.   Lewis 44A
Hegarty, J.D.   List 6-R
Helon, G.G.   List 6-R
Henderson, E.M.   Edinburgh 1 A-58
Henderson, F.M.   Annandale/Eskdale 7A
Henderson, G.M.   Argyll 19B
Henderson, J.M.   Falkirk 22A
Henderson, R.J.M.   Glasgow 16A-95
Hendrie, B.   Ayr 10A
Hendrie, Y.   List 6-D
Hendry, K.E.   Glasgow 16A-130
Herbold Ross, K.M.   Edinburgh 1B
Heriot, C.R.   List 6-R
Herkes, M.   List 6-R
Hetherington, R.M.   Greenock/Paisley 14B
Hewitt, W.C.   Glasgow 16B
Hibbert, F.W.   List 6-D
Hickman, M.R.   Ardrossan 12A
Hickman, M.R.   Ayr 10B
Higham, R.D.   Duns 5B
Hill, J.W.   Edinburgh 1B
Hill, R.E.   Lothian 3A
Hilsley, B.C.   Lothian 3A
Hobson, D.L.   Aberdeen 31A
Hodge, W.N.T.   Angus 30B
Hogg, T.M.   Melrose/Peebles 4B
Hogg, W.T.   Dumfries/Kirkcudbright 8A
Holland, J.C.   List 6-R

Holland, W.   Dumfries/Kirkcudbright 8B
Holt, J.   Edinburgh 1 A-52
Homewood, I.M.   List 6-E
Hood, A.J.J.   Duns 5A
Hood, C.A.   Argyll 19B
Hood, D.P.   Glasgow 16A-90
Hood, E.L.   Greenock/Paisley 14A
Hood, H.S.C.   Argyll 19B
Hood, J.C.   Hamilton 17A-42
Hope, E.P.   Glasgow 16B
Hope, G.H.   Duns 5B
Horne, A.M.   Falkirk 22A
Horne, D.A.   Ross 39B
Horsburgh, A.G.   Lothian 3A
Horsburgh, G.E.   Irvine/Kilmarnock 11B
Hosain Lamarti, S.   Irvine/Kilmarnock 11B
Hosie, J.   List 6-R
Houghton, C.   Kirkcaldy 25B
Houston, E.W.   Dumbarton 18A
Houston, G.R.   Lanark 13B
Houston, T.C.   Glasgow 16B
Houston, W.R.   West Lothian 2A
Howie, M.L.K.   Ardrossan 12B
Howie, W.   List 6-E
Howitt, J.M.   Glasgow 16A-114
Hudson, E.V.   Dumbarton 18B
Hudson, H.R.   Glasgow 16A-48
Huggett, J.A.   Irvine/Kilmarnock 11B
Hughes, B.   Melrose/Peebles 4B
Hughes, D.W.   Hamilton 17A-52
Huie, D.F.   List 6-E
Humphrey, J.W.   Inverness 37A
Hunt, M.J.   Angus 30A
Hunt, T.G.   Inverness 37B
Hunter, A.G.   Glasgow 16B
Hunter, J.E.   Hamilton 17B
Hunter, W.F.   St Andrews 26A
Hurst, F.R.   List 6-E
Hurst, K.   Int. Charges 48A
Hutcheson, N.M.   List 6-D
Hutchison, A.M.   List 6-D
Hutchison, D.S.   Aberdeen 31B

Inglis, A.   Edinburgh 1B
Inglis, D.B.C.   List 6-E
Ingram, J.R.   Dundee 29B
Irvin, S.D.   Edinburgh 1 A-61
Irvine, E.H.C.   Greenock/Paisley 14B
Irving, D.R.   Dumfries/Kirkcudbright 8A
Irving, W.D.   Edinburgh 1B
Izett, W.A.F.   Stirling 23B

Jack, A.M.   Stirling 23B
Jack, J.A.P.   Edinburgh 1 A-22
Jackson, J.A.   List 6-R
Jackson, N.   Ayr 10B
Jackson, W.   Hamilton 17A-5
Jaeger-Fleming, U.   Edinburgh 1 A-39
Jaffrey, A.   Gordon 33A
Jamieson, A.J.   Glasgow 16A-68
Jamieson, D.B.   Dundee 29B
Jamieson, E.M.M.   List 6-D
Jamieson, G.D.   West Lothian 2B
Jamieson, H.E.   Lanark 13A
Jefferson, M.S.   Melrose/Peebles 4A
Jeffrey, E.W.S.   Edinburgh 1B
Jeffrey, K.S.   St Andrews 26B
Jeffrey, S.D.   Inverness 37B
Jenkins, G.F.C.   Dunfermline 24B
Jenkinson, J.J.   List 6-D

Jessamine, A.L.   Dunfermline 24B
Job, A.J.   Falkirk 22B
Johnson, C.I.W.   Dumbarton 18A
Johnston, C.D.   Int. Charges 48B
Johnston, J.E.   Stirling 23A
Johnston, J.P.N.   Aberdeen 31A
Johnston, M.H.   Glasgow 16A-85
Johnston, R.   List 6-R
Johnston, R.W.M.   Glasgow 16B
Johnston, T.N.   Dunfermline 24B
Johnston, W.A.   Orkney 45A
Johnston, W.R.   Ayr 10B
Johnstone, B.   Lewis 44B
Johnstone, H.M.J.   Glasgow 16B
Johnstone, M.E.   Glasgow 16A-25
Johnstone, R.   Caithness 41B
Johnstone, W.   List 6-E
Jones, A.M.   Lothian 3B
Jones, A.M.   Sutherland 40A
Jones, J.O.   Argyll 19A
Jones, R.   Ross 39A
Jones, R.A.   Gordon 33B
Jones, W.G.   Ayr 10A

Kavanagh, J.A.   Glasgow 16A-29
Kay, D.   Greenock/Paisley 14B
Kay, E.   Dundee 29B
Keating, G.K.   Irvine/Kilmarnock 11B
Keddie, D.A.   List 6-R
Keefe, J.A.   Glasgow 16A-100
Keil, A.H.   Edinburgh 1 A-60
Kellas, D.J.   Lochcarron/Skye 42B
Keller, L.   Melrose/Peebles 4A
Kellett, J.M.   Melrose/Peebles 4B
Kellock, C.N.   Lothian 3B
Kelly, E.R.   List 6-D
Kelly, I.J.M.   List 6-R
Kelly, T.C.   Perth 28B
Kelly, W.W.   Dumfries/Kirkcudbright 8B
Kemp, T.   Dumbarton 18B
Kennedy, G.   Edinburgh 1 A-14
Kennon, S.   Melrose/Peebles 4B
Kenny, C.G.   List 6-D
Kenny, E.S.S.   Dunfermline 24B
Kent, A.F.S.   Ayr 10B
Kent, R.M.   Hamilton 17B
Kenton, M.B.   West Lothian 2A
Kerr, A.   Duns 5B
Kerr, A.   West Lothian 2A
Kerr, B.   Lanark 13A
Kerr, H.F.   List 6-D
Kesting, S.M.   Falkirk 22B
Keyes, J.A.   Falkirk 22A
Kimmitt, A.W.D.   Kirkcaldy 25A
Kincaid, J.   List 6-R
Kingston, D.V.F.   Edinburgh 1B
Kinnear, M.A.   Lochaber 38A
Kinninburgh, E.B.F.   Kincardine/Deeside 32B
Kinsey, L.   Aberdeen 31A
Kirk, S.M.   Buchan 34A
Kirk, W.L.   Dumfries/Kirkcudbright 8B
Kirkland, S.R.M.   Glasgow 16A-28
Kirkpatrick, A.H.   Shetland 46B
Kirkwood, G.   Glasgow 16A-81
Kirkwood, J.A.   Dunfermline 24A
Kisitu, T.M.   Edinburgh 1 A-68
Knox, J.W.   Dunkeld/Meigle 27B
Knox, R.A.   Shetland 46B
Kuzma, A.P.   Uist 43A
Kyle, C.A.E.   Hamilton 17A-46

Lacy, D.W.	Irvine/Kilmarnock 11A	
Laidlaw, J.J.	Dundee 29B	
Laidlaw, V.W.N.	Dunfermline 24B	
Laing, D.J.H.	Dundee 29B	
Laing, I.A.	Ayr 10B	
Lamb, A.D.	Kincardine/Deeside 32B	
Lamb, A.H.W.	Lochaber 38B	
Lamont, A.	Argyll 19B	
Lancaster, C.	England 47B	
Landale, W.S.	Duns 5B	
Landels, J.	Stirling 23B	
Lane, M.R.	Edinburgh 1 A-35	
Lang, I.P.	Glasgow 16B	
Langlands, C.H.	England 47B	
Lawrie, B.B.	Melrose/Peebles 4B	
Lawrie, D.R.	Hamilton 17A-43	
Lawrie, R.M.	List 6-D	
Lawson, D.G.	Int. Charges 48A	
Lawson, J.B.	Perth 28B	
Lawson, K.C.	Edinburgh 1B	
Lawson, R.G.	Perth 28B	
Ledgard, J.C.	List 6-D	
Lees, A.P.	Dumbarton 18A	
Legge, R.	Gordon 33A	
Leishman, J.S.	List 6-D	
Leitch, D.G.	Dunfermline 24B	
Leitch, M.	Greenock/Paisley 14B	
Lennox, L.I.	Ayr 10B	
Levison, C.L.	Glasgow 16B	
Liddell, M.	List 6-R	
Liddiard, F.G.B.	List 6-D	
Lillie, F.L.	Glasgow 16A-111	
Lincoln, J.	Ross 39B	
Lind, G.K.	Irvine/Kilmarnock 11A	
Lind, M.J.	Argyll 19B	
Lindsay, D.G.	Duns 5B	
Lindsay, W.D.	List 6-D	
Lines, C.	Irvine/Kilmarnock 11A	
Linford, V.J.	Melrose/Peebles 4A	
Lithgow, A.R.	List 6-D	
Livesley, A.	Inverness 37B	
Livingstone, A.	Perth 28A	
Lloyd, J.M.	Glasgow 16B	
Lochrie, J.S.	Ayr 10B	
Locke, D.I.W.	Buchan 34A	
Lockerbie, C.R.	Shetland 46A	
Lodge, B.P.	Greenock/Paisley 14B	
Logan, A.T.	Edinburgh 1B	
Logan, D.D.J.	Dumfries/Kirkcudbright 8A	
Logan, R.J.V.	List 6-D	
Logan, T.M.	List 6-D	
London, D.	Angus 30A	
Lough, A.J.	Perth 28A	
Lovett, M.F.	England 47B	
Low, J.E.S.	Perth 28B	
Lowey, M.	Glasgow 16A-102	
Lugton, G.L.	England 47B	
Lunan, D.W.	Glasgow 16B	
Lunn, D.I.M.	England 47A	
Lust, A.S.	Hamilton 17B	
Lyall, D.	List 6-D	
Lyall, M.G.	Hamilton 17A-70	
Lynn, J.	List 6-E	
Lynn, R.	Ayr 10B	
Lyon, A.	Inverness 37B	
Lyon, M.	Falkirk 22A	
Lyons, E.D.	Wigtown/Stranraer 9A	
Macalister, E.	Gordon 33B	
Macarthur, A.I.	Lochcarron/Skye 42B	
Macaskill, D.	List 6-E	
Macaulay, G.	Falkirk 22B	
MacBain, I.W.	Glasgow 16B	
MacColl, J.	Greenock/Paisley 14B	
MacColl, J.C.	Greenock/Paisley 14B	
Macdonald, C.D.	Glasgow 16A-17	
Macdonald, F.A.J.	Edinburgh 1B	
MacDonald, G.	Falkirk 22A	
MacDonald, I	Edinburgh 1 A-32	
Macdonald, I.	Uist 43B	
MacDonald, I.D.	Orkney 45A	
Macdonald, I.M.M.	Uist 43A	
Macdonald, I.U.	List 6-R	
MacDonald, J.M.		
	Irvine/Kilmarnock 11B	
MacDonald, J.W.	Perth 28B	
MacDonald, K.	Glasgow 16B	
MacDonald, M.	Falkirk 22A	
Macdonald, M.	Hamilton 17A-71	
Macdonald, M.C.	List 6-E	
Macdonald, M.J.	Ross 39A	
Macdonald, N.	Lanark 13A	
Macdonald, P.J.	Edinburgh 1B	
MacDonald, R.I.T.	Ardrossan 12A	
Macdonald, S.	Ross 39A	
Macdonald, W.J.	Edinburgh 1B	
MacDougall, L.I.	Lanark 13B	
MacDougall, M.I.	Lanark 13A	
Macdougall, M.M.	Melrose/Peebles 4A	
MacEwan, D.G.	St Andrews 26B	
MacEwan, J.A.I.	Abernethy 36B	
MacFadyen, A.M.	Glasgow 16B	
Macfarlane, A.G.C..	List 6-E	
MacFarlane, D.C.	Melrose/Peebles 4B	
Macfarlane, J.	Argyll 19B	
Macfarlane, P.T.	England 47B	
Macfarlane, T.G.	List 6-E	
Macgregor, A.	Buchan 34A	
Macgregor, J.	Perth 28A	
MacGregor, J.B.	Glasgow 16A-76	
MacGregor, M.S.	Edinburgh 1B	
MacGregor, N.I.M.	Gordon 33A	
MacGregor, R.M.	Shetland 46B	
Machado, K.	England 47A	
MacInnes, D.	Uist 43B	
MacInnes, D.M.	Glasgow 16A-71	
Macintyre, T.	Shetland 46B	
Maciver, I.	List 6-D	
Maciver, N.	Aberdeen 31B	
MacIver, N.	Uist 43B	
Mack, E.A.	Dumfries/Kirkcudbright 8B	
Mack, J.C.	Gordon 33B	
Mack, K.L.	Lothian 3A	
Mack, L.	Stirling 23A	
MacKay, A.H.	List 6-D	
Mackay, G.C.	Glasgow 16A-49	
Mackay, K.J.	West Lothian 2B	
Mackay, M.H.	Ardrossan 12B	
MacKay, S.A.	Edinburgh 1B	
Mackenzie, A.M.	List 6-D	
Mackenzie, A.R.A.	Edinburgh 1 A-37	
Mackenzie, C.	Edinburgh 1 A-72	
MacKenzie, D.W.	List 6-R	
Mackenzie, G.R.	Glasgow 16B	
Mackenzie, H.M.	Lochcarron/Skye 42B	
MacKenzie, I.C.	Hamilton 17B	
Mackenzie, J.G.	Edinburgh 1B	
Mackenzie, K.	Hamilton 17A-35	
Mackenzie, K.I.	Kincardine/Deeside 32A	
Mackenzie, R.K.	Argyll 19A	
Mackenzie, S.L.	Inverness 37B	
Mackie, J.F.	List 6-E	
Mackinnon, C.	Glasgow 16A-45	
MacKinnon, C.M.	Glasgow 16B	
Mackinnon, R.M.	Ross 39B	
Mackinnon, T.J.R.	List 6-E	
MacLaine, M.	Greenock/Paisley 14B	
MacLaine, M.	West Lothian 2B	
MacLaughlan, G.	Edinburgh 1B	
Maclean, A.G.	Edinburgh 1B	
MacLean, A.T.	List 6-R	
Maclean, D.A.	Lewis 44B	
MacLean, E.J.	Lanark 13A	
MacLean, G.P.	Gordon 33A	
MacLean, M.	Glasgow 16A-53	
MacLean, M.A.	Dundee 29A	
MacLennan, A.J.	Ross 39B	
MacLennan, D.A.	Lewis 44B	
MacLeod, A.V.	Glasgow 16A-124	
MacLeod, C.A.	England 47A	
MacLeod, C.I.	Edinburgh 1 A-30	
Macleod, D.	Glasgow 16B	
MacLeod, I.	Ardrossan 12B	
MacLeod, I.A.	Glasgow 16A-99	
Macleod, J.	Ross 39B	
MacLeod, K.D.	Ross 39A	
MacLeod, M.	Glasgow 16A-51	
MacLeod, N.	Hamilton 17B	
MacLeod, R.	Argyll 19B	
MacLeod, R.A.R.	Lochcarron/Skye 42A	
MacLeod, R.N.	England 47B	
Macleod, W.	Lewis 44B	
MacLeod-Mair, A.T.	Glasgow 16B	
MacMahon, J.P.H.	Glasgow 16B	
MacMillan, A.	Glasgow 16A-58	
Macmillan, G.I.	Edinburgh 1B	
MacMillan, R.M.	Perth 28B	
MacMillan, W.M.	Annandale/Eskdale 7B	
MacMurchie, F.L.	Edinburgh 1B	
Macnaughton, G.F.H.	Orkney 45A	
Macnaughton, J.A.	Glasgow 16B	
Macnee, I.	Buchan 34B	
MacNeill, T.	Lewis 44A	
MacPherson, A.J.	Stirling 23A	
Macpherson, C.C.R.	Edinburgh 1B	
MacPherson, D.A.C.	Inverness 37A	
MacPherson, D.J.	Annandale/Eskdale 7B	
MacPherson, G.C.	List 6-D	
MacPherson, J.	Sutherland 40A	
MacQuarrie, A.	Falkirk 22A	
MacQuarrie, D.A.	Inverness 37B	
MacQuarrie, S.	Glasgow 16B	
MacRae, E.H.	Stirling 23A	
MacRae, G.	Glasgow 16A-37	
Macrae, J.	Lothian 3A	
MacRae, M.H.	Dunkeld/Meigle 27B	
MacRae, N.I.	West Lothian 2B	
MacSween, D.A.	Ross 39A	
MacVicar, K.	Dunkeld/Meigle 27B	
Mailer, C.	List 6-D	
Main, A.	Aberdeen 31B	
Main, A.W.A.	List 6-D	
Main, D.M.	Perth 28B	
Mair, J.	List 6-R	
Mair, M.J.	Edinburgh 1 A-63	
Mair, M.V.A.	Dundee 29B	
Majcher, P.L.	England 47A	
Malcolm, A.	Perth 28B	
Malcolm, D.S.M.	Caithness 41A	
Malcolm, M.	Glasgow 16A-11	
Mallinson, R.	Dundee 29A	

Malloch, P.R.M. Stirling 23B
Malloch, R.J. West Lothian 2A
Manastireanu, D. Glasgow 16A-113
Manders, S. Edinburgh 1 A-46
Mann, J.W. Glasgow 16A-110
Manners, S. Orkney 45A
Manson, E. Greenock/Paisley 14A
Manson, I.A. Inverness 37A
Manson, J.A. Lothian 3B
Marshall, A.S. West Lothian 2A
Marshall, F. Argyll 19B
Marshall, T.E. Irvine/Kilmarnock 11A
Marten, S. Stirling 23A
Martin, G.M. Lochcarron/Skye 42B
Martin, J. Hamilton 17B
Martin, J.A. St Andrews 26A
Martindale, J.P.F. Glasgow 16B
Masih, M. Hamilton 17A-34
Masson, J.D. List 6-D
Mather, J. England 47B
Mathers, A. Falkirk 22A
Mathers, D.L. Falkirk 22B
Mathieson, A.R. Edinburgh 1B
Mathieson, F.M.M. Edinburgh 1 A-8
Mathieson, J.S. Glasgow 16A-41
Matthew, J.C. Ayr 10B
Matthew, J.G. Stirling 23B
Matthews, S.C. Glasgow 16A-89
Maxton, R.M. Falkirk 22B
Maxwell, D. Glasgow 16A-31
Maxwell, F.E. Greenock/Paisley 14A
Maxwell, I.D. West Lothian 2A
May, A.S. Glasgow 16A-34
May, J.S. Edinburgh 1 A-38
Mayes, R. Ayr 10A
Mayne, K.A.L. Greenock/Paisley 14A
McAdam, D.J. List 6-D
McAlister, A.C. List 6-A
McAlister, D.J.B. Dunkeld/Meigle 27B
McAllister, A.C. Irvine/Kilmarnock 11B
McAlpine, J. Hamilton 17B
McAlpine, R.H.M. Irvine/Kilmarnock 11B
McAlpine, R.J. Kirkcaldy 25A
McArthur, M. Dumbarton 18A
McAspurren, A.T. Edinburgh 1 A-36
McBrier, A. Irvine/Kilmarnock 11A
McCabe, G. Hamilton 17B
McCafferty, A. St Andrews 26A
McCallum, A.D. Ardrossan 12B
McCallum, J. Falkirk 22B
McCance, A.M. Ardrossan 12B
McCarthur, M. Glasgow 16A-13
McCarthy, D.J. Perth 28B
McCarthy, I.S. Annandale/Eskdale 7A
McCaskill, G.I.L. Edinburgh 1B
McChlery, L. Glasgow 16B
McClements, L.J.E. Glasgow 16A-26
McClenaghan, L.P. List 6-E
McConnell, N.S. Dundee 29A
McCool, A.C. Greenock/Paisley 14A
McCorkindale, D.G.B. Lochaber 38A
McCormick, A.F. Perth 28B
McCormick, J.A. Argyll 19A
McCormick, M.G. Stirling 23B
McCracken, G.A. Hamilton 17B
McCreadie, D.W. List 6-E
McCree, I.W. Sutherland 40B
McCrorie, W. Ayr 10B
McCrum, R. Perth 28B
McCrum, S. Kirkcaldy 25A

McCulloch, A.J.R. Lochcarron/Skye 42B
McCulloch, J.D. Irvine/Kilmarnock 11B
McCutcheon, J. Dumbarton 18B
McDonald, A. List 6-R
McDonald, A.D. List 6-D
McDonald, A.L. Aberdeen 31A
McDonald, A.P. Lothian 3A
McDonald, E. West Lothian 2A
McDonald, I.G.M. Int. Charges 48A
McDonald, I.R.W. Hamilton 17A-3
McDonald, J.A. Hamilton 17B
McDonald, M. Edinburgh 1 A-11
McDonald, R.J. List 6-D
McDonald, T. Dunfermline 24B
McDonald, W.G. Falkirk 22B
McDonald, W.J.G. List 6-R
McDougall, H.N. Glasgow 16B
McDowall, R.J. Falkirk 22B
McEnhill, P. Greenock/Paisley 14A
McEwan, I. Dumbarton 18A
McFadyen, G. List 6-D
McFadzean, I. Dunkeld/Meigle 27B
McFarlane, R.G. Greenock/Paisley 14A
McGeoch, G.G. Edinburgh 1 A-6
McGill, S. List 6-E
McGill, T. List 6-E
McGillivray, A.G. List 6-D
McGlynn, M. List 6-R
McGowan, A.T.B. Inverness 37A
McGregor, A.G.C. Edinburgh 1B
McGregor, D.J. St Andrews 26B
McGregor, T.S. Edinburgh 1B
McGregor, W. Perth 28B
McGurk, A.F. Ayr 10B
McHaffie, R.D. Jedburgh 6B
McIlroy, I. Wigtown/Stranraer 9A
McIndoe, J.H. England 47B
McInnes, I.M.S. Glasgow 16A-66
McIntosh, C.G. Perth 28B
McIntosh, H.N.M. Stirling 23B
McIntyre, A.G. Greenock/Paisley 14A
McIntyre, G. Dumbarton 18A
McIntyre, G.J. Stirling 23A
McIntyre, J.A. Dumbarton 18B
McIntyre, J.A. Glasgow 16A-92
McIvor, A. Argyll 19B
McKaig, W.G. Greenock/Paisley 14B
McKay, D.M. Dumfries/Kirkcudbright 8B
McKay, E.M. Gordon 33A
McKay, J.R. List 6-D
McKay, M. List 6-D
McKay, V.C.C. Dunfermline 24A
McKean, A.T. Ross 39A
McKean, M.J. List 6-D
McKee, G.D. Moray 35A
McKee, N.B. Hamilton 17B
McKellar-Young, C. West Lothian 2A
McKenna, E.C. Aberdeen 31A
McKenna, S.S. Edinburgh 1 A-44
McKenzie, A. Stirling 23B
McKenzie, M.O. List 6-E
McKenzie, R.D. Hamilton 17B
McKenzie, W.M. Dumfries/Kirkcudbright 8B
McKenzie, W.M. List 6-E
McKeown, M.W.J. Glasgow 16A-11
McKeown, P. Gordon 33A
McKibbin, F.L.J. Hamilton 17A-69
McKichan, A.J. Dumfries/Kirkcudbright 8B

McKillop, A. Hamilton 17A-49
McKimmon, E. St Andrews 26B
McKinnon, E.W. Hamilton 17A-57
McKinnon, L.F. Ardrossan 12A
McLachlan, D.N. Glasgow 16A-87
McLachlan, E. Glasgow 16B
McLachlan, F.C. List 6-D
McLachlan, I.K. Ayr 10A
McLachlan, T.A. Glasgow 16B
McLaren, D.M. Glasgow 16B
McLaren, W. Dundee 29A
McLarty, R.R. St Andrews 26A
McLauchlan, M.C. Dumfries/Kirkcudbright 8B
McLaughlin, C.H. Glasgow 16A-81
McLay, N. Int. Charges 48B
McLean, G. List 6-D
McLean, I.A. Angus 30A
McLean, J. List 6-E
McLean, J.P. St Andrews 26B
McLeish, R.S. Gordon 33B
McLellan, A.R.C. Dunfermline 24B
McLeod, A.G. Kirkcaldy 25B
McLeod, D.C. Dundee 29B
McLeod, T. Ayr 10A
McMahon, E.J. Ayr 10A
McMahon, J.K.S. England 47B
McMillan, C.D. Dundee 29B
McMillan, E.F. Dundee 29A
McMillan, S. Dundee 29A
McMillan, W.J. Buchan 34B
McNab, D.G. Gordon 33A
McNab, J.L. Edinburgh 1B
McNaught, N.A. Ayr 10A
McNaught, S.M. Kirkcaldy 25B
McNaughtan, J. Irvine/Kilmarnock 11A
McNaughton, D.J.H. Perth 28B
McNay, J.J. Ardrossan 12A
McNeil, J.N.R. Stirling 23A
McNeish, D.G. Orkney 45A
McNicol, B. Jedburgh 6B
McNidder, R.H. Ayr 10B
McPake, J.L. Hamilton 17A-30
McPake, J.M. Edinburgh 1B
McPhail, A.M. Ayr 10B
McPhee, D.C. Edinburgh 1B
McPherson, D.C. Hamilton 17B
McPherson, M. Edinburgh 1B
McPherson, S.M. Edinburgh 1 A-10
McPherson, W. List 6-D
McRoberts, S.A. Inverness 37A
McRoberts, T.D. Inverness 37B
McWilliam, A. Glasgow 16A-129
McWilliam, T.M. List 6-D
McWilliams, G. Perth 28A
Mead, J.M. Wigtown/Stranraer 9A
Meager, P. St Andrews 26B
Mealya, H.B. Ayr 10B
Meason, J. Orkney 45A
Mehigan, A.C. Inverness 37A
Meikle, A.A. Falkirk 22A
Melrose, J.H.L. Hamilton 17B
Melville, D.D. List 6-D
Merchant, M.C. Aberdeen 31A
Messeder, L. Stirling 23A
Meyer, M.W. Gordon 33A
Michelin-Salomon, M. Glasgow 16A-60
Michie, M. Perth 28B
Mickelson, J.M. Gordon 33A
Middleton, J.R.H. Argyll 19B
Middleton, P. England 47B

Mill, D.	Argyll 19A	Munro, G.	Perth 28B	Ogston, E.J.	Lochaber 38A
Mill, J.S.	Dumfries/Kirkcudbright 8A	Munro, G.A.M.	Edinburgh 1B	Ogston, S.	Ayr 10A
Millar, A.E.	Perth 28B	Munro, J.A.	Ross 39B	Oliver, G.	List 6-E
Millar, A.M .	Stirling 23A	Munro, J.R.	Edinburgh 1 A-23	Ormiston, H.C.	Dunkeld/Meigle 27B
Millar, J.L.	Lochaber 38B	Munro, M.	Wigtown/Stranraer 9B	Orr, J.K.	Angus 30A
Millar, J.M.	Stirling 23B	Munro, S.	Moray 35B	Orr, J.M.	West Lothian 2B
Millar, M.R.M.	Argyll 19B	Munton, J.G.	Hamilton 17B	Orr, S.	Edinburgh 1B
Millar, P.W.	List 6-D	Murdoch, C.M.	Dumbarton 18A	Osbeck, J.R.	List 6-E
Miller, A.F.	Stirling 23A	Murdoch, I.C.	Hamilton 17A-72	Ostler, J.H.	List 6-D
Miller, E.	Kirkcaldy 25A	Murdoch, J.A.H.	Perth 28A	Oswald, J.	Dunkeld/Meigle 27B
Miller, I.D.	List 6-E	Murdoch, W.M.	List 6-R	Ott, V.J.	Dumfries/Kirkcudbright 8A
Miller, I.H.	Dumbarton 18B	Murning, J.	Greenock/Paisley 14A	Ovens, S.B.	Stirling 23B
Miller, J.D.	Glasgow 16B	Murphy, F.E.	Greenock/Paisley 14A	Owen, C.W.	List 6-D
Milliken, J.	Ayr 10A	Murphy, J.	Hamilton 17B	Owen, J.J.C.	
Milloy, A.M.	Melrose/Peebles 4B	Murray, A.	Inverness 37A		Dumfries/Kirkcudbright 8B
Mills, P.W.	St Andrews 26A	Murray, A.J.S.		Oxburgh, B.H.	St Andrews 26A
Milne, R.B.	Melrose/Peebles 4A		Kincardine/Deeside 32A		
Milton, A.L.	Glasgow 16A-9	Murray, B.I.	Annandale/Eskdale 7A	Pacitti, S.A.	Lanark 13B
Milton, E.G.	Angus 30B	Murray, D.E.	Duns 5B	Page, J.R.	Greenock/Paisley 14B
Minto, J.	List 6-D	Murray, D.R.	List 6-E	Page, R.	List 6-R
Mitchell, A.B.	Stirling 23B	Murray, G.M.	List 6-D	Palmer, G.R.	Hamilton 17A-27
Mitchell, D.	Argyll 19A	Murray, J.W.	Lochcarron/Skye 42A	Palmer, S.W.	Greenock/Paisley 14B
Mitchell, D.R.	Ardrossan 12B	Murrie, J.	Edinburgh 1B	Park, C.	List 6-E
Mitchell, J.	Dundee 29B			Park, P.B.	Argyll 19B
Mitchell, J.	Lothian 3A	Nash, G.P.	Stirling 23A	Parker, C.A.	Stirling 23A
Mitchell, S.M.	Ayr 10B	Neill, B.F.	Duns 5B	Parker, N.	Aberdeen 31A
Moffat, R.	Edinburgh 1 A-66	Neilson, P.	St Andrews 26B	Paterson, A.E.	Dunfermline 24B
Moffat, R.G.	Ayr 10A	Neilson, R.	List 6-D	Paterson, D.S.	Edinburgh 1B
Moffat, T.	Glasgow 16B	Nelson, G.	West Lothian 2B	Paterson, G.	Kirkcaldy 25A
Moir, I.A.	Edinburgh 1B	Nelson, P.	Edinburgh 1 A-64	Paterson, J.H.	Ardrossan 12B
Moir, S.W.	Melrose/Peebles 4A	Nelson, R.C.	Dunkeld/Meigle 27B	Paterson, J.L.	Stirling 23B
Monteith, W.G.	Edinburgh 1B	Nelson, T.	Glasgow 16A-31	Paterson, J.W.	Ayr 10A
Montgomerie, J.B.	Aberdeen 31B	Ness, D.T.	Ayr 10B	Paterson, M.	Kirkcaldy 25B
Moodie, A.R.	List 6-D	Newell, A.M.	List 6-D	Paterson, S.J.	Hamilton 17A-18
Moody, J.H.C.	Glasgow 16A-30	Newell, J.P.	List 6-D	Paterson, W.	Duns 5B
Moore, A.A.	Hamilton 17B	Newlands, G.M.	List 6-D	Paton, A.S.	Hamilton 17A-31
Moore, A.J.	Falkirk 22A	Ngunga, A.T.	Ayr 10A	Paton, I.F.	Perth 28B
Moore, D.T.	Ayr 10A	Nicholas, M.S.	Lothian 3A	Paton, J.H.	Argyll 19A
Moore, N.	Dumbarton 18A	Nicholson, T.S.	Duns 5A	Paton, M.J.	Dundee 29A
Moore, W.B.	Glasgow 16B	Nicol, D.A.O.	Jedburgh 6A	Patterson, A.R.M.	List 6-R
Moore, W.H.	Melrose/Peebles 4B	Nicol, D.M.	Glasgow 16A-105	Patterson, J.	List 6-E
Moran, T.C.	Hamilton 17A-76	Nicol, G.G.	Kirkcaldy 25B	Patterson, P.W.	Perth 28A
Morrice, A.A.	Dunfermline 24A	Nicol, R.D.	Dunkeld/Meigle 27B	Pattison, K.J.	Perth 28B
Morrice, A.M.	Angus 30A	Nicol, R.M.	West Lothian 2B	Peacock, G.J.	
Morrice, W.G.	Edinburgh 1B	Nicol, S.E.C.	Aberdeen 31A		Dumfries/Kirkcudbright 8A
Morrison, A.	Perth 28A	Nicoll, A.N.	England 47A	Peacock, H.M.	List 6-E
Morrison, A.H.	Ayr 10B	Nicolson, F.	Hamilton 17A-23	Pearce, A.S.W.	Lewis 44A
Morrison, A.W.	Argyll 19B	Nicolson, J.N.	List 6-D	Pearson, M.B.	Glasgow 16A-64
Morrison, C.M.	Kirkcaldy 25A	Nimmo, P.W.	Inverness 37A	Pearson, W.	Glasgow 16A-58
Morrison, D.	Lochcarron/Skye 42B	Ninian, E.J.	Glasgow 16B	Peat, D.	Ayr 10A
Morrison, D.J.	Uist 43B	Nisbet, G.C.	Kirkcaldy 25A	Peden, L.	Glasgow 16A-103
Morrison, G.A.	Moray 35A	Niven, G.A.	Irvine/Kilmarnock 11A	Penman, I.D.	List 6-D
Morrison, H.	Inverness 37B	Niven, W.W.	Ross 39B	Penny, R.F.	Dunkeld/Meigle 27A
Morrison, I.C.	West Lothian 2B	Njeru, S.	West Lothian 2A	Perkins, M.	Perth 28A
Morrison, M.B.	Edinburgh 1B	Noble, A.B.	Ardrossan 12A	Perry, J.B.	List 6-R
Morrison, R.H.B.	Dumbarton 18A	Noble, G.S.	Buchan 34B	Perry, M.	Falkirk 22A
Morton, A.J.	Moray 35B	Norman, J.R.		Petrie, I.D.	List 6-D
Morton, A.Q.	List 6-R		Dumfries/Kirkcudbright 8A	Petrie, J.G.	Uist 43B
Morton, A.R.	List 6-R	Norman, N.M.	Melrose/Peebles 4B	Petrie, K.L.	Aberdeen 31A
Morton, G.M.	Moray 35B	Norrie, G.	Angus 30B	Philip, A.J.	Perth 28A
Mowat, G.M.	Dundee 29B	Notman, A.	Dunkeld/Meigle 27A	Philip, G.M.	Glasgow 16B
Mowbray, H.	Dunkeld/Meigle 27A	Notman, J.R.	List 6-D	Philip, M.R.	Perth 28B
Muckart, G.W.M.	List 6-D	Nugent, J.	Caithness 41A	Phillippo, M.	Aberdeen 31B
Muir, E.D.	List 6-D	Nutter, M.A.E.	Dumbarton 18A	Phillips, P.A.	Angus 30A
Muir, F.C.	Glasgow 16B			Picken, S.D.B.	Stirling 23B
Muir, M.A.	List 6-D	O'Leary, T.	List 6-E	Pickles, J.G.	Annandale/Eskdale 7A
Muir, M.T.	Lothian 3A	Obinna, E.O.	Lanark 13A	Pickles, R.G.D.W.	Ross 39A
Muirhead, M.	Lochaber 38B	O'Brien, H.	Perth 28A	Pieterse, B.	List 6-D
Munro, A.	Kirkcaldy 25B	O'Connor, H.	Edinburgh 1 A-23	Pirie, D.	Lothian 3B
Munro, A.W.	England 47B	O'Donnell, B.	Dumbarton 18A	Pitkeathly, D.G.	Annandale/Eskdale 7A
Munro, D.P.	Dumbarton 18B	Ogg, F.	Lochaber 38A	Pitkeathly, T.C.	Int. Charges 48B
Munro, F.	Aberdeen 31B	Ogilvie, C.	Stirling 23B	Plate, M.A.G.	Edinburgh 1B

Pollock, R.E.   Glasgow 16A-97
Pollock, T.L.   Glasgow 16A-119
Polwarth, S.   Ross 39A
Poole, A.M.   Moray 35B
Pope, D.H.N.   Hamilton 17A-53
Pot, J.   Int. Charges 48B
Potts, S.J.   Buchan 34A
Povey, J.M.   West Lothian 2A
Powrie, J.E.   Dundee 29B
Prentice, D.K.   Moray 35A
Prentice, G.   Greenock/Paisley 14B
Prentice, M.   Orkney 45B
Prentice-Hyers, D.B.   Ayr 10A
Price, A.E.   England 47A
Price, P.O.   Hamilton 17B
Provan, I.W.   List 6-D
Prowe, M.   Kirkcaldy 25A
Pryce, S.F.A.   List 6-E
Pryde, W.K.   Stirling 23B
Purnell, D.   Angus 30A
Purves, J.P.S.   List 6-E
Purves, J.S.   Glasgow 16A-67

Quigley, B.D.   Glasgow 16A-104

Raby, S.   Stirling 23A
Rae, A.W.   Melrose/Peebles 4B
Rae, P.C.   Lochaber 38B
Rae, R.   Dundee 29B
Rae, S.M.   Ayr 10A
Raeburn, A.C.   Glasgow 16B
Raeburn, G.   Hamilton 17A-58
Ramage, A.E.   Dumbarton 18B
Ramsay, A.   List 6-E
Ramsay, B.   Angus 30A
Ramsay, M.   Dunkeld/Meigle 27B
Ramsay, P.   Dundee 29A
Ramsay, R.J.   Dundee 29A
Ramsay, W.G.   Glasgow 16B
Ramsden, I.R.   Glasgow 16B
Rankin, D.R.   Perth 28A
Rankin, L.-J.   Jedburgh 6A
Rankine, C.A.   Hamilton 17A-40
Read, P.R.   Annandale/Eskdale 7A
Reamonn, P.   Jerusalem 49A
Redman, M.R.   Dunfermline 24A
Redmayne, D.W.   Dunfermline 24A
Redmayne, G.   Irvine/Kilmarnock 11A
Redpath, J.G.   Perth 28B
Reid, A.A.S.   St Andrews 26B
Reid, A.B.   Angus 30B
Reid, A.D.   Perth 28A
Reid, A.G.   Dunfermline 24B
Reid, D.   Dunfermline 24B
Reid, I.M.A.   Greenock/Paisley 14A
Reid, J.   Kirkcaldy 25A
Reid, J.G.   List 6-E
Reid, R.G.   Dundee 29B
Reid, R.M.C.   Gordon 33A
Reid, S.   Lanark 13A
Reid, W.M.   List 6-R
Rennie, L.   Caithness 41B
Rennie, M.R.   Dunfermline 24A
Rennie, S.M.   Aberdeen 31A
Rennie, J.D.   Melrose/Peebles 4B
Renton, J.P.   Gordon 33B
Renwick, C.C.   Stirling 23A
Rettie, J.A.   Inverness 37B
Reynolds, K.S.   Jerusalem 49A
Ribbons, F.   Kincardine/Deeside 32A
Richardson, T.C.   Aberdeen 31B
Riddell, J.A.   Melrose/Peebles 4B

Riddell, T.S.   West Lothian 2A
Ridland, A.K.   Edinburgh 1B
Risby, L.P.   List 6-D
Ritchie, B.   Inverness 37B
Ritchie, C.A.Y.   Abernethy 36B
Ritchie, G.W.N.   List 6-E
Ritchie, J.M.   Lothian 3B
Ritchie, W.M.   Argyll 19B
Robb, N.J.   St Andrews 26B
Robb, R.P.T.   Inverness 37B
Robertson, A.   Glasgow 16B
Robertson, A.J.   Glasgow 16A-12
Robertson, B.   Glasgow 16B
Robertson, C.   Edinburgh 1B
Robertson, C.J.   Angus 30A
Robertson, D.   Edinburgh 1 A-19
Robertson, E.M.D.   Stirling 23A
Robertson, F.A.   Inverness 37B
Robertson, G.R.   Angus 30B
Robertson, I.A.R.   Dumbarton 18A
Robertson, I.W.
          Dumfries/Kirkcudbright 8B
Robertson, J.H.   Dundee 29B
Robertson, J.M.   List 6-E
Robertson, M.   Dunkeld/Meigle 27B
Robertson, M.   Inverness 37A
Robertson, N.P.   Edinburgh 1B
Robertson, P.   Moray 35B
Robertson, T.G.N.   List 6-E
Robson, A.M.   Argyll 19A
Robson, B.   West Lothian 2A
Robson, G.K.   Dundee 29B
Roddick, J.N.   Glasgow 16A-19
Roderick, M.R.   Stirling 23A
Rodger, M.A.   Gordon 33B
Rodgers, D.M.   Aberdeen 31B
Rodwell, A.S.   Jedburgh 6B
Roger, A.M.   West Lothian 2A
Rogers, J.M.   List 6-R
Rogerson, S.D.   Hamilton 17B
Rollo, G.B.   Moray 35B
Rooney, M.I.G.   Angus 30A
Rose, D.S.   Stirling 23B
Rose, M.E.S.   St Andrews 26A
Rosener, A.N.   List 6-D
Ross, A.C.   Annandale/Eskdale 7B
Ross, D.M.   Glasgow 16B
Ross, D.S.   Buchan 34B
Ross, E.J.   Falkirk 22B
Ross, E.M.   Greenock/Paisley 14A
Ross, F.C.   Ardrossan 12A
Ross, J.   Glasgow 16A-54
Ross, J.   Glasgow 16B
Ross, K.R.   Argyll 19A
Ross, K.W.   Hamilton 17B
Ross, M.Z.   Edinburgh 1B
Ross, S.L.   Hamilton 17A-12
Rowe, C.J.   Glasgow 16A-62
Roy, A.   Kirkcaldy 25B
Roy, A.E.   List 6-D
Roy, A.J.   St Andrews 26B
Roy, I.M.   Ardrossan 12B
Roy, J.A.   List 6-E
Russell, J.   Dunkeld/Meigle 27B
Russell, K.G.   Stirling 23B
Russell, P.R.   Ayr 10B
Russell, S. Dumfries/Kirkcudbright 8A

Salmond, J.S.   Hamilton 17B
Salters, R.B.   List 6-D
Sanders, M.S.   Gordon 33A
Sanderson, A.M.   Ayr 10B

Sangster, E.G.   Stirling 23B
Sarle, A.   Falkirk 22A
Saunders, G.I.M.   Falkirk 22A
Saunders, K.   List 6-D
Sawers, H.   List 6-D
Schluter, L.   Argyll 19A
Schofield, M.F.   Edinburgh 1B
Scotland, R.G.   List 6-D
Scott, A.D.   List 6-R
Scott, D.D.   Lothian 3A
Scott, D.H.   Falkirk 22B
Scott, D.S.   Inverness 37A
Scott, D.V.   Ross 39B
Scott, I.G.   Edinburgh 1B
Scott, J.   Dundee 29B
Scott, J.E.   Edinburgh 1B
Scott, J.F.   Stirling 23B
Scott, M.C.   Edinburgh 1B
Scott, R.   Argyll 19B
Scott, T.T.   Irvine/Kilmarnock 11B
Scoular, J.M.   Stirling 23B
Scoular, S.   Dundee 29B
Scouler, M.D.   Jedburgh 6A
Scouller, H.   List 6-D
Seaman, R.S.   Annandale/Eskdale 7B
Searle, D.C.   Perth 28B
Seath, T.J.G.   Lanark 13B
Sefton, H.R.   Aberdeen 31B
Selemani, E.   Hamilton 17A-25
Sewell, P.M.N.   Stirling 23B
Shackleton, S.J.S.   Glasgow 16B
Shackleton, W.   Glasgow 16B
Shadakshari, T.K.   Lewis 44B
Shand, G.C.   Lanark 13A
Shanks, N.J.   List 6-D
Shannon, W.G.   Dunkeld/Meigle 27B
Sharp, A.   Kirkcaldy 25A
Sharp, J.   Int. Charges 48B
Sharp, S.W.   Falkirk 22A
Shaw of Chapelverna, D.   List 6-E
Shaw, A.N.   Greenock/Paisley 14A
Shaw, C.A.M.   Irvine/Kilmarnock 11B
Shaw, D   West Lothian 2A
Shaw, D.   List 6-E
Shaw, D.W.D.   List 6-D
Shearer, A.F.   Stirling 23A
Shedden, J.   Argyll 19B
Sheppard, M.J. Wigtown/Stranraer 9A
Sheret, B.S.   Aberdeen 31B
Sherrard, H.D.   Duns 5B
Sherry, G.T.   Stirling 23B
Shewan, F.D.F.   Edinburgh 1B
Shewan, M.R.R.   Aberdeen 31A
Shields, J.M.   Duns 5B
Shields, R.B.   Dumbarton 18A
Shirra, J.   List 6-R
Shuttleworth, A.   Dunfermline 24A
Shuttleworth, M.   Stirling 23A
Silcox, J.R.   List 6-R
Silver, R.M.   Glasgow 16A-65
Sime, C.   Dunfermline 24A
Simpson, E.V.   Ayr 10B
Simpson, J.A.   Perth 28B
Simpson, J.H.   Greenock/Paisley 14B
Simpson, N.A.   List 6-R
Simpson, R.R.   Lothian 3B
Sinclair, B.H.   Glasgow 16A-80
Sinclair, C.A.M.   Edinburgh 1 A-50
Sinclair, D.I.   Glasgow 16A-128
Sinclair, J.H.   Stirling 23B
Siroky, S.   Melrose/Peebles 4A
Slater, D.G.   Glasgow 16A-14

Sloan, R.   Dunkeld/Meigle 27B
Sloan, R.P.   Perth 28B
Smart, V.E.   Edinburgh 1 A-17
Smeed, A.W.   Glasgow 16B
Smillie, A.M.   Greenock/Paisley 14B
Smith, A.   Edinburgh 1B
Smith, A.E.   Kincardine/Deeside 32B
Smith, B.D.   Kincardine/Deeside 32A
Smith, D.J.   Falkirk 22A
Smith, E.   Ayr 10B
Smith, E.W.   Glasgow 16A-98
Smith, F.E.   Inverness 37A
Smith, G.S.   Glasgow 16B
Smith, G.W.   West Lothian 2B
Smith, H.C.   Argyll 19A
Smith, H.G.   Angus 30B
Smith, H.M.C.   Moray 35B
Smith, H.W.   Moray 35A
Smith, J.M.   Uist 43B
Smith, J.S.A.   Glasgow 16B
Smith, M.   Moray 35B
Smith, M.   Uist 43B
Smith, N.A.   Edinburgh 1 A-26
Smith, R.   Falkirk 22B
Smith, R.   Ross 39B
Smith, R.C.P.   List 6-E
Smith, R.L.   Aberdeen 31A
Smith, R.W.   List 6-D
Smith, S.J.   Greenock/Paisley 14A
Smith, S.J.   Lochcarron/Skye 42A
Somevi, J.K.   Aberdeen 31B
Sorensen, A.K.   Greenock/Paisley 14A
Souter, D.I.   Perth 28B
Souter, L.M.   Lothian 3A
Speirs, A.   Greenock/Paisley 14A
Spence, E.G.B.   Glasgow 16A-78
Spence, S.M.   Hamilton 17B
Spencer, J.   Glasgow 16B
Spiers, J.M.   Glasgow 16B
Spowart, M.G.   List 6-E
Stalder, W.A.   Gordon 33A
Stark, C.   Hamilton 17A-10
Steel, G.H.B.   Aberdeen 31A
Steele, G.M.F.   Dunkeld/Meigle 27B
Steele, H.D.   Dunfermline 24A
Steele, L.M.   Melrose/Peebles 4B
Steele, M.D.J.   Melrose/Peebles 4A
Steell, S.C.   Greenock/Paisley 14A
Steenbergen, P. Annandale/Eskdale 7B
Stein, J.   Lothian 3B
Stein, M.E.   Lothian 3B
Stenhouse, E.M.   Perth 28A
Stenhouse, W.D.   Perth 28B
Stephen, A.A. Kincardine/Deeside 32A
Stephen, D.M.   Edinburgh 1B
Sterrett, J.B.   Sutherland 40A
Steven, H.A.M.   Dumbarton 18B
Stevens, A.   Int. Charges 48A
Stevens, L.   Angus 30A
Stevenson, D.F.   Moray 35A
Stevenson, G.   Lothian 3A
Stevenson, J.   Edinburgh 1B
Stevenson, J.   Hamilton 17B
Stevenson, S.   Greenock/Paisley 14B
Stewart, A.E.   Perth 28B
Stewart, A.T.   Edinburgh 1 A-13
Stewart, C.E.   Dumbarton 18B
Stewart, D.   Greenock/Paisley 14B
Stewart, D.E.   Glasgow 16B
Stewart, D.J.   Aberdeen 31A
Stewart, F.M.C.   Ross 39A
Stewart, G.G.   Perth 28B

Stewart, H.   Caithness 41B
Stewart, H.M.   Lewis 44A
Stewart, J.   Argyll 19B
Stewart, J.C.   Aberdeen 31B
Stewart, J.C.   Perth 28A
Stewart, L.   Dunkeld/Meigle 27A
Stewart, L.J.   Edinburgh 1 A-29
Stewart, M.G.   Gordon 33A
Stewart, M.L.   List 6-D
Stewart, N.D.   Glasgow 16B
Stewart, R.J.   Perth 28B
Stewart, U.B.   List 6-D
Stewart, W.   Buchan 34A
Stewart, W.T.   Hamilton 17A-36
Steyn, J.J.   St Andrews 26A
Stirling, A.D.   Edinburgh 1B
Stirling, G.A.S.   Inverness 37B
Stirling, I.R.   Ayr 10A
Stitt, R.J.M.   Edinburgh 1B
Stobo, M.J.   Sutherland 40B
Stoddart, A.C.   Lochaber 38A
Stoddart, A.G.   Gordon 33B
Stone, L.   Int. Charges 48A
Stone, W.H.   Edinburgh 1 A-27
Stone, W.V.   List 6-E
Storrar, W.F.   List 6-D
Stott, K.D.   Dundee 29A
Strachan, A.E.   List 6-D
Strachan, D.G.   List 6-D
Strachan, I.M.   List 6-D
Strachan, P.D.   Melrose/Peebles 4A
Strachan, W.   Dundee 29A
Strang, G.   Abernethy 36A
Strickland, A.   Dundee 29B
Strong, C.   St Andrews 26B
Strong, C.A.   Irvine/Kilmarnock 11A
Stuart, A.P.   Glasgow 16A-43
Sturrock, R.D.   Glasgow 16A-82
Stutter, A.   Kincardine/Deeside 32A
Sutcliffe, C.B.   List 6-E
Sutherland, C.A.
                 Dumfries/Kirkcudbright 8B
Sutherland, D.A.
                 Dumfries/Kirkcudbright 8A
Sutherland, D.A.   Glasgow 16B
Sutherland, D.I.   Glasgow 16B
Sutherland, E.W.   List 6-R
Sutherland, I.A.   Dunfermline 24B
Sutherland, S.J.   Dundee 29A
Suzie, S.   Edinburgh 1 A-62
Swan, A.F.   Lothian 3B
Sweetin, B.A.   Angus 30A
Swinburne, N.   Annandale/Eskdale 7B
Swindells, A.I.   Edinburgh 1 A-27
Swindells, S.   Lothian 3A
Swinton, J.   Aberdeen 31B
Symington, A.H.   Ayr 10B

Tait, A.   Orkney 45B
Tait, J.M.   Edinburgh 1B
Tait, T.W.   Dunkeld/Meigle 27B
Tallach, J.   Ross 39B
Tamas, B.   List 6-D
Taverner, D.J.   Duns 5A
Taverner, G.R.   Melrose/Peebles 4B
Taylor, A.S.   Ardrossan 12B
Taylor, A.T.   Argyll 19B
Taylor, B.S.C.   Aberdeen 31A
Taylor, C.   Dundee 29B
Taylor, C.G.D.   Dundee 29A
Taylor, D.J.   List 6-E
Taylor, G.J.A.   Edinburgh 1 A-9

Taylor, I.   Glasgow 16A-3
Taylor, I.   List 6-D
Taylor, J.   List 6-D
Taylor, M.A.   Edinburgh 1 A-41
Taylor, T.A.   Stirling 23A
Taylor, W.R.   Edinburgh 1B
Teasdale, J.R.   Glasgow 16A-70
Telfer, A.B.   Hamilton 17A-65
Telfer, I.J.M.   Edinburgh 1B
Templeton, J.L.   Kirkcaldy 25B
Thain, G.M.   Glasgow 16A-107
Thane, M.   List 6-R
Thom, D.J.   England 47B
Thom, I.G.   Dunfermline 24A
Thomas, M.R.H.   Angus 30B
Thomas, S.A.   Angus 30B
Thomas, W.C.   List 6-D
Thomson, A.   Glasgow 16A-75
Thomson, A.   List 6-E
Thomson, D.M.   Edinburgh 1B
Thomson, G.L.   List 6-E
Thomson, I.U.   Gordon 33B
Thomson, J.B.   Perth 28B
Thomson, J.D.   Kirkcaldy 25B
Thomson, J.M.   List 6-R
Thomson, J.M.A.   Hamilton 17B
Thomson, M.   Ardrossan 12A
Thomson, M.   Ardrossan 12B
Thomson, M.E.   Abernethy 36B
Thomson, R.   Stirling 23B
Thomson, S.   Perth 28A
Thomson, W.   Falkirk 22A
Thorburn, R.J.   Buchan 34A
Thornburn, S.   Perth 28A
Thorne, L.W.   List 6-E
Thornthwaite, A.P.   Dundee 29A
Thrower, C.D.   List 6-D
Tippner, J.   Buchan 34A
Todd, J.F.   Falkirk 22A
Tollick, F.   List 6-D
Tomlinson, B.L.   Kirkcaldy 25B
Torrance, A.J.   St Andrews 26B
Torrance, D.J.   Lothian 3A
Torrance, D.W.   Lothian 3B
Torrance, I.R.   Aberdeen 31B
Torrens, S.A.R.   Edinburgh 1 A-3
Travers, R.   Ardrossan 12B
Trevorrow, J.A.   England 47B
Trgavolá, M.   Orkney 45B
Turnbull, J.   List 6-D
Turnbull, J.S.   List 6-D
Turnbull, S.L.A.   Hamilton 17A-44
Turner, A.   Glasgow 16B
Turner, F.K.   Inverness 37B
Tuton, R.M.   Glasgow 16B
Twaddle, L.H.   Lothian 3A
Tweedie, F.   Edinburgh 1B

Underwood, F.A.   Lothian 3B
Underwood, G.H.   Lothian 3B
Unsworth, R.   St Andrews 26B
Urquhart, J.A.   Irvine/Kilmarnock 11A
Urquhart, J.C.C.   Edinburgh 1 A-15
Urquhart, N.   Irvine/Kilmarnock 11A

Van Sittert, P.   Buchan 34A
Van Welie, D.L.   Falkirk 22A
Varwell, A.P.J.   Lochaber 38A
Vermeulen, C.J.   Ardrossan 12A
Verster, W.M.   Buchan 34A
Vidits, G.   Edinburgh 1 A-69
Vint, A.S.   Glasgow 16A-20

Vischer, J.	Lothian 3A	Wedderburn, A.J.M.	List 6-E	Wilson, G.R.	Dumbarton 18A
Vivers, K.A.	Annandale/Eskdale 7B	Weir, J.J.C.M.	Aberdeen 31A	Wilson, H.	Stirling 23B
		Weir, M.K.	List 6-E	Wilson, J.	Glasgow 16B
Waddell, E.A.	Hamilton 17B	Wells, I.J.	Edinburgh 1 A-56	Wilson, J.H.	Hamilton 17B
Walker, D.K.	Abernethy 36A	Wells, J.R.	Lothian 3A	Wilson, J.L.	Dundee 29A
Walker, I.	West Lothian 2B	Welsh, A.M.	Irvine/Kilmarnock 11B	Wilson, J.M.	Dunkeld/Meigle 27B
Walker, J.B.	St Andrews 26B	Westmarland, C.A.	List 6-E	Wilson, J.M.	Edinburgh 1B
Walker, K.D.F.	Duns 5B	White, C.P.	Glasgow 16B	Wilson, M.	List 6-E
Walker, L.	Glasgow 16B	Whitecross, J.	Ardrossan 12A	Wilson, M.D.	Dunkeld/Meigle 27B
Walker, R.F.	England 47B	Whiteford, A.	Greenock/Paisley 14B	Wilson, P.M.	Falkirk 22B
Wallace, C.	Wigtown/Stranraer 9A	Whiteford, J.D.	Glasgow 16B	Wilson, T.	Kirkcaldy 25B
Wallace, D.S.	England 47B	Whiteman, D.	Ardrossan 12A	Wilson, T.F.	Aberdeen 31B
Wallace, D.W.	Hamilton 17A-33	Whitley, L.A.B.	Glasgow 16A-59	Wilson, W.T.S.	Glasgow 16A-5
Wallace, H.M.	Aberdeen 31A	Whitson, W.S.	Orkney 45B	Winning, A.A.	Lochaber 38B
Wallace, J.H.	Melrose/Peebles 4B	Whittaker, M.	Aberdeen 31A	Wiseman, I.	Ayr 10A
Wallace, J.K.	Perth 28B	Whitton, J.P.	List 6-D	Wishart, E.M.	Lothian 3A
Wallace, M.		Whyte, D.	Moray 35B	Wishart, J.	Orkney 45B
	Dumfries/Kirkcudbright 8B	Whyte, G.J.	Edinburgh 1B	Wood, G.M.	Glasgow 16A-47
Wallace, P.D.	Argyll 19A	Whyte, I.A.	Edinburgh 1B	Wood, J.L.	List 6-D
Wallace, W.F.	Kincardine/Deeside 32B	Whyte, I.H.	Dunfermline 24B	Wood, P.J.	England 47B
Walton, A.	Glasgow 16B	Whyte, J.	Glasgow 16B	Woods, J.M.	Melrose/Peebles 4A
Wandrum, D.C.	Falkirk 22B	Whyte, J.H.	Greenock/Paisley 14B	Wotherspoon, I.G.	St Andrews 26B
Ward, A.H.	Ardrossan 12B	Whyte, M.	Aberdeen 31A	Wotherspoon, R.C.	
Ward, M.J.	England 47B	Whyte, M.A.	Greenock/Paisley 14B		Dumfries/Kirkcudbright 8B
Wark, A.C.	Kincardine/Deeside 32A	Whyte, N.R.	Duns 5A	Wright, D.L.	Moray 35B
Warner, K.	Caithness 41B	Whyte, R.C.	List 6-D	Wright, M.	Dumbarton 18B
Warwick, I.C.	Inverness 37B	Whyte, W.B.	Dunkeld/Meigle 27B	Wylie, J.	Perth 28B
Watson, E.R.L.	Ardrossan 12A	Wigglesworth, J.C.	Edinburgh 1B	Wyllie, H.R.	Hamilton 17B
Watson, I.	List 6-E	Wiley, J.C.	West Lothian 2A	Wynne, A.T.E.	Edinburgh 1B
Watson, J.M.	List 6-D	Wilkie, G.D.	List 6-E		
Watson, M.D.	Lothian 3A	Wilkie, I.	Falkirk 22A	Yorke, K.B.	Ayr 10B
Watson, N.G.	Edinburgh 1B	Wilkie, J.L.	List 6-D	Young, A.W.	Edinburgh 1B
Watson, T.D.	Ardrossan 12A	Wilkie, J.R.	List 6-R	Young, D.A.	Lanark 13B
Watson, V.G.C.	Argyll 19A	Wilkie, R.F.	Perth 28A	Young, D.T.	Dumbarton 18A
Watt, A.G.N.	Angus 30B	Wilkie, W.E.	List 6-E	Young, E.	List 6-D
Watt, H.F.	Inverness 37A	Wilkinson, A.D.	Ayr 10B	Young, J.	Dumfries/Kirkcudbright 8B
Watt, K.	Irvine/Kilmarnock 11B	Wilkinson, W.B.	Argyll 19B	Young, J.N.	Edinburgh 1 A-25
Watt, R.J.	Dunfermline 24B	Williams, J.M.	Edinburgh 1B	Young, R.M.	Ayr 10B
Watt, W.D.	Kincardine/Deeside 32B	Williams, T.C.	Annandale/Eskdale 7B	Younger, A.	Glasgow 16B
Watts, A.	Moray 35B	Williamson, J.		Younger, A.S.	Inverness 37B
Waugh, J.L.	Inverness 37B		Dumfries/Kirkcudbright 8B	Youngson, E.J.B.	Aberdeen 31B
Weatherhead, J.L.	List 6-D	Williamson, M.J.C	Shetland 46B	Youngson, P.	Angus 30B
Weaver, S.G.	Edinburgh 1 A-53	Willoughby, M.F.	Dunfermline 24A	Yule, M.J.B.	Dumbarton 18A
Webster, A.F.	Angus 30B	Wilson, A.G.N.		Yule, R.F.	Buchan 34A
Webster, B.G.	List 6-D		Kincardine/Deeside 32B		
Webster, J.G.	List 6-D	Wilson, A.J.	Perth 28A	Zambonini, J.	Hamilton 17B
Webster, P.	Edinburgh 1B	Wilson, F.A.			
Webster, T.	Ardrossan 12A		Dumfries/Kirkcudbright 8A		

INDEX OF PARISHES AND PLACES

NOTE: Numbers on the right of the column refer to the Presbytery in which the district lies. Names in brackets are given for ease of identification. They may refer to the name of the parish, which may be different from that of the district, or they distinguish places with the same name, or they indicate the first named charge in a union.

Abdie and Dunbog	26	Ardrossan	12	Bearsden	18	Bower	41
Abercorn	2	Armadale	2	Beath	24	Bowling (Old Kilpatrick)	18
Aberdalgie and Forteviot	28	Arngask (Abernethy)	28	Beattock (Kirkpatrick		Bowmore (Kilarrow)	19
Aberdeen	31	Arnsheen Barrhill (St		Juxta)	7	Bracadale and Duirinish	42
Aberdour (Buchan)	34	Colmon)	10	Beauly (Kilmorack)	37	Braemar and Crathie	32
Aberdour (Dunfermline)	24	Arrochar	18	Beith	12	Braes of Rannoch	27
Aberfeldy	27	Ashkirk	4	Belhaven	3	Brechin	30
Aberfoyle	23	Ashton (Gourock)	14	Belhelvie	33	Breich Valley	2
Aberlady	3	Assynt and Stoer	40	Bellie and Speymouth	35	Bressay (Lerwick)	46
Aberlemno	30	Athelstaneford	3	Bellshill	17	Bridge of Allan	23
Aberlour	35	Auchaber	34	Benarty (Lochgelly)	24	Bridge of Earn	
Aberluthnott	32	Auchinleck	10	Benbecula	43	(Dunbarney)	28
Abernethy	36	Auchterarder	28	Bendochy	27	Bridge of Weir	14
Abernethy and Dron and		Auchterderran Kinglassie	25	Bengairn Parishes, The	8	Brightons	22
Arngask	28	Auchtergaven and		Berneray and Lochmaddy	43	Broadford (Strath)	42
Abernyte	29	Moneydie	28	Bervie (Arbuthnott)	32	Brodick	12
Aberuthven and Dunning	28	Auchterhouse	29	Berwick-upon-Tweed and		Broom	16
Aboyne and Dinnet	32	Auchterless	34	Lowick	5	Broughton, Glenholm	
Acharacle	38	Auchtermuchty	26	Biggar	13	and Kilbucho	4
Advie (Cromdale)	36	Auchtertool	25	Bilston	3	Broughty Ferry (Dundee)	29
Airdrie	17	Auldearn and Dalmore	37	Birnie and Pluscarden	35	Broxburn	2
Airth	22	Aviemore		Birsay, Harray and		Brydekirk	7
Aithsting (Sandsting)	46	(Rothiemurchus)	36	Sandwick	45	Buchanan	23
Ale and Teviot United	6	Avoch	39	Birse and Feughside	32	Buchlyvie	23
Alexandria	18	Avonbridge	2	Bishopbriggs	16	Buckhaven and Wemyss	25
Alloa	23	Ayr	10	Bishopton	14	Buckie	35
Alloway	10	Ayton and Burnmouth		Blackbraes and Shieldhill	22	Bucksburn Stoneywood	31
Almondbank Tibbermore	28	(Ayton & Dist.)	5	Blackburn and Seafield	2	Bunessan (Kilfinichen)	21
Alness	39			Blackford	28	Burghead (Alves)	35
Altnaharra and Farr	40	Baldernock	18	Black Mount	13	Burnmouth (Ayton)	5
Alva	23	Balerno (Edinburgh)	1	Blackridge	2	Burnside Blairbeth	16
Alves and Burghead	35	Balfron	23	Blair Atholl and Struan	27	Burntisland	25
Alvie and Insh	36	Balgonie (Kennoway)	25	Blairbeth (Burnside)	16	Burra Isle	46
Alyth	27	Baljaffray (Bearsden)	18	Blairdaff and Chapel of		Burray (South	
Amulree (Dunkeld)	27	Ballantrae	10	Garioch	33	Ronaldsay)	45
Annan	7	Ballater (Glenmuick)	32	Blairgowrie	27	Burrelton (Cargill)	28
Annbank	10	Balloch (Jamestown)	18	Blairingone (Saline)	24	Busby	16
Anstruther	26	Balmaclellan and Kells		Blantyre	17	Bute, The United	
Appin	19	Balmaghie		Boarhills and Dunino	26	Church of	19
Applecross, Lochcarron		(Crossmichael)	8	Boat of Garten, Duthil			
and Torridon	42	Balmedie (Belhelvie)	33	and Kincardine	36	Cabrach (Mortlach)	35
Applegarth, Sibbaldbie		Balmerino	26	Boharm (Keith)	35	Cadder	16
and Johnstone	7	Balquhidder	23	Boleskine (Dores)	37	Caddonfoot	4
Arbirlot	30	Banchory-Devenick –		Bolton(Humbie)	3	Caerlaverock	8
Arbroath	30	(Maryculter)	32	Bonar Bridge (Creich)	40	Cairneyhill	24
Arbuthnott, Bervie and		Banchory-Ternan	32	Bo'ness	22	Cairngryffe	13
Kinneff	32	Banff	34	Bonhill	18	Cairnie (Huntly)	33
Archiestown (Knockando)	35	Bankfoot (Auchtergaven)	28	Bonkle (Newmains)	17	Calder, Kirk of	2
Ardchattan	19	Bannockburn	23	Bonkyl (Duns & District)	5	Calderbank	17
Ardentinny (Strone)	19	Banton	16	Bonnybridge	22	Caldercruix and	
Ardeonaig (Killin)	23	Bargeddie	17	Bonnyrigg	3	Longriggend	17
Ardersier	37	Barr	10	Border Kirk, The	7	Calder, West Kirk of	2
Ardgay (Kincardine)	40	Barra	19	Borgue (Gatehouse)	8	Caldwell	11
Ardgour and Kingairloch	38	Barrhead	14	Bothkennar and		Callander	23
Ardler, Kettins and		Barrhill (St Colmon)	10	Carronshore	22	Cambusbarron	23
Meigle	27	Barry	30	Bothwell	17	Cambuslang	16
Ardnamurchan	38	Barthol Chapel	33	Botriphnie (Keith)	35	Cambusnethan (Wishaw)	17
Ardoch	28	Barvas	44	Bourtie (Meldrum)	33	Cameron	26
Ardrishaig	19	Bathgate	2	Bowden and Melrose	4	Campbeltown	19

Campsie 16
Canisbay 41
Canonbie 7
Caputh and Clunie 27
Cara (Gigha) 19
Cardross 18
Careston (Fern) 30
Carfin (Newarthill) 17
Cargill Burrelton 28
Carinish 43
Carlops 4
Carloway 44
Carluke 13
Carmunnock (Glasgow) 16
Carmyllie 30
Carnbee 26
Carnock and Oakley 24
Carnoustie 30
Carnwath 13
Carradale (Saddell) 19
Carriden 22
Carrington (Cockpen) 3
Carron (Stenhouse) 22
Carronshore
(Bothkennar) 22
Carsphairn 8
Carstairs 13
Castle Douglas 8
Castletown (Olrig) 41
Cathkin (Fernhill) 16
Catrine 10
Cavers and Kirkton 6
Cawdor 37
Cellardyke 26
Ceres, Kemback and
Springfield 26
Channelkirk and Lauder 4
Chapelhall 17
Chapel of Garioch
(Blairdaff) 33
Chapelton 17
Cheviot Churches 6
Chirnside 5
Chryston 16
Clackmannan 23
Cleish 28
Cleland 17
Closeburn 8
Clunie (Caputh) 27
Cluny 33
Clydebank 18
Clyne 40
Coalburn 13
Coalsnaughton (Sauchie) 23
Coatbridge 17
Cockenzie and Port Seton 3
Cockpen and Carrington 3
Coldingham and St Abbs 5
Coldstream 5
Colinsburgh (Elie) 26
Colintraive (Kilmodan) 19
Coll 19
Collace 28
Colliston 30
Colmonell (St Colmon) 10
Colonsay and Oronsay 19
Colvend, Southwick and
Kirkbean 8
Comrie 28
Condorrat
(Cumbernauld) 22
Connel 19

Contin 39
Cookney (Maryculter) 32
Corby 47
Cornhill (Ordiquhill) 34
Corpach (Kilmallie) 38
Corrie (Ardrossan) 12
Corrie (Lockerbie) 7
Corsock and Kirkpatrick
Durham 8
Coupar Angus 27
Cove (Craigrownie) 18
Cowdenbeath 24
Cowie and Plean 23
Coylton 10
Craigie Symington 10
Craignish 19
Craigrownie 18
Crail 26
Crathie (Braemar) 32
Creich 40
Creich, Flisk and
Kilmany 26
Crieff 28
Crimond 34
Croick (Kincardine) 40
Cromar 32
Cromarty 39
Cromdale and Advie 36
Crossbost (Lochs) 44
Crossford 13
Crosshill 10
Crosshouse 11
Crossmichael, Parton
and Balmaghie 8
Cross Ness 44
Croy and Dalcross 37
Cruden 34
Cullen and Deskford 35
Culloden 37
Culross and Torryburn 24
Culsalmond and Rayne 33
Cults 31
Cumbernauld 22
Cumbrae 12
Cuminestown
(Monquhitter) 34
Cumlodden,
Lochfyneside and
Lochgair 19
Cummertrees, Mouswald
and Ruthwell 8
Cumnock 10
Cunningsburgh
(Sandwick) 46
Currie (Edinburgh) 1
Cushnie and Tough 33
Cupar 26

Dailly 10
Dairsie (Cupar:
St John's) 26
Dalarossie (Moy) 37
Dalavich (Kilchrenan) 19
Dalbeattie and
Kirkgunzeon 8
Dalcross (Croy) 37
Dalgety 24
Dalkeith 3
Dallas 35
Dalmally (Glenorchy) 19
Dalmellington 10
Dalmeny (Edinburgh) 1

Dalmore (Auldearn) 37
Dalmuir 18
Dalry (Ardrossan) 12
Dalry (Dumfries and
Kirkcudbright) 8
Dalrymple 10
Dalserf 17
Dalton 7
Dalziel (Motherwell) 17
Darvel 11
Daviot 33
Daviot and Dunlichity 37
Deer 34
Delting 46
Denbeath (Methilhill) 25
Denny 22
Deskford (Cullen) 35
Devonside (Fossoway) 28
Dingwall 39
Dinnet (Aboyne) 32
Dirleton 3
Dollar 23
Dores and Boleskine 37
Dornoch 40
Dornock 7
Douglas Valley Church,
The 13
Doune (Kilmadock) 23
Dreghorn and Springside 11
Dron (Abernethy) 28
Drongan 10
Drumblade
(Strathbogie) 33
Drumclog (Strathaven) 17
Drumelzier (Stobo) 4
Drummore (Kirkmaiden) 9
Drumnadrochit
(Urquhart) 37
Drumoak-Durris 32
Drymen 23
Dufftown (Mortlach) 35
Duffus, Spynie and
Hopeman 35
Duirinish (Bracadale) 42
Dull and Weem 27
Dulnain Bridge 36
Dumbarton 18
Dumfries 8
Dun and Hillside 30
Dunbar 3
Dunbarney and
Forgandenny 28
Dunblane 23
Dunbog (Abdie) 26
Dundee 29
Dundonald 10
Dundonnell (Gairloch) 42
Dundrennan (Rerrick) 8
Dundurn 28
Dunfermline 24
Dunglass 3
Dunino (Boarhills) 26
Dunipace 22
Dunkeld 27
Dunlichity (Daviot) 37
Dunlop 11
Dunnet 41
Dunnichen, Letham and
Kirkden 30
Dunning (Aberuthven) 28
Dunnottar (Stonehaven) 32
Dunoon 19

Dunrossness and St
Ninian's inc. Fair Isle 46
Duns and District
Parishes 5
Dunscore 8
Duntocher 18
Dunure (Fisherton) 10
Durisdeer 8
Durness and
Kinlochbervie 40
Duror 38
Durris (Drumoak) 32
Duthil (Boat of Garten) 36
Dyce 31
Dyke 35
Dysart 25

Eaglesfield (Hoddom) 7
Eaglesham 16
Earlston 4
Eassie, Nevay and
Newtyle 30
East Calder (Kirknewton) 2
East Kilbride 17
East Linton (Traprain) 3
East Mainland 45
Eccles 5
Echt 33
Eday 45
Edderton (Kincardine) 40
Eddleston 4
Eddrachillis 40
Edenshead and
Strathmiglo 26
Edinburgh 1
Edinkillie 35
Ednam (Kelso: North) 6
Edrom (Duns & Dist.) 5
Edzell Lethnot Glenesk 30
Elchies (Knockando) 35
Elderslie Kirk 14
Elgin 35
Elie Kilconquhar and
Colinsburgh 26
Ellon 33
Enzie 35
Erchless (Kilmorack) 37
Errol 28
Erskine 14
Ervie Kirkcolm 9
Eskdalemuir (Langholm) 7
Ettrick and Yarrow 4
Evanton (Kiltearn) 39
Evie 45
Ewes (Langholm) 7
Eyemouth 5

Fair Isle (Dunrossness) 46
Fairlie 12
Falkirk 22
Falkland 26
Fallin 23
Farnell 30
Farr (Altnaharra) 40
Fauldhouse 2
Fearn Abbey and Nigg 39
Fenwick 11
Fergushill 12
Ferintosh 39
Fern Careston Menmuir 30
Fernhill and Cathkin 16
Fetlar (Unst) 46

Fetteresso (Stonehaven) 32
Feughside (Birse) 32
Findhorn (Kinloss) 35
Findochty 35
Fintray Kinellar
 Keithhall 33
Fintry 23
Firth 45
Fisherton 10
Fishwick (Hutton) 5
Flisk (Creich) 26
Flotta 45
Fodderty and
 Strathpeffer 39
Fogo 5
Ford (Glassary) 19
Forfar 30
Forgandenny
 (Dunbarney) 28
Forglen (Turriff) 34
Forres 35
Fort Augustus 38
Forteviot (Aberdalgie) 28
Forth 13
Fortingall and Glenlyon 27
Fortrose and Rosemarkie 39
Fort William 38
Foss and Rannoch 27
Fossoway and
 Devonside 28
Foulden and Mordington
 (Ayton & Dist.) 5
Foveran 33
Fowlis and Liff 29
Fowlis Wester,
 Madderty and Monzie 28
Fraserburgh 34
Freuchie 26
Friockheim Kinnell 30
Fyvie 34

Gairloch and Dundonnell 42
Galashiels 4
Galston 11
Garelochhead 18
Gargunnock 23
Gartcosh 16
Gartmore 23
Gartocharn
 (Kilmaronock) 18
Garvald and Morham 3
Gask 28
Gatehouse of Fleet 8
Gateside (Edenshead) 26
Giffnock 16
Gifford(Humbie) 3
Gigha and Cara 19
Gilmerton (Edinburgh) 1
Gilmerton (Monzie) 28
Girvan 10
Gladsmuir 3
Glamis, Inverarity and
 Kinnettles 30
Glasgow 16
Glass (Huntly) 33
Glassary, Kilmartin and
 Ford 19
Glasserton and Isle of
 Whithorn 9
Glassford 17
Glenaray and Inveraray 19
Glenboig 16

Glencairn and Moniaive 8
Glencoe 38
Glencorse 3
Glendevon 23
Glenelg, Kintail and
 Lochalsh 42
Glenesk (Edzell) 30
Glengarry 38
Glenholm (Broughton) 4
Glenlivet (Tomintoul) 36
Glenlyon (Fortingall) 27
Glenmoriston (Urquhart) 37
Glenmuick (Ballater) 32
Glenorchy and Innishael 19
Glenrothes 25
Glens, The and
 Kirriemuir: Old 30
Glenshee (Kirkmichael) 27
Golspie 40
Gordon 5
Gorebridge 3
Gourock 14
Grange (Keith) 35
Grangemouth 22
Grantown-on-Spey 36
Grantshouse (Ayton &
 Dist.) 5
Grantully, Logierait and
 Strathtay 27
Greenbank (Edinburgh) 1
Greenbank (Glasgow) 16
Greengairs 17
Greenlaw 5
Greenock 14
Gretna, Half Morton and
 Kirkpatrick Fleming 7
Guernsey 47
Gullane 3
Guthrie and Rescobie 30

Haddington 3
Haggs 22
Half Morton (Gretna) 7
Halkirk Westerdale 41
Hamilton 17
Harray (Birsay) 45
Harthill 2
Harwood (Polbeth) 2
Hawick 6
Helensburgh 18
Helmsdale (Kildonan) 40
Heriot (Stow) 4
Hightae (Dalton) 7
Hillside (Dun) 30
Hobkirk and Southdean 6
Hoddom, Kirtle-
 Eaglesfield and
 Middlebie 7
Holytown 17
Hopeman (Duffus) 35
Houndwood (Ayton &
 Dist.) 5
Houston and Killellan 14
Howe of Fife 26
Howe Trinity 33
Howgate 3
Howwood 14
Hoy and Walls 45
Humbie 3
Huntly Cairnie Glass 33
Hurlford 11
Hutton (Lockerbie) 7

Hutton and Fishwick and
 Paxton 5
Inch 9
Inchbrayock (Montrose:
 South) 30
Inchinnan 14
Inchture and Kinnaird 29
Innellan 19
Innerleithen, Traquair
 and Walkerburn 4
Innishael (Glenorchy) 19
Insch-Leslie-Premnay-
 Oyne 33
Insh (Alvie) 36
Inverallochy and Rathen:
 East 34
Inveraray (Glenaray) 19
Inverarity (Glamis) 30
Inveraven (Tomintoul) 36
Inverbervie (Bervie) 32
Invergordon 39
Invergowrie 29
Inverkeilor and Lunan 30
Inverkeithing 24
Inverkip 14
Inverness 37
Inverurie 33
Iona 19
Irongray, Lochrutton
 and Terregles 8
Irvine 11
Isla Parishes, The 30
Isle of Whithorn
 (Glasserton) 9

Jamestown 18
Jedburgh 6
Jersey 47
Johnstone (Applegarth) 7
Johnstone (Greenock
 and Paisley) 14
Jura 19

Keir (Penpont) 8
Keiss 41
Keith 35
Keithhall (Fintray) 33
Kells (Balmaclellan) 8
Kelso 6
Kelso Country Churches 6
Kelty 24
Kemback (Ceres) 26
Kemnay 33
Kenmore and Lawers 27
Kennoway, Windygates
 and Balgonie 25
Kettins (Ardler) 27
Kilarrow 19
Kilbarchan 14
Kilberry (Tarbert) 19
Kilbirnie 12
Kilbrandon and
 Kilchattan 19
Kilbucho (Broughton) 4
Kilcalmonell 19
Kilchattan (Kilbrandon) 19
Kilchoman 19
Kilchrenan and Dalavich 19
Kilchrist (Urray) 39
Kilconquhar (Elie) 26

Kilcreggan
 (Craigrownie) 18
Kildalton and Oa 19
Kildonan (Whiting Bay) 12
Kildonan and Loth
 Helmsdale 40
Kilfinan 19
Kilfinichen and
 Kilvickeon and the
 Ross of Mull 19
Killean and Kilchenzie 19
Killearn 23
Killearnan 39
Killellan (Houston) 14
Killin and Ardeonaig 23
Kilmacolm 14
Kilmadock 23
Kilmallie 38
Kilmany (Creich) 26
Kilmarnock 11
Kilmaronock Gartocharn 18
Kilmartin (Glassary) 19
Kilmaurs 11
Kilmelford (Kilninver) 19
Kilmeny 19
Kilmodan and
 Colintraive 19
Kilmonivaig 38
Kilmorack and Erchless 37
Kilmore (Kilninian) 19
Kilmore and Oban 19
Kilmorich
 (Lochgoilhead) 19
Kilmory 12
Kilmuir and Logie
 Easter 39
Kilmuir and Paible 43
Kilmuir and Stenscholl 42
Kilmun 19
Kilninian and Kilmore 19
Kilninver and
 Kilmelford 19
Kilrenny 26
Kilspindie and Rait 28
Kilsyth 16
Kiltarlity 37
Kiltearn 39
Kilvickeon (Kilfinichen) 19
Kilwinning 12
Kincardine (Boat of
 Garten) 36
Kincardine (Tulliallan) 24
Kincardine Croick and
 Edderton 40
Kincardine-in-Menteith 23
Kinclaven 27
Kinellar (Fintray) 33
Kinfauns (St Madoes) 28
Kingairloch (Ardgour) 38
King Edward 34
Kinghorn 25
Kinglassie
 (Auchterderran) 25
Kingsbarns 26
Kingscavil (Pardovan) 2
Kingswells 31
Kingussie 36
Kinkell (Trinity Gask) 28
Kinloch 44
Kinlochbervie (Durness) 40
Kinlochleven 38
Kinlochspelvie Torosay) 19

Kinloss and Findhorn	35	Largs	12	Lugar	10	Muirhead (Lundie)	29
Kinnaird (Inchture)	29	Larkhall	17	Lunan (Inverkeilor)	30	Muirkirk	10
Kinneff (Arbuthnott)	32	Lasswade and Rosewell	3	Lundie and Muirhead	29	Murroes (Monikie)	29
Kinnell (Friockheim)	30	Latheron, The Parish of	41	Lunnasting (Nesting)	46	Musselburgh	3
Kinnettles (Glamis)	30	Lauder (Channelkirk)	4	Luss	18	Muthill	28
Kinross	28	Laurencekirk	32	Lyne and Manor	4		
Kintail (Glenelg)	42	Law	13			Nairn	37
Kintore	33	Lawers (Kenmore)	27	Macduff	34	Neilston	14
Kippen	23	Lecropt	23	Madderty (Fowlis		Ness (Cross)	44
Kirkbean (Colvend)	8	Legerwood	5	Wester)	28	Nesting and Lunnasting	46
Kirkcaldy	25	Leith (Edinburgh)	1	Manish-Scarista	43	Netherlee	16
Kirkcolm (Ervie)	9	Leitholm (Eccles)	5	Manor (Lyne)	4	Nether Lochaber	38
Kirkconnel	8	Lenzie	16	Markinch and Thornton	25	Nevay (Eassie)	30
Kirkcowan	9	Lerwick and Bressay	46	Marnoch	34	New Abbey (Lochend)	8
Kirkcudbright	8	Leslie (Insch)	33	Maryculter (Banchory-		Newarthill and Carfin	17
Kirkden (Dunnichen)	30	Leslie (Kirkcaldy)	25	Devenick)	32	Newbattle	3
Kirkfieldbank	13	Lesmahagow	13	Mauchline	10	Newbigging (Monikie)	29
Kirkgunzeon		Leswalt	9	Maud and Savoch	34	Newburgh (Foveran)	33
(Dalbeattie)	8	Letham (Dunnichen)	30	Maxton and Mertoun	4	Newburgh (St Andrews)	26
Kirkhill	37	Lethnot (Edzell)	30	Maxwell Mearns Castle	16	Newburn (Largo)	26
Kirkinner	9	Leuchars	26	Maybole	10	New Byth (Monquhitter)	34
Kirkintilloch	16	Leven	25	Mearns (Glasgow)	16	Newcastle	47
Kirkliston (Edinburgh)	1	Levern (Barrhead)	14	Mearns Coastal	32	New Cumnock	10
Kirkmabreck	9	Lhanbryd (St Andrew's)	35	Meigle (Ardler)	27	New Deer	34
Kirkmahoe (Closeburn)	8	Libberton and		Meldrum and Bourtie	33	New Galloway (Kells)	8
Kirkmaiden	9	Quothquan	13	Melness and Tongue	40	Newhills	31
Kirkmichael (Ayr)	10	Liddesdale	7	Melrose (Bowden)	4	New Kilpatrick	
Kirkmichael and		Liff (Fowlis)	29	Menmuir (Fern)	30	(Bearsden)	18
Tomintoul	36	Limekilns	24	Menstrie	23	Newlands (Kirkurd)	4
Kirkmichael, Straloch		Linlithgow	2	Mertoun (Maxton)	4	New Luce (Luce Valley)	9
and Glenshee	27	Linwood	14	Methil	25	New Machar	33
Kirkmichael, Tinwald		Lismore	19	Methilhill and Denbeath	25	Newmains	17
and Torthorwald	8	Liverpool	47	Methlick	33	Newmill (Keith)	35
Kirkmuirhill	13	Livingston	2	Methven and		Newmilns	11
Kirknewton and East		Loanhead	3	Logiealmond	28	New Monkland (Airdrie)	17
Calder	2	Lochalsh (Glenelg)	42	Mid Calder (Kirk of		New Pitsligo	34
Kirk of Calder	2	Lochbroom and Ullapool	39	Calder)	2	Newport-on-Tay	26
Kirk o' Shotts	17	Lochcarron (Applecross)	42	Mid Deeside	32	New Stevenson	17
Kirkoswald	10	Lochend and New		Middlebie (Hoddom)	7	Newton	3
Kirkpatrick Durham		Abbey	8	Midmar	33	Newtonhill	32
(Corsock)	8	Lochfyneside		Milngavie	18	Newton Mearns	16
Kirkpatrick Fleming		(Cumlodden)	19	Milton of Campsie	16	Newtonmore	36
(Gretna)	7	Lochgair (Cumlodden)	19	Mochrum	9	Newtown	4
Kirkpatrick Juxta	7	Lochgelly and Benarty	24	Moffat	7	Newtyle (Eassie)	30
Kirkton (Cavers)	6	Lochgilphead	19	Moneydie		Nigg (Fearn)	39
Kirkurd and Newlands	4	Lochgoilhead and		(Auchtergaven)	28	Norrieston	23
Kirkwall	45	Kilmorich	19	Moniaive (Glencairn)	8	North Berwick	3
Kirn	19	Lochinver (Assynt)	40	Monifieth	29	North Coast Parish, The	41
Kirriemuir	30	Lochmaben	7	Monigaff	9	North Knapdale	19
Kirtle-Eaglesfield		Lochmaddy (Berneray)	43	Monikie and		Northmavine	46
(Hoddom)	7	Lochranza and Pirnmill	12	Newbigging and		North Queensferry	24
Knock	44	Lochrutton (Irongray)	8	Murroes and Tealing	29	North Ronaldsay	45
Knockando, Elchies and		Lochs-Crossbost	44	Monimail	26	North West Lochaber	38
Archiestown	35	Lochs-in-Bernera	44	Monkton and Prestwick:		Noth	33
Knockbain	39	Lochwinnoch	14	North	10		
Kyles	19	Lockerbie, Hutton and		Monquhitter and New		Oa (Kildalton)	19
		Corrie	7	Byth	34	Oakley (Carnock)	24
Ladykirk(Coldstream &		Logie	23	Montrose	30	Oathlaw Tannadice	30
Dist.)	5	Logiealmond (Methven)	28	Monymusk	33	Oban (Kilmore)	19
Laggan	36	Logie Easter (Kilmuir)	39	Monzie (Fowlis Wester)	28	Ochiltree	10
Lairg	40	Logierait (Grantully)	27	Mordington (Ayton &		Old Cumnock	10
Lamlash	12	London	47	Dist.)	5	Old Kilpatrick Bowling	18
Lammermuir (Duns &		Longforgan	29	Morham (Garvald)	3	Old Luce (Luce Valley)	9
Dist.)	5	Longniddry	3	Mortlach and Cabrach	35	Oldmachar (Aberdeen)	31
Lanark	13	Longriggend		Morvern	38	Old Monkland	
Langbank	14	(Caldercruix)	17	Motherwell	17	(Coatbridge)	17
Langholm Eskdalemuir		Longside	34	Mouswald Cummertrees)	8	Olrig	41
Ewes and Westerkirk	7	Lonmay	34	Moy, Dalarossie and		Onich (Nether Lochaber)	38
Langton (Duns & Dist.)	5	Lossiemouth	35	Tomatin	37	Ordiquhill and Cornhill	34
Larbert	22	Loth (Kildonan)	40	Muckairn	19	Ormiston	3
Largo	26	Loudoun (Newmilns)	11	Muckhart	23	Oronsay (Colonsay)	19
Largoward	26	Lowick (Berwick)	5	Muiravonside	22	Orphir and Stenness	45

Orwell and Portmoak 28
Overtown 17
Oxnam (Kelso Country
  Churches) 6
Oxton (Channelkirk) 4
Oyne (Insch) 33

Paible (Kilmuir) 43
Paisley 14
Panbride (Carnoustie) 30
Papa Westray 45
Pardovan, Kingscavil
  and Winchburgh 2
Parton (Crossmichael) 8
Pathhead (Cranstoun) 3
Patna Waterside 10
Paxton (Hutton) 5
Peebles 4
Pencaitland 3
Penicuik 3
Penninghame 9
Penpont, Keir and
  Tynron 8
Perth 28
Peterculter 31
Peterhead 34
Petty 37
Pirnmill (Lochranza) 12
Pitlochry 27
Pitmedden (Udny) 33
Pitsligo 34
Pittenweem 26
Plean (Cowie) 23
Pluscarden (Birnie) 35
Polbeth Harwood 2
Polmont 22
Port Charlotte
  (Kilchoman) 19
Port Glasgow 14
Portknockie 35
Portlethen 32
Portmahomack (Tarbat) 39
Portmoak (Orwell) 28
Portnahaven 19
Port of Menteith 23
Portpatrick 9
Portree 42
Port Seton (Cockenzie) 3
Portsoy 34
Premnay (Insch) 33
Prestonpans 3
Prestwick 10

Quarff (Sandwick) 46
Quarter 17
Queensferry (Edinburgh) 1
Quothquan (Libberton) 13

Rafford 35
Rait (Kilspindie) 28
Rannoch (Foss) 27
Rathen 34
Ratho (Edinburgh) 1
Rathven 35
Rattray 27
Rayne (Culsalmond) 33
Redding and
  Westquarter 22
Redgorton and Stanley 28
Rendall 45
Renfrew 14
Renton 18

Rescobie (Guthrie) 30
Resolis and Urquhart 39
Reston(Ayton & Dist.) 5
Rhu and Shandon 18
Riccarton (Kilmarnock) 11
Rigside (Douglas Water) 13
Roberton (Hawick:
  Teviot) 6
Rogart 40
Rosehall 40
Rosemarkie (Fortrose) 39
Rosewell (Lasswade) 3
Roslin 3
Rosneath 18
Rosskeen 39
Ross of Mull
  (Kilfinichen) 19
Rosyth 24
Rothes 35
Rothesay 19
Rothiemay (Keith) 35
Rothiemurchus and
  Aviemore 36
Rothienorman 34
Rousay 45
Ruberslaw 6
Rutherglen 16
Ruthwell (Cummertrees) 8

Saddell and Carradale 19
St Abbs (Coldingham) 5
St Andrews 26
St Andrew's-Lhanbryd
  and Urquhart 35
St Boswells 4
St Colman 10
St Fergus 34
St Fillan's (Dundurn) 28
St Madoes and Kinfauns 28
St Martins (Scone) 28
St Monans 26
St Mungo 7
St Ninian's
  (Dunrossness) 46
St Ninians (Stirling) 23
St Quivox (Ayr) 10
St Vigeans (Arbroath) 30
Salen and Ulva 19
Saline and Blairingone 24
Saltcoats 12
Saltoun(Humbie) 3
Sanday 45
Sandbank 19
Sandhaven 34
Sandness (Walls) 46
Sandsting and Aithsting 46
Sandwick (Birsay) 45
Sandwick,
  Cunningsburgh and
  Quarff 46
Sandyhills (Glasgow) 16
Sanquhar 8
Sauchie and
  Coalsnaughton 23
Savoch (Maud) 34
Scarista (Manish) 43
Scone and St Martins 28
Seafield (Blackburn) 2
Selkirk 4
Shandon (Rhu) 18
Shapinsay 45
Shieldhill (Blackbraes) 22

Shiskine 12
Shotts 17
Sibbaldbie (Applegarth) 7
Skelmorlie and Wemyss
  Bay 14
Skene 33
Skerries (Whalsay) 46
Skipness 19
Skirling 4
Slamannan 22
Sleat (Strath) 42
Snizort 42
Sorbie 9
Sorn 10
Southdean (Hobkirk) 6
Southend 19
South Knapdale 19
South Queensferry
  (Queensferry) 1
South Ronaldsay and
  Burray 45
South Uist 19
Southwick (Colvend) 8
Spean Bridge
  (Kilmonivaig) 38
Speymouth (Bellie) 35
Spott 3
Springfield (Ceres) 26
Springside (Dreghorn) 11
Sprouston (Kelso: Old) 6
Spynie (Duffus) 35
Stair 10
Stamperland 16
Stanley (Redgorton) 28
Stenhouse and Carron 22
Stenness (Orphir) 45
Stenscholl (Kilmuir) 42
Stepps 16
Stevenston 12
Stewarton 11
Stirling 23
Stobo and Drumelzier 4
Stoer (Assynt) 40
Stonehaven 32
Stonehouse 17
Stoneykirk 9
Stoneywood Bucksburn) 31
Stornoway 44
Stow and Heriot 4
Strachur and
  Strathlachlan 19
Straiton 10
Straloch (Kirkmichael) 27
Stranraer 9
Strath and Sleat 42
Strathaven 17
Strathblane 23
Strathbogie Drumblade 33
Strathbraan (Dunkeld) 27
Strathbrock 2
Strathfillan 19
Strathkinness 26
Strathlachlan (Strachur) 19
Strathmiglo (Edenshead) 26
Strathpeffer (Fodderty) 39
Strathtay (Grantully) 27
Strichen and Tyrie 34
Stromness 45
Strone and Ardentinny 19
Stronsay 45
Strontian 38
Struan (Blair Atholl) 27

Swinton (Coldstream &
  Dist.) 5
Symington (Craigie) 10
Symington (Lanark) 13

Tain 39
Tannadice (Oathlaw) 30
Tarbat 39
Tarbert, Loch Fyne and
  Kilberry 19
Tarbert (Uist) 43
Tarbolton 10
Tarff and Twynholm 8
Tarves 33
Taynuilt (Muckairn) 19
Tayport 26
Tealing (Monikie) 29
Tenandry 27
Terregles (Irongray) 8
Teviot (Ale) 6
Teviothead 6
The Bengairn Parishes 8
The Border Kirk 7
The Douglas Valley
  Church 13
The Glens and
  Kirriemuir: Old 30
The Isla Parishes 30
The North Coast Parish 41
The Parish of Latheron 41
The Stewartry of
  Strathearn 28
The United Church of
  Bute 19
Thornhill (Dumfries and
  Kirkcudbright) 8
Thornhill (Norrieston) 23
Thornliebank 16
Thornton (Markinch) 25
Thrumster (Wick) 41
Thurso 41
Tibbermore
  (Almondbank) 28
Tillicoultry 23
Tingwall 46
Tinwald (Kirkmichael) 8
Tiree 19
Tobermory 19
Tomatin (Moy) 37
Tomintoul, Glenlivet
  and Inveraven 36
Tongue (Melness) 40
Torosay and
  Kinlochspelvie 19
Torphichen 3
Torrance 16
Torridon (Applecross) 42
Torryburn (Culross) 24
Torthorwald
  (Kirkmichael) 8
Tough (Cushnie) 33
Toward 19
Tranent 3
Traprain 3
Traquair (Innerleithen) 4
Trinity Gask and Kinkell 28
Troon 10
Troqueer (Dumfries) 8
Tulliallan and Kincardine 24
Tullibody 23
Tundergarth 7
Turriff 34

Twechar 16
Tweedsmuir 4
Twynholm (Tarff) 8
Tyne Valley Parish 3
Tyninghame (Whitekirk) 3
Tynron (Penpont) 8
Tyrie (Strichen) 34

Uddingston 17
Udny and Pitmedden 33
Uig 44
Uist, South 19
Ullapool (Lochbroom) 39
Ulva (Salen) 19
United Church of Bute, The 19
Unst and Fetlar 46
Uphall 2
Uplawmoor (Caldwell) 14

Upper Clyde 13
Upper Donside 33
Urquhart (Resolis) 39
Urquhart (St Andrew's-Lhanbryd) 35
Urquhart and Glenmoriston (Inverness) 37
Urr 8
Urray and Kilchrist 39

Walkerburn (Innerleithen) 4
Walls (Hoy) 45
Walls and Sandness (Shetland) 46
Wamphray 7
Waterside (Patna) 10
Watten 41

Weem (Dull) 27
Wemyss (Buckhaven) 25
Wemyss Bay (Skelmorlie) 14
Westerdale (Halkirk) 41
Westerkirk (Langholm) 7
Westhill (Skene) 33
West Kilbride 12
West Kirk of Calder 2
West Linton 4
West Mearns 32
Westquarter (Redding) 22
Westray 45
Westruther 5
Whalsay and Skerries 46
Whitburn 2
Whitehills 34
Whitekirk and Tyninghame 3

Whithorn 9
Whiting Bay and Kildonan 12
Whitsome (Coldstream & Dist.) 5
Wick 41
Wigtown 9
Williamwood 16
Wilton (Hawick) 6
Winchburgh (Pardovan) 2
Windygates (Kennoway) 25
Wishaw 17
Wormit 26

Yarrow (Ettrick) 4
Yell 4
Yester, Bolton and Saltoun (Humbie) 3

INDEX OF SUBJECTS

Action of Churches Together in Scotland
(ACTS) 18, 24
Assembly Arrangements Committee 6
Associations (and Societies) 23
Auxiliary Ministers 244

Baptism 40
Bible Societies 28

Central Properties Department 7
Central Services Committee 7
Chaplains to HM Forces 260
Chaplains, Health and Social Care 257
Chaplains, Prison 282
Chaplains, University and College 282
Chaplains, Workplace 281
Chaplains to the Queen 20
Charity Numbers xviii, 285
Child protection 14
Christian Aid xix, 28
Church and Society Council xviii, 3
Church of Scotland Chaplains' Association 27
Church of Scotland Guild 10
Church of Scotland Housing and Loan Fund 10
Church of Scotland Insurance Services xix, 31
Church of Scotland Investors Trust xxii, 11
Church of Scotland Offices xviii
Church of Scotland Pension Trustees xix, 13
Church of Scotland Societies 27
Church of Scotland Trust 7
Church Offices xviii
Church Service Society 27
Churches, Overseas 19
Churches Together in Britain and Ireland 8
Churches in the United Kingdom, other 18
Civil partnerships 40
Climate Change Project, Responding to 3
Committee on Church Art and Architecture 5
Communications Department 8
Community of Protestant Churches in Europe
(CPCE) 9
Conference of European Churches 9
Conforti Institute xix
Congregational Statistics 293
Council Education Committees, Church
Representatives on 282
Council of Assembly xviii, 3
Councils and Committees, List 1
Covenant Fellowship Scotland 27
CrossReach xviii, xix, 5

Deceased ministers 283
Department of the General Assembly 2
Design Services 8
Diaconate, Membership of 246

Discontinued Parish and Congregational
Names 289
Divinity Faculties/Schools, Scottish 22
Ecclesiastical buildings 9
Eco-Congregation Scotland xix, 28
Ecumenical Officer xix, 2, 8
Ecumenical Relations Committee 8
Editorial xxii
Education 3, 4, 25
Elder training 4
European Churches, Conference of 9

Facilities Management Department xviii, 7, 13
Fellowship of St Andrew 24
Fellowship of St Thomas 24
Forward Together 27
Funds (and Trusts) 30
Funeral services: conduct of and fees for 40

Gaelic language xxii, 44
Gartmore House xix
General Assembly (2016) 42
Moderator of 42
Officials 42
General Assembly (2017), date of xix
General Assembly, Department of the 2
General Trustees 9
Glasgow Lodging House Mission xix
Glebes 9
Go For It Fund 4
Grid references for churches 287
Guild, Church of Scotland 10

Healthcare Chaplaincies 257
Her Majesty's Household in Scotland:
Ecclesiastical 20
Highland Theological College UHI 23
Holidays for ministers 36
Housing and Loan Fund 10
Human Resources Department 10
Hymns Ancient and Modern 14

Index of Advertisers 325
Index of Ministers 326
Index of Parishes and Places 337
Industrial Chaplains 281
Information Technology Department 11
Insurance xix, 31
Inter-Church Organisations 24
Investors Trust, Church of Scotland xviii, 11
Iona Community xix, 24

John Knox House Museum xix, 15

Law Department 11

Lay Agents, Retired	282	Principal Clerk	xix, 2, 42
Legal Names of Congregations	285	Priority Areas Committee	4
Legal Questions Committee	12	Priority Areas Office	xix
Life and Work	12, 45	Prison Chaplains	282
Long Service Certificates	36	Properties	7
Lord High Commissioners (list)	20	Pulpit Supply	xix, 40
Marriage	40	Queen's Chaplains	20
Marriage, same-sex	40		
Marriage and Civil Partnership (Scotland)		Readers	262
Act 2014	40	Records of the Church	37
Marriage Services, conduct of	40	Responding to Climate Change Project	3
Media Relations Team: Press Office	xix, 8		
Ministers deceased	283	Safeguarding Service	xix, 14
Ministers not in Presbyteries (practising		Saint Andrew Press	14
certificate)	249	Same-sex marriage	40
Ministers not in Presbyteries (without		Schools of Divinity/Theology	22
certificate)	254	Scotland's Churches Trust	35
Ministers ordained sixty years and upwards	282	Scottish Charity Numbers	xviii, 285
Ministries and Mission contribution	294	Scottish Church History Society	29
Ministries Council	4	Scottish Church Society	27
Ministries Development Staff	277	Scottish Church Theology Society	28
Mission and Discipleship Council	4	Scottish Churches House Legacy Reserve	35
Moderator of the General Assembly (see		Scottish Churches Housing Action	25
General Assembly)	xxii, 42	Scottish Churches Parliamentary Office	xix, 15
Moderators of the General Assembly (list)	21	Scottish Evangelical Theology Society	29
		Scottish Storytelling Centre	xix, 15
Netherbow, The	xix, 15	Social Care Council	xviii, 5
Nomination Committee	12	Societies (and Associations)	23
		Society, Religion and Technology Project	3
Office Manager (121 George Street)	xviii, 13	Statistics, Congregational	293
Offices of the Church	xviii	Statistics, summary	294
Old Churches House, Dunblane	xix	Stewardship and Finance Department	15
Ordained local ministers	242	Stewardship programmes	15
Ordnance Survey National Grid References	287	Student Christian Movement	26
Organist training schemes	25		
Overseas appointments	6, 280	Theological Forum	16
Overseas Churches	19	Trusts (and Funds)	30
Overseas locations	237, 280		
Overseas Resigned and Retired Mission		UCCF: The Christian Unions	26
Partners	281	University Chaplains	282
Overseas vacancies	6		
		Vacancy procedure	40
Panel on Review and Reform	13	Vacancy schedules	40
Parliamentary Office (Scottish Churches)	xix, 15		
Pension Trustees	xix, 13	Workplace Chaplains	281
Personnel Department (Human Resources)	10	World Communion of Reformed Churches	9
Place for Hope	xix, 25	World Council of Churches	8
Practising Certificates	249, 254	World Day of Prayer	26
Precedence	22	World Mission Council	x, 6
Presbytery lists	47		
Press Office: Media Relations Team	xix, 8	Year Book, information on	xix